Orientalism, Assyriology and the Bible

Hebrew Bible Monographs, 10

ORIENTALISM, ASSYRIOLOGY AND THE BIBLE

edited by
Steven W. Holloway

SHEFFIELD PHOENIX PRESS

2007

First published in hardback, 2006
First published in paperback, 2007

Published by Sheffield Phoenix Press
Department of Biblical Studies, University of Sheffield
Sheffield S10 2TN

www.sheffieldphoenix.com

A CIP catalogue record for this book
is available from the British Library

Typeset by CA Typesetting Ltd
Printed on acid-free paper by Lightning Source UK Ltd, Milton Keynes

ISBN 978-1-905048-37-3 (hardback)
ISBN 978-1-906055-33-2 (paperback)

Contents

Visual Perspectives

Of Harems and Heroines

Assyriology and the Bible

Abbreviations

A	Mari collection of the Musée du Louvre, Paris
AB	Anchor Bible
ABD	*Anchor Bible Dictionary*
AfO	*Archiv für Orient Forschungen*
AfOB	Archiv für Orient Forschungen, Beiheft
AJA	*American Journal of Archaeology*
AJSLL	*American Journal of Semitic Languages and Literatures*
ALASPM	Abhandlungen zur Literatur Alt-Syrien-Palästinas und Mesopotamiens
ANET	*Ancient Near Eastern Texts*
ANB	*American National Biography*
AnSt	*Anatolian Studies*
AO	Département des Antiquités Orientales, Musée du Louvre, Paris
AOAT	Alter Orient und Altes Testament
ARM	Archives royales de Mari
ARMT	Archives royales de Mari (texts in transliteration and translation)
ArtB	*Art Bulletin*
ASAE	*Annales du Service des antiquités de l'Egypte*
AuOr	*Aula Orientalis*
BA	*Biblical Archaeologist*
BAR	*Biblical Archaeology Review*
BASOR	*Bulletin of the American Schools of Oriental Research*
BBB	Bonner Biblische Beiträge
BFCT	Beiträge zur Förderung christlicher Theologie
BIE	*Bulletin de l'Institut d'Egypte*
BL/Add MSS 37,449/Hek 2	British Library, Additional manuscripts No. 37,449, volume 2 of the separately numbered Hekekyan papers (24 vols.; manuscript number and volume number vary)
BM, P&D	British Museum, Department of Prints and Drawings
BM, ANE	British Museum, Ancient Near East
BO	*Bibliotheca Orientalis*
Borger, Ash.	R. Borger, *Die Inschriften Asarhaddons, Königs von Assyrien*
BRM	Babylonian Records in the Library of J. Pierpont Morgan
BSOAS	*Bulletin of the Schools of Oriental and African Studies*
BZAW	Beihefte zur Zeitschrift für die alttestamentliche Wissenschaft
CAD	*Chicago Assyrian Dictionary*
CAH^3	*Cambridge Ancient History*, 3rd edn
CANE	*Civilizations of the Ancient Near East*
CBQM	Catholic Biblical Quarterly Monograph Series
CEDEJ	Centre d'études et de documentation économiques, juridiques et sociales, Cairo
CHANE	Culture and History of the Ancient Near East

COS	*Context of Scripture*
DAB	*Dictionary of American Biography*
DDDB^2	*Dictionary of Deities and Demons in the Bible* (2nd edn,1999)
DWQ	Dar-al-Wathaiq al-Qawmiyya (Egyptian National Archives), Cairo: Abhath: Abhath Collection (followed by box number) MMW: Mahfuzat Majlis al-Wuzara (Archives of the Council of Ministers) MA: Maslahat al-Athar (Antiquities Service) NM: Nizarat al-Maarif (Ministry of Education) Fihrist bataqat al-Dar (card file index of the contents of the Egyptian National Archives / Drawer I: Athar (Antiquities)
EB^{11}	*Encyclopaedia Britannica*, 11th edn
EI^2	*Encyclopaedia of Islam* (Brill, 2nd edn, 1960–)
ExpTim	*Expository Times*
FAT	Forschungen zum Alten Testament
FRLANT	Forschungen zur Religion und Literatur des Alten und Neuen Testaments
HAT	Handbuch zum Alten Testament
HSS	Harvard Semitic Studies
ICC	International Critical Commentary
ICO1, Paris	Mémoires du congrès international des Orientalistes, 1re session, Paris, 3 vols. (Paris: Maisonneuve et cie, 1873–76) (language and title of proceedings vary with host city; abbreviation varies according to congress number and host city)
IFAO	Institut français d'archéologie orientale du Caire
ILN	*Illustrated London News*
JAOS	*Journal of the American Oriental Society*
JBL	*Journal of Biblical Literature*
JCS	*Journal of Cuneiform Studies*
JESHO	*Journal of the Economic and Social History of the Orient*
JETS	*Journal of the Evangelical Theological Society*
JNES	*Journal of Near Eastern Studies*
JRAS	*Journal of the Royal Asiatic Society*
JSJ	*Journal for the Study of Judaism*
JSOT	*Journal for the Study of the Old Testament*
JSOTSup	Journal for the Study of the Old Testament Supplement Series
JSS	*Journal of Semitic Studies*
KAT	Kommentar zum Alten Testament
KJV	King James Version
Langdon, VAB 4	S. Langdon, *Die neubabylonischen Königsinschriften*
LAPO	Littératures anciennes du Proche-Orient
LCL	Loeb Classical Library
LIMC	*Lexicon iconographicum mythologiae classicae*
LSTS	Library of Second Temple Studies
MAE	Ministère des affaires étrangeres, Les Archives diplomatiques de Nantes, France
MAOG	Mitteilungen der Altorientalischen Gesellschaft
MAPD	Middle Assyrian Palace Decrees
MARI	*Mari, annales de recherches interdisciplinaires*
MHUC	Monographs of the Hebrew Union College
MT	Masoretic Text
MVAG	Mitteilungen der Vorderasiatischen/Vorderasiastisch-Ägyptischen Gesellschaft

NAA inv	National Anthropological Archives [Smithsonian Institution] inventory number
N.A.B.U.	*Nouvelles assyriologiques brèves et utilitaires*
NCBC	New Century Bible Commentary
NGDO	*New Grove Dictionary of Opera*
NINOL	Uitgaven van het Nederlands Instituut voor het Nabije Oosten te Leiden
OBO	Orbis Biblicus et Orientalis
OEAANE	*The Oxford Encyclopedia of Archaeology in the Ancient Near East*
OED^2	*Oxford English Dictionary* (2nd edn,1989–)
OIP	Oriental Institute Publications
OLA	Orientalia Lovaniensia Analecta
Or	*Orientalia*
OTL	Old Testament Library
PEGLAMBS	*Proceedings Eastern Great Lakes & Midwest Biblical Societies*
PIHANS	Publications de l'Instituut historique-archéologique néerlandais de Stamboul
RA	*Revue d'assyriologie et d'archéologie orientale*
RevHistRel	*Revue de l'histoire des religions*
RANE	Records of the Ancient Near East
SAA	State Archives of Assyria
SAAB	*State Archives of Assyria Bulletin*
SAAS	State Archives of Assyria Studies
SBL	Society of Biblical Literature
SBLABS	SBL Archaeology and Biblical Studies
SBLDS	SBL Dissertation Series
SBLSCS	SBL Septuagint and Cognate Studies Series
SBLSS	SBL Symposium Series
SBLWAW	SBL Writings from the Ancient World
SHCANE	Studies in the History and Culture of the Ancient Near East
SpTU, I	H. Hunger, *Spätbabylonische Texte aus Uruk,* Teil I
SpTU, III	E. von Weiher, *Spätbabylonische Texte aus Uruk,* Teil III
Streck, VAB 7	M. Streck, *Assurbanipal und die letzten assyrischen Könige bis zum Untergange Nineveh's*
TSBA	*Transactions of the Society of Biblical Archaeology*
TUAT	*Texte aus der Umwelt des Alten Testaments*
TVOA	*Testi del Vicino Oriente antico*
USNM	United States National Museum
VAB	Vorderasiatische Bibliothek
VAT	Vorderasiatische Abteilung Tontafel, Staatliche Museen, Berlin
VT	*Vetus Testamentum*
VTSup	Supplements to Vetus Testamentum
WBC	Word Biblical Commentary
WCE	World's Columbian Exposition (Chicago, 1893)
WdO	*Die Welt des Orients*
WMANT	Wissenschaftliche Monographien zum Alten und Neuen Testament
*WWWE*3	*Who Was Who in Egyptology* (3rd edn, 1995)
WZKM	*Wiener Zeitschrift für die Kunde des Morgenlandes*
YNER	Yale Near Eastern Researches
YOS	Yale Oriental Series
ZA	*Zeitschrift für Assyriologie*
ZAW	*Zeitschrift für die alttestamentliche Wissenschaft*
ZDPV	*Zeitschrift des deutschen Palästina-Vereins*

List of Illustrations

Maps

Tables

Contributors

Julia M. Asher-Greve, Basel, Switzerland

Frederick N. Bohrer, Hood College, USA

Donato Esposito, University of Plymouth, UK

Benjamin R. Foster, Yale University, USA

Eckart Frahm, Yale University, USA

Lester L. Grabbe, University of Hull, UK

Lowell K. Handy, American Theological Library Association

Steven W. Holloway, American Theological Library Association

Victor Avigdor Hurowitz, Ben Gurion University of the Negev, Israel

Burke O. Long, Bowdoin College, USA

Donald Malcolm Reid, Georgia State University, USA

Jack M. Sasson, Vanderbilt University, USA

JoAnn Scurlock, Elmhurst College, USA

Elna K. Solvang, Concordia College, Minnesota, USA

K. Lawson Younger, Jr, Trinity International University, Illinois, USA

Introduction: Orientalism, Assyriology and the Bible

Steven W. Holloway

> The unchanged habits of the East render it in this respect a kind of living Pompeii…we know the outward appearances through the forms of actual men, living and moving before us, wearing almost the same garb, speaking in almost the same language, and certainly with the same general terms of speech and tone and manners.
> A.P. Stanley, *Lectures on the History of the Jewish Church* (1863).

This collection of essays began life as a series of papers delivered at the annual North American Society for Biblical Literature meeting of 2002 in a session bearing the same title as this book, though the lion's share of the contributions herein were written after the fact, so to speak.[1] The only word in the title likely to cause scholarly *Angst* is Orientalism. English speakers since the age of Chaucer and the author of *Piers Plowman* have employed the noun and adjective *Oriental* to denote things located east of the Mediterranean and the old Roman Empire, now used of the Near, Middle or Far East. In this sense, *Oriental* has been pressed into service to label things that are both exotic to Europe and highly prized, like Oriental carpets, Oriental (pearls), and Oriental hyacinth, as well as things that incur condemnation or disgust, like Oriental despotism and Oriental sore (cutaneous *Leishmaniasis*). *Orientalist* (noun and adjective) did not figure widely in English usage prior to the eighteenth century, when it came to be applied to savants skilled in Oriental languages, culture or history, European artists inspired by Oriental subjects, or to label schools of art and architecture perceived as falling under Oriental influence. The venerable *Oxford English Dictionary* in its online iteration (September 2004 revision) recognizes three definitions for the noun *orientalism*:

> (1) Oriental style or quality; the character, customs, etc., of oriental nations; an oriental trait, feature, or idiom [the earliest example calls attention to 'orientalism in Homer' (1769)];
> (2) Knowledge of the languages, cultures, etc. of the Orient (*obscure* and *rare*);
> (3) The representation of the Orient (esp. the Middle East) in Western academic

1. Revised versions of the 2002 papers by Younger, Frahm and Sasson appear herein; the fourth, by Peter Machinist, 'Assyriology and the Bible: Benno Landsberger's *Eigenbegrifflichkeit* Revisited', is not yet in press. The essays by Frederick N. Bohrer and Donald Malcolm Reid have been reprinted.

> writing, art, or literature; *spec.* this representation perceived as stereotyped or exoticizing and therefore embodying a colonialist attitude. [citations beginning with E.W. Said, *Orientalism* (1978)].[2]

Historian of British imperialism John M. MacKenzie adduces examples of Orientalism used in the late eighteenth and early nineteenth centuries in the context of British rule in India. The Orientalism espoused by Warren Hastings, William Jones and the early East India Company sought to maintain British domination over the Indian subcontinent though patronage of Hindu and Muslim languages and institutions, rather than through their eclipse by English speech and aggressive European acculturation. This local policy of Orientalism fell afoul of the Anglicist party in the 1820s and 1830s that favored evangelical missions and universal English education designed to replace indigenous cultures, a policy closely associated with the philosopher J.S. Mill and Thomas Macaulay, who was appointed in 1835 President of the General Committee of Public Instruction in India.[3] From the standpoint of Macaulay and his followers, 'Orientalism' branded policy-makers whose approach to colonial governance was deemed conservative, romantic, and ineffectual.

Another negative but quite different usage of the term Orientalism arose out of the unprecedented waves of Eastern European Jewish immigrants seeking asylum in America in the final two decades of the nineteenth century. The highly assimilated American Jewish communities in New York, Chicago and other metropolitan enclaves, enjoying hard-won civil liberties and growing acceptance by the larger Gentile society, struggled visibly with *Yiddishkeit*. In the 1890s, established American Jews, mostly German in origin, employed 'Orientalism' as a derogatory reference to the 'uncivilized' traits of Eastern European immigrants. Orientalism is a 'hydra-headed monster' that could only be extirpated by an 'American education…the weapon with which to fight Orientalism…Reason calls for it, Judaism demands it, and American Patriotism dictates it.'[4]

Other usages of the protean and polarizing term Orientalism could be adduced. It is the purpose of this introduction, and collection of essays, to explore the impact of Orientalism on the disciplines of Assyriology and biblical studies.

2. OED online, *s.v.* oriental, orientalist, orientalism (http://dictionary.oed.com, accessed 10/2/05).

3. John M. MacKenzie, *Orientalism: History, Theory, and the Arts* (Manchester and New York: Manchester University Press, 1995), pp. xii-xiii, 3, 25-28; A.L. Macfie, *Orientalism* (London: Longman, 2002), pp. 3-4, 50-58.

4. Dr J. Silverman, rabbi of Temple Emanu-El in New York City, quoted in Grace Cohen Grossman and Richard E. Ahlborn, *Judaica at the Smithsonian: Cultural Politics as Cultural Model* (Smithsonian Studies in History and Technology, 52; Washington, DC: Smithsonian Institution Press, 1997), p. 58 n. 18. The observation on the usage of Orientalism in the American Jewish community is hers; to my knowledge, it has not figured in any discussion of Orientalism *à la* Said.

1. *Orientalism Up to the Nineteenth Century*

Scholarly Orientalism can be traced to the twelfth century, a complex product of medieval Western Christendom's growing engagement with Islam, widely misunderstood to be a Christian heresy, and an appetite for the treasures of the Islamic philosophical and mathematical tradition whetted by exposure to primary texts. Peter the Venerable, abbot of Cluny monastery in France, commissioned the first Latin translation of the Qur'ān, which was finished in 1143 by the Englishman Robert of Ketton.[5] Other English scholars studied Arabic, mathematics and philosophy in Spain, and the Sephardic exegete Abraham ibn Ezra taught Arabic in London, 1158–59. At that time, the Abbey of St. Victor in Paris brought the works of the rabbinic scholar Rashi of Troyes (1040–1105) into dialogue with more traditional approaches to Christian biblical exegesis, though the enormously influential *postillae* of Nicholas of Lyra (*c.* 1270–1349) did more to bridge the gap between medieval and Reformation-era usage of Jewish biblical scholarship than the works of Hugh, Richard and Andrew of St. Victor. Numerous medieval translations of and commentaries on Avicenna, Averroës, Algazel (al-Ghazzālī), Haly (ʿAli ibn Ridwān) and Rhazes (Abū Bakr Muḥammad ibn Zakarīyā Rāzī) served to assimilate these thinkers into the cultural canon of European intellectual life, mitigating the scandal of their Muslim origins.

European assessments of Islam were challenged by the rise of the Ottoman Empire in the fourteenth century and its eventual absorption of the remnants of the Byzantine Empire and large parts of southeastern and central Europe itself. By the time that Suleiman the Magnificent lay siege to Vienna in 1529, the 'Turks' as the Ottomans were known, had become the dominant power in the Mediterranean. The zenith of Ottoman power coincided with the religious upheavals of the Protestant Reformation, and in consequence the Ottoman Empire came to serve as a safe harbor for persecuted non-Christian refugees and a tool with which one Christian group attacked another, and in so doing lost much of its ideological threat to western Christendom. Some Europeans found things to admire in the new Islamic power. For instance, Ogier Ghiselin de Busbecq, Habsburg ambassador to the Ottoman court in 1554–62, spoke glowingly of the path to high civil and military rank as based on merit rather than birth, as was the case in Europe. Niccolò Machiavelli extolled the efficiency he perceived in the Ottoman administration, ruling without benefit of hereditary privilege, and ascribed to it many of the virtues of the old Roman Empire, while the French jurist Jean Bodin compared the Habsburg Empire invidiously to that of the Ottoman Sultan.[6]

5. C.E. Bosworth, 'The Study of Islam in British Scholarship', in *Mapping Islamic Studies: Genealogy, Continuity and Change* (ed. Azim Nanji; Religion and Reason, 38; Berlin and New York: Mouton de Gruyter, 1997), pp. 45-67 (47-48). This paraphrastic translation was widely reprinted; the Dutch jurist Hugo Grotius was still quoting it in the seventeenth century.

6. Zachary Lockman, *Contending Visions of the Middle East: The History and Politics of Orientalism* (Cambridge and New York: Cambridge University Press, 2004), pp. 43-44.

At that time, the first Arabic grammar based on sound philological principles and written by a European, Thomas Erpenius (1584–1624), was published in 1613.[7] Chairs of Arabic studies were established in 1539 at the Collège de France for the eccentric Guillaume Postel (1510–81), in 1609 in Berlin and in 1638 at Oxford University for Edward Pococke (1604–91), though Frans Raphelengius (1539–97) was teaching courses in Arabic at Leiden as early as 1593.[8] British Levant Company representatives (founded in 1581) were commissioned by Archbishop Ussher to obtain Arabic, Persian, Turkish, Syriac, Hebrew and Samaritan manuscripts; Archbishop Laud, more successful in that wise than his predecessor, donated his extensive Hebrew and Arabic manuscript collection to the Bodleian Library at Oxford in 1639–42. Pococke, who lived in Aleppo for six years, translated Arabic diplomatic correspondence addressed to the crown and ultimately gained the prestigious Regius Chair of Hebrew at Oxford.[9] The Renaissance efflorescence of Semitic language study was driven in part by the perceived benefits of comparative lexicography and grammar for biblical studies, in part by the advent of Arabic typography by 1586, in part by increasing commercial opportunities in the Levant, and in part by the burgeoning diplomatic contacts between the ruling houses of Europe and the Ottoman court. Fascination with the Muslim East had not yet become exoticism as the nineteenth century would know it, but tales and leitmotifs of Islamic ways figured prominently in artistic works such as Marlowe's *Tamburlaine* and Shakespeare's *Othello*. The French playwright Racine, in his 1672 preface to *Bajazet*, defensively emphasized the care with which he had studied Turkish history and translated it into stagecraft; Molière even went to the pains of inserting genuine Turkish dialogue in *Le bourgeois gentilhomme* (1670).[10] The first attempt at a comprehensive encyclopaedia of Islam was the *Bibliothèque orientale* of Barthelémy d'Herbelot de Molainville, published posthumously in 1697.[11]

7. Thomas Erpenius, *Grammatica Arabica, quinque libris methodicè explicata* (Leiden: In Officina Raphelengiana, 1613); Jacques D.J. Waardenburg, 'The Study of Islam in Dutch Scholarship', in Nanji (ed.), *Mapping Islamic Studies*, pp. 68-94 (69).

8. The polyglot Joseph Justus Scaliger (1540–1609) arrived at Leiden in 1593 but had no formal teaching responsibilities.

9. Thomas Hyde (1636–1703), Thomas Hunt (1696–1774) and Joseph White (1745–1814), other successors to both Arabic chairs at Oxford and the Regius Chair of Hebrew, were first and foremost biblical scholars; Macfie, *Orientalism*, pp. 26-27.

10. Maxime Rodinson, 'The Western Image and Western Studies of Islam', in *The Legacy of Islam* (ed. Joseph Schacht and C.E. Bosworth; Oxford: Clarendon Press, 2nd edn, 1974), pp. 9-62 (33-34).

11. Barthélemy d'Herbelot de Molainville, *Bibliothèque orientale, ou Dictionaire universel, contenant généralement tout ce qui regarde la connoissance des peuples de l'Orient. Leurs histoires et traditions véritables ou fabuleuses. Leurs religions, sectes et politique. Leurs gouvernement, loix, coûtumes, moeurs, guerres, & les révolutions de leurs empires. Leurs sciences, et leurs arts... Les vies et actions remarquables de tous leurs saints, docteurs, philosophes, historiens, poëtes, capitaines, & de tous ceux qui se sont rendus illustres parmi eux, par leur vertu, ou*

Intensive application of Arabic language sources for Hebrew lexicography, however, would have to wait for the Christian Hebraists of the seventeenth century. Johannes Buxtorf (1564–1629) published a string of Hebrew and Aramaic grammars, lexica and student manuals that would continue in print well into the nineteenth century. Basing his philological works on the medieval Jewish commentaries of Abraham Ibn Ezra, Rashi, David Kimchi, Saadia Gaon and Levi ben Gerson, Buxtorf brought Arabic lexicography indirectly into the early modern study of the Bible through these sources. Buxtorf endeavored to teach himself Arabic unsuccessfully, and his foundational studies of Semitic philology suffered accordingly.[12] Nevertheless, Wilhelm Gesenius paid him the ultimate compliment of judging his Hebrew grammar the finest written (thus far by 1815) by either Christian or Jew.[13] Christian Hebraism, in keeping with its learned humanistic origins, advocated the broadest possible study of Judaica, including the vast corpus of rabbinical texts and post-Talmudic compositions, as prerequisite to mastery of the intricacies of Hebrew Scripture. The legacy of Buxtorf and other Christian Hebraists led to the curious phenomenon that saw seventeenth-century Lutherans studying rabbinic literature more intensively than any other group of gentiles before or since.[14]

Asher-Greve in her essay meticulously explores the image of the semi-mythical Assyrian queen Semiramis in European arts and letters, tracking a career that ranged from 'prime exemplum of vicious pagan womanhood' in the Middle Ages to membership among the *femmes fortes* in the Age of Reason to a series of idiosyncratic artistic treatments in the past century. During the Baroque Age, when several European women ruled in their own right or as regents, visual representations by such painters as Simon Vouet and Matteo Roselli depicted this 'Oriental queen' as heroine or as an allegory of good rulership, whereas the didactic possibilities of Semiramis as a tragic heroine expanded through the art of Muzio Manfredi, Nicolas Desfontaines and Calderón. Paintings by Anton Raphael Mengs, Guercino (Giovanni Francesco Barbieri) and others portray Semiramis as a Baroque queen—but none of these artistic evocations attempt

par leur savoir. Des jugemens critiques, et des extraits de tous leurs ouvrages (Paris: Compagnie des Libraires, 1697). Although it was based on earlier histories and travelers' tales, it did try to canvass the entirety of Muslim society from North Africa to East Asia.

12. Stephen G. Burnett, *From Christian Hebraism to Jewish Studies: Johannes Buxtorf (1564–1629) and Hebrew Learning in the Seventeenth Century* (Studies in the History of Christian Thought, 68; Leiden and New York: Brill, 1996), p. 127.

13. Wilhelm Gesenius, *Geschichte der hebräischen Sprache und Schrift: Eine philologisch-historisch Einleitung in die Sprachlehren und Wörterbücher der hebräischen Sprache* (Leipzig: Friedrich Christian Wilhelm Vogel, 1815), p. 110.

14. Burnett, *From Christian Hebraism to Jewish Studies*, p. 3, citing Hans Joachim Schoeps for this observation. On the phenomenon of Christian Hebraism, see Frank Edward Manuel, *The Broken Staff: Judaism through Christian Eyes* (Cambridge and London: Harvard University Press, 1992), pp. 66-107.

to contextualize her by dressing her in Turkish costume or surround her with exoticizing furnishings. Instead, the powerfully vital figure of Semiramis was indigenized into European cultural history, serving variously as a positive or negative *exemplum*, but rarely does her Mesopotamian heritage emerge until the nineteenth-century drive for historicism.

The Ottoman Empire's Mediterranean supremacy was shattered by the Battle of Lepanto in 1571, and portions of its Central European territory were surrendered with the Treaty of Karlowitz in 1699, political reverses that contributed to the rise of a more negative image in the eyes of European writers.[15] Former admiration for the perceived nobility, bureaucratic efficiency and justice of the Ottoman administration shifted towards contempt for its imputed dishonor, corruption and immorality, building upon earlier Christian polemic. Turning the Ottomans into targets for European superiority had as much to do with sweeping social and political changes within European society itself as developments in the Ottoman East, not least of which was a growing identification with classical political theory that pitted the freedom of the Greek *polis* against despotic Asia. In *Spirit of the Laws* (1748), the French philosopher and jurist Montesquieu (1689–1755) set Oriental despotism against republican and monarchic modes of government in an iconic formulation, that, though challenged point-for-point by the French Orientalist Anquetil-Duperron,[16] continues to echo in contemporary East-versus-West diatribes like Samuel P. Huntington's influential 1993 *Foreign Affairs* essay, 'The Clash of Civilizations?'[17]

From the late seventeenth century onwards a growing corpus of travelogues combined with the first French translation of *The Arabian Nights* (1704–17) to conjure up an Orient that was alien yet safely distant, enchanted yet frozen in cultural immobility. In the words of Rodinson, commenting on the appearance of *The Arabian Nights* in Europe, 'Thenceforward Islam was no longer seen as the land of Antichrist but essentially that of an exotic, picturesque civilization, existing in a fabulous atmosphere peopled by good or evil, wayward genies—all this for the delight of an audience that had already shown so much taste for European fairy tales.'[18] The notion that the Orient is the cradle of torpid cultures impervious to change has deep roots in European thought. If this dubious premise be granted, it follows that study of the contemporary peoples of the Middle East opens tangible corridors into the past. If indeed the Ottoman Empire is rife with 'living museums', with communities that embody structures of family

15. Norman Itzkowitz, *Ottoman Empire and Islamic Tradition* (Chicago and London: University of Chicago Press, 1972), pp. 34-36.

16. Abraham-Hyacinthe Anquetil-Duperron, *Législation orientale, ouvrage dans lequel, en montrant quels sont en Turquie, en Perse et dans l'Indoustan, les principes fondamentaux du gouvernement, on prouve…* (Amsterdam: Marc-Michel Rey, 1778).

17. Samuel P. Huntington, 'The Clash of Civilizations?', *Foreign Affairs* 72 (1993), pp. 22-49.

18. Rodine, 'Western Studies of Islam', pp. 36-37.

life, agricultural practices, and religious habits essentially unchanged from the Patriarchal period of the Bible, so the argument runs, then it becomes possible to interpret biblical narratives through a selective exercise of modern ethnography. A classic statement of this idea appeared in the seventeenth century. Sir Jean Chardin, a French-born jeweler by trade, traveled to India and Persia twice, residing in Isfahān for four years. He returned to France in 1677, but fled to England in 1681 as a consequence of the Huguenot wars, becoming crown jeweler to Charles II. His lively and erudite travelogue was translated into English in the 1680s and went through numerous editions. In the preface, Chardin notes that

> In fine, consulting the [biblical] Commentators upon such kind of Passages, I found very strange Mistakes in them, and that they had long guess'd at the Sense, and did but grope (as in the Dark) in the search of it. And from these Reflections, I took a Resolution to make my Remarks upon many Passages of the *Scripture*; persuading myself that they would be equally Agreeable and Profitable for use. And the Learned, to whom I Communicated my Design, encouraged me very much (by their commendations) to proceed in it: And more especially when I inform'd them, That it is not in *Asia*, as in our *Europe*, where there are Frequent changes more or less, in the Form of Things, as the Habits, Buildings, Gardenings, and the like. In the *East* they are constant in all Things; The Habits are at this Day in the Same Manner as in the Precedent Ages; So that one may reasonably believe, That in that part of the World, the Exterior Forms of Things (as their Manners and Customs) are the same now, as they were Two Thousand Years since, except in such Changes as may have been Introduced by Religion, which are nevertheless very inconsiderable.[19]

With the accumulation of information about Oriental peoples gleaned by merchants, missionaries, diplomats, and scholars abroad, coupled with the notion that 'in the *East* they are constant in all things', biblical studies in the vestibule of the Enlightenment began to utilize *comparanda* drawn from Middle Eastern societies to an unprecedented degree. So Robert Lowth, in his *De sacra poesi hebraeorum* (1753), for example, drew frequently on the works of eastern travelers like Sir John Chardin, Edward Pococke, and Thomas Harmer (1714–88) to illustrate details in the Hebrew Scriptures, playing down distinctions between the ancient Israelites and modern Oriental peoples.[20] Lowth's defective Hebrew was corrected in an annotated edition by Johann David Michaelis (1717–91), who shared Lowth's novel enthusiasm for the Bible as primitive literature and

19. Jean Chardin, *The Travels of Sir John Chardin into Persia and the East-Indies. The First Volume, Containing the Author's Voyage from Paris to Ispahan: To Which is Added, the Coronation of This Present King of Persia, Solyman the Third* (London: Printed for Moses Pitt…, 1686).

20. Robert P. Gordon, 'The Legacy of Lowth: Robert Lowth and the Book of Isaiah in Particular', in *Biblical Hebrew, Biblical Texts: Essays in Memory of Michael P. Weitzman* (ed. Ada Rapoport-Albert and Gillian Greenberg; JSOTSup, 333; Hebrew Bible and its Versions, 2; Sheffield: Sheffield Academic Press, 2001), pp. 57-76 (58-59).

religious poetry. Michaelis' curriculum at Göttingen, unremarkable in its concentration on Old and New Testament exegesis, so-called Hebrew antiquities, Mosaic law, and comparative Semitic philology, was, however, distinguished by his conviction that the study of contemporary Arab ethnology, especially that of the Bedouin tribes, would unlock the historical mysteries of the Patriarchal narratives and the Mosaic covenant of the Pentateuch. To that end, Michaelis dreamed up a grand scheme for a scientific expedition to Egypt and Arabia to collect firsthand information about the languages, folkways, material culture, geography, and history of the modern natives. The design of his plan was communicated to Frederick V of Denmark who financed the adventure; the gifted surveyor Carsten Niebuhr alone survived to publish an account, *Beschreibung von Arabien* (1772),[21] whose drawings of the royal Achaemenid trilingual inscriptions of Persepolis would materially advance the decipherment of Akkadian.[22] Not incidentally, the elevation of contemporary Middle Eastern ethnology by Michaelis at the expense of more traditional modes of exegesis, including use of medieval Jewish commentators, expedited the ends of his conventional Lutheran anti-Semitism: the perversions of Second Temple Judaism and their rabbinic obfuscations could be circumvented by returning to the primitive nobility of the Mosaic law and study of the closest living analogues to the Patriarchs, the Bedouin sons of the desert.[23]

2. *Nineteenth- and Twentieth-Century Orientalism*

Nineteenth-century Orientalism, rooted in universalizing Enlightenment attitudes towards eastern peoples, altered radically under the impact of the European 'scramble' for colonial possessions and complex social developments

21. Carsten Niebuhr, *Beschreibung von Arabien aus eigenen Beobachtungen und in Lande selbst gesammleten Nachrichten* (Kopenhagen: N. Moeller; etc., 1772); *idem*, *Reisebeschreibung nach Arabien und andern umliegenden Ländern* (Kopenhagen: N. Moeller, 1774) (the Persepolis inscriptions appear in the second volume published in 1778). Niebuhr's publications were dictated in large part by the research objectives authorized by the Danish king at the start of the expedition, and one hundred questions assembled by Michaelis, Johann David Michaelis, *Fragen an eine Gesellschaft gelehrter Männer, die auf Befehl Ihro Majestät des Königes von Dännemark nach Arabien reisen* (Frankfurt: Johann Gottlieb Garbe, 1762). The questions are frankly driven by the concerns of a German theologian and biblical exegete.

22. Michael Harbsmeier, 'Before Decipherment: Persepolitan Hypotheses in the Late Eighteenth Century', in Gunter (ed.), *Construction of the Ancient Near East*, pp. 23-59.

23. Manuel, *The Broken Staff*, pp. 252-62. In this connection, Michaelis produced an edition and Latin translation of Abū al-Fidāʾ Ismāʿīl ibn ʿAlī's (1273–1331) travels to Egypt, and published an Arabic grammar and chrestomathy in 1781; Johann David Michaelis, *Abulfedae Descriptio Aegypti, arabice et latine: ex codice parisiensi* (Göttingen: J.C. Dieterich, 1776), *idem*, *Arabische Grammatik, nebst einer arabische Chrestomathie, und Abhandlung vom arabischen Geschmack, sonderlich in der poetischen und historischen Schreibart* (Göttingen: V. Vosziegel, 2nd edn, 1781).

within Europe itself. The 'Eastern Question', for instance, which took on a new urgency during and after the Greco-Turkish war of the 1820s, with European and American presses staunchly partisan Philhellene, had as much or more to do with Western disenchantment with monarchic government than hatred of 'Oriental despotism.' Napoleon's elaborately publicized expedition to Egypt in 1798 and the gradual publication of the monumental *Déscription de l'Egypte* set the stage for a muscular pursuit of overseas Oriental studies, one that relied on political negotiations at the ambassadorial level—and gunpowder. France under the Directory, anticipating the commercial and diplomatic need for skilled linguists, founded the secular Ecole de langues orientales vivantes in 1795 under the philologist Silvestre de Sacy (1758–1838), in whose biography one discovers a notable correlation between Orientalism as a profession and colonialism. Languages taught at the Ecole included Arabic, Persian and Turkish (1795), Armenian (1812), Hindustani (1830), Chinese (1843), Malay (1844), Javanese (1844), Japanese (1868); later would be added Russian, Siamese, Berber, Mongol, Ukrainian, Hausa, Urdu and Cambodian.[24] Jean-François Champollion's decipherment of hieroglyphic Egyptian by 1824 and the decipherment of Akkadian by Georg Friedrich Grotefend, Henry C. Rawlinson, Edward Hincks and others by the early 1850s laid the groundwork for the disciplines of Egyptology and Assyriology, opening unprecedented comparative sources for biblical studies. The triumph of the scientific method in nineteenth-century Europe and America witnessed the professionalization of Middle Eastern studies, a phenomenon that began with the 'expert amateur', the tourist and the antiquarian, and concluded with university departments for Islamic studies, Assyriology, and Egyptology. Learned societies and publications catering to the novel specialization included the Asiatic Society of Bengal (1784), *Fundgruben des Orients* (Josef von Hammer-Purgstall, 1809–18), the Paris Société asiatique, with its *Journal asiatique* in 1823, *Journal of the Asiatic Society of Bengal* (1832–), *Journal of the Royal Asiatic Society of Great Britain and Ireland* (1834–), the founding of the American Oriental Society (1842), the Deutsche Morgenländische Gesellschaft (1845), *Zeitschrift für ägyptische Sprache und Altertumskunde* (1863–), the Society of Biblical Archaeology (London, 1870), *Journal of Biblical Literature and Exegesis* (1881–), *Revue d'assyriologie et d'archéologie orientale* (1884–), *Zeitschrift für Assyriologie und vorderasiatische Archäologie* (1886–) and the Seminar für orientalische Sprachen (Berlin, 1887).

Oriental studies throughout the nineteenth century suffered from an over reliance on philological acumen as the perceived necessary and sufficient means of gaining access to Eastern cultures. Kant's student Johann Gottfried Herder (1744–1803) insisted that, to fully grasp the *Volkscharakter* and *Volksseele* of a people, it was imperative to study its *Volkslied* through the *Muttersprache*. The

24. Macfie, *Orientalism*, p. 34.

Ecole de langues orientales vivantes in Paris coupled this romantic notion with administrative pragmatism, and indeed the Ecole's founder de Sacy embodied meticulous and exacting philology at the expense of broad cultural exposure, scientific precision and positivist arrogance. European Orientalism created an understanding or representation of the Orient by classifying it through Western conceptions of race, religion, 'manners', art, worldview and other familiar category signifiers, relying for the most part on linguistics, archaeology, art history, and, towards the end of the century, physical anthropology. The Eurocentric notion that civilizations best express their unique essence in the vigor of youth resulted in Islamic studies that slighted the Ottoman East for the age of Muḥammad and biblical historiography that tended to subordinate the post-Exilic era to the wanderings of Abraham and the Exodus, a political strategy that addressed The Eastern and The Jewish Questions by a preoccupation with past ages.

The investment of European biblical specialists in original research in Islamic history and culture, apart from philological and manuscript studies, was never very pronounced, a casualty of a heavily theological curriculum, conventional Islamophobia, and the quickening pace of professional specialization, with Julius Wellhausen (1844–1918) and William Robertson Smith (1846–94) constituting illustrious exceptions. Within the annals of Assyriology, I cannot come up with the name of a single nineteenth-century scholar who generated sustained research in both the Pre-Islamic and Islamic Near East. Most could read Arabic with varying degrees of fluency, one can cite the occasional publication and doctoral dissertation, but the 'bridge' discipline of choice was the Bible.[25]

Nineteenth-century Europeans and Americans entertained paradoxical attitudes towards the Orient. On one hand, Romantic fascination with exoticism passionately embraced the Middle East out of sheer novelty and as a vehicle to explore fault-lines within European society. Literature like Thomas Moore's *Lalla Rookh*, Byron's *Eastern Tales* and Robert Southey's *Curse of Kehama* portrayed failed revolutions in the imagined Orient. French Orientalist paintings and later counterparts among British artists flooded European salons with dazzling landscapes, architecture and societies heretofore unknown as visual stimuli, both reinforcing and shattering Western stereotypes. On the other hand, growing global European technological and economic dominance gave rise to a chauvinist contempt for Islam and Middle Easterners new in intensity. The Islamic scholar Maxime Rodinson captures this artistic evocation of the East:

> a riot of colour; sumptuousness and savage ferocity; harems and seraglios; heads chopped off and women thrown in sacks into the Bosphorus; feluccas and brigantines flying the Crescent banner; roundness of azure domes and soaring whiteness of min-

25. A similar situation prevails in American research universities today, with Near Eastern Languages and Civilizations or Middle Eastern Studies departments staffed by various Islamic and ancient Near Eastern specialists who are rarely the same individual.

> arets; viziers, odalisques, and eunuchs; cooling springs beneath the palms; *giaours* with their throats slit; captive women subjected to the victor's ravenous lust. Such highly coloured pictures provide inexpensive satisfaction to the deeper instincts, the murky sensualism, the unconscious masochism and sadism of the peaceful Western bourgeoisie, as Heine had already discovered. Even when Westerners actually went to the East, this was the image they sought out, ruthlessly selecting what they saw and ignoring what did not fit in with their preconceived picture.[26]

The Enlightenment idealization of Greek antiquity, as spearheaded by the theories of J.J. Winckelmann and epitomized in the artistic productions of Goethe, served to create a heightened sense of cultural divide of Occident versus Orient, *Abendland* versus *Morgenland*. The initial openness to the possibilities raised by Enlightenment ideals of human universality—that Asiatic peoples might be human after all—grew tempered as Herder's romantic notion of *Volksindividualität* collided with the racial and ultimately biological conceptions of *ethnos* and nationhood of nineteenth-century manufacture. Jacob Burckhardt rejected the quest for universal history of his teacher, Leopold von Ranke, in favor of the parochial historical factors that led to the creation of the West, and in so doing created a vision of the Orient that was inherently inimical to the Greek way of life. As Frahm notes, Burckhardt carried the battle into the realm of ancient Near Eastern aesthetics, deriding the recently recovered Neo-Assyrian art and architecture as 'utterly uncouth' and 'slavish.'

Nationalism, the irresistible dynamo of the nineteenth century, impelled the French and English governments in the 1840s to subsidize veritable treasure hunts at the sites of the Neo-Assyrian capitals to acquire monumental artifacts for triumphal display in the Louvre and British Museum. The extent to which early Assyriology served as a pawn on the gaming board of European colonial adventure has been much written about, as has its role in biblical apologetics.[27]

26. Rodinson, 'Western Studies of Islam', p. 48.

27. Frederick N. Bohrer, 'A New Antiquity: The English Reception of Assyria' (PhD dissertation, The University of Chicago, 1989); Mogens Trolle Larsen, 'Seeing Mesopotamia', in Gunter (ed.), *Construction of the Ancient Near East*, pp. 107-32; Giovanni Bergamini, '"Spoliis Orientis onustus": Paul-Emile Botta et la découverte de la civilisation assyrienne', in *De Khorsabad à Paris: La découverte des Assyriens* (ed. Elisabeth Fontan; trans. Florence Cadouot; Louvre, Département des Antiquités orientales: Notes et documents des Musées de France, 26; Paris: Réunion des Musées nationaux, 1994), pp. 68-85; M.T. Larsen, *The Conquest of Assyria: Excavations in an Antique Land 1840–1860* (London and New York: Routledge, 1996); Magnus Thorkell Bernhardsson, 'Reclaiming a Plundered Past: Archaeology and Nationalism in Modern Iraq, 1808–1941' (PhD dissertation, Yale University, 1999), pp. 69-95; Mark W. Chavalas, 'Assyriology and Biblical Studies: A Century of Tension', in *Mesopotamia and the Bible: Comparative Explorations* (ed. Mark W. Chavalas and K. Lawson Younger, Jr; Grand Rapids: Baker Academic, 2002), pp. 21-67; S.W. Holloway, 'The Quest for Sargon, Pul, and Tiglath-Pileser in the Nineteenth Century', in Chavalas and Younger (eds.), *Mesopotamia and the Bible*, pp. 68-87; F.N. Bohrer, *Orientalism and Visual Culture: Imagining Mesopotamia in Nineteenth-Century Europe* (Cambridge and New York: Cambridge University Press, 2003), pp. 66-223.

The spectacular successes of these exploits accelerated the pace of discoveries throughout the region, though the first excavation in Palestine to emphasize pottery chronology, that of W.M. Flinders Petrie at Tell el-Heṣi, would not occur until 1890. Every year from 1871 to 1914, European empires would expropriate territories the size of France in the Middle East and other sectors of the globe, with England occupying Egypt in 1882 and France Tunisia in 1881. Although Germany under Bismarck did not seek Middle Eastern colonies ('the Eastern Question is not worth the bones of a single Pomeranian musketeer'), a combination of nationalistic jealously over the successes of France and England and a thirst on the part of the German public for biblical confirmation led to the founding of the Deutsche Orient-Gesellschaft in 1898 and the most intensive program of archaeological exploration on the part of any European power until the outbreak of World War I, most notably the work of Koldewey at Babylon (1899–1917) and Andrae at Assur (1903–1914).[28] The masterminding of the 'jihad made in Germany' by Max von Oppenheim, Middle Eastern archaeologist, diplomat and head of the Oriental News Department in the Foreign Office, as a means of inciting Muslim revolt against European colonies at the beginning of World War I, a plan materially aided by such distinguished Orientalists as Carl Heinrich Becker, Martin Hartmann, and Ernst Jäckh, is perhaps the most extreme example of the dark marriage between Near Eastern Orientalism and geopolitics,[29] though the military espionage of the early Palestine Exploration Fund (1865–) also rates special mention.[30]

28. The Deutsche Orient-Gesellschaft counted among its founders the bankers von Siemens, Rothschild and Delbrück and the industrialists Krupp, Rathenau and Borsig. Kaiser Wilhelm II became its enthusiastic supporter and financial backer, and reportedly never missed any of its lectures. The Kaiser from the outset craved artifacts in the Berlin museum that would outshine those of the Louvre and British Museum, hence the acquisition and display of the Ishtar Gate of Babylon and the façade from Mshatta. Johannes Renger, 'Die Geschichte der Altorientalistik und der vorderasiatischen Archäologie in Berlin von 1875 bis 1945', in *Berlin und die Antike: Architektur, Kunstgewerbe, Malerei, Skulptur, Theater und Wissenschaft vom 16. Jahrhundert bis heute* (Aufsätze) (ed. Willmuth Arenhövel and Christa Schreiber; Berlin: Deutsches Archäologisches Institut, 1979), pp. 151-92 (158-91); Stefan R. Hauser, 'German Research on the Ancient Near East and its Relation to Political and Economic Interests from *Kaiserreich* to World War II', *Princeton Papers, Interdisciplinary Journal of Middle Eastern Studies* 10–11 (2001), pp. 155-80 (160-61); *idem*, 'History, Races, and Orientalism: Eduard Meyer, the Organization of Oriental Research, and Ernst Herzfeld's Intellectual Heritage', in *Ernst Herzfeld and the Development of Near Eastern Studies, 1900–1950* (ed. Ann Clyburn Gunter and Stefan R. Hauser; Leiden: Brill, 2005), pp. 505-59 (514-18).

29. Wolfgang G. Schwanitz, 'The German Middle Eastern Policy, 1871–1945', *Princeton Papers, Interdisciplinary Journal of Middle Eastern Studies* 10–11 (2001), pp. 1-23 (6-9).

30. Neil Asher Silberman, *Digging for God and Country: Exploration, Archaeology, and the Secret Struggle for the Holy Land, 1799–1917* (New York: Knopf, 1982), pp. 86-127, 147-70; John James Moscrop, *Measuring Jerusalem: The Palestine Exploration Fund and British Interests in the Holy Land* (London and New York: Leicester University Press, 2000).

Reid's chapter in this volume perceptively explores the 'reception' of Egyptology by the Egyptians, a perspective rarely addressed by those interested in the history of Oriental studies.[31] During the reign of Khedive Ismail (1863–79), Rifāʿah Rāfiʿ al-Ṭahṭāwī (1801–73), head of the Egyptian translation bureau and member of an advisory board on state education, wrote Arabic textbooks, one of which was *Anwar tawfiq al-jalil fi akhbar Misr wa-tawthiq Bani Ismail* (Glorious light on the story of Egypt and authentication of the sons of Ishmael, 1868), a history of Egypt spanning the pharaonic, Greco-Roman and Byzantine eras up to the Islamic conquest. The splendor of Egypt under the Pharaohs carried over into later periods in its renown for learning and philosophy. As a hub of Islamic culture, Egypt had delivered Jerusalem from the Crusaders and, more recently, had successfully repulsed the French invaders. Al-Ṭahṭāwī systematically worked through the thirty dynasties of Manetho, identifying the biblical Noah's grandson Misrayim with the mythical founding pharaoh Menes, and identified the pharaoh of the Exodus with Merneptah of the nineteenth dynasty. Citing inscriptional evidence from Saqqara, al-Ṭahṭāwī matched the pharaonic religion with the Sabians of the Qurʾān, a strategy that may have made it easier for modern Egyptian Muslims and Copts to identify with the ancient pharaonic heritage. The *Anwar* succeeded in placing an up-to-date survey of ancient Egyptian history at the disposal of Arabic readers.

In 1869, Khedive Ismail and his Minister of Education Ali Mubarak (1823/4–93) hired the German Egyptologist Heinrich Brugsch (1827–94) to create a 'School of the Ancient Language' (Madrasat al-Lisan al-Qadim) or School of Egyptology to prepare native Egyptians for leadership roles in the Egyptian Museum and Antiquities Service. The school shut down in 1874, probably as a result of the machinations of Auguste Mariette (1821–81), French director of the Egyptian Antiquities Service, who, fearing the loss of his monopoly on excavations, refused to permit Brugsch's students access to Egyptian monuments in order to copy inscriptions.

From 1867 to 1914, all Egyptian postal stamps bore images of pyramids and the Sphinx, a move that 'hammered home the idea of these as national symbols.' Reid notes that a conservative landowner in 1862 wrote his son a manual of advice in Arabic that included a table of Egyptian rulers that led all the way back to the Pharaohs. The Arab renaissance *(al-nahda al-ʿarabiyah)* under Khedive Ismail sought to integrate the pharaonic heritage into modern Egyptian nation-building, a strategy that both utilized a discourse about history shared by Europeans and one that exploited a set of symbols which fostered social and political distance.

Extended allusions to pharaonic Egypt and the kings of ancient Assyria, Babylonia and Persia in the Old Testament stoked the intense European fascination with the study of the ancient Near East. Budge in his eccentric history of Assyriology

31. Exceptionally, Bernhardsson, 'Reclaiming a Plundered Past'.

takes notice of the public popularity of the findings from ancient Mesopotamia whenever a Bible connection cropped up. 'In the decipherment pure and simple, and in the discussions by experts of philological *minutiae*, they [the public] took no interest; but when the translations of the Assyrian monuments were able to tell them facts about Bible personages, or supply information which would supplement the Bible narrative, Assyriology assumed a vital importance in their eyes.'[32] All of the earliest British Assyriologists utilized the Bible as a primary historical referencing tool, a practice that led to difficulties with the likes of King Pul, who refused to materialize in the monuments on schedule.[33]

> ...George Smith ...devoured the contents of every book and paper on any and every branch of the new science that he could lay his hands on; and the mainspring of his eagerness to study it was his fervent desire to know more about the historical books of the Old Testament...He then began to search for texts relating to the kings of Assyria mentioned in the Bible, and he copied all he found. He spent several years in copying and translating the Annals of Ashurbanipal, whose name is mentioned once under the form of 'Asnapper' in the Bible (Ezra iv. 10), because they contained new and authentic information about a king of whom Biblical scholars knew very little.[34]

The lucrative Victorian market for heavily illustrated Protestant Bibles in England and especially America bespoke a growing conception of the trustworthiness of the Bible as a travel guide to the ancient (and modern) Oriental world. Reading the Bible in isolation no longer satisfied: information about the Holy Land and surrounding Bible lands became the necessary picklock to open hidden doors to scriptural truth.

Sir Richard Westmacott, Sr, a Royal Academician sculptor, powerfully objected to the aesthetic of the newly recovered Assyrian sculptural remains, complaining that when spectators would come to view them at the British Museum they 'would look at the Nineveh Marbles and be thinking of their Bible.'[35] The flamboyant prophetic narratives in the Bible that describe the utter desolation of Nineveh and Babylon controlled Middle Eastern travelogues and biblical commentaries in similar fashion, in that the contrast between European prosperity with the decay that seemed to typify Mesopotamia, especially the sites of the former capital cities, 'proved' the prophecies fulfilled. For example, Alexander Keith's *Evidence of the Truth of the Christian Religion* sought the rationalist's high-ground in the apologetic contest by matching the contemporary plight of the Jews and the ruinous fabric of the Middle East with the

32. E.A. Wallis Budge, *The Rise and Progress of Assyriology* (London: Martin Hopkinson, 1925), p. 266.

33. Holloway, 'Quest for Sargon, Pul, and Tiglath-Pileser'.

34. Budge, *Rise and Progress*, p. 267.

35. Quoted in Bohrer, *Orientalism and Visual Culture*, p. 124.

prophecies of the Old and New Testaments.[36] While such arguments were nothing new, Keith, exercised by the perceived assaults on the faith by David Hume, Voltaire, and especially the recently deceased Constantin-François Volney, marshaled his proof-texts chiefly from modern travelers' tales, culling whatever best matched his projections of debased, incorrigible humanity and blasted urban landscapes. An anonymous reviewer of the 1835 Harper edition was particularly smitten with Keith's treatment of Babylon:

> Let any one follow Mr. Keith through a description of ancient Babylon, as drawn by the pens of Herodotus or Diodorus Siculus, and embodied in his work. Let him then listen to the dooms of Babylon, uttered by Isaiah, Jeremiah, and Daniel, when the proud city was in its glory, and when its frowning battlements 'appeared rather like the bulwarks of nature than the workmanship of art.' Then let him go with Porter, Rich, Mignan, or Buckingham, and (through the ample quotations from their travels, found in the book before us) visit fallen Babylon. The votary of romance himself could not find, even in the pages of [Sir Walter] Scott, a theme of more thrilling interest.[37]

When the flow of contact was reversed, and ancient Mesopotamian artifacts began to percolate through Europe in the guise of museum specimens and woodcuts, the response took on the historical complexity of the societies themselves. Bohrer in his essay contrasts the reception of ancient Assyria as exoticism in nineteenth-century England and France, noting that the ways the initial discoveries were disseminated in the two rival countries greatly influenced the subsequent popularity of the Assyrian art. Massive government subvention in France for publication of the excavations modeled along the lines of the nine volumes of *Déscription de l'Egypte* (1809–28) resulted in a magnificent work, the *Monument de Ninive*, that none but the wealthiest could afford, effectively stifling the popular circulation of images of Assyrian artwork. After the fall of Louis-Phillipe's administration and the expiration of the Second Republic, the Second Empire sought to distance itself from the high-profile excavations in Mesopotamia, further constraining the dissemination of images in French soci-

36. *Evidence of the Truth of the Christian Religion, Derived from the Literal Fulfillment of Prophecy* (1823), reaching its thirty-fifth reprint by 1848, was republished as late as 1984. Publication history is based on a WorldCat search (9/23/04). According to John Davis, *The Landscape of Belief: Encountering the Holy Land in Nineteenth-Century American Art and Culture* (The Princeton Series in Nineteenth-Century Art, Culture, and Society; Princeton: Princeton University Press, 1996), p. 76, the 1844 Edinburgh edition became the 'first Bible-affirming book with illustrations [of the Holy Land] from photographs.' For the curious figure of Alexander Keith, see Lionel Alexander Ritchie, 'Keith, Alexander (1792–1880)', in *Oxford Dictionary of National Biography: From the Earliest Times to the Year 2000* (60 vols.; ed. H.C.G. Matthew and Brian Harrison; Oxford and New York: Oxford University Press, 2004), XXXI, p. 56.

37. Anonymous, 'Review of A. Keith, *Evidence of the Truth of the Christian Religion* (New York: J. & J. Harper, 1835)', *The Methodist Magazine and Quarterly Review* 21 (1839), pp. 215-22 (217).

ety. 'In France, then, Assyrian archaeology was both beneficiary and victim of its close political ties.'

In Great Britain, plans for an elaborate publication of A.H. Layard's first campaign in Mesopotamia by the sponsoring agency, the British Museum, came to naught. Instead, Layard had the good fortune of obtaining the services of John Murray III's formidable publication industry, which spent less than £7 for editing Layard's travelogue and more than £300 for engraving and printing services, resulting in the archaeological best-seller of the nineteenth century, *Nineveh and its Remains* (1849). Despite the opposition of Westmacott and others who compared the Assyrian art unfavorably against the Greek canon, Layard, with the help of the influential *Art-Journal* and other agencies, succeeded in 'aestheticizing' the British Museum acquisitions, a crucial step in their popularization. Another factor, not appreciably present in France, was the degree to which the largely Protestant British public thrilled to the material because of its connection with the Bible, precisely what Westmacott had feared. 'The centralized pattern through which Assyrian artifacts were promulgated in France' would continue to limit their impact, as witnessed in art posters and paintings by French artists of Mesopotamian subjects that demonstrate little trace of inspiration from the sculpture housed in the Louvre. In England, by contrast, Victorian artists following the lucrative trend of historical realism painted canvasses that closely imitated numerous compositional elements of the Assyrian reliefs in the British Museum in their desire to win commissions through graphic verisimilitude.

The rapidity with which enterprising publishers of illustrated Bibles seized on the commercial benefits of including recognizable images from Assyria is astonishing. In 1818, one year after the first Babylonian bricks with cuneiform inscriptions were publicly exhibited in America, a Vermont publisher, John C. Holbrook, reissued his illustrated family Bible with a novel modification of its Tower of Babel woodcut—the inclusion of two cuneiform brick inscriptions, replete with exact details of the provenance and size of the objects.[38] The first Bible to be printed in the United States with reproductions of British Museum Assyrian artwork was a 1851 New York edition originally published three years earlier in London.[39] The preface, written by the British Christian apologist Ingram Cobbin in August 1847, captures the dynamic spirit of the ongoing revolution in graphic arts reception and historical consciousness:

38. See S.W. Holloway, 'Austin's Asiatic Antiquities: The First Cuneiform Inscriptions Published in America' [51st Rencontre assyriologique internationale conference volume, forthcoming].

39. *The Holy Bible: Containing the Old and New Testaments according to the Authorized Version with the Marginal References and the Usual Various Readings, also Notes, Reflections, Questions, Improved Readings, Improved Divisions of Chapters, the Chronological Order, Metrical Portions Distinguished, and Various Other Advantages, without Disturbing the Usual Order of the Books, Verses, and Chapters/by The Rev. Ingram Cobbin, M.A.; illustrated with Numerous Descriptive Engravings* (New York: Samuel Hueston, 1851).

> Pictorial Illustrations are now in very general use, and the introduction of real subjects has nearly superceded those fanciful productions which pleased the eye without informing the mind, and which, how much soever they might have displayed the talents of the artist, rendered no aid to the reader, and often served to impress his mind with notions entirely false respecting Oriental manners and customs.

By 1861, over four million copies of the Bible would be published in Great Britain alone; sumptuously illustrated family Bibles tapped into this burgeoning market. In the early 1860s, the Dalziel Brothers, the most celebrated wood-engraving firm in Victorian England, commissioned a number of Royal Academicians to produce an ambitious series of Bible illustrations. In '*Dalziels' Bible Gallery* (1881): Assyria and the Biblical Illustration in Nineteenth-Century Britain', Esposito explores sources of inspiration behind a series of woodcuts that capitalize on the popularity of the British Museum's sculptural reliefs from ancient Assyria. That this popularity was fuelled by motives other than slavish historicism is borne out, for example, by Edward Frederick Brewtnall's *Esther Denouncing Haman*, in which an imaginary Persian court exploits visual signifiers from the palace of Assurbanipal, and not Achaemenid Persepolis, this despite the fact that the British Museum owned authentic Persian reliefs, and excellent drawings of Achaemenid art had been available for over half a century. Handy in his essay provides additional examples of archaeological referencing in the portraiture of biblical King Josiah, in which Neo-Assyrian chariots and royal regalia provide models for illustrating the Judahite king. Other nineteenth-century artistic evocations of Palestine sought to conjure up a vista free of encroaching modern inhabitants that might deflect the viewer from inhabiting a 'biblical' landscape. In *Jerusalem and the Valley of Jehoshaphat from the Hill of Evil Counsel*, an 1854 painting by Pre-Raphaelite English artist Thomas Seddon, the artist has created a topographical narrative devoid of distracting contemporary complications. In the words of Burke Long, 'Seddon transformed Ottoman Jerusalem into a suggestively effulgent space rescued from the backwater inconsequence, even neglect, of modernity.'

An urgency to preserve the past in the face of the presumed indifference of the modern Middle Easterners or the relentless progress of the West filters through many of the 'job descriptions' penned by Orientalists of the era. The Egyptologist Samuel Birch, inaugural president of the Society of Biblical Archaeology, enjoined its members 'to collect from the fast-perishing monuments of the Semitic and cognate races illustrations of their history and peculiarities; to investigate and systematize the antiquities of the ancient and mighty empires and primeval peoples, whose records are centered around the venerable pages of the Bible.'[40] One recipe to staunch this river of destruction and to

40. Cited in Robert William Rogers, *A History of Babylonia and Assyria* (2 vols.; New York: Eaton Mains, Cincinnati: Jennings & Pye, 1900), I, p. 245.

'enter into full communion with the genius of the sacred penmen' was the publication of ancient Near Eastern compendia in translation. The first such in the English language, *Records of the Past: Being English Translations of the Assyrian and Egyptian Monuments*, edited by Birch between 1872–81, initiated a string of European and American publications aimed primarily at the biblical studies market.[41] In his contribution to this volume, Younger analyzes patterns of production and the scope of these fascinating tools for biblical research. It is well to point out that the first edition of *Records of the Past* appeared during the decade that several monumental Victorian translation projects either went to press or commenced research, including the Revised Version of the Bible (1880), and the series The Sacred Books of the East (50 vols., 1879–1910), both Oxford University Press productions.[42] The Orientalist F. Max Müller, editor of The Sacred Books of the East, convinced the press that the risky venture would garner international prestige if not a handsome return on the investment, which it did. The Sacred Books of the East, like the various compendia of ancient Near Eastern texts, legitimated both the science of Orientalism under British auspices (the second Congress of Orientalists would take place in 1874 in London under the leadership of Samuel Birch, a swipe in the eye of the French), through the imprimatur of a respected publisher, and the comparative-literature method as an academic discipline whose time had arrived. The editorship of such compendia was—and is—both lucrative and prestigious. The Assyriologist Archibald Henry Sayce, a university colleague of Müller, wrote a flattering and disingenuous review of the first volume in the series (Müller's translation of the Upanishads); in 1888–92 Sayce would himself oversee the second heavily revised edition of *Records of the Past*.[43]

Through most of the nineteenth century, in the words of Frahm, 'Assyriology remained the *ancilla theologiae*..., a quarry for material that could be used to fill up holes in the venerated house of the Bible. But around 1900, the servant was eventually fed up with her role and ready to overthrow her mistress'.[44]

41. The first such anthology of translations of Egyptian and Akkadian texts that I am aware of in any modern language is J.P. Guillaume Pauthier, *Hymnes sanscrits, persans, égyptiens, assyriens et chinois; Chi-king; ou, Livre des vers* (Bibliothèque orientale: publiée sous la direction d'un comité scientifique international: chefs d'oeuvre littéraires de l'Inde, de la Perse, de l'Egypte et de la Chine, 2; Paris: Maisonneuve, 1872); 'Assyrie: Chantes et invocations', pp. 209-21, was translated by Jules Oppert.

42. In this connection one thinks of the editorial output of the indefatigable Victorians Sir George Grove, *A Dictionary of Music and Musicians*, Macmillan, 1878–89; William Smith, *Dictionary of the Bible*, 1868–70, *idem*, *Dictionary of Christian Antiquities*, 1876–80, *idem*, *Dictionary of Christian Biography*, 1877–87, and, jointly, *An Atlas of Ancient Geography, Biblical and Classical*, 1874, all John Murray publications.

43. Norman R. Girardot, 'Max Müller's Sacred Books and the Nineteenth-Century Production of the Comparative Science of Religions', *HR* 41 (2002), pp. 213-50 (n. 31).

44. A lecture by the Assyriologist Zimmern comes to mind: Heinrich Zimmern, *Die Assyriol-*

In the presence of the Deutsche Orient-Gesellschaft and Kaiser Wilhelm II, the Assyriologist Friedrich Delitzsch delivered a series of lectures between 1902 and 1904 in which he portrayed ancient Mesopotamia as the cultural fountainhead of the ancient Near East, playing down the innovations of other civilizations (for example, Abraham mastered his Ur-monotheism in Babylonia from Babylonian priests), while playing up the extent to which Mesopotamian achievements were dependent on non-Semitic inspiration (Sumerian and Aryan). Much of this program had been pioneered by the so-called Pan-Babylonians—Hugo Winckler, Peter Jensen, and others—who promulgated the extreme argument that all world mythologies could be traced back to their pristine origin in Babylonian astral religion, *ca.* 3000 BCE. Sweeping neo-romantic diffusionist models were in vogue at the time, and very few Assyriologists controlled the arcane sources cited by the Pan-Babylonians, so it was difficult to refute their claims persuasively. Both the Pan-Babylonians and Delitzsch played a cruel but popular hand of anti-Semitism, capitalizing on widely-accepted notions that Semites were incapable of cultural innovation, an iteration of the East-as-stagnant-and-unprogressive topos. Delitzsch's Babel–Bibel lectures garnered enormous publicity—remarkably, he succeeded in capturing something of the urgency of the secularization challenge for mainstream Protestantism through the dry bones of Assyriology—but the Kaiser withdrew his support when Delitzsch denied the inspiration of the Old Testament. The fallout from the refutation of Pan-Babylonism and the Babel–Bibel lectures dealt Assyriology—as a profession—an immense blow to its prestige, and made it nearly impossible to get dissertation committees to sign on to topics that dealt substantively with comparative religions for many decades.[45]

ogie als Hülfswissenschaft für das Studium des Alten Testaments und des Klassischen Altertums: Antritts-Vorlesung, gehalten in der Aula der Königl. Albertus-Universität zu Königsberg i. Pr. am 1. November 1889 (Königsberg i. Pr.: W. Koch, 1889).

45. On Pan-Babylonism and the Babel–Bibel Streit, see Klaus Johanning, *Der Bibel–Babel–Streit: Eine forschungsgeschichtliche Studie* (Europäische Hochschulschriften, Reihe 23, Theologie, 343; Frankfurt am Main: Peter Lang, 1988); M.T. Larsen, 'Orientalism and the Ancient Near East', in *The Humanities between Art and Science: Intellectual Developments, 1880–1914* (ed. Michael Harbsmeier and Mogens Trolle Larsen; Copenhagen: Akademisk Forlag, 1989), pp. 181-202; Reinhard G. Lehmann, *Friedrich Delitzsch und der Babel–Bibel–Streit* (OBO, 133; Freiburg, Schweiz: Universitätsverlag/Göttingen: Vandenhoeck & Ruprecht, 1994); M.T. Larsen, 'The "Babel/Bible" Controversy and Its Aftermath', in *CANE*, I, pp. 95-106; Eckart Frahm, 'Images of Ashurbanipal in Later Tradition', in *Hayim and Miriam Tadmor Festschrift Volume* (ed. Israel Eph'al, Amnon Ben-Tor, Peter Machinist; Eretz Israel, 27; Jerusalem: Israel Exploration Society, 2003), pp. 37*-48*. Among the Pan-Babylonians, the writings of Winckler in particular garnered broad acceptance among contemporary Orientalists. C.H. Becker, founder of *Der Islam* and Prussian Minister of Education, claimed that Wellhausen's *Das arabische Reich und sein Sturz* modeled for him the historian, Ignác Goldziher his Islamic researches, and Winckler's book *Arabisch, Semitisch, Orientalisch: Kulturgeschichtlich-mythologische Untersuchung* (Berlin: W. Peiser, 1901) inspired him almost to the point of reverence; Helmut Ritter, 'Carl Heinrich Becker als Orientalist', *Der Islam* 24 (1937), pp. 175-85 (177-78).

At the same time that Delitzsch strove to prove the cultural aridity of ancient Israel, fervent literary activity in the Hebrew Revival movement (1900–1930) situated Eretz Israel in the mysterious, magical East. Ideal national futures were translated into pseudo-biblical stories that explored the desert as a paradoxical scene of moral tribulation and the creation of the Jewish Bedouin. Orientalist stereotypes functioned both as a means of critiquing Zionist political aspirations as well as pegging the Arabs as fixtures of the backwards East. The Bible itself was Orientalized by linking Pentateuchal narratives to the Palestine of the late Ottoman Empire and early Zionism in Jewish fears and fantasies about an eastern homeland.[46]

In his 1926 inaugural lecture at Leipzig, the great Assyriologist Benno Landsberger lays out a terse manifesto for the study of the ancient Near East, arguing that, while it is humanly necessary to work backwards from analogous processes of law, economics and so forth, unlocking the unique qualities of the civilization itself must always be the goal—Assyriology is certainly not the *Hülfswissenschaft* of the Bible! While his willingness to seek insight from specialists outside the narrow confines of Assyriology was enlightened for the time, the evolutionary schema against which he ordered Mesopotamian history and his reliance on *Sprachgeist* as the key to the *Eigenbegrifflichkeit* or 'conceptual autonomy' rooted his thinking squarely in the German intellectual tradition. In common with early nineteenth-century Orientalism, 'civilizations' for Landsberger were anatomically manifest chiefly through language, and by the painstaking lexicographic decipherment of the genius of Akkadian—as opposed to Hebrew, Arabic or Sumerian—the mind or *Geist* of the ancient Akkadian-speakers could be rendered accessible to modern science. 'Once we have understood the linguistic structure we have obtained immediate access to the structure of the people's mind as well and with it one of the most important determinants of civilization, in so far as it is a creation of the mind. The important insight of Wilhelm von Humboldt is the more easily applied the more alien the people in question is to us.'[47]

The tragically unfinished work by Omar Carena attempted to analyze ancient Near Eastern historiography systematically, situating the work of the individual historians within their social and political milieu; his scattered remarks on 'Indo Germanic mania' during the period of National Socialism are of a preliminary nature but insightful.[48] During the Weimar and National Socialism years in Ger-

46. Yaron Peleg, *Orientalism and the Hebrew Imagination* (Ithaca, NY: Cornell University Press, 2005), pp. 40-99.

47. Benno Landsberger, *The Conceptual Autonomy of the Babylonian World* (trans. Thorkild Jacobsen, Benjamin R. Foster and H. von Siebenthal; Monographs on the Ancient Near East, 1/4; Malibu, CA: Undena, 1976), p. 67 (p. 365 in the German original).

48. Omar Carena, *History of the Near Eastern Historiography and Its Problems: 1852–1985*. Part 1: *1852–1945* (trans. E. Schmitz and L. Tosco; AOAT, 218/1; Kevelaer: Verlag Butzon & Bercker/Neukirchen–Vluyn: Neukirchener Verlag, 1989), pp. 122-33.

many, study of the ancient Near East at the university level was largely limited to art history and philology. Following the pre-war spate of public enthusiasm for fieldwork and the Babel–Bibel Streit, ancient Near Eastern studies fought a losing battle against German prehistory and the classics. Nazi ideology brought to the fore Aryan studies, with the concomitant denigration of 'alien, and therefore not comprehensible races' (Helmut Berve, 1935), which included the Semitic speaking peoples of the ancient Near East. Hittitology, Iranian and Hurrian studies benefited, since they were perceived as racially Aryan in nature. On top of the conventional Orientalism that minimized the accomplishments of Middle Easterners at the expense of the progressive West, Nazi historians concocted pseudo-scientific *völkisch* and *rassisch* definitions of culture.[49] In this volume Frahm traces the baldly racist and political ideologies that prompted historians even before the decipherment of Akkadian to ascribe the military successes of the Semitic Assyrians to Aryan influence. Eduard Meyer and his disciple Ernst Herzfeld denied Babylonian culture any autonomous capacity for creativity in the graphic arts—all of their accomplishments stem from their Sumerian cultural forbearers as well as contact with other non-Semitic races, a position that led Herzfeld to misdate the Tell Halaf sculpture by almost two thousand years.[50] The Nazi ideologue Fritz Taeger disposes of the scandal of the Semitic Neo-Assyrian and Neo-Babylonian empires in his general history of the ancient world by ignoring it completely. Unfortunately, anti-Semitism, specifically Jew-hatred, has dogged modern ancient Near Eastern historiography from its inception, whether biblical or Mesopotamian; Pan-Babylonism was only the most visible manifestation of this virulent disease.[51]

Foster's contribution to this volume chronicles the rise of Assyriology in the United States, 'narrowly defined as a research discipline.' Initial American interest in ancient Mesopotamia and its remains unquestionably stemmed from a profound cultural adoption of the Bible. Travelogues by American missionaries caught up in Layard's infectious excitement at the Assyrian capital cities and a growing trickle of authentic pre-Islamic Mesopotamian artifacts ultimately found their *raison d'être* in America's engagement with biblical narratives. Exposure to the German educational system transformed American institutions of higher learning in the late nineteenth century. By the 1870s or early 1880s, the scepter of Assyriological studies had passed into German hands, and from

49. Renger, 'Geschichte der Altorientalistik', pp. 191-92; Ludmila Hanisch and Hanne Schönig, 'Ausgegrenzte Kompetenz: Porträts vertriebener Orientalisten und Orientalistinnen 1933–1945', *Orientwissenschaftliche Hefte* 1 (2001), pp. 15-141; Hauser, 'German Research on the Ancient Near East', pp. 165-70; Berve is quoted by Hauser on p. 166.

50. Hauser, 'History, Races, and Orientalism', pp. 551-54.

51. On anti-Semitism in early assyriological studies, see Jerrold S. Cooper, 'Posing the Sumerian Question: Race and Scholarship in the Early History of Assyriology', *AuOr* 9 (1991), pp. 47-66, and *idem*, 'Sumerian and Aryan: Racial Theory, Academic Politics and Parisian Assyriology', *RevHistRel* 210 (1993), pp. 169-205.

that point until American research institutions created their own enclave of professional Assyriologists, the high road to assyriological competence lay through study abroad with Eberhard Schrader or Friedrich Delitzsch. The accession of post-Civil War wealth, coupled with a growing spirit of educational philanthropy and a restructuring of university curriculum to incorporate Oriental languages, led to the Wolfe Expedition and departments of Semitic languages and literatures. Flamboyant Orientalists like William Ward Hayes and Edgar James Banks maintained the visibility of Mesopotamian exploration in the fickle public eye even as they sometimes alienated their tenured colleagues. Most of the early PhDs in Assyriology granted to American students went to Protestant ministers or products of seminary training, a fact bespeaking the continuing close association between interest in matters assyriological and the Bible. The first American PhD in Semitic studies was awarded to Cyrus Adler, having written a dissertation on Assurbanipal under Paul Haupt. Adler was a Jew, and historical Semitic studies opened doors to Jewish scholars in America even as the successful candidates had to contend with hiring quotas and Old World-style anti-Semitism.

Foster, who has published a number of entries on American academics in the Oxford *American National Biography*, has included extensive biographies of three American women Assyriologists. Mary Williams Montgomery (d. 1955), probably the first woman in the world to be awarded a PhD in Assyriology, defended her dissertation on Old Babylonian letters in German at Berlin under Friedrich Delitzsch. Her career seems to have been upstaged by that of her husband, Gutzon Borglum, the flamboyant sculptor of Mount Rushmore. Mary Inda Hussey (1876–1952) studied at Berlin and Leipzig but received her doctorate from Bryn Mawr College in 1906. She published excellent textual editions of cuneiform texts in the Harvard Semitic Museum, and was the first woman appointed annual professor at the American Institute for Oriental Research in Jerusalem during her long teaching career at Mount Holyoke College (1913–41). Ettalene Mears Grice (1887–1927) completed her PhD under A.T. Clay at Yale University in 1917, working as his research assistant and supporting herself through a string of post-doctorate positions. Clay put her to work on a Sumerian syllabary and dictionary project that no single individual could humanly expect to finish. Following Clay's death in 1925, she was appointed to assistant professor and acting curator of the Babylonian Collection for a year, with no real chance of becoming a full professor. As Foster observed, it was possible for women become professionally active in Assyriology in early twentieth-century America, but they could not hope to compete with the white (mostly Protestant) male network for tenured positions; in a word, they were casualties of academic sexism.

In the final section of her essay, Asher-Greve examines sexism within the assyriological guild, especially those engaged in fieldwork in Iraq. With few exceptions, women have not led archaeological expeditions in Mesopotamia.

This is in part a function of the vicious circle of academic lack of preferment (since women are rarely granted leadership opportunities by seasoned excavators, they cannot compete with colleagues who *have* such training), in part a function of crude sexism that encompasses spouses as well as potential female expedition leaders. The camp-tales Asher-Greve has unearthed of Koldewey questioning Andrae's scholarly commitment (he committed the fatal indiscretion of marriage) or Katharine Woolley's negative conduct rating by Max Mallowan bespeak attitudes towards gender-difference endemic to nineteenth-century comedy of manners that haunt the academy to this day. The fate of Ettalene Grice, the unmarried helpmeet of A.T. Clay, has all too many parallels in today's academy.

As the concept of social evolution and notions of an objective racial hierarchy struck root in the latter half of the nineteenth century, cultural ties to the contemporary Middle East became an increasing liability to 'moving ahead' in western societies. Pogroms against Russian Jews in the 1880s had brought over 100,000 Jewish refugees to America by 1890, creating a massive social, educational and financial challenge for the established and largely assimilated Jewish community, raising the specter of nativist, anti-Semitic backlash by the gentile majority. Cyrus Adler, hired by the National Commission of the World's Columbian Exposition to recruit Middle Eastern performers for the Midway Plaisance, the fair's entertainment strip, and charged with assembling a collection of 'Religious Ceremonial Objects' for the United States National Museum (today's Smithsonian Institution) in the White City's Government Building, came up with a novel means of influencing public opinion about Judaism. For the 'Street in Cairo' and other Middle Eastern venues on the Midway, he hired numerous Jews from the Ottoman Empire—but their job was to convince the audience that they were Ottoman Muslims, keeping their Jewish identity more or less secret. The ensemble of Judaica and illustrative photographs Adler hastily assembled for the Government Building, in contrast, aggressively marketed mainstream, westernized Ashkenazi Judaism and linked its rituals to the Old Testament, eschewing anything that smacked of *Yiddishkeit* or Oriental Judaism. The 'Orientals' visible in the Religious Ceremonials exhibit were Muslims and members of various eastern Christian traditions. This stratagem was taken further at the Cotton States and International Exposition in Atlanta two years later. Holloway in his essay explores the ways that Adler used popular Orientalist preconceptions to inform and entertain his American audiences though ethnographic displays and 'biblical antiquities', while at the same time doing sophisticated crisis control for the immigration problem.

Sasson in 'Mari and the Holy Grail' summarizes the impact of seventy years' worth of Mari studies on ancient Near Eastern and biblical studies. Within the early years of the publication of the first tablets from Mari, a 'middle chronology' for the ancient Near East would be devised as a result and historical connections between the Amorites and so-called East Canaanites would find general acceptance. Albright fatefully situated the biblical patriarchs in the age of Hammurabi but changed his mind repeatedly over the identities of the kings in Genesis 14, a cautionary tale.

> Quickly the range of comparisons became established: linguistic studies of West Semitic names; analysis of Upper Mesopotamian place names; variety of nomadic experience; vocabulary for ethnic and kinship identity; the office of judges; the types of sacrifice, especially of donkeys; bans on spoils and (alleged) sins on census-taking; fixing of patrimony, and, never least, prophetism and its impact on affairs of state and of faith. Yahweh and his origins were issues that also periodically surfaced.

The 1970s saw the rise of a broad intellectual critique of historical research itself, a tendency that led to a 'paradigm shift' in the last quarter of the twentieth century, culminating within biblical studies in the breakup of the Albright synthesis. Paradoxically, in the same period historical insights into Mari royal chronology, politics and economic relations flourished; especially important have been the lessons in statecraft and diplomacy gleaned from the Mari corpus. Within the last decade, Sasson finds evidence 'for a new drive to historicize Hebrew traditions' underwritten in part by some rather startling Albrightian atavisms by members of the Mari *équipe* that purport to resurrect the patriarchal narratives of Genesis as historical palimpsests. Part of the danger of this tendency is the likelihood that solid historical gains about Amorite culture will be trodden down in the stampede of a new quest for the historical Abraham.

Grabbe begins his study of biblical 'court literature' of the Persian Period by rehearsing a heated exchange between Julius Wellhausen and Eduard Meyer. Wellhausen, characteristically skeptical of the authenticity of the alleged Persian documents in Ezra 4–7, was challenged on the same ground by Meyer; rejoinder and surrejoinder followed. These two emblematic positions regarding the historicity of the book of Ezra continued to divide twentieth-century scholars. Grabbe refocuses the discussion by teasing out a literary pattern that runs through the stories of Joseph, Daniel, Esther, Ezra, that of the Jewish hero's triumph over adversity and elevation to high office; the Aramaic tale of Ahiqar shares the pattern, save for the protagonist's Jewishness. Ezra 1–6 in its narration of the fortunes of the Jewish community as well as the figure of Ezra reveals many of the same pattern-markers found in other biblical court literature. A number of historically tendentious claims in Ezra, such as the importance assigned the province of Yehud and the Jewish people within the Persian empire, situate the incredulous Grabbe in the 'Wellhausen' camp. In closing, he notes that English-speaking scholarship, decisively influenced by Meyer (who was not a biblical scholar) and the Albright school, tended to champion the historicity of the book of Ezra.

Hurovitz brings two Standard Babylonian texts heretofore unconnected with the Bible to bear on the fascinating dream-legend of Jacob's Ladder, Gen. 28.10-22. These Akkadian texts are geographically specific, couched in cosmological language used exclusively for the city of Babylon. Using semantic and conceptual parallels, he argues that 'the account of Jacob's dream contains hardly a detail without some prominent linguistic or thematic parallel to Babylon in general and the myth of its primeval foundation in particular.' By reading the two biblical stories of the Tower of Babel and Jacob's dream together, Babylon figures twice: explicitly and negatively in the Tower-of-Babel vignette, implicitly and by implication positively in Genesis 28. The biblical author, following Mesopotamian precedent, has transferred the temple-ideology of Babylon to Israelite Bethel. As a theological plot, the inability of humans to reach God through the pre-Abrahamic Tower of Babel finds its resolution in the days of Jacob, when a ladder to heaven will stand in Bethel.

The assyriological advances of the mid-nineteenth century significantly impacted the study of Josiah of Judah, though with questionable results. As Handy reveals, the recovery of Assyro-Babylonian deities supplied scholars with new possibilities for identifying the god-images destroyed in the course of Josiah's cultic purge in 2 Kings 23, a reading largely dependent on one's estimate of Judah's political alignment at the time, gravely complicated by the darkness surrounding the fate of Palestine during the final years of Assurbanipal's reign. Was Josiah in open revolt against Assyria, and did Manasseh install representations of the Assyrian state pantheon in Jerusalem? The assyriological data provide no telling indication one way or another. Reconstructions of the borders of Josiah's 'Greater Judah' balloon and contract over the past 120 years largely without reference to Akkadian sources (the maximal expansion, which engulfed the entire Sinai, the dubious creation of Yohanan Aharoni, followed closely upon the heels of the Arab-Israeli 1967 Six-Day War and the annexation of the Sinai Peninsula). One comes away from this survey of engaged biblical and ancient Near Eastern studies with a sense that innumerable opportunities for constructive historiography were shirked due to a combination of confessional presuppositions, Orientalist prejudice, the politics of nationalism, and a distinctly uncritical exercise of comparative religions.

Scurlock in her essay examines a rare genre of Late Akkadian texts, a subversive prophecy dating from the Persian or Seleucid era, the Uruk Prophecy, first published in 1975. Out of a series of eleven unnamed historical kings, Kings II–IX are described negatively, whereas benign King X restores the lost protective goddess of Uruk, and his son's dynasty is prophesized to rule forever. Six scholars have attempted to identify Kings II–IX with various Assyrian and Babylonian rulers, but none believe that an author living in the southern Babylonian city of Uruk could countenance a Sargonid Assyrian monarch who embodied positive rulership. Scurlock argues that good Kings X and XI were originally intended to signify Assurbanipal and his son Sîn-šar-iškun. The reason that this equation has been overlooked heretofore is the deep-seated bias against Assyria, one of those 'modern prejudices which view the defeat of Assyria by Babylonia as the first of a series of epic struggles in which Western democracy and rule of law triumph over Oriental despotism and terror.

Other examples of this Orientalist trope include Alexander the Great's defeat of Darius III at Gaugamela and Publius Cornelius Scipio's victory over Hannibal Barca at Zama.' Cryptic prophecies, like those in biblical Daniel, allow for 'mistakes': if Assurbanipal and Sîn-šar-iškun fail to establish an everlasting dynasty, then perhaps Cyrus and Cambyses, or Darius and Xerxes will succeed where the Assyrians failed. The message is one of sustaining hope: the stolen goddess will someday return, and the reign of evil kings will ultimately cease.

3. *The Orientalism Critique and Its Discontents*

Grounds for re-evaluating traditional academic Orientalism as a tool of western ethnocentrism or out-and-out imperialism stem from a host of twentieth-century political shocks: the Iranian (1905–1911) and Young Turk revolutions (1908–18), the destruction of the Austrian, German, Ottoman and Russian empires in World War I, the first anticolonial revolution in Egypt (1919–22) and the triumph of Kemalist nationalism in Turkey, and developments in the post World-War II era that witnessed the withering of the British (granting of Indian independence, withdrawal from Egypt and Hashemite Iraq, Palestine and Transjordan) and French empires (withdrawal from Syria and Lebanon, granting of Algerian and Indochinese independence). What heretofore had been 'politically correct' (Eurocentrism, conviction of racial superiority, Orientalism in the service of the state), is now tainted (what nation wants to be branded a colonial power these days?), and what was once viewed with suspicion (pluralism, anti-racism, anti-colonialism) now warrants praise.

Numerous voices have been raised in opposition to conventional Orientalism since the late 1960s. Baldly put, most of these critiques take issue with the contention that Islamic civilization is everywhere and always the same (static and despotic), and that Islamism or Islamic revival can be adequately conceptualized as a perennial tendency to address social, political or economic conflict through religious retrenchment (fanaticism). Anouar Abdel-Malek (1924–), an Egyptian sociologist and philosopher, writing from a Marxist perspective, believes that Western Orientalists continue to pursue their studies within the framework of pre-World War II political realities of empire and colony. The easy recourse to essentializing classification of eastern peoples—*homo islamicus*, *homo arabicus*—leads to pre-ordained results that fail to capture the contemporary social realities of the East.[52] Abdul Latif al-Tibawi (1910–81), Palestinian historian and legal expert, a confessing Muslim, finds rampant denigration of Muslim spirituality and beliefs in the works of Western Orientalists, putatively charged with impartially and accurately describing the heart of Islam. Basic ignorance of Islamic fundamentals, coupled with deep-seated anxiety over Arab nationalism, drive not only popular but academic prejudice. When a Muslim intellectual

52. Anouar Abdel-Malek, 'Orientalism in Crisis', *Diogenes* 44 (1963), pp. 103-40.

cannot identify his own image in the mirror created by Oriental scholarship, that scholarship is professionally bankrupt.[53] Bryan S. Turner (1945–), British Marxist sociologist, identifies the fatal flaw in Orientalism with the construal of Islamic society by a series of absences: lack of a middle class, lack of progressive urbanism, lack of democratic liberties, lack of political revolutions. These 'lacks' provide comfortable foils with which to account for Western cultural and economic superiority in the face of chronic third-world underdevelopment. The true causes of North African and Middle Eastern underdevelopment, far from being a result of internal developments within despotic, unprogressive and enervating Islam, says Turner, have everything to do with the relationship of these areas to the global centers of capitalism.[54]

Edward W. Said (1935–2003), Jerusalem-born literary critic, although not a member of the Middle Eastern studies guild, galvanized public and academic awareness of the shortcomings of traditional Orientalism through a series of extraordinarily influential books and essays. Said's *Orientalism* (1978), a polemical work that does not easily reduce to a simple outline, has exerted by far the greatest impact of any of the charter texts challenging academic Orientalism. He vastly augments the scope of the term by equating Orientalism with the Occident's preferred mode of knowing the East, a productive epistemology which is dedicated both to manufacturing 'Europe's collective day-dream of the Orient' and to imposing that day-dream on the Orient. In addition to defining a scholarly field of study, Orientalism is a construct used as a colonialist weapon of power.

> Taking the late eighteenth century as a very roughly defined starting point Orientalism can be discussed and analyzed as the corporate institution for dealing with the Orient—dealing with it by making statements about it, authorizing views of it, describing it, teaching it, settling it, ruling over it: in short, Orientalism as a Western style for dominating, restructuring, and having authority over the Orient.[55]

Said is cognizant that Orientalist scholarship can indeed pierce the cultural partitions of time and space, gaining knowledge of languages, religions, societies, and so forth, but he is adamant to demonstrate the self-interested political nature of all such knowledge, the fact that the 'Orient' created by the work of the Orientalist exists to benefit the West, generally to the detriment of the

53. Abdul Latif al-Tibawi, 'English-Speaking Orientalists: A Critique of their Approach to Islam and Arab Nationalism', *Islamic Quarterly* 8 (1964), pp. 25-45, 73-88; *idem*, 'Second Critique of the English-Speaking Orientalists and their Approach to Islam and the Arabs', *Islamic Quarterly* 23 (1979), pp. 3-54; *idem*, 'On the Orientalists Again', *Muslim World* 70 (1980), pp. 56-61.

54. Bryan S. Turner, *Marx and the End of Orientalism* (Controversies in Sociology, 7; London: George Allen & Unwin, 1978); *idem*, *Orientalism, Postmodernism and Globalism* (London: Routledge, 1994). For an instructive overview of the 'turmoil in the field' leading up to Edward Said's publications, see Lockman, *Contending Visions of the Middle East*, pp. 148-81; Macfie, *Orientalism*, pp. 73-101.

55. Edward W. Said, *Orientalism* (New York: Vintage Books, 1994 [1978]), p. 3.

Easterners under scrutiny. 'The relationship between Occident and Orient is a relationship of power, of domination, of varying degrees of a complex hegemony' (p. 5); 'Orientalism, as a system of knowledge about the Orient, [is] an accepted grid for filtering through the Orient into Western consciousness' (p. 6). The 'collective day-dream of the Orient' that Said finds inscribed in European arts and letters, a more-or-less stable projection across the centuries, conjures up an Islamic civilization that is despotic, irrational, fanatic, incapable of self-government, racially degenerate, decrepit, sexually abandoned, a perennial menace to the West and to itself, in dire need of Western scientific and administrative prowess, in a word, colonial expertise. 'In a sense the limitations of Orientalism are...the limitations that follow upon disregarding, essentializing, denuding the humanity of another culture, people, or geographical region. But Orientalism has taken a further step than that: it views the Orient as something whose existence is not only displayed but has remained fixed in time and place for the West' (p. 108). With rather more nuancing than many of his critics admit, Said illustrates the political, historical and ideological differences between the early racist Orientalists like Sylvestre de Sacy and Ernst Renan, later 'sympathetic' readings by the likes of H.A.R. Gibb and Louis Massignon, and post-World War II flights of anti-Muslim constructions by Gustave von Grunebaum and Bernard Lewis. In his 'Afterword' to *Orientalism* published in 1994, Said acknowledges a number of constructive criticisms (as well as the persistence of unregenerated Orientalist studies), and opines that 'scholars and critics who are trained in the traditional Orientalist disciplines are perfectly capable of freeing themselves from the old methodological straitjacket.'[56]

Indeed, 'few living intellectuals can claim to have written a text that has revolutionized several fields in both social sciences and humanities, and fewer are responsible for the genesis of a whole field of inquiry.'[57] The phenomenal

56. Said, *Orientalism* (1994–), p. 326.

57. Stephen P. Sheehi, 'Edward Said', in *Encyclopedia of Postcolonial Studies* (ed. John C. Hawley; Westport, CT: Greenwood Press, 2001), pp. 392-97 (394-95). On the remarkable figure of Edward Wadiʾa Said, see Bill Ashcroft and D.P.S. Ahluwalia, *Edward Said: The Paradox of Identity* (London and New York: Routledge, 1999); Naseer Hasan Aruri and Muhammed A. Shuraydi (eds.), *Revising Culture, Reinventing Peace: The Influence of Edward W. Said* (New York: Olive Branch Press, 2001); Shelley Walia, *Edward Said and the Writing of History* (Postmodern Encounters; Duxford, Cambridge and Lanham, MD: Icon Books; Totem Books USA, 2001); ʿĀdil Samārah and Aḥmad Ḥusayn (eds.), *Naqd al-thaqāfawīyah al-burjwāzīyah al-kuluniyālīyah fī utruḥāt Idwārd Saʿīd* (Rām Allāh: Markaz al-Mashriq al-ʿĀmil lil-Dirāsāt al-Thaqāfīyah wa-al-Tanmawīyah, 2000) (with English abstract); Valerie Kennedy, *Edward Said: A Critical Introduction* (Oxford and Malden, MA: Polity Press in association with Blackwell, 2000); Homi K. Bhabha and W.J. Thomas Mitchell (eds.), *Edward Said: Continuing the Conversation* (Chicago: University of Chicago Press, 2004). Edward W. Said and David Barsamian, *Culture and Resistance: Conversations with Edward W. Said* (Cambridge, MA: South End Press, 2003) deals primarily with the Palestinians, Israel and international politics.

impact of Said's cultural studies may be gauged by the fact that the very meaning of Orientalism in most English language sources in the 1980s, 1990s and 2000s acquired a strongly negative connotation, in marked distinction to earlier usage. Said's engagement of the poststructuralism of Foucault in Orientalism, and the growing popularity of Foucault-inspired analyses in critical theory scholarship, led to the first sustained use of poststructuralism in Middle Eastern studies, Timothy Mitchell's *Colonising Egypt* (1988).[58] Beginning in the 1980s, the systemic debt owed Said by scholars who have sought to trace the lopsided and often exploitative contact between the East and West through so-called postcolonial studies is profound, and few such studies fail to acknowledge the master's influence.[59] Postcolonial studies follow Said in analyzing the means by which Anglo-European society uses cultural creations, like Orientalist scholarship, to perpetuate its imperial control, but take leave of *Orientalism* though the constructive task of giving voice to the marginalized, whether defined by race, class or gender. Less of an academic discipline than an intellectual stance, postcolonial studies eclectically appropriates tools from literary theory, philosophy, feminist studies, psychology, political science, anthropology and various historical fields, often juxtaposing discordant and contradictory approaches in order to shatter the complacency of traditional modes of representation. For example, the re-reading of 'classic' English literature like Conrad's *Heart of Darkness* through the lens of colonial discourse, arguing whether the texts perpetuate colonialist stereotypes or challenge the entire colonial enterprise, has been one of the more visible manifestations of postcolonial studies on the university campus. Homi K. Bhabha, Gayatri Chakravorty Spivak and the *Subaltern Studies* scholars have sought to read western historiography and other types of colonial discourse 'against the grain', exploring the ambiguities, anxieties and instabilities in texts that superficially seem to provide unalloyed support for the imperial worldview. A number of scholars in the religious studies field have incorporated postcolonial studies into the so-called emancipatory theologies—liberation, black, Minjung, feminist—in the ongoing effort to 'decolonize' their language and discover authentic means of expressing cultural heterogeneity through the creation of 'resistance literature.'[60] The stakes for 'playing' the postcolonial game are costly. One of the best known and possibly the most controversial postcolonial author today is Salman Rushdie, whose *Satanic Verses* (1988) earned him an Iranian *fatwa* condemning him to

58. Timothy Mitchell, *Colonising Egypt* (Cambridge Middle East Library; Cambridge: Cambridge University Press, 1988).

59. Homi K. Bhabha, *The Location of Culture* (London and New York: Routledge, 1994); Leela Gandhi, *Postcolonial Theory: A Critical Introduction* (New York: Columbia University Press, 1998); Bill Ashcroft, Gareth Griffiths and Helen Tiffin, *Post-Colonial Studies: The Key Concepts* (Routledge Key Guides; London and New York: Routledge, 2000).

60. Challenges to postcolonial studies are summed up in S. Shankar, 'Post-Postcolonial Theory', in Hawley (ed.), *Encyclopedia of Postcolonial Studies*, pp. 359-63.

death.[61] The application of postcolonial hermeneutics to biblical studies in the past twenty years traces its pedigree to Said's *Orientalism*, and surely marks his major legacy to ancient Near Eastern studies to date.

His polemical challenge to academic Orientalism has not gone unanswered! Responses to Said's lightning rods range across a spectrum from obsequious hero-worship[62] to the Anglo-American Orientalist Bernard Lewis, who, in a series of acidulated exchanges accused Said of deliberate obfuscation, historical incompetence, and willful promulgation of an agenda that is massively anti-Zionist and anti-Semitic.[63] The notion that academic historiography exists to serve, and to serve up, the vested interests of the history-writers was hardly a novel idea in 1978, and examples abound of Europeans who have written harsh rebukes of European colonialism and imperialism since Bartolomé de Las Casas (1484–1566).[64] The collusion of academic Orientalism with European colonialism can be massively documented, to be sure, and Said's outrage is justified, but the claim that the European study of Near, Middle and Far Easterners exists primarily to denigrate and politically dominate those people assigns an impossible standard of uniformity to academicians—in any field. The chief pitfall of Said's critique, which he shares with social scientific scholarship as a body, is the danger of *patterning*, of imposing a neatly constrained model on the 'blooming, buzzing' confusion of human history. Together with many other critics, I think it is fair to point out that Said's monolithic and perdurable Occident—Occidentalism—falls prey to the same charge of essentialism that he levels at the Orientalists' Orient: there were, and are, a plethora of Occidents and Ori-

61. Antje M. Rauwerda, 'Rushdie Affair', in *A Historical Companion to Postcolonial Thought in English* (ed. Prem Poddar and David Johnson; New York: Columbia University Press, 2005), pp. 431-32. The United Kingdom and Iran issued a joint statement in 1998 bringing the *fatwa* to an end.

62. For example, Asaf Hussain, Robert Olson and Jamil Qureshi (eds.), *Orientalism, Islam, and Islamists* (Brattleboro, VT: Amana Books, 1984).

63. Said for his part had a number of scathing things to say about Lewis in *Orientalism*, pp. 315-21, 332-36, and in subsequent venues, mincing no words that Lewis was an *agent-provocateur* of American foreign policy in maintaining Israeli hegemony over the Palestinians, operating behind the mask of Islamic studies. For the particulars of these exchanges and bibliography, see Lockman, *Contending Visions of the Middle East*, pp. 190-92. The most balanced and constructive assessment of Said's stance towards Zionism that I have encountered remains Marc H. Ellis, 'Edward Said and the Future of the Jewish People', in *Revising Culture, Reinventing Peace: The Influence of Edward W. Said* (ed. Naseer Hasan Aruri and Muhammed A. Shuraydi; New York: Olive Branch Press, 2001), pp. 38-72.

64. Europe is an '*arrogant, aggressive, money-minded* part of the world; it did not spread civilization among the nations, but wherever it could achieve this, the destruction of the rudiments of their cultures.' Herder, quoted in Werner Ustorf, '*Wissenschaft*, Africa and the Cultural Process according to Johann Gottfried Herder (1744–1803)', in *European Traditions in the Study of Religion in Africa* (ed. Frieder Ludwig and Afe Adogame; Wiesbaden: Harrassowitz, 2004), pp. 117-27 (122).

ents, and it is incumbent on the historian of culture to eschew stylish reductionism and delimit them accurately.[65] Recent studies of European imperial history suggest that profound anxiety on the part of the colonial powers can be traced in much of the surviving literature;[66] that Orientalist perspectives varied dramatically, depending upon the author's locus, political nexus and audience (e.g., London versus Calcutta, utilitarian versus Whig);[67] that innumerable works of art and literature on Orientalist themes actually function primarily as imaginative explorations of alternatives to conventional European society, as witness the mystique of the nomadic Bedouin in romantic literature, used as a foil for the blights of industrial civilization.[68] As MacKenzie objects with a formidable monograph of supporting data, traffic between East and West has always been a two-way thoroughfare, with Eastern material and intellectual culture exerting a profound influence on Europe and North America, a point that Said alludes to in *Orientalism* but never develops.[69] The gender politics that seethe beneath Said's male canon of Orientalist sources is, as Melman and others have shown,

65. As of 1976, Said did not envision the creation of a complementary academic field of study, Occidentalism, courses about which are currently taught at some American universities, and for which the glib publish-or-perish market has its answer: James G. Carrier, *Occidentalism: Images of the West* (Oxford and New York: Clarendon Press, 1995); Couze Venn, *Occidentalism: Modernity and Subjectivity* (London and Thousand Oaks, CA: Sage Publications, 2000); Ian Buruma and Avishai Margalit, *Occidentalism: The West in the Eyes of its Enemies* (New York: Penguin Press, 2004).

66. Nigel Leask, *British Romantic Writers and the East: Anxieties of Empire* (Cambridge Studies in Romanticism; Cambridge and New York: Cambridge University Press, 1992); S.W. Holloway, 'Biblical Assyria and Other Anxieties in the British Empire', *Journal of Religion & Society* [http://www.purl.org/JRS] (2001).

67. Peter Hulme, *Colonial Encounters: Europe and the Native Caribbean, 1492–1797* (London and New York: Methuen, 1986); Mary Louise Pratt, *Imperial Eyes: Travel Writing and Transculturation* (New York: Routledge, 1992); Lisa Lowe, *Critical Terrains: French and British Orientalisms* (Ithaca, NY: Cornell University Press, 1994).

68. Mohammed Sharafuddin, *Islam and Romantic Orientalism: Literary Encounters with the Orient* (London and New York: I.B. Tauris, 1994), pp. xiii-xxxv; Kathryn Tidrick, *Heart-Beguiling Araby* (Cambridge: Cambridge University Press, 1981). A far more exotic example of this artifice is literally out of this world: scientists and science-fiction writers alike since the eighteenth century have used the planet Mars to explore contemporary dreams and anxieties surrounding environmental degradation, over-population, social change, industrial blight, and imperialism in their own (terrestrial) societies; see Robert Markley, *Dying Planet: Mars in Science and the Imagination* (Durham, NC and London: Duke University Press, 2005).

69. MacKenzie, *Orientalism: History, Theory, and the Arts*, pp. 2-42. MacKenzie treats at length Said's 'unwillingness to grapple with political economy, with class, and the contrasting economic and social circumstances of different territories; and difficulties in connecting representation to agency, establishing the precise relationship between scholarly Orientalism and imperial instrumentality', p. 11. MacKenzie successfully illustrates the manifold means through which the Orient became a tool of cultural resistance within Western culture itself, providing various means for challenging the conventional and complacent.

more contradictory, ambiguous, and multi-dimensional than he can imagine.[70] The reliance in *Orientalism* on avant-garde concepts like Foucault's concept of discourse, a linguistic construct whose aim is to establish power by creating an authoritative body of knowledge, Derrida's 'European hallucination' and Gramsci's concept of cultural hegemony, and the repetitious use of the argot of literary criticism (e.g., 'hegemonic saturation') is off-putting to readers outside the circle of adepts. Finally, Said's unsystematic and occasionally ahistorical appropriation of sources and his penchant for quoting authors out of context[71] has left a bad taste in the mouth of the historical guild.

Nevertheless, Said's Orientalism thesis has exercised a substantial impact on Middle Eastern studies in the United States, judging by subsequent publications by members of the Middle East Studies Association, who have critically accepted what seemed useful but ignored or reformulated his less convincing ideas. Some high-profile Middle Eastern scholars like Bernard Lewis (Said's *bête noire*), Fouad Ajami, Daniel Pipes and Samuel Huntington, however, have continued to promote a vision of Islam as a more or less unchanging civilization, endowed with a fixed repertoire of core cultural attributes and a frozen mentality that is suspiciously easy to describe.[72] Such tidy dichotomization between East and West has been popularized through the vehicle of the 'clash of civilizations' thesis, the notion that innate Muslim affinity for traditional societies and despotic governments has failed to 'modernize' in the face of the progressive secular West, spawning irrational Muslim rage and acts of terrorism. Since the formal end of the Cold War, and especially following the attack on the

70. Billie Melman, *Women's Orients—English Women and the Middle East, 1718–1918: Sexuality, Religion, and Work* (Ann Arbor, MI: University of Michigan Press, 1992); Joseph A. Boone, 'Vacation Cruises; Or, the Homoerotics of Orientalism', in *Feminist Postcolonial Theory: A Reader* (ed. Reina Lewis and Sara Mills; New York: Routledge, 2003), pp. 460-86; Reina Lewis, *Rethinking Orientalism: Women, Travel and the Ottoman Harem* (London: I.B. Tauris, 2004). In Said's defense, in his *Culture and Imperialism* (New York: Knopf, 1993) and later essays, he comes to acknowledge the importance of gender in postcolonial studies.

71. Asher-Greve in her essay below considers Said's treatment of Semiramis in Dante starkly in error. Paul John Frandsen, 'Aida and Edward Said: Attitudes and Images of Ancient Egypt and Egyptology', in *Assyria and Beyond: Studies Presented to Mogens Trolle Larsen* (ed. Jan Gerrit Dercksen; NINOL, 100; Leiden: Nederlands Instituut voor het Nabije Oosten, 2004), pp. 205-27, excoriates Said's analysis of a modern opera, which—considering that music and belles-lettres were his professional forte—he should have known better.

72. See, for instance, Bernard Lewis, *The Crisis of Islam: Holy War and Unholy Terror* (New York: Modern Library, 2003); Fouad Ajami, *The Dream Palace of the Arabs: A Generation's Odyssey* (New York: Pantheon Books, 1998); Daniel Pipes, *Slave Soldiers and Islam: The Genesis of a Military System* (New Haven: Yale University Press, 1981); *idem*, *Sandstorm: Middle East Conflicts and America* (Lanham, MD and Philadelphia: University Press of America and Foreign Policy Research Institute, 1993); *idem*, *Militant Islam Reaches America* (New York: W.W. Norton, 2002); Samuel P. Huntington, *The Clash of Civilizations and the Remaking of World Order* (New York: Simon and Schuster, 1996).

New York World Trade Towers in September 2001, it has become increasingly common among a wide spectrum of American scholars as well as policymakers and media pundits to accept as established fact that Islamism has replaced communism as the gravest threat facing the West; the continuing international frustration with the bloody Arab-Israeli struggle over East Jerusalem and the West Bank is strongly ingredient in fostering this perception of irrational Islam locked into a fourteen-century-old struggle with a progressive West, culminating in tomorrow's Armageddon.[73]

By contrast, the ancient Near Eastern studies guild has remained stolidly aloof from the Orientalist critique that reverberates throughout the humanities and social sciences today. It is well to recall that the critique arose from the inability of Oriental readers to discover faithful reflections of themselves in Orientalist scholarship; there are no Assyrians, Babylonians, Canaanites or ancient Israelites left to complain of egregious misrepresentation in ancient Near Eastern scholarship. Many reasons can be adduced to account for this indifference or rejection. Some (few) scholars reject the critique after a careful and impartial survey of the arguments. The narrow training of specialists as hard-core philologists and archaeologists tend to leave them unprepared to grapple with broader intellectual issues, like Orientalist bias. After the disasters of Pan-Babylonism, Assyriology has been particularly hostile to abstract theories originating in other disciplines. The impenetrable jargon and rhetoric affected by critical studies authors repel many who might benefit from the core theses. Demonization of Said as an historical dilettante and anti-Semite clinches the argument for others. The academic profession as a whole tends to avoid controversy and reward bland elaboration; the prickly language of modern Middle Eastern politics may be hazardous to your tenure-climb. And, too, the conviction persists that academics in their innocent quest for objective reality have no business in deliberately engaging in politics, noisily declaring their social locations or otherwise wasting valuable time in ephemeral navel-gazing. Both the biblical studies and the assyriological guilds have labored for over a century to divorce their fields of study from the contemporary inhabitants of Western Asia. More sinisterly, one of the perennial strategies by which Western scholars dissociate the 'Holy Land' and the related Bible-lands of the Middle East from the contemporary Arab inhabitants is the trope of the ancient world as the cradle of civilization, establishing an evolutionary trajectory by which supercessionist ancient Israel enters the Greco-Roman world via Christianity and thus forms the deep structure of European civilization, displacing unwanted

73. See Douglas Little, *American Orientalism: The United States and the Middle East since 1945* (Chapel Hill, NC: University of North Carolina Press, 2002); Lockman, *Contending Visions of the Middle East*, pp. 215-72; Irvine H. Anderson, *Biblical Interpretation and Middle East Policy: The Promised Land, America, and Israel, 1917–2002* (Gainesville, FL: University Press of Florida, 2005), pp. 102-38.

claims by indigenous Middle Easterners to their own cultural heritage. Those old-school specialists who take comfort in the glories of ancient Greece as a foil to despotic, stagnant Asia find little to recommend in *Orientalism*. And there is always garden-variety laziness.[74]

4. *The Import of Orientalism for Biblical Studies and Assyriology*

Two recent monographs that utilize Orientalist critiques throughout in the study of the ancient Near East are instructive in this regard, Keith Whitelam's *The Invention of Ancient Israel: The Silencing of Palestinian History* (1996) and Zainab Bahrani's *The Graven Image: Representation in Babylonia and Assyria* (2003).[75]

The Hebrew Bible specialist Whitelam takes as his point of departure the fact that the textbook entity 'ancient Israel' is part of the Orientalist projection of the European nation state into the past. Its scholarly 'recovery' through archaeology and the biblical studies guild continues to function as an effective means by which political claims to Palestine are reinforced. Whitelam argues, with massive quotations from the leading twentieth-century histories of ancient Israel, that there is a sustained interplay between the invention of ancient Israel and the foundation narratives of the modern state of Israel, with the plea that Palestinian history takes its place as an autonomous discipline in the academy.

Drawing explicitly upon the thought of Edward Said, Whitelam situates the occlusion of 'Palestinian history' within the context of European Orientalist discourse. Nineteenth-century European representations of Palestine tended to depict it as a wasteland, its few inhabitants morally debased and politically impotent, or deliberately rendered invisible as in the Zionist slogan 'a land without people for a people without land.' Mainstream biblical scholarship in the guise of the three 'schools' of Alt and Noth, Albright and Bright, and Mendenhall and Gottwald, while utilizing different models for the settlement/conquest/reorganization of Palestine by ancient Israel, all denigrate and nullify the Bronze-Age Canaanite inhabitants using analogies and explanatory constructs that represent European responses to modern Middle Eastern nationalist politics. Until very recently, Israeli archaeology uncritically accepted the internal chronologies and ethnic ascriptions within the biblical narrative in its mapping of 'ancient Israel'; through circular reasoning it could 'find' traces of Israelite occupation in the hill country/West Bank on demand as it were. The use of

74. See especially section E of Stefan R. Hauser, 'Orientalismus', in *Der neue Pauly: Enzyklopädie der Antike* (16 vols.; ed. Hubert Cancik and Helmuth Schneider; Stuttgart: J.B. Metzler, 1996–2003), XV, pp. 1239-43.

75. Keith W. Whitelam, *The Invention of Ancient Israel: The Silencing of Palestinian History* (London and New York: Routledge, 1996); Zainab Bahrani, *The Graven Image: Representation in Babylonia and Assyria* (Archaeology, Culture, and Society; Philadelphia: University of Pennsylvania Press, 2003).

archaeology to create invented pasts has been a potent weapon in the arsenal of the modern European nation-state, and pre- and post-state Israeli efforts that exploit archaeological 'facts on the ground' to legitimate territorial possession represent an unusually successful venture in kind.[76]

Whitelam's 'facts' do not uniformly point to a refraction of biblical historiography through the lens of Zionist ideology and politics, though most of his examples do add up to an exploded vision of ancient Israelite history. He also seems to be uninformed about the intense inner-Israeli debate on these very matters.[77]

Whitelam is troubled that the postcolonial re-envisioning of history, anthropology, ethnography and economics has gained so little purchase in the biblical studies field. Instead,

> The stranglehold on the past achieved by European scholarship has been maintained by American and Israeli scholarship in the latter part of the century in projecting this as the period of Israel's emergence and dominance as a major state in the religion... The theological and political motivation behind the search [for ancient Israel] in the West and in Israel have combined to deny the claims of the indigenous population to representation in history.[78]

Twentieth-century biblical studies has been an integral part of Orientalist discourse; the intended reader is neither Palestinian nor a member of any other non-Western group, but is European, American and Israeli. His panacea to this state of affairs entails a willingness to confront 'the motives and interests which have informed the scholarly enterprise, both its design of research strategies and the subsequent presentation and interpretation of the data' and a determination to disavow retrojections of the modern state of Israel into the biblical past, especially the 'mirage of the Davidic "empire" '.[79] Since the time that Whitelam wrote *The Invention of Ancient Israel*, postcolonial studies have gained a grudging acceptance within the critical canon of the biblical studies guild,[80] but size-

76. See Rami Arav, 'Archaeology in the Service of Ideology in Israel', in *'A Land Flowing with Milk and Honey': Visions of Israel from Biblical to Modern Times* (ed. Leonard J. Greenspoon and Ronald A. Simkins; Studies in Jewish Civilization, 11; Omaha, NE: Creighton University Press, 2001), pp. 85-104, and Nadia Abu El-Haj, *Facts on the Ground: Archaeological Practice and Territorial Self-Fashioning in Israeli Society* (Chicago: University of Chicago Press, 2001).

77. See Yoram Bar-Gal, *Moledet we-geʾografyah be-meʾah šanot ḥinuk Ṣiyoni* (Tel-Aviv: ʿAm ʿOved, 1993); Gideon Aran, 'Return to the Scripture in Modern Israel', in *Les retours aux Ecritures: Fondamentalismes présents et passés* (ed. Evelyne Patlagean and Alain Le Boulluec; Bibliothèque de l'Ecole des Hautes Etudes, Section des Sciences Religieuses, 99; Paris and Louvain: Peeters, 1993), pp. 101-31; Michael Feige, 'ʾArkeʾologyah, ʾantropologyah, wa-ʿirot ha-pitoḥ: ʿiṣovu šel ha-maqom ha-Yisraʾeli', *Zion* (1998), 441-59.

78. Whitelam, *Invention of Ancient Israel*, pp. 224-25.

79. Whitelam, *Invention of Ancient Israel*, p. 231.

80. R.S. Sugirtharajah, *Voices from the Margin: Interpreting the Bible in the Third World* (Maryknoll, NY: Orbis Books, 1991); Pui-lan Kwok, *Discovering the Bible in the Non-Biblical*

able sectors of the guild continue to reject Whitelam's premises and thesis as dilettantish, politically inflammatory, or simply perverse.[81]

In *Graven Image*, the Assyriologist and art historian Bahrani sets for herself the ambitious task of describing the nature of representation in the pre-Islamic civilization of Iraq, drawing heavily on poststructuralist historical criticism and postprocessual archaeological models. In order to escape the snares of Western aesthetic categories, especially the pervasive notion of mimesis, the first part of the book consists of an overview of modern art history and the ancient Near Eastern studies guild from the vantage point of postcolonial studies. Orientalist studies and the amassing of ancient Near Eastern artifacts in European museums flourished in the era of European colonialism, and, in keeping with Said's Orientalism critique, the imperative to maintain stale Western tropes of the East—violent, fanatical, despotic, slothful, hypersexual—continues to recruit willing accomplices in Near Eastern studies. Art history of the ancient world, in the guise of Kantian idealism, originated as a branch of ethnography that imposed an absolute evolutionary hierarchy upon 'primitive' non-Western races. European interest in the ancient Near East developed out of the twin canons of the Bible and classical texts; much of Bahrani's animadversion against art history turns on the distorting lens of the Greek philosophical tradition as a means of

World (Bible and Liberation Series; Maryknoll, NY: Orbis Books, 1995); Michael Prior, *The Bible and Colonialism: A Moral Critique* (The Biblical Seminar, 48; Sheffield: Sheffield Academic Press, 1997); R.S. Sugirtharajah, *The Postcolonial Bible* (The Bible and Postcolonialism, 1; Sheffield: Sheffield Academic Press, 1998); Fernando F. Segovia and Mary Ann Tolbert (eds.), *Teaching the Bible: The Discourses and Politics of Biblical Pedagogy* (Maryknoll, NY: Orbis Books, 1998); R.S. Sugirtharajah (ed.), *Vernacular Hermeneutics* (The Bible and Postcolonialism, 2; Sheffield: Sheffield Academic Press, 1999); Fernando F. Segovia, *Decolonizing Biblical Studies: A View from the Margins* (Maryknoll, NY: Orbis Books, 2000); R.S. Sugirtharajah, *The Bible and the Third World: Precolonial, Colonial, and Postcolonial Encounters* (Cambridge: Cambridge University Press, 2001); R.S. Sugirtharajah, *Postcolonial Criticism and Biblical Interpretation* (Oxford: Oxford University Press, 2002); Pui-lan Kwok, *Postcolonial Imagination and Feminist Theology* (Louisville, KY: Westminster John Knox Press, 2005); Uriah Y. Kim, *Decolonizing Josiah: Toward a Postcolonial Reading of the Deuteronomistic History* (The Bible in the Modern World, 5; Sheffield: Sheffield Phoenix Press, 2005).

81. See William G. Dever, 'The Identity of Early Israel: A Rejoinder to Keith W. Whitelam', *JSOT* 72 (1996), pp. 3-24 for an archaeologist's answer, and James Barr, *History and Ideology in the Old Testament: Biblical Studies at the End of a Millennium* (New York: Oxford University Press, 2000), pp. 61, 84-86, 146, who declares himself satisfied with the review by Ian W. Provan, 'The End of (Israel's) History—A Review Article on K.W. Whitelam's *The Invention of Ancient Israel*', *JSS* 42 (1998), pp. 283-300. Publication of *Invention of Ancient Israel* and subsequent works critical of the status quo have won Whitelam membership among the reviled minimalists, variously defined as 'the Terrible [Thomas L.] Thompson, the Lamentable [Niels Peter] Lemche, the Diabolical [Philip R.] Davies, or the Woeful Whitelam'; Keith W. Whitelam, 'Representing Minimalism: The Rhetoric and Reality of Revisionism', in *Sense and Sensitivity: Essays on Reading the Bible in Memory of Robert Carroll* (ed. Alastair G. Hunter and Philip R. Davies; JSOTSup, 348; Sheffield: Sheffield Academic Press, 2002), pp. 194-223 (198).

accessing the epistemologies of the non-Western past. One of the persistent means of claiming the ancient cultures of Iraq and Iran for the 'cradle of civilization' of the West, while simultaneously denying their connection with the living inhabitants of those countries, is to eschew the use of 'Iraq' and 'Iran' in textbooks and museum exhibits for terms like Mesopotamia, a de-nationalizing strategy carried over from European denigration of the Ottoman Empire and mirrored in biblical geography that avoids use of 'Palestine' in favor of 'Israel.' Bahrani, in keeping with the tenets of postmodern thought, stresses throughout the critical need for awareness of the role of interpretation as a force in the process of accessing the past itself; the dream of positivist, objective knowledge dies hard, but die it must. Her exposure of continuing Orientalist prejudices ring true at many points and her attempts to disengage Near Eastern history from colonial narrative are praiseworthy. Her analysis of colonialism as an omnipresent motivating force, however, lacks nuance (like Said's): Occidentalism is not the solution to Orientalism.

In the second half of the book, the portion where most of her assyriological evidence appears, Bahrani attempts to explicate the conceptual world behind Akkadian *ṣalmu*, inadequately translated as image, using the calculated defacement of royal images and texts as an entry point, and devotes an entire chapter to a single Middle Assyrian cult socle. Building on Jean Bottéro's interpretation of the multivalent Akkadian writing system, a phenomenon in which the pictographic origins of the early cuneiform script continue to 'operate' in the later linguistic environment where most signs share phonetic and ideographic values, this semiotically-mixed writing system in her view constituted the 'ontological' basis of Assyro-Babylonian visual culture. The *ṣalam šarri* in the form of a royal Neo-Assyrian stele or statue in the round is neither a mere visual object nor a mimetic portrait, but functions as an entity in its own right, 'magically' linking the figure of the king with verbal performance, text, and symbolic *pars pro toto* like a royal garment. Hence the elaborate curse clauses tailored to the particular circumstances of these objects, designed to protect them from mischief, and the evidence for ritual defacement of palace reliefs in Nineveh and Mesopotamian royal monuments deported to Elamite Susa. Bahrani's hermeneutics holds considerable promise for unriddling some of the more recondite associations of text and image, and for dealing with an extensive corpus of esoteric Akkadian literature.

Bahrani's efforts to avoid the overlay of Western aesthetic canons in treating visual sources of ancient Iraq, often provocative and constructive, in common with other pioneering endeavors need refinement, testing and revision. Without the operation of something like mimesis within the history of Neo-Assyrian visual arts, it is profoundly difficult to account for the development of narrative technique between, say, the bronze Balawat Gates of Shalmaneser III (ninth century) and Assurbanipal's Battle of Ulai in palace reliefs (seventh century). Bottéro's and Bahrani's quest for *episteme*, the abstract mind of the ancient

Mesopotamian, embodied in a series of almost two dozen civilizations spanning thirty centuries in which at least five languages were spoken, is the sort of enterprise ('the *Zeitgeist* of ancient Israel') that has been largely abandoned by the biblical studies field, with less than a millennium of history, a vastly simpler linguistic milieu, and a fraction of the geographical spread to work with. Criticisms aside, *The Graven Image* deserves a careful reading by the ancient Near Eastern studies guild as a serious attempt to bridge postcolonial studies and ancient aesthetics.[82] Both Whitelam and Bahrani are fervent converts on a crusade to bring the truth of Orientalist critiques to bear against the complacent practitioners of their various fields; the sympathetic reader will make allowance for the heated polemics that enliven these studies.

Elna Solvang's essay in this volume deals critically with the image of the harem in ancient Near Eastern studies and modern scholarship. Perennial fascination with the Islamic harem, with its frisson of forbidden sensuality, imperious masculine power and moral abandonment, may be traced for hundreds of years in European literature and, more recently, in Orientalist paintings—and ancient Near Eastern scholarship. As an empirical check on the fog surrounding western understandings of the harem, Solvang, utilizing autobiographical sources, reconstructs the women's lives within Topkapı Palace in Constantinople, seat of the Ottoman Sultan, and other late nineteenth-century harems. There is no generic harem in Islamic society, defined either as domestic space or the inhabitants therein. Late Topkapı Palace life reveals a highly structured microcosm of women, some of whom attained considerable education, who exercised immense political power beyond the physical boundaries of the harem that, to a considerable extent, projected the very face of the ruling house into the Ottoman Empire. Solvang deals rather charitably with the Assyriologist Ernst Weidner, who naively imposed his model of Islamic harem life upon a first reading of the Middle Assyrian Palace Decrees, because 'everywhere in the Orient where the extension of western civilization could not penetrate, not much had changed up until the twentieth century.' Other Assyriologists like Stephanie Dalley and Joan Goodnick Westenholz either eschew the concept of the harem altogether as a social construct of dubious use or advocate that far more research needs to be done with primary documentation before such modern models are likely to bear fruit. According to Solvang, 'the *harem* analogy applied to Mari and the Neo-Assyrian materials illuminates patterns of royal women's activities and their benefits for the kingdom that are similar to those of the Ottoman women.' These analogies, however, must not be used to blind oneself to the very real differences between the ancient and modern court life, in the manner of Weidner—and some contemporary biblical scholars.

82. I have benefited from the observations of Holly Pittman, 'Review of Zainab Bahrani, *The Graven Image: Representation in Babylonia and Assyria*', *ArtB* 87 (2005), pp. 342-43, and Marian Feldman, 'Review of Zainab Bahrani, *The Graven Image: Representation in Babylonia and Assyria*', *JAOS* 124 (2004), pp. 599-601.

Asher-Greve, in her section on Semiramis in Assyriology, illustrates the methodological dangers entailed in blurring the distinctions between the figure of Greek legends and an historical Assyrian queen, Sammuramat. The word 'queen' (*šarrutu*) was never used of the wife of a contemporary Neo-Assyrian king, nor have we any cuneiform texts that allude to perverse sexual abuses by these women, facts that emphasize the gulf between Greek legend and historical reality. Such factors, however, have not prevented Assyriologists from capitalizing on the lurid nature of the Semiramis legends by serving up 'widespread Orientalist clichés' in the writing of studies purportedly of Mesopotamian sexuality and eroticism.

Reid, in his discussion of the earliest International Congress of Orientalists, notes in passing

> A disquieting note on definitions: Egyptology was, and still is, the study of ancient Egypt. This definition implicitly slights Islamic and modern Egypt. Another Western trope that emphasizes continuity rather than discontinuity in Egypt is also unsettling—the assumption that quintessential fellahin have not changed since ancient times. This assumes an unchanging Orient juxtaposed to an evolving, dynamic West.

As Holloway attempts to show, Cyrus Adler in his publications and exhibitions for the United States National Museum asserted forcefully and repetitiously the 'fact' that the material and cultural reality of ancient Israel was still available for scholarly investigation in the guise of the inhabitants of the Ottoman Empire untouched by Western civilization. Adler capitalized on the common presumption of the 'stability and conservatism of the East' in his exhibits on 'Mohammedanism' at the Chicago and Atlanta expositions, but studiously avoided juxtaposing this idea when dealing with examples of contemporary assimilated European and American Jewry, save for the insistence that westernized Judaism maintains an authentic repertoire of core rituals and customs found in the Old Testament. This exercise in 'scientific' Orientalism, like the cruder manifestations of racism and jingoism on the Midway Plaisance in Chicago and its recreation in Atlanta, reinforced existing stereotypes within American society that persist in many quarters of the academy to this day.

What could be more uncomplicated or politically innocent than a map in an academic work on the Bible? Long's essay in this volume, 'Picturing Biblical Pasts', seeks to account for the convoluted social, political and confessional motives that controlled the choice of geographical images used in two popular English-language histories of ancient Israel, J. Maxwell Miller and John H. Hayes, *A History of Ancient Israel and Judah* (1986), and John Bright, *A History of Israel* (1st–4th edns, 1959–2004). In keeping with Said's dictum that control of the Orient entails constantly converting it into something else, that 'something else' in this instance comprised maps and landscapes, those intricately-coded blueprints of social and ideological investment that richly repay a close reading. 'In this ideational space where publisher and author meet reader, one may inquire into the dynamic processes by which twentieth-century American biblical scholars, who, working within the continuing presence of a European past, have managed West Asia by producing a Christian, Jewish, or biblical "Orient"'.[83]

Long takes exquisite pains to situate these biblical maps within their historical context, rooting them within a tradition of scholarly representation while adducing biographical information that goes far to account for the precise choices of visual subject matter and historiography. In the case of Bright's *History*, ancient Palestine becomes a tableau of realized American Protestant eschatology, a 'socio-theological notion of early Israel's birth [that] easily merges with the simplified myth of America's origin.' Miller and Hayes, in contrast, construct a decentralized Iron-Age Israel that supports a number of tribal groups of diverse ethnic and cultural origins. '[...]Miller and Hayes opened the door to imagining ancient Israel's origins in ways that need not erase the histories of other Iron Age peoples, or foreclose their continuity with both Arabs and Jews who currently assert mutually exclusive claims to ethnic distinction and rights of primogeniture to the land.'

In truth, the Orientalism critique by Said and other scholars figures infrequently in ancient Near Eastern studies outside the growing field of postcolonial studies and biblical interpretation. The Danish Assyriologist Mogens Trolle Larsen has published several essays on the role of Orientalism within ancient Near Eastern studies and a brilliant monograph on the first decade of the French and British exploration of Ottoman Iraq.[84] The Italian Assyriologist Mario Liverani dealt masterfully with the ideologically-charged image of the ancient Near Eastern city in modern historiography.[85] Mark Hamilton published an isolated comparative study of history writing in ancient Judah and Samʾal during the Neo-Assyrian interregnum, explicitly formulating his analytical parameters by invoking Said's *Orientalism*.[86] At the London Rencontre in 2003, Regina Heilmann gave a talk illustrated with a short Italian silent film, *La Regina di*

83. See Burke O. Long, *Imagining the Holy Land: Maps, Models and Fantasy Travels* (Bloomington, IN: Indiana University Press, 2002), pp. 89-163.

84. M.T. Larsen, 'Orientalism and the Ancient Near East'; *idem*, 'Orientalism and Near Eastern Archaeology,' in *Domination and Resistance* (ed. Daniel Miller, Michael R. Rowlands and Christopher Tilley; One World Archaeology, 3; London and New York: Routledge, 1989), pp. 229-39; *idem*, 'Seeing Mesopotamia', in Gunter (ed.), *Construction of the Ancient Near East*; *idem*, 'The "Babel/Bible" Controversy and Its Aftermath', in *CANE*, I, pp. 95-106; *idem*, *Conquest of Assyria.*

85. Mario Liverani, 'Ancient Near Eastern Cities and Modern Ideologies', in *Die orientalische Stadt: Kontinuität, Wandel, Bruch: 1. Internationales Colloquium der Deutschen Orient-Gesellschaft, 9.-10. Mai 1996 in Halle/Saale* (ed. Gernot Wilhelm; Colloquien der Deutschen Orient-Gesellschaft, 1; Saarbrücken: Saarbrücker Druckerei und Verlag, 1997), pp. 85-107.

86. Mark W. Hamilton, 'The Past as Destiny: Historical Visions in Samʾal and Judah under Assyrian Hegemony', *HTR* 91 (1998), pp. 215-50.

Ninive (1911), examining the popularization of ancient Near Eastern discoveries in an explicit Orientalist context.[87] At the last Rencontre assyriologique internationale in 2005, the Cambridge mathematician Eleanor Robson delivered a stunning paper that explored how traditional historical surveys of mathematics privilege 'Euclidian'-type Babylonian texts, systematically distorting Babylonian science through the lens of Greek mathematics. She argued that the motives for this subordination of Babylonian mathematics were due in part to Saidian Orientalism.[88]

Quo vadis? At the conclusion of the Fifty-First Rencontre assyriologique internationale hosted by the University of Chicago, July 2005, a special workshop was held in order to explore the hotly-contested gulf within the academic community regarding the propriety of publishing unprovenanced antiquities from Iraq in the wake of the 2003 American invasion of Iraq. 'The Threat to Iraq's Cultural Heritage—Current Status and Future Prospects', in the course of its detailed presentations by archaeologists, a journalist, museum officials, and representatives of various organizations working directly with the Iraqis in Jordan and elsewhere, elicited impassioned expostulations about the ethics of Western academics publishing unprovenanced Iraqi antiquities, especially inscriptions, and, by investing them with an academic pedigree, incontinently fuelling the looting of archaeological sites. At one point, a well-known Assyriologist made a plea that the Iraqi cultural heritage is the property of the entire world, defining 'everyone's heritage' as a heritage that belongs to Christians and Jews. Will we ever get it right?

87. Regina Heilmann, ' "Those Old Assyrian Legends": Zur Rezeption des Alten Orients im wiederentdeckten Kurzfilm *La Regina di Ninive* (Italien 1991)', in *Nineveh: Papers of the XLIXe Rencontre assyriologique internationale, London, 7-11 July 2003* (2 vols.; ed. Dominique Collon and Andrew R. George; London: British School of Archaeology in Iraq, 2005), I, pp. 257-64. Her 2004 Johannes Gutenberg-Universität dissertation, 'Paradigma Babylon: Rezeption und Visualisierung des Alten Orients im Spielfilm: Ein Beitrag der vorderasiatischen Archäologie zur Orientalismus-Forschung', is to be published by the Deutsches Archäologisches Institut in the series Orient-Archäologie.

88. According to Robson's handout, this lecture will be published as part of the last chapter of her forthcoming book, *Mathematics in Ancient Iraq: A Social History* (Princeton University Press).

Intellectual and Disciplinary Histories

The Beginnings of Assyriology in the United States

Benjamin R. Foster

1. *Introduction*

American Assyriology has been the subject of a bibliographical and biographical study by C. Wade Meade. This collects extensive information about formal study and publication on ancient Mesopotamia and its languages in the United States through the First World War.[1] An American Assyriologist today might approach this study from a different perspective, in that he would not include many of the people treated by Meade as members of his sometimes jealous little guild. Writing an article about Babylonian archaeology or even teaching a course in the Akkadian language does not make a person into an Assyriologist. To take two examples cited by Meade, Charles C. Torrey, Professor of Semitics at Yale (1900–32), and Philip K. Hitti, Professor of Arabic at Princeton (1926–54), taught Akkadian at some point during their academic careers, but no one, including these great scholars themselves, would consider them Assyriologists.[2] Rather, an Assyriologist is now understood to be a research scholar whose primary interests include the languages and civilizations of ancient Mesopotamia. A research scholar, regardless of whether or not he holds an academic appointment in his area of expertise, wants to carry on original investigation in his chosen discipline. Some research scholars teach, some publish, some do both, some do neither, but they have in common an intellectual focus on ancient Mesopotamia and enough technical competence to understand and work independently with its languages and cultural remains. The task at hand, therefore, is to place the development of American Assyriology, narrowly defined as a research discipline, in its cultural and social matrix.

1. C. Wade Meade, *Road to Babylon: Development of U.S. Assyriology* (Leiden: E.J. Brill, 1974).

2. Meade, *Road to Babylon*, pp. 71-72, 122. For Torrey, see Benjamin R. Foster, 'Torrey, Charles Cutler (20 Dec. 1863–12 Nov. 1956)', in *ANB*, XIX, pp. 756-57; for Hitti, see Oleg Grabar in *Luminaries, Princeton Faculty Remembered* (ed. Patricia H. Marks; Princeton, NJ: Association of Princeton Alumni, 1996), pp. 119-24; James Kritzeck and R. Bayley Winder, 'Philip K. Hitti', in *The World of Islam: Studies in Honour of Philip K. Hitti* (ed. James Kritzeck and R. Bayley Winder; London: Macmillan & Co., 1959), pp. 1-37; Fred M. Donner, 'Pioneers in Medieval Near Eastern Studies: Philip K. Hitti', *al-Usur al-Wusta* 8 (1996), pp. 48-52.

2. *Assyriology and the Biblical World*

My first proposition is that the major impetus for American interest in ancient Mesopotamia during the nineteenth century came from biblical study. It is impossible to overestimate the importance of Bible reading in English-speaking and specifically American culture. The Bible has probably been translated into English more times than into all other European languages combined.[3] To choose one American example of this phenomenon, Charles Thomson, friend and associate of Benjamin Franklin, a colonial deal maker with a good Irish dislike for British monarchy, is best remembered today as the secretary of the First Continental Congress. In that capacity he soon gained a perhaps well-deserved reputation for being a crook. Forced from office into a lonely and embittered retirement, he beguiled his sunset years by translating the entire Septuagint into English, a feat few American politicians or deal makers today would think to emulate.[4] Yet this was not surprising in a culture that had enshrined or rejected a whole series of English renderings of Holy Writ and continues to do so, and Thomson's work had its share of reviews.[5]

Between 1777 and 1820, 400 independent editions of the English Bible, complete or New Testament, were printed in various localities in the United States, roughly ten a year, and in the next decade 300 more. By 1840 there were an additional 400, by 1850 another 300, meaning that between 1770 and 1850, a period of eighty years, 1,415 different American Bibles were published, three times what was produced in England, with a much greater population, in the same period. This does not count re-editions of the same publication. A so-called polyglot Bible ran through 120 printings between 1831 and 1880. Moreover, the press runs were staggering: one edition alone of the American Bible Society Bible sold, between 1877 and 1929, over 3,700,000 copies. More people buy, and presumably read, the Bible in the United States than in any other country on earth.[6]

American fascination with Scripture relates to Assyriology in two ways. First, American Bibles, so-called illustrated or parlor Bibles, began to grow

3. David Daniell, *The Bible in English: Its History and Influence* (New Haven and London: Yale University Press, 2003), pp. xiii-xiv.

4. Boyd Stanley Schlenther, *Charles Thomson: A Patriot's Pursuit* (Newark, DE: University of Delaware Press, 1990), pp. 206-12. Thomson could not read Hebrew and believed that the Septuagint, as the version of the Bible in use in the early Christian church, should be translated separately.

5. Peter J. Thuesen, *In Discordance with the Scriptures: American Protestant Battles over Translating the Bible* (Religion in America Series; Oxford: Oxford University Press, 1999); Daniell, *Bible in English,* chapters 38, 39, pp. 701-68.

6. All figures drawn from Daniell, *Bible in English*, chapters 33, 35, 38, 39, pp. 580-603, 624-58, 701-33, 734-68.

large and sumptuous in format, content, and illustration, including all sorts of supplementary matter. Among the illustrations, cuneiform tablets and towers of Babylon appeared early on. In 1818, the Brattleboro, Vermont Bible featured a plate showing not only the Tower of Babel, but two correctly reproduced cuneiform brick inscriptions, one Neo-Babylonian, the other Elamite, brought to the United States in 1817 by a certain Captain Henry Austin.[7]

Mesopotamia was still rather remote for exploration, but Americans, both explorers and missionaries, were publishing extensively on the geography and sites of the Holy Land, Syria, and Asia Minor.[8] The matter-of-fact American attitude towards travel and exploration in the Middle East is exemplified by Commander W.F. Lynch of the United States Navy, who wrote: 'On the 8th of May, 1847, the town and castle of Vera Cruz having some time before surrendered, and there being nothing left for the Navy to perform, I preferred an application to the Hon. John Y. Mason, the head of the department, for permission to circumnavigate and thoroughly explore the Lake Asphaltites or Dead Sea. My application having been some time under consideration, I received notice, on the 31st of July, of a favourable decision, with an order to commence the necessary preparations'.[9] Lynch's wording suggests that he saw two and a half months as a rather long time for the Secretary of the Navy to decide on his application.

Therefore Mesopotamia, as part of the 'biblical world', arrived in the United States long before Assyriology, piggy-backing on the national obsession with the English Bible. American books on Mesopotamia began to appear as well, such as the Englishman James Fraser's *Mesopotamia and Assyria*, published in America in 1845, and James Phillips Fletcher's *Notes from Nineveh* in 1850. These were travelogues. Fletcher's, for example, was about his experiences in the Mosul region, but he obviously chose biblical Nineveh for the title because no one would buy a book called *Notes from Mosul*. Austen Henry Layard's *Nineveh and Its Remains* appeared in the same year, and stimulated various American articles about the discoveries at Nineveh, one of the most interesting a notice from the British Journal *Athenaeum* of Sir David Brewster's work on the Layard lens,[10] an ancient ground eyeglass found at Nineveh, published in the *American Polytechnic Journal* 2 (July-December, 1853), p. 157.[11]

7. For the Brattleboro Bibles, see Daniell, *Bible in English*, pp. 654-55; for the tablets, see William B. Dinsmoor, 'Early American Studies of Mediterranean Archaeology', *Proceedings of the American Philosophical Society* 87 (1943), pp. 70-104 (100), with figure 2.

8. Meade, *Road to Babylon*, chapter 2 (pp. 17-27).

9. William Francis Lynch, U.S.N., *Narrative of the United States' Expedition to the River Jordan and the Dead Sea* (Philadelphia: Lea & Blanchard, 8th rev. edn, 1852), p. 13.

10. *Athenaeum*, No. 1298, Sept. 11, 1852, p. 979.

11. See in general Steven W. Holloway, 'Nineveh Sails for the New World: Assyria Envisioned in Nineteenth-Century America', *Iraq* 66 (2004), pp. 243-56; for the lens and the history of scholarship on it, see Robert K.G. Temple, *Crystal Sun: Rediscovering a Lost Technique of the Ancient World* (London: Arrow, 1999), pp. 10-49.

Actual relics from Mesopotamia began to arrive through the efforts of missionaries and travelers, even special agents of American colleges and seminaries sent out to buy them. The relics included cylinder seals and especially stone reliefs, such as carved stone slabs from Aššur-nāṣir-apli II's palace at Nimrūd.[12] The decipherment of Old Persian cuneiform was duly noted by Edward Salisbury, Professor of Arabic and Sanskrit at Yale, in the first volume of the *Journal of the American Oriental Society*, published in 1849, so this may be deemed America's first article on cuneiform studies.[13] Meade noted that Salisbury's student, James Hadley, Professor of Classics at Yale, read papers before the Society in 1860 and 1862 on 'Remains of Ancient Babylonian Literature in Arabic Translation', but these two papers were focused on the writings of Ibn Wahshiyyah, especially the so-called 'Nabataean Book of Agriculture', which Hadley deemed, following Gutschmied and others, 'the most prodigious specimen the world has yet seen of literary imposture'.[14]

From the foregoing it is clear that many Americans were interested in Mesopotamia and its remains by 1860. There were many Americans in the Middle East, including Mesopotamia; Americans were in the Middle and Far East before the Austins had gone to Texas.[15] The Americans in the Middle East tended to be

12. Sam B. Harrelson, *Asia Has Claims Upon New England: Assyrian Reliefs at Yale* (New Haven: Yale University Art Gallery, 2006); Meade, *Road to Babylon*, p. 27. For slabs from Nineveh, see John Malcolm Russell, *From Nineveh to New York: The Strange Story of the Assyrian Reliefs in the Metropolitan Museum and the Hidden Masterpiece at Canford School* (New Haven: Yale University Press, 1997).

13. For Salisbury, see B.R. Foster, 'Salisbury, Edward Elbridge (6 Apr. 1814–5 Feb. 1901)', in *ANB*, XIX, pp. 206-208.

14. Meade, *Road to Babylon*, p. 26, understandably did not realize that Hadley's papers were published in combined form in an essay, 'The Book of Nabataean Agriculture', *The New Englander* 21 (1862), pp. 505-36, available online at http://cdl.library.cornell.edu/moa/browse.journals/nwng. These were a summary and critique of the Russian Arabist Chwolson's claim that the writings ascribed to a certain Ibn Wahshiyyah preserved Babylonian writings on agriculture, poisons, astrology, and 'the mysteries of the sun and moon.' Hadley was willing to entertain the possibility that the Babylonians had a written literature, even though Herodotus had not mentioned its existence, but agreed with the critics of Chwolson, including Rougemont, Renan, and Gutschmied, that Ibn Waḥshiyya pretended to translate ancient works that in fact he had written himself (citations in Hadley, 'Book of Nabataean Agriculture'). Chwolson dated the Book of Agriculture to 1400 BCE, whereas his critics pushed the date as late as the ninth century CE. Modern scholarship still debates the authority and authenticity of this material and whether or not there really was such a person as Ibn Waḥshiyya (see T. Fahd, *EI*[2] III, pp. 963-65). Hadley's original manuscripts of these papers are preserved in Yale University Archives Record Group 985 box 4 folder 29.

15. James A. Field, Jr, *America and the Mediterranean World, 1776–1882* (Princeton, NJ: Princeton University Press, 1969), p. 443. The missionary movement is presented in chapters 3, 6, and 8, with bibliography. Biographical sketches of some missionaries are presented in David H. Finnie, *Pioneeers East: The Early American Experience in the Middle East* (Cambridge, MA: Harvard University Press, 1967).

highly educated, dedicated people, combining their missionary zeal with enthusiasm for the biblical world and the thrill of travel in distant lands, not to mention the gratification of writing about it, for example, in the widely circulating *Missionary Herald*. Many were notably loyal to their colleges back home, some of which were assembling collections of curiosities, relics, manuscripts and rare books, eventually founding museums, so were suitable beneficiaries of donations of artifacts.[16]

3. *German Professionalism in American Higher Education*

The second important factor in the development of American Assyriology was the transformation of American scholarship and higher education by America's intellectual dependence on Germany, beginning already in the early nineteenth century. Suffice it to say that by 1912, perhaps 10,000 Americans had studied or taken advanced degrees at German universities, returning to form a cohesive academic elite in the United States, especially after the Civil War.[17] There is a certain element of conflict in this story. In Germany, theology was a separate discipline from philology, whereas in America, Oriental philology had its roots in theological study. The battles that had been fought on the European academic scene between theologians and Oriental linguists in the sixteenth century were over and nearly forgotten, but in the United States of 1840, for example, Oriental languages were still widely perceived primarily as the basis for reading the Bible in its various versions rather than as independent scholarly subjects.[18] America's great Semitist of the early twentieth century, Charles C. Torrey, for example, came from Andover Theological Seminary rather than a college, because the colleges had mostly abandoned what little sham Oriental philology they had taught by the early nineteenth century.[19] Indeed, the revival of interest in the languages of the Bible, including Greek and Hebrew, was in theological seminaries, and with the growth of the missionary movement, modern

16. For early collecting in America, see the material assembled by Dinsmoor, 'Early American Studies'.

17. Charles Diehl, *America and German Scholarship 1770–1870* (New Haven: Yale University Press, 1978); Jurgen Herbst, *The German Historical School in American Scholarship: A Study in the Transfer of Culture* (Ithaca, NY: Cornell University Press, 1965); B.R. Foster, 'Yale and the Study of Near Eastern Languages in America, 1770–1839', in *The United States and the Middle East: Cultural Encounters* (ed. Abbas Amanat and Magnes T. Bernhardsson; YCIAS Paper Series; New Haven: Yale Center for International and Area Studies, 2002), pp. 6-16.

18. N.A. Taylor, 'The Theological Seminary in the Configuration of American Higher Education: The Ante-Bellum Years', *History of Education Annual* 17 (1977), pp. 17-30. The sixteenth-century debate over the importance of study of original languages can be approached through Erasmus's 'Apology against the Dialogue of Latomus', in *Collected Works of Erasmus*. LXXI. *Controversies* (ed. J.K. Sowards; trans. Martin Lowry; Toronto: University of Toronto Press, 1993), pp. 31-84.

19. Foster, 'Yale and the Study of Near Eastern Languages', pp. 9-12.

languages of the Middle East were also taught in seminaries, but not in colleges.[20] Therefore many American students and graduates arriving in Germany to study Middle Eastern languages were coming with an interest in divinity education but studied these languages German style, building up understanding of the text from language, rather than reading the 1611 Bible in Hebrew guise, as had been the custom in the American colleges.[21]

German university professors, beginning in the sixteenth century, had developed teaching strategies for Hebrew, with readers and glossaries, so it was only a matter of time before anthologies and readers along the same lines were available for other biblical languages and even for Akkadian.[22] Education in an ancient Semitic language consisted of mastering the anthology or chrestomathy to hand. As late as 1935 the German Aramaicist Franz Rosenthal memorized an Akkadian chrestomathy to prepare for his comprehensive examination with the Assyriologist Bruno Meissner.[23] The first certifiable American product of this system of instruction was Francis Brown (1849–1916), who studied at Berlin with Eberhard Schrader, 1877–79, and then taught Akkadian to divinity students from the same texts Schrader had taught him. Brown was not the first American to read a cuneiform text, however, as that distinction seems to be held by a certain Edward C. Taintor who, in the same year as the Battle of Gettysburg, translated a cuneiform inscription by correspondence with Henry C. Rawlinson and Layard, but I know nothing further of him.[24]

This raises an important point, independent research. In what sense did people who mastered set pieces know the languages of ancient Mesopotamia? This prob-

20. It is difficult to identify what could be called the first program focusing on the modern Middle East in American higher education. In the early twentieth century, for example, there was talk of programs in preparation for foreign service, but I have found little evidence for language training as part of such preparation. In 1905, Yale and Columbia discussed a joint program, at the initiative of the anthropologist Franz Boas, but, so far as I am aware, little came of it (Report of the President, *Bulletin of Yale University*, Second Series No. 7 [June 1906], p. 25).

21. For growth and definition of graduate education in the United States, see Richard J. Storr, *The Beginnings of Graduate Education in America* (Chicago: University of Chicago Press, 1953).

22. For example, Sebastian Münster (d. 1552), for whom see Karl Heinz Burmeister, *Sebastian Münster: Versuch eines biographischen Gesamtbildes* (Basler Beiträge zur Geschichtswissenschaft, 91; Basel and Stuttgart: Helbing & Lichtenhahn, 1963), pp. 46-47, was the first Christian Hebraist to make a clear distinction among a teaching grammar (*Compendium*), a reference grammar (*Absolutissima*), and an elementary work for students (*Epitome*). The standard chrestomathy for Akkadian was Friedrich Delitzsch, *Assyrische Lesestücke mit den Elementaren der Grammatik und vollständigem Glossar*, the first edition of which appeared as *Assyrische Lesestücke: Nach den originalen Theils revidirt Theils zum ersten Male herausgegeben, und durch Schrifttafeln eingeleitet* (Leipzig: J.C. Hinrichs, 1876). This work appeared in four more editions (1878, 1885, 1900, 1912). Bruno Meissner also produced a *Chrestomathie* at Leiden in 1895, but this did not achieve the same popularity.

23. Personal communication.

24. For Brown and Taintor, see Meade, *Road to Babylon*, pp. 28-30, 26.

lem is as old as Oriental studies in Europe. When the thirteenth-century Franciscan Roger Bacon claimed that one could learn Hebrew in a few weeks, what he meant was that one could read in Hebrew a text one already knew in another language.[25] One could learn the alphabet and some paradigms and soon match up Hebrew with Latin words. When printing made possible great polyglot Bibles, scholars read the biblical text they already knew, but in numerous languages, just as Roger Bacon claimed he could read Hebrew, and thereby acquired enviable reputations for learning. Far fewer were the Christian scholars who could read a non-biblical text in Arabic or even Hebrew, and these often had personal crises or felt the need to justify what they were doing, as they could be accused of heresy, undermining faith, or 'Judaicizing'.[26]

Akkadian had the advantage and disadvantage of being one of the first non-biblical Semitic languages studied in America, so instead of reading excerpts from the Bible, the student read excerpts in a reader or anthology. Thus the Americans like Brown who taught from anthologies they had read in Berlin or Leipzig were working within a modernized Renaissance tradition of Oriental scholarship, which did not stress original reading so much as mastery of set pieces. This is a value foreign to the discipline of Assyriology today, which stresses the ability to read independently in all sources available, but lay near the core of the nineteenth-century American version of the discipline.

So it was that when, in the shadow of World War I, Charles C. Torrey in his presidential address to the American Oriental Society called for a declaration of independence from Germany, he cited the dominance of German anthologies in American Oriental studies as one of two issues that concerned him most. The other was what he saw as the increasing anti-Semitism of German biblical

25. *The Greek Grammar of Roger Bacon and a Fragment of his Hebrew Grammar* (ed. Edmon Nolan and Samuel Abraham Hirsch; Cambridge: Cambridge University Press, 1902); S.A. Hirsch, 'Roger Bacon and Philology', in *Roger Bacon Essays* (ed. Andrew George Little; New York: Russell & Russell, 1972 [Oxford University Press, 1914]), pp. 101-51; C.B. Vandewalle, 'Roger Bacon dans l'histoire de la philologie', *La France franciscaine* 11 (1928), pp. 315-409, 12 (1929), pp. 45-90, 161-228.

26. There is no general study of the polyglot phenomenon, which began as a teaching device, though many individual studies of the various authors, of the various polyglot Bibles, and the development of printing and its importance to scholarship. See, in general, Daniel Droixhe, *La linguistique et l'appel de l'histoire (1600–1800): Rationalisme et révolutions positivistes* (Geneva: Droz, 1978). The real significance of polyglottism for the history of scholarship needs further study; the important point is that printing made it possible. Elizabeth L. Eisenstein, *The Printing Press as an Agent of Change: Communications and Cultural Transformations in Early-Modern Europe* (2 vols.; Cambridge and New York: Cambridge University Press, 1979), I, pp. 303-450 discusses printing of the Bible but does not go into polyglot printing. On the issue of anti-Semitism, see Heiko A. Obermann, *The Roots of Anti-Semitism in the Age of the Renaissance and Reformation* (trans. James I. Porter; Philadelphia: Fortress Press, 1984); Bernard Dov Cooperman (ed.), *Jewish Thought in the Sixteenth Century* (Harvard Judaic Texts and Studies, 2; Cambridge, MA: Harvard University Press, 1983); see also below n. 49.

study.[27] The reason a modern Assyriologist will recognize professionally few names in the early chapters of Meade's *Road to Babylon* is because many of them were men, like Torrey, who mastered a teaching grammar and certain set pieces, but did not go further with Assyriology in their careers, even if they sometimes taught Akkadian to seminary or graduate students.

4. *Philanthropy and Assyriology*

The third influence on the development of Assyriology was closely intertwined with the first two. This was the American tradition of philanthropy, as it developed after the Civil War. Prior to 1860, $100,000 was a great fortune, whereas the annual salary of a Yale professor might be $600. Perhaps thirty-five people in America, living in New York and Philadelphia, had as much as $100,000. By the late 1880s, however, there were perhaps 3,000 millionaires living throughout America and a great fortune might be a hundred million dollars or more, with no income tax.[28] Many wealthy Americans felt it their duty to promote culture by endowing colleges, universities, libraries, museums, and concert halls. The academic elite, imbued with German-style philology as a high academic goal, was not slow to see the possibilities of American munificence. Although professorships in Oriental languages had always been the prestige appointments in American colleges and deemed the hallmark of a nascent university, before the Civil War the colleges were too under-endowed and their curriculum too inflexible to admit non-Classical languages anyway.[29]

The new university programs, created atop of the old colleges like Harvard and Yale and Pennsylvania, were dominated by German-educated scholars who believed that Oriental languages, including Akkadian and ancient Egyptian, were an essential part of the new American higher education. Even Hebrew was reinvented as a secular, philological discipline and taught as a graduate course, because in this same period divinity schools were gradually moving from the ideal of a book-educated clergy to an ideal of the clergyman as social servant,

27. Charles C. Torrey, 'The Outlook for Oriental Studies', *JAOS* 38 (1918), pp. 107-20.

28. Oscar Handlin and Mary F. Handlin, *The Wealth of the American People: A History of American Affluence* (New York: McGraw-Hill, 1975), p. 162.

29. The first professorship endowed by an American was the Hancock Professorship of Oriental Languages at Harvard, first held by Stephen Sewall (d. 1804), for whom see Thomas J. Siegel, 'Professor Stephen Sewall and the Transformation of Hebrew at Harvard', in *Hebrew and the Bible in America: The First Two Centuries* (ed. Shalom Goldman; Brandeis Series in American Jewish History, Culture, and Life; Hanover, NH: University Press of New England for Brandeis University Press & Dartmouth College, 1993), pp. 228-45. Ezra Stiles considered a professorship in Oriental languages one of the highest priorities for Yale, and his successor, Timothy Dwight, began the process of expanding Yale by appointing a professor in Hebrew, even though there were insufficient funds available to pay him a professor's salary, Chandos M. Brown, *Benjamin Silliman: A Life in the Young Republic* (Princeton, NJ: Princeton University Press, 1989), p. 126.

and Hebrew had long since been desacralized. The new American research universities, Johns Hopkins and the University of Chicago, championed German scholarly principles, and they, like their college counterparts, were also the products of philanthropy.[30]

Philanthropy made possible the first American expeditions to Mesopotamia, notably the Wolfe Expedition (see below), paid for by Catherine Lorillard Wolfe, and the University of Pennsylvania expedition to Nippur, paid for by various donors.[31] Neither of these expeditions was funded by invoking a biblical connection; rather, it was the same adventurous spirit that had sent the under-employed U.S. Navy to the Dead Sea. In 1884, Miss Wolfe was prepared to pay $5,000 for reconnaissance in Mesopotamia, no strings attached, and the Nippur expedition was not excavating a site mentioned in the Bible or even a Classical author. American philanthropy was the envy of the British, for example, who chafed under the modest budgets available through the British Museum.[32] On the other hand, the United States had no national museum, as did the French and British. Lynch seems to have been the only explorer to get U.S. government support for work in the Middle East, and this was before the great age of Mesopotamian archaeology had begun.

5. *The Expert Amateur*

Sometimes Americans learned in Mesopotamian languages did not follow orthodox academic careers but maintained nonetheless strong academic inter-

30. Richard J. Storr, *Harper's University: The Beginnings; A History of the University of Chicago* (Chicago: University of Chicago Press, 1966); James P. Wind, *The Bible and the University: The Messianic Vision of William Rainey Harper* (Atlanta, GA: Scholars Press, 1987); briefly in *idem*, 'Harper, William Rainey (24 July 1856–10 Jan. 1906)', *ANB*, X, pp. 131-34. For the early history of Johns Hopkins, see Hugh Hawkins, *Pioneer: A History of the Johns Hopkins University, 1874–1889* (Ithaca, NY: Cornell University Press, 1960); for a general history, see John C. French, *History of the University Founded by Johns Hopkins* (Baltimore, MD: The Johns Hopkins University Press, 1946).

31. Catherine Wolfe (1828–87), reputed in her time to be the wealthiest single woman in the world, inherited $12,000,000 and was the leading philanthropist of her generation, William Bristol Shaw, 'Wolfe, Catharine Lorillard (March 1828–Apr. 4, 1887)', in *DAB*, XX, pp. 449-50; Saul E. Zalesch, 'Wolfe, Catharine Lorillard (8 Mar. 1828–4 Apr. 1887)', in *ANB*, XXIII, pp. 728-29. For the Nippur expedition, see Bruce Kuklick, *Puritans in Babylon: The Ancient Near East and American Intellectual Life, 1880–1930* (Princeton, NJ: Princeton University Press, 1996), pp. 26-27.

32. E.A. Wallis Budge, *The Rise and Progress of Assyriology* (London: Martin Hopkinson & Co., 1925), p. 260: 'All this has been made possible by the generous gifts and benefactions of wealthy citizens…they have worked faster and on a bigger scale than their British colleagues because, unlike them, they were not hampered at every turn by the want of money.' This theme was often taken up by German correspondents with A.T. Clay of Yale in the terrible years after World War I; for example, Deimel wrote, 'Printing is very dear & we have not such funds, as your milliardains can give them' (1921, archives of Yale Babylonian Collection).

ests at a professional level. William Hayes Ward (1835–1916) is an interesting example of this pattern.[33] His father, a clergyman, imposed on him a linguistic education worthy of John Stuart Mill. Young Ward began the study of biblical Hebrew at the age of six and had read through the entire Bible by nine. Then he was set to Greek and by his twelfth year had read through the entire Greek Bible. Finally he was set to Latin and by the age of fifteen had read the entire Bible again in that language. His formal education culminated in graduation from Amherst College in 1856, followed by brief stints at Union, Yale, and Andover seminaries in preparation for the ministry. Disappointed in their hope to serve as missionaries abroad, Ward and his wife spent two years doing mission work in Kansas instead. Ward next taught school for some years and served as professor of Latin and natural science at Ripon College in Wisconsin (1865–67). He was then invited to join the staff of the *New York Independent*, which gave him his livelihood for the rest of his life. Ward was very well read in the Assyriology of his day and published various articles in the *Independent* on archaeology in Mesopotamia, together with translations of cuneiform texts.

Ward was a member of the American Oriental Society and joined an informal group of Society members formed to investigate the possibilities of an American archaeological expedition in Mesopotamia. When Catherine Wolfe offered funds to send out a group to explore for a possible site, Ward was chosen as leader. The team made a broad reconnaissance in Mesopotamia (1884–85), evidently deciding that sites in the north were too heavily excavated, so recommended a site in the Sumerian south, ancient Nippur. Ward did not take part in the subsequent excavations at Nippur, carried out by the University of Pennsylvania and its newly founded University Museum.[34] He also turned down the offer of a professorship in Oriental languages at Harvard in 1879, on the grounds that he was not qualified.

Ward was a man of broad culture, with a keen interest in poetry.[35] His most substantial scholarly publications were two volumes of Mesopotamian cylinder seals, *Cylinders and Other Ancient Oriental Seals in the Library of J. Pierpont*

33. George A. Barton, 'Ward, William Hayes (June 25, 1835–Aug. 28, 1916)', in *DAB*, XIX, pp. 442-43; Morris Jastrow, 'In Memoriam: William Hayes Ward (1835–1916)', *JAOS* 36 (1916), pp. 233-41; [New York] *Independent*, June 28, 1915; June 19, 1916; October 18, 1915; September 11, 1916; December 28, 1918. Ward's last book, *What I Believe and Why* (New York: Charles Scribner's Sons, 1915), contains scattered autobiographical remarks, especially on his experiences in Kansas, but is mostly a defense of his religious beliefs.

34. Kuklick, *Puritans in Babylon*, pp. 35-57, and Richard L. Zettler, 'Excavations at Nippur, The University of Pennsylvania, and the University's Museum', in *Nippur at the Centennial: Papers Read at the XXXVe Rencontre assyriologique internationale, Philadelphia, 1988* (ed. Maria deJong Ellis; Occasional Publications of the Samuel Noah Kramer Fund, 14; Philadelphia: University Museum, 1992), pp. 325-36.

35. *Poems of Sidney Lanier: Edited by His Wife, with a Memorial by William Hayes Ward* (New York: Charles Scribner's Sons, 1884).

Morgan (1909) and *The Seal Cylinders of Western Asia* (1910), the latter based on his own superb collection, now in the Yale Babylonian Collection. Ward willed his library to Albert T. Clay's project of an American School for Oriental Research in Baghdad, but the books were apparently never delivered by his heirs.[36] His son, Herbert D. Ward, married one of nineteenth-century America's most successful and renowned woman writers, Elizabeth Stuart Phelps (1844–1911), and published jointly with her a now-forgotten historical novel based in ancient Mesopotamia, *The Master of the Magicians* (1890). The reader will suspect that it is mostly his work, as it contains a fair amount of late nineteenth-century Assyriology, in one form or another, including translations of cuneiform texts and some very strange ideas, among them that the Babylonian family of Egibi was made up of Jewish exiles (Egibi = Jacob). Space was even found in the narrative for a calculation of the number of bricks needed to build the wall of Babylon, Imgur-Bēl, 'eighteen thousand seven hundred and sixty-five millions, or twice the amount of masonry used in building the great Chinese wall', indeed, 'Four Parises or two Londons could encamp therein'.[37] I have not sought to trace the Assyriological background of this novel, but expect that a considerable amount of it may have been drawn from the elder Ward's newspaper articles and the younger Ward's *Kinderstube*.

Ward is an outstanding instance of a man suited by temperament and training to an academic and research career, but whose energies and talents led him in other directions. He was on excellent terms with the leading Orientalists of his day and noted particularly as a popular archaeological writer, collector, and scholar of cylinder seals.

The case of Edgar James Banks (1866–1945) is more complex.[38] Banks graduated from Harvard in 1893 (M.A. 1895), where he studied Semitic languages, and took a doctorate at Breslau on some bilingual hymns of the Hellenistic period from Uruk (*Sumerisch-babylonische Hymnen der von Georg Reisner herausgegebenen Berliner Sammlung umschrieben: übersetzt und erklärt*, Leipzig, 1897).[39] His energetic personality suited him to be an explorer,

36. Jerrold S. Cooper, 'American School of Oriental Research in Baghdad', in *The Oxford Encyclopedia of Archaeology* (5 vols.; Oxford: Oxford University Press, 1997), I, pp. 92-94 (93).

37. Elizabeth Stuart Phelps and Herbert D. Ward, *The Master of the Magicians* (Boston: Houghton, Mifflin & Company, 1890), p. 215. The authors sign the book's somewhat defensive prefatory note in reverse order and observe that 'Modern Assyriology has become a rapid and complex series of discoveries. To dogmatise, is to be unscientific. The enthusiastic research of to-morrow may overthrow the theory of today…'

38. The fullest published account of Banks' life is Meade, *Road to Babylon*, pp. 66-70; see also *New York Times*, May 9, 1945 [p. 23]. His archaeological publications have a strongly autobiographical quality. He was included in neither the *Dictionary of American Biography* nor the *American National Biography*.

39. This work is a good example of the doctoral dissertation in Assyriology of this period, both in Germany and the United States. It consisted of deciphering and editing texts that had already

and he is said to be the first American to climb Mount Ararat (1912); he also crossed the Arabian desert by camel the same year. Hoping to mount an expedition to Mesopotamia, Banks applied to be U.S. Consul there, and received the post in 1897. His hopes were frustrated, however, as he had been unaware of the Ottoman policy that foreign government officials could not undertake archaeological exploration. He traveled extensively in southern Iraq and commenced a life-long career of buying antiquities. He resigned his post in 1899 and tried to raise funds for an expedition to Ur. With the help of Ward, William Rainey Harper, and John P. Peters, former director of the Nippur excavations, Banks raised money for a season and traveled to Constantinople, but his application was rejected.

Undeterred, Banks applied to excavate at Borsippa, but this proposal too was rejected. He made another application, but this was rejected as well. In the meantime, his supporting committee fell apart and then disbanded. Finding himself without funds, Banks taught ancient history at Roberts College (1902–1903). Finally, Banks was chosen as director of a project mounted by the University of Chicago through its Oriental Fund, a gift of $100,000 from John D. Rockefeller. Robert Francis Harper was made director of the Babylonian section of this fund and he worked out with Banks an expedition to Adab, an important Sumerian site.

Banks' excavations at Adab were amateurish, even by the standards of the day, as he had no knowledge of or experience with field archaeology, but they were richly rewarded with tablets and other finds, including a statue he perversely insisted was the 'oldest statue in the world'.[40] His reputation for acquiring and smuggling antiquities eventually aroused the Ottoman authorities, his project was terminated, and in 1906 the University of Chicago abandoned the excavation and dropped him from its faculty. Although Banks continued to hold an academic post at the University of Toledo, Ohio, as Professor of Oriental Languages (1909), he was *persona non grata* in American scholarship, to the extent that his correspondence was purged from some university files.

He continued to deal in tablets and antiquities for the rest of his life, selling small collections of tablets with highly enthusiastic labels to schools, libraries, and seminaries. These labels show that he knew enough cuneiform to date and identify the subject matter of a Sumerian administrative tablet. After publication of his book on Adab (see below), Banks published no more of the inscriptions he had discovered there, presumably because he had been denied access

been published in copy, in this case by George A. Reisner. Banks edited eight of these hymns for his degree, Dienemann two, and Hussey (see below) five. Since there were no dictionaries of Akkadian or Sumerian at the time, translating texts was much more difficult than today, as one had to search published texts and the secondary literature for parallel passages and lexical data.

40. See Yang Zhi, 'The Excavation of Adab', *Journal of Ancient Civilizations* 3 (1988), pp. 1-21. The site has been extensively looted since 1991 and many more tablets from there have appeared on the antiquities market.

to them after his association with the University of Chicago came to an end. His later books include *The Bible and the Spade* (1913), *Armenian Princess: A Tale of Anatolian Peasant-Life* (1914), and *The Seven Wonders of the Ancient World* (1917).

Whatever his strengths in terms of energy and devotion to archaeology, Banks was incautious and a tireless self-promoter: his book on Adab was subtitled 'A Story of Adventure, of Exploration, and of Excavation among the Ruins of the Oldest of the Buried Cities of Babylonia'.[41] Although smuggling of antiquities out of the Ottoman provinces in Mesopotamia was normal practice, archaeologists working in the name of scholarly institutions were not supposed to be involved in this aspect of the trade, which was dominated by local dealers. Banks himself describes his collector's impulse (p. 21: 'coin fever'). He saw the goal of digging as finding 'valuable treasures' (p. 332). He wrote of his efforts to buy antiquities and of his association with forgers. Although stating openly 'Antiquities are contraband in Turkey; not only is it forbidden to buy and sell them but it is sometimes dangerous to possess them' (p. 362), in the same context he narrated with relish his purchase of a statue stolen from the German excavations at Assur. No American institution, including the University of Chicago, had strong scruples about buying illegally exported antiquities, but Banks was made an example of, for reasons that are now obscure, perhaps in part because he was too open about his interests. He protested vigorously, but to no avail. In his later years, Banks tried speculation in real estate, and had a second career as a filmmaker, specializing in biblical epics (Sacred Films, Inc., Seminole Films Co., Inc.). None of these films is known to have survived.[42]

6. *German-Style Professionalism in American Assyriology to 1918*

The combination of public and scholarly interest made Assyriology a sought-after discipline in the new American departments of Semitic Languages & Literatures of the 1880s. After its failure with Ward, Harvard appointed a professor of Semitic languages in 1880, Crawford Toy, and his first objective was to create an additional professorship in Assyriology. He pinned his hopes on his student, David G. Lyon, whom Toy urged to go to Leipzig to become a profes-

41. E.J. Banks, *Bismya, or The Lost City of Adab* (New York: J.P. Putnam's Sons, 1912).

42. I am indebted for some of this information to the researches of Ewa Wasilewska of the University of Utah, who kindly sent me material from her forthcoming study 'The Forgotten American Indiana Jones', a biography of Banks (a version of which is available online at http://www.worldandi.com/Public/2000/August/indy.html [accessed September 28, 2006) and to a curriculum vitae of Banks in the Cuneiform Collection of the Columbia University Rare Book and Manuscript Library. Banks was closely associated with Clay in the antiquities trade, specializing in Umma and Drehem tablets, sometimes in lots of a thousand or more; his extensive correspondence with Clay on the antiquities trade is preserved in the Yale Babylonian Collection, and is probably one of the best available sources for its operation in the period 1914–25.

sional Assyriologist.[43] Johns Hopkins appointed the Leipzig Assyriologist Paul Haupt to a professorship in Semitics in 1883.[44] The University of Pennsylvania appointed another Leipzig Assyriologist, Hermann V. Hilprecht, to a professorship of Assyriology in 1886 and a second professor, Morris Jastrow, also an Assyriologist, to a professorship of Semitics. Yale, like Harvard, was unwilling to appoint a foreigner to a professorship, so recruited William Rainey Harper, a well-known proponent of the study of Hebrew for everyone, to a professorship in 1886. Harper offered Akkadian, among other languages, but soon turned that over to his brother, Robert Francis Harper, who, unlike William, had studied in Germany and had taken his degree in Assyriology at Leipzig.[45]

All this transplantation of Leipzig to the United States did not, however, serve to make Assyriology a discipline independent of biblical studies. This is best gauged from the graduate student constituency for Assyriology prior to 1920. To take the case of Yale, her first doctorate in a Near Eastern subject was in Assyriology in 1889, directed by William Rainey Harper. Prior to 1920, nine Yale graduate students took doctorates in Assyriology. Of these, eight were ordained Protestant ministers, had at least studied in a divinity school, or later became professors of Bible. The only exception to this pattern was a woman, Ettalene Grice.[46]

43. See David Gordon Lyon in the section 'Semitic, 1880–1929', in Samuel Eliot Morison, *The Development of Harvard University since the Inauguration of President Eliot, 1869–1929* (Cambridge, MA: Harvard University Press, 1930), pp. 231-40.

44. For Haupt, see B.R. Foster, 'Haupt, Paul (25 Nov. 1858–15 Dec. 1926)', in *ANB*, X, pp. 320-21.

45. For Harper at Yale, see Frank Knight Sandars, 'The Yale Period', *The Biblical World* 27 (1906), pp. 177-81 and, briefly, Wind, *Bible and the University*, pp. 46-48.

46. Frank Knight Sandars (1889), 'The Noun Formation of the Asshurbanipal Texts', became Woolsey Professor of Biblical Literature at Yale (1894–1901) and Dean of the Yale Divinity School (1901–1905); Lester Bradner (1891), 'The Order of the Sentence in the Assyrian Historical Inscriptions' [published as *Hebraica* 8 (1891), pp. 1-14], became an Episcopalian minister; Carl Elofson (1891), 'The Attributive Adjective in the Assyrian Historical Inscriptions', became a Swedish Lutheran clergyman; Charles Foster Kent (1891), 'Annexion in Assyrian', became Professor of Biblical Literature at Brown University (1898–1901) and later Woolsey Professor of Biblical Literature at Yale (1901–25); Clarence Elwood Keiser (1912), 'Cuneiform Labels and Tags from the Third Millennium B.C.' [published as *Babylonian Records in the Library of J. Pierpont Morgan* 3 (1914)], became a Lutheran minister; Henry Frederick Lutz (1916), 'Early Babylonian Letters from Larsa' [published as *YOS, Babylonian Texts* 2 (1917)], a graduate of Chicago Lutheran Theological Seminary, became Professor of Egyptology and Assyriology at the University of California, Berkeley (1929–55, first appointed 1921); Ettalene Mears Grice (1917), 'Tablets from Ur and Larsa, Dated in the Larsa Dynasty' [published as *YOS, Babylonian Texts* 5 (1919)]; Raymond Philip Dougherty (1918), 'Temple Records from Erech, Reign of Nabonidus, 555–538 B.C.' [published as *YOS, Babylonian Texts* 6 (1920)], was a graduate of Bonebrake Theological Seminary, later became Professor of Biblical Literature, Goucher College (1918–26), then William M. Laffan Professor of Assyriology and Babylonian Literature and Curator of the Babylonian Collection, Yale (1926–33); Arch Tremayne (1919), 'Temple Records from Erech, Reign of Cyrus, 538–529 B.C.' [published as *YOS, Babylonian Texts* 7 (1925)], became a Meth-

The early Yale faculty in Semitics and Assyriology, including William Rainey Harper, Charles C. Torrey, and A.T. Clay, as well as their successors, Ferris Stephens and Raymond Dougherty, were either Protestant ministers or had studied in divinity schools. They mostly taught in secular graduate programs, and the majority of their students had divinity backgrounds. Even at schools where there was less of an American Protestant spirit, such as the University of Pennsylvania and Johns Hopkins, the early graduate student body was probably dominated by people with Protestant divinity backgrounds, though I have no means of checking this.

7. *Assyriology and Jewish Learning*

In the years after World War I, when Charles C. Torrey interviewed students for graduate courses, he noted with surprise that many of them were Jews.[47] This leads to the fourth aspect of the development of American Assyriology that needs to be stressed, its connection with Jewish learning. The term 'Jewish learning' embraces two different concepts. First is scholarship originally at home in Judaism, such as study of the Talmud. Second, some researchers use the term to refer to branches of learning in which Jewish scholars could develop professional academic careers outside of synagogues and Jewish institutions of higher learning, and here Oriental studies in general and Assyriology in particular were important entry points.[48]

The relationship between Oriental language study and Judaism was not self-evident in the nineteenth-century United States. This was because of the well-established Christian tradition, given new and emphatic voice by Martin Luther, that Jews by their very refusal to accept Christianity were thereby unqualified to read and interpret the Hebrew Bible correctly, even if their formal knowledge of Hebrew was superior to that of a Christian scholar.[49] The American version of this went through various phases; suffice it to say here that the debate over the authenticity and authority of the vowel points in the Hebrew Bible was raging in America long after it was settled elsewhere.[50] A

odist clergyman. This information is drawn from a Yale University publication, *Doctors of Philosophy 1861–1960* (New Haven, 1961), and my research in the alumni files of Yale University, for access to which I thank the Office of Alumni Affairs.

47. Unpublished diaries of Charles C. Torrey, used with the kind permission of his daughter, Nancy T. Frueh.

48. Paul Ritterband and Harold S. Wechsler, *Jewish Learning in American Universities: The First Century* (Modern Jewish Experience; Bloomington, IN: Indiana University Press, 1994).

49. For Luther, see Jerome Friedman, *The Most Ancient Testimony: Sixteenth-Century Christian-Hebraica in the Age of Renaissance Nostalgia* (Athens, OH: Ohio University Press, 1983); Léon Poliakov, *The History of Anti-Semitism*. I. *From the Time of Christ to the Court Jews* (trans. Richard Howard; New York: Vanguard, 1965), pp. 216-26.

50. For a good introduction to the vowel point controversy in Europe of the sixteenth and seventeenth centuries, see Richard A. Muller, 'The Debate over the Vowel Points and the Crisis in

treatise on the study of Oriental languages, published at Andover, Massachusetts, in 1821, gives a fairly mild assessment of Jewish ignorance of the true meaning of Scripture:

> 'The Jewish teachers have, it is true, preserved some knowledge of the Hebrew tongue... Not unfrequently they assign to words a meaning which is deduced from their philosophical tenets; sometimes they sport with serious things by eking out mystical meanings from the letters; and finally, they every where show that they stand upon uncertain ground ... the Jewish Rabbins bear such a relation to the ancient Hebrews, as the Scholastics of the middle age do to the ancient Latins. As the latter are not competent witnesses in respect to the ancient *usus loquendi* of the Latins, so neither are the Rabbins as to that of the ancient Hebrews, from whom they are very remote...'[51]

The American Jewish community was not well represented in the early colleges. Even in the 1920s, Jews could not expect to receive faculty appointments in most disciplines, such as Classics, History, or English; this is why Jastrow's appointment in Semitics at the University of Pennsylvania had been of some significance, as a more likely career path for him would have been the rabbinate. Jastrow was by inclination an Assyriologist, author of a vast survey of Mesopotamian religion, for example, and co-editor of a major manuscript of the Epic of Gilgamesh.[52] Secular Semitics was, therefore, a path into the American academy for learned Jews, such as Jastrow, and such as the Semitist Richard Gottheil at Columbia.[53] Both Columbia and the University of Pennsylvania seem to have been more open to Jewish scholars than either Harvard or Yale.

On the other hand, professional American Assyriology included virulently anti-Semitic men. The first to comment on this publicly was the Assyriologist Samuel Noah Kramer, who revealed in his autobiography the blunt anti-Semitism of his department chairman at the Oriental Institute of the University of

Orthodox Hermeneutics', *The Journal of Medieval and Renaissance Studies* 10 (1980), pp. 53-72. In the United States, the debate continued well into the nineteenth century, but the tide turned with the Andover Hebraist Moses Stuart's reading of Gesenius (see Foster, 'Yale and the Study of Near Eastern Languages', p. 11). For his pre-Gesenius approach, see Moses Stuart, *A Hebrew Grammar without the Points; Designed as an Introduction to the Knowledge of the Inflections and Idiom of the Hebrew Tongue* (Andover: Flagg & Gould, 1813), pp. 9-15.

51. Johann Jahn, 'A View of Studying Languages', in *Dissertations on the Importance and Best Method of Studying the Original Languages of the Bible by Jahn and Others, Translated from the Originals, and Accompanied with Notes* (trans. Moses Stuart; Andover: Flagg & Gould, 1821), p. 19. Jahn was a Catholic biblical scholar.

52. Harold S. Wechsler, 'Pulpit or Professoriate: The Case of Morris Jastrow', *American Jewish History* 74 (1985), pp. 338-55.

53. For Gottheil (appointed to Columbia in 1887), see Marianne Sanna, 'Gottheil, Richard James Horatio (13 Oct. 1863–22 May 1936)', in *ANB*, IX, pp. 323-24; for Jewish faculty teaching Jewish learning, see Ritterband and Wechsler, *Jewish Learning in American Universities*, p. 237 n. 5.

Chicago in the 1920s.[54] Nor was this unique: Daniel Luckenbill could comment on what he saw as Jastrow's 'Jew pushiness' and Edward Chiera could write to Dougherty to inquire if a Jewish job candidate for a post at Chicago had particularly 'oriental features' or not.[55] Yale had a quota on Jewish undergraduate students and eventually turned down the offer of a professorship in Judaica made in 1924.[56] Yale did, however, through the good offices of A.T. Clay, accept the gift of a superb collection of Judaica from the Kohuts in 1915, as well as funds to support research in Semitic subjects.[57] Clay, like other American Assyriologists, including Jastrow, was anti-Zionist, but had no anti-Jewish bias; in fact, he had been the leading proponent of the abortive effort to create a professorship in Judaic studies at Yale.

Thus even if Assyriology was one way for Jews to aspire to faculty positions in American research institutions in the 1920s, they could expect to encounter crude and cruel anti-Semitism along the way. At the same time, Jewish immigration from Europe was transforming the formerly Protestant-dominated graduate programs, which were more open than the colleges, with an infusion of Jewish students. These included students who already knew Hebrew and Aramaic at entry better than the more advanced Protestant students had ever learned them. The typical destiny of Jewish scholars in the American academy, outside of Jewish institutions, was to occupy subordinate positions in the academic underclass, moving from place to place and maintaining themselves on lower salaries than their Christian contemporaries.[58]

8. *Three American Woman Assyriologists*

Although American graduate schools were open to women already in the nineteenth century, despite irritating restrictions,[59] women had far more limited career choices after getting their degrees then men, typically school teaching or teaching in women's colleges, or librarianship. Following any professional

54. Samuel Noah Kramer, *In the World of Sumer: An Autobiography* (Detroit, MI: Wayne State University Press, 1986), p. 50.

55. Unpublished correspondence, Yale Babylonian Collection.

56. Dan A. Oren, *Joining the Club: A History of Jews and Yale* (New Haven: Yale University Press, 1985), pp. 46, 67 188-90, 192, 205-206, 413, 416-17; I have also used the unpublished diary of Charles C. Torrey, October 22, 1924, courtesy of his daughter, Nancy Frueh.

57. The Kohut Collection of Judaica was first acquired by Yale in 1915, added to in 1923. The Alexander Kohut Fellowship was established in 1919 by George Kohut in memory of his father, Alexander, along with a fund to launch the *Yale Oriental Series*. George Kohut continued to add to the publication funds and increased the endowment of the fellowship from $11,000 to $20,000 in 1928 (Yale News Release, October 28, 1928, Yale University Archives). The first recipient of the fellowship was to be an Assyriologist, Ettalene Grice (see below).

58. See above n. 48.

59. In the 1930s, for example, women could not study in the Harvard Library in the evening.

career path was usually viewed as excluding marriage. While it is of interest to note that American women earned degrees in Assyriology earlier than women of other nationalities, these women could not realistically expect to receive academic posts in research universities, even if their qualifications had been equal to those of their male counterparts. Meade's history of Assyriology in America mentions only one of them in passing.

Figure 1. Mary Williams Montgomery (1874–1955), the first American and woman of any nationality to earn a doctorate in Assyriology. Photo (taken *ca.* 1910) courtesy of Robin Borglum Carter.

The first American and, so far as I am aware, the first woman of any nationality to receive a doctorate in Assyriology, was Mary Williams Montgomery. She was born in in 1874 in Mar'ash, Turkey, the child of American missionaries, her father being Giles Montgomery, her mother Emily Redington. She grew up speaking Turkish. Her family moved to Adana in 1883. Montgomery went to high school in New Haven, Connecticut, and graduated from Wellesley College (1896), where she majored in Classics, with a strong minor in German and French, returning to Turkey thereafter. She next studied Assyriology at Berlin, where she attended the lectures of Friedrich Delitzsch, Eberhard Schrader, Eduard Sachau, and others.

Delitzsch was clearly taken with the bright young American woman and presented her with an inscribed copy of his *Lesestücke*, to the admiration of her fellow students. She made rapid progress with cuneiform and Delitzsch initially may have thought she would copy tablets from the great collections in Constantinople. However, he changed his mind and sent her to the British Museum in 1900, with a letter from Schrader introducing her to Budge.

Budge was fascinated to meet a smart young American woman interested in Assyriology. He told her that Delitzsch was a 'black character' who had tried to bribe museum staff into showing tablets that he was not supposed to see and that he had deliberately given her a list of museum numbers that included such items. He went further, suggesting that she leave Berlin, as Delitzsch's reputation was declining, to take a degree at Leipzig or Heidelberg. This was confusing and discouraging for a graduate student, even though Delitzsch had already warned her that his name was not honored in England. Budge did allow Montgomery to see some tablets, however, so her efforts were not lost.

Budge proposed that she change her thesis topic to dream omens or to an investigation of whether or not the Babylonians believed in spirits like the Egyptians. When Montgomery asked him about studying in the United States, Budge summoned no less a figure than Robert Francis Harper, who was then working in the Museum. Harper, who had studied with Delitzsch, had nothing good to say about him and urged Montgomery to take her degree at Chicago. As a visitor from an American institution, she could see whatever she wanted at the British Museum. Her dissertation, which he would help her with, could be published under the auspices of the University of Chicago without charge. Meanwhile, Delitzsch continued to bombard her with lists of tablets to copy and both Harper and Budge insisted on reading his letters to her. Hers was a baptism of fire in the jealousies of Assyriology. Sachau finally settled her doubts, setting her *Hauptfach* as Semitic languages (examiners, Delitzsch and himself), her *Nebenfach* as either Turkish or Coptic (for which her examiner would be Erman). She also had to offer philosophy.

Deciding to remain in Berlin, Montgomery edited some Old Babylonian letters published in volume II of the series *Cuneiform Texts from Babylonian Tablets in the British Museum* (1892, copies by Theophilus G. Pinches), some of which she collated but without correcting mistakes in the copies (Old Babylonian letters were little known at the time). The 'opponents' at her dissertation defense, November 9, 1901, were 'Miss Ransom, Herr W.S. McNeill, Herr Dr. Schlössinger', before whom she defended three theses: 'Es ist wahrscheinlich, dass die

Babylonier eine Art Geldprägung kannten', 'Hammurabi war gleich den übrigen Königen der ersten babylonischen Dynastie kanaanäischen Geblütes', and 'Das Assyrische erweist sich in immer gesteigertem Grade als die dem Hebräischen nächst verwandte semitische Sprache'.[60]

Definitive publication of her dissertation was announced for Delitzsch's periodical *Babylonische Beiträge* (IV/4), along with a companion work by Gottfried Nagel, but this never appeared. She returned to the United States in 1902, where she first taught French and German at a private school in New Haven, then moved to New York City, where she translated works from Hebrew and wrote on Arabic subjects for the Jewish Encyclopedia. She edited the volume on Turkey for the *Historian's History of the World* (vol. 24, 1905, her name not mentioned in the publication). She also published, jointly with Mrs. Izora Chandler, a collection of stories translated from Turkish entitled *Told in a Garden of Araby* (1905). Also in 1905 she started a literary agency with two other women, but this soon became solely Montgomery & Co., with offices at 96 Fifth Avenue, when her two partners married and left the enterprise. This firm soon closed its doors and she became manager for Singer & Co., a publisher.

In 1901, while still a student, she had met on shipboard an energetic, talented painter and sculptor named Gutzon Borglum, a native of Idaho. They married in 1909 and settled on an estate near Stamford, Connecticut. During World War I, this estate became the training ground for Czech soldiers eager to return to Europe to fight, and it is said that the first flag of this brigade, which Mrs. Borglum made herself, is still preserved in the Prague Museum. Borglum was a man of immense drive and vision. He began a prodigious monument to the Confederacy, sculpted from a mountain at Stone Mountain, Georgia, then later achieved considerable fame for designing and executing the largest sculptures ever made, at Mount Rushmore, South Dakota, plus numerous other works, including a monument to Wilson in Poland and another to Atatürk in Turkey. He was a man of strong opinions and much in the public eye, especially after his vigorous investigation of corruption and waste in early aircraft production during World War I. Small wonder, then, that Mrs Borglum had no time for Assyriology after returning from Berlin. In a Wellesley Reunion Book (1926) she described her occupation as 'Buffer—like a buffer state,' and in another she wrote 'I don't seem able to dominate the circumstances of my life'. Until her husband's death in 1941, she was immersed in his complicated activities and the raising of their two surviving children. She was co-author of a biography of her husband called *Give the Man Room: The Story of Gutzon Borglum* (1952, with Robert J. Casey). She died in 1955.[61]

60. *Briefe aus der Zeit des babylonischen Königs Hammurabi (ca. 2250 v. Chr.)*, Inaugural-Dissertation Berlin [1901] (Leipzig: A. Pries, 1901). This contains a brief *Lebenslauf*, or autobiography.

61. For information on Mary Montgomery, I am grateful to Wilma Slaight, Wellesley College

The second American woman to receive the doctorate in Assyriology, and the first to study at Leipzig, was Mary Inda Hussey. She was born in New Vienna, Ohio, in 1876, grew up in Richmond, Indiana, and graduated from Earlham College (1896). She then went to Bryn Mawr College as a Friends Scholar (1897–1901), where she studied Semitic languages and history with George Barton, and then at the University of Pennsylvania (1901–1903), presumably with Jastrow and Hilprecht. She spent the summer semester of 1903 at Berlin and three further semesters at the University of Leipzig. She earned her doctorate at Bryn Mawr College in 1906 for 'Some Sumerian-Babylonian Hymns of the Berlin Collection', published in *American Journal of Semitic Languages and Literatures* 23 (1906–1907), pp. 142-76, also separately. In contrast to the standard self-presentation of the graduate student of today, she commented in a letter (April 5, 1918) to A.T. Clay, 'Of course my dissertation is not a great work—it was not designed to be'.

Hussey's first job was instructor at Wellesley College (1907–1909), then she was sustained by fellowships from the Baltimore Association for the Higher Education of Women (1909–10), the American Association of University Women (Alice Freeman Palmer Memorial, 1910–11), and as an assistant at the Harvard Semitic Museum (1911–13). There she copied two large volumes of cuneiform tablets in elegant, accurate copies, *Sumerian Tablets in the Harvard Semitic Museum, Harvard Semitic Series* 3 (1912), and 4 (1915). She was appointed to the faculty of Mount Holyoke College, Department of Religion, in 1913 and remained there until her retirement in 1941. In 1931–32 she was annual professor at the American Institute for Oriental Research in Jerusalem, the first woman to serve in this capacity. From 1917 to 1933 she served as field secretary for the School, primarily for fund-raising for its proposed archaeological projects.

In her years at Mount Holyoke, Hussey found the time to copy and publish various cuneiform texts. She became interested in Babylonian divination and also committed to preparing a volume of hymns and prayers for a projected Yale translation series (see below). So far as I am aware, she never completed this manuscript. In the letter to Clay quoted above, she makes an interesting comment on this project, 'I should be awfully pleased if you could reserve the bilingual and Semitic hymns for me. Let Mr Meek take the building inscriptions!

Archivist. I have drawn on the following sources in the Wellesley College Archives: Class of 1896 Record Books 1900, 1901, 1902, 1903, 1904, 1905, 1906, 1907, 1908, 1909, 1910, 1913, 1916, 1918, 1921, 1926, 1933, 1937; 'Who's Who Among Wellesley Alumnae', No. 7 (*Wellesley Magazine*, March, 1943), plus notices in the same for October, 1941, April, 1948, May, 1952, May, 1955, January, 1956, July 1959, and January, 1960; Scarsdale (NY) *Inquirer*, May 7, 1943, and a brief obituary in the *New York Times*, August 18, 1955. My source for Mary Montgomery's student days and experiences in the British Museum is Robin Borglum Carter, *Mary's Story* (Corpus Christi, TX: privately published, 2005), especially pp. 112-19; my special thanks go to her for providing me with a copy of this book.

That is a much more natural subject for a man than for a woman…' She also began copying tablets of rituals and incantations in the Yale Babylonian Collection. This project took her many years and repeated collations. To expedite matters, Stephens and Goetze loaned the tablets to the Mount Holyoke College Library, so she could consult them locally. Hussey's elegant and accurate copies were eventually published posthumously in *Yale Oriental Series* 11 (1985).[62]

The third American woman to receive a doctorate in Assyriology was Ettalene Mears Grice. She was born in 1887 in Portsmouth, Ohio, only child of William B. Grice, an attorney, and Louise J. (Tomlinson) Grice. Her mother was unusually well educated for her time, holding a college degree, 'and her mind led to literature, and she had a memory of whatever she read that was almost beyond belief, as she could repeat what she had read years before using the exact words' (according to an unpublished tribute by William Grice). Ettalene attended school in Portsmouth and graduated from Western College for Women in 1908. She taught in the Portsmouth schools (1908–12) then was invited to Bryn Mawr College for post-graduation work in biblical literature, where George Barton introduced her to Assyriology. She then entered the doctoral program at Yale and received her PhD in 1917, the first woman to receive a degree in Semitics (now Near Eastern Languages & Civilizations) at Yale. A.T. Clay, her teacher and Yale's dynamic professor of Assyriology, found post-doctoral support for her as Research Fellow and assistant in the Babylonian Collection (1917), then as Lecturer in Assyriology (1919–25) and as Alexander Kohut Research Fellow in Semitics (1919–25). She also helped out as his assistant when he served as treasurer of the American Oriental Society.[63]

Some American Orientalist scholars and institutions of the period had a penchant for grand projects, of which the supreme example was to be the varied scholarly undertakings of the Oriental Institute of the University of Chicago.[64]

62. Obituary, Holyoke [MA] *Transcript-Telegram*, June 23, 1952; press release, Mount Holyoke Press Bureau, December, 1952; Registrar's records, Mount Holyoke College Archives; correspondence with Clay and Grice in the files of the Yale Babylonian Collection. For her year in Jerusalem and travels thereafter, see *Mount Holyoke News*, March 14, 1931. For the projected edition of Mesopotamian hymns, see *Boston Transcript*, Sept. 20, 1924 (with portrait). For a bibliography of her Assyriological publications, see R. Borger, *Handbuch der Keilschriftliteratur* (3 vols.; Berlin: W. de Gruyter, 1967), I, pp. 199-200. I owe my knowledge of the newspaper articles cited here to the biographical collections in the Mount Holyoke College Archives and Special Collections, LD 7092.8. I thank Ralitsa Donkova, Archives Assistant, for her help. Deimel thought Hussey's copies of Pre-Sargonic tablets 'quite excellent' (1921, Archives of Yale Babylonian Collection).

63. For Grice's work for the American Oriental Society, see 'Proceedings of the American Oriental Society at the Meeting in Washington, DC, 1928', *JAOS* 48 (1928), pp. 326-52 (328).

64. James Henry Breasted, *The Oriental Institute of the University of Chicago: A Beginning and a Program* (Oriental Institute Communications, 1; Chicago: University of Chicago Press, 1922), and *idem*, *AJSLL* 38 (1922), pp. 233-328; Mogens Trolle Larsen, 'Orientalism and the Ancient Near East', in *The Humanities between Art and Science: Intellectual Developments,*

Clay, in his own style, was a man of unlimited energy whose mind generated various large projects to be done at Yale. The first of these was to be a syllabary, that is, a list of all cuneiform signs with their pronunciation, for all periods that cuneiform writing was in use. To compile such a work, one had to go through all published cuneiform texts, extract individual signs, note their values, and file them on cards. One also had to index all published ancient sources of a lexical, epigraphic, or philological nature. Miss Grice bore the brunt of this enormous task, filling box after box with thousands of neatly typed and drawn cards of cuneiform signs according to a complicated system. This grew and grew, so that by 1926, Clay's successor, Raymond Dougherty, estimated to Geuthner, a Paris publisher, that 1,500 octavo pages would be needed to publish the finished product. Efforts were made to raise money to send Grice to the British Museum, even Baghdad, to collate tablets, but she was concerned about her father's health and would not leave the country. In addition to this labor, she typed all the cards for the card catalogue of the Babylonian Collection library.

Grice's syllabary project metamorphosed into a second, a Sumerian dictionary and sign list. Clay knew that a similar project was underway at Rome, the work of a team under the leadership of Anton Deimel. Deimel corresponded with Clay about his project, and was enthusiastic about a new printing process that allowed him to reproduce manuscript. It seems that everyone felt that the Yale syllabary, as it started out to be, was no overlap with Deimel's work. The first of Deimel's volumes of his *Šumerisches Lexikon* appeared in 1928, but Grice's Sumerian dictionary never came to pass.[65]

As Miss Grice typed her cards and checked off texts, one by one, Clay came up with another project in 1918, called 'Library of Western Asiatic (later: Semitic) Inscriptions'. This was to include reliable editions and translations of ancient Near Eastern texts, prepared by American and Canadian scholars, for the benefit of non-specialist readers. The only commitments to this project that seemed likely to be submitted soon were by George A. Barton, a volume of early royal inscriptions, and by Samuel A.B. Mercer, an Assyriologist at Toronto, of the Akkadian letters discovered at El-Amarna in Egypt. Miss Hussey, as noted above, committed to a volume of hymns and prayers. Much of the correspondence for this project was carried on by Miss Grice, especially after Clay's untimely death in 1925. Barton's was the only volume in the series as such to appear, and it was no advance over the masterpiece of Thureau-Dangin, on which it was based. Barton was a hasty scholar, prone to change his mind, and with little patience for details, so completion of the book in publishable form was enough of a struggle to make the future of the project doubtful, especially since Mercer's contribution was deemed unsatisfactory, too heavily dependent

1880–1914 (ed. Michael Harbsmeier and M.T. Larsen; Copenhagen: Akademisk Forlag, 1989), pp. 181-202.

65. Anton Deimel, *Šumerisches Lexikon* (4 vols.; Rome: Pontifical Institute Press, 1928–33).

on the German of J.A. Knudtzon's great *editio princeps*.[66] Robert H. Pfeiffer's *State Letters of Assyria*, published by the American Oriental Society in 1935, was the most successful outcome of this project.

Clay also decided to begin a dictionary of Akkadian, to be prepared jointly by himself and William Muss-Arnolt (d. 1927), a German Assyriologist who had been affiliated with Johns Hopkins. Muss-Arnolt had already published a *Concise Dictionary of the Assyrian Language* in two volumes (1892, 1905). Despite their usefulness, these were sorely in need of revision.[67] Nothing came of this proposal, however, so Miss Grice did not begin on an Akkadian dictionary in addition to her other tasks. Realization of the dream of an Akkadian-English dictionary took resources Yale could never muster. The Akkadian dictionary was begun at the Oriental Institute of the University of Chicago, which began collecting materials in 1921, but published the first volume of the dictionary only in 1959.[68]

Clay also proposed an encyclopedia of Assyriology, for which he began to collect material and to assign articles to prospective contributors. Grice was assigned the article on syllabaries, but nothing came of this proposal either, which was obviated by an encyclopedia of Assyriology founded by Erich Ebeling and Bruno Meissner in Berlin, the first fascicle of which appeared in 1928.[69]

When Clay was struck down by cancer in the summer of 1925, Grice's world fell apart. She had published her large volume of copies of Old Babylonian tablets from Larsa, *Yale Oriental Series* 5, in 1919, as well as her study, *Chronology of the Larsa Dynasty*, *Yale Oriental Studies, Researches*, 4/I (1919), but after that her energies had been focused entirely on Clay's projects, plus some teaching (Clay was in Jerusalem, 1919–20 and 1923–24). She offered courses

66. Mercer's book appeared separately as *The Tell el-Amarna Tablets* (2 vols.; Toronto: Macmillan Co. of Canada, 1939). According to him, the translation took ten years (1919–29), and when it was ready in 1930, he submitted the manuscript, 2,240 pages, to the Yale University Press. A subvention of $5,000 was needed to pay the cost of printing the book, half of which he was supposed to but was unable to provide. Some generous donors noted the manuscript in his house in 1936 and offered to pay the cost, the result being 100 luxury copies, called the 'Nile' edition, priced at $100 each, and 900 ordinary copies, called the 'Luxor' edition, priced at $17.50 each, the proceeds committed to fund a scholarship at the University of Toronto in aid of Oriental research, Samuel A.B. Mercer, *A Brief Autobiography* (privately printed, 1958, no pagination), chapter 4.

67. For Muss-Arnolt and his dictionary, see R. Borger, 'Altorientalische Lexikographie: Geschichte und Probleme zur Vollendung von W. von Soden, Akkadisches Handwörterbuch', *Nachrichten der Akademie der Wissenschaften in Göttingen*. I. *Philologisch-historische Klasse* (1984/2), pp. 70-114 (85-90).

68. Erica Reiner, *An Adventure of Great Dimension: The Launching of the Chicago Assyrian Dictionary* (Transactions of the American Philosophical Society, 92/3; Philadelphia: American Philosophical Society, 2002).

69. *Reallexikon der Assyriologie*… (Berlin: W. de Gruyter).

in beginning Akkadian, syllabaries, lexicographical, and grammatical tests, Sumerian grammar and bilingual texts, and early Babylonian contracts. Upon Clay's death she was appointed assistant professor and acting curator of the Babylonian Collection for a year. Her physical deformity, self-effacing nature, and career choice doomed her to a lonely private life, so she spent all her time in the Yale Babylonian Collection, filling out cards, keeping the library current, and answering and filing correspondence. By special arrangement, she kept the Yale Babylonian Collection, then located in the Osborn Zoological Laboratory, open on Sundays, for which she received an emolument of $1.25 a day.

Grice was blessed with a well-organized mind and excellent research skills. In an unpublished tribute to her, the Assyriologist Ferris J. Stephens remarked, 'Absolute precision and accuracy was her watch word from the beginning. She was possessed of a keenly analytical mind as well as a profound determination and extreme patience…' Similarly the British Assyriologist T.G. Pinches wrote of her 'tireless industry in Assyriological research'.[70] Yet Grice never wrote an independent article and published only two book reviews. At Clay's death, she could sit briefly in his chair, but, for good reason, no one seems to have envisaged her as a possible candidate for his successor. By the accident of Clay's death, she was the first woman to be appointed to a ladder rank in the Semitics department at Yale. Even this promotion was not to last long.

In December, 1927, Grice was hospitalized for a mysterious intermittent fever that resisted both diagnosis and treatment. Death came quickly, bringing to an abrupt end her years of lonely, selfless labor in the Yale Babylonian Collection on whatever meager salary could be negotiated for her. Six mourners attended her funeral: Charles C. Torrey, the Doughertys, her fellow Assyriologist A. Tremayne, her father, and a friend, a Miss Percy. Even though Ferris Stephens, a fellow student, was appointed to the Babylonian Collection to carry on her work, the syllabary project languished and none of Clay's plans was realized.[71]

70. T.G. Pinches, 'Review of Grice, *Chronology of the Larsa Dynasty*', *JRAS* (1920), pp. 611-15, quotation from p. 615.

71. My sketch of Grice's career is based on the archives of the Yale Babylonian Collection and Torrey's diary. Basic bibliographic details may be found in the *Yale Alumni Weekly*, December 16, 1927; notices in the *New Haven Register*, December 5, 1927, December 8, 1927, the *New Haven Journal Courier*, December 7, 1927; obituaries in the *New York Times*, December 6, 1927, *New Haven Journal Courier*, December 6, 1927, and *New Haven Register*, December 5, 1927. An article, based on a Yale press release, appeared in the *New York Herald*, October 8, 1925, noting her appointment as acting curator of the Babylonian Collection, 'the most complete of its kind in the world.' Her reviews were of Clay's *Empire of the Amorites*, *Yale Divinity News* 17/4 (May, 1921), p. 3, and W. Lansdell Wardle, *Israel and Babylon*, *American Journal of Archaeology* 30 (1926), pp. 470-71. According to a list of her publications she compiled herself, an article she wrote entitled 'Yale Babylonian Collection' appeared in a periodical called *Little Blue Bulletin*, May, 1922, p. 8; I regret that I have been unable to identify or locate this publication. A full dossier on her life, including a family history compiled by her father, who lived with her from 1917 until her death, is in Yale University Alumni dossier B17dP, Yale University Archives.

Thus Assyriology offered an opportunity for women to become professionally active in a field of higher learning in the United States, but women could not expect to compete for one of the professorships in the field, all of which in 1925 were held by white males. Nearly all of these professors were American Protestants or men of foreign birth and training. For example, the University of Pennsylvania offered the Clark professorship, vacated by Hilprecht, to an Englishman, L.W. King, and finally to a French Roman Catholic priest, Léon Legrain,[72] who became the Clark research professor of Assyriology at the University of Pennsylvania in 1929 (appointed to the University Museum in 1920). The Johns Hopkins University offered Haupt's chair to his student, William F. Albright, an American. Yale, after considering the German Assyriologist, Arthur Ungnad, offered Clay's chair to Clay's student, the American Raymond Dougherty.

9. *American Professionalism in Assyriology, 1914 to 1941*

By the outbreak of World War I, an impressive number of Americans held advanced degrees in Assyriology and were actively contributing to the discipline. A full assessment of the generation of Americans active in Assyriology during this period would require a monograph-length study, though Meade has laid the foundations for one. From an Assyriologist's standpoint, perhaps the fundamental criterion is professionalism: to what extent did men and women of this generation permanently increase the fund of knowledge, the intellectual perspectives, or the sources and research tools of their discipline worldwide?

One perspective is provided by critical comments of a man who knew this generation well. In a centennial address to the American Oriental Society in 1942, Theophile James Meek, professor at the University of Toronto, set forth with some bluntness his views on the state of American Assyriology at the outbreak of the Second World War.[73] Unlike Torrey, who had called for American intellectual independence from Germany in 1914, Meek stated that the center of ancient Near Eastern research had by 1941 shifted from Germany to the New World. Meek did not elaborate on this proposition, so it is not clear at this remove if he was making a statement about American Assyriology of his time or whether he was referring obliquely to the emigration of European scholars threatened by Nazism to the United States, such as Albrecht Goetze, Julius Levy, and A. Leo Oppenheim. Comparing the contributions of these three alone to those of their American contemporaries, even the most ardent Ameri-

72. For Legrain, see S.N. Kramer, 'Léon Legrain (1878–1963)', *AfO* 21 (1966), pp. 261-62; Clyde Curry Smith, 'Some Footnotes to the History of Assyriology: Leonard William King of the British Museum and the University of Pennsylvania', in *If a Man Builds a Joyful House: Assyriological Studies in Honor of Erle Verdun Leichty* (ed. Ann K. Guinan *et al.*; Cuneiform Monographs, 31; Leiden; Boston: Brill, 2006), pp. 431-41.

73. Theophile James Meek, 'The Challenge of Oriental Studies to American Scholarship', *JAOS* 63 (1943), pp. 83-93.

can patriot would agree that these men decisively raised the level of American Assyriological scholarship.

Meek, tactfully avoiding reference to anyone living in 1942, suggested that Americans tended to make things too simple and were often subjective in their approach. American archaeology, as he saw it, made absurd claims about its potential and importance. American Assyriologists, such as Craig and Langdon, were sometimes careless in their work. Meek found Langdon's scholarship 'so inexact in fact that it can never be a sure guide to anything despite the fact that Langdon's innate scholarship was probably unexcelled in his day'.[74] Thus the only volume by an American (Langdon) in the distinguished series *Vorderasiatische Bibliothek* was the lowest in quality and accuracy.

For Meek, Americans needed to do more cooperative work and needed to be more productive. Some prominent Americans (one could here think of Lyon, though Meek named no names here) never published anything after getting their doctorates. Those that did publish were overworked: Meek taught fifteen or more class hours a week with over 100 students and read all their course papers and exams himself, in addition to publishing regularly. Finally, Americans needed to be better spokesmen for their discipline, which was falling victim to cuts and unfair treatment in the competition for resources.

Using one of the parameters used in this essay, one may inquire whether or not American Assyriologists active in this period who were trained in Germany were more professionally competent or productive as a group than Americans trained exclusively in the United States. To a certain extent this might seem a skewed sample, as one would expect a priori that scholars with the energy and dedication to pursue their studies abroad in an alien culture and language would be likely to achieve more than their peers who stayed at home, but, in fact, no pattern emerges. A short list of Americans trained in Germany would include David Gordon Lyon, James Alexander Craig, Ira Maurice Price, and Robert Francis Harper. A short list of contemporaneous American Assyriologists who received all of their advanced training in the United States would include George A. Barton, John D. Prince, Albert T. Clay and Leroy Waterman. Very few Americans studied Assyriology in England or France, the notable exception being Stephen Langdon, who studied Assyriology in Paris and later became professor of Assyriology at Oxford.

Among the alumni of German programs, Lyon (d. 1935)[75] held a comfortable professorship at Harvard and was instrumental in creation of the Harvard Semitic Museum. He published little professional Assyriology after his dissertation (*Keilschrifttexte Sargon's* [1883]), though honorable mention may be made of America's first Akkadian grammar, *An Assyrian Manual, for the Use of Beginners in the Study of the Assyrian Language* (1886). In his later years, much of Lyon's time was taken up with Harvard excavation projects at Samaria

74. Meek, 'Challenge of Oriental Studies', p. 87.

75. Meade, *Road to Babylon*, pp. 30-32, 120-21.

and Nuzi, and the operation of the Harvard Semitic Museum. Craig (d. 1932)[76] published voluminously at the start of his career, including three volumes of texts from the Kuyunjik Collection of the British Museum, and other studies (1895, 1897, 1899). Owing to their numerous errors, these works were not so well received as he had hoped. Denouncing his critics as 'pedantic and impertinent' (*Assyrian and Babylonian Religious Texts* [1895, 1897], II, p. vii), Craig seems to have withdrawn from Assyriological publication after 1899. Price (d. 1939),[77] who taught at Chicago after receiving his doctorate in Leipzig in 1887, became interested in inscribed objects, such as seals, and brought out an edition of the cylinders of Gudea (*The Great Cylinder Inscriptions A & B of Gudea* [1899–1927]). This was scarcely a creditable effort, as the great French Assyriologist F. Thureau-Dangin had published a transliteration and translation of them already in 1905 and 1907, and his cuneiform copies had appeared in 1925 (*Les cylindres de Goudéa*... [1925]). It is therefore hard to see the purpose or value of Price's work, though the copies, which he was obliged to prepare through the glass of the display case in the Louvre, were well executed.

Robert Francis Harper (d. 1914)[78] first published *Cylinder A of the Esarhaddon Inscriptions* (1888). His major early work was *The Code of Hammurabi, King of Babylon about 2250 B.C.* (1904), which remained useful until replaced by that of Driver and Miles (*The Babylonian Laws* [1952, 1955]); he also collaborated on an anthology of Akkadian literature in translation (*Assyrian and Babylonian Literature* [1904], with translations by Harper, Clifton Daggett Gray, William Muss-Arnolt, Preston P. Bruce, Alois Bárta, Ira M. Price, George A. Barton, Christopher Johnston, John M.P. Smith, R. Campbell Thompson, and L.W. King). Next, Harper was entrusted with the publication of a large collection of Neo-Assyrian and Neo-Babylonian letters in the British Museum. This was the most ambitious project of its kind undertaken by any American Assyriologist of his generation, as the sources were fragmentary, often very difficult to understand, and comparatively little was known of their grammar and cultural and historical background. The Akkadian texts of the letters were published in fourteen volumes in cuneiform type (*Assyrian and Babylonian Letters*... [1892–1914]), for well over half a century a standard work in Assyriology), and were long thereafter referred to as the 'Harper Letters'.

Of native-trained Assyriologists, Barton (d. 1942),[79] who received the first Harvard doctorate in Assyriology (1891), was noted for his lack of philologi-

76. Meade, *Road to Babylon*, p. 41.

77. Meade, *Road to Babylon*, p. 40.

78. Meade, *Road to Babylon*, pp. 39-40, 64-66; George A. Barton, 'Harper, Robert Francis (Oct. 18, 1864–Aug. 5, 1914)', in *DAB*, VIII, pp. 284-85.

79. For Barton, see B.R. Foster, 'Barton, George Aaron (12 Nov. 1859–28 June 1942)', in *ANB*, II, pp. 291-92. Deimel commented on his work to Clay, 'All his publications of texts should be redone according to my view & the view of many others' (1921, Archives of Yale Babylonian Collection).

cal rigor but became an energetic copiest of tablets, including three volumes of Ur III tablets (*Haverford Library Collection* [1905–14]), Sumerian literature (*Miscellaneous Babylonian Inscriptions* [1918]), and Sargonic and Pre-Sargonic administrative documents (*Sumerian Business and Administrative Documents* … [1915]). Barton was gifted with a ready pen and was one of the most active and visible members of the Assyriological profession in the United States of his generation.

Clay (d. 1925)[80] studied with Hilprecht at the University of Pennsylvania, and learned from him the 'exact' style of pen-and-ink reproduction of cuneiform tablets, as opposed to free-hand or cuneiform type. Clay had remarkable gifts and energy as an epigrapher and published volumes of beautifully executed cuneiform copies of all periods, from Pre-Sargonic to Hellenistic. As the first, and dynamic and enthusiastic, professor of Assyriology at Yale, and the first curator of its Babylonian Collection, he was determined to make Yale a center for Assyriology like the University of Pennsylvania. He created text and research series along the lines of those founded by Hilprecht, urged his students to copy and edit volumes of cuneiform tablets for their dissertations, planned for a museum at Yale, and tried to mount a series of archaeological expeditions, particularly to find the site of ancient Mari. He was also a key personality in developing American research schools in the Middle East, one at Jerusalem (founded originally by Charles C. Torrey), and another at Baghdad. On the other hand, he was deemed too hasty a philologist by such scholars as his friend Arthur Ungnad, who urged him to think more carefully before bringing his favorite ideas to print, and Torrey, when he edited his work, found it problematic. His theses concerning the importance of the Amorites, while in some respects prescient, found little acceptance in their time, and their philological underpinnings were inadequate. Clay was also a successful teacher, training a whole 'Yale School' of Assyriologists (Keiser [1912], Lutz [1916], Grice [1917], Dougherty [1918, later to be Clay's successor at Yale], Tremayne [1919], Samuel Feigin [1923], Ferris J. Stephens [1925]. All of these published their dissertation work in the form of large volumes of cuneiform copies in one of Clay's cuneiform text series, but these proved to be their major contribution to Assyriology.

Waterman (d. 1972)[81] studied Assyriology with Robert Francis Harper and paid his epigraphic dues with a volume of Old Babylonian tablets (*Business Documents of the Hammurapi Period*… [1916]). He then became involved with his teacher's project of publishing the Neo-Assyrian and Neo-Babylonian letters from Kuyunjuk, and upon Harper's death undertook to publish the promised edition, which appeared in three volumes as *Royal Correspondence of the*

80. For Clay, see B.R. Foster, 'Clay, Albert Tobias (4 Dec. 1866–14 Sept. 1925)', in *ANB*, V, pp. 17-18.

81. For Waterman, see George G. Cameron, 'Leroy Waterman (1875–1972)', *AfO* 26 (1978–79), pp. 244-45, justificatory on the subject of his edition of the Assyrian letters.

Assyrian Empire (1930–36). Although this was a courageous undertaking and underlay all treatments of these texts by other scholars of his generation, such as Pfeiffer's *State Letters of Assyria* (1935), it probably fell somewhat short of what could have been done with these sources. Waterman spent most of his career at the University of Michigan, making it an important center for Assyriology in the United States. He also led an archaeological expedition to Tell Umar (= Ctesiphon, 1927–29) and promptly published the results, which mostly dated to the Parthian period, although some cuneiform inscriptions were found (*Tel Umar* [1931]).

The outbreak of World War II brought dislocation, death and destruction upon Assyriology and Assyriologists worldwide. The Nazi attack on Jews and on Jewish scholarship, politicization of historical scholarship, and the diaspora of Assyriologists to military service, death camps, and into exile, particularly to Turkey and the United States, meant that American Assyriology looked quite different in 1948 from what it had been in 1938.[82] As Meek had seen, the United States had by then become a major center of gravity in the discipline, whereas German scholarship had to be rebuilt from the ruins of her museums and universities and amidst deep personal divisions among those who had survived the war. A new phase in the history of American Assyriology had begun.

82. Ludmila Hanisch and Hanne Schönig, 'Ausgegrenzte Kompetenz: Porträts vertriebener Orientalisten und Orientalistinnen 1933–1945', *Orientwissenschaftliche Hefte* 1 (2001), pp. 15-141; Muazzez Çiğ, 'Atatürk and the Beginnings of Cuneiform Studies in Turkey', *JCS* 40 (1988), pp. 211-16.

Images of Assyria in Nineteenth- and Twentieth-Century Western Scholarship*

Eckart Frahm

Until the late eighteenth century, Western views of ancient history relied exclusively on two groups of sources: the Bible and the literature of the classical world. Both groups had their central topographical reference points: the first one Jerusalem, the second one Athens and Rome. The people of the Middle Ages and early modernity did not conceive of these cities as distant places of a remote and alien past. They regarded them instead as locations of crucial importance for their self-representation: from Jerusalem, their religious beliefs had arisen, from Athens their methods of thinking, and from Rome their political organization. The ancient civilizations outside this familiar sphere were not completely unknown, since cities such as Nineveh, Babylon, or Carthage appeared in biblical and classical texts as well. But they represented a kind of counter-world to that shaped by Judeo-Christian and classical traditions. While Israel, Greece and Rome served as models of identity for the West, Assyria, Babylonia, and Phoenicia were the corresponding embodiments of alterity. The tone was set by the Bible: Babylon was 'the mother of whores and of every obscenity on earth' (Rev. 17.5), and Nineveh 'the bloody city, all full of lies and booty' (Nah. 3.1).[1]

* I am indebted to Kathryn Slanski for reading an earlier version of this paper, making a number of valuable suggestions, and correcting my English.

1. Of course, this statement simplifies what was in fact a somewhat more complex reception of ancient history. Besides disgust, the pre-modern Western world occasionally also showed a certain degree of admiration for the ancient nations of the East. Egypt represents a particularly ambivalent case—thoroughly investigated by Martin Bernal, *Black Athena: The Afroasiatic Roots of Classical Civilization*. I. *The Fabrication of Ancient Greece 1785–1985* (New Brunswick, NJ: Rutgers University Press, 1987). On the one hand, it was the land where a despicable pharaoh had enslaved and humiliated the Israelites. But several Greek authors, most famously Plato, as well as later European scholars such as John Spencer (1630–93) and William Warburton (1682–1759), whose books have recently been discussed by Jan Assmann, *Moses the Egyptian: The Memory of Egypt in Western Monotheism* (Cambridge, MA and London: Harvard University Press, 1997), pp. 55-143, regarded Egypt as a cradle of ancient wisdom. For other European scholars of the seventeenth and eighteenth centuries, Persia was the major source of such *prisca sapientia*: see, for example, Jacques Gaffarel, *Unheard-of Curiosities Concerning the Talismani-*

By the second half of the nineteenth century, this situation had quite dramatically changed. Convenient historical stereotypes that, thanks to the absence of original sources, had never been challenged, came suddenly under attack, and the clear boundaries between 'us' and 'them' became blurred. The resulting confusion is addressed in a famous passage from Friedrich Nietzsche's 'Thus Spake Zarathustra.' In a chapter about 'the land of culture' ('Vom Lande der Bildung'), the German philosopher describes his contemporaries, the 'present-day men', as follows:

> With fifty patches painted on faces and limbs—so sat ye there to mine astonishment, ye present-day men! And with fifty mirrors around you, which flattered your play of colors, and repeated it! Verily, ye could wear no better masks, ye present-day men, than your own faces! Who could—*recognize* you! Written all over with the characters of the past, and these characters also penciled over with new characters—thus have ye concealed yourselves well from all decipherers! ... All times and peoples gaze divers-colored out of your veils; all customs and beliefs speak divers-colored out of your gestures.[2]

Mirrors, masks and veils: Nietzsche refers to an intellectual situation where cultural identity is lost. The old hierarchies are abolished, all times and peoples are equal, and the contemporaries have their features written on their faces in a completely random patchwork fashion—so that, as Nietzsche says, a decipherer trying to read these faces would despair because they represented a palimpsest of undistinguishable texts. Nietzsche describes a nightmare of historicism.[3]

cal Sculpture of the Persians; the Horoscope of the Patriarkes; and the Reading of the Stars. Written in French by James Gaffarel. And Englished by Edmund Chilmead (London: Printed by G.D. for H. Moseley, 1650 [Paris, 1646]). A history of the image of Assyria in historical treatises from the period between the Renaissance and the eighteenth century, when scholars had begun to question the authority of the Bible, still needs to be written.

2. Translation by Thomas Common, *Thus Spake Zarathustra* (New York: Heritage Press, 1970), p. 112. The German text reads:

> Mit fünfzig Klexen bemalt an Gesicht und Gliedern: so saßet ihr da zu meinem Staunen, ihr Gegenwärtigen! Und mit fünfzig Spiegeln um euch, die eurem Farbenspiele schmeichelten und nachredeten! Wahrlich, ihr könntet gar keine bessere Maske tragen, ihr Gegenwärtigen, als euer eignes Gesicht ist! Wer könnte euch—*erkennen*! Vollgeschrieben mit den Zeichen der Vergangenheit, und auch diese Zeichen überpinselt mit neuen Zeichen: also habt ihr euch gut versteckt vor allen Zeichendeutern! ... Alle Zeiten und Völker blicken bunt aus euren Schleiern; alle Sitten und Glauben reden bunt aus euren Gebärden.

3. It appears that Nietzsche here subtly satirizes the famous German 'historicist' historian Leopold von Ranke, who, in his programmatic treatise *Zur Kritik neuerer Geschichtschreiber: Eine Beylage zu desselben romanischen und germanischen Geschichten* (Leipzig and Berlin: G. Reimer, 1824), p. iv, had remarked:

> Wie einem zu Muth seyn würde, der in eine grosse Sammlung von Alterthümern träte, worin Aechtes und Unächtes, Schönes und Zurückstossendes, Glänzendes

It is not without significance that the metaphor of decipherment features so prominently in the passage just quoted. For it was not least of all the decipherment of ancient writing systems that had provided the historical record Nietzsche found so unhealthily overwhelming. Since the second half of the eighteenth century, when J.-J. de Barthélemy had deciphered the Syrian inscriptions from Palmyra and A.H. Anquetil-Duperron had begun to study the Avesta,[4] scholars had restlessly tackled unknown scripts. Their activity resulted in two particularly decisive breakthroughs: the decoding of the writing systems of ancient Egypt and, a little later, those of Mesopotamia.[5] These achievements, 'decipherments', in fact, not only of scripts but of whole civilizations,[6] opened up dimensions of the past hitherto completely unknown. The challenges thereby presented to traditional perceptions of history were immense.

This paper will discuss how the recovery of one specific 'lost' civilization, that of ancient Assyria, influenced the intellectual discourse of Nietzsche's 'present-day men' as well as their successors—and how, in turn, scholarly views of Assyrian culture and history have been shaped during the past 150 years by the changing spirit of the age. It goes without saying that constraints of space make it impossible to offer here much more than a very basic outline of some important trends.

Assyria's traditional image in the West, while largely negative, had not been completely free of contradictions.[7] The Bible presented Assyria as a nation that,

> und Unscheinbares, aus mancherley Nationen und Zeitaltern, ohne Ordnung neben einander läge, so etwa müsste sich auch der fühlen, der sich mit Einem Mal im Anschaun der mannichfaltigen Denkmale der neuern Geschichte fände. Sie reden uns in tausend Stimmen an: sie zeigen die verschiedensten Naturen: sie sind in alle Farben gekleidet.

4. Peter T. Daniels, '"Shewing of Hard Sentences and Dissolving of Doubts": The First Decipherment', *JAOS* 108 (1988), pp. 419-36; Raymond Schwab, *Vie d'Anquetil-Duperron, suivie des usages civils et religieux des Parses par Anquetil-Duperron* (Paris: E. Leroux, 1934).

5. See P.T. Daniels, 'Methods of Decipherment', in *The World's Writing Systems* (ed. P.T. Daniels and William Bright; New York and Oxford: Oxford University Press, 1996), pp. 141-59. With regard to cuneiform, see also Robert William Rogers, *A History of Babylonia and Assyria* (2 vols.; New York and Cincinnati: Abingdon Press, 6th edn, 1915), I, pp. 1-273, and Mogens Trolle Larsen, 'Hincks versus Rawlinson: The Decipherment of the Cuneiform System of Writing', in *Ultra terminum vagari: Scritti in onore di Carl Nylander* (ed. Börje Magnusson *et al.*; Rome: Quasar, 1997), pp. 339-56.

6. See Hans Gerhard Kippenberg, *Die Entdeckung der Religionsgeschichte: Religionswissenschaft und Moderne* (München: C.H. Beck, 1997), pp. 45-51; Kippenberg uses the term 'Entzifferungen unbekannter Kulturen' and calls this period of European intellectual history 'eine orientalische Renaissance.'

7. See the very condensed overview given by Steven W. Holloway, *Aššur is King! Aššur is King! Religion in the Exercise of Power in the Neo-Assyrian Empire* (CHANE, 10; Leiden: E.J. Brill, 2002), pp. 1-9; see also, by the present author, 'Zwischen Dichtung und Wahrheit: Assur und Assyrien in den Augen der Nachwelt', in *Wiedererstehendes Assur: 100 Jahre deutsche Aus-*

having suppressed the entire world as an agent of divine wrath, finally fell to this wrath itself. The classical tradition conveyed a more ambiguous image, one that preserved a certain admiration for Assyria's military, political, and architectural achievements but also stressed its rulers' brutality and decadence. The Assyrians were exotic in a way that could be both praiseworthy and horrifying.[8]

Biblical as well as classical images of Assyria informed the oeuvre of early nineteenth-century artists and poets. Lord Byron, to mention only the most prominent one, draws on the Bible in his 1815 poem 'The Raid of Sennacherib',[9] and on Diodorus and other classical authors in his tragedy 'Sardanapalus', written in 1821.[10] While the former work, renowned for its evocative *incipit* 'The Assyrian came down like the wolf on the fold', presents a dark image of the Assyrians, portraying them as merciless predators, the latter features a rather sensitive Assyrian protagonist who functions in many respects as the *alter ego* of the author.

Such artistic license to freely project onto the Assyrians one's own fears, desires and other emotions became severely limited when, from 1842 onwards, French and British excavators, led by Paul-Emile Botta and Austen Henry Layard, rediscovered the ancient capitals of Nineveh, Nimrūd, and Khorsabad in northern Iraq. These excavations cast light instead on the Assyrians themselves, unearthing thousands of their images carved on stone slabs and tens of thousands of cuneiform texts mostly written on clay tablets.[11] When the texts, which had been buried for almost two and a half millennia, were eventually deciphered, scholars rather than poets began to dominate the cultural discourse about Assyria.[12] Their claim was that with their access to the

grabungen in Assyrien (ed. Joachim Marzahn and Beate Salje; Mainz am Rhein: Philipp von Zabern, 2003), pp. 19-28.

8. Examples for such attitudes are provided in my discussions of the historical-literary 'afterlife' of two of the most important Assyrian rulers, Sennacherib and Assurbanipal; see Eckart Frahm, *Einleitung in die Sanherib-Inschriften* (AfOB, 26; Vienna: Institut für Orientalistik der Universität Wien, 1997), pp. 21-28; *idem*, 'Images of Ashurbanipal in Later Tradition', in *Hayim and Miriam Tadmor Festschrift Volume* (ed. Israel Eph'al, Amnon Ben-Tor, Peter Machinist; Eretz Israel, 27; Jerusalem: Israel Exploration Society, 2003), pp. 37*-48*.

9. Lord Byron, *The Complete Poetical Works* (7 vols.; ed. Jerome J. McGann; Oxford and New York: Clarendon Press/Oxford University Press, 1981), III, pp. 309-10.

10. Byron, *Complete Poetical Works*, VI, pp. 15-128.

11. For an excellent account of the rediscovery of the ancient Assyrian cities, see M.T. Larsen, *The Conquest of Assyria: Excavations in an Antique Land 1840–1860* (London and New York: Routledge, 1996); Larsen also discusses the intellectual repercussions the excavations had.

12. A recent discussion of the history of nineteenth- and twentieth-century scholarship on Assyria is provided by Holloway, *Aššur is King*, pp. 9-79. Holloway focuses on the question of how scholars have assessed the problem of an alleged Assyrian religious imperialism, but provides important insights into many other aspects of modern Assyrian historiography as well. For the period up to World War II, see also Omar Carena, *History of the Near Eastern Historiography and its Problems 1852–1985*. Part 1: *1852–1945* (trans. E. Schmitz and L. Tosco; AOAT, 218/1;

primary sources, they would be able to assess more objectively what the 'real' Assyria had been.[13]

This promise of objectivity, however, was difficult to keep. In fact, Assyria continued to be studied not for its own sake, but for its links with the classical world and even more so with the Bible. One of the most widely read early histories of the ancient Near East was authored by George Rawlinson, who was not only a historian but a clergyman.[14] His brother Henry Creswick Rawlinson, the influential British scholar who had helped to decipher the cuneiform writing system, claimed in 1852, referring to new insights into Assyrian and Babylonian chronology, that 'every new fact which is brought to light from the study of the Cuneiform inscriptions tends to confirm the scriptural account'.[15] What the Rawlinson brothers and like-minded historians hoped for was that the historical texts from the Assyrian capitals would corroborate the reliability of the biblical account of history, which had come under close scrutiny as a result of research on the 'historical Jesus' and Higher Criticism applied to the Old Testament. For a while, the apologists of a Bible-centered world-view had their triumphs. The Assyrian sources provided irrefutable evidence for the historicity of Hebrew kings like Ahab or Hezekiah, and they showed that biblical references to Assyrian history were in many cases more accurate than what the classical sources had to offer.[16]

But the new texts also began to cast serious doubts on certain details of the biblical narratives, and they invalidated the Bible-based chronology that had been reconstructed with great care by Bishop Ussher and others in the seventeenth century.[17] As early as 1847, a member of the Anglican church protested

Kevelaer: Butzon & Bercker/Neukirchen–Vluyn: Neukirchener Verlag, 1989); for the beginnings of American scholarship on ancient Assyria, see Benjamin R. Foster's contribution to the present volume.

13. The opinion shared by almost all scholars that the cuneiform records were more important as sources for a history of the ancient Near Eastern than the Bible and the classical texts is aptly summarized by Rogers, *History of Babylonia and Assyria*, I, pp. 387-88: 'The gain of the Old Testament has been greater from Assyrian studies than the reverse… As sources the Greek and Latin writers once held first place, but are now reduced to a very insignificant position by the native monumental records.'

14. George Rawlinson, *The Five Great Monarchies of the Ancient Eastern World; Or, the History, Geography, and Antiquities of Chaldaea, Assyria, Babylon, Media, and Persia, Collected and Illustrated from Ancient and Modern Sources* (4 vols.; London: John Murray, 1862–67).

15. Henry C. Rawlinson, *Outlines of Assyrian History from the Inscriptions of Nineveh: The Twenty-Ninth Annual Report of the Royal Asiatic Society of Great Britain* (London: John W. Parker & Son, 1852), p. xv.

16. The most important and influential anthology of cuneiform texts related to biblical history published in the nineteenth century was Eberhard Schrader's *Die Keilinschriften und das Alte Testament*, published in its first edition in 1872 in Giessen. An English translation of the second German edition, prepared by Owen C. Whitehouse, appeared under the title *The Cuneiform Inscriptions and the Old Testament* (London and Edinburgh: Williams and Norgate, 1885–88).

17. See Larsen, *Conquest of Assyria*, pp. 157-76.

against the further prosecution of the excavations in Assyria, being alarmed at the idea that the annals of the Assyrian kings might test the credibility of biblical history.[18] So while offering support for the reliability of the Bible in some respects, the discovery of Assyria created, at the same time, a considerable amount of historical confusion. This confusion contributed to an increasingly widespread feeling of what György Lukács described as 'transcendental homelessness.'[19] Ever since the sixteenth century, when Copernicus invalidated the notion that the earth was the centre of the universe, there was a growing uneasiness among people in the West about the position of the human race in the cosmos, once firmly established by the Bible. This uneasiness reached new peaks in the middle of the nineteenth century when Darwin's discoveries put into question the presumption on the part of men that they possessed a divine soul and a divine descent. The recovery of primary sources from the ancient Near East that challenged the reliability of the *historia sacra* outlined in scripture made the traditional, Bible-based world-view even more dubious.[20]

In the first decades after the rediscovery of the Assyrian capitals, it was not only the historical inscriptions of kings whose names were mentioned in the Bible that drew attention, but also the monuments of Assyria, especially the sculptures and reliefs from the palaces at Khorsabad, Nineveh, and Nimrūd. With no pictorial evidence from biblical Israel available, the model for the visual record was set by the classical art of ancient Greece. Yet comparison between the newly discovered Eastern artifacts and the 'canonical' art of the West yielded, again, quite ambivalent results. While some authors tried to prove the complete inferiority of the Assyrian works, others saw in the Assyrian sculptures worthy predecessors of the classical masterpieces.[21]

Among the former was the cultural historian Jacob Burckhardt, whose judgment of Assyrian art and architecture was extremely severe. In his 'Reflections on History', originally conceived between 1868 and 1871, Burckhardt derides 'the utterly uncouth royal fortresses of Nineveh, [t]he meanness of their ground-plan and the slavishness of their sculptures.'[22]

18. Larsen, *Conquest of Assyria*, p. 164.

19. György Lukács discusses this concept extensively in his *Theorie des Romans* (*Theory of the Novel* [trans. from the German by Anna Bostock; Cambridge, MA: M.I.T. Press, 1971]).

20. Sigmund Freud referred to 'three blows' that undermined human narcissism in the modern age, the Copernican and the Darwinian revolutions and his own new insight that the 'ego is not master in its own house' (see the 18th chapter of his *Vorlesungen zur Einführung in die Psychoanalyse*, in *Gesammelte Werke*, 18 vols. [ed. Anna Freud *et al.*; London: Imago Publishing Co., 1940 (1917)], XI, pp. 294-95). He could also have mentioned the 'disenchantment' caused by historical and philological investigations of ancient history and sacred texts.

21. The debate in nineteenth-century Europe about ancient Near Eastern art is the subject of Frederick N. Bohrer, *Orientalism and Visual Culture: Imagining Mesopotamia in Nineteenth Century Europe* (Cambridge, UK and New York: Cambridge University Press, 2003), and his contribution to this volume.

22. Jacob Burckhardt, *Reflections on History* (trans. M.D. Hottinger; Indianapolis, IN: Liberty

The qualification of Assyrian sculpture as 'slavish' shows where Burckhardt's criticism was rooted. For him, Assyrian art was nothing but a sad reflection of the 'Oriental despotism' that ruled the East. Burckhardt, Renaissance expert and citizen of Switzerland, an admirer of individual freedom and creativity, had no sympathy for an art that, as he saw it, achieved little more than the celebration of tyrants 'who conquered and enslaved and plundered and pillaged far and wide, who, followed by their booty and their slaves, entered Thebes or Nineveh in triumph and were regarded by the people as the beloved of God.'[23]

Quite different from Burckhardt's attitude was the reception of Assyrian art in the capitals of France and Great Britain. In Paris and London, where the monumental Assyrian sculptures were actually displayed, they received criticism but principally admiration. John Ruskin, like Burckhardt an eminent expert on Italian culture, describes the Nineveh bulls as works of art that combined 'highest magnificence' with 'utmost nobleness.'[24] In the view of the educated French and British middle class, Assyria was not so much an epitome of 'Oriental despotism', but rather the first empire in history—and the heroic appropriation of Assyria's monumental art by the Louvre and the British Museum reflected the imperial ambitions France and Britain had themselves.

Summarizing the historical attitudes towards Assyria prevalent in the period between 1850 and 1871, it seems safe to say that there was not only an 'antiquarian' approach, representing the historicist spirit of the age, but also a 'monumental' one, as in the case of Ruskin, and a 'critical' one, exemplified by Burckhardt.[25] It is interesting to note that no coherent 'romantic' vision of ancient Assyria arose during the period in question. Paintings and drawings

Classics, 1979), p. 126. The original text reads: 'Die größten technischen und künstlerischen Genies vermochten an den ganz ungeschlachten Königsburgen von Ninive nichts zu ändern; die elende Anlage und die knechtische Skulptur regierten die Jahrhunderte hindurch weiter' (J. Burckhardt, *Weltgeschichtliche Betrachtungen* [ed. Jakob Oeri; Berlin and Stuttgart: W. Spemann, 1905], p. 86). The critical attitude Burckhardt and other modern students of universal history (Karl Marx, Eduard Meyer, Max Weber, V. Gordon Childe, Karl Polanyi) maintained with regard to the Assyrian city and urban space in the Middle East in general is discussed by Mario Liverani, 'Ancient Near Eastern Cities and Modern Ideologies', in *Die orientalische Stadt: Kontinuität, Wandel, Bruch: 1. Internationales Colloquium der Deutschen Orient-Gesellschaft, 9.-10. Mai 1996 in Halle/Saale* (ed. Gernot Wilhelm; Colloquien der Deutschen Orient-Gesellschaft, 1; Saarbrücken: Saarbrücker Druckerei & Verlag, 1997), pp. 85-107.

23. Burckhardt, *Reflections on History*, p. 67. The passage precedes Burckhardt's famous statement that 'power is in itself evil' ('die Macht an sich böse ist').

24. John Ruskin, *The Stones of Venice*, vol. 3, ch. 3, § 69, in *The Works of Ruskin* (39 vols.; ed. Edward T. Cook and Alexander Wedderburn; London: G. Allen; New York: Longmans, Green, & Co., 1903–12), XI, p. 188; the first edition of *The Stones of Venice* had appeared in 1851. See Bohrer, *Orientalism and Visual Culture*, pp. 165-66 for a fuller quotation and an extended discussion.

25. This classification takes up the historiographic categories introduced by Nietzsche in his 1874 essay 'On the Use and Abuse of History for Life.'

from the time showing Western excavators in Oriental garb or featuring turban-wearing Arabs who gaze, with horror and fascination, at human-headed bull-colossi as they emerge from the rubble[26] romanticize the excavations but not Assyrian civilization itself. Historians writing on ancient Assyria did not follow the example of F. Max Müller, the famous Oxford-based Sanskritist, who had claimed that the ancient texts from India revealed elements of the 'authentic' and true original religion of mankind.[27] Assyrian culture, in spite of its great age, never attracted such comments in the early age of Assyriology.

The most important reason for this rather reserved attitude was the nature of the cuneiform texts that were deciphered in the first three decades after the excavations had started. The bulk of them were royal inscriptions glorifying Assyria's bloody conquests. Highlighting the humiliation, torture, and killing of enemy combatants and civilians,[28] these accounts of the military triumphs of a ruthlessly expansionist state were unsuitable for a 'mystical' reading in the tradition of Müller. Deities appeared in the texts almost exclusively as supporters of a militaristic king who would, in return for their favors, build them temples, and as agents of wrath in the concluding curse formulas. Assyrian 'spirituality' was largely absent from them.

But slowly, literary and religious texts from the library of the Assyrian king Assurbanipal at Nineveh were deciphered as well, and the excavations in the Mesopotamian South enlarged the corpus of cuneiform documents and expanded the horizon to earlier periods of Mesopotamian history. On December 3, 1872, George Smith, a brilliant cuneiformist who worked as an assistant in the British Museum, reported his identification of a Nineveh tablet with the story of the deluge to the Society of Biblical Archaeology in London. Smith presented to his audience, which included the British Prime Minister, William Gladstone, one of the first major texts illustrating non-military aspects of Assyrian civilization.[29] Newspaper announcements in the *London Times* brought Smith's pioneering work worldwide attention.[30]

26. See, for example, the watercolor painting of Layard in Bakhtiari dress, and Layard's drawing of Arabs in an excavation pit; these two images are reproduced in Larsen, *The Conquest of Assyria*, p. 91 and pl. 1.

27. On Max Müller see Kippenberg, *Entdeckung der Religionsgeschichte*, pp. 70-73.

28. Aššur-nāṣir-apli II, for example, boasts in his annals that after conquering the city of Tela, he 'gouged out the eyes of many troops', 'burnt their adolescent boys and girls', and 'razed, destroyed, burnt, and consumed the city' (RIMA II, pp. 201-202: i 117–ii 1).

29. For an account of the meeting, see Rogers, *History of Assyria and Babylonia*, I, pp. 278-80.

30. George Smith, 'The Chaldean History of the Deluge', *The* [*London*] *Times*, no. 27551, December 4, 1872; and 'The Chaldean Story of the Deluge', *The* [*London*] *Times*, no. 27552, December 5, 1872. In January 1873, Edwin Arnold, the editor of *The Daily Telegraph*, arranged with Smith that he should go to Nineveh at the expense of that journal to carry out new excavations and look for additional fragments of the flood story.

Again, though, as in the case of the Assyrian historical inscriptions, this attention had to do with the Bible. The cuneiform flood story did not find interest for its own sake, but because of its close parallels with the story of Noah. The public was fascinated because it could indulge in the recognition of semblance (or ἀναγνώρισις, to use the famous Aristotelian term),[31] the reference point being the sacred book of Genesis. When W.H.F. Talbot, one year later, published his translation of another mythological text from Assurbanipal's library, 'Ištar's Descent to the Netherworld',[32] people were intrigued because they believed the text revealed that the Assyrians believed in the concept of an immortal soul.[33] Once more, Christian doctrine determined the way Assyrian religious texts were received.

Assyriology remained the *ancilla theologiae* for almost three more decades, a quarry for material that could be used to fill up holes in the venerated house of the Bible. But around 1900, the servant was eventually fed up with her role and ready to overthrow her mistress. The act that marks this intellectual rebellion most prominently was a widely discussed lecture on 'Babel and Bible' which the German Assyriologist Friedrich Delitzsch gave in Berlin on January 13, 1902 in the presence of emperor Wilhelm II.[34] Delitzsch turned over the traditional hierarchy between the Bible and the Mesopotamian texts, which by then formed an impressive corpus. He no longer believed, as George Rawlinson had,[35] in a Hebrew 'Ur-monotheism.' Instead, using the romantic argument that greater age meant greater purity, he claimed that the Hebrew Bible offered little more than a distorted rewriting of stories and theological concepts that had originated in Mesopotamia.[36] Later, Delitzsch even suggested that the Old Tes-

31. The concept of ἀναγνώρισις is discussed in chapter 14 of Aristotle's *Poetics*; it refers to a structure of recognition in which the subject of consciousness finds the comfort of identity and self-sameness.

32. 'The Legend of Ishtar Descending to Hades', *TSBA* 2 (1873), pp. 179-212.

33. See, for example, Jules Oppert, 'L'immortalité de l'âme chez les Chaldéens', *Annales de philosophie chrétienne* 87 (1874), pp. 210-33, and the articles by Talbot discussed by Holloway, *Aššur is King*, p. 34 (with exact references). The idea that 'Ishtar's Descent' is related to Christian pneumatology was eventually given up by most scholars, but has been recently revived by Simo Parpola in his *Assyrian Prophecies* (SAA, 9; Helsinki: Helsinki University Press, 1997), pp. xxxi-xxxvi. Parpola's approach to Assyrian religion and culture will be discussed at the end of this paper.

34. Friedrich Delitzsch, *Babel und Bibel: Ein Vortrag* (Leipzig: J.C. Hinrichs, 1902). For an English translation of the lecture, see *idem*, *Babel and Bible: A Lecture on the Significance of Assyriological Research for Religion. Delivered before the German Emperor* (trans. Thomas J. McCormack; Chicago: Open Court Publishing Co., 1902).

35. See Holloway, *Aššur is King*, p. 35.

36. For Delitzsch and the Babel-Bible debate see Reinhard G. Lehmann, *Friedrich Delitzsch und der Babel–Bibel–Streit* (OBO, 133; Freiburg, Switzerland: Universitätsverlag/Göttingen: Vandenhoeck & Ruprecht, 1994) and Klaus Johanning, *Der Bibel–Babel-Streit: Eine forschungsgeschichtliche Studie* (Europäische Hochschulschriften, Reihe 23, Theologie, 343; Frankfurt a.M.: Peter Lang, 1988).

tament, because of its derivative nature, should be completely abolished by the Christians of the modern age.[37]

Delitzsch had called his lectures 'Babel and Bible', not 'Assyria and the Bible.' But his choice of title was clearly guided more by the desire to offer a clever alliterative wordplay and to stress the importance of the German excavations in Babylon begun in 1899[38] than by the wish to exclude Assyria from his presentation. Much of the material discussed by Delitzsch was in fact Assyrian.[39] With its autocratic political system and somewhat 'Prussian' militarism, both Delitzsch and his friend the Kaiser found a lot to admire in ancient Assyria.[40]

Delitzsch gave his lectures as a new ideological trend was gaining momentum: racism. Race-based thinking had already informed, in the later decades of the nineteenth century, a debate among scholars of the ancient Near East about Semites and Sumerians, with anti-Semitic zealots generalizing about the cultural sterility of the Semitic Babylonians and Assyrians, who had taken over civilization—and most prominently, the art of writing—from the non-Semitic Sumerians.[41] Delitzsch himself was not free of such prejudice; in fact, his anti-Semitism had an ever-increasing impact on his historical perception.[42] To rec-

37. Delitzsch, *Die große Täuschung: Kritische Betrachtungen zu den alttestamentlichen Berichten über Israels Eindringen in Kanaan, die Gottesoffenbarung vom Sinai und die Wirksamkeit der Propheten* (Stuttgart: Deutsche Verlags-Anstalt, 1920).

38. In 1899, Delitzsch wrote in the *Illustrierte Zeitung*, no. 113: 'Nineveh, the palace of Sardanapalus—England's fame is forever entwined with these names. Babylon, the royal city of Nebuchadnezzar—might it be a mission worthy of Germany to be associated with these names?' (quoted in Bohrer, *Orientalism*, p. 272).

39. At the beginning of the twentieth century, most of the cuneiform texts that had been published came from Assyria, which remained in the center of many histories of the ancient Near East.

40. Wilhelm II was deeply interested in the history of the ancient Near East. When in exile after World War I, he wrote a book on kingship in Mesopotamia in which he celebrated the Assyrian ruler Assurbanipal as a 'redeemer king' ('Erlöserkönig') whose reign had brought about a new 'spring of the nations' (Wilhelm II, *Das Königtum im alten Mesopotamien* [Berlin: W. de Gruyter, 1938], p. 41).

41. See Jerrold S. Cooper, 'Posing the Sumerian Question: Race and Scholarship in the Early History of Assyriology', *AuOr* 9 (1991), pp. 47-66; *idem*, 'Sumerian and Aryan: Racial Theory, Academic Politics and Parisian Assyriology', *RevHistRel* 210 (1993), pp. 169-205. The debate is reminiscent of the 'Aryan turn' that had started to affect the discipline of classics in the late eighteenth century, with scholars maintaining that Hellenic civilization was superior because of the 'race' of the Greeks; see Bernal, *Black Athena*, I, pp. 189-366. The Aryan ideas that permeated nineteenth-century classical studies can be explained at least partly as a reaction of Western scholars to the 'narcissistic blow' they had received when it became more and more obvious that the 'foreign' civilizations of Egypt and the ancient Near East, which could claim genealogical precedence over Israel, Greece, and Rome, were highly sophisticated.

42. See Bill T. Arnold and David B. Weisberg, 'Babel und Bibel und Bias: How Anti-Semitism Distorted Friedrich Delitzsch's Scholarship', *Bible Review* 18 (2002), pp. 32-40.

oncile this resentment with his positive view of the Assyrian empire, Delitzsch had to downplay the Semitic character of the Assyrians and to claim that the Assyrian people had received significant Indo-European infusions. Ironically, Delitzsch went back, with this claim, to ideas about the Assyrians from the days when cuneiform had not yet been deciphered and only biblical and classical sources were available.[43] Since Mesopotamian texts did not provide any evidence for an Indo-European background of the Assyrians, Delitzsch turned to the completely unfounded and rather desperate argument that Assurbanipal's wife was depicted, on a stone relief from Nineveh, with Aryan features and blond hair.[44]

Delitzsch's new approach to the history of the ancient Near East received a lot of criticism both from colleagues and from the Christian establishment of his time. The 'Pan-Babylonism' he and other German Assyriologists advocated was rightfully dismissed,[45] and for quite a while, any research on cultural contacts between Mesopotamia and the Levant seemed discredited. After World War I, influential scholars claimed for the first time that the civilizations of ancient Mesopotamia should be studied within their own cultural framework, an approach that found its most prominent expression in Benno Landsberger's famous concept of 'Eigenbegrifflichkeit' ('conceptual autonomy'), introduced in his inaugural lecture as a professor at the University of Leipzig in 1926.[46] The

43. In a book about the Phoenicians published in the middle of the nineteenth century (*Die Phönizier* [2 vols.; Bonn and Berlin: Eduard Weber, 1841–50]), F.C. Movers had expressed his admiration for the brutal Assyrian conquerors and had theorized that their military prowess had to be due to 'white' influences (II/1, pp. 300-303, 420); see Bernal, *Black Athena*, I, p. 360. Following Movers, the openly racist Arthur Gobineau, in his *Essais sur l'inégalité des races humaines* from 1853–55, explained the domination the Assyrians had exercised in antiquity by claiming: '[Q]u'à proportion où je m'élève vers le nord, je rencontre les éléments blancs dans un meilleur état de pureté et avec une abondance incomparable. Or les États assyriens étaient, de toutes les fondations chamo-sémites, les plus reculées dans cette direction. Ils étaient sans cesse atteints par des immigrations, latentes ou déclarées, descendues des montagnes du nord-est. C'est donc là qu'était la cause de leur longue, de leur séculaire prépondérance' (Gobineau, *Oeuvres* [3 vols.; ed. Jean Gaulmier and Jean Boissel; Bibliothèque de la Pléiade, 306; Paris: Gallimard, 1983], I, pp. 407-408).

44. '[A]ugenscheinlich ist diese Gemahlin Sardanapals eine Prinzessin arischen Geblüts und blondhaarig zu denken' (Delitzsch, *Babel und Bibel: Ein Vortrag*, pp. 19-20). It may seem surprising that Delitzsch's audience took such statements seriously. But Delitzsch, in his earlier career, had tackled other problems, particularly in the field of Akkadian grammar, with great methodological rigor, which provided him with a scholarly authority difficult to challenge.

45. For a brief overview of Pan-Babylonism see Jürgen Ebach, 'Panbabylonismus', in *Handbuch religionswissenschaftlicher Grundbegriffe* (4 vols.; ed. Burkhard Gladigow, Hubert Cancik and Karl-Heinz Kohl; Stuttgart: W. Kohlhammer, 1998), IV, pp. 302-304.

46. Benno Landsberger, 'Die Eigenbegrifflichkeit der babylonischen Welt: ein Vortrag', *Islamica* 2 (1926), pp. 355-72; an English translation was published as *The Conceptual Autonomy of the Babylonian World* (trans. Thorkild Jacobsen, Benjamin R. Foster and H. von Siebenthal; Monographs on the Ancient Near East, 1/4; Malibu: Undena, 1976).

period after World War I also marks the discovery that Assyrian history, which in the early decades of Assyriology had been regarded as almost synonymous with the history of the Neo-Assyrian empire, possessed a *longue durée* hitherto little known. Thanks to the publication of texts from the Assyrian capital at Assur and from Kültepe in Turkey, the site of the ancient city of Kaneš, which had housed a large Assyrian trade colony in the first centuries of the second millennium, the significance of the Old Assyrian and Middle Assyrian phases of Assyrian history became increasingly understood,[47] and it became clear that the Assyrians had started their historical mission not as military conquerors, but as traders and businessmen operating from a small city-state.[48]

But in spite of these new perspectives, some of the old questions retained a prominent place on the scholarly agenda. Delitzsch's racist ideas continued to find resonance in Germany.[49] The discovery of the mid-second millennium state of Mitanni with its Indo-Aryan ruling class provided the eagerly expected Indo-Europeans, which fostered speculations, again poorly founded, that the creation of the Middle-Assyrian territorial state and its institutions was the consequence of an Indo-European influx. Even an eminent scholar like Wolfram von Soden followed this line of argumentation. In a 1937 paper on the 'historical problem posed by the rise of the Assyrian empire',[50] he claimed that a work like the Tukulti-Ninurta epic, a celebration of warfare and individual courage from late thirteenth-century Assyria, was unthinkable without assuming some Indo-Aryan background. The Semitic Assyrians alone, according to von Soden, could not have possessed the creative capacity and heroic character necessary to create such a text.[51]

47. See the overviews on the archaeological excavations at Assur by Roland W. Lamprichs and Kaneš by Tahsin Özgüç in *OEAANE* I, pp. 225-28 and III, pp. 266-68, respectively.

48. An insight so surprising that it remained highly contested for a long time. When Hildegard Lewy wrote the chapter about the early history of Assyria, 'Assyria c. 2600–1816 B.C.', for *CAH*[3] I/2, pp. 729-70, she still maintained that there had been an Old Assyrian empire.

49. For an overview of the history of ancient Near Eastern studies in Berlin, the center of some of the most important debates that took place during the period between 1875 and 1945, see Johannes Renger, 'Die Geschichte der Altorientalistik und der Vorderasiatischen Archäologie in Berlin von 1875 bis 1945', in *Berlin und die Antike: Architektur, Kunstgewerbe, Malerei, Skulptur, Theater und Wissenschaft vom 16. Jahrhundert bis heute* (Aufsätze) (ed. Willmuth Arenhövel and Christa Schreiber; Berlin: Deutsches Archäologisches Institut, 1979), pp. 151-92.

50. *Der Aufstieg des Assyrerreiches als geschichtliches Problem* (Der Alte Orient, 37/1-2; Leipzig: J.C. Hinrichs Verlag, 1937).

51. Von Soden wrote

> Diese Verächtlichmachung einer im Orient durchaus gebräuchlichen und sonst auch als unanstößig empfundenen Kampfform [the defensive tactics of the Babylonians] kommt uns in einer semitischen Dichtung sehr unerwartet und erinnert ebenso wie viele andere Eigentümlichkeiten der Kampfesschilderung an die Heldendichtung indogermanischer Völker. Der Gedanke, daß mit einer solchen Erinnerung mehr als nur zufällige Ähnlichkeiten aufgedeckt sein sollen, erscheint zunächst abwegig; er

To some extent, the weak foundation of his arguments must have been obvious even to von Soden himself, who in later publications never repeated his racial explanation for the spirit of the Middle-Assyrian age.[52] In his books and articles on Akkadian lexicography and grammar, the fields to which he made his great contributions, von Soden did not succumb to the temptation of complying with Nazi ideology; his numerous references to his Jewish teacher Landsberger led in fact to heavy attacks on him by his colleague Carl Frank, who was an unshakable Nazi.[53] Historians who followed the Nazi ideology wholeheartedly had their own way to solve the problem of the 'heroic' bellicosity of the Assyrians, so incompatible with the prevailing ideas about the nature of the Semites: they just ignored Assyria. In F. Taeger's history of the ancient world,[54] written in 1939, the author, after having covered ancient Near Eastern history up to the invasions by the Sea Peoples, immediately switches to the Greeks, without ever penning a single word about the Neo-Assyrian and Neo-Babylonian empires.

In the period after World War II, the attitude towards Assyria among scholars in the Western world changed again. The Semitic character of the Assyrians was no longer a problem, but their bellicosity, imperial ambitions and auto-

> wird aber unabweisbar, wenn wir zugleich an die jahrhundertelange Herrschaft der mindestens seit 1500…von Ariern geführten Churrier bzw. Mitanni in Vorderasien denken, die uns...zu der Frage nötigte, ob wir im Assyrervolk seit der Mitannizeit nicht auch mit einem gewissen arischen und damit nordrassigen Einschlag zu rechnen haben… Daß das Epos nicht ausschließlich oder doch überwiegend durch das Semitentum bestimmt ist, zeigt ja übrigens auch die Tatsache, daß diese Art von Dichtung im 1. Jahrtausend, in dem die Semiten die arischen Volkssplitter sich restlos angeglichen hatten, offenbar nicht mehr gepflegt wurde (*Aufstieg*, pp. 26-27).

52. The question in how far certain institutions of the Middle-Assyrian state were influenced by Hittite-Mittani traditions is still debated, but scholars now focus on political and cultural contact, not on racial influx. Walter Mayer, a student of von Soden, maintains, in his *Politik und Kriegskunst der Assyrer* (ALASPM, 9; Münster: Ugarit-Verlag, 1995), pp. 220-27, that the influence was strong, while Andreas Fuchs, in his review of Mayer's book in *AfO* 44–45 (1997–98), pp. 409-17, argues that many innovations that took place in Assyria in the Middle-Assyrian period can be explained as internal developments.

53. In *Lamastu, Pazuzu und andere Dämonen: Ein Beitrag zur babylonisch-assyrischen Dämonologie* (MAOG, 14/2; Leipzig: Otto Harrassowitz, 1941), p. 24, Frank writes that another German scholar, Erich Ebeling, had published the difficult text VAT 10057 'without help from Jewish or any other side' ('ohne jüdische oder sonstige Hilfe'), while von Soden, in his own—deficient—edition, had profited from support received from his 'gratefully honored Jewish teacher and co-editor': 'Trotz der sehr weitgehenden Unterstützung, die der Verfasser [von Soden] auch hier wieder von seinem dankbar verehrten jüdischen Lehrer und Mitherausgeber angenommen hat, ist diese Neubearbeitung alles andere als fehlerlos…' On von Soden's personal implications with Nazism, see R. Borger's obituary of him, 'Wolfram von Soden (19. 6. 1908–6. 10. 1996)', *AfO* 44–45 (1997–98), pp. 588-94.

54. Fritz Taeger, *Das Altertum: Geschichte und Gestalt* (3 vols.; Stuttgart: W. Kohlhammer, 1939), I; Carena, *History of the Near Eastern Historiography*, pp. 75, 131.

cratic political system, earlier regarded as legitimate and laudable, were now seen as highly objectionable. In the democratic societies of the post-war period, the Assyrians were quite unsuitable to serve as a role model. The disgust some scholars felt when they had to deal with Assyria was strong. In *The Treasures of Darkness*, a widely read history of Mesopotamian religion, the Danish-American Assyriologist Thorkild Jacobsen banished the religions of the first millennium, when Assyria reached its imperial peak, to an 'epilogue' of thirteen pages, and justified this treatment by saying:

> In terms of insight and depth, the second millennium B.C. can rightly be said to mark the high point of ancient Mesopotamian religious achievement. The millennium that followed contributed no major new insights, rather, it brought in many ways decline and brutalization. [55]

According to Jacobsen, the 'only real religious insight that can be credited to the first millennium in Mesopotamia' was the 'quietistic piety' of the Aramean tribesmen, which the Assyrian and Babylonian kings of this age applied to war—'often to ruthless and cruel war.'[56]

Jacobsen's exclusion of Assyrian religion from the annals of history may appear extreme,[57] but his assessment of Assyria as an empire of unrelenting violence that had nothing to contribute to the world in terms of intellectual or spiritual achievement was not untypical. The idea that Assyria was a brutal, superstition-ridden autocratic state with an army engaged in constant attacks on defenseless opponents was widespread and found its way into many general books on Mesopotamian history.[58] Scholars who specialized in Assyrian studies during the time between 1950 and 1985 left such views largely unchallenged.

55. Jacobsen, *The Treasures of Darkness: A History of Mesopotamian Religion* (New Haven, CT and London: Yale University Press, 1976), p. 223. Jacobsen's preference for the earlier history of Mesopotamia, which was, of course, the period he studied most intensively, is already apparent in his article 'Primitive Democracy in Ancient Mesopotamia', *JNES* 2 (1943), pp. 159-72.

56. Jacobsen, *Treasures of Darkness*, p. 238.

57. The god Aššur is mentioned only very rarely in the book (pp. 159, 167, 232, 234) and almost exclusively in the context of references to the Assyrian version of *Enūma eliš*, where Aššur replaces the Babylonian god Marduk.

58. See, for example, Hartmut Schmökel, *Geschichte des alten Vorderasien* (Handbuch der Orientalistik. 1 Abt., Der Nahe und der Mittlere Osten; 2. Bd., 3. Abschnitt; Leiden: E.J. Brill, 1957), p. 249: 'Sie (the Assyrians) kennen weder Geländeschwierigkeiten noch Skrupel, geschweige denn menschliche Gefühle gegenüber ihren Feinden, die sie foltern, schinden, pfählen… Sklaverei und Deportation bedeutet… Milde. Grausamste Massenexekutionen sind… Dienst an Staat und Gott… Es liegt eine blutige Folgerichtigkeit in diesem Jahrhunderte währenden Schreckensregime, das das Urbild für die apokalyptischen Greuel der Bibel abgegeben hat.' On a lighter note, see Larry R. Gonick's widely read *Cartoon History of the Universe, Book 1* (San Francisco: Rip Off Press, 1978), which claims that 'the Assyrian priesthood, addicted to mumbo-jumbo, had let the practice of medicine slide from a reasonable high level into a mess of magic spells' and presents an Assyrian king who asks himself in despair: 'O dear! Wot shall it be today? Flay, flog, mutilate, impale, or put them on leashes in doghouses?'

Primarily philological in nature, their work was concerned with establishing a better understanding of the Assyrian lexicon and Assyrian grammar[59] and not so much with writing history—although there were some notable exceptions: Hayim Tadmor and his students tried to provide a more sophisticated evaluation of Assyrian power and propaganda, and the so-called Italian school, rooted in the intellectual and social upheavals of the late sixties, applied structuralist and semiotic approaches to the study of Assyria.[60]

The past two decades have brought some notable new developments in Assyrian studies. Perhaps most important is the publication of large numbers of Assyrian texts in reliable new editions. A Helsinki-based project, *State Archives of Assyria*, directed by Simo Parpola, has published thousands of Assyrian letters and legal documents,[61] and the Toronto-based *Royal Inscriptions of Mesopotamia* project has produced, under the direction of A. Kirk Grayson, editions of the inscriptions of all the Assyrian kings who ruled before 745 BCE.[62] Old Assyrian studies have also seen a remarkable resurgence.[63] The publication of

59. Here, the contributions of Karlheinz Deller are of particular importance; for a bibliography of Deller's works, see Gerlinde Mauer and Ursula Magen, 'Schriftenverzeichnis Karlheinz Deller', in *Ad bene et fideliter seminandum: Festgabe für Karlheinz Deller zum 21. Februar 1987* (ed. Gerlinde Mauer and Ursula Magen; AOAT, 220; Kevalaer: Butzon & Bercker/Neukirchen–Vluyn: Neukirchener Verlag, 1988), pp. 1-23, with additions at http://assyriologie.uni-hd.de/Deller.pdf.

60. Good examples for the approaches of these schools are Hayim Tadmor and Moshe Weinfeld (eds.), *History, Historiography, and Interpretation: Studies in Biblical and Cuneiform Literatures* (Jerusalem: Magnes Press, 1984) and Frederick Mario Fales (ed.), *Assyrian Royal Inscriptions: New Horizons in Literary, Ideological, and Historical Analysis. Papers of a Symposium held in Cetona (Siena), June 26-28, 1980* (Orientis antiqui collectio, 17; Rome: Istituto per l'Oriente, 1981).

61. S. Parpola (general editor), *State Archives of Assyria* (Helsinki University Press, 1987–). So far, 18 volumes have appeared. Additional publications of the project include a journal: *State Archives of Assyria Bulletin* (1987–2001, 13 volumes), a series of monographic studies: *State Archives of Assyria Studies* (The Neo-Assyrian Text Corpus Project, 1992—, 16 volumes), and the *Prosopography of the Neo-Assyrian Empire* (The Neo-Assyrian Text Corpus Project, 1998–, 3 volumes).

62. A.K. Grayson, *Royal Inscriptions of Mesopotamia: Assyrian Periods* (3 vols.; Toronto: University of Toronto Press, 1987–96). New publications of inscriptions of later kings include Hayim Tadmor, *The Inscriptions of Tiglath-pileser III, King of Assyria: Critical Edition, with Introductions, Translations, and Commentary* (Jerusalem: Israel Academy of Sciences and Humanities, 1994), A. Fuchs, *Die Inschriften Sargons II. aus Khorsabad* (Göttingen: Cuvillier Verlag, 1994), and R. Borger, *Beiträge zum Inschriftenwerk Assurbanipals: Die Prismenklassen A, B, C = K, D, E, F, G, H, J und T sowie andere Inschriften* (Wiesbaden: Harrassowitz Verlag, 1996).

63. See Cécile Michel, *Old Assyrian Bibliography of Cuneiform Texts, Bullae, Seals and the Results of the Excavations at Aššur, Kültepe/Kaniš, Acemhöyük, Alişar and Boğazköy* (Old Assyrian Archives, Studies, 1; PIHANS, 97; Leiden: Nederlands Instituut voor het Nabije Oosten, 2003).

Assyrian archival texts and monumental inscriptions has clearly made great progress in recent years.

At the same time, some influential scholars have created yet another new 'image' of Assyria. Somewhat surprisingly, this image is not so much based on Assyrian politics, economics or military matters, all areas for which a lot of new material has become available through the editorial projects just described. Instead, it emphasizes Assyrian culture and religion. In a complete reversal of Jacobsen's approach, the scholars in question have portrayed Assyria as a cradle of civilization, a source for ideas and institutions that influenced both the Biblical world and classical Greece. Recent books such as Stephanie Dalley's *Legacy of Mesopotamia*[64] and Martin West's *East Face of Helicon*,[65] with their long catalogues of cultural borrowings from Assyria, represent prominent examples of this neo-diffusionist approach. West forcefully claims that the Homeric epics were influenced by Assyrian royal inscriptions and literary texts from Assurbanipal's famous library,[66] while Dalley and Uehlinger credit the Assyrians with the construction of such legendary buildings as the 'hanging gardens of Babylon' and the biblical 'tower of Babel', architectural marvels that they believe were mistakenly attributed, by classical and biblical authors, to the Babylonians.[67] The influential *Melammu* project, originating in Helsinki, has held a number of conferences gathering scholars from all over the world to discuss the impact that Mesopotamian, and especially Assyrian culture had on neighboring civilizations, and to evaluate its legacy in the Western world.[68]

64. Stephanie Dalley, *The Legacy of Mesopotamia* (Oxford and New York: Oxford University Press, 1998).

65. M.L. West, *The East Face of Helicon: West Asiatic Elements in Greek Poetry and Myth* (Oxford: Clarendon Press, 1997).

66. West, *The East Face of Helicon*, pp. 334-437.

67. On the Hanging Gardens and their possible location in Nineveh, see S. Dalley, 'Nineveh, Babylon and the Hanging Gardens: Cuneiform and Classical Sources Reconciled', *Iraq* 56 (1994), pp. 45-58, and Karen Polinger Foster, 'The Hanging Gardens of Nineveh', *Iraq* 66 (2004), pp. 207-20 (with a full bibliography). On the story of the tower of Babel reflecting the construction of Dūr-Šarrukēn by Sargon II of Assyria, see Christoph Uehlinger, *Weltreich und 'eine Rede': Eine neue Deutung der sogenannten Turmbauerzählung (Gen 11, 1-9)* (OBO, 101; Freiburg, Switzerland: Universitätsverlag/Göttingen: Vandenhoeck & Ruprecht, 1990).

68. So far, the following conference volumes have been published: Sanna Aro and Robert M. Whiting (eds.), *The Heirs of Assyria: Proceedings of the Opening Symposium of the Assyrian and Babylonian Intellectual Heritage Project, Held in Tvärminne, Finland, October 8-11, 1998* (Melammu Symposia, 1; Helsinki: The Neo-Assyrian Text Corpus Project, 2000); R.M. Whiting (ed.), *Mythology and Mythologies: Methodological Approaches to Intercultural Influences: Proceedings of the Second Annual Symposium of the Assyrian and Babylonian Intellectual Heritage Project, Held in Paris, France, Oct. 4-7, 1999* (Melammu Symposia, 2; Helsinki: The Neo-Assyrian Text Corpus Project, 2001); Antonio Panaino and Giovanni Pettinato (eds.), *Ideologies as Intercultural Phenomena: Proceedings of the Third Annual Symposium of the Assyrian and Babylonian Intellectual Heritage Project, Held in Chicago, USA, October 27-31, 2000* (Melammu Symposia, 3; Milan: Università di Bologna/Roma: IsIAO, 2002); Robert Rollinger and Christoph

Like earlier attitudes towards Assyria, the neo-diffusionist trends that the *Melammu* project and the aforementioned books reveal seem to be related to certain developments in the contemporary world. In the increasingly globalized economy of the post-communist period, it has become more urgent to ask questions about cultural contacts and the migration of technologies and ideas—and research projects addressing such topics have been more likely to obtain funding.[69] There is no doubt that Assyriologists engaged in this kind of inquiry have made valuable contributions to ancient Near Eastern studies, but some of their results require more discussion.

It is important to stress that Dalley and West do not claim that it was Assyria alone whence civilization radiated; they credit Babylonia and other ancient states with a number of cultural 'firsts' as well. Simo Parpola, however, the third major advocate of neo-diffusionism in ancient Near Eastern studies, has in effect propagated what could be called a somewhat 'Pan-Assyrian' model, one that seems in many respects similar to the Pan-Babylonism that thrived one hundred years ago—and perhaps even not too far away from the mystical philology of F. Max Müller. Possibly inspired by his encounters with Neo-Aramean Assyrian Christians[70] Parpola has tirelessly claimed in numerous articles written during the past fifteen years that central concepts of both the Western and the Eastern worlds, such as monotheism, mysticism, the idea of redemption, gnosticism or Zoroastrianism, are all ultimately rooted in Assyria.[71] So far, most

Ulf (eds.), *Commerce and Monetary Systems in the Ancient World: Means of Transmission and Cultural Interaction: Proceedings of the Fifth Annual Symposium of the Assyrian and Babylonian Intellectual Heritage Project, Held in Innsbruck, Austria, October 3rd-8th 2002* (Melammu Symposia, 5; Stuttgart: Steiner, 2004).

69. See the remarks by Liverani, 'Ancient Near Eastern Cities', p. 107.

70. See Parpola, 'Assyrians after Assyria', *Journal of the Assyrian Academic Society* 12/2 (2000), pp. 1-16, and available online at http://www.aanf.org/America/assyrians/assyrians_assyria.htm, accessed September 28, 2006. Note that the Assyrian Academic Society is a sponsor of the *Melammu* project.

71. See especially: Parpola, 'The Assyrian Tree of Life: Tracing the Origins of Jewish Monotheism and Greek Philosophy', *JNES* 52 (1993), pp. 161-208; *idem*, *Assyrian Prophecies*, pp. xiii-cviii; idem, 'Monotheism in Ancient Assyria', in *One God or Many? Concepts of Divinity in the Ancient World* (ed. Barbara Nevling Porter; Transactions of the Casco Bay Assyriological Institute, 1; [Chebeaque, ME:] Casco Bay Assyriological Institute, 2000), pp. 165-209; *idem*, 'The Originality of the Teachings of Zarathustra in the Light of Yasna 44', in *Sefer Moshe: The Moshe Weinfeld Jubilee Volume: Studies in the Bible and the Ancient Near East, Qumran, and Post-Biblical Judaism* (ed. Chaim Cohen, Avi Hurvitz and Shalom M. Paul; Winona Lake, IN: Eisenbrauns, 2004), pp. 373-83. Parpola's scholarly agenda brings to mind again what Benno Landsberger wrote 80 years ago: 'Thus the scholar [in the field of Assyriology] faces his own subject unmoved and aloof, and precisely those men to whom our science owes most look for more rewarding research problems outside their field. They are trying—and this was the impulse which brought Assyriology into existence—to make dead things alive by connecting them up with ideas that are still of importance to us or to civilizations close to us' (*Conceptual Autonomy of the Babylonian World*, p. 6).

scholars who have taken a closer look at Parpola's ideas have at least partly dismissed them,[72] but the debate is certainly not yet over.

Summarizing this all too superficial overview[73] of how the scholarly discourse on ancient Assyria meandered along in the West during the past two centuries, it is evident that specific ideological agendas—the religious and imperial ideas of the nineteenth century, the racial views of the first half of the twentieth, the democratic and globalist perspectives of the period that followed World War II—all had their impact. At the same time, the 'image' of Assyria was adapted and readapted to new textual and archaeological discoveries, by scholars who had specific personal interests and idiosyncrasies, and who never ceased to be occupied, intrigued, and irritated by the question of how to position Assyria in the context of 'their own' biblical and classical tradition.

What a modern scholar can learn from an investigation of the history of his discipline is critical awareness of the contingency of his own intellectual approach. The Assyriologist who looks back at the scholarship of his predecessors may realize that he is probably well advised to show a certain degree of skepticism with regard to overly essentialist statements about ancient Assyria. Such skepticism is all the more warranted in the light of the many transformations Assyrian civilization experienced during its long history. *Assur* was a city that served as a trade hub in the Old Assyrian period, an aggressive territorial state in the Late Bronze age, and an empire in the first millennium—what can be said without qualification is that Assyria was a political entity that successfully reinvented itself again and again.[74]

72. See, for example, the review articles on Parpola's *Assyrian Prophecies* by J.S. Cooper, 'Assyrian Prophecies, the Assyrian Tree, and the Mesopotamian Origins of Jewish Monotheism, Greek Philosophy, Christian Theology, Gnosticism, and Much More', *JAOS* 120 (2000), pp. 430-44, E. Frahm, 'Wie "christlich" war die assyrische Religion?', *WdO* 31 (2000–2001), pp. 31-45, and Manfred Weippert, '"König, fürchte dich nicht!" Assyrische Prophetie im 7. Jahrhundert v. Chr.', *Or* 71 (2002), pp. 1-54. Among those who believe that Parpola is right is Ithamar Gruenwald; see his '"How Much Qabbalah in Ancient Assyria?"—Methodological Reflections on the Study of a Cross-Cultural Phenomenon', in *Assyria 1995: Proceedings of the 10th Anniversary Symposium of the Neo-Assyrian Text Corpus Project, Helsinki, September 7-11, 1995* (ed. S. Parpola and R.M. Whiting; Helsinki: The Neo-Assyrian Text Corpus Project, 1997), pp. 115-27.

73. Among the many important topics not addressed in this paper is the question of how different scholars have assessed the impact that Babylonian culture had on Assyrian civilization.

74. It is noteworthy, though, that the mercantile spirit of the beginnings seems never to have disappeared completely. As recently shown again by Karen Radner, 'Traders in the Neo-Assyrian Period', in *Trade and Finance in Ancient Mesopotamia: Proceedings of the First MOS Symposium (Leiden 1997)* (ed. J.G. Dercksen; PIHANS, 84; Istanbul: Nederlands Historisch-Archaeologisch Instituut te Istanbul, 1999), pp. 101-26 (with earlier literature), Assyrian merchants continued to play a prominent economic role during the first millennium, complementing the 'tributary mode of production' that otherwise dominated the age of Assyrian imperialism with trade connections based on exchange. This mercantile spirit may help to explain why Neo-Assyrian royal inscriptions sometimes display a care reminiscent of a diligent accountant's bookkeep-

At times, it is the nature of the practice of history to reduce cultural complexity. But historians also have to question the myth of cultural homogeneity. Both on the synchronic and on the diachronic level, every civilization, Assyria included, is characterized by a number of inherent contradictions. The present author has the impression that recent scholarship has focused too much on the cultural achievements of Assyria, and too little on the dark side of this remarkable state.[75] Few will deny any more that the sculptures from Nineveh and other Assyrian capitals have impressive aesthetic qualities,[76] and nobody will question that the Assyrians, by creating their provincial system, implemented a political order that had a great future. But we should not forget, in our late discovery of the beauty of the artwork and our admiration for the administrative skills of the Assyrians, that their rulers, in order to achieve their goals—even apparently noble goals such as establishing unity and order—, waged extremely aggressive wars, deported whole populations from one end of their realm to the other, and killed large numbers of civilians.[77]

ing when they inventory the numbers of killed, maimed or deported enemies and indicate the amounts of booty and tribute delivered to the king (see Marco De Odorico, *The Use of Numbers and Quantifications in the Assyrian Royal Inscriptions* [SAAS, 3; Helsinki: The Neo-Assyrian Text Corpus Project, 1995], pp. 8-12 and *passim*). Pictorial representations of the atrocities the imperial Assyrian armies committed during their campaigns in the Neo-Assyrian period seem to be imbued with such a bookkeeping spirit as well: several palace reliefs show images of scribes carefully counting severed enemy heads (see, for example, WA 124945, from the palace of Assurbanipal in Nineveh, reproduced on the cover of F.M. Fales and J.N. Postgate, *Imperial Administrative Records, Part II* [SAA, 11; Helsinki: Helsinki University Press, 1995]). Even the Bible is aware of the commercial ambitions of the Assyrians; it mentions Assyrian merchants in Ezek. 27.23. If Karl Marx had known more about the history of the ancient Near East, he would probably have looked with great interest at the close relationship that existed in Assyria between capitalism and imperialism.

75. Even a work like Mayer's *Politik und Kriegskunst der Assyrer* is no exception; its title, with its characterization of the Assyrian war strategy as an art, implies a certain degree of esteem, on the part of the author, for the military machine of Assyria.

76. Although it needs to be said that quite a number of distinguished students of ancient Near Eastern art from the second half of the twentieth century have provided rather critical assessments of the Assyrian artistic record. André Parrot, for example, has claimed that Assyrian art never moves us, presents us with lifeless stereotypes, and lacks the expressive variety necessary to produce a powerful emotional response in the spectator (*Nineveh and Babylon* [trans. Stuart Gilbert and James Emmons; The Arts of Mankind, 2; London: Thames & Hudson, 1991], pp. 12-13). For similarly negative statements on Assyrian art by scholars such as Richard D. Barnett, Eva Strommenger, and H.W.F. Saggs, see Leo Bersani and Ulysse Dutoit, *The Forms of Violence: Narrative in Assyrian Art and Modern Culture* (New York: Schocken Books, 1985), pp. 6-7. For a more appreciative view, see, for example, John Malcolm Russell, 'Bulls for the Palace and Order in the Empire: The Sculptural Program of Sennacherib's Court VI at Nineveh', *ArtB* 69 (1987), pp. 520-39.

77. It goes without saying that other ancient nations, both in the East and in the West, behaved brutally as well, and that even the Bible, as recently shown by John J. Collins ('The Zeal of

When the Assyrian king Esarhaddon reports that he raged 'like an angry whirlwind' to destroy his enemies[78] and presents himself as a ruler who can claim: 'Before him, cities; behind him, ruins',[79] he does not appear much like 'a saviour king who...restored the cosmic harmony', as a modern scholar has recently characterized him.[80] On the contrary, Esarhaddon projects an image of a violent storm reminiscent of Walter Benjamin's famous description of Paul Klee's painting 'Angelus novus.' That painting, Benjamin writes,

> shows...the angel of history. His face is turned towards the past. Where we perceive a chain of events, he sees one single catastrophe which keeps piling up wreckage upon wreckage and hurls it in front of his feet. The angel would like to stay, awaken the dead, and make whole what has been smashed. But a storm is blowing from Paradise; it has got caught in his wings with such violence that the angel can no longer close them. The storm irresistibly propels him into the future to which his back is turned, while the pile of debris before him grows skyward. This storm is what we call progress.[81]

Phineas: The Bible and the Legitimation of Violence', *JBL* 122 [2003], pp. 3-21), indulges repeatedly in the celebration of the killing of enemy civilians and other brutal acts. The degree to which the Assyrians were fixated on violence, in deeds, words, and images, seems, however, unparalleled.

78. *kīma ezzi tīb meḫî ina birīšunu* [*azīq*], see R. Borger, *Die Inschriften Asarhaddons, Königs von Assyrien* (AfOB, 9; Graz: im Selbstverlage des Herausgebers, 1956), p. 65, §28 Nin. E. ii 18. On the ubiquity of the wind metaphor in Assyrian royal inscriptions, see Albert Schott, *Die Vergleiche in den akkadischen Königsinschriften* (MVAG, 30; Leipzig: J.C. Hinrichs, 1925), pp. 83-85.

79. *pānuššu ālumma arkēšu tīlu*, see Borger, *Inschriften Asarhaddons*, p. 97, §65 Mnm. A. rev. 13 (the correct reading of this passage was established by B. Landsberger, 'Einige unerkannt gebliebene oder verkannte Nomina des Akkadischen', *WZKM* 57 [1961], pp. 1-23 [2 n. 8]).

80. Parpola, *Assyrian Prophecies*, p. xliv.

81.

> Es gibt ein Bild von Klee, das Angelus Novus heißt. Ein Engel ist darauf dargestellt, der aussieht, als wäre er im Begriff, sich von etwas zu entfernen, worauf er starrt. Seine Augen sind aufgerissen, sein Mund steht offen und seine Flügel sind ausgespannt. Der Engel der Geschichte muß so aussehen. Er hat das Antlitz der Vergangenheit zugewendet. Wo eine Kette von Begebenheiten vor *uns* erscheint, da sieht *er* eine einzige Katastrophe, die unablässig Trümmer auf Trümmer häuft und sie ihm vor die Füße schleudert. Er möchte wohl verweilen, die Toten wecken und das Zerschlagene zusammenfügen. Aber ein Sturm weht vom Paradiese her, der sich in seinen Flügeln verfangen hat und so stark ist, daß der Engel sie nicht mehr schließen kann. Dieser Sturm treibt ihn unaufhaltsam in die Zukunft, der er den Rücken kehrt, während der Trümmerhaufen vor ihm zum Himmel wächst. Das, was wir den Fortschritt nennen, ist *dieser* Sturm.

Walter Benjamin, *Über den Begriff der Geschichte* IX, in *Gesammelte Schriften* (7 vols.; ed. Rolf Tiedemann and Hermann Schweppenhäuser; Frankfurt a.M.: Suhrkamp, 1972–89), I/2, pp. 697-98.

The Assyrians, who started their expansion from their capitals on the Tigris, one of the four rivers of the biblical Eden, represent Benjamin's storm well. Their empire indeed brought 'progress', but the price was a vast mountain of debris in its wake—cities devastated, lives destroyed, cultures derailed—almost as high as the wrecked remains before Benjamin's 'angel of history.'

The Smithsonian Institution's Religious Ceremonial Objects and Biblical Antiquities Exhibits at the World's Columbian Exposition (Chicago, 1893) and the Cotton States and International Exposition (Atlanta, 1895)

Steven W. Holloway

Although the roaring 1890s is commonly reckoned as the decade that saw America embark on the road to empire, imaginative control of the 'Holy Land' began years before through the production of fine arts, spectacles such as international expositions, missionary and travel writings, commercial reports, and Orientalist academic research. As industriously as Americans etched or classified Eastern peoples and lands, domestic anxieties surrounding slavery, immigrant minorities, and colonial aspirations governed the choice of subject matter and, to a degree rarely acknowledged, dictated the results. 'Biblical antiquities' were no less a site of national and racial self-definition than Orientalist paintings and American 'Egyptomania'. This chapter explores the means by which Cyrus Adler's traveling Smithsonian exhibits served to define populist American Orientalism. In like manner, we will examine how enduring Orientalist myths like the 'unchanging Orient' and the concomitant notion of the modern Middle East as a living museum influenced the organization of a museum exhibit staged for millions of largely Protestant Americans drawn to two international expositions.[1]

1. There are many works that analysis the great world fairs from the standpoint of imperial praxis; see, for example, Richard D. Altick, *The Shows of London* (Cambridge, MA: Belknap Press, 1978); Robert W. Rydell, *All the World's a Fair: Visions of Empire at American International Expositions, 1876–1916* (Chicago: University of Chicago Press, 1984); Paul Greenhalgh, *Ephemeral Vistas: The Expositions universelles, Great Exhibitions, and World's Fairs, 1851–1939* (Studies in Imperialism; Manchester: Manchester University Press, 1988); R.W. Rydell, 'A Cultural Frankenstein? The Chicago World's Columbian Exposition of 1893', in *Grand Illusions: Chicago's World's Fair of 1893* (ed. Neil Harris, *et al.*; Chicago: Chicago Historical Society, 1993), pp. 142-70; Timothy Mitchell, 'Orientalism and the Exhibitionary Order', in *The Visual Culture Reader* (ed. Nicholas Mirzoeff; London and New York: Routledge, 1998), pp. 293-303; Peter H. Hoffenberg, *An Empire on Display: English, Indian, and Australian Exhibitions from the Crystal Palace to the Great War* (Berkeley: University of California Press, 2001); Pieter van Wesemael, *Architecture of Instruction and Delight: A Socio-Historical Analysis of World Exhibitions as a Didactic Phenomenon (1798–1851–1970)* (Rotterdam: 010 Publishers, 2001).

1.0 *The Chicago World's Columbian Exposition and the Smithsonian*

In 1853, the first American exposition (a copycat reproduction of the 1851 London Crystal Palace Exposition), introduced the American public to commercialized ethnographic spectacle. Under the adroit management of Phineas T. Barnum, the New York exposition boasted Shantytown, a rambling mile of amusements that included a Wild Man of Borneo, Fijian cannibals, a Pennsylvania oil well, and a village of some 300 Native Americans drawn from fifty tribes. Deliberate recruitment of exotic 'primitives' and their orchestrated exhibition on an urban circuit was pioneered by the famed German animal trainer Carl Hagenbeck in the 1870s. By the early 1890s, European and American expositions routinely mounted displays of industrial prowess, symbolizing mastery over nature, and exhibits of exotic peoples transported from the periphery to the center, uprooted with contextual trappings, symbolizing mastery over primitives. 'Exhibition techniques tended to represent those peoples as raw materials; within the regnant progressivist ideology they occupied the same category'.[2]

Progress was indeed the watchword. The costliest, most elaborate and assiduously promoted public exhibition staged in nineteenth-century America was the Chicago World's Columbian Exposition of 1893 (WCE). Officially created to celebrate the four-hundredth anniversary of Christopher Columbus' contact with the West Indies, the mighty fair not only enshrined a wonderland vision of American technological and economic prowess, it defined the very social reality it sought to promote. In the words of Robert Rydell, 'The Chicago world's fair, generally recognized for its contributions to urban planning, beaux-arts architecture, and institutions of the arts and sciences, just as importantly introduced millions of fairgoers to evolutionary ideas about race—ideas that were presented in a utopian context and often conveyed by exhibits that were ostensibly amusing'.[3] For intellectual leadership, the WCE National Commission turned to the Smithsonian Institution, specifically enlisting the services of George Brown Goode, Associate Director of the United States National Museum (USNM) since 1881. The Smithsonian by this juncture had gained a reputation 'as the one bureau of the Government whose special function is that of exhibition',[4] and Goode had worked assiduously in mounting impressive displays from the holdings of the USNM at every major American exposition since the Philadelphia Centennial Exposition of 1876. Goode's populist philosophy of the role of the museum and the exposition in American society dovetailed along the theme of public education. 'The exhibition of the future', predicted Goode, 'will be an exhibition of ideas rather than of objects, and nothing

2. Curtis M. Hinsley, 'The World as Marketplace: Commodification of the Exotic at the World's Columbian Exposition, Chicago, 1893', in *Exhibiting Cultures: The Poetics and Politics of Museum Display* (ed. Ivan Karp and Steven Lavine; Washington, DC: Smithsonian Institution Press, 1991), pp. 344-65 (345).

3. Rydell, *All the World's a Fair*, pp. 40-41.

4. Richard Rathbun(?), quoted in Rydell, *All the World's a Fair*, p. 43.

will be deemed worthy of admission to its halls which has not some living, inspiring thought behind it, and which is not capable of teaching some valuable lesson'. The didactic lesson which Goode crafted the WCE to inculcate turned on the idea of progress, illustrating 'the steps of progress of civilization and its arts in successive centuries, and in all lands up to the present time'.[5]

Otis T. Mason, who became the first curator of the Smithsonian's Bureau of American Ethnology in 1884, would provide decisive guidance for Goode in the organization of 'Department M' (ethnology). In 1889, Mason and Thomas Rau, curator of prehistoric anthropology, attended the Tenth Congrès internationale d'anthropologie et d'archéologie préhistoriques in Paris, toured the capital's museums, and experienced the Exposition universelle. Mason, impressed by the Exposition's colonial city where some 182 Asians and Africans had been housed in 'villages' designed to simulate their native surroundings, was most smitten by the Histoire de l'habitation display which laid out the social history of human communities in an evolutionary continuum from the most primitive to the most advanced.[6] In its 1890 proposal to the United States Congress, the Smithsonian officials offered 'to show the physical and other characteristics of the principal races of men and the very early stages of the history of civilization as shown by the evolution of certain selected primitive arts and industries'.[7]

Goode could have no objection to such a system, ideally adapted as it was to illustrate the Exposition's overarching theme of cultural progress. Thomas W. Palmer, president of the WCE National Commission, had attended the Exposition universelle himself and was aware that the colonial villages boosted attendance dramatically, netting the Exposition sponsors the equivalent of $700,000 American dollars. The most popular of the 'living villages' was the Rue de Caire, a deliberately chaotic collection of stalls and shops designed to imitate the medieval city, with Parisians in Oriental costumes hawking perfumes, savories and tarbooshes; donkeys carried passengers up and down the streets at a franc a ride.[8] An Egyptian visitor to the Eighth International Congress of Orientalists who detoured through the Paris Exposition, remarked that the verisimilitude extended to making the paint look grimy.[9] Palmer recommended that the mile-long strip of Chicago land connecting Jackson and Washington parks,

5. Quoted in Rydell, *All the World's a Fair*, p. 45.

6. Alfred Picard, *Exposition universelle internationale de 1889 à Paris: Rapport general.* II. *Travaux de l'Exposition universelle de 1889* (Paris: Imprimerie nationale, 1891), pp. 243-62.

7. Quoted in Rydell, *All the World's a Fair*, p. 56.

8. Picard, *Exposition universelle*, II, pp. 218-19. Those who had visited both the original and the Parisian simulacrum 'admiraient la fidélité du tableau et le talent avec lequel les organisateurs de l'exposition avaient restitué des specimens d'un art si remarquable et souvent si pur.' Of the 225 souls who staffed the display, one part consisted of traders, the other of 'indigenes' one half of whom were recruited from the streets of Paris.

9. Timothy Mitchell, 'The World as Exhibition', *Comparative Studies in Society and History* 31 (1989), pp. 217-36 (217).

known as the Midway Plaisance, should be given over to ethnological exhibits and other live entertainment venues that would charge admission fees.[10] This lucrative concession came to define the nature of the White City quite as powerfully as the monumental beaux-arts structures and the prestigious World's Parliaments. The Exposition universelle in 1889 added the trappings of scientific objectivity to the human panorama on display, together with a clearly articulated program of racial progress, and the spice of Orientalizing intrigue courtesy of the Rue de Caire. Chicago resolved to do Paris one better.

1.1. *Anthropology at the WCE and the Midway Plaisance*

Frederick Ward Putnam, director and curator of the Peabody Museum of American Archaeology and Anthropology at Harvard University, was hired in 1891 by the WCE National Commission to supervise the creation of the Department of Ethnology and Archaeology. Both Putnam and his assistant Franz Boas worked closely with the Smithsonian scientists in order to avoid duplication and to carry out their coveted opportunity to educate the American public about the nascent field of physical anthropology. There would be essentially four avenues of dissemination of ideas: static exhibits mounted in a great hall devoted to ethnography, the Anthropology Building in the White City; a separate exhibit under the direction of the Smithsonian staff, mounted in the United States Government Building, also in the White City; various living villages scattered across the Exposition grounds; and the Midway attractions.[11] Of these, Putnam ostensibly controlled all save for the Smithsonian exhibit, but in fact the organization of the Midway fell under the management of twenty-one-year-old Sol Bloom.[12]

10. In fact, the Chicago Corporation had been approached considerably in advance of 1890 by numerous entertainment vendors, dining establishments, circus acts, and other amusement brokers for concession space at the fair; R. Reid Badger, 'Chicago 1893: World's Columbian Exposition', in *Historical Dictionary of World's Fairs and Expositions, 1851–1988* (ed. John E. Findling and Kimberly D. Pelle; New York: Greenwood Press, 1990), pp. 122-32 (127).

11. Rydell, *All the World's a Fair*, p. 57. Putnam and Boas supervised some fifty-five fieldworkers prior to the Exposition who submitted massive amounts of data, photographs and artifacts from North, Central and South America. As opening day approached, the Exposition directors repeatedly reduced the dimensions of the Anthropology Building in favor of more presumptively popular exhibits, leaving Putnam with less than 60% of the space originally promised; the building opened one month after the fair's start date. Hinsley, 'World as Marketplace', p. 349.

12. The anthropologist Putnam originally had charge of the Midway, but, as sponsor commitment to the role of public science dimmed and the entertainment focus of the area grew paramount, the young impresario Sol Bloom was given charge of the actual installations. Bloom had visited the Paris Exposition and, vastly impressed by the wealth-making potential of the orientalizing tableaus, had obtained the future concession rights to the Algerian Village, and added it to the stew of ethnic spectacles on the Midway. In his autobiography, Bloom, reflecting on the administration of the Midway half a century back, wryly observed that placing Putnam in charge of the Midway was like hiring Albert Einstein to run Barnum and Bailey's Circus. Bloom's hierarchy of human achievements was at odds with those of Putnam and the other scientific racists in Department M: 'a tall, skinny chap from Arabia with a talent for swallowing swords expressed

If the monumental faux-marble façades of the White City succeeded in evoking a fantasy-vista of the Italian Renaissance, the Midway Plaisance created an equally fantastic *Erehwon* where the racial and cultural paradoxes of post-Reconstruction America could be explored through a different wonderland of engaged tourism and carnival excess. Kasson draws attention to the fact that the crowds preferred to pay admission prices for amusements on the Midway Plaisance than to stroll through the uplifting neoclassical buildings and edifying exhibits of the White City—for free. '...[T]he dominant monument of the Midway was no allegorical figure of civic virtue in classical garb like [Daniel Chester] French's statue "The Republic", but the gigantic, spare wheel designed by George W.G. Ferris especially for the Exposition, a striking instance of modern machine engineering in the service of pleasure'.[13] In the shadow of the Ferris wheel stretched a mélange of living ethnographic installations, variety shows, strolling musicians, camel-mounted Bedouin marriage processions, honkey-tonk concessions, packed performances for the 'danse du ventre' of Little Egypt (Fahreda Mahzar), baffling escape acts of the Houdini Brothers, and rigged feats of muscle-magic staged by Eugene Sandow, billed as the strongest man on the earth, adroitly managed by a young prestigitator named Florenz Ziegfeld, Jr.[14] The combination of ethnic displays, amusement rides, restaurants and variety acts proved irresistible to the twenty-seven million fairgoers who visited the WCE, establishing a commercial blueprint imitated by subsequent expositions, amusement parks, and touring circuses.

Appearances to the contrary, the apparent chaos of the Midway ensemble possessed an underlying principle of organization. The contemporary literary critic Denton J. Snider probably caught a glimpse of Putnam's original design of a 'sliding scale of humanity', in the embedded ethnological displays. Closest to the White City were stationed two German and Irish villages, representing the (white) Teutonic and Celtic races. In the center, occupying the largest space, was the Ottoman Empire and Asia. At the farthest removes from the White City, 'we descend to the savage races, the African of Dahomey and the North American Indian, each of which has its place…the best way of looking at these races is to behold them in the ascending scale, in the progressive movement; thus we can march forward with them starting with the lowest specimens of humanity, and reaching continually upward to the highest stage'.[15] The African American press generally excoriated the Exposition's refusal to appoint representatives to the commissions that

a culture which to me was on a higher plane than one demonstrated by a group of earnest Swiss peasants who passed their days making cheese and milk chocolate', quoted in Rydell, *All the World's a Fair*, p. 62.

13. John F. Kasson, *Amusing the Million: Coney Island at the Turn of the Century* (American Century Series; New York: Hill & Wang, 1978), p. 26.

14. Edo McCullough, *World's Fair Midways: An Affectionate Account of American Amusement Areas from the Crystal Palace to the Crystal Ball* (New York: Exposition Press, 1966), pp. 41-48.

15. Quoted in Rydell, *All the World's a Fair*, p. 65.

governed the fair. Frederick Douglass expressed outrage over the racism inherent in the Midway's treatment of Africans: 'as if to shame the Negro, the Dahomians are also here to exhibit the Negro as a repulsive savage'.[16] A member of Putnam's staff went on record to state that the Native American Indian exhibits deliberately attempted to deceive the American public by depicting them either as incorrigible savages or amenable to progressive education only through government agencies. Native American villages on the Midway were subjected to torrents of abuse.[17] The Midway Plaisance conspicuously bolstered the utopian message of the White City by portraying the non-Caucasian world as emotional, primitive, static, balkanized, and ultimately clueless in the cultural march to modernity. American audiences took comfort in the signs of their mastery over technology and economic capital in the White City even as the didactic lesson of the Midway reinforced their sense of Manifest Destiny. The history of Chicago's 'Street in Cairo' was a case in point.

Figure 2. Street in Cairo, Midway Plaisance, WCE, Chicago, 1893. Unnumbered plate from *Midway Types*.[18]

16. Quoted in Grace Cohen Grossman and Richard E. Ahlborn, *Judaica at the Smithsonian: Cultural Politics as Cultural Model* (Smithsonian Studies in History and Technology, 52; Washington, DC: Smithsonian Institution Press, 1997), p. 43.

17. Rydell, *All the World's a Fair*, p. 63.

18. *Midway Types* caption: A GROUP OF NATIVES: 'Here we have them in a lump—Cairo Street types caught by a sun-flash—magnate and subordinates, camel driver, donkeys, donkey

1.2. *Orientalism on the Midway*

European fascination with the Middle East gained momentum with the knowledge explosion set off by the efforts of Napoleon's savants in Egypt. In contrast, the Holy Land held seemingly enduring claims on the American imagination through its Protestant self-definition as the New Canaan. By 1893, Americans had missionized the Middle East for over seventy years, seen the publication of Mark Twain's *Innocents Abroad* amidst a host of Holy Land travelogues, evolved their own school of Orientalist painters, and institutionalized the study of Mediterranean geography through the formation of uniform Sunday School curricula. The professionalization of Semitic studies in American universities and the mounting of American expeditions to the Middle East were indicative of nationalistic jealousy over British and Continental successes in such ventures; if Americans could not colonize the lands of the Bible, they could possess them symbolically through the production of knowledge and stock visual images. And they could domesticate the Middle East through public spectacle.

A cartoon entitled 'Human Natur', captures the allure of Orientalism for the Chicago fairgoers, and also establishes the perceived interchangeability of the Oriental village and the Holy Land. In the first scene, a portly man wearing a tarboosh and 'bloomers' stands outside the Turkish Theater. The placard beside the door reads 'LIFE IN THE HOLY LANDS! SCENES FROM BIBLICAL DAYS!!! THE HISTORIC EAST AS IT IS AND WAS!!! A MORAL SHOW!!!' There were no customers. Next frame. With a change in advertising, male white 'preachers and Sunday-School teachers' of advanced years stampede through the doorway beside the smirking proprietor. The placard now reads 'LIFE IN THE HAREM!! DREAMY SCENES IN THE ORIENT!!! EASTERN DANCES!!! THE SULTAN'S DIVERSIONS!'[19]

drivers and the elusive urchins who were adding American tricks to their native ingenuity in passing the plate for contributions. Looking at this group and its background of shops below, and latticed windows above, it will require a harsh reality to convince you that they were on Chicago earth, and that you are not contemplating an Oriental scene on an Oriental street. No magician in Arabic legend produced a vision so wonderful for its seeming improbability as was done by the hand of the realist who put the people of this group on the sandy beach of Lake Michigan.' *Midway Types: a Book of Illustrated Lessons about the People of the Midway Plaisance, World's Fair, 1893* (Chicago: American Engraving Co., 1893), unnumbered plate.

19. Cartoon and analysis appear in Barbara Kirshenblatt-Gimblett, 'A Place in the World: Jews and the Holy Land at World's Fairs', in *Encounters with the 'Holy Land': Place, Past and Future in American Jewish Culture* (ed. Jeffrey Shandler and Beth S. Wenger; Brandeis Series in American Jewish History, Culture, and Life; Philadelphia & Hanover: National Museum of American Jewish History, Center for Judaic Studies; University of Pennsylvania Library; distributed by University Press of New England, 1997). pp. 60-82 (60-61). A poster outside the Luksor Temple hammered home the linkage between Pharaonic Egypt and the Bible: 'Egyptological exhibit. Don't fail to visit the EGYPTIAN TEMPLE OF LUKSOR, Built by the Israelites when in captivity, by order of Ramses II., 3400 years ago. The Temple is adorned with paintings and with the royal Mummies of Ahmon I., Seti I., Ramses II., Ramses III., Hirbor I., father-in-law of King

Explicitly Middle Eastern exhibits on the Midway Plaisance included the famed Street in Cairo,[20] the Algerian village, the Persian Palace, the Wild East Show, the Moorish Palace,[21] and the Turkish Theater, part of the Turkish Village, encompassing the Ottoman Empire from Morocco to Iran and Egypt to Turkey.[22] Of these installations, the Turkish village was the largest on the entire Midway, boasting a contingent of some two hundred souls. Recent scholarship suggests that most of them were Oriental Jews and Americans in Muslim drag. According to eye-witness Isador Lewi, '...about four-fifths of the inhabitants of the Turkish village on the Midway Plaisance at the Chicago Exposition were Jews. Merchants, clerks, actors, servants, musicians, and even the dancing girls, were of the mosaic faith, though their looks and garb would lead one to believe them Mohammedans'.[23] Denton Snider corroborated this by noting complaints from some fairgoers that the Turkish village was a 'purely speculative enterprise of some Oriental Jews'. Worse, the management of the Turkish village also hired

Solomon, &c.' 'Mummy of Nessi-Ta-Neb-Asher, the sister-in-law of King Solomon.' Chicago Historical Society photograph no. 25187.

20. *Midway Types*: CAIRO STREET, LOOKING EAST: 'Looking down Cairo Street from the West end, one saw a bewildering complication of objects in the fantastically decorated and shaped buildings, and in the motley dressed throngs of it inhabitants and visitors. In the distance the eye catches the shadows of the Egyptian Café, where were sold lager beer and peanuts, and where a lonesome Egyptian girl wandered about selling flowers. The minaret of the mosque of Abou Bake Mazhar [*sic*], from whose heights the muezzin called the faithful to prayer, rises to the right like a dainty carving on the sky. The street, which was a combination of the peculiarities of various streets of old Cairo, and not a reproduction of any one in particular, was honeycombed on its sides with over fifty shops, none of them over six feet square, in which were displayed the work of the quaint artisans of Egypt. From the window of the ticket seller to the front door of the Temple of Luxor was a varied succession, a laughable jumble of the sublime and the ridiculous.'

21.

> The Moorish Palace contains: The Palm Garden; The Magic Maze; The Reproduction of Spain's Alhambra; the Devil's Cave; The Ride on a Razor; The Room of a Thousand Reflections; The Bottomless Well; The Moorish Harem; The Optical Illusion Theatre; The Guillotine that Executed Marie Antoinette; The Finest Collection of Art in Wax in the World, from Castan's Panopticon of Berlin...The Harem: This represents one of the private apartments of the Padishah, richly decorated with fine antique oriental tapestries. The Sultan is seen surrounded by his favorites of the harem. An odalisque [*sic*] of the famous style of oriental beauty is amusing his Turkish majesty by a graceful dance, while a typical eunuch is keeping guard at the entrance of this most secluded part of the Turkish house. We cannot enjoy this private family scene forever and finally turn away. But strange! We find ourselves again in a bewildering labyrinth of colonnades and nooks...

The Moorish Palace and its Startling Wonders—The Chief Attraction of Midway Plaisance—World's Columbian Exposition 1893 (Chicago: Metcalf Stationery Co., 1893).

22. Rydell, 'A Cultural Frankenstein?', p. 163.

23. Quoted in Barbara Kirshenblatt-Gimblett, *Destination Culture: Tourism, Museums, and Heritage* (Berkeley: University of California Press, 1998), p. 97.

young American men and women for service situations, some of whom refused to don 'bifurcated garments' in the interest of verisimilitude.[24] The one place on the Midway where Jews openly identified themselves as such was in Putnam's photographic album, *Portrait Types of the Midway Plaisance*.[25] The caption beneath the full-length portrait of Robert J. Levy reads in part 'Mr. R.J. Levi, a Jewish resident of Constantinople, and by profession a chef and caterer, was the manager and chief proprietor of the Turkish Village and Theatre. Many of the vendors of Oriental wares in this village were Jews and personal friends of Mr. Levi; and all returned to the Orient at the close of the Fair well paid for their enterprise in coming to Chicago...Mr. Levi is unusually tall and handsome, and he appeared at the Fair in fanciful garb that gave him a striking appearance'.[26]

Figure 3. 'An obscure shop', Street in Cairo, Midway Plaisance, WCE, Chicago, 1893. Unnumbered plate from *Midway Types*.[27]

24. Kirshenblatt-Gimblett, 'A Place in the World', p. 70.

25. Frederick W. Putnam, *Oriental and Occidental, Northern and Southern Portrait Types of the Midway Plaisance: A Collection of Photographs of Individual Types of Various Nations from All Parts of the World Who Represented, in the Department of Ethnology, the Manners, Customs, Dress, Religions, Music and other Distinctive Traits and Peculiarities of their Race, with Interesting and Instructive Descriptions Accompanying Each Portrait* (Portrait Types Art Series; St. Louis: Thompson Publishing Co., 1894); *Midway Types*.

26. Putnam, *Portrait Types of the Midway Plaisance* (no plate numbers). 'Monahan Levi, Isaac Cohn and H. Hondon. (Turkish Jews.)' 'The Turkish village, like many another village on the Midway which was primarily intended to depict certain national characteristics and peculiarities, contained within its walls a good many things which were by no means Turkish... Mr. R[obert] Levi, a Jew, was the holder of the concession for the Turkish village, and Mr. Monahan Levi, whose portrait appears above and whose first name has a somewhat Celtic twang to it, is his brother.'

27. 'AN OBSCURE SHOP: The "Street of Cairo" was not half seen by the myriads of people

The firm of Souhami, Sadhullah & Co. held the lucrative Turkish Village concession; Cyrus Adler in his official capacity as WCE Commissioner to Turkey, Persia, Egypt, Tunis, and Morocco, hired its director, Robert J. Levy of Constantinople, to manage the Midway installation.[28] Souhami, Sadhullah & Co. had two American partners, undoubtedly a positive factor in its selection. In his fifteen months abroad as Commissioner, Adler actively 'networked' with Jewish communities in Constantinople, Damascus, Jerusalem, Cairo, Tunis, Algiers, and Tangier, and assigned most of the concessions accordingly.[29] Adler's experience in cosmopolitan Constantinople was that the resident Jews were visibly indistinguishable from other ethnic groups, and therefore he felt at liberty to hire Oriental Jews to come to Chicago in *their* official capacity as Turks.[30]

Adler's installation of invisible Jews on the Midway Plaisance to signify Muslims and concomitant refusal to create a 'Jewish Village'[31] or a 'Street in Jerusalem', served the ends of his larger enterprise to represent Judaism as a universal religion on a par with Christianity and, of equal weight, to create a barrier in the public mind between the established and highly assimilated American Jewish community and the influx of Jewish immigrants from Russia. Following the assassination of Czar Alexander II in 1881, over 135,000 Jews from the Russian Pale, Galicia, Romania, and other Eastern European locales fled to America in the face of state-sponsored pogroms. These Yiddish-speaking refugees from the Orthodox *shtetlach* of Ashkenazi Europe generated grave anxieties among the Jews of America, mostly of German ancestry and mostly Reform, who justifiably feared a nativist, anti-Semitic backlash from Gentile xenophobia and did not

who crowded and crushed one another on the narrow way. The little shops gave no hint of the life and work behind them; the inhabitants told no stories of their living. Those visitors who lingered over the grotesque bits of brass ware, offered here and there, did not behold the toiler at his labor. In giving the picture of the brass-workers at their tasks, there is offered something that was seen by only a few. The stolid, swarthy men, the manner of their work, their tools and partially manufactured goods, and their dismal workroom, will be revelations to our modern worker in metals, where machinery does the work of many hands and the wonders of the brain find speedy expression in the voice and forms of the marvelous work produced.' Caption, *Midway Types*, unnumbered plate.

28. A condescending profile of Robert Levy in *Midway Types*, emphasizing his smug self-satisfaction at the profitability of the Turkish Village, suggests that the American author was peeved by the foreigner's commercial success; letterpress for A TYPICAL TURK, unnumbered plate.

29. Cyrus Adler, *I have Considered the Days* (Philadelphia: The Jewish Publication Society of America, 1941), pp. 83-167.

30. Kirshenblatt-Gimblett, *Destination Culture*, p. 100.

31. *Pace* Kirshenblatt-Gimblett, there existed any number of Oriental Jewish communities, urban enclaves and institutions that might have been successfully represented on the Midway. Apparently Adler chose not to do so, for good reason. There is one savagely anti-Semitic portrait of a 'visible Jew' in *Midway Types*: the money changer. 'Cool, calculating, versed in exchange, unscrupulous and crafty, few made bargains with him and came out the gainer.' Most of the caption quotes the New Testament account of Jesus's expulsion of the money-changers from the Jerusalem Temple, driving home the lesson that such negative Jewish characteristics are two thousand years old and counting.

wish to be saddled with the social and financial burden of caring for destitute refugees.[32] While in Constantinople in 1891, Adler in his autobiography describes a conversation he had with Kiamil Pasha regarding the plight of the Russian Jews. Early Zionist plans to resettle these refugees in Palestine or other Ottoman territories faced opposition from the Ottoman administration and held the peril of offending American sensibilities by a seeming lack of patriotism.[33]

Adler seized a unique opportunity to shape American public perceptions about the very nature of Judaism. Key to his strategy was the extraction of Jews from their perilous role in traditional Christian supercessionism by abandoning the modern Middle East, including the biblical Holy Land, to its political identity as the Ottoman Empire. Given the sweeping cultural politics of the WCE, almost any nationality with a face on the Midway could not by definition share in the luminous triumph of progress embodied by the White City; the cause of Jewish American emancipation would not be served by linking Jewish exhibits to Ottoman bazaars and Dahomian drummers.[34] Instead, in his office as Honorary Assis-

32. Nathan Glazer, *American Judaism* (Chicago: University of Chicago Press, 2nd edn, 1972), pp. 60-78; Howard Morley Sachar, *The Course of Modern Jewish History* (A Delta Book; New York: Dell, 1981), pp. 305-22.

33. Jerrold S. Cooper, 'From Mosul to Manila: Early Approaches to Funding Ancient Near Eastern Studies Research in the United States', in *The Construction of the Ancient Near East* (ed. Ann Clyburn Gunter; Culture & History, 11; Copenhagen: Akademisk Forlag, 1992), pp. 133-64 (150-52). Richard Wheatley, 'The Jews in New York', *The Century Magazine* 43 (1892), pp. 323-42, an article that provided Adler with drawings of assimilated American Jews wearing derby and silk hats for the WCE exhibit, devotes many pages to the 'Slavic problem' 'hordes barbarous in speech, alien in habits, and in many cases broken-spirited by tyrannical and foul treatment' who 'demand the wisest and most persistent endeavor to harmonize their inner life with American currents of thought, and to identify them with all that is proper to our republican civilization' (p. 324).

34. It has been pointed out that the Orientalizing architecture of the laboriously constructed winding streets, kiosks, covered bazaars, mosques and theaters of the Middle Eastern exhibits on the Midway Plaisance powerfully reinforced the message of the progressivist triumph of the White City; see Zeynep Çelik and Leila Kinney, 'Ethnography and Exhibitionism at the Expositions Universelles', *Assemblages* 13 (1990), pp. 34-59. The frozen western imagery of Orientalist visual discourse was consciously manipulated by the Ottoman government itself. Represented by costly displays at the Woman's Building and various industrial installations, the chief architectural exhibit, the Ottoman Pavilion, replicated the Sultan Ahmed fountain, a prominent eighteenth-century Constantinople construction. Inside one encountered the statutory Oriental carpets, silk hangings, and intricate polychrome woodwork, with an Ottoman living room in the center. As Çelik observes, the Turkish government opted for stock Orientalizing clichés in the Chicago Pavilion instead of reproducing the Europeanizing Dolmabahçe Palace, constructed in Istanbul in 1856, which was based on the same beaux-arts principles of the White City, with its imposing French Second Empire style façade and exquisite European furnishings. American fairgoers expected to encounter water pipes, octagonal tables and cushions scattered over Turkish carpets in Turkish living spaces, and the Ottoman government gratifyingly obliged at the Pavilion, but contested that image elsewhere. See Z. Çelik, 'Speaking Back to Orientalist Discourse at the

tant Curator of the Sections of Oriental Antiquities and Religious Ceremonial Objects of the USNM, Adler harnessed Jews and Judaism to the Bible through their role as custodians of a religion unchanged in essentials from biblical times.

1.3. *Adler at the Smithsonian*

In February of 1887, Cyrus Adler, an engaging twenty-four-year-old who last week had earned the country's first PhD in Semitics at Johns Hopkins University, sought out a display of photographs of cuneiform tablets he had heard about at the USNM in Washington, DC. The display had been withdrawn. Nothing daunted, Adler found the curator of the exhibit, Otis T. Mason, who invited Adler into his office. By the conclusion of their conversation, Adler had volunteered his services in assisting the National Museum to form a collection of casts of ancient Near Eastern objects. One month later, Paul Haupt, Adler's dissertation advisor, would send a letter to Spencer F. Baird, Secretary of the Smithsonian Institution, recommending that the USNM add a section devoted to Oriental archaeology, with especial attention paid to the study of the Bible, and expressed the willingness of the Semitics faculty at Johns Hopkins to assist in the good work. One year later in February 1888, The Department of Ethnology formally added a Section of Oriental Antiquities, listing Paul Haupt as the honorary curator and Cyrus Adler as assistant honorary curator.[35] Although Haupt's name would continue to appear in conjunction with annual reports of the Section of Oriental Antiquities, it was Adler's hand that governed the organization of the collection and the philosophy behind its acquisition.[36]

World's Columbian Exposition', in *Noble Dreams, Wicked Pleasures: Orientalism in America, 1870–1930* (ed. Holly Edwards; Princeton, NJ: Princeton University Press and Sterling and Francine Clark Art Institute, 2000), pp. 76-97 (77-76, 85-86).

35. On the convoluted history of Haupt's relationship with the USNM and his rather devious imperialism, see Cooper, 'From Mosul to Manila', pp. 133-64, and Paul Haupt, 'Excavations in Assyria and Babylonia', in *Report of the U.S. National Museum, under the Direction of the Smithsonian Institution, for the Year Ending June 30, 1888* ([Washington, DC]: Smithsonian Institution, 1890), pp. 95-104.

36. Grossman and Ahlborn, *Judaica at the Smithsonian*, pp. 1, 36. Adler's subsequent career combined leadership roles within the Conservative Jewish movement and academic administration. Raised in an energized German Jewish elite community in Philadelphia, Adler received intellectual demanding training from Rabbi Sabato Morais, head of Mikveh Israel Congregation, who would provide an effective role-model for the religiously observant Adler, and from Samuel Hirsch and the lexicographer Marcus Jastrow. Adler took his B.A and M.A. from the University of Pennsylvania, and entered the newly inaugurated Semitics program at Johns Hopkins in 1883.

The emergent secular discipline of Semitic studies at American research institutions, with its emphasis on philology, archaeology, history, and comparative religions, offered a variety of attractions to Jewish American intellectuals. It facilitated a relatively safe way openly to study the Bible within an overwhelmingly Protestant society in a manner that was free of sectarian controversies, yet the scope of its competencies rivaled traditional rabbinic scholarship in terms of breadth and technical rigor. It folded seamlessly into the *Haskalah* project of the *Wissenschaft des Judentums*,

Catering to the scholarly community, the collection of Oriental Antiquities grew out of a desire that the USNM should become a clearinghouse for information on ancient Near Eastern antiquities in the United States, primarily Assyro-Babylonian.[37] Since there was little hope of ever matching the holdings of the great European museums, plaster replicas and photographs would supplement the meager specimens of genuine antiquities.[38] Working through the auspices of

which sought to defuse Gentile prejudice against Judaism through rational exposition using the categories of Enlightenment historiography. Adler's dissertation on the inscriptions of Assurbanipal was never published, and his scholarly publications were relatively few in number. He did, however, remain active in the American Oriental Society throughout his life, and was appointed president in 1923. In the 1926 Festschrift for Paul Haupt, Adler published an important history of Semitic studies in nineteenth-century America; Adler, 'The Beginnings of Semitic Studies in America', in *Oriental Studies Published in Commemoration of the Fortieth Anniversary (1883–1923) of Paul Haupt as Director of the Oriental Seminary of the Johns Hopkins University, Baltimore, MD* (ed. C. Adler and Aaron Ember; Baltimore, MD: Johns Hopkins Press, 1926), pp. 317-28.

Adler taught as an instructor at Johns Hopkins from 1887 through 1892, leaving the position when Smithsonian Secretary Samuel P. Langley appointed him librarian of the Smithsonian Institution. By the time that Adler withdrew from the Smithsonian as honorary curator and assistant secretary, he had served as editor of the American Jewish Yearbook (1899–1905) and had begun work as a department editor for the great Jewish Encyclopedia (1901–1909). In 1906 Adler, impressed with the notion that American Judaism needed a united voice, became a cofounder of the American Jewish Committee. In 1908 Adler became president of Dropsie College in Philadelphia and acting president of the Jewish Theological Seminary in 1915, to be appointed to the presidency of the latter following the death of Solomon Schechter in 1924. Adler remained president of both institutions to his death. Although opposed to Zionism in his early life, he worked to secure immigration opportunities for European Jews under the conditions of the Balfour Declaration, and attempted to secure political haven for Jews in America fleeing Nazi Germany. For a comprehensive list of Adler's publications, through 1933, see Edward D. Coleman and Joseph Reider, 'A Bibliography of the Writings and Addresses of Cyrus Adler 1882–1933', in *Lectures, Selected Papers, Addresses, by Cyrus Adler, with a Bibliography* (Philadelphia: privately printed, 1933), pp. 364-445, and James A. Montgomery and Joseph Reider, 'Cyrus Adler, 1863–1940', *JAOS* 61 (1941), pp. 193-94. Primary sources for his life include the excellently edited Adler and I. Robinson, *Selected Letters* (2 vols.; Philadelphia and New York: Jewish Publication Society of America and Jewish Theological Seminary of America, 1985), and Adler's own autobiography, *I Have Considered the Days*, in which he engages in considerable self-fashioning. Secondary studies include Jonathan D. Sarna, 'Cyrus Adler and the Development of American Jewish Culture: the "Scholar-Doer" as a Jewish Communal Leader', *American Jewish History* 78 (1989), pp. 382-94, I. Robinson, 'Adler, Cyrus (13 Sept. 1863–7 Apr. 1940)', in *ANB Online* (Oxford University Press, 2005), and the hagiographic Abraham A. Neuman, *Cyrus Adler: A Biographical Sketch* (Philadelphia: The Jewish Publication Society of America, 1942).

37. While Adler recognized the importance and aesthetic attractiveness of Egyptian artifacts to a biblically-literate constituency, his research focus and the influence of his Doktor-Vater insured that assyriological materials would dominate the collection.

38. American art fanciers, including George Washington, begin to acquire plaster reproductions of Greco-Roman antiquities in the eighteenth century. Most nineteenth-century American collections of Mediterranean and Middle Eastern antiquities contained large numbers of reproductions thought perfectly suitable for display and study purposes. See William B. Dinsmoor,

the American Oriental Society, Adler issued a call in October 1887 for Assyro-Babylonian antiquities residing in the United State to be loaned to the USNM for the purpose of reproduction in plaster.[39] Most of his annual reports included several paragraphs detailing the 'discovery' of this or that object in an American collection, and the successful efforts to have a copy made for accessioning into the Smithsonian collection. But the Section of Oriental Antiquities also served the larger Smithsonian program for popular education. With the enthusiastic backing of Goode, Adler attempted to address a felt need for the National Museum to offer exposure to a collection 'corresponding to those known in London as Biblical archaeology'.[40] W. Edward Earll, in his official report on the Smithsonian installation at the 1888 Ohio Exposition, put the matter thus:

> Owing to the wide-spread interest in biblical studies, Dr. Cyrus Adler, Assistant Curator of the Section of Oriental Antiquities, was called upon to prepare an exhibit which should enable Bible students (of whom it is estimated that there are already more than four millions in the Sunday-schools of the United States) to see something of the results of the work of the numerous specialists who have devoted their time and energies to the study of the people of Bible lands, and to become familiar with some of the interesting objects which have been collected and studied, with a view to the better understanding of the language, history, art, social life, and religion of these people.[41]

The figure of four million may have been an invention of Adler's, but Protestant American enthusiasm for the study of the Bible was not.

Once the Section of Oriental Antiquities was officially in place in February 1888, Adler's first major task was preparation of a biblical archaeology exhibit for the Centennial Exposition of the Ohio Valley and Central States, Cincinnati Ohio, July 4–November 8, 1888. The Smithsonian was allotted 12,000 square feet of exhibit space at the Cincinnati Centennial Exposition of 1888—and one month to plan, transport, and assemble the entire exhibit! The exhibit ensemble canvassed prehistoric anthropology, general ethnology, the Bureau of Ethnology, biblical archaeology, transportation, naval architecture, graphic arts, photography, mammals (systematic exhibit), mammals (extermination series),

'Early American Studies of Mediterranean Archaeology', *Proceedings of the American Philosophical Society* 87/1 (1943), pp. 70-104.

39. Adler, 'Report on the Section of Oriental Antiquities…1888', pp. 93-94; Adler, 'On a Study-Collection of Casts of Assyrian and Babylonian Antiquities in the National Museum at Washington', *JAOS* 13 (1889), p. ccxxxiv.

40. Goode, 'The Collection of Oriental Antiquities, and The Collection of Religious Ceremonial Objects', in *Annual Report of the Board of Regents of the Smithsonian Institution, Showing the Operations, Expenditures, and Condition of the Institution for the Year Ending June 30, 1893* (1895), pp. 135-37 (135).

41. R. Edward Earll, 'Report upon the Exhibit of the Smithsonian Institution, including the U.S. National Museum, at the Centennial Exposition of the Ohio Valley and Central States, held at Cincinnati, Ohio, in 1888', in *Report of the U.S. National Museum, under the Direction of the Smithsonian Institution, for the Year Ending June 30, 1889* ([Washington, DC]: Smithsonian Institution, 1891), pp. 154-89 (165).

birds, insects, mollusks, marine invertebrates, botany, and mineralogy. The biblical archaeology section was assigned 280 square feet of exhibit space. Earll described the biblical archaeology exhibit as follows:

> The exhibits were arranged by countries, including Assyria and Babylonia, Egypt, Elam, and Palestine. They contained objects from a period beginning 3800 years B.C., and continuing to the present time, including royal seals and impressions of same, casts of obelisks and tablets containing pictorial and historical inscriptions, photographs of the Egyptian pyramids, sphinxes, sculptures, mummies of noted kings, with specimens of plants, shells, lamps, and costumes collected in the several countries named. Among the more interesting objects were the casts of the Black Obelisk of Shalmaneser II, the Rosetta Stone, the Moabite Stone, and the Siloam Inscription.[42]

Following the model of earlier Smithsonian exposition displays, at the close of the Ohio Valley Centennial the biblical archaeology materials were shipped back to Washington to form the core of the Oriental Antiquities installation at the National Museum. The new exhibit opened March 2, 1889, a date designed to coincide with the inauguration of President Benjamin Harrison. Between March 2–5, over 100,000 visitors toured the USNM, a remarkable crowd for the age. The number of objects on display numbered 425, which included 150 photographs. Among the specimens were several items of European Judaica, including a *shofar* (ram's horn).[43]

Although no mention of efforts to assemble Judaica figure in Adler's first two reports to the Smithsonian, it is evident that, with Goode's backing, he intended to amass such a collection from the beginning. Indeed, a letter to Sabato Morais dated November 1889 indicates that the Smithsonian, on behalf of Adler, had already commissioned Harry Friedenwald to procure Judaica in Italy for the National Museum collection.[44] A smattering of pieces were donated, purchased, and exhibited prior to 1892, but the great push begin with preparations for the WCE in 1893. In September 1892, Adler received permission to travel to several East Coast cities in order to open negotiations with various owners of Judaica collections with a view to purchasing them for the Smithsonian exhibit in Chicago. Several valuable items were procured; however, the bulk of the Judaica on exhibit in the Government Building in Chicago belonged to Hadji Ephraim Benguiat, whose collection of forty-four objects was installed in the USNM following the fair and remained on loan to the Smithsonian Institution until deaccession in 1924.[45] In 1893, the Section of

42. Earll, 'Centennial Exposition of the Ohio Valley', p. 165.

43. Adler, 'Report on the Section of Oriental Antiquities in the U.S. National Museum, 1889', in *Report of the U.S. National Museum, under the Direction of the Smithsonian Institution, for the Year Ending June 30, 1889* ([Washington, DC]: Smithsonian Institution, 1891), pp. 289-92; Grossman, *Judaica at the Smithsonian*, p. 38.

44. Adler and Robinson, *Selected Letters*, I, p. 10, though the date given is 1887; see Grossman, *Judaica at the Smithsonian*, p. 39.

45. Adler, 'Report on the Section of Oriental Antiquities in the U.S. National Museum, 1892',

Religious Ceremonial Objects was established, with Adler appointed Custodian of the Section until 1903–1904, when he became its honorary curator.[46]

1.4. *The Smithsonian's Religious Ceremonials Exhibit at the White City*

Proposals had been floated in 1881 and 1889 for establishing a comparative religions exhibit at the National Museum,[47] but Adler's plan for the WCE caught the fancy of his superiors at the Smithsonian. His proposal to Goode in May of 1892 recommended that Judaism, Islam, Buddhism, Hinduism, Egyptian, Babylonian, Greek and four Native American religions be represented in Chicago. An accompanying note revealed that the Smithsonian's holdings of Islamica was next to nil. For around $400, Adler was confident that he could acquire ritual items associated with the mosque, costumes, and illustrative photographs adequate for a creditable exhibit. The exhibit ultimately sponsored by the Smithsonian Institution in the White City differed substantially from the May proposal. The official catalogue prepared for the United States Government Building states that 'this exhibit [Religious Ceremonials] is limited to a selection from the religions of the nations inhabiting the Mediterranean basin, with special regard to the ceremonials as forming the starting point for a comparative study of religions'. The religions treated were, in the order printed in the catalogue, Assyro-Babylonian, Judaism, Islam, Greek, Roman, and Oriental Christian.[48]

By 1893, Adler had acquired hundreds of photographs from the leading studio photographers in the Middle East—the Maison Bonfils, Abdullah Frères, Hippolyte Arnoux, Constantine Zangaki—as well as extensive stock from the Palestine Exploration Fund. Their portfolios of *cartes-de-viste* and cabinet-sized reproductions consisted of shots of the Egyptian pyramids with western tourists scrambling up the stones, Holy Land landscapes and cityscapes peopled by 'biblical' looking natives, genre portraits of stock Oriental types, soft pornography in the guise of dancing girls and harem interiors, and artfully contrived street scenes. The creation of montages assembled from unrelated negatives, and the fabrication of otherwise impossible voyeuristic exploits (like harem scenes) by utilizing paid models and the bric-a-brac of the portrait studio, guaranteed that the companies would turn a profit by reinforcing western visual expectations of the Ottoman East.[49] Adler's Middle Eastern photo-

in *Report of the U.S. National Museum, under the Direction of the Smithsonian Institution, for the Year Ending June 30, 1892* ([Washington, DC]: Smithsonian Institution, 1893), pp. 111-13 (112); Grossman, *Judaica at the Smithsonian*, pp. 50-55.

46. Goode, 'The Collection of Oriental Antiquities, and The Collection of Religious Ceremonial Objects', in *Annual Report of the Board of Regents of the Smithsonian Institution, Showing the Operations, Expenditures, and Condition of the Institution for the Year Ending June 30, 1893* (1895), pp. 135-37; Grossman, *Judaica at the Smithsonian*, p. 63.

47. Goode, 'Collection of Oriental Antiquities and Religious Ceremonial Objects', p. 136.

48. Reprinted in Grossman, *Judaica at the Smithsonian*, pp. 96-97.

49. Louis Vaczek and Gail Buckland, *Travellers in Ancient Lands: A Portrait of the Middle*

graphic collection was in no wise unusual, and could be counted on to unfold a desertified Orient punctuated by grand architectural ruins, populated with cultural fossils that were both picturesque and gratifyingly impoverished. His photographic ensemble for the Judaica collection took an altogether different tack.

Figure 4. Religious Ceremonials Exhibit, Government Building, White City, WCE, Chicago, 1893. Adler's framed photographs hang on the walls above the glass cases. Smithsonian Institution Archives, Record Unit 95, Box 61, Folder 11, image no. 12350. Used by permission.

Jewish ceremonial art dominated the display, with major divisions between objects associated with synagogue, home, and life-cycle events. In order to provide a living context, the Judaica was accompanied by a series of photographs, engravings and art reproductions of synagogues, rabbis, worship and domestic life in the ghetto. The choice of illustrations strategically influenced the reception of Adler's Judaica exhibit, and should be evaluated within the larger context of ethnic and racial representation at the WCE. Adler plundered Bernard Picart's exquisitely executed copper engravings in *Cérémonies et coutumes religieuses de tous les peuples du monde.* 1. *Cérémonies des juifs & des chrétiens catholiques* (1723) for examples of Jewish rituals.[50] Most of Picart's illustrations are of the assimilated Jewish community in Amsterdam. However, one

East, 1839–1919 (Boston: New York Graphic Society, 1981), pp. 132-33; Paul Faber, Anneke Groeneveld, and Hein Reedijk, *Beelden van de Oriënt: Fotografie en toerisme, 1860–1900 = Images of the Orient: Photography and Tourism, 1860–1900* (Amsterdam: Fragment in samenwerking met Museum voor Volkenkunde Rotterdam, 1986), p. 22.

50. Bernard Picart, *Cérémonies et coutumes religieuses de tous les peuples du monde.* I. *Cérémonies des juifs & des chrétiens catholiques* (Amsterdam: J.F. Bernard, 1723),

of the Picart plates that has survived in the Smithsonian collection, 'cérémonie nuptiale des juifs allemands', shows a tableau on a German cobblestone street of the veiled bride receiving her ring in a circle of well-dressed bourgeoisie wearing tricorn hats and frock coats, to the accompaniment of musicians playing hammered dulcimer and violins.[51] With the exception of the ritual objects, rites, and synagogue appointments, the Jews in these illustrations were indistinguishable from their Gentile fellow Germans or Dutchmen.[52]

mentations of
Jeremiah it is
sympathetic,
sorrowful, and
steeps the
heart in pro-
foundest grief.
The ornamen-
tation of wrap-
pings, which

As in all other orthodo
are male. The deep, ric
is exquisitely fine. Wo
church, as orthodox ra
do; but they do not l
joyed the restraint. T
ful, plaintive, passionat
the entire scale of hu
from David's harp, S
Oriental composers ble
Beethoven, Mendelsso
nal melodies of the gif
Chief Rabbi Jacob
head of eighteen larg
lower part of the city.
posed of Slavonic Jews
long gabardine, bear
tokens of orthodo
now is due t
stripped the
acteristics a
izing proce
into the s
with the l
reft of th
not the fi
who ha
with

THE ABODAH.

Figure 5. 'The Abodah'. Illustration by Irving R. Wiles in Richard Wheatley, 'The Jews in New York' (1892), p. 330.[53]

51. Reprinted in Grossman, *Judaica at the Smithsonian*, p. 51, fig. 14.

52. On the career of Bernard Picart (1673–1733), see Maxime Préaud, 'Picart, Bernard', in *Grove Art Online* (Oxford University Press, 2005). Other pieces of Picart's copperplate Judaica in Adler's collection include NAA inv 08645700 and 08645800. I wish to thank Lorain Wang, Reference Archivist for the National Anthropological Archives of the Smithsonian Institution, for access to the holdings of NAA photo lot 97.

53. NAA inv 04054000, a photographic enlargement with the surrounding text cropped, was erroneously labeled 'The Day of Atonement.' Other illustrations from this popular *Century Magazine* article are also to be found in the Adler corpus.

Another collection of prints is of a popular series of paintings by the portraitist Moritz Daniel Oppenheim (1799–1882). In *Bilder aus dem altjüdischen Familienleben* (1880),[54] Oppenheim crafted a vision of German Jewish life in the ghetto by using highly romanticized images of cosy, middle-class homes with families fulfilling the Sabbath injunction or celebrating holidays. The eighteenth-century anachronism of the paintings does not detract from the essentially European architecture and society they powerfully project.[55] An 1892 *Century Magazine* article, 'Jews in New York' furnished Adler with sketches of contemporary well-to-do Jewish men in frock coats and stylish haberdashery reading from the Torah in synagogue or praying the Abodah (fig. 5). In none of this artwork does one find a hint of the Eastern European *Yiddishkeit* that was causing the progressive American Jewish community such *Angst* in the 1890s.[56] With relatively few exceptions, the Smithsonian's scientifically-labeled collection of Judaica at the Chicago fair consisted of eighteenth- and nineteenth-century pieces of European manufacture. Displayed in conjunction with the Picart and Oppenheim illustrations, Adler adroitly furnished Judaism in the United States Government Building with an impeccably middle class, Western European locus. Aside from some of the fairgoers, the only documented Oriental Jews at the fair were running the most popular concessions on the Midway, but they were supposed to be invisible. 'Taken together the diverse forms of Jewish participation at the Chicago fair illuminate the paradoxes of diaspora and the theatricality of race, which needed to be staged to be seen. That staging also offered a place to hide'.[57]

Adler's religious ceremonials display at the fair did in fact openly exhibit two types of Orientals. One was identified as Mohammedan. That exhibit, which held a distant second in richness to the Jewish tableau, boasted a Qur'ān, a reading stand, crescent, lamps, ewer and basin, costumes of a Persian imam and a dervish, and photographs of Mecca and pilgrims, mosques, fountains, religious persons and feasts, and burial places. An extensive word-picture of the Smithsonian exhibit was published in the *New York Evening Post* 6 September 1894. The news writer undoubtedly interjected his own biases in the essay, but something of the way that Adler shaped his presentation of Islam emerges from the

54. Moritz Daniel Oppenheim, *Bilder aus dem altjüdischen Familienleben: Nach Original-Gemälden von Moritz Oppenheim. Mit Einführung und Erläuterungen von Rabbiner Dr Emil Levy* (Berlin: L. Lamm, 1913).

55. Ruth Dröse, *Der Zyklus 'Bilder aus dem altjüdischen Familienleben' und sein Maler Moritz Daniel Oppenheim* (Hanau: CoCon-Verlag, 1996), is unavailable to me.

56. The only pictures that I saw in the Adler NAA corpus of ostensibly Oriental Jews were either of the Samaritan community (NAA inv 04056500 and others) or a pair of Palestine Exploration Fund photographs of a group of seven Ashkenazi Jews in Jerusalem (NAA inv 04056800 and 04056900, both of which bore exhibit labels 'Group of Jews, at Jerusalem' but both of which also bore handwritten legends on the back 'Polish Jews.'

57. Kirshenblatt-Gimblett, *Destination Culture*, p. 105.

description of the items highlighted. 'The Mohammedans treat the Koran with at least great outward veneration…Its reading is preceded by legal ablution and the usual prayer, "I seek protection with God against Satan, the accursed"…In the back of the case are hung many silver cases for charms against evil spirits, witchcraft, or disease, a belief in the efficacy of these charms being very general throughout the East'.[58] Numerous Picart copperplates of Islamic functionaries and various drawings of Muslims at prayer in the Smithsonian archives bear the marks of Adler's handiwork. His presentation of Islam in Government Building was scholarly for the time and surely more balanced than anything most Chicago fairgoers had encountered. At the same time, it served up hackneyed images of Islam as a faith focused on externals and the Ottoman Empire as a land filled with a people that time had forgotten.[59]

58. The newspaper article was appended to Adler's address on comparative religions in museum exhibits, Adler, 'Museum Collections to Illustrate Religious History and Ceremonials', in *Report of the U.S. National Museum, under the Direction of the Smithsonian Institution, for the Year Ending June 30, 1893* ([Washington, DC]: Smithsonian Institution, 1893), pp. 757-68 (766-68), which is reprinted in Grossman, *Judaica at the Smithsonian*, pp. 98-99. NAA inv 04128900, a drawing, bears a handwritten legend on the back: 'chapter of "Koran" carried as Talisman and a Voodoo bag.' NAA inv 04036500, a photograph of an eye-of-Horus amulet, bore the legend 'Egyptian charm against evil eye and opthalmia.'

59. A series of nineteen photographs of the famous Arbeely family from Syria in the Adler corpus bear comment. Joseph Arbeely (Yusuf Awad Arbili), a medical doctor and president of the Patriarchal Syrian College of the Greek Church, immigrated to America in 1878 with his six sons, Ibrahim, Khaleel, Fadlallah, Nageeb, Habeeb and Nasseem. Nageeb J. Arbeely, naturalized as an American citizen in Tennessee, was hired as a medical examiner for Ellis Island and was detailed for dealing with Arabic- and French-speaking nationals. Arab-American histories of the period are fulsome with praise for Nageeb's tireless humanity in the face of the brutal assembly-line processing of immigration screening. He also taught French for a short time at Maryville College, Tennessee. His older brother, Abraham Joseph (Ibrahim Yusuf) Arbeely, also an MD, president of the Orthodox Benevolent Society of New York, published an English grammar in Arabic designed to assist immigrants in negotiating assimilation into American society. The two brothers founded the first Arabic newspaper printed in America, the *Kowkab Amrika* (1892–), printing three pages in Arabic and one in English per issue. The editorial position adopted by the Arbeely brothers was said to have been consistently loyal to the Ottoman sultan. In 1885, the newly elected President Grover S. Cleveland dismissed the irascible (and Republican) U.S. Consul in Jerusalem, Selah Merrill, and appointed Nageeb J. Arbeely in his stead. Unfortunately for Nageeb, the Ottoman administration could not countenance a former subject as both a naturalized U.S. citizen and Consul, so he was recalled to Washington 11 November 1887. At about this time, a series of studio photographs of the strikingly handsome Nageeb, his brother Habeeb and Hanna Arbeely, relation unknown, were made with the intent of casting the subjects in a variety of stock Islamic poses and roles, including that of Bedouins, scholars, soldiers, and, naturally, prayerful Muslims. The purpose behind the photogenic playacting must remain speculative. It is virtually certain, however, that Adler had personal dealings with Nageeb. In 1893, both Nageeb and I.M. Casanowicz, Adler's protégé at the USNM, joined the elect company of the American Oriental Society, in which Adler was active, probably through his sponsorship. See NAA inv 04085000, 04086000, 04086100, 04086200, 04086300 ('Nageeb and Habeeb Arbeely and Hanna

Figure 6. 'Nageeb and Habeeb Arbeely and Hanna from Damascus in Costume, Demonstrating Prayer Positions (Lectures on Palestine) 1887'. National Anthropological Archives of the Smithsonian Institution, Photographic Lot 97, Division of Ethnology Collection, NAA inv 04087000. Used by permission.

The other Orientals on display in the Smithsonian exhibit were Christians—Greek and Russian Orthodox. A collection of Russian Orthodox copper icons and Greek Orthodox crosses, scepters, embroidered vestments and other liturgical objects filled a glass case next to the Judaica collection, some of which the Smithsonian had purchased from an expert on gems who had acquired the items in Russia with an eye to their marketability in America. Other items on display

from Damascus in Costume, Demonstrating Fight with Swords, Shields, and Daggers [Lecture on Palestine]'), 04086400, 04086500, 04086600, 04086700, 04086800, 04086900, 04087000, 04087100 ('Nageeb and Habeeb Arbeely and Hanna from Damascus in Costume, Demonstrating Prayer Positions [Lectures on Palestine]'), 04087200, 04087300, 04087400, 04088600, and 04088700; Ruth Kark, *American Consuls in the Holy Land, 1832–1914* (America-Holy Land Monographs Series; Detroit, MI: Wayne State University Press, 1994), p. 326; Gregory Orfalea, *Before the Flames: A Quest for the History of Arab Americans* (Austin: University of Texas Press, 1988), pp. 9-10, 76; Samir Khalaf, 'The Background and Causes of Lebanese/Syrian Immigration to the United States before World War I', in *Crossing the Waters: Arabic-Speaking Immigrants to the United States before 1940* (ed. Eric J. Hooglund; Washington, DC and London: Smithsonian Institution Press, 1987), pp. 17-35 (24); Adele L. Younis and Philip M. Kayal, *The Coming of the Arabic-Speaking People to the United States* (Staten Island, NY: Center for Migration Studies, 1995), pp. 118-19; Alixa Naff, *Becoming American: The Early Arab Immigrant Experience* (Middle East Research Institute Special Studies; Philadelphia: Middle East Research Institute, University of Pennsylvania Press, 1985), pp. 104-105, 130-31, 295, 320.

represented the Armenian, Coptic, and Ethiopian Christian traditions.[60] The *New York Evening Post* writer captures the essential otherness of the exhibit for his Protestant American constituency: The items on display represent 'the Greek church, of which the Czars of all the Russias have since Peter the Great been the head. The full title of the Greek Church is the Holy Oriental Orthodox Catholic Apostolic Church… The doctrine of the Greek Church is substantially like the Roman, though the government is a patriarchal oligarchy…[a] piece was bought at Nizhui Novgorod for Tiffany & Co. in 1891, and is said to be the finest icon in the United States'.[61]

From internal evidence of the correspondence exchanged between Adler and other Smithsonian officers, it is clear that the Smithsonian was ambivalent about displaying Christian ecclesiastical art in its exhibit in the White City. Goode had acquired pieces of Catholic liturgical art in Italy that Adler knew about, but no effort was made to add them to the display. In point of fact, Adler had received unsolicited offers for loans of Christian art for exhibition purposes which he did not follow up. Was this an instance of the Smithsonian fearing public backlash should Catholic or Protestant liturgical art be treated like museum curiosities? Perhaps. Another possibility is that, by aggressively advertising Judaism as a universal religion whose 'endusers' are assimilated Europeans, as opposed to Muslim and Christian Orientals, Adler adroitly extricated Judaism from its negative role in Christian *Heilsgeschichte* and dangerous cultural associations with the modern Orient, whether Russia or Ottoman Empire. Instead, the invisible conversation partner of assimilated Judaism becomes mainstream American Protestantism: both traditions stand apart from and are superior to their Oriental co-religionists. Within the explicit progressivism of the WCE, the evolutionary schema of the Smithsonian Institution exhibit of religious ceremonials culminates in the western Judeo-Christian tradition. Over twenty-one million entrance tickets were sold for the fair; millions of Americans had the opportunity to experience Adler's display in Government Building.[62] This formula of Judeo-Christian tradition versus the unchanging Orient would be articulated

60. Grossman, *Judaica at the Smithsonian*, pp. 51-52, 97.

61. Adler, 'Museum Collections to Illustrate Religious History and Ceremonials', p. 767. *Midway Types* supplies a picture of two 'Christians from Bagdad' with predictably negative copy: 'As to the merits of the religion of the Christians it is unquestionably greatly below the requirements in this country in consequence of a lower standard of education, as well as by reason of the constant friction against and contamination by other and antagonistic beliefs.'

62. To be sure, Adler's Religious Ceremonials exhibit could not compete with displays of Krupp armaments in the White City and the blandishments of the Midway Plaisance. Having scoured the photographic holdings of the Chicago Historical Society, the Smithsonian Institution, and a host of oversized illustrated souvenir books, I have identified exactly one photograph of the exhibit. It just wasn't very sexy. I wish to thank Kirsten van der Veen of the Dibner Library of the History of Science & Technology, and Ellen Alers, Assistant Archivist, Smithsonian Institution Archives, for help in separating the chaff from the grain.

in greater detail in the biblical antiquities exhibit Adler mounted at the Cotton States and International Exposition two years later.

2.0. *Biblical Antiquities at the Cotton States and International Exposition*

In the midst of the financial depression of 1893, a group of Atlanta businessmen incorporated the Cotton States and International Exposition Company. Many southern states believed themselves to have been grievously under-represented at the WCE, a residual token of Reconstruction-era legislation. Too, there was also a frank objective to establish advantageous trade relations with Latin America, coupled with the desire to put Atlanta, reborn from the ashes of the Civil War, on the map of progressive American cities. The Atlanta fair, like other southern international expositions,[63] sought to construct an ideology of the New South as a cornucopia of mineral and agricultural wealth ripe for investment, led by a progressive oligarchy of Anglo-Saxon plutocrats adept at matching the evolving social realities with industrial processes. Like the White City in Chicago, the Atlanta fair scripted its visible hierarchy of class and race through the trappings of science, especially evolutionary anthropology. But unlike the White City, and in common with other southern expositions, the Atlanta fair actively projected an image of white and African American racial harmony through the creation of 'Colored Departments' 'Negro Buildings' and sponsorship of prominent African American leaders like Booker T. Washington who publicly lent their approbation to the proceedings. In the words of E.A. Burke, Director-General of the New Orleans World's Industrial and Cotton Exposition of 1885: 'It [the Colored Department] was designed by the management of the Exhibition, through this exhibit, to reach out our hand to our brother in black; to shed upon that unfortunate race the sunlight of science and invention, and implant in him the desire to come out of the slough of ignorance and make a manly effort to occupy with us the improved farm, the workshop, and the factory'.

The Cotton States and International Exposition ran from September 18 to December 31, 1895; paid attendance at the fair topped 779,000,[64] though it is claimed that total attendance exceeded 1,285,000.[65] The federal government constructed a 58,000 square-foot building to house representative exhibits from all departments; the Smithsonian claimed 5,300 square feet for itself, with a

63. New Orleans World's Industrial and Cotton Exposition (1885), Atlanta Cotton States and International Exposition (1895), the Tennessee Centennial Exposition (1897), the South Carolina Interstate and West Indian Exposition (1901–1902), and the Jamestown Tercentenary Exposition (1907).

64. Walter Gerald Cooper, *The Cotton States and International Exposition and South, Illustrated: Including the Official History of the Exposition* (Atlanta, GA: The Illustrator Company, 1896), p. 88.

65. Rydell, *All the World's a Fair*, p. 102.

congressional budget allocation of $22,000.[66] Cyrus Adler and his assistant Immanuel Moses Casanowicz[67] mounted a major exhibit called variously 'Section of Biblical Archaeology' and 'Biblical Antiquities' for the Atlanta fair. Fortunately, Adler and Casanowicz published an extensive catalogue of the exhibit, complete with over forty plates, thus making it possible to describe the 'Biblical Antiquities' in substantial detail 110 years after the fact.

Figure 7. Section of Biblical Archaeology Exhibit, Government Building, Cotton States and International Exposition, Atlanta, 1895. Neo-Hittite relief casts line the wall behind the ziggurat model; a large relief map of Palestine is partially obscured by the left-hand glass case. The case below the Shabbat lamp contains stuffed animals. The free-standing case on the left is labeled 'Jewish religious ceremonials'. In the case on the right, 'Palestinian archaeology', one can make out a pair of slippers and a sheepskin, presumably part of a garment. Smithsonian Institution Archives, Record Unit 95, Box 61, Folder 11, image no. 12666. Used by permission.

66. Bessie Nicholls Croffut, 'Exposition, Cotton-States and International', in *Appleton's Annual Cyclopaedia and Register of Important Events of the Year 1895: Embracing Political, Military, and Ecclesiastical Affairs; Public Documents; Biography, Statistics, Commerce, Finance, Literature, Science, Agriculture, and Mechanical Industry* (42 vols.; New York: D. Appleton & Company, 1868–1903), XXXV, pp. 269-77; Goode, 'Cotton States and International Exposition at Atlanta, Ga.', in *Annual Report of the Board of Regents of the Smithsonian Institution, Showing the Operations, Expenditures, and Condition of the Institution for the Year Ending June 30, 1895* (1897), pp. 47-48; Russell Duncan, 'Atlanta 1895: Cotton States and International Exposition', in *Historical Dictionary of World's Fairs and Expositions, 1851–1988* (ed. John E. Findling and Kimberly D. Pelle; New York: Greenwood Press, 1990), pp. 139-41.

67. Casanowicz, like Adler, earned a PhD in Semitic studies from Johns Hopkins University.

2.1. *Geology, Flora and Fauna*

The Atlanta exhibit displayed the Smithsonian's 'Oriental Antiquities' and Judaica as a joint collection 'which, for want of a better name, may be called Biblical Antiquities'.[68] In the official Smithsonian bulletin prepared for the Cotton States Exposition, it is claimed that, despite space limitations, the exhibit 'may fairly be said to constitute a miniature Biblical Museum'.[69] A polychrome relief map of Palestine, prepared from the Palestine Exploration Fund's Survey of Western Palestine, heads the exhibit, with '[t]he Old and New Testament sites... marked in red'. A curious group of oddments called GEOLOGY consisted of dust from Jerusalem, water from the Jordan, a small shell from Tyre, and granite from Jebel Musa. Adler apologetically notes that these pilgrims' trophies 'possess a sentimental interest merely'. The prose descriptions of the items follows the customary oscillation between scientific facts, extra-biblical historical information, and biblical narrative made familiar to the American reading public by popular works devoted to illustrating the Bible through biblical antiquities. A smattering of biblical floral and faunal specimens occupied their own glass case, a collection readily assembled from various departments of natural history in the Smithsonian; no information on provenience is provided.[70]

2.2. *Palestinian Antiquities*

The collection of so-called Palestinian antiquities bore West Semitic inscriptions; evidently, anepigraphic objects were not deemed sufficiently arresting or educational to warrant exhibition. All of the items were casts of originals. At the head of the lot was the Moabite Stone, the discovery of which in 1868 garnered

68. Adler and Casanowicz, 'Biblical Antiquities: A Description of the Exhibit at the Cotton States International Exposition, Atlanta, 1895', in *Report of the U.S. National Museum, under the Direction of the Smithsonian Institution, for the Year Ending June 30, 1896* ([Washington, DC]: Smithsonian Institution, 1896), pp. 953-1023 (953).

69. Goode, *The Exhibit of the Smithsonian Institution at the Cotton States Exposition, Atlanta, 1895* (Washington, DC: Smithsonian Institution, 1895), Department of Oriental Antiquities and Religious Ceremonial (no pagination).

70. Examples of flora included carob seed pods, the sycamore from Palestine ('The sycamore of the Bible has no natural alliance with the maple sycamores of Europe and North America'), Sodom apples ('The Orientals describe the *Asclepias gigantea* as a plant containing an astringent milky juice'), an unripe pomegranate from Palestine, Cedar of Lebanon cones, etc. Faunal examples include mammals: the ape ('The ape was not native to Palestine. It was mentioned in the Bible among the commodities brought to Solomon by the ships of Tarshish.') the bat, 'coney', young camel, rock-badger, etc.; birds: the cock ('No mention is made of the cock in the Old Testament, but in the New Testament he is referred to in connection with Peter's denial of Jesus, when Jesus said to Peter, "The cock shall not crow this day until thou shalt thrice deny that thou knowest me"'.), turtledove, quail, griffon vulture etc.; reptiles: frog, lizard, viper ('It is assumed that the viper that fastened on the hand of the Apostle Paul was the *Vipera aspis*'); insects: horsefly, breeze flies, sacred scarabaeus, hornet, locust, moth. Adler and Casanowicz, 'Biblical Antiquities', pp. 955-68.

vast publicity in the American press. Adler and Casanowicz describe in some detail how the inscription passed from the possession of the Beni Humaydah, 'a wild Arab tribe east of the Jordan', who, believing the stone 'to be possessed of supernatural power', shattered it and dispersed the fragments, thence into the hands of the scholar Clermont-Ganneau, who had prudently prepared a squeeze beforehand and gallantly gathered the remnants together for the Louvre. Other items included casts of the Siloam inscription, a Lachish tablet, the seal of Haggai, son of Shebaniah, an ancient Hebrew weight, and an inscribed bead.[71]

2.3. *Musical Instruments*

An entire glass case was devoted to modern musical instruments from the Middle East. This unexpected ethnographic collage was intended to address the fact that the Bible preserves virtually no details on the construction of musical instruments or the techniques by which they were played. Instruments from contemporary indigenous cultures can illustrate the Bible because 'it may be assumed that the musical instruments of the Hebrews resembled those of the nations with which they came in contact, and that, considering the stability and conservatism of the East, the instruments still used in Palestine, Syria, and Egypt differ but little, if at all, from those employed in ancient times'.[72] Eight accompanying plates illustrate percussion, wind and string instruments from modern Syria, Palestine, Egypt, and North Africa, with photographs of musicians on Neo-Assyrian and Neo-Hittite reliefs. There is also a photograph of the Arch of Titus in Rome illustrating two trumpets captured from the Temple of Jerusalem. The exhibit labels are severely professional, with brief descriptive name of object, native name in transliteration, museum accession number, provenience, and name of donor or lender.[73] Wind instruments (pl. 2 in Adler and Casanowicz, 'Biblical Antiquities'), includes a *shofar* from Adler's own collection, one of only two plates in the publication that combines items of Middle Eastern provenience and Judaica. We are not told what ethnic group possessed any of the musical objects photographed; the accompanying text only identifies the country and sometimes the city of origin. However, although the descriptive narrative ranges widely across the ancient and modern worlds, the first sentence or sentences 'assist' the reader by contrasting the Hebrew name with the modern Arabic name and object provenience, as, for example, 'FLUTE OR PIPE (Hebrew, *Halil*; Revised Version, flute.) Damascus, Syria. (See plate 2,

71. Adler and Casanowicz, 'Biblical Antiquities', pp. 968-73.

72. Adler and Casanowicz, 'Biblical Antiquities', p. 973. Adler and Casanowicz uncritically accept the Chronicler's figure of thousands of musical Levites organized for the Jerusalem temple cultus in the reign of Solomon. Rather illogically, they extrapolate that the 'idolatrous' kings of Israel and Judah neglected sacred music. Sacred music revived following the Exile, and 'it is known that it continued to form a prominent feature of Jewish worship' (p. 974).

73. So, for instance, object number 1 on plate 11, 'Eastern ornaments', is identified as 'Necklace (*anaq*) (Cat. No. 151757, U.S.N.M. Bagdad, Turkey. Collected by Rev. Dr. John P. Peters.)'.

fig. 4.) The pipe or flute now called in Syria *Shubab*, was a favorite instrument of the ancients…'[74] The object in pl. 2 fig. 4 (Adler and Casanowicz, 'Biblical Antiquities') may or may not have been created in an Arab workshop in Damascus, but the implication is that it is Arabic in origin, just as it was assumed by most Chicago fairgoers that the Middle Easterners dressed up as Turks on the Midway Plaisance were Muslim, not Jewish. While Adler and Casanowicz labor to document the historical continuity between the *shofar* of the Bible and the *shofar* used in modern Jewish ritual, the visual thrust of the musical instruments exhibit links the expansive Holy Land of the Smithsonian Oriental Antiquities collection with the modern Islamic Middle East.[75]

Figure 8. 'Women Grinding Corn by Hand Mill'. Photograph made by H. Phillips, Palestine Exploration Fund, Jerusalem, 1865. Adler and Casanowicz, 'Biblical Antiquities', pl. 13.

2.4. *Clothing and Domestic Realia*

This tendency was carried still further in the section devoted to clothing and domestic realia: 'The fashion of dress and ornament, as well as the form of household utensils, are, it may be assumed, in the "unchanging East" essentially

74. Adler and Casanowicz, 'Biblical Antiquities', p. 977.

75. The Adler corpus of photographs in the NAA collection is rich in group portraits of Middle Easterners playing exotic musical instruments, including a series of shots taken on the Midway Plaisance in front of the 'Luksor Temple' in which the intruding images of the audience have been cropped, yielding an authentic-looking ethnographic image; NAA inv 04030900, 04030800, 04030700, 04030600, 04030500, 04030400, 04030300.

the same at the present day as in the Bible times, and the collection shown of objects of modern life and industry in the Orient explain or illustrate many allusions in the Scriptures'.[76] A sheepskin coat from Syria apparently illustrates the fact that 'skins of animals were the primitive material used for clothing' and that pelisses of sheepskin 'still form an ordinary article of dress in the East'. Exhibits of male and female costumes of Baghdad, at least for Adler and Casanowicz, illustrate the essential interchangeability of clothing worn in Neo-Hittite and Neo-Assyrian reliefs with designs prevalent in the current Middle East, a fantastic lapse in empirical observation.[77] In common with hundreds of popular stereographic illustrations of the Holy Land, the Smithsonian Cotton States exhibition boasted an iconic photograph of seated women grinding grain, gazing directly at the intrusive camera.[78] A misleading quote from Layard's mid-century archaeological classic and travelogue, *Discoveries in the Ruins of Nineveh and Babylon*, establishes the locus of the unidentified women in the picture as Arabs: 'The wandering Arabs have no other means of grinding their corn than by hand mills, which they carry with them wherever they go…'[79] The setting of the photograph is clearly urban. In truth, the photograph, part of a set made by H. Phillips in 1865 for the Palestine Exploration Fund, is titled 'Grinding Corn in Jerusalem'.[80] Adler and Casanowicz suppressed the datum of provenience

76. Adler and Casanowicz, 'Biblical Antiquities', p. 988.

77. Adler and Casanowicz, 'Biblical Antiquities', pp. 989-90. The authors engage in blanket generalizations at other points in the catalogue narrative: 'The doors of Eastern houses, which are usually small and low…' (p. 993).

78. NAA inv 04052800, 04052900, 04053000. The actual exhibit label consisted of a bland description of the mechanics of hand-mill operation lifted from Edwin Cone Bissell, *Biblical Antiquities: A Hand-Book for Use in Seminaries, Sabbath-Schools, Families and by All Students of the Bible* (Green Fund Book, 5; Philadelphia: American Sunday-School Union, 1888), p. 65. For a stereoscopic example of women grinding grain, compare Burke O. Long, *Imagining the Holy Land: Maps, Models, and Fantasy Travels* (Bloomington, IN: Indiana University Press, 2003), pp. 113-14, fig. 31.

79. Quoted in Adler and Casanowicz, 'Biblical Antiquities', p. 991.

80. H. Phillips (dates unknown) produced over 400 6' × 9' collodion images between 1865 and 1867 for the Palestine Exploration Fund. A corporal in the Royal Engineers, he accompanied Captain Charles W. Wilson (1836–1905) in 1865–66 on a four-month journey from Baalbek and Damascus south through the Galilee and Hebron to Jerusalem. A second trip paired him with Lieutenant Charles Warren (1840–1927) in Jerusalem for six months. The Palestine Exploration Fund offered a selection of 334 photographs for sale in 1867 at 1s. 6d. apiece; Adler presumably acquired 'Grinding Corn in Jerusalem' in summer 1892 when he purchased photographs for the Smithsonian from the Anglo-Jewish Historical Exhibition collection. On Phillips's Middle Eastern photographic career, see Nissan N. Perez, *Focus East: Early Photography in the Near East (1839–1885)* (New York and Jerusalem: Harry N. Abrams, in association with The Domino Press & The Israel Museum, Jerusalem, 1988), pp. 40-41 and 204-205, fig. 17; Vaczek and Buckland, *Travellers in Ancient Lands*, p. 69. A photograph of Phillips in the field with Warren appears in John James Moscrop, *Measuring Jerusalem: the Palestine Exploration Fund and British Interests in the Holy Land* (London & New York: Leicester University Press, 2000), p. 76, fig. 4.

and with it the potential inference on the part of the fairgoers that the subjects were Oriental Jews. In the one instance where a Jewish object is photographed alongside jewelry from Mesopotamia, Palestine and Egypt, it is clearly labeled as such; the provenience is Philadelphia (pl. 11 fig. 2, Adler and Casanowicz, 'Biblical Antiquities').

Figure 9. 'Passover Plate. Constantinople'. Adler and Casanowicz, 'Biblical Antiquities', pl. 19.[81]

2.5. *Jewish Ritual Objects*

Jewish ritual objects had their own glass case. They derived from Philadelphia, Germany, and cosmopolitan Constantinople; it is unlikely that the Judaica exhibit was accompanied by photographs of Oriental Jews.[82] The items figure in a biblical

81. The inscription, described by Adler and Casanowicz as Arabic in Hebrew characters, is neither Hebrew nor any other language written in Hebrew characters, like Ladino. The decoration is highly unusual for a *seder* plate. Finally, since it was purchased on the antiquities market, a provenience of Constantinople or Turkey is guesswork. Grossman, *Judaica at the Smithsonian*, p. 106

82. The catalogue lists the following items: Torah scroll, Torah pointer, Torah breastplate, veil of the Torah ark, Sabbath lamp, Kiddush cloth, spice box, Passover platter, Omer tablet, lulav and ethrog, Megillah Esther, Hanukkah lamp, circumcision knife and cup, fringed garment,

antiquities exhibition because 'they had their origins in and are based upon Biblical ordinances'.[83] The textbook-correct descriptions were skillfully geared for a Protestant audience possessed of little if any familiarity with modern Jewish practices and beliefs. Illustrative Old and New Testament passages are quoted at length; references to the Talmud eschew tractate and section subdivision. The living Judaism that pervades the catalogue narrative is strictly Orthodox Ashkenazi, Adler's own tradition, although the term Ashkenazi never appears. There is an oblique philological aside on Ladino,[84] one explicit allusion to 'Jews of the Orient' whose *tallit* patterns differ from the normative Ashkenazi praxis,[85] and an erroneous notice that a Passover platter from Constantinople bore an Arabic inscription in Hebrew characters,[86] but otherwise the Judaism on display in the glass cases at the Cotton States Exposition was staunchly that of the assimilated Orthodox households and synagogues of the major East Coast cities. There was no talk of Yiddish usage, no references to the Eastern European *shtetl*s, or Hasidic courts, or rabbinically dubious rituals such as *kapparot*, nor were there displays of Jewish amulets or micrographic *sefirot* trees, or photographs of Jews praying before the Western Wall in Jerusalem. By not specifying the loci of the specific Jewish communities that observe the rituals that underlay the Judaica exhibit, Judaism is powerfully communicated as a universal religion, largely free of contemporary 'Oriental' associations.[87] Adler and Casanowicz build an impeccably strong case for the continuity between the Bible and living Jewish practice, even as they sever Judaism's Orientalizing ties to Eastern Europe and the modern Middle East. By abstracting Jewish ceremonial objects from the modern Orient and Holy Land, and linking them to Christianity through numerous New Testament citations, Adler masterfully aligns Judaism with western Christianity against the alien East.

2.6. *Gems and Numismatics*

A glass case at the Cotton States Exposition held eye-catching examples of the gemstones assigned the breastplate of the Israelite high priest, together with other precious stones mentioned in the Bible (Exod. 28.17-20, Ezek. 28.13, Rev. 21.19-20). The catalogue lists three tables, with Hebrew and Greek biblical names, scientific Latin name if known, and common English terms.[88]

phylacteries, silk prayer shawl, wedding ring, marriage contract, Mizrach, slaughterer's knife and sheathe.

83. Adler and Casanowicz, 'Biblical Antiquities', p. 993.

84. Adler and Casanowicz, 'Biblical Antiquities', p. 995, in context of the orthography of *omer*.

85. Adler and Casanowicz, 'Biblical Antiquities', p. 998.

86. Adler and Casanowicz, 'Biblical Antiquities', p. 995.

87. In this regard, the authors meet the challenge of Jewish circumcision directly by citing historical and comparative religions examples, concluding with '[i]t is a common rite among Mohammedans everywhere', Adler and Casanowicz, 'Biblical Antiquities', p. 997.

88. Adler and Casanowicz, 'Biblical Antiquities', pp. 979-82.

Figure 10. 'Mummy and Cover of Coffin. Luxor, Egypt'. Adler and Casanowicz, 'Biblical Antiquities', pl. 23.

2.7. *Egypt Exhibit*

Atlanta fairgoers primed to encounter colossal Assyrian guardian figures and Egyptian mummies at a biblical antiquities exhibit were not disappointed. By 1895, the USNM, largely through Haupt's efforts abroad, had acquired token life-size reproductions of several iconic sculptures and reliefs, including a spread of Neo-Hittite reliefs recently excavated by the Deutsche Orient-Gesellschaft, which had captured the imagination of the popular American press. Among the sculptural casts of Seti I, Rameses II and Tirhakah figured a genuine adult mummy from Luxor, acquired in 1886 by Samuel Sullivan Cox (1824–89), the U.S. ambassador to Turkey at the time. The mummy, a rather plain affair with a face painted by encaustic appliqué and amulets lodged in the expected places, was exhibited in its wooden coffin together with the carved cover. Adler and Casanowicz rehearse details in Herodotus and Diodorus Siculus on embalming techniques; images of human bodies steeping in natron with myrrh, cassia and other costly aromatics filling the empty cavities increased the 'exoticness' of the spectacle.[89] The following exhibit, fragmentary mummified dog(?), cat, crocodile, and other animals, amplified the uncanniness of the ancient Egyptians even as it struck a familiar cord by the presence of animals commonly domesticated in American households.

In the catalogue for the Cotton States Exposition, Adler and Casanowicz express curiosity about the racial identity of both the ancient Egyptians and the Hittites. In their description of photographs of the mummy of Rameses II taken immediately after its unwinding in 1886, they opine that

> The typical physiognomy of the native Egyptian, as exhibited on the numerous monuments, shows a head often too large in proportion to the body, a square and somewhat low forehead, a short and round nose, eyes large and wide open, the cheeks filled out, the lips thick, but not reversed, and the mouth somewhat wide. Contrasting the features of Ramses II with these, some scholars have assumed that he was of Semitic descent or at least had Semitic blood in his veins.[90]

The unspoken but heavily implied identification is between the ancient Egyptians and black Africans as opposed to the normative Caucasians.

Although George R. Gliddon (1809–57), former United States vice-consul in Cairo, lectured to packed audiences on ancient Egypt and occasionally unwrapped mummies as part of the entertainment,[91] the first American cred-

89. Adler and Casanowicz, 'Biblical Antiquities', pp. 1001-1003.

90. Adler and Casanowicz, 'Biblical Antiquities', p. 1001. In a lengthy footnote that quotes the president of the Institut égyptien Gaston Maspero's eye-witness account of the exposure of Ramses II's mummy, he notes that '…it may be said the face of the mummy gives a fair idea of the face of the living king. The expression is intellectual, perhaps slightly animal, but even under the somewhat grotesque disguise of mummification, there is plainly to be seen an air of sovereign majesty, of resolve and of pride' (p. 1000 n. 4).

91. Scott Trafton, *Egypt Land: Race and Nineteenth-Century American Egyptomania* (Durham, NC and London: Duke University Press, 2004), pp. 41-45.

ited with publicly unwrapping an Egyptian mummy (1821) was John Collins Warren (1778–1856), first professor of anatomy and surgery at Harvard University.[92] The exposure of ancient Egypt in America, however, came at a fearful price exacted by a legacy of African slavery. Apparent archaeological confirmation of the majestic achievements of the biblical kingdom of Egypt, and depictions of non-Caucasians in Egyptian royal funerary art, led antebellum and post-bellum immigrant Americans alike to scrutinize their relationship to African Americans through the lens of racialized anthropology, popular culture (including expositions), and of course biblical studies.

Ponderous mid-nineteenth century phrenological and ethnological studies sought to exploit Egyptian art and antiquities in the construction of human polygenesis in order to avoid the white scandal of a single genealogical line originating in black Africa. For example, Glidden and Josiah Clark Nott, the latter an Alabama doctor and slavery advocate, argued that the ancient Egyptian ruling classes, Caucasian in race for the most part, routinely enslaved inferior black Africans.[93] Yet Afrocentric voices challenged this interpretation, using the raw materials of Egyptology and a racialized reading of Genesis 1–11 to evoke a vibrant black Egypt from whose superfecondating Nile flowed the founding waters of western civilization.[94] This fiercely contested intellectual space between Egyptology and racial ideologies, white supremacism and black Orientalism, is one of the least known facets of ancient Near Eastern studies in nineteenth-century America, and must ultimately be factored into the reception of any high profile exhibit of Egyptian antiquities.

And in truth, the issue of race relations pervaded the Atlanta Cotton States and International Exposition, especially between African Americans and whites. The

92. Gerry D. Scott III, 'Go Down into Egypt: the Dawn of American Egyptology', in *The American Discovery of Ancient Egypt* (ed. Nancy Thomas; Los Angeles and New York: Los Angeles County Museum of Art; distributed by Harry N. Abrams, 1995), pp. 36-47 (43).

93. 'We thus obtain proof [from a relief at Medinet Habu] that the Negro has remained unchanged in Africa, above Egypt, for 3000 years; coupled with the fact that the same type, during some eight or ten generations of sojourn in the United States, is still preserved, despite of transplantation.' Josiah Clark Nott and George R. Gliddon, *Types of Mankind: Or, Ethnological Researches Based upon the Ancient Monuments, Paintings, Sculptures, and Crania of Races, and upon their Natural, Geographical, Philological and Biblical History: illustrated by Selections from the Inedited Papers of Samuel George Morton and by Additional Contributions from L. Agassiz, W. Usher, and H.S. Patterson* (Philadelphia: J.B. Lippincott Grambo & Co., 6th edn, 1854), pp. 249-50. See the discussion in Malini Johar Schueller, *U.S. Orientalisms: Race, Nation, and Gender in Literature, 1790–1890* (Ann Arbor, MI: University of Michigan Press, 1998), pp. 33-38.

94. Martin Robison Delany, *Principia of Ethnology: The Origin of Races and Color, with an Archaeological Compendium of Ethiopian and Egyptian Civilization, from Years of Careful Examination and Enquiry* (Philadelphia: Harper, 1879), and its treatment in Trafton, *Egypt Land*, pp. 72-84. On the highly charged *topos* of Afrocentrism in African American reconstructions of antiquity, I recommend Jacob Shavit, *History in Black: African-Americans in Search of an Ancient Past* (London and Portland, OR: Frank Cass, 2001).

most famous speech at the fair was delivered by the scientist and educator Booker T. Washington of the Tuskegee Normal Institute on racial accommodation, arguing that facilitating black advancement in industry and agriculture, while maintaining segregation, would avoid the social upheavals in the North blamed on European immigrants.[95] Curious visitors packed the 'Negro Building', first of its kind in United States exposition history, which sported exhibits of patented inventions, industrial institutions, sculpture, paintings, books and newsprint, and a draft copy of the Emancipation Proclamation.[96] Throughout the fair, segregation of auditoriums, toilet facilities and hospital arrangements was strictly enforced, and many restaurateurs refused to admit blacks to their concessions.

Adler and Casanowicz's Egyptian exhibit at the Atlanta Cotton States fair followed a well-trodden path in its construction of ancient Egyptian race, 'discovering' black Africans in the 'typical physiognomy of the native Egyptian', but groping for other racial signifiers for the Pharaohs.[97] Given their tutelage under Haupt, it is not surprising that the Biblical Antiquities resumé of the Atlanta fair bears traces of the regnant Pan-Babylonian notion that high Egyptian culture arose from contact with Sumerian civilization.[98] There is, however, considerable evidence that the Smithsonian's Biblical Antiquities tailored itself to the themes and expectations of the larger fair. For example, in their Egyptian exhibit, Adler and Casanowicz provided a vigorous discussion of the botanical history of the cotton plant, citing archaeological findings of seed, analyses of mummy shrouds, and the opinions of various authors, ancient and modern, as to range and date of cultivation.[99] Far from challenging the status quo, the portrayal of race in ancient Egypt sponsored by the Smithsonian served to maintain the contemporary racial hierarchies hard-wired into the design of the Atlanta Cotton States and International Exposition.[100]

95. Text in Cooper, *Cotton States and International Exposition*, pp. 98-99.

96. Cooper, *Cotton States and International Exposition*, pp. 57-63.

97. They cement the cultural continuity between Pharaonic and modern Egypt by exhibiting a Dynastic-era brick from Thebes with a modern counterpart, which is 'of the same general make and character as the ancient specimen'; Adler and Casanowicz, 'Biblical Antiquities', pp. 1004-1005.

98. 'It is assumed that these [Babylonian] temple towers were the prototype of the later Egyptian pyramids, the stories disappearing in the latter by filling up the platforms of the different stages, which produced an uninterrupted slope on all sides.' Adler and Casanowicz, 'Biblical Antiquities', p. 1007. For a contemporary Pan-Babylonian perspective on Egypt, see, for example, Fritz Hommel, *Der babylonische Ursprung der ägyptischen Kultur, nachgewiesen* (München: G. Franz, 1892).

99. Adler and Casanowicz, 'Biblical Antiquities', pp. 1005-1006.

100. American contempt for black Egyptians creams over in a *Midway Types* portrait of 'An Egyptian Chambermaid'. 'It provokes a laugh to speak of bed-making and room-caring in the land of the sphinx and the crocodile…The chambermaid, as shown by the type on the Midway, was not a hard worker, and, as our old-fashioned country people say, passed over her labors with "a lick and a promise"'.

Figure 11. 'Model of a Babylonian Temple Tower'. Notice the pair of Assyrian winged human-headed bulls flanking the main stairway, a cultural howler (the Babylonians did not use this motif in their monumental art). Adler and Casanowicz, 'Biblical Antiquities', pl. 26.

2.8. *Assyria and Babylonia Exhibit*

The Assyria and Babylonia exhibit at the Cotton States Exposition consisted of a model and reproductions of objects that capitalized on popular associations with the Bible. A free-standing polychrome plaster model of Ezida, the ziggurat (temple-tower) of Borsippa, called 'Model of a Temple Tower of Babylon', is said to represent the original on a scale of ¼ inch to the foot (fig. 11). Adler and Casanowicz valorize the model by conspicuously removing it from its Middle Eastern context. Although the biblical Tower of Babel has been associated both by 'Arab tradition' and European archaeologists with the ruins of Birs Nimrud, it is the latter who, together with the Greek historian Herodotus, provide the accurate blueprints for its reconstruction by a German scholar working under the direction of Haupt. The scientific facticity of Henry Rawlinson's excavations, the learned Orientalism of Professor Haupt and fine German craftsmanship, and not 'Arab tradition', breathe life into the garbled reports of Herodotus and yield a repristinated Babylonian ziggurat, the probable inspiration for the biblical Tower of Babel.[101]

Once again, a faithful reproduction, the 'Chaldean Deluge Tablet', is created by a German scholar working under the expert supervision of Haupt, together with casts from the British Museum.[102] Without venturing directly into the dangerous territory of textual dependency, Adler and Casanowicz diplomatically note that 'the narrative of the Deluge [Tablet] closely accords both in matter and language with the biblical account', leaving open the possibility that the Babylonian story is based on Genesis and not the other way around. It is unlikely

101. Adler and Casanowicz, 'Biblical Antiquities', pp. 1006-1007.

102. Friedrich Wilhelm Rudolph Zehnpfund, the craftsman in question, wrote a 1891 Leipzig dissertation on the temple archives of Nabonidus.

that Haupt's students personally believed in a West-to-East transmission, but the Southern Protestant Evangelicals attending the Atlanta Exposition might have been exercised by the usual Pan-Babylonian fare.

No exhibit of Assyro-Babylonian antiquities could be complete without a scale reproduction of a colossal human-headed winged bull or lion. The Smithsonian model of a winged human-headed lion from the British Museum, an imposing eleven-by-nine foot plaster model, replicated the signature image of ancient Assyria in popular imagination, made famous through the circulation of countless illustrations in periodicals, picture Bibles and biblical study aids.[103] The popular associations are pandered to by linking the model to the stop-press names British Museum, Austen Henry Layard, and Nineveh, despite the fact that the original was excavated at Nimrūd. Stale biblical and comparative religious parallels to lions and monsters are repeated.[104] The same cast of the British Museum's Black Obelisk of Shalmaneser III that graced the Smithsonian's Ohio Valley Centennial exhibit in 1888 traveled to Atlanta in 1895. One of the most widely reproduced 'biblical antiquities' to this day, the Black Obelisk is discussed in terms of the novel information it imparts about biblical personalities and events, constituting an unsubtle plug for continuing archaeological exploration of the Middle East, a dream nurtured by both Adler and Haupt.[105]

Figure 12. 'Hittite Lion Chase. Saktschegözu'. Adler and Casanowicz, 'Biblical Antiquities', pl. 36.

103. See Frederick N. Bohrer, *Orientalism and Visual Culture: Imagining Mesopotamia in Nineteenth-Century Europe* (Cambridge and New York: Cambridge University Press, 2003), pp. 125-26, 139-42; Henrietta McCall and Jonathan Tubb, *I Am the Bull of Nineveh: Victorian Design in the Assyrian Style* (London: PDC Publishers [privately printed], 2003); and Steven W. Holloway, 'Nineveh Sails for the New World: Assyria Envisioned by Nineteenth-Century America', *Iraq* 66 (2004), pp. 243-56 (248-56).

104. Adler and Casanowicz, 'Biblical Antiquities', p. 1008.

105. Adler and Casanowicz, 'Biblical Antiquities', pp. 1008-1009. They incorrectly ascribe the unique contents of the Kurkh Monolith of Shalmaneser III to 'another inscription…in the rocks of Armenia' (p. 1009). Adler's scholarship for the Smithsonian expositions is curiously sloppy even when dealing with his primary research focus. On Adler and Haupt's ambitions for the federal government to bankroll their Middle Eastern excavations, see Cooper, 'From Mosul to Manila', pp. 133-64, and Haupt, 'Excavations in Assyria and Babylonia', pp. 95-104.

2.9. *Hittite Exhibit*

Ten casts in the round of (Neo-)Hittite sculpture and reliefs conclude the exhibit collection of biblical 'monuments'.[106] Haupt had procured them on behalf of the Smithsonian while traveling through Europe in 1888.[107] Reasons for the extensive collection include a flurry of British historical publications of the 1880s, recent newsworthy Deutsche Orient-Gesellschaft excavations and, notably, earlier American initiatives: 'Of late there have been added to the Biblical, Egyptian, and Assyrian sources numerous monuments which were discovered throughout Asia Minor and Northern Syria, and which are by some scholars attributed to the Hittites. The beginning was made by two Americans, Mr. J. Augustus Johnson, of the United States consular service, and Rev. S. Jessup, who in 1870 found Hittite inscriptions at Hama, in Syria'.[108] The fascination with largely Neo-Hittite visual sources evinced by the Smithsonian exhibition at the 1895 Cotton States Exposition photographs is the correlative to recent efforts to record the many 'Hittite' hieroglyphic inscriptions of Western Asia. One of the first American publications of such a text appeared in the second number of the Palestine Exploration Society in 1873. The Palestine Exploration Society, organized in New York in 1870 by some of the same individuals who would later found the Archaeological Institute of America, the Society of Biblical Literature, and the American School of Oriental Research, sought to bring fame to American Orientalists through a program calculated to match the successes of the British Palestine Exploration Fund by surveying Trans-Jordan.[109] 'The Hamath Inscriptions', by William Hayes Ward, included folding illustrations of five short inscriptions from Hamath. Ward freely admitted that 'the problem of deciphering these inscriptions is much more difficult [than Assyrian cuneiform], and seems to me, at present, not very hopeful'.[110] The first number of the Palestine Exploration Society published a drawing of the reconstructed Moabite

106. On the Neo-Hittite civilization, see now H. Craig Melchert (ed.), *The Luwians* (Handbuch der Orientalistik. Erste Abteilung, Nahe und der Mittlere Osten, 68; Leiden and Boston: Brill, 2003).

107. Cyrus Adler, 'Report on the Section of Oriental Antiquities in the U.S. National Museum, 1889', in *Report of the U.S. National Museum, under the Direction of the Smithsonian Institution, for the Year Ending June 30, 1889* ([Washington, DC]: Smithsonian Institution, 1891), pp. 289-92 (291).

108. Adler and Casanowicz, 'Biblical Antiquities', p. 1010. Jeremiah Augustus Johnson was United States Consul-General in Syria (1867–70). Reverend Samuel Jessup served as an American Board of Commissioners for Foreign Missions missionary in Syria, brother of the better-known Henry Harris Jessup.

109. On the history of the organization, see Warren J. Moulton, 'The American Palestine Exploration Society', *Annual of the American Schools of Oriental Research* 3 (1928), pp. 55-78, and Thomas W. Davis, *Shifting Sands: The Rise and Fall of Biblical Archaeology* (Oxford and New York: Oxford University Press, 2004), pp. 16-18.

110. W.H. Ward, 'The Hamath Inscriptions', *Palestine Exploration Society* 2 (1873), pp. 19-26 (24).

Stone with translation and details about its discovery,[111] and there can be little doubt that the men who organized the Society anticipated American discoveries of epigraphic objects of equal fame.

In 1895, Adler and Casanowicz located Neo-Hittite art in an evolutionary framework. It is 'of a primitive, rude character', evoking 'the early art of Babylonia, Greece, and Phenicia [*sic*]'. In keeping with the conflation of race, language and culture common to late nineteenth-century anthropological thought, they build a case for the Hittites as racial members of the Mongolian or Turanian family, citing the opinion of A.H. Sayce and other British Orientalists for support.[112] The one sculpture bearing a decipherable inscription, the so-called Panammu Inscription, leads to a discussion of the 'Hittite' and West Semitic pantheons, with a synopsis of the text. Three of the remaining reliefs depict Neo-Hittite figures engaged in hunting, warfare and music-making, while the rest are of gods or apotropaic beings.[113]

2.10. *Biblical Manuscripts and Bibles*

The Smithsonian Cotton States exhibit concludes with a handsome spread of biblical manuscripts, ancient and modern Bible versions, and American first editions. Notable specimens include a facsimile of the Aleppo Codex, some Cairo Genizah fragments, Haupt's Polychrome edition of the Old Testament, a Coptic New Testament, Eliot's Indian Bible in facsimile reprint, Joseph Avery's Hieroglyphic Bible, and Thomas Jefferson's bowdlerized Gospel.[114]

3.0. *Models for the Smithsonian's Exhibits*

Precedents for Adler's Oriental Antiquities and Religious Ceremonial Objects exhibitions were many. In the nineteenth century, most East Coast American universities accumulated cabinets of ancient coins and objects through alumni initiative, especially from missionaries; one thinks of the Nineveh Cabinet at Amherst College, a significant collection of materials from Nimrūd and other

111. Howard Crosby, 'The Moabite Stone', *Palestine Exploration Society* 1 (1871), pp. 17-21.

112. A.H. Sayce, *The Hittites: The Story of a Forgotten Empire* (London: Religious Tract Society, 4th rev. and enlarged edn, 1888); William Wright *et al.*, *The Empire of the Hittites* (London: James Nisbet & Co., 1884); John Campbell, *The Hittites: Their Inscriptions and their History* (London: J.C. Nimmo, 1891), all cited in Adler and Casanowicz, 'Biblical Antiquities', p. 1011.

113. Adler and Casanowicz, 'Biblical Antiquities', pp. 1011-13.

114. Adler and Casanowicz, 'Biblical Antiquities', pp. 1016-23. Adler himself recognized the unusual nature of Jefferson's pastiche, arranged through his pull as Smithsonian Librarian to have it printed by the Government Printing Office, and wrote it an introduction; Thomas Jefferson and Cyrus Adler (ed.), *The Life and Morals of Jesus of Nazareth, Extracted Textually from the Gospels in Greek, Latin, French, and English* (Washington, DC: Government Printing Office, 1904).

Mesopotamian sites assembled under the auspices of Henry Lobdell, MD.[115] Egyptian, Greco-Roman and Mesopotamian antiquities entered the country through private donations and reached the public through such venues as the American Philosophical Society (1743), the first of the Peale museums (Philadelphia, 1784), the Massachusetts Historical Society (1791), New-York Historical Society (1804), and the Boston Athenaeum (1807).[116] The first modern American museums with substantial ancient Near Eastern holdings were the Metropolitan Museum of Art (1870) and the Museum of Fine Arts, Boston (1876). The first major American expedition to the Middle East was the Wolfe Expedition to Asia Minor and Babylonia (1884), organized under W.H. Ward for the American Institute of Archaeology.[117] The Babylonian Exploration Fund of the University of Pennsylvania fielded its first expedition in 1889, undoubtedly a contributing factor behind the Smithsonian's mounting of a 'Biblical Antiquities' exhibit in Atlanta.

The Chautauqua program, a popular continuing education institution established at Chautauqua, New York in 1874, grew out of the Methodist church camp revival movement under the guidance of Bishop John Heyl Vincent, a leading exponent of Protestant Sunday-School curriculum.[118] Study of the Bible, especially with heavy emphasis on the archaeological exploration of the territories covered by the Bible, linked up with a curious bent for experiential learning and amateur theatricals, as witness the creation of Palestine Park, a loosely scaled model of Palestine set near the principal landing dock on Lake Chautauqua.[119] J.E. Kittredge formed the Chautauqua Archaeological Society as part of the Chautauqua School of Theology in 1880. In 1881 a museum was established in Oriental House at Chautauqua to exhibit a collection of biblical antiquities that included casts of Nineveh reliefs from the British Museum, reportedly the first in the country, accomplished with a flourish of nationalistic flag-waving. The British Egypt Exploration Fund donated unwanted finds,

115. Edward Hitchcock, *Reminiscences of Amherst College, Historical, Scientific, Biographical and Autobiographical; Also, of Other and Wider Life Experiences* (Northampton, MA: Bridgman & Childs, 1863). pp. 104-109; see Selah Merrill, 'Assyrian and Babylonian Monuments in America', *Bibliotheca Sacra* 32 (1875), pp. 320-49.

116. Dinsmoor, 'Early American Studies of Mediterranean Archaeology', pp. 70-104.

117. See Neil Asher Silberman, 'Between Athens and Babylon: The AIA and the Politics of American Near Eastern Archaeology, 1884–1997', in *Excavating our Past: Perspectives on the History of the Archaeological Institute of America* (ed. Susan Heuck Allen; Colloquia and Conference Papers, 5; Boston: Archaeological Institute of America, 2002), pp. 115-22.

118. Andrew Chamberlin Rieser, *The Chautauqua Moment: Protestants, Progressives, and the Culture of Modern Liberalism* (New York: Columbia University Press, 2003).

119. See John Davis, 'Holy Land, Holy People? Photography, Semitic Wannabes, and Chautauqua's Palestine Park', *Prospects* 17 (1992), pp. 241-71; *idem*, *The Landscape of Belief: Encountering the Holy Land in Nineteenth-Century American Art and Culture* (The Princeton Series in Nineteenth-Century Art, Culture, and Society; Princeton, NJ: Princeton University Press, 1996), pp. 89-94; Long, *Imagining the Holy Land*, pp. 28-41.

Mount Union College loaned a mummy, and, together with dried specimens of Middle Eastern flora, fauna, costumes, agricultural and domestic implements, the Chautauqua Archaeological Society Museum strove to bring the Bible to life for mostly liberal white Protestants during the summer vacation months.[120] Adler certainly knew of the existence of the summer Chautauqua and found its brand of triumphalist Protestant biblical study repellent. However, he never spoke of his Oriental Antiquities Section at the National Museum in connection with the Chautauqua, so it is unlikely that the chaotic Chautauqua Archaeological Society Museum served as a model.[121]

3.1. *Anglo-Jewish Historical Exhibition, London 1887, and Musée Guimet, Paris*

There can be no doubt that the Smithsonian exhibit of religious ceremonial objects was markedly influenced by Adler's exposure to the Anglo-Jewish Historical Exhibition in London in 1890, while en route to the Middle East on WCE business. Although the exhibit ran its course at the Royal Albert Hall in 1887, Adler made the acquaintance of one of the chief organizers and lenders, Lucien Wolf, and purchased installation photographs of the exhibit in summer of 1892 that are now in the Smithsonian collection. As Appendix II to his address, 'Museum Collections to Illustrate Religious History and Ceremonials' which he delivered at the anthropology conference at the WCE, Adler included the classification scheme of the Anglo-Jewish Exhibition.[122] The London exhibition itself comprised some 2,500 items of Judaica and antiquities borrowed from 345 sources, undoubtedly the most comprehensive such collection mounted up to that time. The organization of the material followed what would be called 'the Jewish plan', the ritual settings pertaining to synagogue, home, and life-cycle events. With its heavy emphasis on wholesome family life, exquisite ritual objects, and westernized piety, the Gentile Victorian audience would have found much to admire. Of notable interest is the fact that the 'antiquities' section of the exhibition included biblical manuscripts, replicas of ancient inscriptions, a model of the Temple of Solomon, and a spread of objects

120. See J.E. Kittredge, 'Archaeological Museum', *Chautauqua Assembly Herald* 6 no. 16 (1881), p. 5; Anonymous, 'Chautauqua: 1882', *The Chautauquan; A Weekly Newsmagazine* 2 (1882), pp. 368-70 (368-69); J.E. Kittredge, 'Chautauqua's Archaeological Society', *Chautauqua Assembly Herald* 8/12 (1883), pp. 6-7; Theodore Morrison, *Chautauqua: A Center for Education, Religion, and the Arts in America* (Chicago: University of Chicago Press, 1974), pp. 35-36; Rieser, *The Chautauqua Moment*, pp. 152-53.

121. An article published in the *The Chautauquan* on the U.S. Government exhibit at the WCE passes over the Smithsonian's Religious Ceremonials Exhibit without comment. Here of all places, one would expect an expression of interest in Adler's handiwork; Charles Worthington, 'Our Government Exhibit at the World's Fair', *The Chautauquan; A Weekly Newsmagazine* 16/1 (January 1893), pp. 393-98.

122. Grossman, *Judaica at the Smithsonian*, p. 49.

on loan from the ubiquitous Palestine Exploration Fund.[123] This combination of Judaica and 'biblical antiquities' closely foreshadowed Adler's comprehensive design for the Smithsonian Institution. Another source of inspiration for Adler was the Musée Guimet in Paris.[124] Both Goode and Mason had already visited the Musée Guimet and expressed enthusiasm for its treatment of the history of religions; Goode was favorably disposed to back Adler's plans for a comparative religions exhibit on the strength of it. Adler, while impressed with the character of the collections, disapproved of the traditional organization along the lines of geography and, most damning, a general failure to 'furnish an intelligent train of thought to the mind of the average visitor'.[125]

3.2. *Adler's Definition of the Holy Land*

Adler's positivist conception of biblical archaeology ran true to his course of study under the Semiticist Haupt:

> By Biblical archaeology is understood the study of the language, history, social life, arts, and religion of the Biblical nationalities. This study is not a part of dogmatic theology; its results can command the same acceptance accorded to a new fact reported from a physical laboratory; its problems should be faced in the same spirit of fearless investigation into the truth as obtains in other departments of scientific research.[126]

The geographical locus of study is drawn with equal bravura: 'Roughly speaking, it would require that one point of a compass be placed in Jerusalem, and a radius of a thousand miles be selected to describe a circle which would include all of the peoples with whom the Israelites came in contact during

123. 'In the department of antiquities there were the objects lent by the Palestine Exploration Fund, the elaborate model of the Temple, designed by Mr. T. Newbury, and the collection of ancient Jewish coins, the largest and one of the most interesting ever brought together. The collections of rare MSS. lent by Lord Crawford and Sir Julian Goldsmid also deserve notice.' *Papers Read at the Anglo-Jewish Historical Exhibition, Royal Albert Hall, London. 1887* (Publications of the Anglo-Jewish Historical Exhibition, 1; London: Office of the 'Jewish Chronicle', 1888), p. 295; see also Kirshenblatt-Gimblett, *Destination Culture*, pp. 85-86. The Lord Crawford in question was James Ludovic Lindsey, twenty-sixth Earl of Crawford (1847–1913). Together with his father, Lord Crawford managed to amass a library of over 200,000 volumes at his death. Joseph Jacobs and Lucien Wolf, *Catalogue of the Anglo-Jewish Historical Exhibition, 1887, Royal Albert Hall* (London: Office of the *Jewish Chronicle*, 1888) is unavailable to me.

124. The Musée Guimet, founded in Lyon in 1878 but relocated to Paris in 1885, was formed to exhibit the materials collected by the colonial officer Emile Guimet who had been commissioned by the Ministry of Public Instruction to study Oriental religions. By the time of Adler's visit, the Musée Guimet boasted a superb collection of Egyptian and Assyro-Babylonian artifacts; L. de Milloué, *Petit guide illustré au Musée Guimet* (Paris: Ernest Leroux, 1894); Grossman, *Judaica at the Smithsonian*, p. 50.

125. Grossman, *Judaica at the Smithsonian*, p. 50.

126. Adler, 'Report on the Section of Oriental Antiquities in the U.S. National Museum, 1888', in *Report of the U.S. National Museum, under the Direction of the Smithsonian Institution, for the Year Ending June 30, 1888* ([Washington, DC]: Smithsonian Institution, 1890), pp. 93-95 (94).

their national existence'. However, in spite of the geographical and temporal sweep of Adler's vision, in practical terms the balance of the antiquities and reproductions in the collection consisted of material from Pharaonic Egypt to the west, and the Assyro-Babylonian civilizations indigenous to Mesopotamia. Adler's exhibit foci were largely those of his teacher, Haupt, whose 'soft' Pan-Babylonism privileged the study of Assyria and Babylonia over ancient Persia, certainly.[127] Greco-Roman civilization made a token showing in his exhibit at the WCE, perhaps in partial deference to the omnipresent neoclassicism of the White City, but had only the slenderest of presences in the permanent exhibit in Washington.

3.3. *Adler on the Unchanging East*

Adler shared with generations of westerners the conviction that the Orient plays host to homogeneous cultures that remain unchanged in essentials from high antiquity to the present. Granted the dubious premise, it follows that one can illustrate an exhibit of 'Biblical Antiquities' with modern musical instruments manufactured in North Africa and Syria, and a modern photograph of women grinding grain by hand (Jerusalem provenience suppressed). 'Owing to the intense conservatism of oriental peoples, a careful study of the modern inhabitants of western Asia may exhibit in a new aspect the manners and customs of former times'.[128] '...[I]t may be assumed that the musical instruments of the Hebrews resembled those of the nations with which they came in contact, and that, considering the stability and conservatism of the East, the instruments still used in Palestine, Syria, and Egypt differ but little, if at all, from those employed in ancient times'.[129] He reiterates this trope *ad nauseum* in his official reports and descriptive materials published to accompany the four traveling exhibits he mounted for the Smithsonian.[130] Such items were placed on display 'for the purpose of enabling the student or visitor to place himself in the position of one who lived in the times and the lands in which the books of the

127. Adler, 'Two Persepolitan Casts in the U.S. National Museum', in *Report of the U.S. National Museum, under the Direction of the Smithsonian Institution, for the Year Ending June 30, 1893* ([Washington, DC]: Smithsonian Institution, 1893), pp. 751-53 described two Persepolis casts obtained by Truxton Beale, U.S. ambassador to Persia, and listed twelve other casts from Achaemenid Persepolis housed in the USNM. None apparently were sent to the Chicago or Atlanta expositions.

128. Adler, 'Report on the Section of Oriental Antiquities...1888', p. 94.

129. Adler and Casanowicz, 'Biblical Antiquities', p. 973.

130. Adler and Casanowicz organized a smaller exhibit for the Tennessee Centennial Exposition in Nashville (1897); it included 'objects intended to illustrate Brahmanism and Buddhism, the principal religions of eastern Asia, Mohammedanism, the literary history of the Bible, and the religious ceremonials of the Jews'. Catalog quoted in Grossman, *Judaica at the Smithsonian*, p. 64.

Bible were composed'.[131] It is unclear to this author whether Adler personally believed in a culturally homogeneous and changeless Orient, but the rationale was trotted out regularly in print and certainly must have flattered the visitors to the White City and Washington, whirring hubs of industrial, economic and social progress.

Conclusion

Cyrus Adler's operative belief in the 'intense conservatism of oriental peoples' rooted him in the mainstream of American biblical studies, an instance of 'populist Orientalism'. Use of studio photographs and *realia* of contemporary Middle Easterners was a shopworn device in the academy and satisfied a public yearning to visualize the Orient as a static and homogeneous culture, useful for illustrating biblical commentaries and suitable for exhibition both on the Midway Plaisance and in a biblical antiquities glass case.[132] Adler's pedagogical goals for his religious ceremonial objects display were manifold and subtle. By linking the Smithsonian's display of Judaica closely to the Bible, Old and New Testaments, he sought to severe living Judaism from traditional Christian denigration and triumphalism. And, by excluding any trace of Eastern Jewry from his exhibits, Adler did his part in managing the crisis of massive Eastern European Jewish immigration to America. Much of his strategy entailed reorienting visual representations of living Judaism away from the Ottoman Holy Land and Eastern Europe, both of which savored of 'the Orient'; instead, by adroit use of exhibit captions and art prints, he retrained the spectator's eyes to perceive the immediate antecedents of American Jews among highly assimilated Jewish communities from Germany and other western European states. Within this construct, the westward-looking Judaism of Europe and America shares full membership with American Protestant culture in the White City, or Atlanta, or Washington DC.

In classic *Wissenschaft des Judentums* fashion, Adler's progressive Judaism retains its authentically biblical roots but sheds the trappings of cultural stagnation that, within the Orientalist preconceptions he promoted, typify the tradition-shackled peoples of the Middle East. The 'unchanging East', like the living

131. Adler, 'Biblical Antiquities', p. 958.

132. Examples from the captions in *Midway Types* abound. THE WATER CARRIER: 'In dress, figure, face action and burden she represented the water carrier of old—the woman who figures in the stories of the Bible and in the narratives of travelers in the East both of ancient and modern times.' AN EGYPTIAN GIRL: 'People who had only read about the veiled women of the Orient here had an opportunity to study the reality of costume, going back as far as Biblical history.' BORN TO DRUDGERY: 'The type above is a fellah woman. The social and intellectual conditions of this class have undergone scarcely any change during centuries of misrule. If they are no longer subjects to the hazards of the highest bidder, they are still the sad, living symbols of a system of drudgery older than the Pyramids'.

villages of the Midway Plaisance, constituted a laboratory for the anthropologist to observe primitives *in vivo* and the biblical specialist to capture salient background data that survives in the folkways of these cultural fossils. The dominant racial hierarchies of the Cotton States Exposition went unchallenged in the Smithsonian's explicit treatments of ancient peoples and implicit treatments of Islam. To be sure, Adler appears to have been no more racist or imperialistic than his other professional colleagues at the Smithsonian, and one should be mindful of the forces of anti-Semitism that he sought to contain. His conception of the modern Middle East and the 'Egyptian question', however, couched in a popular Orientalizing idiom, carried his exposition of the Bible into the mythical geography of the unchanging East and racial anthropology, beguiling to the fairgoers but perilous for all.

Egyptology under Khedive Ismail: Mariette, al-Tahtawi, and Brugsch, 1850–82[1]

Donald Malcolm Reid

> And on those stones is writing in the ancient temple script which no Egyptian knows how to read, although some Europeans in this thirteenth [nineteenth] century have deciphered its riddles to a certain extent.
>
> al-Tahtawi, *Anwar tawfiq al-jalil fi akhbar Misr wa-tawthiq Bani Ismail*

Less than two years after writing these lines, al-Tahtawi had the satisfaction of seeing a school opened in Cairo to teach Egyptians how to read ancient Egyptian. The distinguished German Egyptologist Heinrich Brugsch became its director. Mariette's hostility was a major factor in forcing the school to close five years later, but not before it had started Ahmad Kamal and one or two others of the younger generation down the road to Egyptology.

During these same years under Said and Ismail, Mariette was setting up the Antiquities Service and Egyptian Museum. The usual celebration of him as the founder of these institutions ignores the abortive earlier attempt associated with Muhammad Ali and Rifaa al-Tahtawi in 1835.[2] In any case, Mariette had to start over in 1858. Mariette's career frames the era covered in this chapter: he first set foot in Egypt in 1850 and died there in January 1881, a year and a half before the British occupation. Table 1 juxtaposes the European Egyptologists active during this era with the Egyptians relevant to this narrative.

During these years, the old and new nations of Greece and Italy were also bringing excavation under national control and building up national museums. Unlike them, however, Egypt—on the wrong side of the Mediterranean and Muslim—was marked out for European imperial domination. Like scores of

1. Reprinted from chapter three of Donald Malcolm Reid, *Whose Pharaohs? Archaeology, Museums, and Egyptian National Identity from Napoleon to World War I* (Berkeley: University of California Press, 2002), pp. 93-136. Used by permission of University of California Press. No attempt was made by the editor to add diacritics to the many Arabic and Turkish sources cited in Reid's chapter.

2. Mohamed Saleh and Hourig Sourouzian, *The Egyptian Museum Cairo: Official Catalogue* (trans. Peter Der Manuelian and Helen Jacquet-Gordon; Cairo: Organisation of Egyptian Antiquities, the Arabian Republic of Egypt/Mainz: Verlag Philipp von Zabern, 1987), p. 9, however, do give credit for the earlier effort.

other officials, Mariette was both an employee of the khedivial government and a patriotic citizen of a European imperial power that was steadily undermining Egyptian autonomy.

Table 1. Egyptologists Active 1850–82

Egyptologists		Egyptian Egyptologists and Other Scholars		Rulers	
Wilkinson	1797–1875	Rifaa al-Tahtawi	1801–1873	Abbas I	r. 1848–1854
Leemans	1809–1893	Joseph Hekekyan	1807–1875	Said	r. 1854–1863
de Rougé	1811–1872	Mahmud al-Falaki	1815–1885		
Mariette	1821–1881	Ali Mubarak	1823–1893		
H. Brugsch	1827–1894			Ismail	r. 1863–1879
Amelia Edwards	1831–1892				
Duemichen	1833–1894				
Ebers	1837–1898				
Naville	1844–1926	Ahmad Najib	1847–1910		
Grébaut	1846–1915	Ahmad Kamal	1851–1923		
Maspero	1846–1916			Tawfiq	r. 1879–1892

Meanwhile, in Paris, London, Berlin, and New York, national museums were emerging as both expressions and shapers of industrial capitalism, nationalism, and democracy. In Egypt as in other colonies, the Egyptian Museum and Antiquities Service served as instruments of European penetration and domination. More obvious instruments of imperial intrusion included railroads and steamships, the Suez Canal, and the telegraph; the cotton trade, international loans, tourism, missionary work, the Capitulations, the Mixed Courts, and Western military power. Museums in semicolonial and colonial lands like Egypt, however, were not simply or exclusively 'tools of empire'. Europeans promoted and visited them out of varied motives, and so did Egyptians.

World's fairs, which offered more ephemeral exhibits than museums, also came of age in the decades after London's Great Exhibition of 1851. The fairs developed in tandem with the mass tourism epitomized by Thomas Cook. Ancient, Islamic, and modern Egypt figured in almost every great world's fair of the next sixty years. But who represented Egypt at these Western celebrations of nationalism, imperialism, industrial capitalism, and consumerism, and with what intentions and what results? Mariette organized Egypt's displays for two *expositions universelles* in Paris; dispatched displays to exhibitions in London, Vienna, and Philadelphia; and helped orchestrate the extravaganza celebrating the opening of the Suez Canal. After the British occupation of 1882, representations of Egypt at world's fairs were mostly a case of Western and Levantine entrepreneurs marketing 'the Orient' to Western consumers.

Until mid-century, learned societies and academies, museums, and leisured circles of wealth and privilege had provided the prime patronage for Egyptology in Europe. Now, Egyptology began changing into an academic discipline, with German universities leading the way. In Egypt, with a Western-style university still half a century in the future, Khedive Ismail and Minister of Education Ali Mubarak set up a specialized school of Egyptology. Al-Tahtawi wrote his history of ancient Egypt in Arabic, and Mubarak's topographical encyclopedia *Al-Khitat al-tawfiqiyya* paid careful attention to pharaonic sites. *Al-Ahram*, which survives today as the leading daily newspaper, seized on 'the Pyramids' for its name, and every postage stamp used from 1867 to 1914 projected a pyramid and the Sphinx as symbols of Egypt.

Two European-dominated learned societies emerged in Egypt as forums of archaeological discussion. The Institut égyptien, founded in Alexandria in 1859, and—to a lesser extent—the Khedivial Geographical Society, established in 1875 in Cairo to foster Ismail's African empire, supplemented the museum and Antiquities Service in disseminating the fruits of Egyptology. Members of these societies joined the international congresses of Orientalists and geographers, which began meeting in Europe in the 1870s. Many Egyptians were still preoccupied with their own circles of Arabic-Islamic learning, but al-Tahtawi, Ali Mubarak, and astronomer Mahmud al-Falaki encouraged their countrymen to participate in these Western-dominated—but potentially universal—institutions of expanding knowledge.

1. *Ismail's Precarious Renaissance*

Official patronage of the Arabic renaissance *(nahda)* peaked under Khedive Ismail (r. 1863–79). The financial, political, and socioeconomic catastrophe that engulfed Egypt toward the end of his reign led to his deposition, the Urabi revolution, and the British conquest, events that overshadowed the cultural advances of a small elite. Ismail made mistakes, but given that European empires would on the average annex an area the size of France each year from 1871 to 1914,[3] blaming him personally for the disaster is superficial.

3. Michael Adas, *Machines as the Measure of Men: Science, Technology, and Ideologies of Western Dominance* (Cornell Studies in Comparative History; Ithaca, NY: Cornell University Press, 1989), p. 143. On Egypt under Ismail, see F. Robert Hunter, *Egypt under the Khedives: From Household Government to Modern Bureaucracy, 1805–1879* (Pittsburgh: University of Pittsburgh Press, 1984); Abd al-Rahman al-Rafii, *Asr Ismail* (2 vols.; Cairo: Maktabat al-Nahda

Like his contemporaries in Istanbul and Tunis, Ismail's predecessor, Said, started down the treacherous path of European loans in the 1850s. The North's blockade of Southern ports during the American Civil War had sent the prices for Egyptian cotton soaring by the start of Ismail's reign, encouraging a euphoric sense of prosperity. Eager to project himself as an enlightened, European-style ruler, Ismail tried to do everything at once—expand his African empire, finish the Suez Canal, remake Cairo *à la parisienne*, erect Abdin and other palaces, dig irrigation canals, build railroads, elaborate a state school system, and overhaul the courts. European officials hired for their presumed expertise in the customs department, police, post office, railroads, telegraphs, Mixed Courts, and army proved to be entering wedges of imperialism. When the bill came due, Ismail's desperate sale of Egypt's dearly bought Suez Canal shares to Britain barely slowed the plunge into bankruptcy.

Searching for roots of the nineteenth-century *nahda* in the works of Azhari scholars such as Hasan al-Attar[4] and perhaps al-Jabarti provides a salutary corrective to stereotypes of a dynamic West awakening a stagnant East. But as the century wore on, the renaissance flourished not at al-Azhar but in such new or reformed milieus as the press, state and missionary schools, study missions to Europe, telegraph offices, translation bureaus, and the offices of judges, lawyers, and import-export merchants. Al-Tahtawi, Ali Mubarak, and Mahmud al-Falaki were both products of Muhammad Ali's educational reforms and proponents of further change.

In 1840–41, the British-led rollback of Muhammad Ali's dominance in the Levant ushered in an era of retrenchment, which continued under Abbas I. Then Said reversed course and flung wide the door to European fortune-seekers. De Lesseps was first in the door with his Suez Canal proposal. The Institut égyptien, Antiquities Service, and Egyptian Museum were all products of this intensified European influx. Ismail decreed one new cultural institution after another—the Khedivial Library, the Khedivial Geographical Society, the opera house, a state theater, the Dar al-Ulum teachers college, and other schools at all levels. A half-hearted attempt to reform al-Azhar met resistance, so Ismail and Ali Mubarak bypassed it in 1867 with a decree for a state school system, which became the cultural centerpiece of the reign. Arabic replaced Turkish as the official language of administration, and both the Arabic and Western press in Egypt came of age.

al-Misriyya, 2nd edn, 1948); Juan Ricardo Cole, *Colonialism and Revolution in the Middle East: Social and Cultural Origins of Egypt's Urabi Movement* (Princeton: Princeton University Press, 1993); Georges Douin, *Histoire du règne du khédive Ismaïl* (3 vols. in 4; Cairo: Reale Società di geografia d'Egitto, 1933–39); David S. Landes, *Bankers and Pashas: International Finance and Economic Imperialism in Egypt* (Harvard University. Research Center in Entrepreneurial History. Studies in Entrepreneurial History; Cambridge, MA: Harvard University Press, 1958).

4. Peter Gran, *Islamic Roots of Capitalism: Egypt 1760–1840* (Modern Middle East Series, 4; Austin: University of Texas Press, 1979).

By the end of the reign, the press and the Majlis al-Nuwwab (Chamber of Deputies) were developing minds of their own. The charismatic reformer Jamal al-Din al-Afghani had taught on the fringes of al-Azhar, attracting not only young Muslims like Muhammad Abduh and Sa'd Zaghlul but also Syrian Christian journalists. Ahmad Faris al-Shidyaq's Istanbul-based Arabic paper, *Al-Jawaib*, brought in news of the ferment in Istanbul, which culminated in the Ottoman constitution of 1876 and the parliamentary experiment of 1876–78.

Al-Tahtawi, Ali Mubarak, and Ahmad Kamal—each representing a different generation—were critically involved with Egyptology under Ismail. Beneficiaries of the educational reforms set in motion under Muhammad Ali, each learned at least one European language—increasingly a prime key to bureaucratic advancement. They began thinking not only in terms of Islamic loyalties but also of an Egyptian nation rooted in the pharaonic past.

Al-Tahtawi was sixty-two when Ismail ascended the throne, Ali Mubarak forty, and Ahmad Kamal a schoolboy of twelve. In al-Tahtawi's youth, Quran schools and al-Azhar were almost the only formal schooling available, but as already seen, his appointment as chaplain to a student mission to Paris in 1826 enabled him to add on a liberal education in France. Mubarak's al-Azhar-educated father hoped his son would follow in his footsteps, but the rebellious boy ran away to a new state school. Chancing to see an official as dark-skinned as himself in an influential post, Mubarak had jumped to the conclusion that high state service need not be restricted to Turks. His educational path to the top led through a provincial primary school, the Cairo Preparatory (Tajhiziyya) School and School of Engineering, the Egyptian school in Paris, the French military academy at Metz, and a year's service in the French army.[5]

For some years, al-Tahtawi's and Mubarak's careers proceeded on nearly opposite trajectories. Abbas I exiled al-Tahtawi to Khartoum and rewarded Mubarak for drastically pruning the school system that al-Tahtawi had helped to build. Mubarak fell from favor under Said, who shipped him off to the Crimean

5. On al-Tahtawi, see Gilbert Delanoue, *Moralistes et politiques musulmans dans l'Egypte du XIXᵉ siècle (1798–1882)* (2 vols.; Textes arabes et études islamiques, 15; Cairo: Institut français d'archéologie orientale du Caire, 1982), II, pp. 383-487, 618-30, 651-54. See also Anouar Louca, *Voyageurs et écrivains égyptiens en France au XIXᵉ siècle* (Etudes de littérature étrangère et comparée, 61; Paris: Didier, 1970), pp. 55ff.; Salih Majdi, *Hilyat al-zaman bimanaqib khadim al-watan: Sirat Rifaa Rafii al-Tahtawi* (ed. Jamal al-Din al-Shayyal; Cairo: Maktabat Mustafa al-Babi al-Halabi, 1958); and Ahmad Badawi, *Rifaa Rafii al-Tahtawi* (Cairo, 2nd edn, 1959). Ali Mubarak's autobiography appears in his *Al-Khitat al-tawfiqiyya al-jadida* (20 vols.; Cairo: al-Matbaʿah al-Kubra al-Amiriyah, 1305–1306/1886–89), IX, pp. 37-61. Secondary sources include Delanoue, *Moralistes*, II, pp. 488-558; Darrell I. Dykstra, 'A Biographical Study in Egyptian Modernization: Ali Mubarak (1823/4–93)' (2 vols.; Unpublished PhD dissertation, University of Michigan, 1977); Stephan Fliedner, *Ali Mubarak und seine Hitat: Kommentierte Übersetzung der Autobiographie und Werkbesprechung* (Islamkundliche Untersuchungen, 140; Berlin: K. Schwarz, 1990); Hunter, *Egypt*, pp. 123-38.

War and then alternated minor appointments with abrupt dismissals. Said rescued al-Tahtawi from Khartoum and made him director of a military school, but later al-Tahtawi also suffered from Said's capriciousness. Under Ismail, al-Tahtawi and Mubarak flourished in tandem, although not at the same level. Friends with Ismail since their student days in Paris, Mubarak became a pasha and cabinet minister, variously in charge of public works, education, *awqaf* (charitable endowments), communications, and railways; al-Tahtawi never rose above bey, but he had a productive final decade directing a revived translation bureau, writing textbooks, overseeing Arabic instruction in the schools, and editing *Rawdat al-madaris* (Garden of the schools).

Al-Tahtawi and Mubarak were renaissance men, with Egyptology merely one interest among many. Benefiting from the schools Mubarak and al-Tahtawi had helped to build, the younger generation of Ahmad Kamal had the possibility of specialization. Kamal would have come across al-Tahtawi's textbooks in school, and he owed his vocation to the School of Egyptology, which Ismail and Mubarak founded. Unlike these two elders, Kamal long knew the West only indirectly through books and resident Europeans; he traveled in Europe only briefly and rather late in life. If al-Tahtawi ever met Kamal, it would provide a personal link across the century between al-Tahtawi's awakening to antiquity in the 1820s and the refounding of Cairo's School of Egyptology in 1923, the year Kamal died. Kamal's career coincided with the heyday of the British occupation and is treated in chapter 5.[6]

2. *(Re-)Founding the Antiquities Service*

Born two years after Mubarak in Boulogne-sur-Mer, Mariette (1821–81) turned eleven the year that Champollion died. Jacques-Joseph Champollion-Figeac published his brilliant younger brother's uncompleted works but could not advance Egyptian philology. Nestor l'Hôte and I. Rosellini followed their mentor Champollion to early graves. Champollion's successor at the Louvre, Léon Dubois, cut colored pictures of the gods out of papyri for framing and discarded the texts as unreadable scraps. Only at mid-century did Emmanuel de Rougé, who took over as curator of Egyptian antiquities in 1849, and Mariette put French Egyptology back on track.[7]

6. Reid, *Whose Pharaohs?*, pp. 172-212. For the biography of Ahmad Kamal, see *Al-Muqtataf* 63 (November 1923), pp. 273-77; Tawfiq Habib, 'Tarikh al-kashf an al-athar al-misriyya wa amal al-marhum Ahmad Kamal Basha', *Al-Hilal* 32 (1 November 1923), pp. 135-41; Zaki Fahmi, *Safwat al-asr fi tarikh wa rusum mashahir rijal fi Misr* (2 vols.; Cairo: Matbaʿat al-Iʿtimad, 1926), I, pp. 331-36; Jamal al-Din al-Shayyal, *A History of Egyptian Historiography in the Nineteenth Century* (Alexandria University. Faculty of Arts. Publication, 15; Alexandria: Alexandria University Press, 1960), pp. 60-63; Tawfiq Habib, 'Dars al-athar fi al-Jamia al-Misriyya', *Al-Muqtataf* 72 (1928), pp. 438-39; *WWWE*3, p. 224. Dia M. Abou-Ghazi, 'Ahmed Kamal 1849–1923', *ASAE* 64 (1981), pp. 1-5, lists his articles.

7. *WWWE*3, pp. 130-31. On L'Hôte, Rosellini, Dubois, and de Rougé, see *WWWE*3, pp. 253-

Mariette earned a *baccalauréat ès-lettres* at Douai and tried teaching and journalism. Inheriting his relative Nestor l'Hôte's papers turned him toward Egyptology, but he struggled with Coptic and hieroglyphics for seven years in provincial isolation before winning a minor temporary post at the Louvre in 1849. Envious of the manuscripts Robert Curzon and Henry Tattam had obtained from Coptic monasteries for the British Museum in the 1830s, the Louvre sent Mariette to Cairo in 1850 for early Christian manuscripts. The Coptic patriarch remembered Curzon and Tattam only too well and refused to cooperate.[8]

Mariette gambled his funds and future instead on finding the Serapeum described by the Greek traveler Strabo. He traced to Saqqara sphinxes he saw in European gardens in Alexandria and Cairo and hit on the avenue of sphinxes leading to the sepulchre of the Apis bulls. In its enthusiasm the French Chamber back in Paris voted credits for transporting the finds to the Louvre before Abbas had agreed to their export. The angry pasha dispatched guards to stop Mariette from digging. British consul general Charles Murray, Prussian-born Anglican missionary Reverend Rudolf Lieder, and Austrian consul general Baron de Huber—all antiquities collectors themselves—lobbied Abbas against Mariette. Mariette had an assistant manufacture fake votary tablets to fob off on Abbas and kept on digging, secretly, at night. French consul general Arnaud Lemoyne finally brokered a compromise. Mariette could send 515 pieces to the Louvre and keep on digging, but future finds would stay in Egypt.[9] Just before his funds ran out and he headed home, Mariette discovered Khafra's valley temple near the Giza sphinx.

The Louvre rewarded Mariette with an assistant curatorship, but with his superior de Rougé only in his early forties, further promotion was blocked. Mariette found himself daydreaming of his adventures at Saqqara and decided he preferred art to philology. In 1857, he leapt at the chance to excavate antiquities for Said, who had succeeded Abbas I, to present to Prince Napoleon on a projected visit. Said had given away the remnants of the state collection to Archduke Maximilian of Austria in 1855. (These objects are now in the Kunst-

54, 362-63, 130-31, 365-66. See also Diane Sarofim Harlé, 'The Unknown Nestor L'Hôte', in *Travellers in Egypt* (ed. Paul Starkey and Janet Starkey; London: I.B. Tauris, 1998), pp. 121-29.

8. On Mariette, see Elisabeth David, *Mariette Pacha 1821–1881* (Paris: Pygmalion and G. Watelet, 1994); Gaston Maspero, 'Mariette (1821–1881): Notice biographique', in Auguste Mariette, *Oeuvres diverses* (Paris: E. Leroux, 1904), I, pp. i-ccxxiv (Mariette's *Oeuvres diverses* is vol. 18 of the series Bibliothèque égyptologique, contenant les oeuvres des égyptologues français, ed. Gaston Maspero, 40 vols. [Paris, 1893–1915]); Edouard Mariette, *Lettres et souvenirs personnels (avec un portrait de Mariette Pacha)* (Paris: H. Jouve, 1904); and Jean Sainte Fare Garnot, *Mélanges Mariette* (IFAO, Bibliothèque d'études, 32; Cairo: Institut français d'archéologie orientale, 1961). For his own account of the Serapeum discovery, see Auguste Mariette-Pacha, *Le Sérapeum de Memphis* (Paris: F. Vieweg, 1882). On Curzon and Tattam, see *WWWE*3, pp. 113, 410-11.

9. DWQ/Abhath B118: Athar/F: Mariette/Le Moyne to Stéphan Bey, 9 June 1851, begins a series of letters on the Serapeum dispute. Le Moyne to Stéphan Bey, 4 February1852, concludes the series with thanks to the viceroy for the gift of 515 pieces.

historischen Museum in Vienna).[10] De Lesseps and Consul General Raymond Sabatier persuaded the impressionable Said that he could not afford to be less generous to France. Said furnished Mariette a steamer and corvée labor, and the delighted archaeologist set gangs digging simultaneously at Giza, Saqqara, Abydos, Thebes, and Elephantine. Prince Napoleon's visit fell through, but Said went ahead and presented the discovered objects to the Louvre.

With Napoleon III's backing, de Lesseps, Sabatier, and Nubar Pasha (Said's Armenian secretary and director of communications and railways) persuaded the viceroy to have Mariette refound the Egyptian Antiquities Service. Said's Alsatian secretary and former tutor König Bey worked out the details, and on 1 June 1858—a year before Alexander Cunningham founded the Archaeological Survey of India[11]—Mariette became *mamur al-antiqat* or *directeur des monuments historiques de l'Egypte et du musée* at 18,000 francs (£720) a year.[12] His Service des antiquités was variously called Maslahat Antiqat, Maslahat Antikhana, and Maslahat al-Athar in Arabic. Mariette became a bey second class, with exclusive excavation rights throughout the country, a steamboat, and authorization to levy corvée labor. Maspero's imperialist simile on the appointment says it all: 'This was like taking possession of Egypt for the cause of science'.[13]

Bonnefoy and Gabet, two obscure Frenchmen whose first names remain unknown, assisted Mariette early on, and the Louvre seconded Théodule Devéria to copy inscriptions. Luigi Vassalli long worked under Mariette, and Heinrich Brugsch's younger brother Emile began his long Antiquities Service career at this time.[14] Mariette set gangs to work at six sites from Giza to Aswan. The first entry in the museum's *journal d'entrée* dates from June 1858.[15] Mariette at first suggested a force of 2,380, including 200 at Karnak, 500 to 1,000 at Edfu, 750 at Esna, and 400 at Giza but cautioned that the estimate was provisional—archaeology was not like digging a canal.[16] At one time he had authorization for seven thousand laborers.[17]

The victims of Mariette's forced labor may also have associated archaeology with the ongoing digging of the Suez Canal. Both were miseries inflicted by Europeans, Said, and Ismail without tangible benefit to the workers. The *reises*

10. Gaston Maspero, *Guide du visiteur au Musée du Caire* (Cairo: Imprimerie de l'Institut français d'archéologie orientale, 4th edn, 1915), p. x; Abou-Ghazi, 'Egyptian Museum', *ASAE* 67 (1991), p. 9.

11. Bernard S. Cohn, *Colonialism and its Forms of Knowledge: The British in India* (Princeton Studies in Culture/Power/History; Princeton, NJ: Princeton University Press, 1966), p. 9.

12. DWQ/Abhath B118: Athar/F: Mariette/Mariette to König (viceregal secretary), 18 April 1858, begins a series negotiating Mariette's appointment and reporting on his early activities as director. Mariette to König, 26 December 1859, concludes the series.

13. Maspero, 'Mariette', p. xcvi.

14. Maspero, 'Mariette', p. xcvi.

15. May Trad, 'Journal d'entrée et catalogue général', *ASAE* 70 (1984–85), pp. 352-57.

16. DWQ/Abhath B118: Athar/F: Mariette/Mariette to König Bey, 18 April 1858.

17. *WWWE*3, p. 276.

(foremen) who recruited the corvée gangs did well, however. Mariette's foremen would levy the richest men in a village, accept bribes to exempt them, and move on down until the poorest had to serve.[18]

Like Paul Emile Botta and Austen Henry Layard in Mesopotamia a few years before, Mariette employed huge gangs to dig for art objects and inscriptions. Attention to stratigraphy, field notes, and detailed scientific publication were not yet the order of the day. Heinrich Schliemann's treasure hunts at Troy and Mycenae in the 1870s were no better. In 1864, Mariette had a thousand men clearing temple walls to give de Rougé access to inscriptions on an upcoming visit.[19] Flinders Petrie later complained that, except at nearby Giza and Saqqara, Mariette left European assistants or Egyptian *reises* digging on their own for months on end. Antiquities from Mariette's digs leaked onto the market, because he would not pay individual *bakhshish* for finds. *Reises* even kept up Mariette's interest in unpromising sites by salting it with antiquities bought on the market.[20] By the 1860s in Italy, Giuseppe Fiorelli and Pietro Rosa were pioneering more scientific digging at Pompeii and Rome, and in the 1870s in Greece, Alexander Conze of Austria and Ernst Curtius of Germany were elaborating techniques which left Mariette far behind.

In Egypt, excavation by other Europeans ceased when Mariette enforced his monopoly and the ban on export without a permit. Periodic orders to officials to enforce the ban on digging and report any finds confirm, however, that Egyptians kept on digging fertilizer *(sabakh)*, selling antiquities, and burning temple stones to produce lime. No, Mariette told a village petitioner in 1880, he could not quarry the Giza pyramids to build a house.[21]

In 1861, Said's foreign debt reached £8 million and he fled to his yacht to escape European creditors. He had already mortgaged revenues far in advance, laid off officials, slashed the army to twenty-five hundred, and sold off military equipment. Mariette implored Paris to beat out London in advancing a new loan: 'Whoever makes the loan to viceroy will have put the cord around the neck (the words of the viceroy himself), and in other words will be master of Egypt'.[22] Napoleon III seized the chance to press Mariette to obtain Said's help in finding new sources for a biography he was writing on Julius Caesar and in obtaining manuscripts from Coptic monasteries. Mariette ignored Napoleon's remark that the antiquities Mariette was assembling in Bulaq would be better off in the Louvre. Although British and German, rather than French, financiers eventually made the new loan, Said was so relieved that he made Mariette bey first class, promised

18. W.M. Flinders Petrie, *Seventy Years in Archaeology* (London: S. Low, Marston & Co., 1931), p. 46.

19. Maspero, 'Mariette', p. cxliv.

20. Petrie, *Seventy Years*, pp. 52-53.

21. Garnot, *Mélanges*, pp. 1-2.

22. Mariette, *Oeuvres*, p. cxxv. For this paragraph, see pp. cxxiii-cxxxi; and Landes, *Bankers*, pp. 108-109.

more publication and museum subsidies, awarded him a pension, and made him commissioner-general to the London International Exhibition of 1862.

Despite Mariette's success in stanching the flow of antiquities from Egypt, he could not prevent the loss of two more obelisks. In the 1820s Muhammad Ali had offered both Britain and France one of Alexandria's two obelisks. The French traded theirs for a better one from the Temple of Luxor, which they took in 1831–32 for re-erection in the Place de la Concorde. Wilkinson warned of national disgrace if the French got their obelisk first, but his friend Robert Hay said it would be a disgrace to *take* the proffered obelisk, since France had gotten a finer one. Wilkinson later opposed bringing the obelisk to London on the vaguely sinister grounds that its original purpose was unknown. Thackeray mocked the whole project:

> Then we went to see the famous obelisk presented by Mehemet Ali to the British Government, who have not shown a particular alacrity to accept this ponderous present... If our country takes the compliment so coolly, surely it would be disloyal upon our parts to be more enthusiastic. I wish they would offer the Trafalgar Square Pillar to the Egyptians; and that both of the huge, ugly monsters were lying in the dirt there, side by side.[23]

Only in 1877 did the physician Sir Erasmus Wilson finally finance the obelisk's transportation to London and its erection at the Embankment on the Thames the following year.

This spurred on the Americans, to whom Ismail offered the remaining Alexandria obelisk in appreciation for the Civil War veterans serving in his army. This was too much for Mariette, who protested that only five obelisks still stood in Egypt, which now had

> two Museums. One is the Museum of Boulaq. The other is all of Egypt... It is moreover a principle universally adopted in all Museums. Namely that if a Museum can receive, it cannot ever give away. That Egypt requests of the Louvre Museum the Venus de Milo, of the Museum of London the Rosetta Stone, of the Museum of New York a monument from the Abbott Collection, for nothing in the world would they make it this gift. Why treat Egypt differently? ... The time when Lord Elgin carried off the bas reliefs of the Parthenon is passed. Egypt has the oldest extant archives in human history. These are the deeds of her ancient nobility, and she intends to keep them.[24]

The Egyptian cabinet reluctantly honored Ismail's promise, even though he lost his throne a few months before the Americans loaded the monolith late in 1879. It went up in Central Park, New York, in January 1881, the month that Mariette died. At least Mariette had extracted a cabinet resolution that 'hereafter no

23. William Makepeace Thackeray, *The Paris Sketch Book of Mr M.A. Titmarsh: The Irish Sketchbook; and Notes of a Journey from Cornhill to Grand Cairo* (New York, n.d.), p. 714. For the rest of the paragraph, see Jason Thompson, *Sir Gardner Wilkinson and his Circle* (Austin: University of Texas Press, 1992), pp. 192-93. On the removal of the Paris, London, and New York obelisks, see Labib Habachi, *The Obelisks of Egypt: Skyscrapers of the Past* (Cairo: American University in Cairo Press, 1984), pp. 152-82.

24. Mariette. Contrary to academic convention, I have decided to keep this quotation, although I have mislaid my notecard and cannot check the original source, which was probably in MAE.

Egyptian monument shall be given to any Power or to any city whatever not forming a part of the Egyptian territory'.[25]

3. *The Egyptian Museum: Mariette at Bulaq*

Over the course of the century, three very different east Mediterranean states—Greece, the Ottoman Empire, and Egypt—developed antiquities departments and national archaeological museums. An impetus from northwest Europe was critical in each case, but the museums were also arenas in which local citizens began forging their modern identities.

Greece was first, with the Aigina National Museum of 1829, even before the European powers had finished forcing the Ottomans to concede Greek independence. The powers imposed Otto I of Bavaria on the fractious little state. He arrived from Munich, where neoclassicism was in full swing. The founders of the Greek Antiquities Service (1833) and National Archaeological Museum (1834) were also German. The National Archaeological Museum, in Athens, was housed in the Hephaisteion until 1874, when it began moving into its new German-designed neoclassical edifice. Most Greeks identified more easily with Byzantium and Greek Orthodoxy than with the distant classical past extolled by western Europeans and Americans. Reconciling these two legacies became a central issue in the negotiation of a modern Greek national identity.[26]

The antiquities museums of Istanbul and Cairo began in makeshift quarters, as in Athens, but had more fitful starts. Neither the Cairo collection, begun in 1835, nor the Istanbul one, started in the former Byzantine church of Saint Irene in 1845, was open to the public. The Imperial Ottoman Museum, decreed in 1869 under a British director named Goold, was quickly abolished but reemerged three years later under a German, Dethier. He transferred the collection to the Çinili Kiosk in the Topkapi Palace, drafted an antiquities law, and in 1875 opened the museum daily to the public, with Wednesdays reserved for women.

25. DWQ/MMW/NA/MA 1/4: Matahif 1879–1914/F: al-Hukumat al-ajnabiyya wa al-athar al-misriyya/subdossier: Talab dawlat Amrika li-masilla, extracts from Council of Ministers, 20 October 1879, incl. in Cherif to Farman, 18 March 1879; U.S. National Archives, Records of Department of State, Microfilm T41, Roll 7, Cairo Consuls to State Dept., 10 November 1879, Farman to Evarts enclosing a translation from *Gazette des Tribunaux*, 4 November 1879, showing Europeans' opposition to removing the obelisk. The September 1879–January 1880 correspondence on the obelisk shows it was the American consul's major concern that fall. Farman to Evarts, 20 January 1880, is a forty-one-page letter on the history of the obelisk, including a translation of its texts.

26. Maria Avgouli, 'The First Greek Museums and National Identity', in *Museums and the Making of 'Ourselves': The Role of Objects in National Identity* (ed. Flora E.S. Kaplan; London: Leicester University Press, 1994); Yannis Hamilakis and Eleana Yalouri, 'Antiquities as Symbolic Capital in Modern Greek Society', *Antiquity* 70 (1996), pp. 117-29; Maria Mouliou, 'Ancient Greece, its Classical Heritage, and the Modern Greeks: Aspects of Nationalism in Museum Exhibitions', in *Nationalism and Archaeology* (ed. John A. Atkinson, Iain Banks and Jerry O'Sullivan; Scottish Archaeological Forum; Glasgow: Cruithne Press, 1996), pp. 174-99.

The Cairo and Istanbul museums survived national bankruptcies in the late 1870s and, in 1881, the deaths of their European directors. Thereafter, their paths diverged. The Ottomans under Sultan Abdulhamid II retained enough independence to have an indigenous antiquities director, the Turkish painter Osman Hamdi. In British-occupied Egypt, however, the French maintained their grip on the museum and Antiquities Service.[27]

Mariette assembled his Bulaq collection in the former quarters of the overland transit company, which the railroad had just put out of business. The riverside location—near the present-day Television Building and the Ministry of Foreign Affairs—was convenient for off-loading heavy antiquities floated down the Nile.

Mariette initially envisioned building his promised permanent museum in Alexandria.[28] But the railroad cut Alexandria-Cairo travel time to a few hours, making it easy for arrivals by sea to move inland to the capital. Mariette now set his sights on the Ezbekiyeh quarter of Cairo, where Shepheard's, other hotels, and shops and cafes drew crowds of Europeans.

Said's death in January 1863 at forty-one took Mariette aback, but Ismail hastened to reassure him. As Maspero put it, Mariette was delighted to meet in Ismail 'someone with an imagination even more fantastic than his own'.[29] 'Improvising ever grander projects as he became intoxicated with his own words', Ismail spoke of a huge complex at Ezbekiyeh with museums for Greek, Arab, and pharaonic antiquities. Inclusion of the Institut égyptien, with a full-time director, librarian, and library, would make the complex 'the true scientific center of Egypt'. The new Ismailiyya quarter, laid out on the eve of the Suez Canal ceremonies, began drawing the fashionable residents westward toward the Nile, and Mariette changed his ideal site to the southern tip of Gezira,[30] the undeveloped island facing Bulaq and the Qasr al-Nil barracks. (See map 1.)

Meanwhile, Mariette remodeled the Bulaq premises for a modest temporary museum. By the summer of 1860, the foundations had been laid, and he expected an Italian construction firm to finish within a year. The decorative ironwork for a *'belle façade mauresque'* had already arrived in Alexandria from Paris. Later he wrote:

> You would no longer recognize our old court at Boulak. At the center now is a vast monument, in ancient Egyptian style, consisting of a dozen rooms built to my plans. This is our provisional museum. I don't say we will be lodged there like kings, but at least we will have an ensemble of galleries while we await the definitive museum. On the interior as on the exterior, all is decorated *à l'égyptienne*, and the monuments

27. On developments in Istanbul, see Tülay Ergil, *Museums of Istanbul/Istanbul Müzerleri* (Istanbul: Istanbul Egitim ve Kültür Vakfi, 1993). On Osman Hamdi, director of the museum and Antiquities Service from 1881 until his death in 1910, see Mustafa Cezar, *Müzeci ve ressam Osman Hamdi Bey* (Türk Kültürüne Hizmet Vakfi sanat yayinlari, 1; Istanbul: Türk Kültürüne Hizmet Vakfi, 1987).

28. DWQ/Abhath B118: Athar/F: Mariette/Mariette to König, 29 April 1858.

29. Maspero, 'Mariette', pp. cxxiv-cxxv, for this and the following two quotations.

30. Maspero, 'Mariette', p. cxcii.

> will soon begin to take their places... The inauguration of these new constructions will take place Oct. 1.[31]

Mariette's detractors charged that the structure had cost hundreds of thousands of francs. Maspero put the sum at under sixty thousand, with Mariette paying part out of his own pocket.[32]

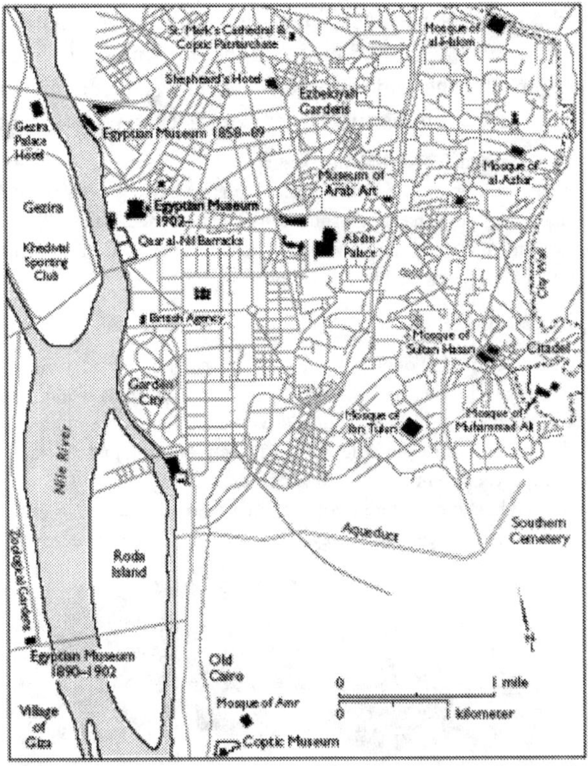

Map 1. Cairo *c.* 1914.

Ismail opened the Bulaq Museum on 16 October 1863, in the presence of a French museum curator and a senator close to Napoleon III. This may have been Egypt's first building in neopharaonic style. It had a court for the museum and one for Mariette's residence and the garden where his pet gazelle sported.

31. Maspero, 'Mariette', p. cxxxvii. On the Bulaq Museum generally, see Auguste Mariette-Bey, *Notice des principaux monuments exposés dans les galeries provisoires du Musée d'antiquités égyptiennes de S.A. le Vice-Roi à Boulaq* (Alexandria and Cairo, 1st–6th edn, 1864–76) (title varies; hereafter, particular editions cited by year); Maspero, *Guide du visiteur*, pp. vii-xx; Etienne Drioton, 'Le Musée de Boulac', *Cahiers d'histoire égyptienne* 3/1 (November 1950), pp. 1-12; and *Album de musée du Boulaq* (Cairo: Mourès, 1871), photos by Hippolyte Délié and Emile Béchard, text by Mariette.

32. Maspero, 'Mariette', p. cxxxix.

Mariette later convinced Ismail that two additional display halls would impress the Europeans attending the Suez festivities.[33]

Mariette organized displays along the lines of de Rougé's Egyptian materials in the upper level of the Louvre, with divisions for religious, funereal, civil, and historical monuments. (He later displayed Greek, Roman, and Christian objects in a fifth section). Lepsius's rather similar arrangement in Berlin had historical, civil, and mythological series. Mariette was proud that in contrast with Egyptian collections in Europe, he had recorded the provenance of every object.

Mariette admitted that he sometimes fell back on aesthetic rather than 'scientific' arrangements, defending this as an attempt to attract Egyptians (see figure 13):

> Certainly as an archaeologist, I would be disposed to deplore these useless arrangements of no use to science; but if the Museum thus arranged pleases those for whom it is intended, if they come back often and in so doing are inoculated without knowing it with a taste for the study and, I would almost say, the love of the antiquities of Egypt, my intention will have been accomplished.[34]

Mariette explained that

> the Museum of Cairo is not only intended for European travelers; the viceroy intends that it should above all be accessible to the natives (*indigènes*) whom it is charged to instruct in the history of their country. I would not be maligning the civilization introduced to the banks of the Nile by the dynasty of Mehemet-Ali in saying that Egypt is still too young in the new life which she has just received to have a public easily impressed in matters of archaeology and art. Some time ago, Egypt destroyed its monuments; she respects them today; tomorrow she should love them.[35]

Figure 13. Aesthetic arrangement in Mariette's Bulaq Museum. Although dismissing such arrangements as 'useless to science', Mariette said he used them to catch the attention of Egyptians. In Auguste Mariette-Bey, *Album de musée du Boulaq* (1871), pl. 37. Photograph by Hippolyte Délié and Emile Béchard.

33. Félicien de Saulcy, 'Musée du Caire', *Revue archéologique* NS 9 (May 1864), pp. 313-22; Maspero, 'Mariette', pp. cxxxix-cxl, clxxviii.

34. Mariette, *Notice*, 1868, pp. 10-11.

35. Mariette, *Notice*, 1868, p. 10.

Abdallah Abu al-Suud, a pupil and younger colleague of al-Tahtawi's, translated Mariette's museum guidebook into Arabic. It opens with a *bismillah* invocation, evokes the Prophet, and declares its purpose: to explain the contents of the museum Mariette created to Egyptians so that they will know about their ancestors.[36] Little is yet known of what the Egyptian public made of the museum. An intriguing picture by a German artist shows veiled Egyptian women and a Western woman tourist and girl looking at the sphinxes in the forecourt (see figure 14).

Figure 14. *Court of the Museum of Antiquities at Boolak*, illustration by W. Gentz, in Georg Ebers, *Egypt* (1878–79), II. Mingling of veiled Egyptian women and Western tourists.

36. Auguste Mariette-Bey, *Furjat al-mutafarrij ʿalá al-Intiqih Khanah al-Khidiwiyah al-ka'inah bi-Bulaq Misr al-mahamiyah, wa-hiyya ʿibarah ʿan wasf nukhbat al-athar al-qadima al-misriyya al-mawjuda fi khazinat al-tuhaf al-ilmiyya al-misriyya* (Cairo: Matbaʿat Wadi al-Nil, 1286/1869), p. 4. A title page, but nothing more, of the original French version is bound in with this Arabic translation: *Une visite au musée de Boulaq ou description des principaux monuments conservés dans les salles de cet établissement* (Paris: A. Franck, 1869).

Mariette had European as well as Egyptian audiences in mind when he emphasized that ancient Egyptians were not idolatrous polytheists but believers in 'a sole God, immortal, uncreated, invisible and hidden in the inaccessible depths of his being; he created all that exists..'.[37] The perplexing variety of lesser gods merely personified attributes of this creator.

Said's and Ismail's personal attitudes toward antiquities remain elusive. Once Said took Mariette aboard the royal steamboat and asked where he might dig for antiquities. To the viceroy's annoyance, nothing was found. Said visited the embryonic museum only once, when escorting the comte de Chambord, the legitimist claimant to the French throne. Said and the French consul passed the forty-five-minute visit in the courtyard on silk divans, talking and smoking, and never followed the *comte* in to see the collection.[38]

According to Maspero, Ismail would not enter the museum with his French guests on inauguration day: 'Like the true Oriental he was, the horror and fright which he had for death kept him from entering an edifice containing mummies. While the ceremony took place inside, he remained in the garden, amusing himself with the grimaces of the apes and the gamboling of Finette, the archaeologist's gazelle'.[39] The Orientalist wrap of such anecdotes may reveal as much about Mariette, Maspero, and their Western audiences as it does about Said and Ismail.

4. *Al-Tahtawi's History of Pre-Islamic Egypt*

In his campaign to interest his compatriots in ancient Egypt, al-Tahtawi drew heavily on Mariette's works. Shortly after his accession, Ismail made al-Tahtawi head of a revived translation bureau and member of an advisory board on education. Later, he also oversaw Arabic instruction in the schools and edited the educational magazine *Rawdat al-madaris*.

In 1838–39, Abdallah Abu al-Suud and two of al-Tahtawi's other students had translated a French history of ancient Egypt into Arabic as *Bidayat al-qudama* (Primer of the ancients). Al-Tahtawi revised it and added a preface.[40]

37. Mariette, *Notice*, 1868, pp. 20-21.

38. Mariette, *Mariette*, pp. 32-33; Maspero, 'Mariette', pp. cxxvii-cxxviii.

39. Maspero, 'Mariette', p. cxl.

40. *Bidayat al-qudama wa hidayat al-hukama* (trans. Mustafa al-Zawarbi, Muhammad Abd al-Raziq and Abdallah Abu al-Suud; Bulaq: Dar al-Tibaʿah al-Amiriyya, 1254/1838; 2nd edn, 1282/1865). Delanoue, *Moralistes*, II, pp. 623-24. Abu al-Futuh Radwan, *Tarikh Matbaat Bulaq: wa-lamhat fi tarikh al-tibaʿah fi buldan al-Sharq al-Awsat* (Cairo: al-Matbaʿah al-Amiriyya, 1953), p. 468, lists a *Tarikh al-Misriyyin*, or *Tarikh qudama al-Misriyyin* by al-Tahtawi published in 1254/1839; Ayda Ibrahim Nusayr, *Kutub al-arabiyya nushirat fi Misr fi al-qarn al-tasi ashar* (Cairo: American University in Cairo Press, 1990), p. 252, lists al-Tahtawi as translator of *Tarikh qudama al-Misriyyin*, 1254/1838. These probably both refer to *Bidayat al-qudama*. I have been unable to locate a copy of this work. On Abu al-Suud, see Jamal al-Din al-Shayyal, *History*, pp. 41-43; Cole, *Colonialism*, pp. 127, 225, 314 n. 37.

Abu al-Suud returned to the subject in 1864–65 with his translation of Mariette's *Aperçu de l'histoire d'Egypte depuis les temps les plus reculés jusqu'à la conquête musulmane (Kitab Qudama al-Misriyyin).* Ismail had commissioned this textbook sketch, Abu al-Suud explained, because 'the Khedive wants to waken us from this torpor by the study of the history of our ancestors so that we can revive their glorious virtues and follow their example in working together as true Egyptians and true patriots, for the renaissance of Egypt'.[41]

Love of country, Abu al-Suud explained, meant working together for the good of fellow citizens regardless of origin or race. Abu al-Suud legitimated Ismail's empire by rejecting the First Cataract at Aswan as Egypt's southern boundary and endorsing a civilizing mission to the 'pagan savages' to the southernmost reaches of the Nile basin.[42] The title of the journal Abu al-Suud launched in 1867 with a subsidy from Ismail—*Wadi al-Nil* (The valley of the Nile)—reflects an Egyptian consciousness that comfortably embraced both pride in the pharaohs and the renewed Sudanese empire. Abu al-Suud, who taught history at Dar al-Ulum and wrote for *Rawdat al-madaris*, also translated Mariette's museum guide into Arabic.

Al-Tahtawi conceived his history of ancient Egypt, *Anwar tawfiq al-jalil fi akhbar Misr wa-tawthiq Bani Ismail* (Glorious light on the story of Egypt and authentication of the sons of Ishmael, 1868), as the first volume of a longer survey. The volume covered the pharaonic, Greco-Roman, and Byzantine eras up to the Islamic conquest. The year after al-Tahtawi's death in 1873, his son Ali Fahmi Rifaa brought out the unfinished sequel, *Nihayat al-Ijaz fi Sirat Sakin al-Hijaz*, which held the life of the Prophet Muhammad up for emulation.[43]

As he had done three decades earlier in writing of Paris, al-Tahtawi prefaced *Anwar* with endorsements in hopes of warding off conservative attacks. Shaykh al-Azhar Mustafa al-Arusi noncommittally praised al-Tahtawi's grace in the historical arts, but Azhari professor Muhammad al-Damanhuri praised the book for holding up models of virtuous men who had served the Egyptian fatherland across the millennia. Khedive Ismail's private secretary Ahmad Khayri noted that European hieroglyphic scholarship enabled al-Tahtawi to dispense

41. Quoted in Arthur Rhoné, *L'Egypte à petites journées: Le Caire d'autrefois* (Paris: Société générale d'éditions, new edn, 1910), p. 3.

42. Auguste Mariette, *Aperçu de l'histoire d'Egypte depuis les temps les plus reculés jusqu'à la conquête musulmane (Kitab Qudama al-Misriyyin)* (Alexandria: Imprimerie de Mourès, Rey, 1864), pp. 3, 5. The copy consulted had Mariette's French original bound together with Abu al-Suud's Arabic translation. Shayyal, *History*, pp. 41-43, gives different Arabic titles for both the AH 1281 translation of *Aperçu* (*Qannasat ahl al-asr fi khulasat tarikh Misr)* and the AH 1286 guide *(Mutafarrij ala al-Antikhana al-Khidaywiyya).*

43. Delanoue, *Moralistes*, II, p. 630; Rifaa Rafi al-Tahtawi, *Anwar tawfiq al-jalil fi akhbar Misr wa-tawthiq Bani Ismail*, in *Al-Amal al-kamila li-Rifaa Rafi al-Tahtawi.* III. *Tarikh Misr wa al-arab qabla al-Islam* (ed. Muhammad Amara; Beirut: al-Mu'assassah al-ʿArabiyah lil-Dirasat wa-al-Nashr, 1974).

with uncritical lore from Arabic sources pertaining to the Jews (Israiliyyat). Ali Mubarak also praised the book's use of evidence from European archaeology and philology rather than merely repeating old legends. Al-Tahtawi opened with a Quranic quotation validating human reason and flattered Ismail as 'the guardian of the Egyptian land, the restorer of its former splendour and the renewer of the Islamic community'.[44]

Setting aside divine history 'written in the books of heaven', al-Tahtawi divided human histories into universal ones that treat all nations *(umam)* and particular ones that focus on a single *umma*, such as Egypt, 'the ancient Iraqis and the Kurds', Phoenicia, Persia, India, or Greece. He boasted that Egypt, unlike other nations, had not just shone in a single era and then gone into eclipse but had kept its luster across seventy centuries. 'At the time of the pharaohs it was the mother of all the nations of the world', and under Alexander, the Ptolemies, and the Romans, it won fame for its learning and philosophy. Egypt then became a pole of Islamic culture, defeating the kingdoms of the Franks, delivering Jerusalem from the crusaders, and even capturing the king of France. Egypt played a leading role in spreading civilization to the West, defeated the French invaders at the beginning of the present century, and was now flourishing under the beneficent Muhammad Ali dynasty.[45]

A dozen preliminary chapters treated the geography and sources of the Nile, the annual flood, Nilometers, ancient Egyptian agriculture, canals and lakes, flora, fauna, minerals, and geopolitics. A three-page chapter on antiquities, emphasized the uniqueness of pyramids, obelisks, sphinxes, hieroglyphic inscriptions, and the monumental column in Alexandria.[46] Al-Tahtawi mentioned France's taking of an obelisk to Paris. Although from the region himself, he disposed of the wondrous ruins of the Said (Upper Egypt) in a mere three lines. He cited Muhammad Ali's order of 1835 to collect antiquities, again with a Quranic justification.

Identifying Noah's grandson Misrayim, the son of Shem, with the legendary founding pharaoh Menes carried al-Tahtawi from Quranic and biblical tradition to the dynastic framework Manetho had elaborated for his Greek-speaking Ptolemaic overlords. Al-Tahtawi followed Mariette's long chronology in placing Menes at 5626 before the Hijra (5004 BCE), although he noted that some European scholars would lower this by two or three millennia.[47]

Al-Tahtawi marched reign-by-reign through Manetho's thirty dynasties, with thematic summaries at the end of each era. He noted that the Europeans'

44. Youssef M. Choueri, *Arab History and the Nation-State: A Study in Modern Arab Historiography 1820–1980* (Exeter Arabic and Islamic Series; London: Routledge, 1989), pp. 9-11. These prefatory endorsements were omitted from the later edition of *Anwar* available to me.

45. al-Tahtawi, *Anwar*, pp. 14-15, 18-19.

46. al-Tahtawi, *Anwar*, pp. 33-70. The antiquities chapter is pp. 63-66.

47. al-Tahtawi, *Anwar*, p. 70.

decipherment of hieroglyphics had revealed the correct names of the three pyramid builders of Giza, though whether they came before or after Abraham was still in dispute.[48] *Anwar*'s references to Herodotus, Strabo, and Diodorus Siculus were presumably filtered through Champollion, Mariette, and other modern Europeans. Al-Tahtawi followed Mariette in pointing out where evidence from the monuments confirmed, augmented, or contradicted Greek literary sources. He departed from Mariette in his literary flourishes and moral lessons from the Quran and such Arabic writers as al-Masudi, al-Maqrizi, Ibn Abd al-Hakam, and al-Suyuti.

Anwar necessarily reflected the limitations of European scholarship at the time. It lacked evidence from the monuments for the first two dynasties, the Fifth Dynasty, and the First Intermediate Period following the Old Kingdom. Al-Tahtawi considered the Hyksos 'Shepherd Kings' Arabs. He knew little of Hatshepsut or Amenhotep IV's (a modern editor's note points out that this was Ikhnaton) religious revolution and the move of the capital to Tell el-Amarna. He followed Mariette in identifying Rameses II as the Sesostris of the Greeks and accepting Herodotus's inflated account of his conquests. Al-Tahtawi noted that some equated Rameses-Sesostris with Hermes Trismegistus, the Quranic Idris. He reviewed arguments over the pharaoh of the Exodus, favoring Merneptah of the Nineteenth Dynasty.[49]

Al-Tahtawi felt no need to give Gregorian equivalents for his 'before the Hijra' dates. Not until around 1900 did including both Gregorian and Islamic dates become common in Arabic publications in Egypt. Like Mariette in his *Aperçu*, al-Tahtawi gave pre-Hijra rather than BC and early AD dates, but pointed out that these were counted in solar years. Thus '2314 before the Hijra' means 2,314 *solar* years before the Hijra, even though the Hijri calendar is lunar. The editor of a twentieth-century edition of *Anwar* adds BC and AD equivalents and points out that by not allowing for the overlap of Manetho's dynasties, long chronologies overestimated the length of the pharaonic period by two millennia.[50]

Citing inscriptions on the pyramids of Saqqara, al-Tahtawi identified the ancient Egyptians religiously as Sabi'a, or Sabians. *Anwar*'s modern editor identifies the Sabians as practitioners of a pre-Islamic religion from Ḥarrān in northern Iraq, who revered the stars and planets. 'Sabians' is also applied to two little-known gnostic groups in early Islamic times, one Christian and one pagan.[51] Since the Quran mentions Sabians along with Christians and Jews as monotheistic 'people of the Book', assimilating ancient Egyptians to the Sabians made it easier for modern Egyptian Muslims—and perhaps Copts as well—to identify with the pharaonic heritage.

48. al-Tahtawi, *Anwar*, pp. 64, 74.
49. al-Tahtawi, *Anwar*, pp. 73-74, 80, 90, 94-95, 100-105, 110-13.
50. al-Tahtawi, *Anwar*, pp. 73.
51. T. Fahd, 'Sabi'a', *EI*², VIII, pp. 675-78.

Ending the volume with the Islamic conquest of Egypt in 640 CE/AH 18 reflected the Muslim vision of the mission of the Prophet Muhammad as the great historical divide. But then, without acknowledging any discrepancy, al-Tahtawi followed Mariette in speaking of two main eras of pre-Islamic Egyptian history, the 'heathen' *(jahili)* period up to Theodosius's decree of AD 391–241 solar years before the Hijra—banning pagan cults and closing the temples, and the 'Christian' period of 259 years until the Islamic conquest. This was fine for Mariette, but for a Muslim it seems to imply that Egypt's 259 years of Christian rule were not part of the *jahiliyya.* In speaking of Egypt's 'middle centuries' as beginning with the Islamic conquest, he also imported, perhaps unconsciously, the West's tripartite ancient-medieval-modern model without appreciating its problems when applied to Islamic history.[52]

The publication of *Anwar* put a solid survey of pharaonic history at the disposal of Arabic readers, but this takes up less than a fifth of the volume. Al-Tahtawi devoted nearly as many pages to each of four subsequent eras—Alexander and the Ptolemies, the Romans up to Theodosius, the Byzantines from Theodosius to the Islamic conquest, and—shifting the geographical focus to Arabia—the pre-Islamic Arabs. Egypt's Greco-Roman-Byzantine millennium thus received nearly three times as much space as the whole pharaonic era.

In 1865, the Bulaq Press received orders to print five hundred copies of al-Tahtawi's *Tarikh Misr* for the schools. Since *Anwar* came out only in 1868, this may refer to a reprinting of *Bidayat al-qudama.* Muhammad Abduh recommended *Anwar* as a text for young Egyptians, but further information about its reception is lacking.[53] It was not reprinted until 1971.

With al-Tahtawi as editor, contributors to the magazine *Rawdat al-madaris* included at least four scholars firmly committed to promoting the pharaonic legacy among modern Egyptians—al-Tahtawi, Ali Mubarak, Abdallah Abu al-Suud, and Heinrich Brugsch. Half a dozen Egyptians and Brugsch sat on the board,[54] Mubarak and Abu al-Suud were among the contributors, and al-Tahtawi's son, Ali Fahmi Rifaa, assisted his father. Al-Tahtawi had had previous journalistic experience as chief editor of the government's *Al-Waqai al-Misriyya.* Taking *La Revue encyclopédique* and *Le Journal asiatique* loosely as models,[55] *Rawdat* ranged through the humanities and the social and natural sciences. Its initial press run was 350, later rising to 700.

Having opened the School of Egyptology several months earlier, H. Brugsch was on hand for *Rawdat*'s birth. He published in it, in Arabic translation, a

52. al-Tahtawi, *Anwar*, pp. 20-21.

53. Khalil Sabat, *Tarikh al-tibaa fi al-sharq al-arabi* (Maktabat al-dirasat al-tarikhiyah; Cairo: Dar al-Ma'arif, 2nd edn, 1966), p. 186; Cole, *Colonialism*, pp. 42, 294 n. 43.

54. Muhammad Abd al-Ghani Hasan and Abd al-Aziz al-Disuqi, *Rawdat al-madaris: Nashatuha wa ittijahatuha al-adabiyya wa al-ilmiyya dirasah naqdiyya tahliliyya* (Cairo: Al-Hay'a al-Misriyya al-Amma lil-Kitab, 1975), pp. 44-45.

55. Louca, *Voyageurs*, p. 73.

study on the history of coinage and the text of lectures he delivered at the fledgling Dar al-Ulum.[56] One of his students, a Muhammad Ali, contributed Arabic translations of hieroglyphic texts, and Coptic journalist Mikhail Abd al-Sayyid offered the study 'Customs of the Ancient Egyptians'.[57]

5. *Egyptological Rivalries in Cairo: France, Germany, and the Rest*

Said's and Ismail's affinity for French culture, de Lesseps's canal, Mariette's triumphs, and Napoleon III's prestige converged to make the 1860s France's decade in the Egyptian sun. The word 'imperialism' caught on in English in the 1850s, often in connection with the Second French Empire.[58] Napoleon's assertiveness in the Crimea, Mexico, Indochina, and Egypt fostered its association with overseas expansion. The 1860s were the only decade when more Egyptian guidebook editions came out in French than in English.[59] Empress Eugénie starred at the Suez ceremonies in November 1869, an apogee of French prestige on the Nile.

Ten months later, Prussia shattered the French army and Second Empire at Sedan, clearing the way for Bismarck to unify Germany under Prussia as the Second Reich. The German siege trapped Mariette in Paris for months, and when freed at last he hurried back to Bulaq to head off any German challenge to France's archaeological preeminence there.[60]

Mariette had little to fear from British Egyptology. French had been the first language to coin words for the new field. *Egyptologue* (Egyptologist) cropped

56. Hasan and al-Disuqi, *Rawdat*, pp. 219-20, 363-65.
57. Hasan and al-Disuqi, *Rawdat*, pp. 222, 227, 363-65, 381.
58. *OED*²; *Grand Larousse de la langue française* (Paris: Larousse, 1971–78).
59.

Table 2. Egyptian Guidebook Editions, by Language

Dates	English	French	German	Other
1830s	1	1	0	0
1840s	3	1	1	0
1850s	4	1	1	0
1860s	4	8	0	1 Italian
1870–1882	5	2	3	0
1883–1889	2	0	2	0
1890–1899	19	4	3	0
1900–1914	31	15	9	1 Russian

Table 6, Reid, *Whose Pharaohs?*, p. 299. Source: Compiled from Oleg V. Volkoff, *Comment on visitait la vallée du Nil: les 'Guides' de l'Egypte* (Recherches d'archéologie, de philologie et d'histoire, 28; Cairo: IFAO, 1967), pp. 103-19. His list is not exhaustive. Guides to a single city, region, or museum have not been counted.

60. Maspero, 'Mariette', pp. clxxx–clxxxii.

up in 1827, the year Champollion opened the Egyptian section at the Louvre, and *égyptologie* followed around 1850. Not until 1856 did an English writer try out 'Egyptologue' as a loan word from the French. 'Egyptology' followed in 1859 and began to catch on in the 1860s. Even without a word for their new field, however, Salt, Wilkinson, Hay, and Lane had forcefully represented it on the Nile in the 1820s and 1830s. By Mariette's day, Samuel Birch was the leading British Egyptologist. He would share the founding-father honors on the facade of the Cairo Museum of 1902 with Champollion, Lepsius, and Rosellini, yet he never set foot in Egypt. British diplomats, merchants, and financiers were hardly so passive. It augured ill for France—and for Egypt—that 66 percent of the tonnage passing through the French-built Suez Canal the year after it opened was British. By 1880 the figure had risen to 79 percent, and the British were taking 80 percent of Egyptian exports and supplying 44 percent of its imports.[61]

'The German problem' preoccupied French patriots after 1870, but they could not agree on how to meet the challenge. Georges Clemenceau deplored overseas imperialism as a distraction from the German frontier and rebuilding at home. In contrast, Jules Ferry's fragile Opportunist republican cabinets of the early 1880s and the *parti colonial*—a coalition of seaport, military, *colon*, missionary, and geographical society interests—seized on overseas empire as the very tonic needed to spark regeneration at home.[62]

France's *mission civilisatrice* took on new urgency after 1870, with Mariette in the forefront. It must have been difficult for him to hear his old comrade H. Brugsch often mentioned in rumors of a German bid to take over the Antiquities Service and museum. Brugsch's experience at Cairo's Prussian consulate, his presence now at the School of Egyptology, and his scholarly stature briefly gave German Egyptology a prestige in Cairo unknown since Lepsius's day.

Back in Europe after Lepsius's return to Berlin in 1846, Germans were soon in a position to challenge French leadership in Egyptology. With a dual base in Berlin's Egyptian Museum and the University of Berlin, Lepsius trained most of the next generation of German Egyptologists. Kaiser Wilhelm I had him over for tea, and the scholar's dazzling circle included Orientalist F. Max Müller, the Grimm brothers, geographer Karl Ritter, historian Leopold von Ranke, classical archaeologist Ernst Curtius, naturalist Alexander von Humboldt, philosopher

61. D.A. Farnie, *East and West of Suez, 1854–1956* (Oxford: Clarendon Press, 1969), pp. 751-52; A.G. Hopkins, 'The Victorians and Africa: A Reconsideration of the Occupation of Egypt, 1882', *Journal of African History* 27 (1986), p. 379. For the new vocabulary relating to Egyptology, see *Dictionnaire de la langue française* (Paris, 1988), p. 609; *OED*², V, p. 97.

62. Christopher M. Andrew and A.S. Kanya-Forstner, *The Climax of French Imperial Expansion 1914–1924* (Stanford: Stanford University Press, 1981); Mathew Burrows, '"Mission civilisatrice": French Cultural Policy in the Middle East, 1860–1914', *Historical Journal* 29 (1986), pp. 109-35.

Friedrich Schelling, and Roman historian Theodor Mommsen.[63] Even Maspero hailed Lepsius as 'the master of us all'.[64]

While Bismarck was unifying Germany under Prussia and German research seminars and laboratories were becoming the envy of the world, Egyptology was establishing itself as an academic discipline. Chairs of Egyptology proliferated across Germany: Göttingen (1868, H. Brugsch); Strasbourg (1872, Johannes Duemichen); Heidelburg (1872, August Eisenlohr); and Leipzig (1875, Georg Ebers). The names of Brugsch, Duemichen, and Ebers joined that of Lepsius on the Cairo Museum facade.[65] Brugsch carried this German Egyptological florescence to Cairo. He was seventeen years younger than Lepsius, who treated him not as a protégé but as an upstart rival. Brugsch took his doctorate from Berlin but considered his Egyptian more self-taught than learned from Lepsius. After further studies in Paris, Brugsch won a Prussian fellowship to Egypt, where he worked at Saqqara alongside Mariette for eight months. After undertaking a diplomatic mission to Persia and founding the first lasting journal of Egyptology *(Zeitschrift für ägyptische Sprache und Altertumskunde)* in 1863, he returned to Cairo as Prussian consul. An Egyptology chair finally opened up for him at Göttingen in 1867, but two years later he was back in Cairo to direct the new School of Egyptology.[66]

In 1864, an incident aggravated Mariette's relations with the Germans. Duemichen had copied a king list Mariette's workmen had uncovered at Abydos and sent a copy to Lepsius. Lepsius published it without acknowledging Mariette. National honor seemed at stake in the ensuing uproar, and Duemichen was on the point of challenging Mariette to a duel.[67]

Mariette and Brugsch's friendship weathered the storm, and late in June 1870 they shared an Alexandria-Marseilles steamer on their way home for the summer. When Mariette reached Paris on 6 July, Louis-Adolphe Thiers was making a last futile effort to prevent the French assembly from declaring war on Prussia. In a later distant echo of the Franco-Prussian War, an old Sudanese shaykh 'knew well that the King of the Germans had only acquired the resources to vanquish the French, through the treasures which the Howadji Lepsius had found at Meroe and sent back to his native land'.[68] Mariette's enemies

63. Georg Ebers, *Richard Lepsius: A Biography* (trans. Z.D. Underhill; New York: W.S. Gottsberger, 1887), pp. 275-76; Suzanne L. Marchand, *Down from Olympus: Archaeology and Philhellenism in Germany, 1750–1970* (Princeton, NJ: Princeton University Press, 1996), pp. 49, 108.

64. Ebers, *Lepsius*, p. 300.

65. For the dates of these chairs, see the *WWWE*3 entries on these individuals.

66. Heinrich Brugsch, *Mein Leben und mein Wandern* (Berlin: Allgemeiner Verein für Deutsche Literatur, 2nd edn, 1894 [1893]); Louis Keimer, 'Le Musée égyptologique de Berlin', *Cahiers d'histoire égyptienne*, ser. 3, fasc. 1 (November 1950), pp. 30-36. See also *WWWE*3, pp. 67-68.

67. Maspero, 'Mariette', pp. cxlvi-cli.

68. Ebers, *Lepsius*, p. 157.

deplored his long absence from Bulaq during the siege of Paris, urging Ismail to replace him with Brugsch. Brugsch dissociated himself from the intrigue, and Mariette replied:

> For me you are not a German, you are Brugsch; and you have no need to explain yourself with regard to such events. They have been able to affect my heart as a Frenchman; they have not been able to modify my heart as a man, especially vis-à-vis you. I love you as a true friend and have always loved you deeply with a natural sympathy that nothing has destroyed and that nothing will destroy.[69]

Two years later Mariette took on Brugsch's younger brother Emile as a photographer for what proved to be a long career in the Antiquities Service.

De Rougé's death in 1873 opened vacancies at the Collège de France and the Louvre, but Mariette was not interested. Maspero and François Chabas could carry the ball in Paris, he said; his duty was to hold on 'in Egypt against German influence which is being pushed by all means'.[70]

When George Bancroft, 'the illustrious author of the History of the United States, the Thucydides of America', toured Egypt, Mariette found him too pro-German even to concede France's help in winning American independence.[71] Later, as ambassador to Berlin, Bancroft joined the Lepsius circle. Such 'Anglo-Saxon' ties to Germanic cousins were not unusual. Two Britons—sculptor Joseph Bonomi and architect James Wild—had joined the Lepsius expedition. Prussian diplomat Baron von Bunsen, an ardent promoter of Egyptology and an anglophile, had an English wife and served as Prussian ambassador in London.[72]

An Italian bid to take over the Antiquities Service in Cairo was out of the question. Italian was still the lingua franca of the eastern Mediterranean in the first half of the nineteenth century, and in 1845 *Lo Spettatore egiziano* became the first Egyptian journal of note after the short-lived journals of the French expedition and the official *Al-Waqai al-Misriyya.* Three more Egyptian-based Italian journals joined *Lo Spettatore* in the 1850s, when three French journals also sprang up.[73] As late as the 1860s, the French still considered Italian the main language of merchants and missionaries in the eastern Mediterranean.[74] An Italian company ran the postal service in Egypt, and Italians headed the sanitary and statistical services. But in 1867 French replaced Italian as the second

69. Maspero, 'Mariette', p. clxxxii.

70. Maspero, 'Mariette', p. cxc.

71. Mariette, *Mariette*, pp. 117-19.

72. On Bonomi, Wild, and Bunson, see *WWWE3*, pp. 53-54, 442, 73.

73. Angelo Sammarco, *Gli italiani in Egitto: il contributo italiano nella formazione dell'Egitto moderno* (Alexandria: Edizioni del fascio, 1937), pp. 151-53.

74. Burrows, '"Mission civilisatrice"', pp. 111-12, speaking of the Ottoman Empire; Jean-Jacques Luthi, *Le français en Egypte: Essai d'anthologie* (Beirut: Maison Naaman pour la Culture, 1981).

language on Egyptian stamps, and in the 1870s French won out as the working language of the Mixed Courts, the Anglo-French 'Dual Control' over the Egyptian government, and cosmopolitan high society.

Rosellini, Luigi Vassalli, and Amadeo Peyron made up the rather spotty Italian contingent honored on the facade of the Egyptian Museum in 1902. Peyron had published a Coptic dictionary in 1835 before concentrating on Greek studies, and Rosellini's early death had cut short his promising work. Vassalli (1812–87) assisted Mariette at the museum but was older than he and an unlikely successor.[75] The real plum for Italian archaeology was Guiseppe Botti's appointment in 1892 to direct Alexandria's Greco-Roman Museum, which became an Italian cultural enclave.

6. *Egyptology for the Egyptians: Brugsch and the School of Egyptology*

Ismail and Ali Mubarak wanted to produce Egyptologists to work alongside Europeans in the Egyptian Museum and Antiquities Service. Mariette opposed this, fearing for his own position. Franco-German rivalry, however, opened a crack in European solidarity, enabling Egyptians to try for a toehold in Egyptology. In the fall of 1869, Mubarak offered Heinrich Brugsch a five-year contract to direct a 'School of the Ancient Language' (Madrasat al-Lisan al-Qadim) or School of Egyptology at five hundred francs a month.[76] The 1871–72 budget earmarked £E1,009 for three professors and £E112 for student scholarships.[77]

Ismail and Ali Mubarak personally welcomed Brugsch back to Cairo, Ismail reminiscing about student days in Paris and Mubarak reporting on the progress of his encyclopedia, *Al-Khitat al-tawfiqiyya.* As a board member and contributor to *Rawdat al-madaris*, Brugsch would have known al-Tahtawi, its editor, and their paths probably also crossed at the Institut égyptien.

Brugsch opened the school in a rat- and bat-infested villa near the Bulaq Museum, with ten students selected from other state schools for their high marks in French.[78] Instructions to recruit them from among pupils as dark-skinned

75. *L'egittologo Luigi Vassalli (1812–1887): disegni e documenti nei Civici Istituti Culturali Milanesi* (Milan: Edizioni ET, 1994).

76. DWQ/Fihrist Bataqat al-Dar, Drawer No. 1: Athar/15 Safar 1289, Order to Diwan al-Maliya, Daftar 1939, Doc. No. 140, p. 145. Brugsch's account is from his *Leben*, pp. 275-82. The best secondary account is Ahmad Izzat Abd al-Karim, *Tarikh al-talim fi Misr min nihayat hukm Muhammad Ali ila awail hukm Tawfiq 1848–1882* (3 vols.; Cairo: Matbaʿat al-Nasr, 1945), II/2, pp. 569-73.

77. Amal Hilal, 'Les premiers égyptologues égyptiens et la réforme', in *Entre réforme sociale et mouvement national: identité et modernisation en Egypte (1882–1962): Actes du colloque 'Réforme social en Egypte' qui s'est tenu du 10 au 13 décembre 1992 à l'Institut français d'archéologie orientale, Le Caire* (ed. Alain Roussillon; Cairo: CEDEJ, 1995), p. 346.

78. Abd al-Karim, *Tarikh*, II/2, pp. 570-71, gives their names; Ahmad Kamal and Ahmad Najib later became the most prominent.

as the southernmost Upper Egyptians and Sudanese are puzzling,[79] recalling Muhammad Ali's failed attempt to fill his new army with Sudanese. Brugsch commented on the light skins of some students, suggesting that they must have had Turkish mothers. Though French was the language of instruction, Brugsch hired his younger brother Emile to teach German. Brugsch taught Egyptian, the patriarchate sent a Copt to teach Coptic,[80] and a shaykh taught Arabic. Brugsch occasionally took his students on field trips to Upper Egypt. Once, while on medical leave, he took two students to Europe to widen their horizons, leaving lesson plans for the rest. Humidity in the Bulaq building was a problem, so the school moved into a wing of the educational complex in Darb al-Jamamiz.

Like Mariette and al-Tahtawi, Brugsch tried to make the Egyptian pantheon palatable to Muslims. Finding that some epithets of Amon of Thebes, Ptah of Memphis, and other divinities were identical to Islam's ninety-nine 'names' or attributes of God, he emphasized that a single divine being underlay the surface pluralism of the ancient religion.[81]

Meanwhile, Ismail and Ali Mubarak also turned to a German to direct the Khedivial Library they founded in 1870, a few months before the Franco-Prussian War reversed the relative prestige of France and Germany in Cairo. In 1872, Brugsch's former student Ludwig Stern became director of the library. Stern had studied Egyptology at Göttingen while also taking Hebrew, Arabic, and Ethiopic and would end his career as a Celtic specialist and keeper of manuscripts in the Berlin Royal Library.[82] Four more German Orientalist directors followed Stern at the library, turning it into a sphere of German influence until 1914.

Brugsch's appointment as Egyptian commissioner for the 1873 Vienna Exposition diverted some of his energy from the School of Egyptology; in 1876 he served as commissioner again, to the Philadelphia world's fair. The Egyptian government's decision, in the wake of the Franco-Prussian War, to introduce German into the schools also undercut the School of Egyptology. Brugsch's students were among the few Egyptians who had made a start on German, and it was suggested that he take five of them to Prussia or Austria for preparation to teach it. They did not go, but in 1872 Ahmad Kamal and six other Egyptology students were appointed translators and assistants in the Ministry of Education. Brugsch was abroad late in 1874 when the School of Egyptology closed, its five remaining students being transferred to posts in the railroad administration and Ministry of War.[83]

79. Quoted in Abd al-Karim, *Tarikh*, II/2, p. 569.

80. Abd al-Karim, *Tarikh*, II/2, p. 569, says Mikhail Jirjis taught them *'al-lugha al-Habashiyya'*, probably meaning Coptic rather than Ethiopic.

81. Brugsch, *Leben*, p. 299.

82. *WWWE*3, p. 404.

83. Abd al-Karim, *Tarikh*, II/2, p. 572, says that Amin Sami, *Al-Talim fi Misr fi sanatay 1914 wa 1915: wa-bayan tafsili li-nashr al-taʿlim al-awwali wa-al-ibtida'i bi-anha' al-diyar al-Misriyya,*

Brugsch's absence due to the Vienna Exposition was the ostensible reason for the closure,[84] but Mariette's hostility probably doomed the school from the start. Brugsch's report calls into question Mariette's commitment to interesting Egyptians in their ancient past:

> The Viceroy was highly satisfied with my work, the minister of education [Ali Mubarak] was delighted, and the director of government schools almost burst with envy...my old friend Mariette worried that it might lead the Viceroy to have it up his sleeve to appoint officials who had studied hieroglyphics to his museum. No matter how much I tried to set his mind at ease, he remained so suspicious that he gave the order to museum officials that no native be allowed to copy hieroglyphic inscriptions. The persons in question were thus simply expelled from the Temple.[85]

A Swiss inspector rated most of the School of Egyptology's students deficient in language, history, and 'scientific adaptability' and at best suitable for only minor museum and antiquities posts.[86] Mariette's refusal to consider them at all undercut the school's raison d'être. Years later, Petrie met an alumnus in Benha who 'spoke very fair English'. The fellow had been a secretary to a British engineer and administrator of the district where Memphis was situated but was currently unemployed.[87] Kamal and Ahmad Najib did make it back to Egyptology, but for a time Mariette seemed to have derailed Egypt's first try at training its own Egyptologists.

7. *Ancient Egypt and the Egyptian Public*

Outside the Antiquities Service, museum, and School of Egyptology, scattered indicators show a modest but growing interest in ancient Egypt among the Egyptian public. In August 1876, the newspaper *Al-Ahram* appeared, with two pyramids and the Sphinx on its masthead. Its editors, Salim and Bishara Taqla, were Syrian Christian immigrants with francophile leanings. The first issues gave a rather garbled history of the pyramids of Giza, mentioning speculations that the pyramids were built to preserve knowledge before the Flood, to store grain, or to observe the stars. Chephren, the son of Cheops I was said to have laid the cornerstone of the Great Pyramid, which was completed in the reign of a Cheops II.[88]

mumahhadan la-hu bi-shadharat min kitab al-taʿlim (Cairo: Matbaʿat al-Maʿarif, 1917), appendix, p. 91, is mistaken in saying the school lasted until December 1876.

84. Maspero, 'Mariette', pp. clxxvi, clxxxvi; Abd al-Karim, *Tarikh*, II/2, p. 572.

85. Brugsch, *Leben*, p. 282.

86. James Heyworth-Dunne, *Introduction to the History of Education in Modern Egypt* (London: Luzac, 1968), p. 355.

87. Petrie, *Seventy Years*, p. 64.

88. Yunan Rizk, 'Al-Ahram: A Diwan of Contemporary Life', *al-Ahram Weekly*, 12-18 August 1993; Ibrahim Abduh, *Jaridat al-Ahram: Tarikh wa fann 1875–1964* (Cairo: Mu'assasat Sijill al-ʿArab, 1964).

In 1867, a pyramid-and-sphinx design replaced the calligraphy and arabesques that had decorated Egypt's first postage stamps the year before. At least at first, the pyramid and sphinx probably reflected European ideas of appropriate Egyptian national symbols, but Khedive Ismail would have had to ratify the choice. Italians had run Egypt's private postal system until the state post office opened in 1865 under G. Muzzi, the director of the old private company. The ubiquitous pyramid-and-sphinx stamp design on every letter mailed from 1867 to 1914 hammered home the idea of these as national symbols (see figure 15). Coins did not share in the new symbolism. Being one of the traditional symbols of Islamic sovereignty and inherently more conservative, they bore the name of the Ottoman sultan down to 1914, when Britain severed Egypt's nominal link to Istanbul and declared it a British protectorate.[89]

Figure 15. Pyramid-and-sphinx postage stamp. From 1867 to 1914, all regular Egyptian postage stamps projected the pyramid and sphinx as symbols of Egypt.

Even Persian-born Jamal al-Din al-Afghani, famous for his pan-Islamic activism, occasionally appealed to local patriotic pride in ancient Egypt: 'Look at the pyramids of Egypt, the temples of Memphis, the remains of Thebes, the shrines of Siwa, and the fortresses of Dimyat, all testifying to the invincibility of your fathers and the might of your grandfathers!'[90] Less surprising was a series of

89. On the stamps, see 'Egypt', in *Scott 2000 Standard Postage Stamp Catalogue, Countries of the World.* II. *Countries C-F* (Sidney, OH: Scott Publishing Co., 156th edn, 2000). For coins, see 'Egypt' and 'Turkey' in the most recent editions of Krause Publications' *Standard Catalog of World Coins, 1801–1900* (Iola, WI: Krause, 2nd edn, 1998); *Standard Catalog of World Coins, 2001* (Iola, WI: Krause, 2000). On the postal system, see *Les postes en Egypte: Notices publiées à l'occasion du X*[e] *Congrès Postal Universel et du soixante-dixième anniversaire de la fondation des postes égyptiennes* (Cairo: Imprimerie nationale, 1934).

90. Charles Wendell, *The Evolution of the Egyptian National Image: From its Origins to*

articles that Afghani's Egyptian disciple Muhammad Abduh published in 1876 linking the glory of ancient Egypt with the renaissance under Ismail.[91]

In 1862 an Egyptianized landowner of central Asian background wrote his son a manual of advice in Arabic. He grumbled about the intrusion of European clothes, manners, medicine, and ideas. He backed traditional dress unless state service required Westernized effendi garb, preferred the Islamic calendar, and advised studying Islamic before European languages. Yet his table of Egyptian rulers and governors went back not just to the Islamic conquest but all the way to the pharaohs.[92] Even such a conservative member of the landed elite was already assimilating ancient Egypt as an integral part of the national heritage.

8. *Egyptology at the Institut égyptien and Khedivial Geographical Society*

In 1859, with the founding of the Institut égyptien, European residents transplanted a Western-style learned society to Egyptian soil. For its first four decades and less intensely thereafter, the Institut was a significant forum for discourse on ancient Egypt.

In Europe, such academies and learned societies were often nationalist and internationalist at the same time. Eighteenth-century *philosophes* had taken for granted a pan-European 'republic of letters'—Voltaire's 'Grande Republique'.[93] In the nineteenth century, Western socialist, religious, and learned communities had to struggle to keep international bridges open across moats of competing nationalism. Even dedicated internationalists often imagined their communities as only Western.

Egypt's semicolonial status complicated the picture at the Institut égyptien. The viceroy officially sponsored the Institut, but Europeans dominated it just as they were increasingly dominating the state. Here Europeans had to interact with other European nationals far more than did their counterparts in nationally framed learned societies at home. Members extolled 'pure science' but never lost sight of where each individual fit into the Anglo-French, Franco-German, and other European rivalries pervading the scene.

Ahmad Lutfi al-Sayyid (Berkeley: University of California Press, 1972), p. 169, quoting Muhammad Rashid Rida, *Tarikh al-Ustadh al-Imam al-Shaykh Muhammad Abduh: wa-fihi tafsil siratuhu wa-khulasat sirat muqiz al-Sharq al-hakim wa-al-Islam Jamal al-Din al-Afghani* (3 vols.; Cairo: Matbaʿat al-Manar, 1324–50/1906–31), I, pp. 46-47.

91. Angelo Sammarco, *Histoire de l'Egypte moderne depuis Mohammed Ali jusqu'à l'occupation britannique (1801–1882)* (Cairo: Imprimerie de L'Institut français d'archéologie orientale, 1937), p. 324.

92. Cole, *Colonialism*, pp. 33-35. The manuscript 'Irshad al-Walad' by Kaçïfzade Mehmet Aqïl Buharalï, also signed in Arabized form as Muhammad Aqil ibn Muhammad Kashif, is in the Egyptian National Library.

93. David C. Gordon, *Images of the West: Third World Perspectives* (Totowa, NJ: Rowman & Littlefield, 1989), p. 15.

Behind intra-European rivalries loomed issues of imperialism and racism. Was the ideal of international 'science' really meant for Westerners alone, or was it universal? Could an 'Oriental' join the privileged club of Orientalists or an Egyptian that of Egyptologists?

Fittingly, the Institut came into being in 1859, the year work on the Suez Canal began. The canal accelerated the influx of Europeans and the resulting proliferation of their churches, schools, hospitals, periodicals, clubs, and benevolent societies. At the Institut égyptien, Antiquities Service, Egyptian Museum, Khedivial Library, Khedivial Geographical Society, and government offices, the less tribally inclined tested the limits of their internationalism, but national and European-Egyptian fault lines were never far beneath the surface.

The founders of 1859 looked back to Bonaparte's Institut d'Egypte (patterned on the Institut de France back in Paris) and less explicitly to the Egyptian Society of 1836. The Institut de France had several state academies, each with a fixed number of seats. Entry was by election, usually upon the death of a member. A majority of the Egyptian Society's members had been Britons, but its membership was more open, at least to Western men. Eighty-three-year-old Jomard was a living link between the Institut d'Egypte, which disappeared from Cairo in 1801, and the Institut égyptien.[94] He wrote from Paris accepting an honorary membership in the latter and in 1861 became honorary president. Linant de Bellefonds may have been the only veteran of the Egyptian Society to join the new Institut.[95]

Despite this second Institut's Egyptian-state sponsorship and avowed internationalism, membership lists document the enduring predominance of Frenchmen and the marginality of Egyptians for decades. Prince Napoleon topped the list of honorary members in 1859. Four Frenchmen and a gallicized Egyptian Armenian (Yaqub Artin) followed each other as honorary presidents from 1861 to 1917. The French also had the edge in the regular presidency and vice presidency for the first thirty years. English, Italian, and German were acceptable languages at the Institut, but the lingua franca was French.

As table 3 indicates, in 1859 60 percent of the Institut's honorary members were French, as were 43 percent of resident members and 38 percent of corresponding members outside the Middle East. Italians—on the eve of Italian unification—were a distant second. Antonio Colucci, physician to the khedivial family, was vice president for five years and president for ten. Mariette stood

94. Jomard, only twenty-one in 1798, had not actually been a member of the first Institut d'Egypte but had worked closely with it. J.-E. Goby, 'Travaux de premier Institut d'Egypte (1798–1801)', *Bulletin de la Société française d'égyptologie* 66 (March 1973), p. 36.

95. Jacques Ellul, *Index des communications et mémoires publiés par l'Institut d'Egypte (1859–1952)* (Cairo: IFAO, 1952), is the reference for the following observations on the articles in the *Bulletin de l'Institut d'Egypte (BIE);* for the officers, see the unnumbered appendices. For lists of members, see *BIE* 2 (1859), pp. 7-12; ser. 3, 1 (1890), pp. 200-22; ser. 5, 3, fasc. 2 (1909), pp. 176-79.

out among the European founders of the Institut. Naming König Bey, Said's Alsatian secretary and former tutor, the first president assured royal patronage. Said visited the Institut and, in a familiar cliché, praised it for 'reviving on the banks of the Nile the knowledge which was the glory of our ancient Egypt, the cradle of letters, sciences, and arts'.[96] Mariette was one of two founding vice presidents, a Briton being the other.

Table 3. *Membership in the Institut égyptien and the Khedivial Geographical Society*[97]

	Institut égyptien, 1859:			Khedivial Geographical Society:
	Honorary Members	Resident Members	Corresponding Members[98]	Honorary, Founding and Regular Members, 1881
French	38	21	16	27
British	8	3	2	15
German	4	2	2	5
Italian	3	9	8	37
Austro-Hungarian	3	0	1	8
Russian	2	1	1	2
Swedish	1	0	1	0
Swiss	0	0	2	4
Belgian	1	0	0	3
Dutch	0	0	0	2
Greek	1	3	0	6
Egyptian	1	7	9	25
USA	0	0	0	6
Other	1	4[99]	21[100]	0
Total:	63	49	63	140

96. *BIE* 1 (1859), p. 2.

97. Table 10, Reid, *Whose Pharaohs?*, p. 303. Sources: *BIE* 2 (1859), pp. 7-12; *Bulletin de la Société khedivial géographique* 12 (May 1881), p. 52.

98. Corresponding members are counted as citizens of the country of residence. Nationality of several resident members is speculative. Khedivial Geographical Society figures include 11 honorary, 48 founding, and 81 regular members.

99. Unknown.

100. From the Middle East outside Egypt (including one Egyptian).

The Institut's first seat was Alexandria, the main port of entry and location of the largest European colony. Muhammad Ali had revived the port, and the Suez Canal put the Mediterranean back in the mainstream of world trade. The new Cairo-Alexandria railroad made it feasible for Cairenes like Mariette to join the Institut égyptien as resident members. Of course, the requisite rhetoric invoked the memory of ancient Alexandria's museum and library.

With a Comtean summons to 'Union and Progress', the Institut declared itself open regardless of race or caste—gender had not crossed its horizon—and to all fields of knowledge. Like the first Institut égyptien and the Saint-Simonians, who had tried to colonize Egypt in the 1830s, the second Institut proposed to give practical advice to the government on crops, animals, and human diseases.[101] The Institut met monthly from fall to spring, when wealthy residents often left to summer in Europe.

The Institut survived the financial and political upheavals of 1875–82 with difficulty. In 1880, it revised its statutes and moved to Cairo to its current building at the north end of Qasr al-Ayni Street, across from the American University. There were to be fifty resident members, up to one hundred honorary members, and an unlimited number of corresponding members. President Mariette, who had less than a year to live, complained that the bankrupt state had not paid the Institut's fifteen hundred–franc annual subvention since 1875. Once Britain was installed in Egypt, Vice President Edward Rogers, an official in the Egyptian government, persuaded financial advisor Auckland Colvin to double the annual subvention.[102]

What of Egyptian members? Seven founding resident members (14 percent) were Egyptians, including future prime minister Nubar, astronomer Mahmud al-Falaki, and al-Tahtawi.[103] Al-Falaki was the sole Egyptian on the original eighteen-man board. Al-Tahtawi served two years alongside two Europeans on the publications committee, where al-Falaki later took a turn. Ali Mubarak joined the Institut later but did not play an active role.[104]

Surprisingly, an 'Armenian gentleman resident in Cairo, whose name is mentioned in almost every book or letter written about that city' in the 1860s, did not belong.[105] Joseph Hekekyan had relished Western company in the Egyptian

101. *Livre d'or de l'Institut égyptien: Publié à l'occasion du centenaire de la fondation de L'Institut égyptien, 6 mai 1859–5 mai 1899* (Le Mans: Imprimerie de l'Institut de bibliographie, 1899), p. 3.

102. DWQ/Abhath B132/Institut d'Egypte/June 29 1947, pres. of Institut égyptien to Adli Bey Andraws, enclosing Annexe F: Mariette to ministers of the interior and finance, 6 February 1880; *BIE*, ser. 2, 4 (1883), p. 256.

103. The others were J. Hazan, the grand rabbi of Alexandria, medical doctors Shafii Bey and Muhammad Ali, and Abdallah Said Effendi, director of the commercial office at Alexandria.

104. *BIE*, ser. 2, 5 (1884–85), p. 167, lists him as a member without the date he joined.

105. BL /Add MSS 37,463/Hek 16: 427, undated and unsigned, probably Russell, correspondent of the *Times*, 1869. For the rest of the paragraph, see 37,462/Hek 15: 55; 37,460/Hek 12: 759; 37,472/Hek 24 :75; 37,470/Hek 22: 308; 37,462/Hek 15: Hekekyan to de Lesseps, 26 April 1869.

Society, and his alienation from his adopted country of Egypt and his eagerness to lay bare its secrets to Europeans have already been noted. After the Indian 'Mutiny' of 1859, he wrote a British friend: 'You must disarm India. Compel the people to make railways and electric telegraphs and canals of navigation in every direction. Stock the rivers with steamers. I would not have a native in the army. You must maintain 100,000 Englishmen in the mountains—ready—by rail—to descend into the valley like mountain torrents...'[106] Hekekyan made friends with Mariette while digging at Memphis and wrote Edouard Naville and H. Brugsch introductions to de Lesseps. He corresponded with Sir Charles Lyell on geology, sent Lucie Duff Gordon an Arabic dictionary, and met the Prince of Wales on his Egyptian tour. Explorer Henry Stanley even asked Hekekyan for a character reference to the family of a Greek woman he hoped to marry! Hekekyan's nephew Yaqub Artin later relished a similar mediating role, as did Marcus Simaika.

The Institut égyptien's emphasis on ancient Egypt began with Vice President Mariette's reading of several reports at the very first session. Mariette was president for seven of the Institut's first twenty-one years and honorary president for eleven more. He and his successors at the Antiquities Service used the Institut regularly to announce their discoveries. H. Brugsch read a paper there; and Lepsius, three. A non-Egyptologist briefly followed as president after Mariette's death, then Maspero assumed the mantle until his return to France in 1886.

Two of Mahmud al-Falaki's five papers at the Institut égyptien involved Egyptology, one on an ancient branch of the Nile and one on classical Alexandria. Al-Falaki served as vice president for a dozen years. An astronomer—the meaning of 'al-Falaki'—he had won a belated chance to study in France when his former engineering student Ali Mubarak commended him to Abbas I. Al-Falaki stayed in Europe nine years, returning home the same year the Institut was founded. Al-Falaki's publications in French in scattered European journals included articles on the calendar of the pre-Islamic Arabs, weights and measures in Islamic Egypt, excavating and mapping ancient Alexandria, and pyramid chronology in relation to the star Sirius. He was minister of education in the same cabinet as Urabi during the 1882 crisis but survived the British occupation politically, making his way back to the same post in Nubar's 1884–85 cabinet before dying in office. President Artin praised al-Falaki alongside Mariette, Maspero, and Georg Schweinfurth as Institut members who were worthy successors of Monge, Jacques Lepère, and Claude Berthollet of Bonaparte's Institut d'Egypte.[107] After al-Falaki, Egyptians dropped out of the Institut's Egyptological discourse until Ahmad Kamal's election in 1904.

106. BL /Add MSS 34,463/Hek 16: 76, Hekekyan to Nassau Senior.

107. *Livre d'or*, p. 9. On al-Falaki, see Pascal Crozet, 'La trajectoire d'un scientifique égyptien au XIXe siècle: Mahmoud al-Falaki (1815–1885)', in *Entre réforme sociale*, pp. 285-310.

Egyptology was more marginal in the other main learned society of the day—the Khedivial Geographical Society. Nevertheless the society deserves mention as a prominent feature of the cultural scene and a minor forum for Egyptology. Ismail founded it in 1875 to promote and legitimize his expanding empire in Africa. The German explorer and naturalist Georg Schweinfurth was its first president. He also served as president of the Institut égyptien and wrote the 'Origin and Present Condition of the Egyptians' for Baedeker.[108]

Early Geographical Society membership differed from that of the Institut égyptien in two ways: the prominence of Italians and the presence, at first, of Americans. As table 3 shows, Italians outnumbered the second-place French among the founders. Two Italians long monopolized the leadership of the society—Dr. Onofrio Abbate as president (1890–1915) and Federico Bonola as salaried secretary-general (1881–1912). Italian advisers were close to the ruling dynasty for most of its history; Abbate was personal physician to the family from Said on. He also was one of the Institut égyptien's two vice presidents from 1882 to 1910.[109]

The Institut included no Americans, but the American advisers in Ismail's army were prominent in the Geographical Society for its first eight years. Americans helped explore and map the Sudan, and General Charles Stone became chief of staff of the Egyptian army. Ismail's bankruptcy forced him to dismiss most American officers, but Stone stayed on and presided over the Geographical Society from 1879 to 1883. He did not return home until the British occupation made it clear that there was no longer a place for him in the Egyptian army.[110]

Twenty-five of the society's 140 founders were Egyptians. An index of the *Bulletin de l'Institut égyptien* for 1881–87 shows that Egyptians read four papers out of thirty-two. Mahmud al-Falaki attended the International Geographical Congress at Venice in 1881, was twice vice president of the Geographical Society, and succeeded Stone as president.

Like early geographical societies in the West, the Khedivial Geographical Society began as a collection of amateurs with a sprinkling of professionals from other disciplines. There were occasional Egyptological papers. H. Brugsch spoke on the Nubian language and pharaonic quarrying in Wadi Hammamat. A few months before his death, Mariette was made an honorary member alongside de Lesseps and others.[111] The 1888–93 index of the *Bulletin de la Société khédivial géographique* lists five papers on pharaonic and Ptolemaic Egypt out of a total of thirty-two.[112]

108. On the Khedivial Geographical Society see, Donald Malcolm Reid, 'The Egyptian Geographical Society: From Foreign Laymen's Society to Indigenous Professional Association', *Poetics Today* 14 (1993), pp. 539-72.

109. On Abbate and Bonola, see L.A. Balboni, *Gl'Italiani nella civiltà Egiziana de secolo XIX: Storia–biografie–monografie* (3 vols.; Alexandria: V. Penasson, 1906), III, pp. 28-30, 30-34.

110. On Stone, see David Shavit, *The United States in the Middle East: A Historical Dictionary* (New York: Greenwood Press, 1988), p. 337.

111. *Bulletin de la Société khédivial géographique*, no. 8 (May 1880), p. 34.

112. *Bulletin de la Société khédivial géographique*, no. 6 (November 1879), p. 5; no. 8 (May 1880), p. 34; ser. 3, no. 12 (July 1893), pp. 847-49.

Unlike the European-driven Institut d'Egypte and Geographical Society, the Jamiyyat al-Maarif (Society of Knowledge), which was founded with Ismail's blessing in 1868, sprang from local initiative and was not concerned with Egyptology. The *jamiyya* collected subscriptions, bought its own press, and published Arabic and Islamic classics. It fell apart, however, when Ismail won a change in the succession law in favor of his own sons, and several members of the losing court faction had to flee to Istanbul.[113]

9. *Representing Egypt: World's Fair Fantasies of Pharaoh*

In the second half of the nineteenth century, many Westerners got their most vivid impressions of Egypt at world's fairs. Mariette and H. Brugsch played central roles in organizing Egyptian exhibits at several of these celebrations of industrial progress, capitalism, and consumerism. In 1851, London's Great Exhibition of the World's Industry inaugurated these extravaganzas, which the British call universal exhibitions; the French, *expositions universelles;* and Americans, world's fairs. Reaching a far wider public than scholarly societies or museums, these events were part museum, part market, and eventually part amusement park. They also served as either a substitute for or a prelude to foreign travel.

Britain's Royal Society of Arts had displayed manufactured goods at national fairs since 1756, and French national expositions went back to 1797. Prince Albert, president of the Royal Society of Arts, and civil servant and writer Henry Cole moved to an international stage with the Great Exhibition of 1851. Manchester-school free enterprise was riding high, and public subscriptions, private companies, and entry fees paid most of the cost. Conservatives feared popular rowdiness, but working-class 'shilling people' attended quietly in droves. At the opening and closing ceremonies in Joseph Paxton's Crystal Palace of glass and steel, Queen Victoria proceeded to her private lounge down the main axis, receiving the symbolic imperial homage of the strategically situated Indian exhibit at the transept. British displays were spread throughout the building, and other Western nations had their own national courts. The exhibition took in six million visitors in 140 days before closing and moving to Sydenham, where the Crystal Palace exhibits remained until the building burned in 1936. Historicism ran riot in the decorations at Sydenham, with Greek, Roman, Pompeian, Byzantine, Romanesque, Gothic, Renaissance, Chinese, Moorish, Assyrian, and Egyptian courts.[114]

113. Al-Rafii, *Asr Ismail*, I, pp. 242-43.

114. For the exhibitions generally, see *The Books of the Fair: Materials about World's Fairs, 1834–1916, in the Smithsonian Institution Libraries,* intro. Robert W. Rydell, Smithsonian Institution Libraries Research Guide No. 6 (Chicago: American Library Association, 1992). Paul Greenhalgh, *Ephemeral Vistas: The Expositions Universelles, Great Exhibitions, and World's Fairs, 1851–1939* (Studies in Imperialism; Manchester UK: Manchester University Press, 1988), is a useful survey. For colonialist implications, see Timothy Mitchell, 'The World as Exhibition', *Comparative Studies in Society and History* 31 (1989), pp. 217-36; Timothy Mitchell, *Colonising Egypt*

Tunisia and 'Turkey'—as Europeans insisted on calling the Ottoman Empire—sent commissioners to the Great Exhibition,[115] and the shah of Persia came in person. Egyptian exhibits were unofficial. The Ottomans may have discouraged separate Egyptian participation, and Abbas I presumably felt little compulsion to impress the West with antiquities, art, and proofs of progress. The official catalogue began a display on taxidermy and ethnological models with 'Egyptian embalmers'. There were printed books from the Bulaq Press, cloth, saddles, food crops, and slabs of 'Oriental alabaster'. 'It is agriculture and commerce, not manufactures, that nature has assigned to Egypt in the territorial division of labor', intoned the catalogue.[116] Pharaonic antiquity came into its own only with the move to Sydenham. An avenue of lions preceded a Ptolemaic-style temple facade that proclaimed in hieroglyphics that 'in the seventeenth year of the reign of Victoria, the ruler of the waves, this Palace was erected and furnished with a thousand statues, a thousand plants, etc., like as a book for the use of men of all countries'.[117] Joseph Bonomi's stunning replica of two colossal statues from Abu Simbel dominated the Egyptian court (see figures 16 and 17).

France's riposte to the Great Exhibition was Napoleon III's Exposition universelle on the Champ de Mars in 1855. Saint-Simonian Frederic Le Play elaborated a complex sociological scheme for arranging the products of human industry. The death of Prince Albert overshadowed London's second international exhibition in 1862, when Egypt and Japan sent official exhibits for the first time. As Said's commissioner-general for the fair, Mariette sent objects from the collection he was assembling in Bulaq for his as yet unopened museum. Mariette escorted Said to Paris and stayed with him in the Tuileries, then took him on to London to see the exhibition.[118]

(Cambridge Middle East Library; Cambridge UK: Cambridge University Press, 1988); Robert W. Rydell and Nancy Gwinn (eds.), *Fair Representations: World's Fairs and the Modern World* (European Contributions to American Studies, 27; Amsterdam: VU University Press, 1994); and Zeynep Çelik, *Displaying the Orient: Architecture of Islam at Nineteenth-Century World's Fairs* (Comparative Studies on Muslim Societies, 12; Berkeley: University of California Press, 1992). On the Great Exhibition, see *History and Description of the Great Exhibition of the World's Industry* (4 vols.; London: Tallis, 1851); C.R. Fay, *Palace of Industry: A Study of the Great Exhibition and its Fruits* (Cambridge: Cambridge University Press, 1951); Jeffrey A. Auerbach, *The Great Exhibition of 1851: A Nation on Display* (New Haven: Yale University Press, 1999). Owen Jones and Joseph Bonomi, *Description of the Egyptian Court Erected in the Crystal Palace* (London: Crystal Palace Library and Bradbury & Evans, 1854), describe this court at Sydenham.

115. *History and Description of the Great Exhibition*, I, p. 46.

116. *History and Description of the Great Exhibition*, III, p. 150. Vol. III, pp. 147-52, describes the Egyptian section before the move to Syndenham; III, p. 257 mentions the embalmers.

117. As quoted in Nicholas Warner (ed.), *An Egyptian Panorama: Reports from the 19th Century British Press* (Cairo: Zeitouna, 1994), p. 19, from *ILN*, 5 August 1854.

118. David, *Mariette*, pp. 144-46. See also C.J. Campbell, *Campbell's Visitor's Guide to the International Exhibition and Handy Book of London* (London: C.J. Campbell, 1862).

Figure 16. World's fair fantasies of Pharaoh: entrance to the Egyptian Court, Crystal Palace, Sydenham, London, 1854. *ILN*, 5 August 1854, p. 112.

Figure 17. Reproductions of the Abu Simbel colossi of Rameses II, Crystal Palace, Sydenham, London, 1854. Replicas by Joseph Bonomi. *ILN*, 22 July 1854, p. 72.

The Paris Exposition universelle of 1867 was a triumph for Napoleon III, urban renewal maestro Baron Haussmann, Khedive Ismail, and Mariette. This time Le Play had an outer ring of machinery in the main building and an inner ring parading evolutionary progress of civilization from the Stone Age to the present. The Egyptian pavilions, the serail of the bey of Tunis, Turkish baths, an Ottoman kiosk, and a Chinese tea house clustered together in an Oriental section of the park.[119]

Ismail, eager to flaunt his new khedivial title and greater autonomy from Istanbul, enlisted Mariette to organize a striking display. Ancient, medieval, and modern Egypt each had a pavilion, as did de Lesseps's rapidly progressing Suez Canal. Mariette modeled the pharaonic pavilion on Emperor Trajan's kiosk at Philae, with eclectic Old and New Kingdom and Ptolemaic touches thrown in. An avenue of sphinxes led into the pavilion, which boasted the famous diorite statue of Chephren and the wooden 'sheikh al-balad' from the Bulaq Museum.

The ornate Islamic *selamlik*, or men's reception room, was decorated with mosque lamps, a gold crescent at the top, and busts of Ismail. Mahmud al-Falaki had furnished relief maps of ancient and modern Alexandria, and other maps highlighted geology, industry, commerce, and hydrology. A collection of Arabic and Turkish books, mostly printed on the Bulaq Press, represented enlightenment and revival under the reigning dynasty. The third pavilion was a *wikala*, or caravansary, with *mashrabiyya* screens stripped from Cairene houses. Ten painted scenes showed men and women engaged in agriculture and industry. The neopharaonic Suez pavilion had a diorama of the isthmus and relief maps of the canal towns.

What was real and what was showmanship? Egyptian craftsmen, two camels, and two donkeys populated the *wikala*. Khedive Ismail and de Lesseps played themselves in the drama. De Lesseps held court in the Suez pavilion, and Ismail received Napoleon III and Empress Eugénie in the *selamlik*. The empress declined Ismail's present of a luxury *dahabiyya, Daughter of the Nile*, which ended up with Prince Napoleon instead. Although he later attended the Suez Canal ceremonies in Egypt, romantic writer Théophile Gautier declared that his visit to the exposition was his real Egyptian trip. In Paris, Gautier watched the opening of a mummy and saw five hundred skulls that had been removed from

119. On the 1867 exposition, see Auguste Mariette, *Description du parc égyptien: Exposition universelle de 1867* (Paris: Dentu, 1867); Charles Edmond (Karol Edmund Chojecki), *L'Egypte à l'exposition universelle de 1867* (Paris: Dentu, 1867); G. Douin, *Histoire de la règne du Khédive Ismail*, vol. 2: *L'Apogée 1867–1873* (Rome: Istituto poligrafico dello stato per la Reale societá di geografia d'Egitto, 1934), pp. 1-20; Louca, *Voyageurs*, pp. 181-90; and Mehrangiz N. Nikou, 'Egypt's Architectural Representation in the 1867 Paris International Exposition and Napoleon III's Aspiration for a French Arab Kingdom', unpublished paper presented at the convention of the Middle East Studies Association, Orlando, Florida, 16-19 November 2000. Mitchell, *Colonising*, p. 17, notes that Sulayman al-Harayri's *Ard al-Badi' al-Amm* (Paris, 1867) is the first Arabic account of a world exhibition.

mummies and arranged chronologically according to current anthropological theory!

When Empress Eugénie coveted the jewelry of Queen Iahotep and some pharaonic statues, Ismail referred her to Mariette. She offered him directorship of the French imperial press or the Bibliothèque national, a senatorial seat, a conservatorship at the Louvre, or a role in writing her husband's biography of Caesar. At the cost of temporarily forfeiting her favor, Mariette flatly refused to give her any treasures from the Bulaq Museum. Mariette, Ismail, de Lesseps, and Ali Mubarak went back to Egypt with ideas for staging the opening celebration for the Suez Canal two years later.

The festivities Khedive Ismail, de Lesseps, Mariette, and Ali Mubarak staged for the inauguration of the Suez Canal in the fall of 1869 were something of an Egyptian answer to the great exhibitions. Like the fairs, the festivities mobilized state and private resources to impress the world, entailed breakneck construction of ephemeral pavilions, and drew an international cast of stars. Mariette wrote a special guidebook and personally escorted the European royalty on an Upper Egyptian tour. He also proposed the plot for what became Verdi's *Aida*. Drawing on events from Rameses III's reign and patterning costumes after scenes from the pharaoh's tomb, Mariette also personally painted watercolor backdrops for the December 1871 world premier at the Cairo Opera House.[120]

In 1873 Vienna staged the Germanic-speaking world's only major international exposition. Ismail named H. Brugsch, who had helped Mariette at Paris in 1867, Egypt's commissioner-general. Having taken the precaution of sending only reproductions and originals of minor value to the exposition this time, Mariette relaxed as he escorted Habsburg empress Augusta through the Egyptian exhibit. A cholera epidemic turned this world's fair into something of a failure.

Exhibition mania crossed the Atlantic with Philadelphia's Centennial Exhibition of 1876. Smithsonian Institution anthropologists arranged the main building's exhibits on racial lines, with American and British 'Anglo-Saxons', Latins (especially France), and Teutons in prime locations. Denied their own exhibits, American blacks figured in demeaning roles in depictions of the South. Crowds of white ruffians harassed Turkish, Egyptian, Spanish, Japanese, and Chinese visitors.[121] Egypt, Tunisia, and the Ottoman Empire had all scraped up resources for their exhibits despite looming bankruptcy. Brugsch organized the Egyptian exhibit under the slogan 'The Oldest People to the Youngest'. The pavilion had the facade of an ancient temple, and books from the Bulaq Press again suggested modern progress.

120. On *Aida*, see David, *Mariette*, pp. 201-204.

121. Robert W. Rydell, *All the World's a Fair: Visions of Empire at American International Expositions 1876–1916* (Chicago: University of Chicago Press, 1984), pp. 9-32; Ibrahim el Mouelhy, 'L'Egypte à l'exposition de Philadelphie (1876)', *Cahiers d'histoire égyptienne* 1 (1948), pp. 316-26; and Kenneth J. Perkins, 'Three Middle Eastern States Helped America Celebrate its Centennial in Philadelphia', *Aramco World* (November–December 1976), pp. 9-13.

The Paris Exposition universelle of 1878 continued an eleven-year cycle of French fairs that culminated in 1900. Eager to forget for the moment nightmares of the Franco-Prussian War, the Paris Commune, and President MacMahon's attempted coup of 1877, France went all out with a building in the Champ de Mars that covered fifty-four acres. Pavilions in varied styles lined the Avenue des Nations for nearly half a mile. Thirteen million visitors came.[122]

With the Turco-Russian War straining his already exhausted treasury, Ismail almost withdrew from the fair. Mariette's dream of ancient, medieval, and modern pavilions remained only a dream. De Lesseps's Suez Canal Company came through with a neopharaonic pavilion, and Egypt obtained space for modest displays in the Palais Trocadéro. There were copies of tomb scenes from Beni Hasan, a head of Chephren, and a model of ancient artisans' houses. A house facade with *mashrabiyya* balconies, illuminated Qurans, pottery, and swords and armor were classified as medieval. Jewels, rugs, and brocade work were presented as modern—'the country has no industry at all, properly speaking', explained the guidebook.[123] Artifacts and maps boasted of Egypt's annexation of Sudanese Equatoria even as Egypt itself teetered on the brink of Western conquest.

10. *Representing Egyptology: International Congresses of Orientalists*

The transportation and communication revolutions that made world's fairs and Cook's tourism possible also underpinned the international congress movement, which reached its stride in the 1870s. The other prerequisite was networks of national organizations—in this case, Asiatic, Oriental, and geographical societies—that had sprung up since the 1820s. By 1870, national geographical societies, the Asiatic Societies of Paris (1822) and Great Britain and Ireland (1823), and the American (1842) and German (1845) Oriental Societies were all well-established. With its Antiquities Service, Egyptian Museum, Institut égyptien, and Geographical Society, Ismail's Egypt was ready—or at least its European residents were—for the international congress movement.

The idea for an International Congress of Orientalists (ICO) crystallized in the Société d'ethnographie de Paris,[124] and it was in that city that the First ICO assembled in 1873. Egyptology constituted an important section of the meetings for a century after ICO's founding. Twentieth-century usage usually separates 'Egyptology' from 'Orientalism', although institutions like the American Oriental Society, the Institut français d'archéologie orientale du Caire (IFAO),

122. Auguste Mariette-Bey, *Exposition universelle de Paris 1878: La galerie de l'Egypte ancienne à l'exposition rétrospective du Trocadéro* (Paris: F. Pichon, 1878); Louca, *Voyageurs*, pp. 190-92.

123. Mitchell, *Colonising*, pp. 8-9.

124. K. Vollers, 'Le IXme congrès international des orientalistes tenu à Londres du 5 au 12 septembre 1892', *BIE*, ser. 3, 3 (November 1892), p. 193.

and the University of Chicago's Oriental Institute keep the older overlapping terminology alive. In 1973, Egyptologists seceded from the International Congress of Orientalists, which itself bowed to changing times by renaming itself the International Congress of Asian and North African Studies.

'Orientalist', in the sense of one versed in Oriental languages and literatures, first appeared in English in 1781. 'Egyptologist' did not appear until 1859 and only became common in the 1870s, when the field began to set itself apart as a distinct discipline.[125]

Around the middle of the nineteenth century, European Egyptologists working in Egypt began to change their habits of dress. Pioneer Orientalists-Egyptologists Champollion, Rosellini, Wilkinson, Lane, and Prisse d'Avennes wore beards and Turkish garb. This was useful, protective coloration in their day, although when they displayed themselves in such garb back home, other questions about identity, disguise, and claims of expertise on foreign cultures came into play. As Egyptology became a distinct discipline, and Western ascendancy in Egypt grew, Egyptologists like Maspero and Petrie no longer presented themselves in 'Oriental' dress. Egyptologists did not need fluent Arabic to establish their credentials. Orientalists, however, who sometimes tested themselves by trying to disappear temporarily into a still-living 'other' society, kept the urge to disguise longer.

A disquieting note on definitions: Egyptology was, and still is, the study of ancient Egypt. This definition implicitly slights Islamic and modern Egypt. Another Western trope that emphasizes continuity rather than discontinuity in Egypt is also unsettling—the assumption that quintessential fellahin have not changed since ancient times. This assumes an unchanging Orient juxtaposed to an evolving, dynamic West. This seems to be the implication of an Orientalist photograph posing a fellah with his head tilted to resemble a just-excavated mummy at Thebes (see figure 18).

The First International Congress of Orientalists in Paris in 1873 included seven papers on Egyptology and one on Coptic studies. Seven of the eight presenters were French, including Maspero and Chabas; the eighth was Samuel Birch. German troops still occupied French soil until 16 September 1873, so the hosts were in no mood for papers by Germans. Thirty-five Germans nevertheless subscribed to the congress (not all of the 1,064 'subscribers' attended), and Lepsius spoke up from the floor. Khedive Ismail, Mahmud al-Falaki, Yaqub Artin, and six other Egyptians were among the twenty subscribers listed from Egypt. Three of the eleven others were Egyptologists—Mariette, H. Brugsch, and Albert Daninos. Curiously, Schweinfurth was listed as representing the Khedivial Geographical Society, which had not yet been founded.[126]

125. *OED*^{2}, X, p. 931; V, p. 97.

126. *Mémoires du congrès international des Orientalistes, 1re session, Paris* (3 vols.; Paris: Maisonneuve, 1873–76) (hereafter, *ICO1*, Paris, etc.), I, pp. 114-15; III, pp. cvii, cxxxviii-xi, 42-43. Unless otherwise specified, references to ICOs come from the proceedings of the congresses for the years cited. Title and language vary with host city.

Figure 18. Unchanging Egypt? An Orientalist whimsy. 'Momies trouvées dans un tombeau à Thebes', photograph by Félix Bonfils, 1878. Courtesy of the Bibliothèque nationale de France, Paris. Jean-Claude Simoën, *Egypte éternelle* (1993), p. 104, gives the photograph's date as 1860.

Scholars disagree on Egyptian reactions to representations of their country at world's fairs and International Orientalist Congresses. Timothy Mitchell, using a Saidian or postmodern approach, emphasizes Egyptian dismay and embarrassment, while Carter Findley finds Egyptian and Ottoman reactions more positive and nuanced. Mitchell and Findley draw their main evidence from the ICO held jointly in Stockholm and Christiania (now Oslo) and the Paris Exposition universelle of 1889, which falls in the period taken up in chapter 6.[127]

Already at the first ICO, an energetic Japanese scholar blurred the categories for anyone who presumed that only Western Orientalists were qualified to dis-

127. Reid, *Whose Pharaohs?*, pp. 213-57; Louca, *Voyageurs*, pp. 181–208; Mitchell, *Colonising*, pp. 1-2, 180-81; Carter Findley, 'Ottoman Occidentalist', *American Historical Review* 103 (1998), pp. 15-49.

cuss 'Orientals'. The Persian ambassador, General Nazar Aga, lauded Orientalists for discovering that the language of Firdawsi, Cyrus, Darius, and Xerxes was kin to those of Europe. 'Thanks to the progress of comparative philology', he effused, 'Persians can today say—what they had not suspected—that they belong to the same race as the Europeans, that they are brothers to the noble nation which inaugurated this year the grand and magnificent international work of the Congress of Orientalists'.[128]

Egyptologist Samuel Birch took the chair at the Second International Congress of Orientalists in London in 1874 (see table 4 and figure 19).[129] Mixing imperial pride and scholarly internationalism, he pronounced London

128. *ICO1*, Paris, II, p. 315. For the Japanese scholar, see II, pp. 111 ff.

129.

Table 4. *World's Fairs and International Congresses, 1851–82*

Date	World's Fairs	Geographical Congresses	Orientalist Congresses	Other Congresses
1851	London			1. Sanitary, Paris
1853				1. Statistical, Brussels
1855	Paris			
1862	London			
1863				Red Cross, Geneva
1865				1. Telegraphic Union, Paris
1866				1. Anthropology and Prehistoric Archaeology, Neuchatel
1867	Paris			2. Sanitary, Istanbul
1870				
1871				
1872		1. Antwerp		
1873	Vienna		1. Paris	1. Postal Union, Bern
1874			2. London	
1875		2. Paris		
1876	Philadelphia		3. St. Petersburg	
1877				
1878	Paris		4. Florence	
1881		3. Venice	5. Berlin	
1882				

Reid, *Whose Pharaohs?*, p. 304. Sources: International Geographical Union, Commission on History of Geographic Thought, *Geography through a Century of International Congresses*

> distinguished for its extent as well as for its devotion to the study of the East, and connected by a thousand ties, the interests of commerce, the spread of civilization, missionary labors, and the duties of governing Oriental Dependencies of various tongues and sites in the East...
>
> Orientalists, too, are all, so to say, men born of the same family...as students, all the distinctions of race, creed, and nationality disappear or are forgotten. Even criticism ought neither to be nor become personal, in as much as Science places for its object the highest scope of the mind—truth, which is in most cases difficult to find, and no reproach to miss.[130]

Alongside the Archaeological and Ethnological sections, Semitic, Hamitic, Turanian, and Aryan sections reflected prevailing linguistic-racial categories. Birch announced: 'The Hamitic Section will represent the progress made in Egyptology since the first discovery of the mode of deciphering and reading this pictorial language of Ancient Egypt in 1817'.[131] The date implied recognition of Thomas Young and a swipe at Champollion, but no Frenchmen were present to protest. Lepsius and five other Germans dominated the Egyptology section as thoroughly as the French had in Paris the year before. H. Brugsch officially represented Egypt. Birch, still the lone British Egyptologist presenting, invited his seven colleagues to a workshop at his home.[132]

The Third International Congress of Orientalists moved east in 1876 to Saint Petersburg. Mariette represented Egypt as a corresponding member of the organizing committee. At the Fourth International Congress of Orientalists in Florence in 1878, Franco-German rivalry was muted. Maspero chaired the 'Egyptology and African Languages section', which in practice included only Egypt. A German, a Swiss (Naville), and two Italians (one was Ernesto Schiaparelli) read papers, but no Egyptian or foreign resident of Egypt did so.[133]

(Caen: International Geographical Union, 1972); the proceedings of the various International Congresses of Orientalists; Henry Richard Tedder, 'Societies, Learned', in *EB*[11], XXV, pp. 309-19; F.S.L. Lyons, *Internationalism in Europe 1815–1914* (Aspects européens, 14. Série C. Etudes politiques; Leiden: Sijthoff, 1963). Note: numbers before city names indicate the number within that series of congresses.

130. Samuel Birch, 'Inaugural Address', *ICO2*, London, *Transactions*, pp. 1-3.

131. Birch, 'Inaugural Address', p. 13.

132. The eighth person was Jens Lieblein, a Norwegian. *ICO2*, London, *Report* (1874), p. 57; *WWWE*3, p. 255.

133. *ICO3*, Saint Petersburg, *Travaux*, II, p. xvi; *ICO4*, Florence, *Congresso*, I, pp. 1 ff., II, pp. 338-44, 355.

Figure 19. An 'Oriental' at the International Congress of Orientalists, London, 1874. Samuel Birch explains the Rosetta Stone to Western scholars as a beturbaned man looks on. *ILN*, 26 September 1874, p. 292.

Thus, down to the British occupation in 1882, international congresses of Orientalists provided the emerging discipline of Egyptology an important forum. With specialists of the caliber of Maspero, Birch, Lepsius, and Brugsch setting the tone, few amateurs ventured papers. Franco-German rivalry was pervasive, on stage and off. Egyptians lacked a voice in the ICO's Egyptology section; there were as yet no Egyptian Egyptologists.

11. *The Gathering Storm: Ismail and Mariette in the 1870s*

Mariette and Ismail both celebrated triumphs early and later endured many tribulations. How could one top discovering the Serapeum, founding the Antiquities Service and Egyptian Museum, orchestrating the sensational Egyptian display at the Paris Exposition universelle of 1867, or opening the Suez Canal? The tragedies in the archaeologist's private life were appalling. Cholera carried off his wife in 1865, six of their ten children died before him, and he fought diabetes for years before it killed him.[134]

Mariette's job was never secure. 'For better or worse', as one Frenchman put it, 'Mariette Bey is part of the viceregal household, on a level with the head of the stables and the chief black eunuque. One has an Egyptologist in the way

134. See the family tree in David, *Mariette*, pp. 274.

that one's forebears had an astrologist, a master of parades, awkwardly placed between the fool and the physician'.[135] Not until 1883, after Mariette's death and the beginning of the British occupation, did inclusion of the Antiquities Service in the Ministry of Public Works end its precarious dependence on khedivial goodwill.

Mariette's rivals whispered that he was merely an agent of French control, secretly sold antiquities, and was assembling the Bulaq collection only to advance his personal fortunes. Briefly heeding the slander, Ismail took back Mariette's steamboat and revoked his right to corvée.[136] Mariette soon got the steamboat back, but with a leaner budget and without the right of corvée. By 1867 he had funds only to pay several hundred laborers.

By 1873 there was almost no money for excavation, and none for publications or museum expansion. Mariette's salary was in arrears, and he again temporarily lost his steamboat. He wrote a popular book, *Itinéraire de la haute Egypte* (2 vols., 1878–80), to pay the bills. In 1878, the French minister of public works in Nubar's cabinet squeezed out £E1,000 for Mariette's most pressing excavation and surveillance needs, and the French Ministry of Public Instruction contributed an emergency subvention of 10,000 francs.[137]

Mariette's publication dreams were as gargantuan as his initial Antiquities Service excavations, but most fell through for want of funds and time. Excavation, museum work, travel, planning world's fairs, escorting famous visitors, and ventures into diplomacy left little time for scholarship. Devéria's early death deprived him of much-needed assistance with the publication of inscriptions.

Ignoring looming bankruptcy, the government let bids in March 1873 for the foundations of a great new museum on Gezira. The work was to be finished by 1 October at the cost of 186,000 francs. In Paris, the Académie des inscriptions et belles lettres set a prize of twenty thousand francs for a design of the facade. After news of the true state of Egyptian finances broke that summer during the Vienna Exposition, the proposed new museum—like the School of Egyptology—disappeared from view.[138]

According to Cromer, 'The nadir both of financial chaos and of popular misery was reached in the summer and autumn of 1878'.[139] France and Britain stripped Ismail of his family estates and forced him to install Nubar as prime minister, with a Briton at finance and a Frenchman at public works. The Nile flood that reduced some peasants to starvation rampaged through the Bulaq Museum and Mariette's living quarters in October 1878, destroying or damaging books, manuscripts, squeezes, and antiquities. A proposal to move the

135. Quoted in David, *Mariette*, pp. 233–34.

136. Maspero, 'Mariette', p. xcliii.

137. Maspero, 'Mariette', pp. ccii, ccxiii.

138. Maspero, 'Mariette', pp. cxccvi-cxccvii.

139. Earl of Cromer, *Modern Egypt* (2 vols.; New York: Macmillan, 1908), I, p. 28.

museum to the unfinished Girls School building in the compound of the Ministry of Public Works—apparently the quarters the Institut égyptien obtained in 1880—remained a dead letter.

In the summer of 1879, Britain and France forced Sultan Abdulhamid II to depose Ismail in favor of his son Tawfiq. Mariette doggedly cleaned and repaired the Bulaq premises and in 1880 reopened the museum. He was not quite sixty when he died of diabetes in January 1881, a year and a half before the Urabi revolution precipitated the British occupation. His last years did have a few bright spots, such as election in 1878 to the Académie des inscriptions et belles lettres and becoming a pasha on 5 June 1879, just weeks before Ismail's deposition. On Mariette's deathbed, the Brugsch brothers told him of the wonderful pyramid texts in the pyramid of Unas at Saqqara.

The flamboyant age of Ismail and Mariette was over. After the turbulent ensuing year of the Urabi revolution and the British conquest, Cromer and Maspero, with the independent-minded Petrie in the wings, would work out new parameters for Egyptian archaeology under colonial rule. Anglo-French rivalry in Egypt entered a new stage, with France on the defensive in archaeology and elsewhere. With al-Tahtawi dead, Ahmad Kamal and several colleagues took up the uphill battle to establish an Egyptian Egyptology.

Mari and the Holy Grail

Jack M. Sasson

The news from Mari, as all of you know, has never failed to be less than interesting, ever since the French dug at Tell Hariri in the early 1930s and resurrected Mari. Especially in the past two decades, however, the news from Mari has become positively spectacular. In fact, with practically no exception, Mari documentation—not to say also the archaeology of Mari—is now the most densely published in cuneiform scholarship. So, with information on Mari readily available, why would someone like me pontificate before specialists like you on Mari and what it might mean for our studies?

Inquiring into this question, in fact, lies at the heart of my presentation. Keeping in mind the old adage that history—political, cultural, religious, or the like—is seldom written or read in a vacuum, I want to describe to you what Mari meant to the generations immediately after its discovery and tell you what it has come to mean in recent times. Naturally enough, given our Society of Biblical Literature hospices, I will focus on the reciprocal stimulation between Mari and the Bible. In the process, I will share with you some details about recent discussions, in the hopes of steering you towards archives that are a mother-lode for research. So let me tackle the story.

1. *Resurrecting Mari*

The French had earned the right to excavate Mari because just after World War I they had quickly snuffed out a native push for independence, keeping Syria under mandate until 1945. A year after the Second World War, the French left Syria but continued control over the archaeology and epigraphy of Mari. Despite regional conflicts, their stewardship has proven productive and, within reason, fair.

Excavations began exactly 70 years ago in December 1933, with almost instantaneous discoveries. The first campaigns were not particularly scientific: tablets were removed with scarcely any inventory taken at the field; tablets were baked at the grounds, some of them fracturing into pieces; no epigrapher stood by until the 5th campaign. The harvest was rich and in 1935 and 1936 Thureau-Dangin and his team offered samples that created a fuss. An inscription found *in situ* delivered the ancient name of the city, but scholarship being also an exercise in tenacity, the dispute about the location of Mari continued. Some were sure that Mari should be in the Upper Euphrates or near Elam. I.J. Gelb was dismissive, writing in 1935, 'In my opinion the identification of Mari with Tell el-Hariri, or any other single site, is of the same value as the identification of ancient Latium with modern Tivoli or Frascati.'[1]

In 1937, Thureau-Dangin cited textual evidence for making Hammurabi a younger contemporary of Samsi-Addu I. At once the lawmaker dropped about three centuries from his previous chronological perch, and with enormous consequences.[2] Albright quickly placed Hammurabi around 1800 BCE and Sidney Smith gave him the familiar but hardly plausible middle chronology slot of 1792–1750 BCE.[3] Also in 1937, Georges Dossin excerpted a now famous passage (from A.482) that detailed the power balance of the time:

> There is no king who, just by himself, is truly powerful. From ten to fifteen kings follow Hammurabi of Babylon, as many do Rīm-Sîn of Larsa, as many Ibāl-pî-El of Ešnunna, as many Amūd-pî-El of Qaṭna; twenty kings follow Yarim-Lim of Yamḫad [Aleppo].[4]

Dossin also cited A.186, in which a prince from Ugarit asks to visit Mari, effectively bridging two cultures in Canaan and Mesopotamia that heretofore had not been deemed a unity.[5] In those days, folks differentiated between Amorites, individuals styled MAR.TU in Ur III texts, and East Canaanites, individuals recorded in Old Babylonian tablets without the label MAR.TU. The last were themselves distinguished from the Canaanites we know and love from the Bible. Mari onomastics cast powerful doubt on the distinctions, but they did not completely die until 1968, when Gelb published an Old Babylonian text from Tell Asmar (Ešnunna) with oodles of West Semites labeled MAR.TU.[6]

1. I.J. Gelb, 'Mari', *AJSLL* 52 (1935), pp. 43-44 (43).

2. F. Thureau-Dangin, 'Iasmaḫ-Adad', *RA* 34 (1937), pp. 135-39.

3. Overview in O. Neugebauer, 'The Chronology of the Hammurabi Age', *JAOS* 61 (1941), pp. 58-61.

4. Georges Dossin, 'Les archives épistolaires du palais de Mari', *Syria* 19 (1938), pp. 105-25 (117) [= *Recueil Georges Dossin: Mélanges d'assyriologie, 1934–1959* (*Akkadica.* Supplementum, 1; Leuven: Peeters, 1983), p. 102-32 (114)]. See the comments of Bertrand Lafont, 'Relations internationales, alliances et diplomatie au temps des royaumes amorrites: Essai de synthèse', in *Mari, Ebla, et les Hourrites: Dix ans de travaux, deuxième partie: Actes du colloque international (Paris, mai 1993)* (ed. Jean-Marie Durand and Dominique Charpin; Amurru, 2; Paris: Éditions Recherche sur les civilisations, 2001), pp. 213-328 (222-24).

5. G. Dossin, 'La correspondance de Zimrilim, dernier roi de Mari (vers 2000 avant J.-C.)', in *Comptes-rendus des séances de l'Académie des Inscriptions et Belles-Lettres, année 1937* (Paris: Auguste Picard, 1937), pp. 12-20.

6. I.J. Gelb, 'An Old Babylonian List of Amorites', *JAOS* 88 (1968), pp. 39-46. See also William L. Moran, 'The Hebrew Language in its Northwest Semitic Background', in *The Bible and the Ancient Near East: Essays in Honor of William Foxwell Albright* (ed. G. Ernest Wright; New York: Doubleday, 1961), pp. 59-84.

2. *Mari and the Bible*

To get back to our story: On the eve of World War II, Mari and its archives were making waves, but the discussion remained largely within the confine of Assyriology even if many of its practitioners were more savvy about the Hebrew Bible than most of us. One reason was that despite the rich serving of appetizers, few Mari documents were published in any density. Another reason is that there was an overload of resources, from Ugarit, Alalakh, and Nuzi, that kept the attention of the biblicists fixed elsewhere.

In Europe, the Mari tablets inspired Assyriologists toward a richer tableau of Akkadian culture. But in America, where James Henry Breasted was finding internationalism in the 'Fertile Crescent' of the Amarna Age, such scholars as Ephraim A. Speiser and Cyrus H. Gordon busily drew on social practices displayed in the Nuzi tablets to authenticate a Late Bronze setting for the patriarchs. But the regional dominance of the Amorites that Mari was describing encouraged a few scholars to embed Abraham within their bosom. Albrightianism, by which I mean the drive to privilege historical research in authenticating biblical events, predated Albright of course, especially among Protestants for whom Genesis 14 had become the link with true history. Albright himself readily jettisoned his old reliance on the Hyksos as guide to dating the patriarchs. Increasingly, he favored the age of Hammurabi as a setting. But in his long career he proved restless in making equations between historical personalities and the names of Eastern kings 'recorded' in Genesis 14. As with others (for example Böhl)[7] Albright identified Arioch of Ellasar with a vassal of Zimri-Lim named Ariyyuk, and was willing to find an Elamite equivalent to Chedorlaomer.[8] Interestingly enough, in his last years, when he had donkey caravaneering on his mind, Albright eschewed a facile correspondence between Amraphel of Shinar and Hammurabi of Babylon, or even with Amūd-pî-El of Qaṭna, both within linguistic contortion. Rather, he connected the latter with Emudbal, allegedy Yamud-pala, the latter not a king but a region frequently mentioned in Mari and other Old Babylonian texts.[9]

7. F.M.Th. Böhl, *King Hammurabi of Babylon in the Setting of his Time (about 1700 B.C.)* (Amsterdam: Noord-Hollandsche uitgevers maatschappij, 1946), p. 17; see W.F. Albright's review in *BO* 5 (1948), pp. 125-27.

8. Parenthetically, now that we have this vassal's dossier (see ARM, XXVIII, textes 153-57), he has proven to be a minor scrambler who sold his allegiance to the lowest bidder, not at all what we consider a major player. Still, Dominique Charpin and Nele Ziegler have this to say, 'Il ne me semble pas exclu qu'Ariyôk soit à identifier à Arriyuk, un lieutenant des Élamites qui finit par devenir roi au nord-est du Sindjar et…se rallia finalement à Zimri-Lim'; *Mari et le Proche-Orient à l'époque amorrite: Essai d'histoire politique* (Florilegium marianum, 5; Mémoires de N.A.B.U., 6; Paris: SEPOA, 2003), p. 226.

9. W.F. Albright, *Yahweh and the Gods of Canaan: A Historical Analysis of Two Contrasting Faiths* (Winona Lake, IN: Eisenbrauns 1990 [1968]), pp. 68-69 n. 37; see his 'Abram the

After the war, the publication of Mari documents began in earnest. Because they were in autograph copies, widespread knowledge of the contents of the letters did not come until they were transliterated and translated. For the purpose of our story, however, the stunner came in 1948 when Dossin published the first of a stream of letters from dreamers and prophets, in which the will of the gods was communicated to Zimri-Lim.[10] While Mari was by no means the first to give evidence of such manifestations, the wealth as well as the antiquity of the material from Mari simply gave proof of the special connection between Mari and the Bible, intensifying inspection of the archives for more evidence of the same.

So during the 1950s and 1960s occurred the greatest conjunctions between Mari and the Bible, with many fine scholars participating in the proposed equations. Mari documents streamed forth, albeit at a sane pace, with good commentaries by Maurice Birot, Jean Bottéro, Georges Boyer, and Madeleine Lurton Burke, and their works helped unlock many mysteries behind the social, economic, and palatial systems at work. Administrative texts gave backbones to the testimony of letters, confirming the broad network of political connections that included such Mediterranean towns as Hazor, Ugarit, Ṭūba, and Qaṭna. Still, because in those years we had but the grossest chronologies internal to the reigns of Mari kings, choreographing the great events mentioned in the texts was an adventure of the greatest imagination. Elsewhere, I have written how in those year we crafted a life for Zimri-Lim that made of him a *juste souffrant*, a portrait that was so sentimentally verisimilar that we have a hard time parting from it ever since.[11]

Some remarkable works helped ease the linkage between Mari and the Bible. Unsung is the great achievement of Bottéro and André Finet who in 1954 jointly produced ARMT, XV, full of indexes and rich in lexicographic and grammatical details that permitted access to Mari's vast rich resources.[12] In the same year Bottéro edited a *Rencontre assyriologique internationale* volume on the *Ḫabirus*.[13] He cited Mari material that forced their connection with the Hebrew back into the Middle Bronze Age. Most influential was Jean-Robert Kupper's 1957 book on the nomads in the Mari age.[14] Though occasionally

Hebrew: A New Archaeological Interpretation', *BASOR* 163 (1961), pp. 36-54, especially pp. 49-50.

10. G. Dossin, 'Une révélation du dieu Dagan à Terqa', *RA* 42 (1948), pp. 125-34 [= *Recueil Georges Dossin*, pp. 169-79].

11. J.M. Sasson, 'The King and I: A Mari King in Changing Perceptions', *JAOS* 118 (1998), pp. 453-70.

12. Jean Bottéro and André Finet, *Répertoire analytique des tomes I à V* (ARM, XV; Paris: Imprimerie nationale, 1954).

13. J. Bottéro, *Le problème des Ḫabiru à la IVe Rencontre assyriologique internationale* (Paris: Imprimerie nationale, 1954).

14. Jean-Robert Kupper, *Les nomades en Mésopotamie au temps des rois de Mari* (Biblio-

misread and its subtleties commonly missed, Kupper's book gave impetus to a wide discussion on second millennium nomadism. So many tribes roaming in and around the river valleys, including the Balikh where Israel had set the origins of its ancestry simply invited biblical comparison. Parrot could imagine tribal descendents of Terah and Abraham halting by Mari on their way from Ur and Ḫarrān and Albright could muse about Israel's ancestors founding Hammurabi's dynasty.[15] Quickly the range of comparisons became established: linguistic studies of West Semitic names; analysis of Upper Mesopotamian place names; variety of nomadic experience; vocabulary for ethnic and kinship identity; the office of judges; the types of sacrifice, especially of donkeys; bans on spoils and (alleged) sins on census-taking; fixing of patrimony, and, never least, prophetism and its impact on affairs of state and of faith. Yahweh and his origins were issues that also periodically surfaced.[16] In all this, none but the most Scripture-committed ever drew direct historical inferences; but the implications of the exercises were never lost. So, as we entered the 1970s, Mari had become a backdrop for buttressing the legitimacy, even the validity, of Hebrew traditions; not through direct historical synchronism mind you, but in the same way as Ugarit helped to chart the rise of monotheism or Nuzi helped to explain such social oddities as husbands and wives who could label themselves 'brothers and sisters.'

3. *The Historicity of the Patriarchs*

1971 was calamitous for our field, for among the great scholars who died then were William Foxwell Albright and Roland de Vaux. Their deaths robbed scholarship of broad knowledge, dominant convictions, and sustained lobbying for comparative research. Within a few years the historical constructs they worked for (or against) faced multiple challenges. Books by John Van Seters and Thomas L. Thompson in the mid-1970s are generally credited with compromising Albrightianism; but in fact paradigmatic shifts were weakening reliance on historical research. In the wake of global wars, history came to be mistrusted as an instrument for political, social, class, and gender abuse. History was no longer charted linearly and progressively, but fractured into a kaleidoscope of visions and perspectives. The consequences were more rapid and drastic for Israel than for allied fields, probably because solid evidence for the

thèque de la faculté de philosophie et lettres de l'Université de Liège, 142; Paris: Société d'Edition «Les Belles Lettres», 1957).

15. André Parrot, 'La vie d'un chef d'état au IIe millénaire', in *Institut de France: Séance publique annuelle mardi 25 octobre 1966* (Paris: Firmin-Didot et Cie, 1966), pp. 3-11 (8); Albright, *Yahweh and the Gods of Canaan*, p. 81.

16. See, most forcefully, A. Finet, 'Yahvé au royaume de Mari', in *Circulation des monnaies, des marchandises et des biens* (ed. Rika Gyselen; Res orientales, 5; Bures-sur-Yvette: Groupe pour l'étude de la civilisation du moyen-orient, 1993), pp. 15-22.

historicity of its traditions was never quite there, tools had been imported from other disciplines, methodologies were in dispute, and, above all, motivations remained suspect. As a result in the final quarter of the twentieth century people in droves abandoned researching biblical history in favor of biblical historiography. Despite the tom-tom beats of the *Biblical Archaeology Review*, the discussion since then on where Hebrew traditions and controllable history meet has continued to slip and the skirmishes for a demarcation line are now joining deep into the Monarchic period.

4. *Mari without Patriarchs*

Interestingly enough, during the same two decades, knowledge of Mari became more historically reliable and intricate. In 1978, Birot established a sequence for the year-date formulas of Zimri-Lim and so allowed us to reconstruct a more trustworthy formulation of events, each with its background and aftermath.[17] When Jean-Marie Durand took over care-taking the archives in 1981, he brought into being a team of incredibly dedicated and hard-working French scholars. Mari research became better focused, better published, and better integrated with the information that was spilling forth from contemporaneous archives, such as those form Tell Šimšāra (Šušarrā), Rimah (Qaṭṭara), Tell Leilān (Šubat-Enlil), Chagar Bazar, Tell al-ʿAšāra (Terqa), and Tell Biʿa (Tuttul). True enough, the change was so sudden and the material so dense that until recently few outside the team have kept a sustained familiarly with it. The textual results have appeared in a rich assortment of journals, contributions to *Festschriften* and specialized studies; but if you are seeking a single source to give you a broad perspective on what Mari is now about, you cannot do better than Durand's three volumes in the series *Littérature du Proche-Orient*, with translations of almost 2000 collated letters and with generous if also idiosyncratic comments and overviews: a masterpiece of the genre.[18]

So what have we learned about Mari in the recent decades? The range of textual material has not expanded much, in that it remains overwhelmingly administrative and epistolary, with pockets of cultic and juridical texts. True, we do have now the earliest examples of treaties and can follow in detail the intricate processes by which they were formulated and put into effect.[19] Still unpublished but cited in fragments is also the earliest attested royal epic, this one honoring Zimri-Lim, written seconds after he took over the throne, and so proving that sycophants could also have a taste for literature.[20] Reports are that a library of

17. M. Birot, 'Données nouvelles sur la chronologie du règne de Zimri-Lim', *Syria* 55 (1978), pp. 333-43.

18. J.-M. Durand, *Les documents épistolaires du palais de Mari* (3 vols.; LAPO, 16-18; Paris: Les Éditions du Cerf, 1997–2000).

19. See Lafont, 'Relations internationales', pp. 213-328.

20. The epic is as yet unpublished; but some of its lines have been cited in diverse publica-

learned scribes has been found; but with nothing yet published, we still miss having the practical compilations that explain how to read the omens, understand words, make beer, prepare perfume, heal the sick, cure animals, or succeed in love—the last genre most missed.[21]

In all other ways, however, our knowledge of the Mari age has deepened. We now know better how the palace functioned and have recovered intimate details about the world of women within it. We have a pretty good handle on the major moments in the reigns of successive kings, even in we cannot always grasp the motivations behind their political maneuverings.[22] We have learned much about the operation of kingship, at least during the Zimri-Lim period, and can reconstruct his activities for good chunks of his reign.[23] We now know how he came to power (by first conquering Tuttul) and how he maintained it, via alliances, diplomatic marriages, wars, bribery, consultation with the gods, travel to such distant places as Ugarit, and a generous table where loyalty was forged and maintained.[24] Although we lack introspective comments from Zimri-Lim, Samsi-Addu, Yasmaḫ-Addu and Išme-Dagan, or any other ruler of the time, each nevertheless acquires personality through the countless messages they received and penned and we can now deliver psychological profiles about their hopes and fears. The great law-giver himself, Hammurabi of Babylon, is now an individual for the many personal quirks he displays and Yarim-Lim of Yamḫad reveals the profound insight into providence and destiny that is so well exposed in the Bible.[25]

Among the more enriching recoveries from recent publications from Mari is the world of statecraft and diplomacy as reflected in the archives. Old Babylonian diplomacy was a major tool of expansion and confirmation of power, obeying a Byzantine etiquette for acceptable behavior. [26] How Zimri-Lim's

tions. A helpful compilation is now available in Nathan Wasserman, *Style and Form in Old-Babylonian Literary Texts* (Cuneiform Monographs, 27; Leiden: Brill and Styx, 2003), p. 189.

21. My opinion is that divination as practiced in Mari was learned practically and did not depend on learned texts; see Sasson, 'About "Mari and the Bible" ', *RA* 92 (1998), pp. 91-123 (118-19).

22. See now Charpin and Ziegler, *Mari et le Proche-Orient à l'époque amorrite*.

23. Aside from the study of Charpin and Ziegler, cited above, see Sasson, 'The King and I', pp. 453-70.

24. On this last topic see J.M. Sasson, 'The King's Table: Food and Fealty in Old Babylonian Mari', in *Food and Identity in the Ancient World* (ed. Cristiano Grottanelli and Lucio Milano; History of the Ancient Near East. Studies, 9; Padua: S.A.R.G.O.N. Editrice e Libreria, 2004), pp. 179-215.

25. On Hammurabi, see now D. Charpin, *Hammu-rabi de Babylone* (Paris: Presses universitaires de France, 2003) and Marc van de Mieroop, *King Hammurabi of Babylon: A Biography* (Blackwell Ancient Lives; London: Blackwell Publishing, 2004). On Yarim-Lim, see Robert M. Whiting, 'Amorite Tribes and Nations of Second-Millennium Western Asia', in *CANE*, II, pp. 1231-42 (1237).

26. Bertrand Lafont, 'International Relations in the Ancient Near East: The Birth of a Complete Diplomatic System', *Diplomacy and Statecraft* 12 (2001), pp. 39-60.

diplomats almost botched the purchase of land near Alalakh in Northwest Syria is one of the most wonderful of the dossiers recently published.[27] Mari vassals and ambassadors, we have discovered, can be exceptionally garrulous, their prose matching well with what we find in biblical narratives, both sharing lively phrasing, vivid pacing, and fine sense of structure. I truly believe that in this shared feeling for words we bring Mari and the Bible to some of their closest proximities. We cannot but be impressed by the literary instinct (whether the speaker's or the scribe's) that is displayed in such evocative passages as when a vassal reminds Zimri-Lim of the conversations they had long ago in the gardens of Carchemish.[28] Or when: a diplomat (Buqāqum) feeds Zimri-Lim salacious tidbits about the wife of another leader (ARM, XXVI, 488); a majordomo gingerly reports on a Qaṭna princess dancing herself sick under a brutal mid-day sun (ARM, XXVI, 318) advisers brutally remind a neglectful king that rivers cannot reverse death that comes from thirst (ARM, XXVI, 171.14-15); a chieftain gives three different accounts on the death of an enemy just to drive home a lesson on theodicy.[29] I could go on, but let me come back to the main thread of this presentation.

We have seen how for the past couple of decades 'Mari and the Bible' have missed making the best conjunctions. True, such veteran scholars as Abraham Malamat or Moshe Anbar never lost their keen interest in finding parallels between the two corpora on in reporting on Mari's connection with Western Asia. Truth to tell, however, while the majority of biblical scholars has simply not kept up with the dramatic reshaping of our knowledge about Mari, members of the Mari team have trained as historians rather than as biblical scholars or as semiticists; until very recently for the most part, they have shown little interest in biblical research. Still, something interesting has happened in the past decade and I devote my final remarks to it.

5. *Renewed Connections*

In 1983, the new Mari *équipe* held a colloquium on the occasion of Mari's fiftieth resurrection.[30] The program was hard-core Mariology, with only one paper, by André Lemaire, reviewing what could be said about Mari and the Bible.

27. J.-M. Durand, *Le culte d'Addu d'Alep et l'affaire d'Alahtum* (Florilegium marianum, 7; Mémoires de N.A.B.U., 8; Paris: SEPOA, 2002); .J.M. Sasson, 'The Trouble with Nūr-Sin: Zimri-Lim's Purchase ofAlahtum'; forthcoming contribution to a Festschrift.

28. J.-R. Kupper, 'Dans les jardins de Carkémish...', in *Recueil d'études à la mémoire d'André Parrot* (ed. D. Charpin and J.-M. Durand; Florilegium marianum, 6; Mémoires de N.A.B.U., 7; Paris: SEPOA, 2002), pp. 195-200.

29. J.M. Sasson, 'On Reading the Diplomatic Letters in the Mari Archives', in *Mari, Ébla, et les Hourrites* (Amurru, 2), pp. 329-38.

30. Proceedings published as Actes du colloque internationale du C.N.R.S. 620, 'A propos d'un cinquantenaire: Mari, bilan et perspectives' (Strasbourg, 29, 30 juin, 1er juillet 1983), J.-M. Durand and J.-Cl. Margueron (edn), in *MARI* 4 (1985).

(At that stage, not an enormous amount was new, except for Lemaire's linkage to the Hebrew phenomenon via the Arameans of the Late Bronze Age.[31]) Ten years later, in 1993, another colloquium was mounted by the team, accentuating correspondences in trans-Euphratene Syria and upper Mesopotamia.[32] Again, Lemaire was alone with a biblical topic, not surprisingly, on prophecy.[33] Within four years, however, in 1997, the *équipe* held a 'table ronde' on 'Amorite traditions and the Bible', the papers for which were published a couple of years later in several issues of the *Revue d'Assyriologie*.[34] Participants were again members of the Mari team, but there were also a few strays, including Daniel Fleming, Eckart Otto, and myself. Dominique Charpin gave an exciting tour of the Beqaʿ valley in which troops from Mari and Qaṭna held a joint military campaign.[35] Most of the other papers, however, made more or less congruous connections between Mari and the Bible on such issues as sacrifice, war, palace life, kingship, and legal formulae, the goal being to expand our grasp of practices or institutions without committing to definite channels of transmission or chronology. The Mari material was dealt with much subtlety but, as is not uncommon in these enterprises, the biblical texts brought into comparison were generally read flat. There was the requisite review of the prophetic material (by Lemaire) as well as the obligatory warning about misuse of Mari documentation (my own essay). All very bracing and rewarding. Two papers, however, went beyond thematic analogies: Durand's 'Réalités amorrites et traditions bibliques', and Daniel Fleming's 'Mari and the Possibility of Biblical Memory.'[36] They deserve a few more words.

6. *Amorites and their Memory*

Ever since he took the helm of the Mari *équipe*, Durand and his team have made remarkable progress in reconstructing the culture of Mari, with special attention on reign of Zimri-Lim, where our evidence is very full. Early in 1992, Durand

31. A. Lemaire, 'Mari, la Bible et le monde nord-ouest sémitique', *MARI* 4 (1985), pp. 549-58 (553-54).

32. Proceedings published in *Mari, Ébla, et les Hourrites: Dix ans de travaux, première partie: Actes du colloque international (Paris, mai 1993)* (ed. J.-M. Durand; Amurru, 1; Paris: Éditions Recherche sur les civilisations, 1996), and Durand and Charpin (eds.), *Mari, Ébla, et les Hourrites* (Amurru, 2).

33. A. Lemaire, 'Les textes prophétiques de Mari dans leurs relations avec l'Ouest', in *Mari, Ébla, et les Hourrites* (Amurru, 1), pp. 427-38.

34. *RA* 92/1-2 (1998) and 93/1 (1999).

35. D. Charpin, 'Toponymie amorrite et toponymie biblique: la ville de Ṣîbat/Ṣobah', *RA* 92 (1998), pp. 79-92; see Charpin and Ziegler, *Mari et le Proche-Orient à l'époque amorrite*, pp. 101-102.

36. J.-M. Durand, 'Réalités amorrites et traditions bibliques', *RA* 92 (1998), pp. 3-39, and Daniel E. Fleming, 'Mari and the Possibility of Biblical Memory', *RA* 92 (1998), pp. 41-78.

wrote the most forceful reassessment of nomadism in the Mari texts since Kupper's 1957 study.[37] The famous Ḫana, once regarded as a major tribal coalition of the time disappears, its name shown to be generic for such tribal confederations as the Yaminites ('Southerners') and the Simalites ('Northerners'), themselves just two of many Amorite tribes in the region. Durand is confident that diverse forms of governance and associations could be detected for each of these two major groups, the Yaminites and the Simalites, and, not without success, he has detailed a technical vocabulary for each of them. For Durand, the Lim dynasty, to which Zimri-Lim belonged, was Simalite although his own mother was Yaminite, a fact that did not stop Zimri-Lim from waging war against them. Politics remained fluid and tribes easily floated between settled and non-settled status. Remarkably, however, individuals could shift allegiance from one tribe to another after the requisite donkey sacrifices. Yet, as we learned more about tribes, the terminology of linkage between Amorites and Israel has proved slippery, they seem to share etymology but not application: for example Amorite *ga'um/gâyum* ('clan') seems closest *not* to Hebrew *gôy* but to *mišpaḥâ*, whereas Hebrew *gôy* parallels Amorite *ummatum* and not *ga'um*.[38]

Daniel Fleming has depended heavily on Durand's reformulation of tribal context in the Mari age, using it to test the quality of biblical memory. That Zimri-Lim was a Simalite ruling at an urban center allows Fleming to make phenomenological equivalence with what obtained as David was forging a kingdom. However, there is a problem in conception. Leaving aside the biblical material, there is a slighting of a fundamental insight drawn long ago from the Mari records: namely that no matter who ruled at Mari there was always continuity among administrators and bureaucrats. It is difficult, therefore, to claim that Zimri-Lim governed differently from his predecessors, Simalites or otherwise. This is not to say that political situations remained stagnant, that rulers shared the same governing style, or that events did not require changes of tactics; rather, it is possible to argue that the organs of government did not shift appreciably enough for us to imagine a radically different rule for Zimri-Lim. I can also cast doubt about Fleming's reading of the Simalite material. (He presumes correspondents meant Simalites when they mentioned Ḫana.) In fact, Zimri-Lim has been shown to own a double allegiance to tribe and city ever since Kupper published ARM, VI, 76 fifty years ago, with a message urging the king to please both his urban and tribal constituencies.

Fleming next resurrects an old discussion about the value of place names that seem shared in the Bible and in Mari. His insight here is that Mari's Yami-

37. J.-M. Durand, 'Unité et diversités au Proche-Orient à l'époque amorrite', in *La circulation des biens, des personnes et des idées dans le Proche-Orient ancien* (ed. D. Charpin and F. Joannès; Actes de la XXXVIIIème Rencontre assyriologique internationale, Paris, 8-10 juillet 1991; Paris: Éditions Recherche sur les civilisations, 1992), pp. 97-128.

38. On these points see Sasson, 'About "Mari and the Bible" ', pp. 104-105.

nite tribes occupied such North Mesopotamian places as Ḫarrān and Nāḫôr, and this is reflected in the Biblical preoccupation with the tribal origins of Benjamin and with its setting of the patriarchs in the Balikh region. He connects one Amorite tribal term, *ḫibrum*, with Hebrew *ʿibrî*. Whether or not Fleming succeeds in saying anything useful on this matter is not at issue here; more relevant to me is that Fleming's willingness to lean on such evocative mosaics may itself be a harbinger for a new drive to historicize Hebrew traditions. If so, 'Why now?' would be an interesting issue to explore. It could be because the combats between so-called minimalists and maximalists demand reaction by historians, in biblical studies always the arbiters of Hebraic veracity. But there is also in Fleming an interest in other themes that are also patently American in their exploration, not least among them is the notion that nomadic ideals included a primitive form of democracy that just begs ferreting out. That such ideals were shared among Israel's ancestors continues to be an attractive notion for some scholars.[39]

7. *Nimrod, Chedorlaomer, and Amraphel*

The other article to similarly reopen older issues is Durand's 'Réalités amorrites et traditions bibliques.' For him, the blossoming of Amorite political power was relatively short lived, being practically coeval with the Mari age.[40] But the Amorites have proven themselves homologous precursors of the Hebrews, for

39. Fleming has a book on the subject: Daniel E. Fleming, *Democracy's Ancient Ancestors: Mari and Early Collective Governance* (Cambridge and New York: Cambridge University Press, 2004). The classic argument is in Thorkild Jacobsen's 'Primitive Democracy in Ancient Mesopotamia', *JNES* 2 (1943), pp. 159-72, reprinted in *Toward the Image of Tammuz and Other Essays on Mesopotamian History and Culture* (ed. W.L. Moran; HSS, 21; Cambridge, MA: Harvard University Press, 1970), pp. 157-70. The argument was quickly followed by C. Umhau Wolf, 'Traces of Primitive Democracy in Ancient Israel', *JNES* 6 (1947), pp. 98-108. See also Robert Gordis, 'Democratic Origins in Ancient Israel: The Biblical *ʿēdāh*', in *Alexander Marx: Jubilee Volume on the Occasion of his Seventieth Birthday* (New York: Jewish Theological Seminary of America, 1950), pp. 369-88; G.E. Mendenhall, 'Ancient Oriental and Biblical Law', *BA* 17 (1954), pp. 26-46; Norman K. Gottwald, *All the Kingdoms of the Earth: Israelite Prophecy and International Relations in the Ancient Near East* (New York: Harper and Row, 1964).

The argument for Israel as a source for democratic ideals has had a long history in America; see J.M. Sasson, 'On Choosing Models for Recreating Israelite Pre-Monarchic History', *JSOT* 21 (1981), pp. 3-24. The notion continues to be developed; see Daniel J. Elazar, 'Kinship and Consent in the Jewish Community: Patterns of Continuity in Jewish Communal Life', *Tradition: A Journal of Orthodox Jewish Thought* 14/4 (Fall 1974), pp. 63-79; *idem*, 'Covenant as the Basis of the Jewish Political Tradition', in *Kinship and Consent: The Jewish Political Tradition and its Contemporary Uses* (ed. D.J. Elazar; Ramat Gan: Turtledove, 1981), pp. 21-56, and D.J. Elazar and Stuart A. Cohen, *The Jewish Polity: Jewish Political Organizations from Biblical Times to the Present* (Bloomington, IN: Indiana University Press, 1985).

40. Durand, 'Réalités amorrites et traditions bibliques', pp. 7-8.

the memory of their culture and institutions is well reflected in biblical lore. For Durand, Mari letters and biblical narratives shared the same sensibilities, including outrage at the abuse of hospitality, a morbid concern with blood vengeance, and interest in consecrating *betyls* as a covenantal act. But Durand goes two steps further. He proposes that behind the Nimrod of Genesis 10 may well the great Samsi-Addu, with his capitals Ekallātum and Šubat-Enlil recalled in the mysterious Rĕḥōbōt-ʿÎr and Resen. This particular issue is frankly not worth debating. Durand's other proposal, however, rises from a different matrix and may be more significant and, because it is now adopted by Charpin in a recent article in German (hence likely more accessible to biblical scholars) as well as by Charpin and Ziegler in their masterly book on the history of Mari; we may need to linger a bit on it.[41]

For reasons that cannot be pursued at this forum, the Mari team has created a veritable morality tale out of events that ended Mari's life.[42] History (as Jimmy Durante sang in 'The Day I Read a Book') has plot. At the fall of Samsi-Addu's empire, Zimri-Lim made ready alliances with other Amorite leaders, principally Hammurabi of Babylon. Their first enemy was Ešnunna, a power that regarded itself heir to Agade. A first war ended in a cold peace. But soon, another war broke out, this time instigated by Ešnunna's old nemesis, Elam. Elam, in the opinion of the *équipe*, was the *éminence grise* of the time. Its people were not Semites, its mores were distinctive and its leaders were arrogant and aggressive. The Amorite coalition foolishly participated in the humbling of Ešnunna, whetting Elam's appetite. Its ruler turned against Babylon and, seeking influence far to the West, plotted with Qaṭna, thus threatening Yarim-Lim of Aleppo. Elam's march was reversed, its defeat resulting from a 'holy war' mounted against her.[43] For some members of the Mari team, the memory of the trauma lasted and was recalled in Genesis: Chedorlaomer of Elam is Kudušuluš (Šulšikudur) of Susa, Amraphel is Amūd-pî-El of Qaṭna (never mind Shinar), and Ariyôk is Arriyuk, a minor player in the drama, yet a supporter of Elam.[44]

41. D. Charpin, '"Ein umherziehende Aramäer war mein Vater": Abraham im Lichte der Quellen aus Mari', in *'Abraham, unser Vater': Die gemeinsamen Wurzeln von Judentum, Christentum und Islam* (ed. Reinhard Gregor Kratz and Tilman Nagel; Göttingen: Wallstein Verlag, 2003), pp. 40-52; Charpin and Ziegler, *Mari et le Proche-Orient à l'époque amorrite*, pp. 226-27; see above n. 8.

42. This is sharply drawn in D. Charpin and J.-M. Durand, 'La suzeraineté de l'empéreur (*sukkalmaḫ*) d'Elam sur la Mésopotamie et le "nationalisme" amorrite', in *Mésopotamie et Elam: Actes de la XXXVIème Rencontre assyriologique internationale*, Gand, 10-14 juillet 1989 (ed. L. De Meyer and H. Gasche; Mesopotamian History and Environment, Occasional Publications, [IV]/I; Ghent: The University, 1991), pp. 59-66.

43. See Michaël Guichard, 'Les aspects religieux de la guerre à Mari', *RA* 93 (1999), pp. 27-48.

44. Durand, 'Réalités amorrites et traditions bibliques', pp. 16-20. See also Charpin and Ziegler, *Mari et le Proche-Orient à l'époque amorrite*, p. 226.

All of this is rather surprising, especially since it comes from eminent Assyriologists with remarkable flair for historical reconstruction, albeit without the necessary heavy investment in biblical research. I can object to a proposal that does not explore the role Genesis 14 plays within the saga of the patriarchs. I can lament the crafting of such an ambitious proposal out of fragments of history. I can puzzle over the conceit that the documentation we master as scholars is the key to solving other mysteries. But above all I worry lest such pronouncements, themselves delivered cautiously as opinions within vastly more consequential contributions, might nevertheless encourage resumption of the historicizing effort that so distorted the study of the Bible until a generation ago.

8. *Why now? Why again?*

You might still ask, 'Why now? Why again?' It is possible, of course, that these scholars are accurately gauging the memory of events behind Genesis 14 and are giving us keys to understand early episodes in Israel's history. I leave it to you to judge. But it is also possible, as we have learned fifty years ago, that any reconstruction of Amorite culture will always bring with it a powerful urge to make linkage, not just with history as extracted from Mari letters buried in their own time, but also with biblical memories that continue to haunt us centuries into their formation. Still, if we are once more readying to chase that most elusive of Grails, the quest for the historical Abraham, for one I am glad that Mari is there to deliver the necessary clues.

The Production of Ancient Near Eastern Text Anthologies from the Earliest to the Latest

K. Lawson Younger, Jr

1. *Historical Overview*

At the beginning of the nineteenth century, the ancient Near East had as its chief witness the text of the Hebrew Bible. Relatively insignificant was the evidence recovered from sources outside the Bible; and that which had been discovered had not been sufficiently understood to serve as a reliable historical source. But by the mid-nineteenth century, with the decipherments of Egyptian hieroglyphic texts and cuneiform tablets, scholars suddenly had documentary material dating to the time of the stories of the Hebrew Bible. In fact, many of these written sources dated considerably earlier than the Old Testament texts. In many ways, these new discoveries were unquestionably superior to the paucity of the classical sources (e.g. Josephus, Philo, Herodotus, etc.), many of which contained obviously corrupted versions of the ancient records.

Nevertheless, there were different reactions to the discoveries of material contemporaneous to or earlier than the biblical documents. Some scholars of the nineteenth century saw this material as a means of vindicating the biblical record, especially as over against the attacks of a growing number of higher critics.[1] Some other biblical scholars feared that these discoveries might be used to contradict the biblical accounts and undermine their authority,[2] a fear that materialized in the efforts of some scholars to deny Israel any innovation.[3] Thus from the beginning, comparative studies were hampered by either apol-

1. See Steven W. Holloway, *Aššur is King! Aššur is King! Religion in the Exercise of Power in the Neo-Assyrian Empire* (CHANE, 10; Leiden: E.J. Brill, 2002), pp. 431-32; and Joel Sweek, 'The Monuments, the *Babel–Bibel Streit* and Responses to Historical Criticism', in *The Pitcher is Broken: Memorial Essays for Gösta W. Ahlström* (ed. S.W. Holloway and L.K. Handy; JSOTSup, 190; Sheffield: Sheffield Academic Press, 1995), pp. 401-19.

2. Mark W. Chavalas, 'Assyriology and Biblical Studies: A Century of Tension', in *Mesopotamia and the Bible: Comparative Explorations* (ed. M.W. Chavalas and K.L. Younger, Jr; JSOTSup, 341; Sheffield: Sheffield Academic Press, 2002), pp. 21-67, esp. pp. 24-25.

3. Frederick E. Greenspahn, 'Introduction', in *Essential Papers on Israel and the Ancient Near East* (ed. F.E. Greenspahn; New York and London: New York University, 1991), pp. 1-14 (7).

ogetic concerns or deep-rooted skepticism and suspicions. Early on, comparisons between the two were often done in connection with religious polemic.[4] In such an environment, overstating or understating the evidence characterized many of the initial attempts at comparative work. Therefore from the start, the production of compendia was interlinked to a greater or lesser extent with the issues of the place and role of comparative studies.

In addition, since the languages utilizing the cuneiform script were not fully understood, errors in reading and interpreting the documents plagued early studies. Moreover, the *Babel-Bibel* controversy of Friedrich Delitzsch and the radical Pan-Babylonism movement only further polarized the opinions of many about the value of all these ancient Near Eastern texts.[5]

There can be no doubt that the movers and shakers of Assyriology, to a degree equal to their biblical studies brethren, encoded their pre-understandings of political, religious and intellectual reality into their scholarship. While it is much easier to visualize this process the farther one is removed from the scholarship in place and time, it is much harder—and perhaps politically more hazardous—to describe such 'bias' in the age in which oneself is embedded. 'Methods' that appeared to be flawless exercises of empirical objectivity are revealed through time to exclude and suppress information that challenge the aforesaid pre-understandings.

In spite of these problems, as more and more archives and individual texts were discovered and published, important strides were being made. In the last decades of the nineteenth and the early decades of the twentieth centuries, the discoveries of many West Semitic inscriptions, including extrabiblical Hebrew inscriptions, fueled further advances in the comparative study of the biblical texts, opening a window into the development of the alphabet and the scripts of the biblical world.

Excavations between the two World Wars and immediately after the second saw the discoveries of numerous additional texts, but perhaps more importantly the discoveries of archives of texts written in peripheral Akkadian (e.g. Mari, Alalaḫ) as well as in newly deciphered languages (e.g. Ugaritic from Ugarit,

4. In terms of religion, see Th. C. Vriezen, 'The Study of the Old Testament and the History of Religion', in *Congress Volume: Rome 1968* (VTSup, 17; Leiden: E.J. Brill, 1969), pp. 1-24. For two early examples, see Archibald Henry Sayce, *The 'Higher Criticism' and the Verdict of the Monuments* (London: SPCK, 1893); William St. Chad Boscawen, *The Bible and the Monuments: The Primitive Hebrew Records in the Light of Modern Research* (London: Eyre & Spottiswoode, 1895).

5. See Mogens Trolle Larsen, 'The "Babel/Bible" Controversy and its Aftermath', in *CANE*, I, pp. 95-106; Reinhard G. Lehmann, *Friedrich Delitzsch und der Babel–Bibel–Streit* (OBO, 133; Freiburg, Switzerland: Universitätsverlag, Freiburg Schweiz/Göttingen: Vandenhoeck & Ruprecht, 1994); David B. Weisberg, 'The Impact of Assyriology on Biblical Studies', in *COS*, III, pp. xliii-xlviii, esp. pp. xliii-xliv; Chavalas, 'Assyriology and Biblical Studies', pp. 32-34; J. Sweek, 'The Monuments, the *Babel–Bibel Streit* and Responses to Historical Criticism', pp. 401-19.

Hurrian from Nuzi). The period following 1945 saw a significant increase in comparative studies (Ugaritic studies alone producing a plethora of books and articles).[6] Many of these studies were characterized by generally positive assessments of the biblical material through comparisons with the ancient Near Eastern data. Scholars such as William Foxwell Albright, E.A. Speiser, Cyrus H. Gordon, Roland de Vaux and others saw various biblical motifs, customs, etc. being vindicated by comparative analysis with these ancient texts. Unfortunately, some of the studies from this period indulged in great excesses in over-emphasizing the comparisons. This indiscriminate use of the comparative method has especially occurred when new discoveries are first published, and such excesses undercut the importance of the comparative process.[7]

This general trend in comparative analysis continued throughout the 1950s, 1960s and early 1970s. But all along there had been opposition to comparative studies coming from different quarters and for different reasons. For example, in Assyriological circles, certain scholars (e.g. Benno Landsberger)[8] felt that such studies made cuneiform scholarship a handmaiden to biblical studies. The discipline needed to be divorced from the study of the Bible and studied on its own terms. Within biblical studies, there was a growing opposition that felt that many of the comparative studies of the period were flawed because: (1) they overstated the evidence, (2) they were frequently agenda-driven (trying to 'prove the Bible'), and (3) they simply lacked methodological controls. Reaction to these three problems led to different responses.

First, the feeling that comparative studies overstated the evidence led to an increasing disillusionment with comparative studies as a valid enterprise in the study of the Bible. Co-joined with the fact that biblical studies as a discipline in the 1970s and 1980s was beginning to struggle with methodological issues

6. Mark S. Smith, *Untold Stories: The Bible and Ugaritic Studies in the Twentieth Century* (Peabody, MA: Hendrickson, 2001), pp. 51-128; *idem*, 'Ugaritic Studies and the Hebrew Bible, 1968–1998 (with an Excursus on Judean Monotheism and the Ugaritic Texts)', in *Congress Volume: Oslo 1998* (ed. André Lemaire and Magne Sæbø; VTSup, 80; Leiden: E.J. Brill, 2000), pp. 327-52.

7. The tendency has been to overemphasize the importance of new discoveries to the Old Testament, and then when the flaws become obvious, approach comparative data from the standpoint of skepticism, causing many to completely ignore comparative material altogether. See J.J.M. Roberts, 'The Ancient Near Eastern Environment', in *The Hebrew Bible and its Modern Interpreters* (ed. Douglas A. Knight and Gene M. Tucker; Philadelphia: Fortress Press/Chico, CA: Scholars Press, 1985), pp. 75-121 (96).

8. Benno Landsberger, 'Die Eigenbegrifflichkeit der babylonischen Welt: Ein Vortrag', *Islamica* 2 (1926), pp. 355-72; reprinted as vol. 142* of the series *Libelli* (Darmstadt: Wissenschaftliche Buchgesellschaft, 1965), pp. 1-18, together with a short 'Nachwort' by the author (p. 19) = *The Conceptual Autonomy of the Babylonian World* (trans. Thorkild Jacobsen, Benjamin R. Foster and H. von Siebenthal; Monographs on the Ancient Near East, 1/4; Malibu, CA: Undena, 1976). See the discussion of William W. Hallo, 'Sumer and the Bible', in *COS*, III, pp. xlix-liv.

in philosophical hermeneutics, moving away from author-oriented readings toward, at first, text-oriented readings and then toward reader-oriented readings, this disillusionment created an environment in which large numbers of Hebrew Bible scholars turned away from comparative studies altogether.

There can be little doubt that biblical scholars have been more prone to search for comparative data than Assyriologists. The two disciplines must be pursued independent of each other and, in fact, presently are in large measure. Nevertheless, it must be recognized that there is an intimate relationship between the two.[9] The ancient Near Eastern and Israelite traditions should be seen as two contemporary systems in the ancient Near East, though not necessarily exclusively in context with each other. The ancient Near East and Israel were part of a greater cultural continuum.[10]

Second, those who objected to comparative studies because they felt these were often attempts to 'prove the Bible' began to expose the excesses and errors in many of these studies. Some of the comparative studies of the patriarchal materials were especially weak and these were addressed by scholars like Thompson[11] and Van Seters.[12] They exposed the excesses of previous scholarship through analyses of the comparative material. Thus there was not a rejection of comparative studies as a valid approach to the biblical material; rather there was a critique of earlier scholarly assumptions and assessments. While the work of these scholars to reveal methodological problems in earlier studies is quite laudable, their critiques succumbed to the criticism by different scholars that they considered *late* comparative evidence to the exclusion of earlier sources; hence they tended to produce studies that seemed to be driven by a 'disprove the Bible' agenda.

The situation described in the previous paragraph highlighted a greater need for methodological controls. This had been the third objection to earlier studies. Some scholars, most notably William W. Hallo, began to address this issue. Over the last two decades of the twentieth century, a number of scholars have taken up the challenge of appropriate comparative methodology,[13] although

9. H.W.F. Saggs, *The Encounter with the Divine in Mesopotamia and Israel* (Jordan Lectures in Comparative Religion, 12; London: Athlone Press, 1978), p. 5.

10. Karel van der Toorn, *Family Religion in Babylonia, Syria and Israel: Continuity and Changes in the Forms of Religious Life* (SHCANE, 7; Leiden: E.J. Brill, 1996), p. 4.

11. Thomas L. Thompson, *The Historicity of the Patriarchal Narratives* (BZAW, 133; Berlin: W. de Gruyter, 1974).

12. John Van Seters, *Abraham in History and Tradition* (New Haven: Yale University Press, 1975).

13. Nili Sacher Fox, *In the Service of the King: Officialdom in Ancient Israel and Judah* (MHUC, 23; Cincinnati: Hebrew Union College Press, 2000), pp. 9-42; Greenspahn, 'Introduction', pp. 1-14; W.W. Hallo, 'Biblical History in its Near Eastern Setting: The Contextual Approach', in *Scripture in Context: Essays on the Comparative Method* (ed. Carl D. Evans, W.W. Hallo and John B. White; Pittsburgh Theological Monograph Series, 34; Pittsburgh: Pickwick

querulous voices were raised from the beginning, as witness Francis Brown's *Assyriology: Its Use and Abuse in Old Testament Study* (New York: Charles Scribner's Sons, 1885).

In the present-day context, in spite of its wide availability, many interpreters of the Hebrew Bible continue to choose to ignore ancient Near Eastern material. In part this is due to a reader-oriented tendency among many modern biblical literary critics. This approach, as Simon B. Parker has recently observed,[14] puts the reader rather one-sidedly in control of the literature. Rather than seeking to let the literature of ancient Israel address us on its own terms—however remote from ours and however we may finally judge them—it too easily makes of biblical literature a reflection of our own concerns at the beginning of the

Press, 1980), pp. 1-26 (1-12); *idem*, 'Compare and Contrast: The Contextual Approach to Biblical Literature', in *The Bible in the Light of Cuneiform Literature: Scripture in Context III* (ed. W.W. Hallo, Bruce William Jones and Gerald L. Mattingly; Ancient Near Eastern Texts and Studies, 8; Lewiston: Edwin Mellen Press, 1990), pp. 1-30; *idem*, *The Book of the People* (Brown Judaic Studies, 225; Atlanta, GA: Scholars Press, 1991), chapter 3, 'The Contextual Approach', pp. 23-34; Richard S. Hess, 'Ancient Near Eastern Studies', in *Interpreting the Old Testament: A Guide for Exegesis* (ed. Craig C. Broyles; Grand Rapids, MI: Baker Academic, 2001), pp. 201-20; Tremper Longman, *Fictional Akkadian Autobiography: A Generic and Comparative Study* (Winona Lake, IN: Eisenbrauns, 1991), pp. 30-36; Peter Machinist, 'The Question of Distinctiveness in Ancient Israel: An Essay', in *Ah, Assyria…: Studies in Assyrian History and Ancient Near Eastern Historiography Presented to Hayim Tadmor* (ed. Mordechai Cogan and Israel Ephʿal; Scripta hierosolymitana, 33; Jerusalem: Magnes Press, 1991), pp. 196-212; Meir Malul, *The Comparative Method in Ancient Near Eastern and Biblical Legal Studies* (AOAT, 227; Kevelaer: Butzon & Bercker/Neukirchen–Vluyn: Neukirchener Verlag, 1990); Dennis Pardee, 'Review of Carl D. Evans, W.W. Hallo and John B. White (eds.), *Scripture in Context: Essays in the Comparative Method*', *JNES* 44 (1985), pp. 220-22; *idem*, 'Ugaritic Studies at the End of the 20th Century (review of W.G.E. Watson and N. Wyatt [eds.], *Handbook of Ugaritic Studies*)', *BASOR* 320 (2000), pp. 49-86; *idem*, 'Review of S.B. Parker (ed.), *Ugaritic Narrative Poetry*', *JNES* 60 (2001), pp. 142-45; Simon B. Parker, 'The Ancient Near Eastern Literary Background of the Old Testament', in *The New Interpreter's Bible* (ed. Leander E. Keck; Nashville: Abingdon Press, 1994), I, pp. 228-43; *idem*, *Stories in Scripture and Inscriptions: Comparative Studies on Narratives in Northwest Semitic Inscriptions and the Hebrew Bible* (New York and Oxford: Oxford University Press, 1997); Roberts, 'The Ancient Near Eastern Environment', pp. 75-96; H.W.F. Saggs, 'Assyriology and Biblical Studies', in *Dictionary of Biblical Interpretation* (ed. John H. Hayes; Nashville: Abingdon Press, 1999), I, pp. 69-83; Jack M. Sasson, 'Two Recent Works on Mari', *AfO* 27 (1980), pp. 127-35; *idem*, 'About "Mari and the Bible" ', *RA* 92 (1998), pp. 91-123; Shemaryahu Talmon, 'The 'Comparative Method' in Biblical Interpretation—Principles and Problems', in *Congress Volume: Göttingen 1977* (ed. John A. Emerton; VTSup, 29; Leiden: E.J. Brill, 1978), pp. 320-56; Jeffrey H. Tigay, 'On Evaluating Claims of Literary Borrowing', in *The Tablet and the Scroll: Near Eastern Studies in Honor of William W. Hallo* (ed. Mark E. Cohen, Daniel C. Snell and D.B. Weisberg; Bethesda, MD: CDL Press, 1993), pp. 250-55; Klaas R. Veenhof, ' "Seeing the Face of God": The Use of Akkadian Parallels', *Akkadica* 94–95 (1995), pp. 33-37; and K. Lawson Younger, Jr, 'The "Contextual Method": Some West Semitic Reflections', in *COS*, III, pp. xxxv-lxii.

14. Parker, *Stories in Scripture and Inscriptions*, p. 4.

twenty-first century, whether secular or theological. While the different reading strategies employed today have provided many new and valuable insights (some to greater or lesser degrees), such interpretations of a work without any knowledge of its literary background permit for a high degree of arbitrariness. In addition, since the Bible is understood by some to be

> a direct communication from God to us, many believe that the Bible must be comprehensible on its own, without having to read the literature of cultures that Israel—indeed God—condemned. In addition, some feel an anxiety about discovering the Bible's human dimension or historical rootedness, which, in their view, might lessen the divine character of the message.[15]

Among Christians, the dominant theologies, both before and after the Reformation, tended to depreciate an interest in or need for establishing the literary context for the diverse texts of the Old Testament, seeing the New Testament as the interpretive key to the Old Testament.[16] In fact, many Christian interpreters of many different denominations and theological persuasions have practiced a Christocentric hermeneutic[17] that virtually eliminates the need for understanding the Hebrew Bible's literary context.

But undoubtedly the response of ancient Near Eastern peoples to many of the features of the ancient documents must have been different from ours. Their rhetoric was designed to create a certain impression on the hearer or reader, and that impression is lessened or confused by a reader's ignorance of the ancient rhetorical devices and the presuppositions that these texts employ. Some apprehension of the ancient culture and social environment that their rhetoric presupposed and addressed—in which the composer made his or her choices—is essential for a comprehension of the text.

It seems apparent—at least to me—that one of the best ways to improve one's literary competence in reading the Hebrew Bible is to read as much of the literature under consideration as possible within the Bible in order to gain generic competence, but also and especially within the ancient Near East. Adequate understanding, explanation, and assessment of ancient texts require attention to all dimensions of the text—literary and historical, internal and external, intellectual and social.

2. *The Compendia*

As one can see from the table at the end of the essay, there have been quite a few compendia produced from roughly the last quarter of the nineteenth century until now. In a short article like this, it is impossible for me to say something

15. Parker, 'The Ancient Near Eastern Literary Background of the Old Testament', p. 229.

16. For Rabbinic Judaism, the Talmud became the key or filter for interpreting the Hebrew Bible.

17. E.g. Origen, Luther, Bultmann—just to name a few.

meaningful about all of them. Nevertheless, I hope that what I have selected out will demonstrate some of the common issues that compilers of such compendia have faced, as well as some of the pitfalls.

1872 was a red-letter year.[18] In Germany, Eberhard Schrader, Professor of Oriental Languages at the University of Giessen, published his *Die Keilinschriften und das Alte Testament.* It enjoyed great popularity and in 1883, a second, revised edition appeared—nearly double the size of the first. This second edition also appeared in an English translation in two volumes, the first published in 1885, the second in 1888. Schrader arranged his work in the form of a commentary in which the cuneiform material that was illustrative of the Old Testament was collected under the biblical passages in transliteration and translation. He adopted the form of a commentary deliberately, believing that such an unassuming form did less to prejudice the judgment of the reader (preface to second edition). Schrader gave a transliteration and translation of the appropriate part of the cuneiform text that he was citing to illustrate the biblical text.

Thus the reader could look up a biblical passage and find whatever cuneiform material might elucidate it. So for example, if one looked up 1 Kings 16.29, where the name of Ahab first occurs in the book of Kings, one would find a transliteration and translation of the passage from Shalmaneser III's Kurkh Monolith that mentions 'Ahab, the Israelite'. Schrader gave a full philological discussion of this passage in the Monolith followed by a discussion of the historical context. For another example, one could look up 1 Kings 16.23 where the name of Omri first occurs, and find a detailed philological comment on Omri's name in the cuneiform sources. But here Schrader also included transliterations and translations of all of the passages in cuneiform texts known to him at the time that contained the name Ḫumri/Ḫumria. The advantage of such a commentary-type arrangement is obvious to the one studying a particular biblical passage. The disadvantage, however, is that one doesn't have, in a number of instances, the whole context of a passage; in fact, in most instances one could not study the individual inscriptions themselves because they are only given in bits and pieces scattered throughout the commentary. So, for example, it is impossible to study *Enūma eliš* or the inscriptions of Shalmaneser III as integral compositions.

Schrader's *Die Keilinschriften* also included an eighty-plus-page glossary of Hebrew words with Akkadian and other cognate equivalents. The impact of Schrader's work was enormous. One scholar of the time noted that 'every student of Hebrew or of Assyrian consulted it, every Old Testament commentator quoted from it or made reference to it; (and) its influence was incalculable'.[19]

18. For the following discussion, see the Table at the end of this essay.

19. Robert William Rogers, *Cuneiform Parallels to the Old Testament* (New York: Eaton & Mains, 1912), p. xvii.

Twenty years later in 1903, with the work now a classic, Schrader's compendium was completely rewritten and updated based on a new plan by two leading Assyriologists of the time, Heinrich Zimmern and Hugo Winckler. In this new edition, far more learned than the former and crowded with matter of high importance, the original texts as Schrader had given them were omitted and their place supplied by elaborate discussions of all the questions involved. The additional matter was so great in amount that the book was, in reality, a complete rewrite.

In 1873, coterminous with Schrader's *Die Keilinschriften*, the initial volume of a work entitled *Records of the Past: Being English Translations of the Assyrian and Egyptian Monuments* began publication in England under the editorship of Samuel Birch. Eventually, over the next eight years, twelve volumes were published through the sponsorship of the British Society of Biblical Archaeology. The differences between the first German compendium and the first compendium in English are significant. Whereas Schrader organized his work as a commentary on the biblical text, the English work was organized more along the lines of genre. In Schrader's *Die Keilinschriften*, there was plentiful scriptural referencing and philological comment; in Birch's *Records of the Past*, there was little of either. Birch's work included Egyptian texts; Schrader's did not. The translators of the Assyrian texts in Birch's edition included Archibald Henry Sayce, W.H. Fox Talbot, George Smith, and Henry C. Rawlinson, Britain's best Assyriologists of the day.

A year after the first volume of Birch's *Records of the Past* was published (i.e. in 1874), Joachim Ménant published an anthology of Assyrian historical inscriptions. In his twelve-page introduction, Ménant discussed in some depth the relationship between the biblical and Assyrian texts, but throughout the rest of the volume, the translations have few biblical references.

In the years 1888 through 1892, *Records of the Past* underwent a complete revision. A.H. Sayce, who had been one of the translators for the first edition, provided vigorous editorship for the second edition. The necessity of a new edition of *Records* involved both significant advances in understanding of the cuneiform script as well as the significant increase in the number of newly discovered texts. Concerning the former issue, Sayce commented: 'Indeed there are certain cases in which the progress of knowledge has shown the tentative renderings of a few years ago to be so faulty, if not misleading, that it has been determined to replace them by revised translations in the series which is now being issued'.[20] Concerning the latter issue, the inclusion of the newly discovered Mesha inscription and Siloam Tunnel inscription are of special note. Sayce's edition contained fuller introductions and notes concerning the history, geography and theology of the texts, and it contained more scripture referencing than the first edition.

20. A.H. Sayce, (ed.), *Records of the Past: Being English Translations of the Ancient Monuments of Egypt and Western Asia. New Series* (6 vols.; London: Samuel Bagster & Sons, 1888), I, p. vi.

In 1877, four years before the completion of the first edition of *Records of the Past*, and eleven years before the beginning of its second edition, another compendium in English appeared. William Harris Rule, who was encouraged in his project by none other than Samuel Birch, published his *Oriental Records. Monumental. Confirmatory of the Old Testament Scriptures*, for the purpose of, as he put it, collating 'some of the most ancient monumental records with Holy Scripture as to show that they confirm those portions of Sacred History with which they correspond; and sometimes to show that they throw fresh light thereon'.[21] However, unlike Birch's *Records of the Past*, but like Schrader's *Die Keilinschriften*, Rule's compendium is in the form of a commentary on the biblical text; but unlike Schrader, he utilized a topical arrangement. Thus the chapter headings are 'The Creation', 'The Antediluvians', 'The Deluge', 'The Tower of Babel', etc. The strong apologetic nature of the work is evident throughout. The fact that Rule's work was published by the same company that printed both editions of *Records of the Past* and, that Rule's work was *even* published before the completion of the first edition of *Records of the Past* illustrates the public demand in England for such compendia.

In fact, the power of the print media and its role in the sensationalism that accompanied many of the discoveries surrounding the cuneiform texts cannot be underestimated. George Smith's translation of the 'Assyrian' account of the flood and his description of the extrabiblical account of creation published in London's *Daily Telegraph* (March 4, 1875) generated great interest among biblical scholars in the new science of Assyriology, as well as eliciting popular support for further excavation and research.[22] In fact, the proprietors of the *Daily Telegraph*, at their own expense, sent Smith to Nineveh to recover, if possible, further fragments of the 'ancient Babylonian legends!'

I don't know any Assyriologist today who has received payment from Rupert Murdoch, or any other print media mogul, to go find more fragments of any text. But when one remembers that, in those days, the power of the press was significant enough to actually cause nations to go to war, the sensationalism connected to the cuneiform text discoveries must have had a far greater impact than what we are accustomed to today. Not that there isn't still today a great deal of sensationalism created by the print media. I cannot help but think of the *New York Times* and *Newsweek* articles that led me as an undergraduate to attend lectures where the epigraphist of the newly discovered Tel Mardikh/Ebla archives and a major biblical studies professor announced—with

21. W.H. Rule, *Records. Monumental. Confirmatory of the Old Testament Scriptures* (London: Samuel Bagster & Sons, 1877), p. i.

22. Smith had already delivered an important paper on the subject in 1872 to the Society of Biblical Archaeology. In 1876, he published a book titled: *The Chaldean Account of Genesis, Containing the Description of the Creation, the Fall of Man, the Deluge, the Tower of Babel, the Times of the Patriarchs, and Nimrod: Babylonian Fables, and Legends of the Gods from the Cuneiform Inscriptions* (New York: Scribner, Armstrong & Co., 1876).

great fanfare—the supposed occurrences of the patriarchal name 'Abram' and the cities of 'Sodom and Gomorrah' in the Eblaite tablets. Or perhaps, more recently, one might think of the recent hoopla over an ossurary.[23]

Certainly underlying this power of the print media was a strong public interest in proof of the biblical record (note again the sub-title to Rule's compendium 'Confirmatory of the Old Testament Scriptures'). All of the first generation of Assyriologists were, without exception, biblically engaged, and sought, to varying degrees, to harmonize the emerging contours of the Neo-Assyrian Empire with the Assyria enshrined in the Old Testament. Thus, as Steven W. Holloway has noted, a H.C. Rawlinson could confidently harmonize biblical, classical and historical Assyria into 'a richly woven tapestry of scriptural confirmation', which was, in fact, a constantly evolving understanding that incorporated all of the latest revelations from the 'monuments'.[24] Such 'a richly woven tapestry of scriptural confirmation' could be used to confound the extremes of the higher critics.

But in many ways, a much greater driving force, not only in Britain, but also in France and Germany, was nationalism, which was more or less the same as imperialism. In the nineteenth century, European archaeology worked hand-in-glove with national rivalry. The French opened the first permanent display of Assyrian antiquities in May of 1847 at the Louvre. The success of the French excavations at Khorsābād and their triumphant display constituted an affront to British imperial supremacy. For the restoration of British honor, it was imperative for the British Museum to mount a display—which it did in August of 1847—that surpassed the 'French Nineveh'. And it is evident that the Deutsche Orient-Gesellschaft was founded in 1898 out of a sense of imperialistic rivalry with France and Great Britain. Thus it was European nationalism and imperialism, rather than disinterested scientific curiosity, that provided the necessary financial backing, safety for its citizens abroad and leverage on the Turkish government for assyriological advancement in the nineteenth century.[25] Certainly, as it has been clearly documented, this component of the *Zeitgeist* impacted the translations and interpretations of the cuneiform literature.

In 1892, Hugo Winckler produced a compendium, which in 1903, at the same time that he and Heinrich Zimmern were re-working Schrader's, appeared in a second edition. A third edition followed in 1909. This was a smaller compendium (the 2nd edition had only 130 pages). It contained historical and mythological texts and was arranged according to genre. It had no illustrations and few scripture references. But Winckler did give both transliterations and translations of the cuneiform texts.

23. Hershel Shanks, 'The Storm over the Bone Box', *BAR* 29 (2003), pp. 27-39, 83.

24. Holloway, *Aššur is King! Aššur is King!*, p. 432.

25. Holloway, *Aššur is King! Aššur is King!*, p. 428 n. 1.

Winckler, of course, was one of the chief champions of 'Pan-Babylonism', arguing that all the world myths were reflections of Babylonian astral religion which had developed about 3000 BCE, including Israelite monotheism, imported from Mesopotamia by the patriarch Abraham. In the late nineteenth century, the new 'science' of comparative religion espoused an evolutionary view of religion. This view so pervaded late nineteenth-century scholarship that many assumed religion was still progressing higher and higher to an ultimate goal. Both Christian supercessionism and European racism found in this evolutionary thought a convenient vehicle for demoting Semitic religions.[26] Hence, Pan-Babylonism found fertile ground.

The impact of Pan-Babylonism as a motive for the production of a compendium can perhaps be most clearly seen in the work of Alfred Jeremias who published the first edition of his compendium in 1904. Jeremias was committed to the mythological form of presentation and the mythological system as developed by Winckler (see the preface to his first German edition). He reaffirmed this commitment in the second edition of 1906 where he greatly amplified the astral motifs. He devoted two full chapters (over 100 pages) to introductory essays on the Babylonian astral motifs traced throughout world religions. The popularity of this work can be judged by the fact that it went through two more editions. But interestingly, in the third edition (1916) and the fourth edition (1930), these two introductory chapters were removed. They were published as a separate work in 1913 entitled *Handbuch der altorientalischen Geisteskultur*.[27] Like the works of Schrader and Winckler before him, Jeremias' work was in the form of a commentary on the biblical text, although it is more of a topical arrangement that follows the biblical order, similar to Rule's compendium, but with much greater depth. After Jeremias, all compendia under discussion have been arranged according to genre.

In 1901, one of the pioneer American Assyriologists, Robert Francis Harper published a compendium containing translations by an international array of scholars like Clifton Daggett Gray, William Muss-Arnolt, Preston P. Bruce, Alois Bárta, Ira Maurice Price, George A. Barton, Christopher Johnston, John M.P. Smith, R. Campbell Thompson, L.W. King, and Harper himself. Harper felt that a compendium of the cuneiform inscriptions was 'more interesting and valuable than that written on the papyri and monuments of Egypt', not only because of its general historical value, but 'because of its striking similarities to the Hebrew, and because of the help it brings to an understanding of the biblical text.[28]

26. For further discussion, see Bill T. Arnold and D.B. Weisberg, 'A Centennial Review of Friedrich Delitzsch's "Babel und Bibel" Lectures', *JBL* 121 (2002), pp. 441-57, esp. p. 450.

27. Alfred Jeremias, *Handbuch der altorientalischen Geisteskultur* (Leipzig: J.C. Hinrichs, 1913).

28. Robert Francis Harper (ed.), *Assyrian and Babylonian Literature: Selected Translations.*

Back in Germany, only three years after Jeremias' second edition appeared (1906) and in the same year that Winckler published the third and final edition of his compendium (1909), Hugo Gressmann widened the scope of such works still further by introducing the pictorial element in 'Ancient Near Eastern Texts and Pictures to the Old Testament', in a two-volume work. While Jeremias and Robert William Rogers (see below) included photographs and line-drawing illustrations in their works, Gressmann's was on a completely different scale. The first volume contained the translations, and the second the pictures. This was also the first German compendium to include translations of relevant Egyptian texts (done by Hermann Ranke).[29] The work quickly became a standard reference for biblical scholars. In 1926–27, a second edition appeared. The discoveries of new texts and improved understanding of the old ones warranted an entirely new edition. The quantity of translations was almost doubled, and there was rich philological comment. The significance of this work can be seen in the evaluation of James B. Pritchard who, in the preface to the first edition of *Ancient Near Eastern Texts*, stated: 'This work has remained until now as the most useful collection of extrabiblical material bearing upon the Old Testament'.[30]

Through the first decade of the twentieth century, German scholarship had produced the majority of compendia. The appeal of these works of synthesis, however, was by no means limited to a German-speaking readership. Besides the two editions of *Records of the Past*, Rule's compendium and Harper's anthology, the compendia of Schrader and Jeremias were translated into English. At this same time, German scholarship, both biblical and ancient Near Eastern, was having a profound impact in the English-speaking world through more personal, direct means: British and particularly American students coming to Germany for graduate and post-graduate study on the one hand, and on the other, German scholars coming to American universities to teach.[31]

This influence is particularly acknowledged by the American scholar, Rogers, who published the first edition of his *Cuneiform Parallels to the Old Testament* in 1912. In this work, Rogers attempted to offer 'a complete corpus of all the Assyrian, Babylonian and Persian inscriptions which are parallel to or illustrative of the Old Testament'.[32] He included transliterations of the texts so that students would have access to the widely scattered original texts and could exercise their own judgment upon them. In this connection, he quipped: 'It would be a most useful reformation in much of our academic, and even

With a Critical Introduction (The World's Great Books, Aldine edition; New York: D. Appleton & Company, 1901), p. iii.

29. Arthur Ungnad translated the Babylonian, Assyrian and North-West Semitic texts. Gressmann was responsible for the photos and illustrations.

30. James B. Pritchard, 'Introduction', in *ANET* (1950), pp. xiii-xviii (xiv).

31. Hallo, 'Preface', in *COS*, I, pp. xi-xii.

32. Rogers, *Cuneiform Parallels to the Old Testament*, p. xviii.

of our graduate teaching, if our pupils were compelled to do a little more for themselves'.[33]

Even in 1912, the enormity of such a project for one individual was realized by Rogers' frank admission that the project had exhausted him. 'It has, indeed, cost so much that my early hopes and enthusiasm for it have slipped away, and, like Johnson with his Dictionary, "I therefore dismiss it with frigid tranquillity, having little to fear or hope from censure or from praise" '.[34]
Rogers adopted a general generic arrangement of the translations:

- mythological texts—these included many of the by-then-well-known texts like *Enūma eliš*, the Epic of Gilgamesh, etc., but also included Greek and Latin sources for Berossus;
- hymns and prayers;
- liturgical texts;
- chronological materials;
- historical texts—these included a number of Old Babylonian letters; the Amarna letters; the Gezer cuneiform tablets that had recently been discovered;
- and legal texts—these included a *kudurru*-stone, an adoption text, a marriage contract and the Code of Hammurabi.

He deliberately made few references to scripture. He felt that the reader should be the one to make these connections.

Another American scholar who followed closely on the heels of Rogers was George A. Barton. He published the first edition of his *Archaeology and the Bible* in 1916. This work was very successful, going through seven editions, the last being published in 1937.

In 1924, Charles-François Jean published an anthology in French of Babylonian and Assyrian texts. This edition continued the tradition started by Ménant, though greatly improved in both the number of texts included and the quality of the translations.

No doubt due to the Great Depression and the Second World War, the 1930s and 1940s were devoid of the appearance of any new compendia. Moreover, the days of a single author producing a compendium were over. Thus it was in 1950 that J.B. Pritchard edited the first edition of *Ancient Near Eastern Texts Relating to the Old Testament* (frequently referred to by the acronym *ANET*). This work quickly established itself as the pre-eminent compendium

33. Rogers, *Cuneiform Parallels to the Old Testament*, p. xix.

34. Rogers, *Cuneiform Parallels to the Old Testament*, p. xviii. In the preface to the second edition (p. xxiv), Rogers states: 'I should have wished to do more but for the high cost of all the work of our brothers, the printers. I have no reason to believe that their rewards are too great, but the compensation of scholars and teachers has not always kept even pace with them, and the publication of learned books is hardly so easy as it was when this book first saw the light.' It doesn't seem that much has changed in this regard since the days of Rogers!

of its kind in the post-war period. Pritchard used Gressmann as his proximate and most recent model, both in the initial selection of texts (preface to the first edition) and in the creation of a companion volume of pictures which was his own work based on his archaeological training and interests, a work which appeared in 1954 under the title *The Ancient Near East in Pictures* (*ANEP*).[35]

Pritchard's collection has served as the standard for English readers since 1950. According to Hallo,[36] comparable efforts by British, French and even German teams made no attempt to replace it, but rather to offer complementary works answering to different requirements. Thus, for example, the British Society for Old Testament Study published *Documents from Old Testament Times* in 1958 on the occasion of its fortieth anniversary. But David Winton Thomas, its editor, had no intention of matching or even approaching the scope of *ANET* (which was freely cited in the volume). The 1975 work of the German scholars, Hellmut Brunner and Walter Beyerlin, along with its English translation in 1978 edited by Beyerlin, was an anthology of primarily religious texts. The more recent German project that started in 1982 and saw its completion in 2001, *Texte aus der Umwelt des Alten Testaments*, edited by Otto Kaiser and others, is a four-volume work that is very ambitious in scope. It combines the older tradition of German compendia with some of the best features of the newer ones. But in spite of its title, it makes little or no reference to biblical parallels or contrasts.

In 1991, with a second edition appearing in 1997, Victor H. Matthews and Don C. Benjamin produced a reader-oriented translation anthology. It has received popular use, but isn't of the breadth and depth of other recent compendia.

Exactly one hundred and twenty-five years after Schrader published the first compendium of ancient Near Eastern texts related to the Hebrew Bible, the first volume of *The Context of Scripture* was published (1997). The second volume appeared in 2000, and the third and final volume in 2002.

In the remainder of this essay, I would like to focus on some of the similarities and differences between *ANET* and *The Context of Scripture*. In many ways the overall purpose of each is the same. Pritchard stated that *ANET*'s purpose was 'to make available to students of the ancient Near East—serious students of the Old Testament, we believe, are necessarily such—the most important extrabiblical texts in translations which represent the best understanding which present-day scholarship has achieved'.[37] According to Hallo, the purpose of *COS* is 'to assem-

35. J.B. Pritchard (ed.), *The Ancient Near East in Pictures Relating to the Old Testament* (Princeton, NJ: Princeton University Press, 1954); and *idem* (ed.), *The Ancient Near East: Supplementary Texts and Pictures Relating to the Old Testament* (Princeton, NJ: Princeton University Press, 1969).

36. Hallo, 'Introduction: Ancient Near Eastern Texts and their Relevance for Biblical Exegesis', in *COS*, I, pp. xxiii-xxviii (xxiv).

37. Pritchard, 'Introduction', in *ANET* (1950), p. xiii.

ble the existing renderings [of ancient Near Eastern texts], update them where necessary, and indicate their relevance for biblical scholarship'.[38]

But *COS*'s aims are more ambitious and nuanced.[39] Reflecting a half-century's worth of discussion on the place of ancient Near Eastern texts in the study of the Bible, *COS*, as Hallo points out, intends to combine 'an intertextual and a contextual approach'. No longer are biblical and ancient Near Eastern texts simply to be lined up and 'compared', on a one-to-one basis, as many did in the first one hundred years of producing compendia. Now, scholars of the contextual approach speak of understanding the Bible's context in both a vertical and a horizontal dimension. The horizontal dimension is roughly the synchronic one—i.e. the geographical, historical, religious, political and literary setting in which a given text was created and disseminated[40]—whereas the vertical dimension is roughly the diachronic (or 'intertextual') one—'a vertical axis between the earlier texts that helped inspire it and later texts that reacted to it'.[41] This diachronic dimension functions on the text-critical level (where there are multiple copies and editions of the same text) as well as for purposes of comparison and contrast of different texts that are related genre-wise.

ANET accounted very well for the horizontal dimension, but not as self-consciously as *COS* for the vertical one. For example, in *ANET* (1950), Theophile J. Meek's translation of Hammurabi's law code is done from the Louvre stela, supplemented in a few cases by one tablet from Nippur,[42] but large gaps nevertheless remain in the resulting text, whereas in *COS*, Martha Roth's translation takes into account some fifty different versions and almost no gaps remain. In addition, *COS* comments much more in its introductions about relations among the various law codes from different periods and polities—Lipit-Ishtar, Eshunna, Hammurabi, Middle Assyrian, Neo-Babylonian and Hittite—than does *ANET*.

COS is a larger project than *ANET*, containing more texts and a greater number and variety of contributors. *ANET* began with eleven contributors in 1950 and grew to eighteen by the third edition of 1969. In contrast, *COS* includes a total of 63 contributors: 37 in volume I; 33 in volume II (22 of these new); and 17 in volume III (4 new). *ANET*'s three editions came to a total of 735 folio-sized pages, while *COS*' three volumes come to 1,551 equally large-sized pages. *COS* has extensively larger introductions, bibliographies, explanatory notes, scripture references,[43] and indexes. *ANET*'s translations in many

38. Hallo, 'Introduction: Ancient Near Eastern Texts', in *COS*, I, p. xxv.

39. D.M. Howard, Jr, 'Review of Hallo and Younger (eds.), *The Context of Scripture*', *JETS* 47 (2004), pp. 137-40.

40. Hallo, 'Introduction: Ancient Near Eastern Texts', in *COS*, I, p. xxv.

41. Hallo, 'Introduction: Ancient Near Eastern Texts', in *COS*, I, p. xxvi.

42. Theophile James Meek, 'The Code of Hammurabi', in *ANET* (1950), pp. 163-80.

43. Rogers deliberately left out scripture references feeling that the reader should be the one to make the connections. This was perhaps a realistic decision at that time. But in these days, students and scholars are often not as familiar with the Bible as in Rogers' day, and so there is a

places manifested a feeling of reading the King James Version of the Bible; *COS*' translations do not.

The first organizing principle in *ANET* was genre. This was based, according to Pritchard, on the assumption that

> the greatest number of readers will approach this work (*ANET*) from an interest in the Old Testament rather than primarily from an interest in one of the other linguistic or cultural areas. For those whose interest is regional or linguistic, there has been compiled a second table of contents listing the texts according to languages.[44]

In the case of *COS*, the first organizing principle is Hallo's threefold taxonomy: canonical compositions, monumental inscriptions, and archival documents. This served as the breakdown of the texts into the three volumes. Some reviewers of the first *COS* volume were especially critical of the use of the term 'canonical', failing to understand that the term was not used as it is in biblical scholarship, but rather as in literary scholarship; hence, for example, Shakespearan canon, Western canon, Assurbanipal's canon, etc. Nevertheless, of course, one can still disagree with such a taxonomy (as I know Harry Hoffner would for the generic division of Hittite texts);[45] but from a purely pragmatic point of view, when one can no longer put all the ancient Near Eastern text translations into a single volume, there must be some kind of division and, in my opinion, Hallo's taxonomy works as well as any other that can be conceived.[46]

The second organizing principle in *COS* is linguistic: each volume is divided into Egyptian, Hittite, West Semitic, Akkadian and Sumerian, along the lines of *ANET*. The third principle is genre.

3. *Conclusion*

The making of compendia has not ended with the production of *COS*; nor should it. While there will always be those who are agenda-driven, wanting to use the ancient Near Eastern texts to prove or disprove the Hebrew Bible, there will likewise always be a need for up-to-date translations of all of the relevant and most recently discovered texts for those who are interested in seeking to gain better understandings of the *complexities* of the relationships of the ancient Near Eastern texts and the various texts of biblical literature. Ancient Near Eastern texts have served and will continue to serve as bits of evidence that call for *integrity* in the interpretive process. So, the role of compendia will continue to contribute to this process.

greater need to supply references. Furthermore, it is not possible for anyone to remember all the various occurrences of words, phrases, motifs, etc.

44. Pritchard, 'Introduction', in *ANET* (1950), p. xv.

45. Harry A. Hoffner, Jr (personal communication).

46. See the further comments of Hallo, 'Introduction: The Bible and the Monuments', in *COS*, II, pp. xxi-xxvi.

Table 5. Compendia of Ancient Near Eastern Texts Related to the Old Testament[47]

	Work		Com.	Gen.	Ill.	Scrip.
1a	Schrader, Eberhard.					
	1872	*Die Keilinschriften und das Alte Testament* (Giessen: J. Ricker).	•			H
	1883	*Die Keilinschriften und das Alte Testament* (2. umgearb. und sehr vermehrte Auflage; Giessen: J. Ricker).	•			H
	1885, 1888	*The Cuneiform Inscriptions and the Old Testament* (2 vols.; trans. Owen C. Whitehouse from the 2nd German edn; Theological Translation Fund Library, 33, 38; London and Edinburgh: Williams & Norgate).	•			H
1b	Schrader, Eberhard, Heinrich Zimmern and Hugo Winckler.					
	1902–1903	*Die Keilinschriften und das Alte Testament.* I. *Geschichte und Geographie.* II. *Religion und Sprache* (3. Auflage mit Ausdehnung auf die Apokryphen, Pseudepigraphen und das Neue Testament; Berlin: Reuther & Reichard).	•			H
2a	Birch, Samuel (ed.)					
	1873–81	*Records of the Past: Being English Translations of the Assyrian and Egyptian Monuments* (12 vols.; London: Samuel Bagster).		•		L
2b	Sayce, Archibald Henry (ed.)					
	1888–92	*Records of the Past: Being English Translations of the Ancient Monuments of Egypt and Western Asia.* New Series (6 vols.; London: Samuel Bagster & Sons).		•		L
3	Ménant, M. Joachim.					
	1874	*Annales des rois d'Assyrie, traduites et mises en ordre sur le texte assyrien* (Paris: Maisonneuve).		•		L

47. *Com* = Commentary-type arrangement; *Ill.* = Illustrations; *Gen.* = Generic arrangement; *Scrip.* = Scripture referencing (H: heavy; M: moderate; L: light).

4	Rule, William Harris.					
	1877	*Oriental Records: Monumental. Confirmatory of the Old Testament Scriptures* (London: Samuel Bagster & Sons).	•			H
5	Winckler, Hugo.					
	1892	*Keilinschriftliches Textbuch zum Alten Testament* (Hilfsbücher zur Kunde des alten Orients, 1; Leipzig: E. Pfeiffer).		•		L
	1903	*Keilinschriftliches Textbuch zum Alten Testament* (Hilfsbücher zur Kunde des alten Orients, 1; 2. neu bearbeitete Auflage; Leipzig: J.C. Hinrichs).		•		L
	1909	*Keilinschriftliches Textbuch zum Alten Testament* (Hilfsbücher zur Kunde des alten Orients, 1; 3. neubearbeitete Auflage mit einer Einführung; Leipzig: J.C. Hinrichs).		•		L
6	Harper, Robert Francis (ed.)					
	1901	*Assyrian and Babylonian Literature: Selected Translations. With a Critical Introduction* (The World's Great Books, Aldine edition; New York: D. Appleton & Company)		•	•	L
7	Jeremias, Alfred.					
	1904	*Das Alte Testament im Lichte des alten Orients: Handbuch zur biblisch-orientalischen Altertumskunde* (Leipzig: J.C. Hinrichs).	•		•	H
	1906	*Das Alte Testament im Lichte des alten Orients: Handbuch zur biblisch-orientalischen Altertumskunde* (2. neu bearbeitete Auflage; Leipzig: J.C. Hinrichs).	•		•	H
	1911	*The Old Testament in the Light of the Ancient East: Manual of Biblical Archaeology* (2 vols.; ed. C.H.W. Johns; trans. C.L. Beaumont from the 2nd German edn; Theological Translation Library, 28-29; London: Williams & Norgate; New York: Putnam).	•		•	H

	1916	*Das Alte Testament im Lichte des alten Orients* (3. völlig neu bearbeitete Auflage; Leipzig: J.C. Hinrichs)	•		•	H
	1930	*Das Alte Testament im Lichte des alten Orients* (4. völlig erneuerte Auflage; Leipzig: J.C. Hinrichs).	•		•	H
8	Gressmann, Hugo (ed.)					
	1909	*Altorientalische Texte und Bilder zum Alten Testamente* (Tübingen: J.C.B. Mohr [Paul Siebeck]).		•	•	M
	1926–1927	*Altorientalische Texte und Bilder zum Alten Testament* (2. völlig neugestaltete und stark vermehrte Auflage; Berlin and Leipzig: W. de Gruyter).		•	•	M
9	Rogers, Robert William.					
	1912	*Cuneiform Parallels to the Old Testament* (New York: Eaton & Mains).		•	•	L
	1926	*Cuneiform Parallels to the Old Testament* (2nd edn; New York: Abingdon Press).		•	•	L
10	Barton, George A.					
	1916	*Archaeology and the Bible* (Philadelphia: American Sunday-School Union).		•	•	H
	1937	*Archaeology and the Bible.* Part I: *The Bible Lands, their Exploration, and the Resultant Light on the Bible and History;* Part II: *Translations of Ancient Documents Which Confirm or Illuminate the Bible* (7th revised edn; Green Book Fund, 17; Philadelphia: American Sunday-School Union).		•	•	H
11	Jean, Charles-François.					
	1924	*La littérature des babyloniens et des assyriens* (Paris: Libraire orientaliste Paul Geuthner).		•		L
12	Pritchard, James B. (ed.)					
	1950	*Ancient Near Eastern Texts Relating to the Old Testament* (Princeton, NJ: Princeton University Press).		•	•	L

	1954	*The Ancient Near East in Pictures Relating to the Old Testament* (Princeton, NJ: Princeton University Press).		•	•	L
	1954	*The Ancient Near East in Pictures Relating to the Old Testament* (Princeton, NJ: Princeton University Press).		•	•	L
	1955	*Ancient Near Eastern Texts Relating to the Old Testament* (2nd edn; Princeton, NJ: Princeton University Press).		•		L
	1969	*Ancient Near Eastern Texts Relating to the Old Testament with Supplement* (3rd edn; Princeton, NJ: Princeton University Press).		•		L
	1969	*The Ancient Near East: Supplementary Texts and Pictures Relating to the Old Testament* (Princeton, NJ: Princeton University Press).		•	•	L
13	Thomas, D. Winton (ed.)					
	1958	*Documents from Old Testament Times* (London and New York: Thomas Nelson and Sons).		•		L
14a	Brunner, Hellmut and Walter Beyerlin (eds.)					
	1975	*Religionsgeschichtliches Textbuch zum Alten Testament* (Grundrisse zum Alten Testament. Das Alte Testament Deutsch, 1; Göttingen: Vandenhoeck & Ruprecht).		•		L
14b	Beyerlin, Walter (ed.)					
	1978	*Near Eastern Religious Texts Relating to the Old Testament* (OTL; trans. John Bowden; Philadelphia: Westminster Press).		•		L

15	Kaiser, Otto *et al.* (eds.)					
	1982–2001	*Texte aus der Umwelt des Alten Testaments* (4 vols.; Gütersloh: G. Mohn).		•		L
16	Matthews, Victor H. and Don C. Benjamin.					
	1991	*Old Testament Parallels: Laws and Stories from the Ancient Near East* (New York: Paulist Press).		•	•	H

	1997 *Old Testament Parallels: Laws and Stories from the Ancient Near East* (2nd fully rev. and expanded edn; New York: Paulist Press).		•	•	H
17	Hallo, William W. and K. Lawson Younger, Jr (eds.) 1997–2002 *The Context of Scripture*. I. *Canonical Compositions from the Biblical World*; II. *Monumental Compositions from the Biblical World*; III. *Archival Documents from the Biblical World* (Leiden: E.J. Brill).		•		H
18	Arnold, Bill T. and Bryan Beyer (eds.) 2002 *Readings from the Ancient Near East: Primary Sources for Old Testament Study* (Grand Rapids, MI: Baker Academic).		•		H

Visual Perspectives

INVENTING ASSYRIA: EXOTICISM AND RECEPTION IN NINETEENTH-CENTURY ENGLAND AND FRANCE[1]

Frederick N. Bohrer

> Since the Elgin marbles were brought to England, no similar arrival has occurred so calculated to excite the interests of artists and archaeologists, as these Assyrian-Babylonian remains...
>
> Sidney Smirke, 1847[2]

> Among the interesting questions which have arisen along with the recently discovered [Assyrian] monuments, it is certainly quite surprising to find those concerning art for its own sake...
>
> Musée de Ninive, *L'illustration* 1847[3]

The sudden archaeological discovery, starting in 1843, of a wealth of artifacts of the ancient Neo-Assyrian empire brought to the attention of Europeans a form of artistic production that was unique and unexpectedly striking to many contemporary eyes. Roughly comparable arrays of ancient Assyrian artifacts found by both French and English excavators were put on display almost simultaneously in the Louvre and British Museum, starting in 1847. Yet, even as Assyrian art received a (literal) place in the ranks of ancient art, it was problematic and difficult to assimilate into established artistic and cultural discourse. As we shall see, Assyria presented an unsettling addition to a history of ancient art and cultures whose primary touchstones had been objects from ancient Egypt and the Greco-Roman world.

The interplay of Assyrian archaeology with nineteenth-century Western art and visual culture has never been fully assessed. The study of the Western reception of Assyrian art has focused largely on two portions of the phenomenon: a largely positivist narrative of archaeological progress and a narrowly defined 'influence' on aspects of European art.[4]

1. Previously published in *ArtB* 80 (1998), pp. 336-56. Reprinted by permission of the author. All translations are by the author unless otherwise noted.

2. London, Royal Institute of British Architects Archives, Sidney Smirke to Joseph Scoles, 28 June 1847.

3. 'Musée de Ninive', *L'Illustration* (15 May 1847), pp. 167-70 (169).

4. For archaeology, see, e.g. Seton Lloyd, *Foundations in the Dust: The Story of Mesopotamian Exploration* (London and New York: Oxford University Press, rev. edn, 1980); Glyn Daniel, *A Hundred and Fifty Years of Archaeology* (London: Gerald Duckworth, 1978). For some

My goal here will be, to adopt a term of Walter Benjamin, to brush these histories of continual progress, discovery, and innovation 'against the grain'.[5] As we shall see, the varied and contradictory associations impressed upon Assyria not only predate the archaeological discoveries themselves but also were decisively shaped by the particular institutional, ideological, aesthetic, and national arenas within which they circulated. Indeed, tracking the different significations of Assyria provides almost a snapshot of structures of power and knowledge active at the time, as well as some of the conflicts and contradictions involved in Western cross-cultural representation. This is a case-study, then, in a given cultural moment, of the principle stated by Johannes Fabian, that '...our ways of making the Other are ways of making ourselves'. Further, as it represents an overlap between the concerns of art history and postcolonial studies, I will draw on the resources of both fields.[6]

suggestive 'revisionist' treatments which engage the specific concerns of the Near East, see Neil Asher Silberman, 'Promised Lands and Chosen Peoples: The Politics and Poetics of Archaeological Narrative', in *Nationalism, Politics, and the Practice of Archaeology* (ed. Philip L. Kohl and Clare P. Fawcett; Cambridge and New York: Cambridge University Press, 1995), pp. 249-62; Curtis M. Hinsley, 'Revising and Revisioning the History of Archaeology: Reflections on Region and Context', in *Tracing Archaeology's Past: The Historiography of Archaeology* (ed. Andrew L. Christenson; Publications in Archaeology [Southern Illinois University at Carbondale. Center for Archaeological Investigations]; Carbondale, IL: Southern Illinois University Press, 1989), pp. 79-96; Bruce G. Trigger, 'Alternative Archaeologies: Nationalist, Colonialist, Imperialist', *Man* NS 19 (1984), pp. 355-70. For studies of Assyrian 'influence', see Robert L. Alexander, 'Courbet and Assyrian Sculpture', *ArtB* 47 (1965), pp. 447-52; Hannelore Künzl, *Der Einfluss des alten Orients auf die europäische Kunst besonders im 19. und 20 Jh.* (Cologne [Inaug.-Diss.], 1973); Robert Burge, 'Pablo Picasso's *Man with a Sheep*', *Source: Notes in the History of Art* 2 (1982), pp. 21-26; Evelyn Silber, *The Sculpture of Epstein: With a Complete Catalogue* (Oxford: Phaidon, 1986); Vojtech Jirat-Wasiutyński, 'Gauguin's Self Portraits and the Oviri: The Image of the Artist, Eve, and the Fatal Woman', *Art Quarterly* ns 2 (1979), pp. 172-90 (189), and Ziva Amishai-Maisels, *Gauguin's Religious Themes* (Outstanding Dissertations in the Fine Arts; New York: Garland, 1985).

5. Walter Benjamin, 'Theses on the Philosophy of History', in *Illuminations* (trans. Harry Zohn; New York: Schocken Books, 1969), p. 257.

6. Johannes Fabian, 'Presence and Representation: The Other and Anthropological Writing', *Critical Inquiry* 16 (1990), pp. 753-72 (756). While I cannot begin to summarize the varieties of contemporary postcolonial criticism, my own approach has been informed by the following works (in addition to the works cited elsewhere in this study), among others, (as well as by the arguments between them): Mary Louise Pratt, *Imperial Eyes: Travel Writing and Transculturation* (London and New York: Routledge, 1992); Edward W. Said, *Culture and Imperialism* (New York: Knopf, 1993); Michael T. Taussig, *Mimesis and Alterity: A Particular History of the Senses* (New York: Routledge, 1993); Homi K. Bhabha, *The Location of Culture* (London and New York: Routledge, 1994); Nicholas Thomas, *Colonialism's Culture: Anthropology, Travel, and Government* (Princeton, NJ: Princeton University Press, 1994); Iain Chambers and Lidia Curti (eds.), *The Post-Colonial Question: Common Skies, Divided Horizons* (New York: Routledge, 1996).

My primary focus, then, is not ancient Assyria itself or its excavation, but rather what was made of it within nineteenth-century Europe. I thus approach nineteenth-century Assyrian exoticism as a phenomenon of reception.[7] I am concerned not with distinguishing 'authentic' versus 'inauthentic' representations of Assyrian culture or its artifacts, but rather of articulating the (Western) processes through which all such representations take place, from Courbet's fanciful 'Assyrian' beard to Ford Madox Brown's more painstaking recreation of the interior of an Assyrian palace.

Parallel to the dynamic of imperialist power involved in Mesopotamian archaeology itself, the European reception of Assyria presents a series of conflictual power relations. As we shall see, the establishment of Assyria in the cultural and artistic discourse of the West consistently illuminated, often precisely as it challenged, established norms of cultural discourse. To be more specific, I want to show here how the Assyrian discoveries were involved in a consistent process of identification by means of binarism and bifurcation. The most obvious binary pairing is that in which the West defined itself against its nebulous 'Other'. At the same time, juxtaposing different works of art and moments of reception ultimately undermines the binary logic which underwrites the Western construct of a timeless 'exotic' East. It instead reveals that the exotic subject takes on a variety of forms and roles in the nineteenth century, encompassing a broad array of artistic production.

As we shall see, France and England asserted themselves directly against each other in their representations of Assyria in a way that paralleled the nations' rivalry to gain Assyrian antiquities. Further, though they can only be briefly touched on here, other sorts of bifurcated oppositions were also involved. The distinction between judging an object a work of art or an antiquarian artifact was clearly invoked to evaluate Assyria, by partisans of both positions. Even the conventional roles of male and female were a bit unsettled by the case of Assyria.

7. 'Isn't exoticism primarily a phenomenon of reception?' Jean-Pierre Leduc-Adine, 'Exotisme et discours d'art au XIXe siècle', in *L'exotisme: Actes du colloque de Saint-Denis de la Réunion* (ed. Alain Buisine, Norbert Dodille and Claude Duchet; Paris: Diffusion Didier-Erudition, 1988), pp. 457-65 (461). This suggestive essay deserves wider attention. On the general methodological range of reception theory, see Robert C. Holub, *Reception Theory: A Critical Introduction* (London and New York: Methuen, 1984); Susan R. Suleiman, 'Introduction: Varieties of Audience-Oriented Criticism', in *The Reader in the Text* (ed. Susan R. Suleiman and Inge Crosman; Princeton, NJ: Princeton University Press, 1980), pp. 3-45. For some specific ramifications of these approaches to visual material, see Wolfgang Kemp, 'Review of John Shearman, *Only Connect: Art and the Spectator in the Italian Renaissance*', *ArtB* 76 (1994), pp. 364-67; Michael Ann Holly, *Past Looking: Historical Imagination and the Rhetoric of the Image* (Ithaca, NY: Cornell University Press, 1996), pp. 195-208: Dario Gamboni, 'Histoire de l'art et "reception": Remarques sur l'état d'une problematique', *Histoire de l'art* 35-36 (October 1996), pp. 9-14.

Finally, I must add a note on context. I use the term *exoticism* with a full sense of its complex history.[8] Indeed, I use it for that very reason: to underline the contestable and problematic nature of 'non-Western' representation.[9] There are pressing reasons, both historical and contemporary, to question the putatively objective accounts that circulate in the West of the world beyond it. A critical analysis of Assyrian exoticism is part of that project. Nonetheless, the overwhelming majority of postcolonial studies, both in art history and elsewhere, are devoted to European representations of lands contemporary to the artist. This study moves instead toward the (less often examined) implications for understanding the involvement of historical subjects in the representation of exoticist difference.[10]

1. *Martin and Delacroix:* *The Image of Ancient Assyria in the Early Nineteenth Century*

What did ancient Assyria represent in France and England during the earlier nineteenth century? Consideration of a key artistic monument from each country will allow us to focus on Assyria's primary associations in the period in which the impetus to excavate first developed. To begin, though, we must locate Assyria, and Mesopotamia, both geographically and temporally.[11]

Mesopotamia refers to the land between the Tigris and Euphrates rivers in what is modern-day Iraq. In antiquity, it was for millennia the site of many

8. For a range of definitions, compare the mocking treatment of the term in Aimé Césaire, *Discourse on Colonialism* (trans. Joan Pinkham; New York: MR, 1972), *passim*, with the largely expository presentation of Vincenette Maigne, 'Exotisme: Evolution en diachronie du mot et de son champ sémantique', in *Exotisme et création: Actes du colloque internationale (Lyons 1983)* (Paris: L'Hermès, 1985), pp. 7-16.

9. This is a founding tenet of postcolonial theory, starting with Edward W. Said, *Orientalism* (New York: Pantheon Books, 1979). Most recently, see the formulation of exoticism in Roger Célestin, *From Cannibals to Radicals: Figures and Limits of Exoticism* (Minneapolis, MN: University of Minnesota Press, 1996).

10. A pioneering study in this direction is Johannes Fabian, *Time and the Other: How Anthropology Makes its Object* (New York: Columbia University Press, 1983). For a range of treatments of time in more recent postcolonial studies, see Paul Carter, *The Road to Botany Bay: An Essay in Spatial History* (New York: Knopf, 1987); Homi K. Bhabha 'DissemiNation: Time, Narrative, and the Margins of the Modern Nation', in *Nation and Narration* (ed. H.K. Bhabha; London and New York: Routledge, 1990), pp. 291-322; Chambers and Curti (eds.), *Post-Colonial Question*, pp. 65-120.

11. For a detailed account of these regions in antiquity, see Amélie Kuhrt, *The Ancient Near East c. 3000–330 B.C.* (2 vols.; Routledge History of the Ancient World; London: Routledge, 1995). Among the extensive bibliography of the region's more recent history, a useful comprehensive source is Albert Hourani, *A History of the Arab Peoples* (Cambridge, MA: Harvard University Press, 1991).

and varied cultures, chief among them the Assyrian empire centered in northern Mesopotamia and the Babylonian kingdom of southern Mesopotamia. The best-known capitals of these two ancient kingdoms were Nineveh and Babylon, respectively. The names of both resounded in Western discourse (and also blended to some extent), largely through accounts circulated by Greco-Roman writers as well as biblical sources.[12] The view of Mesopotamia communicated to the West derived from the accounts of peoples central to Western self-definition, the ancient Hebrews and those of classical antiquity. That is, Mesopotamia was seen not on its own terms, but rather via those of its historical antagonists. Through these accounts, largely considered documentary in the earlier nineteenth century, Mesopotamia was taken as a cautionary tale, a site of sloth, sin, violence, and transgression: the West's first great 'Other'.[13]

In the nineteenth century, the area was a province at the far eastern edge of the Ottoman empire, a region of semi-autonomous *pashaliks* each governed primarily by a local *pasha*, though officially under the control of the Ottoman ruler in Istanbul. Seen by Western travellers as a remote and unwelcoming locale of largely unrelieved desert, Mesopotamia was not part of the itinerary of the Grand Tour, which preferred the more impressive and accessible monuments of Egypt, Palestine, Greece, and the Turkish lands. In a telling turn of illogic, the relatively few nineteenth-century travelogues of the area that existed often used the seemingly 'wasted' state of the land and its current inhabitants to emphasize the notable evils ascribed to its ancient population. Mesopotamia's current state was seen as a lasting trace of the divine punishments said to have rained upon its ancient rulers Sardanapalus of Assyria and Nebuchadnezzar of Babylon.[14] What was not there was taken to prove what had been. Here, then, is the

12. C.J. Gadd, *The Stones of Assyria: The Surviving Remains of Assyrian Sculpture, their Recovery, and their Original Positions* (London: Chatto & Windus, 1936), pp. 2-9; Béatrice André-Salvini, ' "Où sont-ils ces remparts de Ninive?" Les sources de connaissance de l'Assyrie avant les fouilles', in *De Khorsabad à Paris: La découverte des Assyriens* (ed. Elisabeth Fontan and Nicole Chevalier; Louvre, Département des Antiquités Orientales: Notes et documents des Musées de France, 26; Paris: Réunion des musées nationaux, 1994), pp. 22-43; Stephanie Dalley, 'Nineveh, Babylon, and the Hanging Gardens: Cuneiform and Classical Sources Reconciled', *Iraq* 56 (1994), pp. 45-58.

13. François Hartog, *The Mirror of Herodotus: The Representation of the Other in the Writing of History* (trans. Janet Lloyd; New Historicism, 5; Berkeley: University of California Press, 1988); Wilfried Nippel, 'Facts and Fiction: Greek Ethnography and its Legacy', *History and Anthropology* 9 (1996), pp. 125-38 (125-31).

14. Thus James Fletcher, a missionary who visited Mesopotamia in the 1840s described the scene: 'Yet what a moral might be derived from the present condition of the capital of Assur. In lieu of lofty palaces and gorgeous temples, the eye surveys only the mounds composed of their dust, or the miserable collections of huts which have arisen on their site. The gardens where Sardanapalus revelled are wasted and desolate, the sounds of soft and luxurious music that once floated on the soft Assyrian breezes have yielded to the silence of devastation or decay'. James Phillips Fletcher, *Notes from Nineveh, and Travels in Mesopotamia, Assyria and Syria* (2 vols.;

first and most obvious binarism involved in the constructed image of Assyria, in which Western achievement is contrasted with Eastern ruin, and taken as an index of the morality of the former versus the immorality of the latter.

The Western image of Assyria in the early nineteenth century thus subsumed present to past, consistently invoking ancient events supposed to have led to the reputedly wasted state of the region during the nineteenth century. More than any other work of its kind, John Martin's tremendously popular *Fall of Nineveh* attempted to document in detail such moments in the inherited narrative of ancient Assyria. Martin had made his name with another work of Mesopotamian imagery, *Belshazzar's Feast* of 1821. Seven years later, in *The Fall of Nineveh*, he returned to the subject, creating a work that exemplifies what Morton Paley has termed 'the apocalyptic sublime'.[15] Though perceptions of Assyria and Babylonia were frequently intermingled, and the similarities may have been seen as greater than the differences, *Belshazzar's Feast* (as Martin seems to have realized) is a subject which took place in Babylon, while *The Fall of Nineveh* allows us to address specifically the conception of Assyria.[16]

London: Henry Colburn, 1850), I, p. 206; See also Asahel Grant, *The Nestorians, or the Lost Tribes: Containing Evidence of their Identity, an Account of their Manners, Customs, and Ceremonies, together with Sketches of Travel in Ancient Assyria, Armenia, Media, and Mesopotamia and Illustrations of Scripture Prophecy* (London: John Murray, 2nd edn, 1843 [New York, 1841]), p. 27; Robert Mignan, *Travels in Chaldœa, Including a Journey from Bussorah to Bagdad, Hillah, and Babylon, Performed on Foot in 1827: With Observations on the Site and Remains of Babel, Seleucia, and Ctesiphon* (London: Henry Colburn & R. Bentley, 1829), *passim*. Significantly, the *topos* is repeated by Eugène Flandin in an account of Botta's archaeological activity, 'Voyage archéologique à Ninive: L'architecture assyrienne', *Revue des deux mondes* 10/2 (1845), pp. 642-60, and 'Voyage archéologique à Ninive: La sculpture assyrienne et les bas-reliefs de Khorsabad', *Revue des deux mondes* 10/2 (1845), pp. 768-85.

This 'denial of coevalness', which essentializes the contemporary Mesopotamian land and its inhabitants as moral and historical inheritors of ancient forebears, is a common *topos* of exoticist description and has received considerable attention in postcolonial analysis. See Fabian, *Time and the Other*, p. 35; Ali Behdad, *Belated Travellers: Orientalism in the Age of Colonial Dissolution* (Post-Contemporary Interventions; Durham, NC: Duke University Press, 1994), p. 46; Pratt, *Imperial Eyes*, p. 64.

15. Morton D. Paley, *The Apocalyptic Sublime* (New Haven: Yale University Press, 1986); for *Belshazzar's Feast*, see esp. pp. 128-38. On Martin, see also Thomas Balston, *John Martin 1789–1854: His Life and Works* (London: Gerald Duckworth, 1947); William Feaver, *The Art of John Martin* (Oxford: Clarendon Press, 1975); Hazlitt, Gooden and Fox, *John Martin 1789–1854* (London, 1975: exhibition catalogue). The original oil painting of *The Fall of Nineveh*, of 1828, was formerly in the Royal Collection, Cairo, Egypt (Balston, *John Martin*, p. 276; Feaver, *Art of John Martin*, pp. 223-24). The work is known now from the many mezzotints Martin produced of it around 1830.

16. *A Description of the Picture, Belshazzar's Feast, Painted by Mr J. Martin...* (London, 42nd edn, 1825).

Figure 20. John Martin, *The Fall of Nineveh*, mezzotint, 1829 (photo: British Museum, London).

A huge painting (measuring 84" by 134"), *The Fall of Nineveh* was a vast spectacle of destruction, a panorama of violent disorder in an elaborately detailed setting. In it, the capital of the Assyrian empire is laid waste by invading armies. Martin detailed, to an explicit internal scale, 100-foot walls and a gateway twice that size. At the far right he created the tomb of Ninus, the legendary founder of Nineveh. In the middle ground, the armies of the siege set upon soldiers and citizens of Nineveh, who are in various stages of capitulation. Further, in the same area are civilian fighters, described by Martin as 'Fathers and husbands defending their children and wives'. By contrast, many of the Ninevite soldiers have broken rank, and flee in terror before the well-ordered invaders. A sea of vast columns connects foreground and background, a hybrid order combining Egyptian and Indian architectural features.

Among the most striking features of *The Fall of Nineveh*, a key to both its legibility and profitability, was Martin's descriptive brochure, which circulated with the work. The brochure describes the architecture as 'invented as the most appropriate for a city situate [*sic*] betwixt the two countries [Egypt and India] and necessarily in frequent intercourse with them'.[17] As we approach the foreground of the image, looking down omnisciently upon a wing of the royal palace, we can make out the figure the descriptive brochure puts at the heart of the drama. At the edge of the steps, gesturing toward the pyre being

17. *Descriptive Catalogue of the Picture of The Fall of Nineveh* (London: George Woodfall, 1828), p. 14. Norah Monckton, 'Architectural Backgrounds in the Pictures of John Martin', *Architectural Review* 104 (1948), pp. 81-84.

built for him at left, is Sardanapalus, the legendary final king of Assyria, said to have 'exceeded all his predecessors in sloth and luxury'. As his leaderless army broke apart, the king, we are told

> retired into his palace, in a court in which he caused a vast pile of wood to be raised; and, heaping upon it all his gold and silver, and royal apparel, and at the same time enclosing his eunuches and concubines in an apartment within the pile, he set fire thereto, and so destroyed himself and the rest.[18]

This quotation in the brochure, from a nineteenth-century reference source, largely distills the facts from ancient accounts. But it does not precisely account for Martin's picture, in which the pyre is not located in an apartment within the palace but rather in open space adjoining the city itself.

This sort of disjuncture abounds between the image and the texts purported to explain it. Thus while one portion of the text acknowledges that there is no biblical description of the scene, a quote from the book of Nahum is nonetheless used specifically to justify the action of the queen (also unmentioned in ancient accounts). In Martin's conception she 'casts a farewell look of love and regret upon the king' before being led off to safety, in the opposite direction from the king, together with her maids and advisers. Similarly, in another sort of disjuncture, some of the architectural decoration of Nineveh is justified by Herodotus's description of a temple located not in Nineveh but in Babylon.[19]

Beyond serving mere factual explanation, Martin's brochure testifies to a certain referential obsession, a need to justify. Assembling a bulwark of authoritative sources comes to be more important than demonstrating any internal consistency among them. The brochure is choked with a variety of heterogeneous texts, including much of the biblical book of Nahum, contemporary reference works, various classical citations, and a poetic account of the incident. But they too are as much pretexts for Martin's inventions as factual validations of the proffered spectacle.

Martin's image of ancient Nineveh exemplifies both the particular subject and judgmental tone that dominated the popular conception of Assyria in the early nineteenth century. The sheer sublime charge of Martin's huge, animated image holds in check, or at least disguises, the jarring discontinuities of the sources from which it is fashioned. In all, the work testifies to a need both to construct and justify an ancient Assyrian 'other'.

Martin's work was well known in France. Throughout the later 1820s and early 1830s Martin's elaborate prints after his oil paintings circulated widely in France, to critical, popular, and even royal acclaim, receiving a gold medal from Charles X in 1829. His painting *The Deluge* made a sensation and won a

18. *Descriptive Catalogue*, pp. 8; 10-11.

19. *Descriptive Catalogue*, pp. 11, 15, 14. Sardanapalus is mentioned in numerous ancient sources, but by far the most detailed and influential account is that of Diodorus Siculus, 2.23-27.

further gold medal at the Salon of 1834.[20] But while Martin's image was circulated among overlapping French and English audiences, to assess its implications more fully it must be seen in counterpoint to a French work of the same subject, begun the year before Martin's *Fall of Nineveh*.

Eugène Delacroix's *The Death of Sardanapalus* stands today as the most famous representation of Assyria of the nineteenth century.[21] The work caused a sensation at the Salon of 1827–28. As with Martin's image, there is further evidence of the work's continuing popularity. Several engravings of the painting exist, as well as a number of copies both by the artist himself and later followers. A further parallel to the cross-channel currency of Martin's image is that Delacroix's work in the 1820s embraced a number of English sources, notably Shakespeare and Byron. Byron's *The Tragedy of Sardanapalus*, first published in 1821, has often been considered an inspiration for Delacroix's painting.[22] Thus, while Delacroix's work, like Martin's, suggests a certain common interest in Assyria in France and England, the considerable difference between the two images testifies also to the remarkable degree of invention and variety allowed by the subject. However paradoxical, this 'mobility' of subject consistently coexists with the referential exactitude of both Martin and Delacroix. [23]

Indeed, the treatment by the classically-educated Delacroix of the subject corresponds more precisely to the description quoted above from Martin, as the scene is now set inside, within the king's palace, in a locale controlled by his gaze. The smoke of the conflagration already has begun to fill the chamber, and the room is littered with the concubines, servants, animals, and other treasures being destroyed as the king watches.

20. John Gage, *Goethe on Art* (London and Berkeley: Scolar Press, 1980), p. xv calls Martin 'the rage of England and the continent in the 1820s'. Jean Seznec, *John Martin en France* (All Souls Studies, 4; London: Faber & Faber, 1964); Paley, *The Apocalyptic Sublime*, pp. 142-43; Balston, *John Martin*, p. 90.

21. The basic sources for this work are Jack J. Spector, *Delacroix: The Death of Sardanapalus* (Art in Context; New York: Viking Press, 1974); Lee Johnson, *The Paintings of Eugène Delacroix: A Critical Catalogue* (7 vols.; Oxford: Clarendon Press, 1981–2002), I, pp. 114-21. See also Eric-Henry Berrebi, 'Sardanapale, ou l'impossible étreinte', *L'écrit-voir, revue d'histoire des arts* 8 (1986), pp. 37-49.

22. The similarities and differences between Delacroix's treatment of the subject and Byron's are summarized by Johnson, *The Paintings of Eugène Delacroix*. On the Byronic affinities of the work, see especially Spector, *The Death of Sardanapalus*, pp. 59-73; Alain Daguerre de Hureaux and Stéphane Guégan, *L'ABCdaire de Delacroix et l'orient* (Paris: Flammarion: Institut du monde arabe, 1994), p. 38; Rana Kabbani, *Europe's Myths of Orient* (Bloomington, IN: Indiana University Press, 1986), p. 75. Byron was named as inspiration also in Delacroix's time: Maurice Tourneux, *Eugène Delacroix devant ses contemporains, ses écrits, ses biographes, ses critiques* (Bibliothèque internationale de l'art; Paris: Librairie de l'art, 1886), p. 48.

23. On exoticist mobility, see Frederick N. Bohrer, 'Eastern Medi(t)ations: Exoticism and the Mobility of Difference', *History and Anthropology* 9 (1996), pp. 293-307. See also the discussion of Behdad's 'principle of discontinuity' below n. 29.

Figure 21. Eugène Delacroix, *The Death of Sardanapalus*, 1827–28. Paris, Musée du Louvre (photo: Art Resource, New York).

But Delacroix's scene cannot be taken as a closer transcription of a textual source. To the contrary, this work also maps itself on a field of overlapping and discontinuous textual referents. First, Byron's soulful conception of Sardanapalus is not compatible with that of the classical historians. Byron's play, in fact, does not even include this scene of brilliant immolation. Beyond the divergence between the classical and Byronic conceptions, a third text further problematizes the precise subject. This text is contemporary with Delacroix, and one to which his work clearly was meant to refer. An unattributed paragraph, in quotation marks, was published in the Salon catalogue accompanying the work's original exhibition. Its description of Sardanapalus and his setting follows approximately the account of Diodorus Siculus (the major classical authority for the incident), but also mentions two other characters, including a Bactrian woman, Aïscheh, who is mentioned nowhere else among the established sources of the legend, and does not seem clearly identifiable within Delacroix's image.

Visually, the same sort of referential calculus is at work here as in Martin's image. Delacroix again creates Assyria again through citations from a wide and heterogeneous range of sources, always substantiating the most imaginary and sensational by including elements agreed to be authentic and attested. But whereas Martin explicitly claimed to have invented a single period style used more or less consistently in the setting, Delacroix employs a pastiche of visual references from a variety of ancient and contemporary cultures. In Delacroix's attempt to pass off details of architecture, costume, and implements as Assyrian, convincing cases have been made for his painstaking transposition of archaic Greek, Mughal Indian, Etruscan, and Egyptian sources in various aspects of the painting.[24]

Delacroix's work, like Martin's, creates a network of references to authoritative texts and artifacts. But the considerable differences between the two images, renditions of the same subject drawn from common sources of a given historical moment, only serve to further undermine the claim of each to objectivity. Ancient Assyria, then, serves as a mirror which reflects the different preconceptions and desires of the representer as much as it does any objective subject being represented. Western artists and audiences, while partaking of a widely accepted network of established references, also differently construe the imagery of a foreign culture in a way related to their own cultural differences. The subject of the fall of Nineveh thus floats on a sea of references without being precisely tied to any one. It is strikingly open to individual manipulation.

Delacroix's conception of the subject, with its explicit violence, sexuality, and cruelty contrasts sharply with the mock-heroic and sentimentalized conception of Martin. Martin's placement of the king bestows a certain privilege, as he engages in a grand pointing gesture that elevates him above the height of the crowd. Delacroix's king, by contrast, lies in darkness outside the main focus of the composition. Rather than acting he watches impassively.

Further, there is a remarkable difference between the two images in the treatment of gender relations. Martin presents active, loving, familial relations between the sexes. We have seen this already between king and queen, and the fathers fighting to defend their daughters. Even the king's favorite concubine, who is to follow him to her death, leans her head gently on his bosom. Delacroix's Sardanapalus, of course, who watches calmly as his concubines are abjectly murdered, could not be more different.

The differing gender conceptions of Martin and Delacroix reflect different social norms, but also reflect different imaginations. More than a decade ago, Linda Nochlin described *The Death of Sardanapalus* as 'a fantasy space' into which the artist's own erotic and sadistic desires could be projected. As she wrote '[it is not] Western's man power over the Near East that is at issue, but

24. Beatrice Farwell, 'Sources for Delacroix's *Death of Sardanapalus*', *ArtB* 40 (1958), pp. 66-71; Lee Johnson, 'The Etruscan Sources of Delacroix's *Death of Sardanapalus*', *ArtB* 42 (1960), pp. 296-300; *idem*, 'Toward Delacroix's Oriental Sources', *Burlington Magazine* 120 (1978), pp. 144-51; Donald Rosenthal, 'A Mughal Portrait Copied by Delacroix', *Burlington Magazine* 119 (1977), pp. 505-506; William A. Steinke, 'An Archaeological Source for Delacroix's *Death of Sardanapalus*', *ArtB* 66 (1984), pp. 318-20; Helen Whitehouse, lecture, Association of Art Historians meeting, Brighton, England, April 1986.

rather, I believe, contemporary Frenchmen's power over women...'[25] This was a decisive move away from interpreting the work purely in terms of the objective conditions of its visual and textual sources, locating the work as well in the subjectivity of the Western artist. Looking more closely at the dynamics of gender in Delacroix's work from the standpoint of reception aesthetics, however, it hardly seems that admitting one interpretation excludes the other.[26] Rather, these two forms of power—Western man's power over the Near East and that of the contemporary Frenchman over women—are related within the work.

Delacroix's *Sardanapalus* thematizes viewing itself. Drawing on the method of reception aesthetics, we can locate the work's 'implied viewer' and then construct a relationship between this viewer and the figures in the work. Especially when seen, as Nochlin suggests, specifically within its masculine-dominated milieu of reception, the work clearly employs both forms of power-relations. The decentered position of the king gives way to the even more privileged view of the women's bodies, and other objects, offered the (presumed male) viewer.[27] To extend Nochlin's observation, the viewer's relation to the women, like that of Sardanapalus to the women, can stand for the power of the contemporary Frenchman over women. Yet at the same time, the relation of this same implied viewer to Sardanapalus, as like genders engaged in the same action of viewing, reflects on just the same level the power of West over East. For even as the viewer is intimately present in the room with Sardanapalus, he is also in a position of superiority to the doomed, effeminate ruler. The viewer is thus in a position to validate the excoriating description of Sardanapalus by an early nineteenth-century critic as 'a prince whose name has become synonymous with debauchery and passivity of the most degraded and notorious sort'.[28]

Considering Delacroix and Martin together, we can see that while relations of gender in conceptions of Assyria may vary, this power of West over East is common to both images. The viewer's closeness to Delacroix's Sardanapalus, and even participation with him in the same activity of viewing, is countered by the infamy of the king's name, and the fate that awaits him. In Martin's work,

25. Linda Nochlin, 'The Imaginary Orient', in *The Politics of Vision: Essays on Nineteenth-Century Art and Society* (Icon Editions; New York: Harper & Row, 1989), pp. 33-59 (42).

26. As suggested in another context in Zeynep Çelik and Lila Kinney, 'Ethnography and Exhibitionism at the Expositions Universelles', *Assemblages* 13 (1990), pp. 34-59. On gender in exoticist representation and its relation to other forms of difference, see also Reina Lewis, *Gendering Orientalism: Race, Femininity and Representation* (Gender, Racism, Ethnicity; London and New York: Routledge, 1996); Anne McClintock, *Imperial Leather: Race, Gender and Sexuality in the Colonial Contest* (London and New York: Routledge, 1995).

27. An assumption not only of Nochlin. See Kabbani, *Europe's Myths*, pp. 67-85; Joanna de Groot, '"Sex" and "Race": The Construction of Language and Image in the Nineteenth Century', in *Sexuality and Subordination: Interdisciplinary Studies of Gender in the Nineteenth Century* (ed. Susan Mendus and Jane Rendall; London and New York: Routledge, 1989), pp. 89-128.

28. Tourneux, *Eugène Delacroix*, p. 48.

while the conception and composition are vastly different from Delacroix, the relation of viewer to subject is comparable. The high, omniscient viewpoint now insulates the viewer from the threat of the action while providing a panoramic view. Even if Sardanapalus is identifiable among the crowd, he is only slightly larger than the rest of the doomed multitude in the distant, roiling sea of the battle. The closest figures to the viewer are the 'rulers' of the state (unattested by any literary source), gesturing toward the heavens and cursing Sardanapalus for ignoring their counsel. Their rebuke is a metaphor for the Western viewer's own stance toward the scene.

More generally, then, the pattern of commonalities and divergences between the two paintings both confirms and complicates the conventional binarist model of exoticism. Each work clearly reinforces the conception of Assyria as a moralizing and cautionary tale, a counterexample to Western 'progress': a place picturesque, violent, sensual, and, perhaps most significant, doomed. Each work clearly looks down upon its subject, in the directed, imperialistic power relation between West and East dominant at the time. At the same time, the palpable differences we have noted mitigate against finding this binary situation completely adequate as an explanation. There is neither a single Assyria nor a single, given West. Instead, as we have seen, the subject metamorphoses as it circulates among different cultural nodes within the West. The enormous differences of subject, setting, treatment, and even style between Martin and Delacroix testify to the heterogeneity of the Western audience. This in turn has major importance for theorizing nineteenth-century exoticism.

The features we have examined here in the representation of Assyria seem to confirm a judgment that has only recently emerged in postcolonial studies. Rather than a single dominant monolith, the Western conception of 'the East' was multiple, fragmented, and localized. We have found, instead of a closed and coherent system, something closer to what Ali Behdad has recently called Orientalism's 'principle of discontinuity', its dispersion of authority through intermingled but incomplete networks of reference.[29] The authority of exoticist reference in such a system is deferred from an individual representation and taken up, unevenly and idiosyncratically, by a pre-existent repertory of assumptions.

A similar feature has already been noted specifically in connection with nineteenth-century exoticist painting. In her study of Antoine-Jean Gros's *Plague-Stricken of Jaffa*, Darcy Grimaldo Grigsby has observed that 'Orientalist discourse represents its own incompleteness'.[30] It is through just this incom-

29. Behdad *Belated Travellers*, p. 13. On the relation of Said's initial, and seminal, formulation to more recent studies, see Gyan Prakash, '*Orientalism* Now', *History and Theory* 34 (1995), pp. 199-212.

30. Darcy Grimaldo Grigsby, 'Rumor, Contagion and Colonization in Gros's *Plague-Stricken of Jaffa* (1804)', *Representations* 51 (1995), pp. 1-46 (2).

pleteness, this purport to represent what is beyond the validating capability of the Western viewer, that the cultural boundedness of the artistic conception is enunciated. These circumstances are at the heart of the discontinuity of exoticist representation. They are the founding conditions for the exoticist 'mobility' we have noted above.

Images such as those of Martin and Delacroix, then, are clearly evidence of a widespread interest in Assyria. But juxtaposing them uncovers the slippery, subtle working of the exoticist signifier. It is a process, as we have seen, that begins by appealing to a binary relationship between West and East, even while amending the particular subject matter in different ways to fit different situations.

In short, the representation of Assyria must be investigated with a full sense of its Western context, as much as its individual meaning. In precisely this manner, I want to follow Assyria's representational fortunes in France and England through two successive moments. First, we will consider the response to Assyrian archaeological discoveries in the years around 1850, and second, we will look briefly at some representations of Mesopotamia from the years following the discoveries. As we shall see, these discoveries did nothing to 'correct' the imaginative constructions of the earlier artists. Despite new findings based on actual artifacts, Assyria continued to be explicitly infused with the character and expectations of its audience. Further, the debate inspired by its artifacts brought up a new kind of controversy, which emerged from vexing questions about their aesthetic value.

2. *Crises of Discovery: The Motivation and Circulation of Early Assyrian Archaeology*

Following further the European representation of Mesopotamia necessitates a shift from art to archaeology. This underlines the interdependence of the two activities and specifies the contemporary political and cultural conditions under which such representation took place. Like the works of art we have just considered, in their treatment of the actual Mesopotamia (and Mesopotamians) France and England asserted both unique identities and common assumptions. Just as we have noted the overlap of audiences and sources drawn on by Martin and Delacroix, so too the archaeological rediscovery of the ancient Neo-Assyrian kingdom owes much to the projects for geo-political dominance of the two countries. The rivalry of France and England was played out, in part, through the amassing of remains.[31]

31. The acquisition of antiquities is acknowledged by John M. MacKenzie, *Orientalism: History, Theory, and the Arts* (Manchester and New York: Manchester University Press, 1995), p. 53 as 'that ultimate imperial act' even though he is otherwise notably opposed to analysis in the direction inspired by Said and Nochlin.

Already in the 1820s word was circulating in Europe that the remains of the great Mesopotamian kingdoms had been located. The first sentence of Martin's brochure states 'The mighty cities of Nineveh and Babylon have long since passed away, and, till lately, the traveller hath in vain sought for the spot where their dust reposed'.[32] The recent development noted in England was indeed part of a chain that led, ironically, to France's making the premiere discovery.

Three years before Martin's picture, in 1825, a collection of some fifty-odd ancient Babylonian baked clay tablets, bricks, and related objects entered the collection of the British Museum. Assembled by Claudius James Rich, and donated to the museum upon his death at age thirty-four, this modest collection was the first significant assembly of ancient Mesopotamian artifacts. Together with Rich's several popular and detailed publications on the sites of ancient Babylon and Nineveh, they raised the profile of Mesopotamia in European discourse.[33]

Rich's presence in Mesopotamia, and the European public's interest, grew from a distinct, and hardly disinterested, source. Instead, they were a by-product of a strategy to promote colonial interests. Rich had been appointed in 1807 as the British East India Company's first 'resident' in Baghdad, in Southern Mesopotamia. His primary mission was defensive. The success of Napoleon's Egyptian campaign in the previous years (and Britain's own failed occupation of Alexandria in 1807) raised English fears of further French conquests in the region. Rich was to shore up British interests in Mesopotamia, particularly seeing to the maintenance of overland and river routes to India. Mesopotamia thus had a specific function in the map of English interests. The location of Mesopotamia in Martin's brochure as directly between Egypt and India thus bears particular relevance, situating it directly between these contemporary sites of Western power and contention.

As the immediate political threat passed, Rich's interest in the ancient history of Mesopotamia grew. His memoir on Babylon quickly went through four editions and was followed by a second, while a memoir of his visit to Northern Mesopotamia, with a considerable portion devoted to ancient Nineveh, was published posthumously.[34] Thus even in the two decades following his death in

32. *Descriptive Catalog*, p. 5.

33. Thus Byron states in *Don Juan* of 1819–24 (5.62) 'Though Claudius Rich, Esquire, some bricks has got/and written lately two memoirs upon't'. On Rich, see Lloyd, *Foundations*, pp. 12-42, 57-73; Mogens Trolle Larsen, *The Conquest of Assyria: Excavations in an Antique Land 1840–1860* (London and New York: Routledge, 1996), pp. 9-12; Julian E. Reade, 'Les relations anglo-françaises en Assyrie', in Fontan and Chevalier (eds.), *De Khorsabad à Paris*, pp. 116-34 (116-17).

34. Claudius J. Rich, *Memoir on the Ruins of Babylon* (London: Longman, Hurst, Rees, Orme & Brown, 1815); *idem*, *Second Memoir on Babylon: Containing an Inquiry into the Correspondence between the Ancient Description of Babylon and the Remains Still Visible on the Site* (London: Longman, Hurst, Rees, Orme & Brown etc., 1818); *idem*, *Narrative of a Residence*

1821, Rich's work continued to bring to attention both textual and artifactual evidence of ancient Mesopotamia. The last works bearing his name were published in 1839.

The circulation of Rich's findings on ancient history and archaeology do not mark a complete break from the overtly political nature of his earlier work, but rather point to the establishment of archaeology as a new arena of contention for the European powers. Around 1841, a French consulate was opened in Mesopotamia. As Baghdad had been taken by the British, the French placed their toehold nearly two hundred miles to the north, in the city of Mosul—which proved to be located as strategically for archaeology as for any other purpose. Beside its importance for trade and manufacture (notably a delicate textile soon dubbed in French *mousseline*), Mosul also boasted a location directly across the Tigris from the enormous mounds that had been (correctly) presumed by Rich to be the remains of ancient Nineveh.

In 1842, Paul-Émile Botta was named to the newly-created post at Mosul, largely through the backing of Jules Mohl, the driving force behind the Société Asiatique, then the leading organization in France devoted to the study of Near Eastern and Asian languages and the collection of related artifacts. Botta began excavations almost immediately, without official permission from the Ottoman government even to dig much less remove any remains.[35] When little was turned up at the site of Nineveh, Botta moved his entourage to the village of Khorsabad, about fifteen miles to the northeast, and began almost immediately to make spectacular finds. From the start of work on 20 March 1843, as he later put it, 'I had the first revelation of a new world of antiquities'.[36]

Botta's letters to Mohl were published and annotated by the latter in the Société's *Journal Asiatique* the following year. These documents, which

in Koordistan, and on the Site of Ancient Nineveh; with Journal of a Voyage down the Tigris to Bagdad and an Account of a Visit to Shirauz and Persepolis, Edited by his Widow (2 vols.; London: James Duncan, 1836); *idem*, *Narrative of a Journey to the Site of Babylon in 1811: Now First Published: Memoir on the Ruins with Engravings from the Original Sketches* (London: Duncan, 1839).

35. Botta referred to himself as 'only a tool of M. Mohl'. E. Fontan, 'Introduction', in Fontan and Chevalier (eds.), *De Khorsabad à Paris*, pp. 12-15 (13). On Botta's early activities and Mohl's 'nationalistic dream', see Larsen, *Conquest*, pp. 21-33. On Botta, see also Giovanni Bergamini, '"*Spoliis Orientis onustus*": Paul-Emile Botta et la découverte de la civilisation assyrienne', in Fontan and Chevalier (eds.), *De Khorsabad à Paris*, pp. 68-85; Charles Levavasseur, 'Notice sur Paul-Emile Botta', in Paul-Emile Botta, *Relation d'un voyage dans l'Yémen, entrepris en 1837 pour le Muséum d'histoire naturelle de Paris* (Paris: B. Duprat, 1880), pp. 1-34. On Mohl, see also F. Max Müller, 'Notice sur Jules Mohl', in Jules Mohl, *Vingt-sept ans d'histoire des études orientales: Rapports faits à la Société Asiatique de Paris de 1840 à 1867* (2 vols.; Paris: Reinwald, 1879–80), I, pp. ix-xlvii.

36. Paul-Emile Botta in Botta and Eugène Flandin, *Monument de Ninive découvert et décrit* (5 vols.; Paris: Imprimerie nationale, 1849–50), V, p. 5.

constitute Botta's only written work to receive any large public distribution give the first descriptions of Assyrian art published in the West. They were disseminated widely throughout the French and English press, the first dispatches of a remarkable discovery.[37] In Botta's letters, and Mohl's annotations, we find the demands of antiquarian science tied to those of imperialist accumulation.

First, it is clear that a nationalist motivation was central, and that the recovered artifacts were meant from the start to be sent to France and adorn its national collections. Mohl, for instance, assures the reader in an addendum to Botta's letters 'everything admitting of removal will be sent to France, and there form an Assyrian museum, unique throughout the world...[U]ntil the Louvre shall be embellished by a hall of Assyrian Sculptures, Europe cannot profit by the discovery of Khorsabad'.[38] Mohl neatly takes France for all of Europe, the measure of his nationalistic viewpoint. It was also through his efforts that permission from the Ottoman government was ultimately obtained for the French acquisition of the artifacts.

Second, and more pervasive, is the scientific/antiquarian project enunciated in Botta's writings. Botta's letters are primarily dedicated to providing an objective transcription of the carved images and cuneiform texts discovered in the underground chambers of Khorsabad. Botta, trained as a natural scientist by an associate of the naturalist Georges Cuvier, had been previously engaged in the collection of biological and botanical specimens. The positivist, descriptive framework of classificatory science is behind the exhaustive coverage of the letters.

Last, however, one finds in Botta's letters something almost unprecedented from Rich's frame of reference: aesthetic judgment. An Assyrian group is said to be superior to the Achaemenid sculpture of Persepolis with '...more animation in the figures and greater anatomical science in the design...these bas-reliefs give favorable evidence of the tastes and skill of those by whom they were executed'. Another figurative relief is described as 'extremely well sculptured, and the *tout ensemble* has so Grecian an air, that I [almost] doubted its origin...'[39] Once uncovered, the huge, elaborately-sculpted stones of Assyrian art posed an unexpected visual interest, bearing comparison even with ancient Greek sculpture, the paradigm of classicism. Yet while the language of aesthetic evaluation is dispersed throughout Botta's report, it always plays a subordinate role in his descriptions.

37. Paul-Emile Botta, *Lettres de M. Botta sur ses découvertes à Khorsabad, près de Ninive* (Paris: Imprimerie royale, 1845); *idem*, *M. Botta's Letters on the Discoveries at Nineveh, Translated from the French by C.T.* (London: Longman, Brown, Green, & Longmans, 1850). First published irregularly in *Le Journal Asiatique* from 1843 to 1845, the letters were also quoted frequently in magazine dispatches about the discoveries.

38. Botta, *M. Botta's Letters*, pp. 30, 59.

39. Botta, *M. Botta's Letters*, pp. 12, 11.

These three modes of evaluation, then—nationalistic, antiquarian, and aesthetic valuation—attended the introduction of the fruits of Assyrian archaeology to a Western audience. Together, they account for virtually all of the published text of Botta's letters. While they establish discursive norms more generally for the Western evaluation of Assyrian antiquities, just as with Martin and Delacroix, they also present terms used by agents of the different countries to conflict and oppose each other. For the same touchstones will be seen to be of equal relevance, although in different proportions and to very different effect, in the communications of the English discoveries which soon followed those of the French.

The history of English archaeology in Assyria begins not with an official appointment, but rather with the stealthy trip of Austen Henry Layard, then an unofficial aide to the British ambassador at Constantinople, Stratford Canning.[40] In November 1845, with a small grant and strict instructions from Canning, Layard travelled from Constantinople to Mosul, posing as a traveller. Excavating tools were prepared for him in secret, and with a small group he began digging just south of Nineveh in the more remote town of Nimrūd, which featured a mound rivalling that of Nineveh. Layard made discoveries as quickly as Botta, finding on the first day of digging major portions of two separate Assyrian palaces. Layard's work was ultimately as productive as Botta's, if not more.

Like Botta's, Layard's actions too were illegal under Ottoman law, and only later were remedied with retroactive permissions obtained by Canning from the Sultanate. He thus attempted to shield his work as much as possible from the pasha of Mosul (whom he described as a cunning adversary). Equally, at least, Layard hid his actions from Botta. However he conceived Ottoman interests in the artifacts, he clearly recognized the power of a French claim to the discoveries and sought to work against it. Layard's later work, *Nineveh and its Remains*, triumphantly detailed the many maneuvers and subterfuges involved in his activities.[41] In its own way, it is comparable to the travel narratives of Mesopotamia mentioned above. Though enlivened by much description of contemporary Mesopotamian customs and cultures, it is driven by an interest in what was

40. On Layard's activities as archaeologist and publicist, see especially Gordon Waterfield, *Layard of Nineveh* (New York and Washington, DC: Frederick A. Praeger, 1963), pp. 116-77; Larsen, *Conquest*; Frederick Mario Fales and Bernard J. Hickey (eds.), *Austen Henry Layard tra l'Oriente e Venezia: Symposium internazionale, Venezia, 26-28 ottobre 1983* (Roma: 'L'Erma' di Bretschneider, 1987); John W. Swails, 'Austen Henry Layard and the Near East, 1839–1880', PhD dissertation, University of Georgia, 1983; Austen Henry Layard, *Nineveh and its Remains: With an Account of a Visit to the Chaldean Christians of Kurdistan and the Yezidis, or Devil-Worshippers, and an Inquiry into the Manners and Arts of the Ancient Assyrians* (2 vols.; New York: George P. Putnam, 1850 [London, 1849]).

41. Layard, *Nineveh and tts Remains*, I, pp. 31-133.

literally underneath the place itself, which led to conflict with the indigenous inhabitants.

In the reception of the Assyrian discoveries, precisely the same interpretive touchstones were at work in the English situation as in the French. Canning, for one, provided for Layard the same tone of national chauvinism as did Mohl for Botta. He wrote to the Prime Minister to justify his sponsorship of Layard, 'M. Botta's success at Nineveh [*sic*] has induced me to venture in the same lottery, and my ticket has turned up a prize...there is much reason to believe that Montague House [the British Museum] will beat the Louvre hollow'.[42] The antiquarian value of the discoveries was vouched for principally by Henry Creswicke Rawlinson, a leading scholar in the decipherment of Mesopotamian cuneiform since the mid-1830s. It was on Rawlinson's recommendation, together with that of Canning, that the British Museum ultimately agreed to sponsor Layard's excavation.[43]

Rawlinson had acquired the position of Baghdad resident originally created for Rich. Heir to Rich's political/antiquarian position, he also made explicit an inherent nationalistic interest, writing to Layard, for instance:

> It pains me grievously to see the French monopolize the field, for the fruits of Botta's labors, already achieved and still in progress, are not things to pass away in a day but will constitute a nation's glory in future ages.[44]

Layard's approach to the Assyrian works, and much of the tone of his publicization of them, was based directly on the theme we have seen broached by Botta, but only occasionally expressed in his writing: the aesthetic evaluation of the Assyrian objects. In a letter about his discoveries, for instance, he wrote '[the Assyrians'] knowledge of the arts is surprising, and greatly superior to that of any contemporary nation'. He went on, describing one of the colossal winged animals that became the very emblem of the Assyrian discoveries:[45]

42. Stratford Canning, quoted in Stanley Lane-Poole, *The Life of the Right Honourable Stratford Canning Viscount Stratford de Redcliffe: From his Memoirs and Private and Official Papers* (2 vols.; New York: AMS Press, 1976 [1888]), II, p. 149.

43. London, British Museum Archives, Minutes of Trustee Meetings, Sub. Comm., 22 Jan 1848, f. 399-402; Comm., 29 Jan 1848, f. 7443-46.

44. BL / Add MSS 38976, 234. Rawlinson to Layard, 15 October 1845, quoted in H.W.F. Saggs, 'introduction', to Layard, *Nineveh and its Remains* (London and New York: Routledge & Kegan Paul, 1970 [London, 1849]), pp. 1-64 (42).

45. The typological nature of Assyrian art makes it difficult to identify precisely which of the many winged animals Layard may have referred to.

Figure 22. Winged human-headed lion, Assyrian, from Nimrūd, ninth century BCE. London, BM, ANE 118802 (photo: E.A. Wallis Budge, *Assyrian Sculptures in the British Museum* [1914], pl. 4).

> The [colossal winged] lions lastly discovered, for instance, are admirably drawn, and the muscles, bones and veins quite true to nature, and portrayed with great spirit. There is also a great *mouvement*—as the French well term it—in the attitude of the animal, and 'sa pose est parfaite'; excuse the phrase, we have no equivalent. The human head, too, is really grand.[46]

Whereas Botta relied primarily on the language of the antiquarian, Layard most frequently expressed himself in terms redolent of his youthful training as an art connoisseur. Botta had also noted 'mouvement' in the works, but Layard described the works aesthetically at far greater length, and throughout much of his writing, both public and private.[47]

Notably, only in communication with his sponsors did Layard find reason to suppress this aestheticizing tendency. Writing to Canning, just a month after the letter just cited, Layard averred that the sculptures were 'undoubtedly inferior to the most secondary works of Greece or Rome'.[48] The necessity for leaving unquestioned the inherited hierarchies of the established artistic canon was enunciated directly to Layard by Rawlinson.

> I still think the Nineveh marbles are not valuable as works of art... Can a mere admirer of the beautiful view them with pleasure ? Certainly not, and in this respect they are in the same category with the paintings and sculptures of Egypt and India... We have specimens of the very highest art—and anything short of that is, as a work of art...valueless, for it can neither instruct nor enrapture us. I hope you understand this distinction and when I criticise design and execution, will understand I do so merely because your winged God is not the Apollo Belvedere.[49]

46. Austen Henry Layard, *Sir A. Henry Layard, G.C.B., D.C.L., Autobiography and Letters from his Childhood until his Appointment as H.M. Ambassador at Madrid, Edited by the Hon. William N. Bruce, with a Chapter on his Parliamentary Career by the Rt Hon. Arthur Otway* (2 vols. London: John Murray, 1903), II, pp. 166-67, letter of March 22, 1846; cf. II, pp. 161, 175.

47. Cf. Botta's description of two figures in a chariot with the king 'les poses du serviteur et du cocher sont dessinnées...avec une perfection de *mouvement* et une naïveté qu'à mon grand regret mon ignorance du dessin ne m'a permis de bien reproduire', quoted in 'Découvertes archéologiques faites à Ninive, en 1843 et 1845', *Le magasin pittoresque* 12 (1844), pp. 283-86 (285) (emphasis added). On Layard as connoisseur see Layard, *Autobiography*, I, p. 27; Julian E. Reade, 'Reflections on Layard's Archaeological Career', in Fales and Hickey (eds.), *Layard tra l'Oriente e Venezia*, pp. 47-53. Soon after his return to England, Layard became closely involved in the promotion of art, especially early Renaissance art, in England. Layard, *Autobiography*, II, pp. 203-12; Robyn Cooper, 'The Popularisation of Renaissance Art in Victorian England: The Arundel Society', *Art History* 1 (1978), pp. 263-92.

48. Layard to Canning, 4 August, 1847, Quoted in Ian Jenkins, *Archaeologists and Aesthetes in the Sculpture Galleries of the British Museum, 1800–1939* (London: British Museum Press, 1992), p. 157.

49. BL/Add MSS 38977, Rawlinson to Layard, August 5, 1846, quoted in Waterfield, *Layard of Nineveh*, pp. 147-48.

Throughout both France and England, there was little dispute over the antiquarian value of the Assyrian discoveries or the presumed right of European powers to appropriate these artifacts. But Layard's highlighting of the Assyrian artifact as aesthetic object, his concentration on the mode of aesthetic validation kept strictly subordinate by Botta, conflicted with the values of his sponsors. Aesthetic vs. non-aesthetic, work of art vs. antiquarian artifact: this becomes a further binary pairing in which the Western image of Assyria oscillates. Attention to the purely visual appearance of the Assyrian objects, in the aestheticizing framework suggested by Layard, is perceived to upset a tenet of conventional artistic taste: the dominance of the works of classical antiquity. This is a crucial moment in the reception of the Assyrian artifacts, the first intimation that transplanting the objects to Europe would not merely confirm historical and nationalist beliefs but also might have the power to interfere with established aesthetic doctrine.

Emphasis on aesthetic evaluation, or even extended attention to the visual features of Assyrian works, thus posed a threat that other forms of evaluation did not. In England, the aesthetic approach had clear social implications, carrying the works beyond the narrow circle that initially sponsored Layard's excavations. In a piece excerpted in the antiquarian *Athenaeum*, for instance, Layard wrote of Botta's discoveries in a way that honors all three touchstones of evaluation, while defiantly highlighting the aesthetic appeal of Assyrian art

> ...they are immeasurably superior to the stiff and ill-proportioned figures of the monuments of the Pharaohs. They discover a knowledge of the anatomy of the human frame, a remarkable perception of character, and wonderful spirit in the outlines and general execution. In fact, the great gulf which separates barbarian from civilized art has been passed.[50]

Without precisely calling the works equal to Greek art, Layard still clearly sets Assyria above the level of Egypt to which Rawlinson had confined it. A paragraph notice on Botta appeared soon after in the *Penny Magazine*, foremost among the cheap, popular, widely-circulated magazines then proliferating in England. Notably, the *Penny Magazine* cites *Athenaeum* as its source and closely follows Layard's language, but it concentrates almost exclusively on his aesthetic evaluation. It refers to 'exquisite taste', 'remarkable knowledge of anatomy', 'great intelligence and harmony of composition' and similar features of the artifacts.[51] Thus especially through Layard's frame of aesthetic rei-

50. 'Our Weekly Gossip', *Athenaeum* no. 901, 1 February 1845, pp. 120-21; this dispatch was originally written by Layard for *Malta Times*. See London, John Murray Archive, Layard to Murray, 17 May 1847; Saggs, *Nineveh*, p. 40; Waterfield, *Layard of Nineveh*, p. 114.

51. Anonymous, 'Nineveh', *Penny Magazine* 14 no. 851 (1845), p. 264. Circulation of *Penny Magazine* ran as high as two hundred thousand copies per issue in the 1830s. In 1845, its last year of existence, its circulation was forty thousand. *Athenaeum*, by contrast, circulated only five hundred to one thousand copies weekly in the 1830s and is recorded as rising no higher than 7,200 copies

fication, the news of the Assyrian discoveries broke out of the smaller, more rarefied circle represented by *Athenaeum* for the much larger, lower-class readership of the *Penny Magazine*.

The aesthetic challenge of Assyria took further shape as the Assyrian objects began to reach London and Paris in 1847. There they coexisted directly with the same kinds of sources and spoke to the same expectations we have seen earlier in the case of the images of Martin and Delacroix. These European images, as we have seen, were conceived within a network of established textual references to Assyria, as well as a basis in material evidence for conceiving an ancient Near Eastern culture. The discoveries of Layard and Botta were well positioned to aid in the material reconstruction of Assyria. Yet while on both nationalistic and antiquarian grounds the discoveries clearly were welcomed, the aesthetic treatment of the artifacts consistently posed challenges. An overview of the aesthetic interpretation of Assyria will illuminate the forms of aesthetic discourse at work in the two countries, as well as their social dynamic.

The Louvre's Assyrian display, the first ever mounted in the West, opened to the public in the presence of King Louis-Phillipe on 1 May, 1847. In the lengthy notice of the opening in *L'Illustration*, the foremost illustrated magazine of the time in France, the question of the aesthetic valuation of Assyria is deemed 'quite surprising'. This same sentence immediately continues 'but the most important [questions] concern the details of royal usage, of military and domestic life, in a word, of Assyrian customs'.[52] The aesthetic is taken up, only to be deferred in favor of a more directly antiquarian mode of evaluation. In the same way, the question of whether Assyria stood beyond the achievements of Egyptian art, so vexing an assertion to Rawlinson, is also neatly deferred. The article states that when Assyria is compared to Egyptian, as well as to Greek and Etruscan art, it is apparent that 'they have a common origin'.

Still, all these concerns are affected, and overshadowed, by the presence of the king, and perhaps the particular historical moment of Assyria's entry into the French milieu. Louis-Phillipe's government was under severe attack, and was to be overthrown in less than a year in the Revolution of 1848. *L'Illustration* stretched to connect the royalty of contemporary France with what was known of Assyrian kingship. It seized upon the same figures we have seen illustrated above by Martin and Delacroix. 'Nebuchadnezzar, Sardanapalus or even Ninus himself, since we do not know his identity, the Assyrian monarch now sets foot on the banks of the Seine. A new, more worthy, home has been destined for him, the palace of our kings'.[53]

as late as 1854. Richard D. Altick, *The English Common Reader: A Social History of the Mass Reading Public, 1800–1900* (Chicago: University of Chicago Press, 1957), pp. 393-94.

52. 'Musée de Ninive', *L'Illustration*, 15 May 1847, p. 169.

53. 'Musée de Ninive', p. 168.

The focus on kingship reflects not only the reputation of Assyria but also the government's consistent association with the excavation. Yet if the sponsorship provided any brief buttress for the king, the tie was disastrous for Mesopotamian excavation. While excavations had ceased provisionally in 1844, with the revolution the consulate at Mosul itself was suppressed, and the royalist Botta fell into disgrace.[54] He was reassigned to lesser positions, first in Jerusalem and later Tripoli. He died forgotten in 1870, having only returned to Europe two years previously.

The trajectory of Botta's career is matched by the history of its official documentation. Botta's work, and that of the artist Eugène Flandin sent to record his finds, was enshrined lavishly in the huge, magisterial five-volume *Monument de Ninive*.[55] It is arguably the most elaborate publication ever devoted to Mesopotamian archaeology, an ancient Near Eastern successor to the Napoleonic *Description de l'Egypte*. Begun soon after the initial discoveries, it was the product of extraordinary outlays of time and money by Louis-Phillipe's government. Botta and Flandin had each received an enormous honorarium of sixty thousand francs. In all, the government spent almost three times as much on the publication itself as on the entire course of excavations it was meant to describe.[56]

Botta's grand book was the legacy of a very small circle of privileged authorities, whose power was clearly on the wane. While nearly complete (after four years of production) before the revolution, it ultimately appeared in 1849 and 1850, with a press run of only three hundred copies. One of the most telling comments on his book appeared in a publication that had not even existed when Botta began to excavate. *Le Tour du Monde* was one of the new, cheap illustrated magazines of the Second Empire, devoted to the literature and imagery of travel. In 1863, on Botta's work, it opined:

> It may be regretted that the results of [Botta's] labors have not been published in a form which promotes awareness of them and spreads his fame. Such volumes in a gigantic format, whose price runs into the thousands of francs, are no doubt monuments worthy of a great nation, but they are hardly accessible and will never break out of a very narrow circle.[57]

Mohl, Botta's initial sponsor, had protested 'the unwieldy format and exorbitant price' of the book even at the time of its publication, but largely on the grounds of its restricting accessibility to the finds among scholars.[58] Here the writer

54. Larsen, *Conquest*, p. 138. Larsen (p. 14) remarks that Botta 'seems almost to be erased from history'.

55. Botta, *Monument de Ninive*, V, p. 5.

56. Maurice Pillet, *Khorsabad: Les découvertes de V. Place en Assyrie* (Paris: Leroux, 1918), pp. 103-108; Béatrice André-Salvini, 'Introduction aux publications de P.E. Botta et de V. Place', in Fontan and Chevalier (eds.), *De Khorsabad à Paris*, pp. 166-72.

57. 'Ninive', *Le Tour du Monde* 7 (1863), p. 318.

58. Mohl, *Vingt-sept ans*, I, p. 413.

is speaking instead on behalf of the newer and far larger audience of a non-specialist public. Strikingly, the writer pointed to England as a model of such dissemination. 'The wisely practical spirit of our neighbors across the English channel may serve as an example in this regard'.

Botta, then, was both beneficiary and victim of the extraordinary largesse of the July Monarchy. Such a pattern of support had ramifications for the public currency of Assyria itself. This is exemplified by the folio *Monument de Ninive*, a remarkable 'white elephant', as we have seen. But it continues, indeed accelerates, in the image of Assyria in French art after the excavations, as we will examine in the next section. In addition, as we have already begun to see, the contrast with the English coverage of the discoveries could not have been greater.

Much unlike the limited circulation of Botta's words and work in France, news of the Assyrian discoveries pervaded England in the years after Layard's discoveries and was made available at all social levels. Textual and visual information on Assyria appeared throughout the range of publications from the upper-class *Athenaeum* to the popular *Penny Magazine*.[59] The same palpable interest contributed to making Layard's *Nineveh and its Remains*, an account of his first archaeological campaign and related matters, one of the greatest English best-sellers of the entire nineteenth century. This difference of circulation reflects in part the different arrangement by which Layard, as opposed to Botta, received compensation. He got very little direct support from the British Museum or any other governmental sponsor, but he profited greatly from the sale of his book, which was privately published.[60]

As the Assyrian artifacts were promulgated in England, they were frequently made to carry not only nationalistic and antiquarian value, as in France, but also religious significance, a development unique to the English situation. The discussion in both countries, however, nearly always included the inevitably controversial question of the aesthetic value of the works.

For instance, an exhaustive review of Layard's book in the upper-class *Quarterly Review* which covers all the themes mentioned above, is framed with the aesthetic evaluation of the objects. It begins by singling out 'the huge lion and bull' as 'by far the most remarkable and characteristic specimens of Assyrian art'. These works

> impressed us with a strange, gigantic majesty, a daringness of conception, which was in no way debased by the barbaric rudeness of the execution, and on the other hand enhanced by its singular symbolic attributes. It is that kind of statue which it takes away one's breath to gaze on.[61]

59. Frederick N. Bohrer, 'A New Antiquity: The English Reception of Assyria' (PhD dissertation, University of Chicago, 1989), pp. 57-85, 173-211.

60. Frederick N. Bohrer, 'The Printed Orient: The Production of A.H. Layard's Earliest Works', in *The Construction of the Ancient Near East* (ed. Ann Clyburn Gunter; Culture & History, 11; Copenhagen: Akademisk Forlag, 1993), pp. 85-105.

61. [H.H. Milman], 'Review of A.H. Layard, *Nineveh and its Remains*', *Quarterly Review* 84

Forty-odd pages later the reviewer has regained his breath, and adds that Assyrian works are nonetheless inferior to the 'true beauty' and 'exquisite anthropomorphism' of the Greeks. Nonetheless, he counts the discoveries as a new chapter in the history of art.

The *Quarterly Review* writer, reacting viscerally to an object that nonetheless refuses to obey reigning doctrines of sculpture in such matters as scale, finish, subject, and composition, exemplifies a position of ambivalence toward the Assyrian works. The writer is caught in the binary evaluation of the objects, between a tantalizingly aesthetic and a dutifully antiquarian appraisal of the works. Yet this is already a position of far more aesthetic sympathy to Assyria than that of Rawlinson or of others even more closely associated with the British Museum.

The immense popularity of the Assyrian works (and the insistence of the museum's Parliamentary overseers) kept them on public display, ultimately in new galleries designed especially for them.[62] Even so, a number of the museum's own trustees were downright hostile to the works. One trustee deemed them 'a parcel of rubbish' belonging 'at the bottom of the sea'.[63] The testimony of another, Sir Richard Westmacott Sr, elaborates on the position. A professor of sculpture at the British Royal Academy since 1827, Westmacott had served for decades as the 'sculpture advisor' to the museum's trustees. He was present at official meetings and, as the minutes confirm, held considerable sway in decisions about sculptural display. Asked by a Parliamentary commission in 1853 about the artistic worth of the Assyrian discoveries, Westmacott responded with an opinion even more aesthetically denigrating than Rawlinson. Specifically distinguishing them from the Elgin marbles, which are valuable for 'their excellence as works of art', he stated

> The Nineveh Marbles are very curious, and it is very desirable to possess them, but I look upon it that the value of the Nineveh Marbles will be the history that their inscriptions, if they ever are translated, will produce; because if we had one-tenth part of what we have of Nineveh art it would be quite enough as specimens of the arts of the Chaldeans, for it is very bad art... The less people as artists, look at objects of that kind, the better.[64]

no. 167 (1848), pp. 106-53 (107). The *Quarterly Review* was published by John Murray, who also published Layard's books. On the journal, see Roger P. Wallins, '*The Quarterly Review*', in *British Literary Magazines: The Romantic Age, 1789–1836* (4 vols.; ed. Alvin Sullivan; Historical Guides to the World's Periodicals and Newspapers; Westport, CT: Greenwood Press, 1983), II, pp. 359-67.

62. Jenkins, *Archaeologists & Aesthetes*, pp. 158-67; Frederick N. Bohrer, 'The Times and Spaces of History: Representation, Assyria, and the British Museum', in *Museum Culture: Histories, Discourses, Spectacles* (ed. Daniel Sherman and Irit Rogoff; Media & Society, 6; Minneapolis, MN: University of Minnesota Press, 1994), pp. 197-222.

63. BL/Add MSS 38,984, 374, William Vaux to Austen Henry Layard, partially quoted in Edward Miller, *That Noble Cabinet: A History of the British Museum* (London: A. Deutsch, 1973), p. 192.

64. House of Commons 'Minutes of... the Select Committee on the National Gallery', *Par-*

Westmacott's unbridled disapproval, however, was counterbalanced by an enormous outpouring of unqualified aesthetic approval for the artifacts. This was expressed on the part of the same popular audiences that thronged the British Museum (on the days they were allowed in) and purchased Layard's book in record number (especially the cheaper 'popular edition'). As we have seen above with the *Penny Magazine*, these are the same audiences to whom the discoveries first penetrated in large part through the very language of aesthetic valuation.

For instance, in the preface to one of the many cheap, anonymous books on the discoveries, the reception of Layard's finds is described thus

> A city buried for more than twenty centuries offered its remains for comparison with the aspects of modern London or Paris; and the sculptured monuments of a bygone race rose up to offer a contrast with the works of modern art.[65]

Acceptance of Assyria as a contrast to modern art ultimately goes beyond the terms of contention above. Rather merely than arguing over whether Assyrian art is comparable to the Greek, it now can be put to the same use for which the Greek was invoked in the nineteenth century: as a model for evaluating contemporary work, precisely the kind of looking at Assyria explicitly proscribed by Westmacott.

Similarly, one finds significant acknowledgement of Assyria in the central organ of middle-class artistic discourse in England, the *Art-Journal*. *Art-Journal* carried a number of pieces on the Assyrian discoveries, such as an elaborately illustrated article in 1850 stating that 'the beauty of execution in each of these sculptures so strongly speak of their [the Assyrians'] acquirements also in the arts of peace'.[66] The accepted aesthetic achievement of the objects now allows for the superimposition of other values onto the Assyrians. For the first time, the process is not defined by external, textual sources. The image of Assyria offered by *Art-Journal* is not that of the barbarism attributed to them by others, but rather one of cultivation and refinement.

The most significant trace of *Art-Journal*'s approval of Assyrian art came three years later, at about the same time the British Museum opened its Nineveh Gallery. The journal associates its own interest not only with Layard's campaign, but also with a central earlier crusader for a change in aesthetic canons.

liamentary Papers 1852–53 (1853), XXXI, pp. 9050ff. On this exchange, see Francis Haskell, *Rediscoveries in Art: Some Aspects of Taste, Fashion and Collecting in England and France* (Wrightsman Lectures, 7; London: Phaidon Press, 1976), pp. 101-102.

65. [James S. Buckingham], *The Buried City of the East, Nineveh: A Narrative of the Discoveries of Mr Layard and M. Botta at Nimroud and Khorsabad; with Descriptions of the Exhumed Sculptures, and Particulars of the Early History of the Ancient Ninevite Kingdom* (London: Office of the National Illustrated Library, 1851), p. i.

66. 'Nineveh and Persepolis', *Art-Journal* 12 (1850), p. 225.

> ...[I]t is a singular proof of the increased and increasing interest in all things appertaining to ancient Art, that Mr. Bonomi's *Nineveh and its Palaces*, has also achieved a second edition, notwithstanding the deserved popularity of 'Layard's Nineveh'. When we remember the fight poor Haydon had for the Elgin Marbles, we cannot but congratulate ourselves on our 'progress'.[67]

The fight for the legitimation of the Elgin marbles, in the early nineteenth century, had lasted nearly two decades. It involved most authoritative figures of English artistic taste, and undermined the dominant sense of classicism embodied, most of all, by Sir Richard Payne Knight.[68] Despite their ultimate acceptance, Benjamin Robert Haydon, the indefatigable promoter of the Elgin works, committed suicide, penniless, in 1846, while Knight's influence rapidly faded after the affair.

Art-Journal's parallel between the reception of the Elgin marbles and that of the Assyrian artifacts posits an inevitable struggle over the acceptance of a heterodox form of artistic production. In light of the continued aesthetic resistance to the works by figures such as Rawlinson, Westmacott, and the British Museum Trustees, 'our progress' for *Art-Journal* is not that of society as a whole, but the unique portion of the English art audience occupied by the backers of the aesthetic worth of Assyria, that is, the lower- and middle-class audiences of journals from the *Penny Magazine* to *The Illustrated London News* to *Art-Journal* itself. Notably, representatives of both groups can invoke the Elgin marbles for their competing ideals.

In short, England's Assyrian archaeology as a whole had a variety of supporters. While some opinions about the objects were widely shared, the particular question of the aesthetic value of the objects split the public into opposing camps. Assyria's backers ultimately won the conflict in almost every particular. But what is crucial here is not merely the outcome of the situation but the way it forced a widespread debate which juxtaposed Assyria and the demands of art. Only by setting the terms of debate in this way could Assyria win aesthetic validation, as in the extraordinary words of praise for Assyria as art we have

67. 'Reviews', *Art-Journal* 15 (1853), pp. 235-36 (235).

68. On the reception of the Elgin marbles, see Jenkins, *Archaeologists & Aesthetes*, pp. 24-29; Jacob Rothenberg, *'Descensus ad terram': The Acquisition and Reception of the Elgin Marbles* (Outstanding Dissertations in the Fine Arts; London and New York: Garland, 1977); Massimiliano Pavan, 'Antonio Canova e la discussione sugli "Elgin Marbles" ', *Rivista dell'Instituto nazionale d'archelogia e storia dell'arte* ns 11-12 (1974–75), pp. 219-344. Haydon's role is detailed in Frederick Cummings, 'Benjamin Robert Haydon and the Critical Reception of the Elgin Marbles' (PhD dissertation, University of Chicago, 1967). For the central opponent of the works, see *The Arrogant Connoisseur: Richard Payne Knight, 1751–1824: Essays on Richard Payne Knight together with a Catalogue of Works Exhibited at the Whitworth Art Gallery, 1982* (ed. Michael Clarke and Nicholas Penny; Manchester, UK: Manchester University Press, 1982); Andrew Ballantyne, 'Knight, Haydon, and the Elgin Marbles', *Apollo* 128 (1988), pp. 155-59.

noted above. Here too, the contrast with France could not be greater. No debate comparable to the one in England took place in France. Contrasting opinions about Assyria appeared rarely to confront each other. The French (middle- and lower-class) social groups who might have supported the idea of Assyrian artifacts as works of art were marginalized from the discoveries, and the circulation of Botta's work constrained.[69]

By the early 1850s, then, France and England had acquired and placed on display roughly comparable collections of Assyrian artifacts. Yet, as we have seen, the two countries presented considerably different milieus of reception. Moreover, the subsequent archaeological fortunes of the two countries diverged, much to England's advantage. While the French excavation had been halted in the later 1840s, Layard returned to Mesopotamia in 1849 for a remarkable campaign that finally succeeded in unearthing ancient Nineveh itself, within the very mound first examined, and then abandoned, by Botta. In 1853, after the fall of the Second Republic, Mohl finally persuaded the succeeding government of the Second Empire to reopen excavation. Victor Place was sent by the government to continue the work of Botta at Khorsabad. His tenure is most notable for the disastrous loss, through a transport mishap on the Tigris, of a huge cache of Assyrian antiquities entrusted to his care. In what Mohl lamented as 'an irreparable loss', Place's campaign inadvertently deposited on the river's bottom the contents of more than 120 cases of objects from Khorsabad (excavated both by him and Botta), as well as a large array of objects from Layard's excavation at Nineveh, which Place had been allowed to select for acquisition by the Louvre.[70] Subsequent salvage attempts met with only limited success.

In France, then, Assyrian archaeology was both beneficiary and victim of its close political ties. The reproduction and circulation of Assyrian artifacts was constrained by the dominant structure of archaeological sponsorship, largely directed by the small group of scholarly and political figures authorizing the effort. Thus, the essential French monument to Botta's discovery, *Monument de Ninive*, was both extraordinarily lavish and extraordinarily rare, effectively withheld from audiences beyond those of its narrow patronage group. Further, later excavations were hampered by the turbulent history of governmental sponsorship, as well as embarrassing mishaps.

The reception of Assyrian archaeology in England was far more diffuse. Information on the discoveries circulated far and wide in the England, and in a variety of forms. This was aided particularly by the aestheticization of the objects promoted by Layard. Though appealing to many, it also provoked from

69. The discoveries were, however, steadfastly covered in the French counterpart to *The Penny Magazine*, *Le magasin pittoresque* 16 (1848), pp. 131-34; 17 (1849), pp. 193-94; 20 (1852), pp. 241-44. Though anomalous among the French popular press, it may also suggest a certain submerged interest in the discoveries among popular constituencies.

70. Mohl, *Vingt-sept ans*, II, p. 36; cf. I, p. xxxiii; Lloyd, *Foundations*, p. 140; Pillet, *Khorsabad*, pp. 17-70.

some an opposing response. The objects were conceived within a bifurcated opposition as either aesthetically based works of art or as antiquarian artifacts. This aestheticization was crucial for the wide social circulation of the artifacts, for while antiquarian evaluation required a certain level of education and erudition, the aesthetic approach to the artifacts could be more widely shared throughout the social spectrum. At the same time, the aesthetic offered a framework of evaluation more specific and engaged with individual objects than a purely nationalistic (or religious) approach.

3. *Constructing and Controlling Assyrian Imagery in the Later Nineteenth Century*

As we have seen, many of the same assumptions about ancient Assyria were active in France and England in the period before the excavations, even though expressed in different ways. The image of the fall of Nineveh served audiences in both countries as a sort of projection of various cultural identities and fascinations. In the period immediately after the discoveries, the two countries also acted in common, if, again, not in concord. They had clearly rivaled each other in the archaeology of the region (albeit with different degrees of success). Yet, the very different structures for archaeological reception in the two countries—circulating the finds to different audiences, through different media, and differing notably on the aesthetic value of the objects—work to further uncouple the representation of Assyria in the two countries. As the fortunes of France and England in Mesopotamian archaeology came to diverge, so too did their images of the Assyrian past. Art and archaeology, past and present, conspire to underline a last notable bifurcation that has been at work throughout: France vs. England.

To assess this contrast, we turn now to a few key representations of Assyria in France and England in the decades after the discoveries. These are not 'pure' attempts to emulate the formal qualities of Assyrian art. In both countries, such decontextualized emulation dates from the late nineteenth and early twentieth centuries, well after Assyria's initial reception.[71] By contrast, the range of Assyrian representations in the period closer to its initial display reflects the heterogeneous and discontinuous moment in which Assyrian antiquities appeared on the European horizon. Even though London and Paris both displayed considerable collections of relatively similar ancient Assyrian objects, the initial circulation

71. This tendency can be found in a still obscured portion of European 'Primitivism', including works by artists such as Paul Gauguin, Pablo Picasso, and Jacob Epstein. For Gauguin, see Jirat-Wasiutyński, 'Gauguin's Self Portraits', p. 189 n. 48; Amishai-Maisels, *Gauguin's Religious Themes*, p. 276 n. 66. For Picasso, see Künzl, *Der Einfluss des alten Orients*, p. 135; Burge, 'Pablo Picasso's *Man*', pp. 21-26; Jaime Sabartés, *Picasso à Antibes, Paris, 1948*, quoted in *Picasso on Art: A Selection of Views* (ed. Dore Ashton; The Documents of Twentieth-Century Art; London: Thames & Hudson, 1972), p. 115. For Epstein, see Silber, *Sculpture of Epstein*, pp. 130-32.

of the discoveries fostered a vast, hybrid, and even contradictory array of representations and references.[72] Rather than focus the image of Assyria on a newly prominent visual repertory, we find instead the very contrary, as the variation of representations among different milieus (which we have called representational 'mobility'), is now considerably greater than before.

First, there is the question of continuity with the images created by Martin and Delacroix before the discoveries. Neither artist produced anything directly related to the newly visible Assyrian art. Martin died in 1854, one year after the British Museum formally completed its Assyrian galleries. Delacroix lived considerably longer, and even remarked on the extraordinary treatment of animals in Assyrian works.[73] Yet he never revised the imagery of *The Death of Sardanapalus* or otherwise directly used the visual evidence of Assyria. Indeed, the most telling evidence of Delacroix's relation to actual Assyrian art is a brief notation in his journal from 1858 making clear that it is not Delacroix himself, but rather a relative who was 'quite struck' with Assyrian art.[74]

Delacroix's stance toward Assyria exemplifies the nature of its artistic reception in mid-century France, and follows the same pattern as the passage from *L'Illustration*. Assyria is tacitly acknowledged, but also withheld from concerted artistic consideration. Indeed, this process, strictly controlling, and even manufacturing Assyria to the requirements of the audience, accounts for the best-known and longest-lived visual reference to Assyria in nineteenth-century France, the 'Assyrian' profile.

The pose in profile, with a thick beard jutting directly downward from the chin, was claimed perhaps most famously by Gustave Courbet, as in his description of himself at the center of his 1855 Atelier of the Painter, as 'myself painting showing the Assyrian profile of my head'.[75] Many of Courbet's paintings of the 1850s show him from a similar angle.

72. On modes and means of hybridity, see esp. Bhabha, *Location of Culture*, as well as Pratt, *Imperial Eyes*, and Taussig, *Mimesis and Alterity*; Annie Coombes, 'The Recalcitrant Object: Culture Contact and the Question of Hybridity', in *Colonial Discourse/Postcolonial Theory* (ed. Francis Barker, Peter Hulme and Margaret Iversen; The Essex Symposia; Manchester and New York: Manchester University Press, 1994), pp. 89-114. The range of images in this section might be considered as well to exemplify the 'semiotic play' of reception, as described by Norman Bryson, 'Art in Context', in *Studies in Historical Change* (ed. Ralph Cohen; Charlottesville, VA and London: University Press of Virginia, 1992), pp. 18-42. This, in turn, tends to corroborate the structural connection of exoticism and reception suggested by Leduc-Adine, 'Exotisme et discours'.

73. Eugéne Delacroix, 'Des variations du beau', in *Ecrits sur l'art* (ed. François-Marie Deyrolle and Christophe Denissel; Paris: Librairie Séguier, 1988 [1857]), p. 34. 'One is struck above all by the perfection with which animals are rendered'.

74. Eugène Delacroix, *Journal* (3 vols.; ed. André Joubin; Paris: Plon, 1932), III, p. 197, June 20, 1858. 'We go to the museum with my amiable cousin. He is quite struck with Assyrian antiquities'.

75. Gustave Courbet, *Letters of Gustave Courbet* (ed. and trans. Petra ten-Doesschate Chu; Chicago: University of Chicago Press, 1992), p. 132.

Figure 23. Gustave Courbet, *The Meeting*, 1854. Montpellier, Musée Fabre (photo: Art Resource, New York).

Contemporary caricatures also delighted in exaggerating this feature.[76] Much of Assyrian art consists of profile reliefs, and protruding beards are a common characteristic. These contemporary allusions, however, made no attempt to emulate the specific knotting and shaping of Assyrian beards, and Courbet's facial features are not directly comparable to the stylized Assyrian features.[77]

Courbet's 'Assyrian' profile, that is, does not indicate a deep interest in Assyrian art. It would hardly be identifiable as Assyrian on its own. Rather, Assyria offers an occasion for the artist's self-assertion. Courbet almost flaunts his lack of concern with the specifics of antique art, in a manner consistent with his subsumption of all past art to his contemporary concerns.[78]

76. Nadar (Gaspar Félix Tournachon), 'Les contemporains de Nadar: Courbet', *Journal amusant*, 11 December 1858, reproduced in Linda Nochlin and Sarah Faunce, *Courbet Rediscovered* (New York: Brooklyn Museum, 1988: exhibition catalogue), p. 9.

77. '[A]s even a cursory look at the original reliefs shows, Courbet invented the "Assyrian" beard entirely from his imagination—the angle and pointed shape of the French "Assyrian" beard is nothing like the vertical, rectangular true Assyrian examples... Courbet was evidently capitalizing on the reputation of the Assyrian discoveries without ever having looked at them'. John Malcolm Russell, letter to author, 21 February 1997.

78. Alexander, 'Courbet and Assyrian Sculpture', pp. 447-52.

Courbet's 'Assyrian' profile is a casual, even whimsical gesture of self-fashioning, barely acknowledging the actuality of Assyrian art. Yet its off-handedness, its actual neutralization of the particularity of Assyrian art, should be taken seriously as a means of popularizing Assyria. Strikingly, the Assyrian beard achieved a currency of its own in French visual culture, covering over much of the inherited image of ancient Assyria.

Thus Célestin Nanteuil's poster for the 1867 opera *Sardanapale* by Henri Becque and Victorin Jonciéres revisited Delacroix's subject without the slightest use of the repertory of Assyrian objects now available in the Louvre.

Figure 24. Célestin Nanteuil, poster for *Sardanapale*, 1867 (photo: Bibliothèque nationale de France, Paris).

Figure 25. Detail of figure 24.

The world of Sardanapalus was recreated instead with specifically Egyptian features such as curved architraves, swelling 'lotus' capitals, and even hieroglyphics. The cache of pots before the king are, like his costume, of classical form. Most prominent among them is a Greek amphora. This heterogeneous assembly is sanctioned by the king's conspicuously 'Assyrian' beard.

The coining of a certain facial feature as Assyrian stands, then, as a substitute for Assyrian art itself. Thus, in the theoretical terms discussed above, exoticism does not merely convey information but actually constructs its subject, producing an Assyria that is more assimilable to established norms than the actual works. The 'Assyrian' beard is the very emblem of this process of assimilating, denaturing, and ultimately constructing Assyria: a hybrid, second-order visual creation.

Finally, counterbalancing an invented Assyrian feature that had achieved considerable currency, the look of actual Assyrian artifacts was strictly controlled, even erased from artistic contexts in which they had clearly been noted. For instance, in one of Edgar Degas's notebooks from around 1860 are detailed drawings of a number of Near Eastern antiquities, including a portion of an Assyrian relief.[79] They form part of the context of his painting of *Semiramis Constructing a City*.

79. Theodore Reff, *The Notebooks of Edgar Degas: A Catalogue of the Thirty-Eight Notebooks in the Bibliothèque Nationale and Other Collections* (2 vols.; Oxford: Clarendon Press, 1976), I, p. 19.

Figure 26. Edgar Degas, *Semiramis Constructing a City*, *c*. 1860–62. Paris, Musée d'Orsay (photo: Art Resource, New York).

It has been plausibly suggested that the painting was partly inspired by an 1860 production of Rossini's opera *Semiramide*, one which utilized elaborately researched costumes and decor based on the Assyrian discoveries.[80] While Degas would thus seem to have done painstaking preparatory work comparable to that of Delacroix, little in Degas' painting takes up with any specificity the wealth of Assyrian details in these would-be sources. Semiramis, the legendary builder of Babylon, and her party are dressed in neo-classic belted gowns, while the city surveyed by the queen is designed entirely of Greco-Roman architecture. Only the shaped hair of Semiramis and perhaps a chariot just slightly visible bear even a faint resemblance to features that can be found anywhere on Assyrian reliefs.[81] Like Nanteuil's poster, Degas's work largely (though not quite completely) excludes Mesopotamian sources from a Mesopotamian subject.

The examples of Courbet and Degas testify to a fragmentation and marginalization of Assyria in the realist mode that dominated French art of the time of the discoveries. But the pattern is only slightly different in the proto-Symbolist work of their contemporary Gustave Moreau. A considerable portion of Moreau's

80. Roy McMullen, *Degas: His Life, Times, and Work* (Boston: Houghton Mifflin, 1984), pp. 94-96. A photo album of the production is in the Bibliothèque de l'Opéra in Paris, PH 9 (2).

81. The most extensive list of correspondences and contrasts is in *Degas* (New York: Metropolitan Museum of Art, 1988: exhibition catalogue), pp. 89-92. On the creation of the work, see Geneviève Monnier, 'La genèse d'une oeuvre de Degas: *Sémiramis construisant une ville*', *Revue du Louvre et des musées de France* 28 (1978), pp. 407-26.

library was devoted to 'exotic' arts, while the majority of his paintings depict subjects derived from biblical and classical themes.[82] This might seem a set of interests more amenable to Assyria than the contemporary ones favored by Courbet and Degas. Further, Moreau's penchant for covering his canvases with *sgraffito*-like ornamentation is visually comparable to the dense ornamentation and use of cuneiform texts in Assyrian artifacts.

Moreau devoted part of a sketchbook from the 1860s to Assyrian works at the Louvre, and clearly knew of the discoveries through printed sources as well.[83] Yet none of his finished paintings directly employs Assyrian subjects or motifs. Perhaps the closest is a full-scale study for *The Suitors* in which an Assyrian figure in a commonly employed gesture of salute is lightly sketched in among the otherwise classically-garbed figures seeking the hand of Penelope. Clearly identifiable by the horned crown over the head, position of the extended arm, and protruding bracelet, this same figure is absent from the finished work, which is completely classical in conception.[84]

Figure 27. Gustave Moreau, study for *The Suitors* (*Les prétendants*), *c.* 1862. Paris, Musée Gustave Moreau (photo: Art Resource, New York).

82. Pierre-Louis Mathieu, 'La bibliothèque de Gustave Moreau', *Gazette des Beaux-Arts* ser. 6, 91 (1978), pp. 155-62.

83. The sketchbook, dating from 1850 to 1869, is now in the collection of the Musée Gustave Moreau, Paris. There is also in the museum a notebook recording notable articles in *Le magasin pittoresque*, including two described by the artist as 'bas-relief decouvert à Ninive-Sculpture assyrienne' (1844) and 'poids assyriennes' (1861). I am grateful to Mme. Geneviève Lacambre for her continued assistance with this material.

84. This gesture can be found in a variety of Assyrian deity figures conserved in London and Paris and elsewhere, such as the series from Room H of the Northwest Palace at Nimrūd. Gadd, *Stones*, p. 236.

Figure 28. Winged deity facing right and saluting, holding cone and situla, Assyrian, from Nimrūd, ninth century BCE. London, BM, ANE 118876 (photo: E.A. Wallis Budge, *Assyrian Sculptures*, pl. 48 n. 1).

In Moreau's work too, then, Assyria is a very faint visual trace, a source largely excluded. More generally, the seeming solidarity of such different artists as Courbet, Degas, and Moreau in eliding Assyrian references is testimony to the continuing deferral and submersion of Assyria throughout contemporary French art. To look for Assyrian imagery in France is, quite literally, to search for glaring absences as well as almost ghostly presences.

The nature of Assyrian representation is, in part, a legacy of the centralized pattern through which Assyrian artifacts were promulgated in France. As we have seen, Assyria's French publicists were beholden to a small circle, and publications were directed to this privileged group. Furthermore, while the question of the aesthetic value of the artifacts was raised, it was still largely subordinated to historical and antiquarian modes of inquiry. Finally, the complexities and misfortunes of French archaeology contribute also to the low standing of the artifacts. In all, it would seem that the effect of the unprecedented initial discovery and later display and circulation of Assyrian art in France was, paradoxically, virtually to erase its presence from contemporary artistic representation.

The image of ancient Assyria in English art in the decades after the discoveries contrasts enormously with that which we have seen in France. It engages the visual specificity of ancient Assyrian work, rather than largely withholding it, as in the French examples. Paradoxically, the discoveries seem almost to mark an end to the French interest in Assyria, as Delacroix's reaction to the discoveries might suggest. By contrast, the English treatment of Assyria extends the concerns we have found in the pre-discovery imagery of Assyria in both countries. A perfect example is Ford Madox Brown's *Dream of Sardanapalus*.[85] Although Sardanapalus is presented in an 'Assyrian' profile, it is now, unlike in Nanteuil's conception, among the least of a range of Assyrian signifiers within the image. In fact, most of the details of setting and costume in the work come directly and specifically from Assyrian reliefs. Two Assyrian winged animals stand by the sides of the doorway, while the frieze behind the king is filled with figures derived from Assyrian reliefs, most notably the winged, bird-headed genie to the right of the bull. This figure is an Assyrian *apkallu*, a variant of the same figure utilized by Moreau.[86] But Brown, unlike Moreau, presents the image in its entirety, including wings, drapery, and implements.

Figure 29. Ford Madox Brown, *The Dream of Sardanapalus*, 1871, Wilmington, Delaware Art Museum, Samuel and Mary R. Bancroft Memorial (photo: Delaware Art Museum, Wilmington DE).

The more functional features of the scene are equally beholden to Assyrian imagery. Sardanapalus reclines on a couch similar in shape and detailing to that on which the king lies in a famous entertainment scene among the Assyrian finds.

85. On the work and its context, see Ford Madox Hueffer [Ford Madox Ford], *Ford Madox Brown: A Record of his Life and Work* (London: Longmans, Green & Co., 1896), pp. 262, 272; Rowland Elzea, *The Samuel and Mary Bancroft Jr and Related Pre-Raphaelite Collections* (Wilmington, DE: Delaware Art Museum, 1978), pp. 30-31.

86. A prototype is London, British Museum, Department of Ancient Near Eastern Antiquities (hereafter BM, ANE) 98060. All of the Assyrian artifacts referred to here were collected by and displayed at the museum by the early 1850s.

Figure 30. King and queen at banquet, Assyrian, from Nineveh, seventh century BCE. London, BM, ANE 124920 (photo: Hormuzd Rassam, *Asshur and the Land of Nimrod* [1897], facing p. 38).

His earring and armlet derive from features shown on the reliefs. Even the crown that tops the armor he has set aside is that specifically reserved for the king.[87]

Brown's conception, in short, uses a plethora of visual details from Assyrian artifacts to realize what seems an authentic Assyrian setting. Yet, the image is actually no less composite, no less the result of a discontinuous array of references (both visually and textually), than any from before the archaeological discoveries. The Assyrian discoveries, that is, do not lead to a truer or more exact conception of Assyria. Rather, they work to transform the range of terms through which ancient Assyria is construed, opening up new fictive possibilities for Assyrian subjects. In Brown's image, along with the greater dependence on the now unimpeachable sources in Assyrian art, we find a tiled, or even parquet floor, a purely nineteenth-century anachronism. Even more, this same shift toward the authority of ancient visual remains sanctions a turn toward a subject now derived specifically from Byron, dropping the precedent of ancient literary sources on which the earlier works of Martin and Delacroix depended. Brown's image depicts a specific moment (the opening of Act 4, Scene 1) of Byron's *Sardanapalus*. It reflects the quiet, sensitive tone of the play, far from the spectacular, apocalyptic conceptions of Martin and Delacroix. Sardanapalus, in Byron's story, has returned wounded from previously leading his army. His left forearm is bandaged. His Greek slave Myrhha (an invention of the Hellenophile Byron) comforts the king as he lies hallucinating, in a dream that prophesies the end of the Assyrian kingdom.

87. See, for instance BM, ANE 124533 or 124557.

In Brown's *Sardanapalus*, then, the antiquity of the visual details provides an authoritative anchor in tradition which allows the artist to jettison the (previously indispensable) authority associated with ancient texts. In addition, the considerable attention paid to Assyrian art may well be related to the more positive conception of the king. *Art-Journal* remarked, as we have seen, that Assyrian art seemed to speak well of the civilized achievement of the Assyrians. In the same way, Brown's work envisions in detail both an Assyrian ambience and a soulful, sensitive leader. Though Sardanapalus is still doomed, it is now an occasion for pathos rather than judgmental condescension. Even the viewpoint has changed from the earlier conceptions of Martin and Delacroix, as the viewer is now on the same level as the king, sharing this tender, vulnerable moment.

Brown's work pays great attention to the material specifics of Assyrian art. It is the culmination of the historicist tendency toward material validation in the mid-nineteenth-century conception of Assyria. It also marks a change in the very image of Assyria, coinciding with the addition of Assyrian artifactual sources, but also allowing a shift from the more ostensibly authoritative classical and biblical sources of Martin and Delacroix to that of Byron.

A final work from slightly later, Edwin Long's then-famous *Babylonian Marriage Market*, situates Assyrian imagery within a more diverse audience, and reflects further on larger themes of exoticist representation.

Figure 31. Edwin Long, *Babylonian Marriage Market*, 1875. Surrey, Royal Holloway and Bedford New College (photo: Bridgman Art Library, London and New York).

Long's work not only adheres to the general mode of conception of Martin and Delacroix, it also inherits the thematization of vision and the gendered imaginary which we found in the earlier works. Yet even as it seeks to take up the previous gender dynamic, the changed nature of both subject and audience unsettles its unquestioned binarism of male versus female roles.

Long's subject derives from Herodotus. The painting was exhibited at the British Royal Academy with a lengthy quotation from a nineteenth-century popularization of the work. The custom ascribed to the Babylonians, which Herodotus deemed their wisest, was that once a year all eligible females were gathered together in their villages for men who wished to marry. The most beautiful among them was presented first, for purchase by the highest bidder, followed by the others, in decreasing order of beauty and selling for decreasing amounts. Finally, the deformed and ugly were presented, and the money of those who purchased the more beautiful women went to subsidize the takers of the uglier women, so that

> the plainest was got rid of to some cynical worthy, who placidly preferred lucre to looks. By transferring to the scale of the ill-favoured the prices paid for the fair, beauty was made to endow ugliness, and the rich man's taste was the poor man's gain.[88]

Long's subject is the transformation of woman into currency. The characteristic feature of this system is the hierarchical ranking and measurement of the women/commodities. Long's primary innovation lay in setting the scene in a place devoted solely to such ranking, one without a trace of the functional setting of the village mentioned by Herodotus. Instead, Long set the work in an auction house. Some of the male viewers hold boxes of coins and other valuable objects, while a balance stands in front of the auctioneer's podium.

The woven beards, bracelets, earrings, wrapped garments, headwear, and similar features pictured on Assyrian reliefs are transferred to the crowd of male viewers in the picture. The crowd is, though, leavened with some black Africans, a few Italic figures, and a white-bearded, Rembrandtesque Jew. The women, too, notably in their hairstyles, rounded heads, and similarly wrapped garments, are modeled after Assyrian and other ancient Near Eastern sources. The setting is just as consciously historicized, as most of the wall and floor decorations, the pattern on the curtain, and even the relief on the auctioneer's podium derive from Assyrian reliefs and other decorations.[89]

The reception of Long's work, painted in 1875, suggests that Assyria by this time has become assimilated by Western viewers. On the details of setting, the

88. George C. Swayne, *The History of Herodotus* (Edinburgh: William Blackwood & Sons, 1870), pp. 36-37, paraphrasing Herodotus, 1.196. On Long's treatment of the subject, see Richard Jenkyns, *Dignity and Decadence: Victorian Art and the Classical Inheritance* (Cambridge, MA: Harvard University Press, 1992), pp. 119-24.

89. The curtain design at right is derived from an Assyrian floor threshold, such as BM, ANE 118910. The battle scene at far left is closely derived from BM, ANE 124536. The central frieze is closely derived from BM, ANE 118914, 118916. The disposition of the frieze—its coloration and use of the 'sacred tree' motif to take up the wall's edges—suggest the influence not only of the artifacts in the museum, but also Layard's reconstruction of an Assyrian throne room. Layard's design is reproduced in Esin Atil, Charles Newton and Sarah Searight, *Voyages and Visions: Nineteenth-Century European Images of the Middle East from the Victoria and Albert Museum* (Washington, DC: Smithsonian Institution Traveling Exhibition Service/London: Victoria and Albert Museum in Association with University of Washington Press, Seattle and London, 1995), pp. 78-79.

Art-Journal stated 'We accept the archaeological details as presented to us, and without any hesitancy, fix our attention on the rare disposition of figures'.[90] Long's archaeological details are completely credible to *Art-Journal* and also quite unremarkable, merely a prologue for the examination of its figures. Yet just as the look of ancient Assyria becomes commonplace to the English viewer, it highlights larger themes at work throughout the nineteenth-century representation of Assyria. Notably, unlike Brown, but like John Martin before him, Long conflates Assyria and Babylonia. Even more, the primary subject of the work is the display of women, and of men gazing at them with an eye toward possession. This reiterates the gendered power structure of Delacroix's work. The composition again flatters the viewer at the expense of male figures in the scene.

At the far right, a man looks over a fence at the private zone of the women waiting to be displayed. His relation to these women mirrors that of the painting's viewer to the woman being displayed on the stage. In both cases, the male viewer sees the woman from behind and must guess at her appearance. The face of the man at right, and even more his gesture of raised hands (derived from Renaissance painting), testify to his being moved by the sight he sees.[91] This man's gesture also flatters the external viewer, who can see from his privileged perspective (and knowledge of the ritual) that this man appears to have fallen in love with one of the least beautiful of the women. Thus while internal and external viewing are related, the external, contemporary, Western viewer is again established as superior to the internal, historical one.

Long's work, then, refers to the same themes of the power of men over women and of the contemporary West over the Middle East evident in Delacroix's work. Yet the passage of more than forty years from Delacroix's time to Long's, and from France to England, also brought it to a realm where these assumptions were no longer universal. Two comments on Long's work suggest that the work also invited a critique, both of its gender assumptions and of its claim to historical veracity.

A reviewer in *Blackwood's Edinburgh Magazine*, among the older and more refined of middle-class periodicals, wrote of the piece:

> [The woman on display] is evidently the first and finest piece of goods in the collection, and the expression of the crowd of faces all fixed upon her is wonderfully fine and full of variety. The lips parted with that smile of mingled vanity and admiration with which men (out of marriage markets) so often regard the women exposed to their gaze, the gleam of the sensual eye, appear in most of the gazers; but some are pitiful and half tender, with a touch of compassion in them. And if the spectator gazes around him after he has looked at the picture, he will see another picture scarcely less attractive in the curious glances of the living faces that crowd about.[92]

90. 'The Royal Academy Exhibition', *Art-Journal* n.s. 14 (1875), pp. 247-52 (250).

91. Michael Baxandall, *Painting and Experience in Fifteenth Century Italy: A Primer in the Social History of Pictorial Style* (Oxford: Clarendon Press, 1972), pp. 47, 65-66.

92. 'Art in May', *Blackwood's Edinburgh Magazine* 117 (1875), pp. 747-64 (763).

The woman is a 'piece of goods' who offers the spectator a chance to be amused by the varieties of male reactions. This comment would seem to sustain the superiority of external viewer to internal viewer. Yet the implied unity of actual viewers and painted viewers is sundered by acknowledging the explicit gendering of spectatorship. The *Blackwood's* reviewer continues:

> We should not wonder if the young women, flower of English youth, who gather round with a curiosity not unmixed with personal feelings, found something like a revelation in the picture. One sees them glance at each other with a half smile, half blush, sometimes with subdued awe or indignation. 'Is that how they think of us, these men, though they dare not look it?' the girls ask themselves.

The dissimilar composition of audiences, between nineteenth-century England and that attributed to ancient Mesopotamia, presents a confrontation of genders in the work's actual audience that would be inadmissible in the ideal realm of the audience in the picture. The acts of viewing thematized in the work, that is, are thus again illuminated as specifically masculine, voyeuristic activities. Yet such a conception of viewing is distinctly unlike the actual viewing context of the work. The work's ideal male viewer is confronted by a actual female viewer, and thus the perfect binarism within the painting of men viewing and women being viewed is confronted and undermined.

A premise of the *Blackwood's* review is that the painting addresses contemporary England at least as much as ancient Babylonia. But the specific manner in which the structure of gender relations calls into question the painting's claim to historical authenticity was only directly considered by John Ruskin. Ruskin's erudite notice of the work was virtually alone in distinguishing between Assyrian and Babylonian artifacts. Although realizing the work's anachronisms he called it 'A painting of great merit, and well deserving purchase by the Anthropological Society'.[93] But this was not because the work was deemed to represent the ethnographic custom of a pristine past.

> As a piece of anthropology, [Long's work] is the natural and very wonderful product of a century occupied in carnal and mechanical science. In the total paralysis of conception—without attempt to disguise the palsy—as to the existence of any higher element in a woman's mind than vanity and spite, or in a man's than avarice and animal passion, it is also a specific piece of the natural history of our own century; but only a partial one, either of it or of the Assyrian...[94]

To the contrary, Ruskin saw the work as embodying the prejudices of the contemporary viewer. Far from purely exhibiting an extrinsic viewpoint or unusual custom, then, Long's work (for both writers) was a contemporary statement, as much about present as past. At the same time, through this way of approaching the image of the

93. John Ruskin, 'Academy Notes', in *The Works of John Ruskin* (39 vols.; ed. Edward T. Cook and Alexander Wedderburn; London: G. Allen/New York: Longmans, Green, & Co., 1903–12), XIV, pp. 274-77 (274).

94. Ruskin, 'Academy Notes', p. 275.

ancient world, the conventional dominance of the contemporary masculine, Western viewer is again put in doubt. Thus, the image of Assyria clearly brings together past and present concerns, while also presenting an occasion for both Ruskin and the *Blackwood's* reviewer to question conventional gender distinctions.

When looked at over the span of almost fifty years from Delacroix to Long, then, Assyrian archaeology did not simply work to provide more authentic envisioning of preexisting subjects, such as the death of Sardanapalus. To the contrary, art and archaeology functioned as two parts of a larger system of cultural circulation, in a continual process of reinventing ancient Assyria. Although images might have been constructed in accord with archaeological and antiquarian knowledge, they also responded to the varying needs and capabilities of artists and audiences.

The works of Brown and Long continue the sort of exoticist mobility with which Martin and Delacroix worked. But the combination of invented and 'authentic' elements on which mobility depends allows a widening of the conception of Assyria. Brown's use of Assyrian archaeological details allows a turn from dependence on authoritative ancient textual sources to the near-contemporary Byron. As much as the sources for the subject widened, so too did audience assumptions as the play of exoticist representation became more familiar. In the reception of Long's work we even find an explicit critique of the assumptions of power and gender which had dominated the conception of Assyria and the larger exoticist imagination throughout the earlier nineteenth century.

While even the traditional conception of Assyria was thus transformed, the juxtaposition of France and England is key to a much more radical and varied range of reception between the two countries. The varying fortunes of Assyria in France and England disrupted the prediscovery situation, in which both countries shared the same mode of conceiving the subject. Rather, the works of Courbet, Degas, and Moreau (and even Delacroix's lack of interest in the discoveries) suggest a distinctly different atmosphere in France from that of England, one which forecloses on, governs, and ultimately subordinates the aesthetic challenge of ancient Assyrian art.

Tracking the archaeological history and aesthetic debate over Assyria, as we have done, illuminates the fundamental differences between the milieus of reception in France and England. Not only their pragmatic archaeological histories, but also their methods of disseminating information differed sharply. The subsequent French submersion of Assyrian imagery we have noted is remarkably concordant with the troubled history of French Mesopotamian archaeology as well as the constrained circulation of the discoveries to the public. By contrast, in England, with its vigorous public debate on Assyria and its art, the lionizing of Layard as discoverer, as well as numerous publications on the works, an audience was fostered that was prepared to respond to the specific, detailed Assyrian images of artists such as Brown and Long.

For all the amassing of textual and visual evidence of Assyria, for all the energy expended in the antiquarian project of fixing the Assyrian past, the image of Assyria that arose was thus localized and hybridized as it circulated among Western audiences. Courbet's 'Assyrian' beard is no less the fruit of this process of circulation than Brown's painstaking Assyrian decor. Ultimately, then, like many another exoticist subject, Assyria served not only as an object in its own right but also as a distant and distorted mirror in which France and England asserted their respective identities. On these grounds, a most telling observation of the early reception of ancient Assyrian objects is this line from a review of an English production of Byron's *Sardanapalus*, which used elaborate sets and costumes almost directly copied from Layard's reliefs. 'That one performance gave us a better insight into the manners and habits of the Assyrians, than a whole lifetime has enabled us to acquire of the French'.[95]

95. *Lloyd's Weekly Newspaper*, June 15, 1853, quoted in Inge Krengel-Strudthoff, 'Archäologie auf der Bühne—das wiedererstandene Ninive: Charles Keans Ausstattung zu *Sardanapalus* von Lord Byron', *Kleine Schriften der Gesellschaft für Theatergeschichte* 31 (1981), pp. 1-24 (19).

Dalziels' Bible Gallery (1881): Assyria and the Biblical Illustration in Nineteenth-Century Britain*

Donato Esposito

Every painter now…is bound to be an archaeologist.[1]

Dalziels' Bible Gallery (London: George Routledge & Sons, 1881) has long been trumpeted as a milestone of late nineteenth-century book-illustration.[2] Less well-known is the fact that a number of the illustrations in this compendium are among the first products of the British artistic response to the newly unearthed material remains of ancient Assyria. In this connection, recent scholarship has documented a variety of media, including jewelry, ceramics, paintings, literature, and theater-sets.[3] Absent from these considerations is the place of several wood-engraved illustrations that formed a distinctive body of work commissioned by the Dalziel Brothers for their illustrated Bible. Begun in the early 1860s, though not published until 1881, these wood-engravings articulate original responses by artists with varying aesthetic agendas. This essay seeks to explore the genesis of the *Bible Gallery*, outline the designs that show the influence of Assyria, and locate these within the early artistic reception of Assyria in Britain.

1. *Mis-en-scène*

The primacy of the British Museum, both for inspiration and instruction, for British artists for much of the nineteenth century was unassailable. However,

* I would like to thank Jenny Graham, Elizabeth Prettejohn and Douglas Schoenherr for reading early drafts of this essay and making many useful suggestions and comments. I am grateful to Steven Holloway for support and encouragement throughout this project.

1. Remark made by Philip Stanhope, 5th Earl Stanhope (1805–75) at the annual Royal Academy dinner 29 April 1865, in 'The Royal Academy', *The Art-Journal* (June 1865), pp. 161-72 (163).

2. Gleeson White, *English Illustration: 'The Sixties' 1855–70* (London: A. Constable & Co., 1897), pp. 146-47.

3. See Frederick N. Bohrer, *Orientalism and Visual Culture: Imaging Mesopotamia in Nineteenth-Century Europe* (Cambridge and New York: Cambridge University Press, 2003) *passim* for a thorough and sustained analysis of the field, and Henrietta McCall, 'Rediscovery and Aftermath', in *The Legacy of Mesopotamia* (ed. Stephanie Dalley; Oxford: Oxford University Press, 1998), pp. 183-213 for a concise survey.

the rich and varied displays of archaeological material at the British Museum provided but one path towards explorations of historical authenticity, so vital to Victorian audiences. Many painters sought to immerse themselves in the literal landscape of the Bible and set off for extended sojourns in the Holy Land. For some painters, such as Frederick Goodall (1822–1904), the aim was to produce numerous sketches and studies that would serve as the basis for large exhibition paintings to be executed on his return to London. Following his first visit to Egypt in 1858, Goodall exhibited a virtually unbroken sequence of pictures inspired by the topography and associations of biblical Egypt. His first work in this vein was his *Early Morning in the Wilderness of Shur* (1860; Guildhall Art Gallery, London). Goodall was well acquainted with the collections in the British Museum and occasionally inserted objects into his canvases in a vague attempt at historicism, but never shared the passion or inclination towards the archeological exactitude of other artists such as Edward John Poynter or Lawrence Alma-Tadema.[4]

William Holman Hunt (1827–1910), a leading Pre-Raphaelite artist and *Bible Gallery* contributor, undertook three separate visits to the Holy Land, each to invigorate and inform his biblical paintings. He chose to immerse himself, and his art, in the culture and landscape of the modern Middle East in an effort to tap into the biblical epoch and absorb the 'faithful' spirit of his biblical work. He was not therefore, as was Goodall, merely content to amass a group of studies for later use elsewhere but actually began large-scale biblical paintings while abroad. Hunt also added historical and geographical labels to these pictures. To *The Shadow of Death* (1870–73; Manchester Art Gallery), which treats the foretelling of Christ's crucifixion, Hunt inscribed 'Jerusalem' beside the customary signature and date, he had begun the painting in that city in April 1870.[5] Hunt is clearly staking his claim for authenticity by linking his work inextricably with that celebrated biblical city.

Hunt's painstaking method of working meant that many of his biblical pictures took many years to complete. His most ambitious work in this area, *The Finding of the Saviour in the Temple* (1854–60; Birmingham Museums and Art Gallery), reveals the use of many available sources for this complex and richly detailed painting. Begun in Jerusalem in the summer of 1854, Hunt sought separate Jewish models for each of the seventeen foreground figures, sketched views of the Mount of Olives for the background and even

4. See Donato Esposito, 'From Ancient Egypt to Victorian London: The Impact of Ancient Egyptian Furniture on British Art and Design 1850–1900', *Decorative Arts Society Journal* 27 (2003), pp. 80-93 for a discussion of these artists' use of Egyptian archaeological material.

5. Judith Bronkhurst, in *The Pre-Raphaelites* (ed. Leslie Parris; London: Tate Gallery & Penguin Books, 1984), no.143, pp. 221-23 for a discussion of the genesis of the painting. Other pictures that have equivalent inscriptions include *A Street Scene in Cairo: The Lantern-Maker's Courtship* (1854–56, 1860–1861; Birmingham Museums and Art Gallery) and *The Afterglow in Egypt* (1854, 1860–63; Southampton City Art Gallery), both with 'Cairo'.

obtained locally sourced variegated limestone for the temple floor in the picture.[6] Following his return to London in the spring of 1856, Hunt embellished his picture with the lotus-and-bud motif that he would have seen in numerous examples of carved Neo-Assyrian door-sills then on display in the British Museum, as well as other smaller decorative elements, such as the ebony and ivory inlay found in a single surviving example in an ancient Egyptian stool, also in the British Museum.

The excavations by Austen Henry Layard (1817–94) in the mid-1840s unearthed large sequences of stone bas-reliefs that had once adorned a succession of royal palaces, in the Assyrian capitals at Nimrūd and Nineveh. In 1849 a temporary 'Nimroud Room' was installed at the British Museum for the reception of the newly-arriving antiquities and the interest of the public was especially caught by examples of colossal human-headed winged creatures that had flanked the entrances to the monumental gateways.[7] The excitement the Assyrian antiquities aroused in the British artistic community is captured by the young painter Edward Burne-Jones (1833–98) writing home to his father in Birmingham in July 1850:

> Today I went over [to] the British Museum and spent a considerable time in the Nimroud [*sic*] or Assyrian room; they are preparing a splendid apartment for the reception of them. I was quite surprised at the clearness and beauty of the Sculpture. The bas-reliefs seem to be as perfect as when they emerged from the workman's shop.[8]

The extraordinary popularity of the Assyrian exhibits at the British Museum, coupled with cost-effective improvements in the creation and distribution of graphic reproductions, ensured that the 'monuments' from the Bible-land of Assyria would begin to figure in the illustration of Bibles, Bible commentaries and other related art objects marketed in Great Britain. Layard's own publications of his finds, from the late 1840s onwards, brought these to a wide audience.[9] The growth in the distribution of copies of the Bible throughout the mid-nineteenth century was considerable. The British and Foreign Bible Society, for example, saw a rise in distribution of more than three hundred per cent

6. Bronkhurst, in Parris (ed.), *Pre-Raphaelites*, no. 85, pp. 158-60.

7. See Ian Jenkins, *Archaeologists and Aesthetes: In the Sculpture Galleries of the British Museum 1800–1939* (London: British Museum Press, 1992), pp. 158-67 for a lucid history of the display of Assyrian antiquities at the British Museum.

8. Georgiana Burne-Jones, *Memorials of Edward Burne-Jones* (2 vols.; London: Macmillan & Co., 1904), I, p. 45.

9. Especially important were his *Nineveh and its Remains* (London: John Murray, 1849) and *Discoveries in the Ruins of Nineveh and Babylon, with Travels in Armenia, Kurdistan and the Desert: Being the Result of a Second Expedition undertaken for the Trustees of the British Museum* (London: John Murray, 1853), both of which exploited the powerful biblical associations of these locations.

between 1831 and 1861.[10] Indeed, by 1861 nearly four million Bibles were issued annually in Great Britain.[11] London could boast huge bookshops packed with many tens of thousands of Bibles, prayer books and other religious publications. Among the biggest emporia were those located in busy shopping districts in the West End of the city. Advertisements for them placed in the popular weekly *Illustrated London News* attest to their great size; John Field's Great Bible Warehouse at 25 Regent Quadrant (near Piccadilly Circus) had a stock of 50,000 publications, while Parkins and Gotto Bible Warehouse at 24-25 Oxford Street stocked 25,000 examples. It was against this soaring demand that the immediate financial context for the emergence of the Dalziel Brothers' *Bible Gallery* may be seen.

2. *The House of Dalziel*

The wood-engraving firm Dalziel Brothers was founded in 1839 by George Dalziel (1815–1902) and Edward Dalziel (1817–1905).[12] Two other brothers later joined the venture, John (1822–69) in 1852 and Thomas Bolton Gilchrist (1823–1906) in 1860. The elder son of Edward, Edward Gurdon Dalziel (1849–89) was an illustrator and designed biblical work (used in *Art Pictures*). The firm's reputation grew and the Dalziels supplied illustrations to Britain's first dedicated art periodical, *The Art-Journal* (initially *The Art Union*), founded in 1839. Their greatest critical success came in the 1850s with their work in connection with two landmarks in British illustration: William Allingham, *The Music Master: A Love Story: And Two Series of Day and Night Songs* (London: George Routledge & Co., 1855) and Alfred Tennyson, *Poems* (London: Moxon, 1857), for which the Pre-Raphaelite painters Dante Gabriel Rossetti and John Everett Millais famously provided illustrations. The Dalziel Brothers cut the designs for each of the publications.

The Dalziels were far from alone in their venture to capitalize on the rich, and growing, market for Bible illustrations. The publishing magnate Joseph Cundall (1818–95) was intent on producing a collection of artworks comparable to that envisioned by the Dalziel brothers. In 1843–44 he published four volumes of scriptural works, entitled *Bible Events*, aimed at the burgeoning middle-classes as part of his 'The Home Treasury' series.[13] These volumes

10. 'Bibles', *ILN*, 5 October 1861, p. 344. The Society was founded in 1804.

11. 'Bibles', *ILN*, 5 October 1861, p. 344.

12. The single best account of the firm remains that jointly written by Edward and George Dalziel and published as *The Brothers Dalziel: A Record of Fifty Years' Work in Conjunction with Many of the Most Distinguished Artists of the Period 1840–1890* (London: Methuen & Co., 1901), which dispassionately records the victories (and failures) of the family venture that dominated its field for decades.

13. Ruari McLean, *Joseph Cundall: A Victorian Publisher; Notes on his Life and a Check-List of his Books* (Pinner: Private Libraries Association, 1976), pp. 48-49.

were illustrated with prints after the Old Masters, including the later Holbein, Dürer, Raphael and Michelangelo. Cundall did this both to enhance the prestige of the publications by their association with these great names from the art historical canon and, more prosaically, to avoid any issue over copyright. Surviving documentation from one of the artists involved in the *Dalziels' Bible Gallery* illustrates the delicacy of the arrangements, with permission granted solely for specific outlets which did not, for example, permit the sale of photographs of any original artworks in the possession of the Dalziel Brothers.[14] In 1844 Cundall released *The Passion of Our Lord Jesus Christ, Portrayed by Albert* [*sic*] *Dürer* which continued his preference for the use of past artwork long out of copyright. His decision to publish an illustrated Bible with contemporary British painters was therefore unusual and one that would require complex negotiations in order to publish the work of living artists. Cundall approached the same painters that the Dalziel brothers sought for their comparative project. Clearly the two camps were competing for illustrators, and, under mounting pressure, Cundall decided to abandon his plan. Exasperated, the publisher candidly wrote to his rivals in September 1863:

> I find that it is quite impossible for me to carry on my project for an Illustrated [*sic*] Bible without in some degree clashing with yours. We go to the same artists, we are getting the drawings of the same size, and however I may endeavour to steer clear of yours, there must be a certain similarity [remaining] between them.[15]

Cundall then detailed what could be done to resolve the issue. He elected to relinquish his project and to dispose of the drawings already received, together with others in hand, to his rivals for their market value. The Dalziel brothers appear to have taken up his capitulatory offer, as Cundall never did issue an illustrated Bible. Five months later the artist William Dyce died, and the single drawing he had supplied to Cundall, *Jacob and Rachel*, evidently passed into the possession of the Dalziels, which was included in the later edition of their *Bible Gallery*.

The immediate artistic precursors for large-format publications in Victorian Britain which the Dalziel brothers projected included the Nazarene painter Julius Schnorr von Carolsfeld's *Bible Pictures.*[16] The volume originally appeared in 1851 in German and was translated into English in 1860. The full-page illustra-

14. Letter from Ford Madox Brown to Dalziel Brothers, 9 March 1864 (BL/Add MSS 39168, 53-54). Brown was equally demanding about the copyright of his stained glass designs for Morris & Co., for whom Brown worked, retaining the copyright of his cartoon and prominently inscribing his claim below many of his designs. See *The Earthly Paradise: Arts and Crafts by William Morris and his Circle from Canadian Collections* (ed. Katharine A. Lochnan, Douglas E. Schoenherr and Carole Silver; Toronto: Art Gallery of Ontario and Key Porter Books, 1993), no. A8, p. 50. I am grateful to Douglas Schoenherr for this reference.

15. Joseph Cundall to Dalziel Brothers, 7 September 1863 (BL/Add MSS 39168, 50).

16. Julius Schnorr von Carolsfeld, *Schnorr's Bible Pictures: Scripture History Illustrated in One Hundred and Eight Wood Cuts from Original Designs* (London: Williams & Norgate, 1860).

tions were never accompanied by any substantial biblical text or commentary and the illustrations were evidently intended to stand alone. Though the style of Schnorr's designs is markedly different from any in the Dalziels' publication, the German's crisp linear style proved influential upon several painters who specialized in biblical depictions such as William Dyce, a *Bible Gallery* contributor, and John Rogers Herbert (1810–90).[17]

In addition, the work of the French émigré painter and printmaker Gustave Doré (1832–83) may have presented itself as a powerful example. Certainly Doré's phenomenal technical mastery of wood-engraving would have appealed to the Dalziels, and the French painter's substantial (and profitable) biblical *oeuvre* may have guided them in the planning and eventual format of their *Bible Gallery*. The *Doré Bible* (Old and New Testaments), first published in 1866, was reissued as *The Doré Gallery: Containing Two Hundred and Fifty Beautiful Engravings Selected from the Doré Bible, Milton, Dante's Inferno, Dante's Purgatorio and Paradiso, Atala, Fontaine, Fairy Realm, Don Quixote, Baron Munchausen, Croquemitaine...* (London: Cassell, Petter, Galpin & Co, 1870). The *Doré Gallery* represented a formidable body of designs even for an artist as prolific as Doré. The two enormous volumes were accompanied by a revealing comment: 'The artist has no personal knowledge of the [Middle] East, and has therefore been obliged to compile his accessories...from books and museums'.[18] Foremost among the latter were the Musée du Louvre in his native France and the British Museum in London, where he resided intermittently. Doré seems to have relied primarily upon published sources for the Assyrian motifs found in his illustrations. In *Daniel Interpreting the Writing on the Wall*, set in King Belshazzar's palace in Babylon, the human-headed winged bull to the right of the composition has an awkward perspective, with legs oddly aligned along the temple floor; it was probably derived from tracings the artist made from one of Layard's numerous publications. Doré was unconcerned with the archaeological precision that characterized the work of some of his contemporaries on both sides of the Channel. His 'insertion' of winged bulls in Mesopotamian and Persian settings seems to have been the extent of his researches, serving to suggest rather than copy the reconstructions of Nineveh in Layard and elsewhere. Both Schnorr's and Doré's publications included the New and Old Testaments.

3. *Dalziels' Bible Gallery: Format and Production*

Following the publication of *The Parables of Our Lord and Saviour Jesus Christ: With Pictures by John Everett Millais. Engraved by the Brothers Dalziel*

17. Paul Goldman, *Victorian Illustrated Books 1850–1870: The Heyday of Wood-Engraving* (London: British Museum Press, 1994), p. 105.

18. Edmond Ollier, *Doré Gallery*, I, p. 22 (Ollier supplied the letterpress and a 'critical essay').

(London: Routledge, Warne & Routledge, 1864), the Dalziels decided to commission a florilegium of engravings based on the Hebrew Scriptures. These texts held strong narrative possibilities and lay open the chance to incorporate the latest archaeological discoveries in the Near East and make reference to the Assyrian antiquities then newly discovered. The Dalziel brothers utilized the same medium and design as the comparable works by Schnorr and Doré: large, dynamic wood-engravings with only a brief scriptural citation for the legends. The *Bible Gallery* sold in two formats: bound and unbound. Each illustration was printed on *chine collé*, a fine smooth paper originally from China, that provided an ideal surface on which to print minutely detailed relief prints. *Chine collé* was also (confusingly) known as India paper, hence, impressions printed on it were commonly known as India proofs. The bound version, issued in an edition of 1,000 copies, therefore had 'India Proofs' tooled on the front cover. The layout of the pages between formats was identical and where, for example, Thomas Dalziel had two small illustrations on one page this was identical in both formats. The unbound portfolio format, with the illustrations printed on loose sheets, came in an edition of 100 copies. The maximum dimensions of the bound edition were approximately 435 × 350 mm, whereas the unbound portfolio with flaps measured 580 × 410 mm, and thus could only have been consulted comfortably on a large table or portfolio stand. Either bound in vellum and leatherette for five guineas or mounted on hand-made paper in portfolio for ten guineas, the *Bible Gallery* was neither a portable 'democratic' read, nor was it within easy reach of most of the middle class.

The originality of the designs, though not strictly contemporary, was unambiguously guaranteed by a brief statement dated October 1880 and placed at the beginning of the *Bible Gallery*: 'Original drawings made expressly for us, and have never before been published. Dalziel Brothers'. The letterpress beneath each illustration carried the title of the work, the designer and, where applicable their institutional affiliation. The title-page too gave the appropriate senior membership of each contributor. In truth, the publication made much of the artistic membership of its contributors. Paintings occupied a privileged position in the artistic canon. The *Bible Gallery* tended to favor painters who exhibited, and hence achieved membership, in those institutions that championed painting in oils. It is probably for that reason that Edward Frederick Brewtnall's associate membership of the Royal Watercolour Society went unrecorded. The most prestigious 'club' was that of the Royal Academy of Arts in London, whose forty members were called Royal Academicians and who were entitled to add the initials R.A. after their names. The *Bible Gallery* included six Royal Academicians.[19] The only other title in the publication was that of the Dublin-based Irish

19. Edward Armitage, Henry Hugh Armstead, William Dyce, Frederick Richard Pickersgill, Edward John Poynter and George Frederic Watts. When the project began in the early 1860s only Pickersgill and Dyce were already Royal Academicians.

equivalent of the parent institution. Hence, Francis Sylvester Walker's (1848–1916) membership of the Royal Hibernian Academy of Arts (R.H.A.) is highlighted in the list of contributors in order to stack up against his London-based colleagues. The Dalziels took great delight in having the loftiest such accolade possible, a President of the Royal Academy (P.R.A.), the position Frederic Leighton assumed in 1878; he was therefore placed at the head of the listing. Contemporary reviews of the publication also began (invariably) their commentaries with Leighton.

One of the completed designs for *The First Offering of Aaron*, one of Simeon Solomon's submissions for the *Bible Gallery*, is in the Cecil Higgins Art Gallery, Bedford. The size is exactly that of the wood-engraving made from it, and is dated September 1864 in keeping with Solomon's usual habit of precisely dating his work.[20] The print closely follows the drawing, even allowing for cropping of one of the young priests at the left of the composition. Preparatory sketches culminated in the 'finished' design executed in pen and ink on paper, which was then either re-drawn by the artist on the block, or the drawing was glued to the block itself (thereby destroying this 'final' drawing). Before cutting the block, the Dalziels would add their 'signature', 'DALZIEL SC', to the design thereby asserting their mediating artistic presence in the 'reproduction' of drawings.[21] However, from about 1868 onwards photography allowed both the preservation of these 'finished' drawings and freed the contributory artists from fixing the size of their published designs in advance.[22] The early drawings for the project made in the early 1860s were initially drawn to the same scale as the intended published illustrations.

The date of the drawings (where given) varies from Simeon Solomon's *And David Took An Harp* and *Jewish Women Burning Incense* of 1862 to three much later works, William Small's *Cushi Brings to David News of the Death of Absalon*, his *Job Receiving the Messengers* and Francis Sylvester Walker's *Elijah Fed by the Ravens*, all from 1876. The completion of the *Bible Gallery* as issued in 1881 seems to have been done with the close

20. Pen-and-ink drawing, 145 × 184 mm (inv. P. 330), print measures 142 × 184 mm. The '9' in the inscription on the drawing (in Solomon's hand) '9/64' indicates the date of the drawing as September 1864 and is not, as has been suggested, Solomon's reference to the ninth chapter of Leviticus, the subject of the composition. See Evelyn Joll, *Cecil Higgins Art Gallery: Watercolours and Drawings* (Bedford, UK: Cecil Higgins Art Gallery, 2002), p. 242.

21. 'Sc' was the common abbreviation for the Latin word *sculpsit*, for 'engraved', which appeared on prints. This was usually added beside the printmaker's name in the customary lettering in intaglio printmaking, especially engraving. In nineteenth-century Britain it began to be adopted by large firms of wood-engravers, such as the Dalziel Brothers and Joseph Swain (1820–1909) and added within the printing matrix, making it inseparable from the (published) image.

22. Geoffrey Wakeman, *Victorian Book Illustration: The Technical Revolution* (Detroit, MI: Gale Research Company, 1973), pp. 78-79.

intervention of the artist members of the Dalziel family. Thomas Dalziel had seven designs included in the *Bible Gallery*, but none were used in the later 1894 edition. He was clearly out of favor with the new publishers. Unusually these designs are somewhat smaller than the other contributors and often two designs were printed on a single page, diluting their impact and visual clarity. The smaller designs could be engraved with speed and worked upon simultaneously, suggesting Thomas' late inclusion in the project.

4. *Dalziels' Bible Gallery: Artists and Works*

Henry Hugh Armstead (1828–1905) was the sole sculptor chosen for the *Bible Gallery*. He exhibited at the Royal Academy from 1851 onwards and only occasionally made illustrations; his specialty was relief carving, and the flattened perspective of this technique made him well-suited to illustration. He is perhaps best-known for two of the four panels of celebrated figures from history commissioned for the Albert Memorial in Hyde Park, London.

Armstead contributed two designs to the *Bible Gallery*. *The Sun and Moon Stand Still* illustrates the miraculous defeat of the five Amorite kings by Joshua at Gibeon (see figure 32). Joshua stood over the Israelite army and cried: 'Sun, stand thou still upon Gibeon; And thou, Moon, in the Valley of Ajalon' (Joshua 10.12 [KJV]). Armstead depicts the Israelite leader in strong silhouette against a brilliant sunlit sky with a gesturing hand to the sun behind him, while below is conveyed a sense of anguish, chaotic disorder and destruction of tangled horses' legs, crashing chariots, spears and fallen soldiers. The principal focus in the foreground is a chariot rapidly losing control, carrying one of the Amorite kings, wearing a distinctive conical tiara like those worn by the Neo-Assyrian emperors; a tasseled umbrella used to protect the Assyrian kings from the sun falls behind in the general rout. The royal chariot and equipage are based on numerous examples seen in British Museum Assyrian reliefs. Joshua's horse wears a head-dress that was described by Layard in *Nineveh and Its Remains* as 'surmounted by an arched crest and round the neck was an embroidered collar, ending in a rich tassel…' (II, p. 275). In the immediate foreground, an Amorite soldier wearing an Assyrian arched crested helmet supports the sagging weight of a fallen comrade, perhaps even a king, judging from his dress, which is similar to that of the royal rider in the chariot. The illustration drew praise from the critic of the *Athenaeum*, who considered that the design is 'full of movement… and tells the story perfectly'.[23]

23. 'Fine Arts: Gift Books', *Athenaeum*, 13 November 1880, p. 646.

Figure 32. Henry Hugh Armstead, *The Sun and Moon Stand Still*, undated. Wood-engraving touched with Chinese white (now faded), 178 × 158 mm. London, BM, P&D 1913-4-15-201 (654) (photo: British Museum, London).

The Royal Academy has two preparatory studies for the *The Sun and Moon Stand Still* in which Armstead's techniques of resolving black and white and the massing of forms are strongly evident; he designed his illustrations with a sculptor's eye and fondness for sculptural expression. There is also a double-sided sheet of his studies after the celebrated Nineveh banqueting relief of Assurbanipal (see figure 30). An important prototype for Armstead's composition was John Martin's *Sturm und Drang* painting *Joshua Commanding the Sun to Stand Still upon Gibeon*, exhibited at the Royal Academy in 1816 and widely circulated in mezzotint version by the artist. The large scale of the work meant that it would certainly have attracted attention. It was later exhibited at the 1862 International Exhibition in London and Armstead may well have seen it there.[24]

24. The previous year another version of the painting was sold from the collection of Charles Scarisbrick (1800–60), a collector from Lancashire, who also owned a version of Martin's *Fall of*

The 1894 reissue of the *Bible Gallery* revealed the sculptor's proficiency at absorbing other Assyrian motifs into his illustrative work. The adaptation of examples of carved door-sills, with their lotus-and-bud and rosette decorations, form the principal point of interest in one of two newly selected illustrations, *Samuel and Eli*. Here the aged Eli is confronted by the news of impending trouble caused by the actions of his two wayward sons.

The recruitment of Ford Madox Brown (1821–93) and his involvement with the Dalziel *Bible Gallery* can be more precisely detailed because of surviving documentation, which is the most complete of the artists under discussion. Brown's 1865 solo exhibition in a commercial gallery space on Piccadilly, in the heart of London's commercial art district, provides a useful reference point.[25] One-man shows were novel at that time and this particular example is the more extraordinary because the commentary in the accompanying catalogue was written by the artist and provides an unusually rare insight into an artist's working methods and thought processes. It bears direct relevance here since in that exhibition a clutch of three works was labeled as 'first sketches and small works' intended for 'Messrs. Dalziel's [*sic*] illustrated Bible'.[26] Brown cites the dual influence of ancient Egyptian and Assyrian sources for much of the costume in these three designs and 'other nearly contemporary remains'. His borrowings were decidedly eclectic, but his designs for the *Bible Gallery* nonetheless reveal his historical leanings at his most extreme. Brown's involvement with the *Bible Gallery* began in November 1863.[27] The oil painting *Elijah and the Widow's Son*, based on a design for the project of the same title, was commissioned by the Brighton collector John Hamilton Trist (1811–91) in 1864 and completed in time for inclusion in Brown's show the following year.[28] A study for the subject that would later be known as *Joseph's Coat* is clearly dated 1855 and he recycled this for the *Bible Gallery* when the originally intended

Nineveh. The sale at Christie's in London on 17-18 May 1861 was reviewed by the art press of the time, astonishing *The Art-Journal* by the low prices to which some of Martin's 'grand and poetical compositions were knocked down' ('Picture Sales', [July 1861], pp. 214-15 [215]). Martin also mezzotinted this composition as was his usual practice and began issuing them in 1827, thereby reaching a wider audience. That same year, the printmaker Richard James Lane (1800–72) had also made a print of the composition; Christopher Johnstone, *John Martin* (London: Academy Editions: 1974), p. 46. Martin's painting was acquired in 2004 by the National Galley of Art, Washington, D.C.

25. *The Exhibition of Work, and Other Paintings, by Ford Madox Brown, at the Gallery, 191 Piccadilly* (London: Gallery, 1865). The exhibition was held March to June 1865.

26. BL/Add MSS 39168, 55.

27. Mary Bennett, *Artists of the Pre-Raphaelite Circle: The First Generation: Catalogue of Works in the Walker Art Gallery, Lady Lever Art Gallery and Sudley Art Gallery* (London and Liverpool: Lund Humphrie and National Museums and Galleries on Merseyside, 1998), p. 37.

28. See Dianne Sachko Macleod, *Art and the Victorian Middle Class: Money and the Making of Cultural Identity* (Cambridge: Cambridge University Press, 1996), p. 481 for a concise biography of Trist.

sale of the piece was not forthcoming.[29] He had previously worked with the Dalziel Brothers on one of the firm's most celebrated publications to which he designed the *Prison of Chillon* in 1857 for a collection of poetry edited by Rev. Robert Aris Willmott, *Poets of the Nineteenth Century* (London: George Routledge & Co., 1857). Brown was personally known to them and they would frequently call on him, although usually these visits were related to business and the exchange of trial proofs. His son-in-law, Ford Madox Hueffer, considered Brown's *Bible Gallery* submissions 'some of his most dramatic and successful'.[30] The Dalziel Brothers owned the copyright for Brown's *Joseph's Coat* and retained the finished pen-and-ink drawing. Comparable drawings for the other designs, including *The Death of Eglon*, must also have been made but seem not to have survived and remain untraced.

Brown's sporadic diary entries from 1847 to 1868 provide another credible source for the motifs in his designs for the *Bible Gallery*. The diary was a 'working diary' and hence is fashioned with note-like brevity but nonetheless provides valuable written testimony in his 'distinctive spelling'.[31] In 1855 he went 'to the Cristal [*sic*] Palace with whole Family & one servant' in Sydenham and again the following year visited 'the Cristal [*sic*] Palace with Emma'. He is unlikely to have made any sketches or drawings of the displays while in company but would no doubt have been impressed by the larger-than-life reconstructions of ancient architecture, including the so-called Nineveh Court. Brown had much to say in his entry on *The Death of Eglon*:

> The costume and accessories of this cartoon are taken from Assyrian and Egyptian remains of a remote period. These alone, it seems to me, should guide us in Biblical subjects... The Moabites having remained in Palestine from the time of Abraham and Lot, I have [therefore] given a more Assyrian character to Eglon. Ehud on the contrary, I have thought necessary to represent with more of the Egyptian character, the Israelites having come from that country.[32]

Brown mentioned the 'Assyrian [antiquities]... and those of their neighbours, the Egyptians, which we have in the British Museum' available for perusal by interested parties. In a letter of October 1864 he outlined his current and forthcoming submissions for the Dalziel Brothers. *Elijah and the Widow's Son* had

29. See Janet Butler, 'A Pre-Raphaelite Shibboleth: Joseph', *Journal of Pre-Raphaelite Studies* 3/1 (1982), pp. 78-90. Brown may have known of Henry Warren's watercolor *Joseph's Coat Brought to Jacob*, first exhibited at the New Watercolour Society in London in 1849 and engraved by Samuel S. Smith (1810–79) and published by *The Art-Journal* (November 1863), opposite p. 217.

30. Ford Madox Hueffer [Ford Madox Ford], *Ford Madox Brown: A Record of his Life and Work* (London: Longmans, Green & Co., 1896), p. 197.

31. *The Diary of Ford Madox Brown* (ed. Virginia Surtees; New Haven: Yale University Press, 1918), p. xv.

32. Brown, quoted in Kenneth Bendiner, *The Art of Ford Madox Brown* (University Park, PA: Pennsylvania State University Press, 1998), p. 147.

by this time been accepted and his latest design *Joseph's Coat* he wished to be considered 'on the same terms agreed for the Elijah drawing'.[33] He added that the next subjects he 'should like to begin [designing are] Rahab letting the spies down from her window Joshua II.15 [and] Ehud slaying Eglon King of Moab Judges III.17-20', the former of which was not undertaken. Brown was only partly successful with his request, for in the end Frederic Leighton illustrated the former of these subjects, published as *The Spies Escape*. Brown eventually published the latter composition as *The Death of Eglon*, the design for which was complete just five months later when his solo exhibition opened in March 1865. *Elijah and the Widow's Son* and *Joseph's Coat* may have been the 'finished' pen-and-ink drawings that were photographed, transferred to wood-blocks and then cut, thus preserving the original drawings which are both extant.[34] *Joseph's Coat* was in the possession of the Dalziel Brothers until 1893 when it was sold to the British Museum. The drawing is the same size and direction as the published wood-engraving. *Elijah* is in the Victoria and Albert Museum, London.

Figure 33. Ford Madox Brown, *The Death of Eglon*, undated. Wood-engraving touched with Chinese white, 152 × 187 mm. London, BM, P&D 1913-4-15-201 (656) (photo: British Museum, London).

33. BL/Add MSS 39168, 55.

34. The exhibited works were (no. 67) *Ehud and Eglon King of Moab*, (no. 68) *Elijah and the Widow's Son* and (no. 69) *Jacob and Joseph's Coat*.

Despite Brown's knowledge of the collections of the British Museum, he seems to have based his design for *The Death of Eglon* almost entirely on published sources, in particular the numerous small wood-engraved illustrations dotted throughout Layard's *Nineveh and Its Remains*. Eglon's dais and a section of wall behind Ehud is inscribed with the distinctive wedge-shaped cuneiform script commonly found carved or impressed in Assyrian artifacts, although the texts are gibberish. The goat-headed anthropomorph clutching two small goats to the left of the Israelite is entirely the artist's invention, possibly inspired by British Museum reliefs of human-headed genies in profile holding deer and goats. Eglon's thick and tightly curled 'Assyrian' beard partly obscures the emblems hung around his neck that follows Layard's description of 'figures of the sun, moon, and stars, suspended round the neck of the king' seen in several bas-reliefs of Assyrian kings and illustrated in *Nineveh and its Remains* (II, p. 338). The dagger heads protruding from Eglon's ample girth are likely to have been taken from Layard's work which gives a single example of a group of these without citing the source of the illustration. In Brown's composition, two daggers terminate with a chevron pattern, accompanied by a third ending with the head of a horse, exactly, and in the same configuration, as in Layard's illustration (II, opposite p. 228). The reversal of the arrangement suggests that Brown may have made a tracing of the group. The decorative frieze behind Eglon is composed of honeysuckle interspersed with other motifs, again as illustrated from a pattern by Layard from Nimrūd. The throne and footstool are composites from various sculpted examples, though the side-table resembles an example from the Northwest Palace at Nimrūd.

Brown, encouraged by his handling of Assyrian models in his solo exhibition in 1865 won a commission to illustrate Lord Byron's poem *Sardanapalus* (1821) which appeared in *The Poetical Works of Lord Byron* (ed. William Michael Rossetti; London: Moxon, 1870). The design was repeated shortly afterwards in a watercolor *The Dream of Sardanapalus* (1871; Delaware Art Museum, Wilmington, DE; see figure 29). Brown also began an oil version in 1873 and another watercolor of 1875, both of which remain untraced.[35] Like the *Bible Gallery* designs before them, Brown's rare foray into historical pictures proved lucrative for the artist and popular with his patrons, providing further opportunity for Brown's knowledge of Assyrian motifs to be newly explored and reworked in each successive version. No repetitions are

35. Stephen Wildman *et al.*, *Waking Dreams: The Art of the Pre-Raphaelites from the Delaware Art Museum* (Alexandria, VA: Art Services International, 2004), no. 5, pp. 98-99 (98). The watercolor (Sotheby's London, 14 November 1964, lot 83, not illustrated) is known from an etching made after it by George Woolliscoft Rhead (1855–1920) and exhibited at the Arts and Crafts Exhibition Society in London in 1890 (no. 627), an impression of which is in the British Museum (BM, P&D 1916-8-9-26).

known to have been made by Brown of *The Death of Eglon* but, judging from the many made from his other *Bible Gallery* contributions, it seems entirely possible.[36]

The largest group of drawings came from Edward John Poynter (1836–1919) who contributed twelve designs for the *Bible Gallery*. He first began exhibiting at the Royal Academy from 1861 onwards and throughout the next decade built a solid reputation as a leading painter of both the historical genre and history painting proper. His works dealt mainly with Egyptian subject matter, sometimes based on episodes from the Bible. In 1864 he exhibited *On Guard in the Time of the Pharaohs* (1864), which personalized this moment from history by focusing on the dutiful action of one attentive guardsman.[37] In 1867 he showed at the Dudley Gallery *Adoration to Ra* (1867) which again focused on personal self-absorption, here the individual religious ritual of a single devout Egyptian.[38] But the undoubted masterpiece from this time was his *Israel in Egypt* (1867; Guildhall Art Gallery, London) shown to singular praise at the Royal Academy in 1867. This large canvas, over two meters in length, illustrated the biblical book of Exodus; it was crowded with references to antiquities taken primarily from his close study and intimate knowledge of the Egyptian antiquities on display in the British Museum. Throughout his long career, spanning more than six decades, his association with the Royal Academy was close and he eventually rose to become its President in 1896. Poynter later found himself in academic and administrative roles, which saw the tailing off of his artistic practice.[39] In the early 1880s, however, his time was increasingly devoted to art history and he began publishing a number of textbooks focusing on the major schools of European painting.[40]

Poynter's contribution to the *Bible Gallery* project consolidated his reputation during the 1860s, and it was at this time that he exhibited in quick succession a series of history paintings of an ambition rarely seen in British art

36. One design, for example, *Elijah and the Widow's Son*, was reworked into an oil version of 1864 (Birmingham Museums and Art Gallery) and two watercolors, one in 1864 and, until recently, in the collection of Seymour Stein (Sotheby's New York, 11 December 2003, lot 109, illustrated) and the other in 1868 (Victoria and Albert Museum, London).

37. Sotheby's London, 14 June 2001, lot 43, illustrated.

38. Sotheby's London, 19 June 1990, lot 53, illustrated.

39. He became the first Slade Professor of Fine Art at University College London (1871–75), President of the Royal Academy of Art (1896–1918) and Director of the National Gallery (1894–1905).

40. For example, Edward John Poynter and Percy Rendell Head, *Classic and Italian Painting* (Illustrated Text-Books of Art Education; New York: Scribner & Welford/London: Sampson, Low, Marston & Co., 1880), Harry John Wilmot-Buxton and Edward John Poynter, *German, Flemish and Dutch Painting* (Illustrated Text-Books of Art Education; New York: Scribner & Welford/London: Samson Low, Marston, Searle & Rivington, 1881) and Edward John Poynter, *Painting, Classic, Early Christian, Italian and Teutonic* (Illustrated Handbooks of Art History; London: Samson Low, Marston, Searle & Rivington, 1882).

of this time. Poynter was recruited on the strength of a single work that caught the attention of the Dalziel brothers at a small exhibition in 1862. The work was a watercolor, *Egyptian Water Carriers*, which they considered 'small, but charming' and which they promptly purchased.[41] The strongly defined female profiles and the picture's historicist vein must have appealed to Edward Dalziel who purchased the work from the exhibition and later had it translated it into the wood-engraving *The Israelites in Egypt: Water-Carriers*; it remained in his collection until it was sold in 1886.[42] The work is the only one in the entire *Bible Gallery* that is not directly based on a scriptural episode.[43] By May 1863 Poynter's friend from his Parisian student days George Du Maurier (1834–96) wrote that 'Old Poynter… intends to keep himself by 'wood' and 'glass'—he has done two very nice drawings for the illustrated Bible which the Dalziels are bringing out & which promises to be a very crack affair'.[44] Poynter had completed one of these designs by October that same year and which was praised by his friend as the 'best thing he has yet done'.[45] Throughout the period of his engagement with the designs for the *Bible Gallery*, Poynter always lived in close proximity to the British Museum, and for several years literally across the street.[46] Surviving drawings of his, appropriately enough, now held in the British Museum of identifiable Roman and Egyptian antiquities seen there attest to his close study of the collection. Poynter undertook extensive research for this large painting—more than seventy drawings can be associated with it.[47] Other studies related to the same painting document his varied knowledge of Assyrian metalwork.

41. The work was seen in a small exhibition in Newman Street, possibly an exhibition at Leigh's Academy (*Brothers Dalziel*, p. 250). The Dalziel brothers probably worked solely with the watercolor for engraving purposes and may not have had the need to commission from Poynter a pen-and-ink drawing of the composition. It may have been converted into a drawing by one of their own in-house draughtsman, perhaps Thomas Dalziel; Poynter's signature is clumsily drawn, a fact supporting this suggestion.

42. The watercolor was sold from the (partial) sale of Edward Dalziel (Christie's London, 19 June 1886, lot 58, not illustrated) and was recently in the collection of Seymour Stein (Sotheby's New York, 11 December 2003, lot 89, illustrated).

43. The *Bible Gallery* did not give the biblical references with each illustration.

44. Letter to the art critic and writer Thomas Armstrong (1832–1911), in *The Young George Du Maurier: A Selection of his Letters 1860–67* (ed. Daphne Du Maurier; London: Peter Davies, 1951), p. 204. I am grateful to Alison Inglis for this reference. The two designs Du Maurier refers to are *Moses Slaying the Egyptian* and *Moses Keeping Jethro's Sheep*.

45. Du Maurier, *Young George Du Maurier*, p. 215.

46. In 1861–64 he lived on Grafton Street (near Fitzroy Square); then in 1865–66; at 62 Great Russell Street (Poynter's friend Du Maurier lived at 91 Great Russell Street 1863–64); and in 1867–69, at 106 Gower Street. These locations were short walking distances from the British Museum at Great Russell Street.

47. See Alison Inglis, in *Queen of Sheba: Treasures from Ancient Yemen* (ed. St John Simpson; London: British Museum Press, 2002), no. 1, p. 23.

In 1846 Henry Nelson O'Neil (1817–80) exhibited at the Royal Academy *By the Waters of Babylon* (untraced), and re-exhibited the canvas later that same year in Liverpool. The young painter and friend of Poynter and Du Maurier, Philip Hermogenes Calderon (1833–98) exhibited at the 1853 Royal Academy a small picture *By The Waters of Babylon* (1852; Tate, London) in which brightly clad and minutely observed figures are set within an overtly English landscape, clearly in direct reference to the emerging Pre-Raphaelite group of painters.[48] For the same exhibition John Prescott Knight (1803–81) submitted *The Prophet Daniel* with the line 'By the Waters of Babylon' (untraced), appended in the catalogue. In 1850 Joseph Bouvier (fl.1839–88) exhibited *By the Waters of Babylon* (untraced). Later still in the winter of 1858 Simeon Solomon, a *Bible Gallery* contributor, exhibited at the French Gallery *The Waters of Babylon* (untraced).[49] The rage for subject matter of the Israelites' captivity in Babylonia spread beyond the confines of the metropolitan exhibition venues centred on London. Liverpool held an annual exhibition of contemporary art to which many London-based artists contributed in the hope of securing a wider market. Solomon exhibited his early masterpiece *The Mother of Moses* there in 1862, and *Hosannah!* in 1867,[50] both of which were incorporated into the Dalziel project. In 1860 Chester Earles showed at the Liverpool Society of Fine Arts *The Exiles* (untraced), appended to which was a line from Psalm 137.4: 'How shall we sing the Lord's Song in a Strange Land'. The potency of the influence of the Israelites' captivity was felt in other fields beyond the visual arts. In 1865 a new musical score for duet, *By the Waters of Babylon* by F.F. Courtenay, became available for the first time.[51]

48. Calderon maintained his interest in Mesopotamian subject-matter in his unfolding artistic career. In the 1880 Royal Academy his painting *Captives of his Bow and Spear* (untraced) was noted by one art critic for its kneeling supplicants before an 'Assyrian-looking warrior' ('The Royal Academy Exhibition', *The Art-Journal* [June 1880], pp.186-88 [187]).

49. The work was accompanied in the exhibition catalogue by the following quotation: 'They that carried us away captive required of us a song, and they that wasted us required of us mirth. O Daughter of Babylon, who art to be destroyed, happy shall he be that rewardeth thee thou hast served us'. Psalm 137.3,8 (KJV).

50. *Hosannah!* was lent by George Rae (1817–1902), a Liverpudlian banker. He also owned a version of Ford Madox Brown's *Joseph's Coat* (1866; Walker Art Gallery, Liverpool) which he commissioned in 1864. See Macleod, *Victorian Middle-Class*, pp. 463-64.

51. Published by Ollivier & Co, 19 Old Bond Street, London ('New Music', *ILN*, 13 May 1865, p. 459).

Figure 34. Edward John Poynter, *By the Rivers of Babylon*, 1865. Wood-engraving touched with Chinese white (now faded), 224 × 180 mm. London, BM, P&D 1913-4-15-201 (669) (photo: British Museum, London).

Poynter's *By the Rivers of Babylon* illustrates the plight of the Israelite captives in Babylon as recounted in Psalm 137.1–3:

> By the rivers of Babylon, there we sat down, yea, we wept, when we remembered Zion. We hanged our harps upon the willows in the midst thereof. For there they that carried us away captive required of us a song; and they that wasted us required of us mirth, saying, Sing us one of the songs of Zion (KJV).

The three 'Babylonians' engaged with the Israelite harps and harpists are dressed from sandals to diadem or tiara in clothing and ornaments meticulously copied from Neo-Assyrian palace reliefs in the British Museum. The harps themselves replicate those depicted on Assyrian palace reliefs, as do the beards and male coiffeurs. In the absence of comparable remains from the southern Mesopotamian kingdom of Babylonia, artists like Poynter routinely exploited the Assyrian visual repertoire for models for other Mesopotamian civilizations and, as we shall see, even for Achaemenid Persia. The draperies and hairstyles of the women are in keeping with conventional Greco-Roman historicist artworks, although the two rosette bracelets worn by the figure on the far right might have been inspired by Assyrian prototypes. The floral pattern surrounding the doorway replicate characteristic Assyrian ornamental motifs.

Figure 35. Edward John Poynter, *Daniel's Prayer*, 1865. Wood-engraving touched with Chinese white (now faded) and graphite, 191 × 175 mm. London, BM, P&D 1913-4-15-201 (672) (photo: British Museum, London).

Daniel's Prayer (Daniel 6.10-11) locates the prophet in an imaginary chamber opulently carved with repeating patterns of Assyrian rosettes, guilloche, lotus-and-bud, kneeling quadrupeds and, directly above his back, the tableau of the Assyrian king standing before the sacred tree surmounted with the winged solar disk popularly identified with the imperial god Aššur. Despite the presence of relief panels from Persepolis in the British Museum and the wide circulation of excellent on-the-spot drawings of Achaemenid Persia art since the early part of the century, most Victorian-era British artists turned to ancient Assyria when casting about for historicizing images for illustrating biblical stories that were set in Persia.

Simeon Solomon (1840–1905) was one of several artist siblings who from early youth was fascinated by the biblical heritage of his Judaism. He began his career solidly enough by exhibiting at the Royal Academy and his submission of 1860, *The Mother of Moses* (1860; Delaware Art Museum, Wilmington, DE) won him a medal from the Society for the Encouragement of Fine Arts in the category of history painting.[52] This genre, which included work illustrating the Bible, occupied a privileged position in the artistic canon and many aspiring young painters—including many *Bible Gallery* contributors—channeled their initial efforts into this area, until their positions became secure enough to pursue other subjects. Despite this auspicious confirmation, the critical reception of the picture was negative.[53] It was not, however, universally condemned; the novelist William Makepeace Thackeray (1811–68) praised the work publicly while the picture still hung on the walls of Burlington House.[54] The painting was soon bought by the Pre-Raphaelite collector Thomas Edward Plint (1823–61). Solomon later looked elsewhere to exhibit his art, which moved away from any narrative, anecdote or reference to the everyday towards an exploration of the ideal and the beautiful. In 1865 he co-founded (with Poynter and others) the Dudley Gallery, which showcased this 'new' artistic practice. This shift in narrative impulse became evident in his biblical work for the *Bible Gallery*: in one illustration, *Abraham and Isaac*, the cranes in the upper left of the composition recall his awareness of Japanese art with the stylized depictions of these birds in flight. But Solomon's arrest in 1873 for homosexual crimes caused his exclusion from the artistic community and the end of his brilliant career, and even close friends such as Rossetti and Charles Algernon Swinburne turned against him. He supplemented his workhouse living into which he found himself by selling chalk drawings. Solomon's involvement with the Dalziels appears to have

52. 'Society for the Encouragement of the Fine Arts', *ILN*, 19 January 1861, p. 53. The Society was founded in 1858.

53. Roberto C. Ferrari, 'The Unexplored Correspondence of Simeon Solomon', *The Journal of Pre-Raphaelite Studies* NS 12 (Spring 2003), pp. 23-34 (25).

54. 'Roundabout Papers, Vol. V', *Cornhill Magazine* 2 (July 1860), pp. 122-28 (123-24).

been unaffected and six of his designs were published by them in 1881. Solomon's involvement with the *Bible Gallery* project seems to be among the earliest—if not the earliest—documented of any of the published artists.

> Mr. Dalziel has asked me to make him a drawing of the 'Moses' which now belongs to you. I wish to know if you would object at all to my doing it and if not, if you would allow [me] to have the picture for two or three days at my own place.[55]

The work to which Solomon refers was his 1860 exhibit mentioned previously. The painting was sold in March 1862, having been in the collection of Plint for less than a year before Plint's sudden death.[56] The work seems to have quickly found its way into another collection; Solomon was keen on securing it on loan. The *Athenaeum* considered it among his best illustrations, marking the return of Solomon from artistic wilderness, for those who view it will 'recognise with fresh zest Mr. Solomon's skill and just feeling for Biblical subjects'.[57]

Concerning Solomon's painting *Hosannah!* which he exhibited in 1861, the *Athenaeum* critic described it as 'a youth, of the highest Jewish type, is seen bearing the immemorial ten-stringed harp, such as we find sculpted on the Ninevite bas-reliefs'.[58] The Dalziels singled out this design which they considered a 'very beautiful work. What joy and fervour of music are expressed in the drawing!' and remembered the painting from its exhibition at the Royal Academy in 1861.[59]

Edward Frederick Brewtnall (1846–1902) painted primarily genre subjects and rarely ventured into biblical work, which marks his singular contribution to the *Bible Gallery* unusual in his *oeuvre*. He began his professional career providing illustrations for leading popular publications such as *The Graphic* and the *Illustrated London News*. The circumstances of his adoption into the *Bible Gallery* project are unknown, but it was probably through these wood-engraved illustrations that he came to the professional attention of the Dalziels. Brewtnall began public exhibition of his work from 1868 onwards with his first watercolor *Post Time* (untraced) at the Society of British Artists. He may well have been recruited solely on the strength of his published work alone; in any event, he was one of the youngest artists selected. He probably joined the project after much of it was already in hand, perhaps even as late as the 1870s. Having found that his skill was in watercolor he began to exhibit at the Royal Watercolour Society, became a member and eventually showed more than two hundred works there.

55. Ferrari, 'Correspondence of Simeon Solomon', p. 26.
56. Ferrari, 'Correspondence of Simeon Solomon', p. 26.
57. 'Fine Arts: Gift Books', *Athenaeum*, 13 November 1880, p. 646.
58. 'Fine Arts: Royal Academy', *Athenaeum*, 25 May 1861, pp. 698-700 (698).
59. *Brothers Dalziel*, p. 254.

Figure 36. Edward Frederick Brewtnall, *Esther Denouncing Haman*, undated. Wood-engraving touched with Chinese white (now faded), 227 × 177 mm. London, BM, P&D 1913-4-15-201 (667) (photo: British Museum, London).

Brewtnall's *Esther Denouncing Haman* is a superb illustration of a dramatic episode from the book of Esther (Esther 7.8; see figure 36). The book of Esther was fertile ground for dramatic scenes, and the exposure of Haman and his treachery in the court of the Persian King Ahasuerus was a favorite subject for both Old Master and Victorian painters alike. In 1865 Edward Armitage (1817–96) exhibited at the Royal Academy and Liverpool *Esther's Banquet* (untraced), which now is known only from contemporary engravings. The tableau is the same as that of Brewtnall's and takes place in Esther's bed-chamber, the walls of which are decorated with Assyrianizing reliefs of warfare. In the background can be seen a chariot hunting down lions from the Northwest Palace at Nimrūd (BM, ANE 124579). Haman, the king's favorite, pleads for forgiveness to no avail. Ahasuerus bursts into the room, but Esther does not yield to Haman's pleas. The picture garnered universal praise.[60] It featured as a full-page illustration in the *Illustrated London*

60. This canvas is untraced; another, modified version was presented to the Royal Academy of Arts by Armitage as his diploma picture when he became a Royal Academician in 1872. *The Art-Journal* asserted about the Liverpool exhibition 'but two pictures that are likely to excite attention—the 'Esther', by Armitage, and 'Treading Out the Corn' by [Richard] Ansdell', in 'Art in Scotland and the Provinces' (December 1865), p. 371. *The Times* enthused that *Esther* displayed 'vigorous and masterly drawing, well studied composition, and that largeness of treatment which

News, the same periodical in which the unfolding news of Assyrian discoveries and their British Museum installations were avidly reported.[61] Brewtnall's depiction was probably executed after the exhibition of Armitage's impressive canvas and may well have inspired him to treat the subject himself. The suite of furniture, the couch upon which Esther reclines and the side-table beside it are taken directly from a carved bas-relief depicting Assurbanipal and his queen at a banquet from the North Palace, Nineveh, ca. 645 BCE, and acquired by the British Museum in 1856 (see figure 30). Relatively little Persian art was on display at the British Museum at this time, so Brewtnall, in keeping with his contemporaries, conjured up the Achaemenid court using Neo-Assyrian visual elements familiar to museum visitors and widely circulated in the English-speaking press. The side-table, formed of intersecting cross-bars with a single central support, the two bands of incised decoration, lion's paws supported upon a bar and in turn terminating in conical feet, is exactly as in the celebrated Assurbanipal relief. The background of the chamber has *sgraffito*-like figurative panels intended to suggest sculpted bas-reliefs. Haman's sandals and rosette bracelet are lifted from numerous sculpted examples in the British Museum's collection. The glowering Ahasuerus, with full square-cut beard and peaked headpiece, unmistakably mimics an Assyrian king in full royal regalia.[62]

Arthur Murch (fl.1859–77) is not known to have exhibited any work, and his two contributions to the *Bible Gallery* are the only examples of his work extant in the near exhaustive collections of British art held in the Tate, Victoria and Albert and British Museums. He was a friend of Frederic Leighton, perhaps from the latter's sojourn in Rome in the 1850s when many young British artists gathered there (including Poynter), and Murch is thought to have lived there. His wife is known to have exhibited at the Grosvenor Gallery in London in the 1880s and listed her address as Rome.[63] The painter Walter Crane (1845–1915) remarked that Murch was in Capri in 1872 when he passed through and later noted what a 'painstaking artist' he was and how little he seemed to produce as a consequence.[64] Crane was impressed by his two designs for the *Bible Gallery*, which he described as 'strik-

rightly entitles a picture to the title of "historic" ', 'Royal Academy Exhibition (Third Notice)', 18 May 1865, p. 6. The *Athenaeum* noted that 'there is not in the whole Exhibition [at the Royal Academy] a more manly picture than this one', in 'Fine Arts: Royal Academy', 6 May 1865, pp. 626-29 (627). 'Fine Arts: Exhibition of the Royal Academy', *ILN*, 6 May 1865, p. 439 maintained that it was the 'best oil picture the artist has exhibited'.

61. *ILN*, 28 October 1865, p. 424.

62. This illustration may well have influenced another later treatment of the same subject by the history painter Ernest Normand (1857–1923). In 1888 he exhibited at the Royal Academy a large, opulent, work *Esther Denouncing Haman to King Ahasuerus* (1888; Sunderland Museum and Art Gallery). Normand's work is studded with references to Assyrian art from the British Museum's collection. The treatment of the costume and furniture is exquisitely painted and abounds in rich detail derived from close study of Assyrian prototypes.

63. Exhibited 1880–81 and 1885.

64. Walter Crane, *An Artist's Reminiscences* (London: Methuen, 1907), p. 142.

ing' and compared them in spirit to the work of Poynter in the same publication.[65] Both Murch and Poynter shared a fascination with fastidious archaeological referencing. In the late 1860s, Murch, like Poynter, lived in close proximity to the British Museum and was on friendly terms with the American expatriate painter James McNeill Whistler (1834–1903) Murch allowed Whistler to stay in his apartment on Great Russell Street—directly opposite the British Museum—when he was away.[66] Murch, like Whistler, was a member of The Arts Club between 1865 and 1877 and he is thought to have died sometime before 1891.[67]

Figure 37. Arthur Murch, *The Flight of Adrammelech*, before 1872. Wood-engraving, 215 × 173 mm. London, BM, P&D 1913-4-15-201 (665) (photo: British Museum, London).

65. Crane, *Reminiscences*, p. 142.

66. Letter from Whistler to Charles Augustus Howell (1840–90), 7 January 1869, University of Glasgow Library (MS Whistler LB 11/19).

67. This was because his wife Edith (*née* Edenborough) (1850–1920) later married, in 1891, the landscape painter Matthew Ridley Corbett (1850–1902) (http://www.whistler.arts.gla.ac.uk/correspondence viewed 22 September 2005). Crane, *Reminiscences*, p. 239, records that Arthur and Edith Murch and Corbett were living in Rome in the early 1880s, among a larger group of British expatriates. It is likely that Edith and Corbett met there.

Crane's comment about Murch's habits was perceptive. The most remarkable illustrations in the entire *Bible Gallery* were contributed by Murch: *The Flight of Adrammelech* (2 Kings 19.37) and *The Arrow of Deliverance* (2 Kings 13.17). *The Flight of Adrammelech* captures the moment of high drama when, having murdered their father Sennacherib in cold blood in the temple of 'Nisroch, his god', Adrammelech and another brother, Sharezer, flee for their lives. The tableau is a brilliant compendium of British Museum artifacts and reconstructions of Neo-Assyrian architecture lifted from the pages of Layard and James Fergusson. The most prominent visual presence is the colossal engaged lion sculpture which originally guarded the gateway leading into the temple of Ištar bēlet nipḫa at Nimrūd (BM, ANE 118895). Frederick Charles Cooper, one of the artists assigned to Layard by the British Museum, made a watercolor of the newly-excavated lions and flanking tall crenellated altars,[68] which undoubtedly served as the key organizing architectural elements in Murch's *The Flight of Adrammelech.* The sculpted carpet under the assassins' feet replicates the designs of several such objects excavated at Nineveh and Nimrūd. Several examples of the human- and bird-headed genies or *apkallu* in Murch's composition figured in the British Museum display, and many others had been published in the 1840s and 1850s from the French and British excavations of the ancient Assyrian capital cities. The elevated clerestorey with the chevron-adorned square pillars and coffered ceiling owes more to the fanciful architectural reconstructions of James Fergusson than the mudbrick palaces and temples built by the Assyrians, but the design was adopted for the popular polychrome 'Nineveh Court' at the Sydenham Crystal Palace, and Murch probably followed Fergusson's lead in this matter.[69] Murch's exquisite attention to atmosphere in *The Flight of Adrammelech* includes the shadow of an otherwise unseen bird of prey in flight at lower left, evoking in striking chiaroscuro the headlong flight of the parricides.

68. Austen Henry Layard, *Discoveries in the Ruins of Nineveh and Babylon; With Travels in Armenia, Kurdistan and the Desert: Being the Result of a Second Expedition Undertaken for the Trustees of the British Museum* (London: John Murray, 1853), p. 360. Cooper exhibited at the Royal Academy and the British Institution. Concerning his interesting role in the circulation of paintings of contemporary Middle Easterners, see Bohrer, *Orientalism and Visual Culture*, pp. 183-84, 187-91.

69. James Fergusson, *The Palaces of Nineveh and Persepolis Restored* (London: John Murray, 1851).

Figure 38. Arthur Murch, *The Arrow of Deliverance*, before 1872. Wood-engraving touched with Chinese white (now faded) and graphite, 215 × 159 mm. London, BM, P&D 1913-4-15-201 (664) (photo: British Museum, London).

In *The Arrow of Deliverance*, Murch illustrates the narrative moment when, at the behest of the dying prophet Elisha, King Joash of Israel is instructed to take bow and arrow and open a window that faces east. 'Then Elisha said, "Shoot". And he shot. And he said, "The arrow of the LORD's deliverance, and the arrow of deliverance from Syria: for thou shalt smite the Syrians in Aphek, till thou have consumed them" ' (2 Kings 13.17 [KJV]). Behind Joash the wall is carved with an illegible inscription imitating an early Northwest Semitic script, surrounded by an Egyptianizing lotus-and-papyrus design, historicizing elements that situate Israel in the Egyptian *Kulturkreis*.[70] While the dying prophet

70. The Moabite Stone, discovered in 1868 and widely published thereafter, probably supplied Murch with a template for his convincing—and accurate—archaic script, and is now in the Musée du Louvre, Paris (AO 5066).

rests in shadow, covered with a garment that suggests the stripes of a Jewish prayer shawl, the sunlit Israelite king wears a fringed tunic and bears arms more in keeping with Assyrian examples. Many British artists of the 1860s and 1870s engaged in illustrating the Old Testament elected to dress their evocations of Israelite and Judahite kings in the style of the Assyrian emperors; this despite the fact that the only Assyrian relief image of an Israelite king, Jehu, identified as such since 1853, bore no particular similarity in royal apparel to the figure of Shalmaneser III before whom he bows.

Murch may have been influenced in his choice of subject by William Dyce, who painted *King Joash Shooting the Arrow of Deliverance* (1844; Kunsthalle, Hamburg). The work was first shown at the Royal Academy in 1844 and again in 1871, when Murch may have seen it in person or in reproduction.[71] Frank William Warwick Topham (1838–1924) exhibited in 1864 *An Arrow of Deliverance* (untraced) in Liverpool and he may too have been inspired to treat this subject after Dyce's canvas.

5. *Afterlife*

In the October 1880 issue of *The Art-Journal*, the stalwart monthly periodical, notice was given that the *Bible Gallery* was nearing completion and was due for imminent publication.[72] Many of the reviews date from late autumn 1880, when advance copies were circulated to the leading periodicals and newspapers of the time, such as the *The Times*, the *Athenaeum*, *Magazine of Art* and *The Art-Journal* copies must also have been sent at this time to the contributors.[73] Poynter's copy is inscribed, 'Professor E.J. Poynter R.A. with regards and many thanks from Dalziel Brothers Octr 1880'.[74] The popular weekly *Illustrated London News* commended the work as a suitable festive gift and considered it the 'crowning work of their successful career' and thought the publication of the 'noblest proportions'.[75] *The Art-Journal* remarked that 'many fine works may be issued this Christmas,

71. A proof of a wood-engraving, by an unknown printmaker, modeled after the painting, is in the British Museum (BM, P&D 1976-6-19-29). It is not known where the print was published, if at all. *The Art-Journal* held that Dyce's two 'well-known pictures, 'Jacob and Rachel' (59), and 'Joash Shooting the Arrow of Deliverance' (99), both lent by Mr. [Gustav Christian] Schwabe, take their place in the gallery as a learned academic Art' ('The Royal Academy: Second Exhibition of Works by Old, and Deceased, Masters', [February 1871], pp. 49-50 [50]).

72. 'Art Notes', *The Art-Journal* (October 1880), pp. 317-19 (319).

73. *The Times*, 28 December 1880, p. 9. *The Art-Journal*'s press-copy is now in the collection of Birmingham Museums and Art Gallery, inv. P713'[19]20 (1). It is inscribed 'To the Editor of the Art Journal with Messrs. Dalziels' Comp[limen]ts'; see Tessa Sidey, *Prints in Focus: Birmingham Museums and Art Gallery* (Birmingham: Birmingham Museums and Art Gallery, 1997), no. 48, p. 47.

74. Gordon N. Ray, *The Illustrator and the Book in England from 1790 to 1914* (New York: Pierpont Morgan Library, 1976), no. 158, pp. 95-96 (96).

75. 'Fine Arts', *ILN*, 27 November 1880, p. 518.

but none of them will surpass 'Dalziel's [*sic*] Bible Gallery'.'[76] *The Times* appears to have carried the first advertisement for the *Bible Gallery* in its 'New Books and New Editions' section on 18 November 1880.[77] It proceeded to list the contributors, beginning with Frederic Leighton, continuing with the Royal Academicians and concluding with the remaining 'eminent living artists' such as Brown and Hunt, who found themselves outside of the orbit centred on Burlington House.

Yet the *Dalziels' Bible Gallery*, having earned such lofty critical accolades, was commercially ruinous. The Dalziel Brothers themselves candidly described the publication as a 'dead failure'.[78] The engraving firm lost thousands of pounds over the venture, a significant factor that contributed to the financial embarrassment of the company, forced into receivership in 1893.[79] Then, too, the engravings, though newly published for the first time in the *Bible Gallery*, were not new, most of them dating from at least twenty years before, and most of which had been exhibited in one form or another. By 1893, the craft of wood-engraving, the technology that underlay the vast commercial success of the *Illustrated London News* and other heavily-illustrated publications of the 1860s and 1870s, had fallen prey to the invasion of photography and the displacement of wood-engraving as an economical means of replicating artistic designs.

The failure to secure George Grove (1820–1900) as editor of the publication was cited by the Dalziels as one of the main reasons the project floundered.[80] In a letter of 1863, Grove expressed his reservations about the Dalziels' *Bible Gallery* project. He was particularly unhappy that any notes he may have provided would be subsumed by the illustrations, many of which were already in hand, and worried that their relationship would be an uneasy marriage.[81] It seemed to Grove that the project was essentially a series of illustrations by promising young artists, aimed at the artistically literate, inspired by the Bible and evidently intended to stand alone. The introduction of extraneous letterpress would mar, Grove contended, the pictorial clarity of the group. Grove seemed well-placed in biblical circles to have undertaken the editorship for the Dalziels. In 1865, for example, he was closely associated with a committee charged with the cartographic and archaeological survey of the Holy Land, acting as the committee's honorary secretary.[82] Grove was celebrated in the late nineteenth century

76. 'Dalziel's [*sic*] Bible Gallery', *The Art-Journal* (December 1880), pp. 365-66 (366).

77. *The Times*, 18 November 1880, p. 12.

78. *Brothers Dalziel*, p. 256.

79. In late 1893 the Dalziel Brothers had begun to dispose of their vast holdings of 'finished' drawings, uncut blocks, proofs and other materials related to sixty years of business.

80. *Brothers Dalziel*, p. 260, and Betty Elzea, *Frederick Sandys 1829–1904: A Catalogue Raisonné* (Woodbridge, Suffolk: Antique Collectors' Club, 2001), no. 2.B.76, pp. 224-25.

81. *Brothers Dalziel*, p. 260.

82. *ILN*, 6 May 1865, p. 443. This association bore fruit when he co-edited and authored a number of atlases that specialized in biblical geography and thus brought order to a daunting task; see, for example, Samuel Clark and George Grove, *The Bible Atlas of Maps and Plans to Illus-*

as the author of numerous dictionaries of music and musicians that still bear his name.

The Society for Promoting Christian Knowledge (SPCK) reissued the *Bible Gallery* in 1894, merely a year after the Dalziel Brothers had gone into receivership, having bought the copyright for reproduction and issued it as *Art Pictures from the Old Testament: Sunday Reading for the Young: A Series of Ninety Illustrations from Original Drawings* (London: Society for Promoting Christian Knowledge, 1894). The number of illustrations rose from the sixty-two of the *Bible Gallery* to ninety. But the increase was not primarily due to the addition of illustrations that could not be accommodated in the 1881 edition; the illustrations by Solomon expanded from six in the *Bible Gallery* to twenty in *Art Pictures.*[83] The choice of title outlined the lofty ideals of the re-issue, which hoped that *Art Pictures* would 'serve not only to give dramatic interest to the most important events recorded in the Old Testament, but also help to cultivate the artistic taste of those into whose hands they may come. The association of artistic treatment with events which excel all others in interest will give to this work, it is hoped, a special value' (preface). The copyright of the illustrations had passed to the publishers Herbert Virtue & Co. when the Dalziels came to publish their reminiscences in 1901.[84]

The national collections of graphic art housed in the British Museum and the South Kensington Museum (later the Victoria and Albert Museum) were keen to secure representative examples for their collections of the Dalziels' work, in particular that related to the *Bible Gallery* which had by then become their undisputed masterpiece. The Dalziel Brothers had accumulated many 'finished' drawings, both on wood-blocks and paper, trial proofs, touched proofs, and each of the cut wood-blocks for each illustration. Both institutions acquired material from this diverse cache. The British Museum was limited to the purchase of material from deceased artists and, since many of the artists involved were still alive in 1893, their selection was somewhat limited. Brown's 'finished' pen-and-ink drawing *Joseph's Coat* and the uncut wood-block preserving the original brush-and-pencil drawing of *The Chronicle Being Read to the King* by Arthur Boyd Houghton (1836–75) were added to the Department of Prints and Drawings in October 1893.[85] The Victoria and Albert Museum was free

trate the Geography and Topography of the Old and New Testaments and the Apocrypha, with Explanatory Notes (London: Society for Promoting Christian Knowledge, 1868) and William Smith and George Grove, *An Atlas of Ancient Geography, Biblical and Classical: To Illustrate the Dictionary of the Bible and the Classical Dictionaries* (London: John Murray, 1874).

83. Stephen Wildman, *Visions of Love and Life: Pre-Raphaelite Art from the Birmingham Collection, England* (Alexandria, VA: Art Services International, 1995), no. 52, pp. 185-87.

84. Beneath each plate from the *Bible Gallery* is the lettering 'By permission of Messrs. Herbert Virtue & Co. Ltd'.

85. Paul Goldman, 'The Dalziel Brothers and the British Museum', *The Book Collector* 45 (1996), pp. 341-50 (343).

to purchase work by living artists, and accordingly bought in September 1893 a group of seven 'finished' pen-and-ink drawings, among them Brown's *The Death of Eglon* and *Elijah Restoring the Widow's Son*, Poynter's *Joseph Distributes Corn*, *Joseph Presents his Father* and *Joseph before Pharaoh*, Leighton's *Samson at the Mill* and Pickersgill's *Rahab and the Spies*. In 1924 Gilbert Dalziel (1853–1930) donated proofs of the *Bible Gallery* to the Tate Gallery. These three collections have both by gift and purchase continued to add to their holdings of material associated with the Dalziels' great biblical projects. In June 1924 Gilbert also sold a group of important letters to the British Museum's Department of Manuscripts (now part of the British Library). Including letters by Brown, Burne-Jones, Watts and Cundall, the collection records valuable information about the early gestation of the project. In April 1913 Gilbert sold the unique set of touched proofs of the 'Bible Gallery' to the British Museum's Department of Prints and Drawings, which the contributing artists had corrected and which provided the illustrations for this essay. Large metropolitan centers outside of London, particularly Birmingham, have amassed an impressive group—the entire suite of cut wood-blocks for the *Bible Gallery*—including those commissioned but not originally used in the 1881 publication.

Dalziels' Bible Gallery and the artistic reception of Assyria by its illustrators underscores the primacy of the British Museum as a site of artistic discovery, and its special relationship with biblical art. The project succeeded in forging an authentic visual history which satisfied the nineteenth-century demands of archaeological exactitude in the visual arts. The *Bible Gallery* cast a long shadow over the later artistic reception of Assyria from which British artists found it difficult to escape.

Picturing Biblical Pasts

Burke O. Long

1. *Introduction*

To investigate aspects of Orientalism and biblical scholarship, I have chosen to focus on the intersection of narrative and visual images—pictorial art and maps—in two recent treatments of biblical history. In this ideational space where publisher and author meet reader, one may inquire into the dynamic processes by which twentieth-century American biblical scholars, who, working within the continuing presence of a European past, have managed West Asia by producing a Christian, Jewish, or biblical 'Orient'.[1]

I follow Edward Said in taking 'Orientalism' to mean a controlling representation of a subaltern 'Orient' which, produced from a position of exteriority, is always 'converting the Orient into something else'.[2] That process of conversion has proven to be extraordinarily complex as other scholars, decisively influenced by Said's work, opened up global, regional, and local variability in the cultural productions of Orientalism, including resistance to its colonialist dispositions of power and powerlessness.[3]

Frederick N. Bohrer richly documented that complexity for West Asia by reconstructing the processes of display, circulation, interpretation, and emulation that created multiple versions of Assyria (and more broadly, Mesopotamia) for nineteenth-century Europeans.[4] In these cultural realizations, the creation

1. See Keith W. Whitelam, *The Invention of Ancient Israel: The Silencing of Palestinian History* (London and New York: Routledge, 1996), and Burke O. Long, *Imagining the Holy Land: Maps, Models and Fantasy Travels* (Bloomington, IN: Indiana University Press, 2003), pp. 89-163.

2. Edward W. Said, *Orientalism* (New York: Vintage Books, 1978), p. 67.

3. For example, *Orientalism and the Postcolonial Predicament: Perspectives on South Asia* (ed. Carol A. Breckenridge and Peter van der Veer; New Delhi and New York: Oxford University Press, 1994); John M. MacKenzie, *Orientalism: History, Theory, and the Arts* (Manchester and New York: Manchester University Press, 1995); Judith Snodgrass, *Presenting Japanese Buddhism to the West: Orientalism, Occidentalism, and the Columbian Exposition* (Chapel Hill, NC: University of North Carolina Press, 2003); R.S. Sugirtharajah, *Imagining Hinduism: A Postcolonial Perspective* (London and New York: Routledge, 2003); Bryan S. Turner, *Orientalism, Postmodernism and Globalism* (London and New York. Routledge, 1994).

4. Frederick N. Bohrer, *Orientalism and Visual Culture: Imagining Mesopotamia in Nineteeth-Century Europe* (Cambridge, UK and New York: Cambridge University Press, 2003).

of an 'exotic' subject, or subaltern other, was 'not a matter of limpid *transmission*, but rather one of representational *transformation*'.[5] Bohrer showed that as fresh discoveries reached Europe, scholars, museum-goers, entertainers, fashion designers and news reporters served up malleable representations of Assyria, each one a fusion of materiality and concept, and each one assimilated in different ways to pre-existent cultural norms and expectations.

For this essay, I have found it useful to consider pictorial art in biblical history textbooks as evidence of similarly transformational systems of promulgating, circulating and appropriating West Asia. Even if the limited availability of archival sources greatly limits my effort, these illustrations nonetheless repay inquiry into the ways in which historians, publishers, and illustrators managed an unruly 'Orient' by transforming it into a westerner's dream: ancient 'Israel', the Land of the Bible, and protean source of true religion and most valued things Western.

To put the matter differently—and this reveals a second line of my indebtedness—to deploy an image of ancient 'Israel' in history textbooks, is to configure human space as a nexus of memory, invention and geography. Invention must take place if recollection occurs. And invention is at the heart of geography, which I take to mean a socially constructed and maintained sense of place. Insights into human life and history, though often soaring on the wings of poetic and scientific language, are as often tethered to the profound existential significance of place, space, and landscape.[6]

In historical geography, for example, maps of Palestine typically represent an objective world as it really was at a certain time, but without disclosing the geographer's social practices, the value-laden choices by which that world came to be and the particular interests it served, both in production and reception. 'Maps are never value-free images', historian and geographer John B. Harley has argued, and 'except in the narrowest Euclidean sense, they are not in themselves true or false'. Rather, maps are purposeful and partial articulations of reality that often imply a particular national memory. They structure human space that is 'biased toward, promoted by, and exerts influence upon particular sets of social relations'.[7] In such cases, salient interrogations of maps and map-

5. Bohrer, *Orientalism*, p. 12. Emphasis in original.

6. See Edward W. Said, 'Invention, Memory, and Place', *Critical Inquiry* 26 (Winter, 2000), pp. 175-92; Derek Gregory, *Geographical Imaginations* (Oxford: Blackwell 1994); David N. Livingstone, *The Geographical Tradition: Episodes in the History of a Contested Enterprise* (Oxford and Cambridge, MA: Blackwell, 1992); *idem*, *Putting Science in its Place: Geographies of Scientific Knowledge* (Chicago: University of Chicago Press, 2003); Edward W. Soja, *Postmodern Geographies: The Reassertion of Space in Critical Theory* (London and New York: Verso, 1989); *idem*, *Thirdspace: Journeys to Los Angeles and Other Real-and-Imagined Places* (Oxford: Blackwell, 1996).

7. John B. Harley, 'Maps, Knowledge and Power', in *The Iconography of Landscape: Essays on the Symbolic Representation, Design and Use of Past Environments* (ed. Denis Cosgrove and

making will seek to uncover individual features as well as the historical, political and ideological entanglements that lie beneath a map's epidermis of settled fact.[8]

However, as geographer Edward Soja has argued, it is not enough to tease out conceptual biases. One should also consider how people and communities enact socially constructed and maintained senses of place. Symbols, concepts, maps, visual images, even architecture, arise in social interactions that endow place with particular meanings and intent. These spatial practices, of which cartography is but one mode, constitute multiple social realities in which different people imagine and actualize competing intentions and meanings—spaces—that they associate with any given place.

Consider, for example, the physical and cultural realms permitted and prohibited to women in Victorian society and art.[9] Parse the production of various holy lands in early photographs of Palestine.[10] Explore the Anglo-European realizations of Assyria in the nineteenth century.[11] Travel through the overlapping social and spatial realities of modern Los Angeles.[12] Such practices of lived spatiality—often creating subaltern 'others'—enact real-imagined spaces of Woman, Holy Land, Decadent Orient, and Modern City. Laden with concept and intention, these practices build what Neil Smith called 'deep space', that is, physical extent infused with social intent.[13]

For purposes of this essay, I regard visual illustrations in tandem with biblical historiography as artifacts of such socio-spatial practices. They offer evidence of culturally realized transformations of West Asia through which historians and readers constituted themselves in relation to the real-imagined places of antiquity.

In this context, I analyze two recent biblical histories, the one co-authored by J. Maxwell Miller and John H. Hayes, and the other written by John Bright.[14]

Stephen Daniels; Cambridge Studies in Historical Geography, 9; Cambridge: Cambridge University Press, 1988), pp. 277-312 (278). See also John B. Harley, 'Historical Geography and the Cartographic Illusion', *Journal of Historical Geography* 15 (1989), pp. 80-91.

8. See Burke O. Long, 'Bible Maps and America's Nationalist Narratives' [forthcoming].

9. Bram Dijkstra, *Idols of Perversity: Fantasies of Feminine Evil in Fin-de-Siècle Culture* (Oxford and New York: Oxford University Press, 1986).

10. Yeshayahu Nir, *The Bible and the Image: The History of Photography in the Holy Land 1839–1899* (Philadelphia: University of Pennsylvania Press, 1985); Nissan N. Perez, *Focus East: Early Photography in the Near East, 1839–1885* (New York and Jerusalem: Harry N. Abrams, in association with The Domino Press and The Israel Museum, Jerusalem, 1988).

11. Bohrer, *Orientalism.*

12. Soja, *Thirdspace.*

13. Neil Smith, *Uneven Development: Nature, Capital, and the Production of Space* (Oxford: Blackwell, 1990).

14. J. Maxwell Miller and John H. Hayes, *A History of Ancient Israel and Judah* (Philadelphia: Westminster Press, 1986); John Bright, *A History of Israel* (Louisville, KY: Westminster/John Knox Press, 1959; 3rd edn, 1981, reissued unrevised as 4th edn, 2000). Requirements for

By dismantling neatly packaged pictures of the biblical past, I try to insert consciousness of socio-spatial practices into the objectifying discourse of historiography. At its fullest, that task—which requires abundant archival sources and extensive research—would entail thickly textured descriptions of the production, distribution, and reception of various ideas of 'biblical' Israel. The challenge, surely one that is better met by a team rather than one researcher, is to situate those processes in the broadest and most local of cultural, historical, and material circumstances. Within the limits of this essay, however, I can only make what I hope will be received as a suggestive start at such a comprehensive project.

Of course, approaching biblical historiography as an artifact of socio-spatial practices is an occasion for me to construct resistive space. I stand within a real-imagined place that tries, through analysis and example, to subvert the hegemonic power of representation that is habitually claimed by biblical historians. I do this as a historian, of course, and partially, as one who emphasizes the socially configured textuality of historiography and the cultural aspects of knowledge making. It is for others to help mitigate any commanding and utopian elements that remain in my own critical practice.

2. *Imagining Biblical Israel*

In 1967, three years after earning his PhD from Emory University, J. Maxwell Miller joined the faculty of Candler School of Theology, a graduate center affiliated with the United Methodist Church. Shortly thereafter, Miller published a number of essays in which he pointedly avoided theology and biblical apologetics in trying to reconstruct biblical history.[15] In this regard, Miller's approach was notable for refusing the consensus built by William Foxwell Albright who, since beginning his career in the late 1920s, had used archeological data to clarify the Bible's meaning, defend its historical trustworthiness, and chart its role in the evolution of Christian monotheism.[16] By the late 1970s, when the formi-

the length of this essay prevented my considering Iain W. Provan, V. Philips Long, and Tremper Longman III, *A Biblical History of Israel* (Louisville, KY: Westminster/John Knox Press, 2003). In any case, this textbook offered only one illustration on its cover, and no maps, and so was not well suited to my particular line of inquiry.

15. J. Andrew Dearman, 'J. Maxwell Miller, Scholar and Teacher: a Sketch', in *The Land That I Will Show You: Essays on the History and Archaeology of the Ancient Near East in Honor of J. Maxwell Miller* (ed. J.A. Dearman and M. Patrick Graham; JSOTSup, 343; Sheffield: Sheffield Academic Press, 2001), pp. 16-35 (21-23); J. Maxwell Miller, 'The Fall of the House of Ahab', *VT* 17 (1967), pp. 307-24; *idem*, 'The Rest of the Acts of Jehoahaz (I Kings 20 22.1-38)', *ZAW* 80 (1968), pp. 337-42; *idem*, 'Jebus and Jerusalem: A Case of Mistaken Identity', *ZDPV* 90 (1974), pp. 115-27.

16. William Foxwell Albright, *From the Stone Age to Christianity: Monotheism and the Historical Process* (Baltimore, MD: The Johns Hopkins University Press, 1940; 2nd edn, Garden

dable influence of Albright was waning, Miller spoke plainly: joining Bible, theology and archaeological research to produce a critical biblical history was much more problematic than Albright and many of his followers were prepared to acknowledge.[17]

By this time, John Hayes had arrived at the Candler School of Theology. Shortly thereafter, he and Miller collaborated in a multi-authored volume aimed at reviewing the sources for writing a biblical history, assessing current debates in the field, and reconstructing the ancient history of Israel and Judah.[18] The result was distinctly non-Albrightean, chiefly because the contributing authors refused Albright's apologetics and did not mix theology with historiography.

A decade later, Miller and Hayes clearly articulated their own guiding principles.[19] Professional historians above all value *primary* sources (the Bible is already a *secondary* narrative of the past), and they seek naturalistic explanations for events, since 'modern historians have trouble with miracles' even if the biblical writers did not. Suspicious of literary artifice, idealistic simplification, and theological language, Miller and Hayes weighed evidence from external archaeology and epigraphy, invoked models and analogy, and applied their own 'threshold of credibility' to biblical reports before arriving at a coherent narrative. Even so, they admitted, they engaged in a 'considerable amount of intuitive speculation'.[20]

These matters are important when considering the Miller-Hayes *History* as an artifact of socio-spatial practice. The authors resist the Bible's ethnocentric memory of ancestral 'Israel', united by blood and divine election and set apart from, or in deadly opposition to, neighboring groups. Instead, Miller and Hayes imagine inchoate beginnings. They write of decentralized village dwellers who, scattered in the highlands of Iron Age Palestine and the trans-Jordan, are hardly dissimilar from other peoples in the region. The authors do not envision formative 'Israel' as a unified national and theological subject, and thus do not track this 'Israel' on maps which span the centuries from ancestral wanderings to settlement in Canaan.

City, NY: Doubleday, 1957); *idem*, *Archaeology and the Religion of Israel* (Baltimore, MD: The Johns Hopkins University Press, 1942; 5th edn, Garden City, NY: Doubleday, 1969); David Noel Freedman, 'W.F. Albright as an Historian', in *The Scholarship of William Foxwell Albright: An Appraisal* (ed. Gus W. Van Beek; HSS, 33; Atlanta, GA: Scholars Press, 1989), pp. 33-43; Burke O. Long, *Planting and Reaping Albright: Politics, Ideology, and Interpreting the Bible* (University Park, PA: Pennsylvania State University Press, 1997).

17. J. Maxwell Miller, 'The Israelite Occupation of Canaan', in *Israelite and Judean History* (ed. John H. Hayes and J. Maxwell Miller; OTL; Philadelphia: Westminster Press, 1977), pp. 213-84; *idem*, 'W.F. Albright and Historical Construction', *BA* 42 (1979), pp. 37-45.

18. John H. Hayes and J. Maxwell Miller (eds), *Israelite and Judean History* (Philadelphia: Westminster Press, 1977).

19. Miller and Hayes, *History*.

20. Miller and Hayes, *History*, pp. 59 and 76-77.

At the same time, Miller and Hayes interrupt a long tradition of cultural biography in which religious and national communities present themselves as cultural heirs to a biblical 'Israel' that is primarily imagined as theological subject. Right down to the present day, these histories of early Israel—for popular and scholarly audiences—tell of faithful ancestors who, as part of a community that was both time-bound and anchored in eternity, transmitted the truths of God. These insights, preserved in a genealogy of witness and cultural affinity, mark Christian and Jewish audiences as authorized cultural descendants of that theological entity, Israel, whose timelessly available essence fused—and fuses—contingent materiality with the eternal verities of God. By enacting such a real-imagined place of time-eternity, biblical historians make 'Israel' (attached to God and the land of inheritance) forever accessible to those who seek instruction from the Holy Book and who locate themselves within a narrative that culminates in the politically consequential destinies of Christian and Zionist redemption.[21]

John Bright—historian, Presbyterian churchman, biblical theologian, Professor at the Union Theological Seminary in Virginia—fully identified with this cultural tradition. Like many of those who studied with Albright in the 1940s and 1950s, Bright eagerly sought to make the views of his revered teacher widely accessible to students, churches and pastors. 'I never grew away from Albright', Bright recalled much later, but 'I added an interest in biblical theology'.[22] Bright might just as well have said the same thing about his *History of Israel*. The history textbook, which was intended especially for theological students, elegantly bespoke Albright on historical matters and articulated theological themes aimed at revitalizing the role of the Old Testament in Christian churches. Bright folded the Bible, archaeology, and ancient Near Eastern history into a work that located theism within the historical experience of ancient 'Israel'—in this he followed his teacher Albright. Yet as Bright told his readers,

21. For example, as cited in Hayes and Miller (eds), *Israelite and Judean History*, pp. xxvii-xxviii: Humphrey Prideaux, *The Old and New Testament Connected in the History of the Jews and Neighbouring Nations, from the Declension of the Kingdoms of Israel and Judah to the Time of Christ* (2 vols.; London: R. Knaplock & J. Tonson, 1716–18); Samuel Shuckford, *The Sacred and Profane History of the World Connected, from the Creation of the World to the Dissolution of the Assyrian Empire at the Death of Sardanapalus, and to the Declension of the Kingdoms of Judah and Israel under the Reigns of Ahaz and Pekah* (2 vols.; London: R. Knaplock & J. Tonson, 1728–30); H.H. Milman, *The History of the Jews, from the Earliest Period down to Modern Times* (3 vols.; London: John Murray, 1829). Among authors who have written more for the general reader, see Lyman Coleman, *An Historical Text Book and Atlas of Biblical Geography* (Philadelphia: J.B. Lippincott, 1854); Jesse Lyman Hurlbut, *Manual of Biblical Geography: A Text-Book on Bible History* (Chicago: Rand McNally, 1884); Leon James Wood, *A Survey of Israel's History* (Grand Rapids, MI: Zondervan, 1970); Michael Avi-Yonah (ed.), *A History of Israel and the Holy Land* (New York and London: Continuum, 2001).

22. John Bright, unpublished interview with Burke O. Long, 1990.

he was not interested primarily in the 'mere facts of Israel's history', or even a generalized history of religion. He wished, rather, to chronicle a 'history of (Israel's) faith' and make that history a part of the genealogy of modern Christian communities.[23] Perfectly suited for this task was the notion of redemptive drama, or 'salvation history', a theological rubric that was popular at the time among American Protestants, especially Presbyterian G. Ernest Wright, and avidly promoted by that denomination's Westminster Press.[24]

Wright, the only student of Albright to have made substantial contributions to both biblical archaeology and Christian theology in mid-twentieth century America, believed that one must present biblical history as a narrative of both factual events (supported with the evidence of archaeology) and God's redemptive actions in and through those selfsame events. A biblical archaeologist/theologian therefore is to construct a critically evaluated narrative of the wondrous acts of God that constituted and sustained not only a people of antiquity, but continues to nurture Christians, the cultural heirs to that ancient Israelite community of faith.[25]

Fully accepting this mandate, John Bright deployed data from the Bible, archaeology and non-biblical inscriptions in a narrative that was centered on a people 'united in covenant with Yahweh', distinguished in religion and morals from their environment, and embarked on a 'long pilgrimage of faith' toward, as finally noted in an epilogue, 'Christ and his Gospel'.[26] In this way, Bright implicitly spoke to age-old debates among Christians about the status of the Hebrew Bible in the life of the churches. He aided efforts to provide renewed justification for accepting that unwieldy, sometimes alien anthology of Hebrew writings as the *Old* Testament, which, rooted in factual history, led toward the *New* Testament.[27]

The political gesture was not limited, however, to anxious debates about the place of the Old Testament in Christian congregations. Bright's *History* became a strategic text in the activities of the Biblical Colloquium, a private by-invitation-only group which in the 1950s consisted mostly of Albright's former students. Founded by G. Ernest Wright, the group met annually to share original research and initiate publishing ventures that would amplify Albright's voice in American biblical studies. As Wright later recalled, from its beginning in

23. Bright, *History* (4th edn, 2000), p. 75. All quotes taken from the unrevised 4th edn. See also Kurt L. Noll, 'Looking on the Bright Side of Israel's History: Is There Pedagogical Value in a Theological Presentation of History?', *Biblical Interpretation* 7 (1999), pp. 1-27 (6-14).

24. Brevard S. Childs, *Biblical Theology in Crisis* (Philadelphia: Westminster Press, 1970), pp. 13-50.

25. G. Ernest Wright, *The God Who Acts: Biblical Theology as Recital* (Studies in Biblical Theology, 8; London: SCM Press, 1952); G. Ernest Wright and Reginald H. Fuller, *The Book of the Acts of God: Christian Scholarship Interprets the Bible* (Christian Faith Series; Garden City, NY: Doubleday, 1957).

26. Bright, *History* (4th edn, 2000), pp. xvii, 459, 464.

27. Noll, 'Looking on the Bright Side', p. 21.

1950, the Colloquium sought to preserve 'his [Albright's] ideal...his identity, his ideas, his school'.[28]

Bright was responsive to that collective ambition, despite some initial reluctance to take on the task of writing a new biblical history.[29] Members of the Colloquium discussed the *History* in its early stages, and Bright asked both Albright and Wright to review specific chapters. On one occasion, referring to his treatment of the Israelite ancestors, Bright wrote to his teacher, 'I hope that what I have done will pass muster and will be no great discredit to the position (that is, your own position) which I have tried to represent'.[30]

From its first printing, Bright's *History* had included a selection of maps taken from the best-selling *Westminster Historical Atlas to the Bible*, also a project of the Albright school.[31] This particular combination was formidable testimony to both the strength of Albright's appeal and the ambitions of the Biblical Colloquium. In two handy textbooks, the Bible, cartography and biblical history were now successfully integrated with Christian theology and made available to many thousands of students, teachers, and Christian ministers. After publication, the Albrighteans energetically promoted Bright's *History*, which, despite mixed reviews from biblical scholars, rang up strong sales, finally selling over 100,000 copies.[32]

Several generations of readers would thus come to know a factually presented ancient West Asia. It met cultural expectations in America that this part of the world be an exclusively biblical space. But the space was also infused with the not-so-public desire to advance Albright's scholarship, recover the Old Testament as vital scripture, and formulate Christian theology in the legitimating language of historical knowledge. Bright imagined ancient Palestine as the locus of revelation, and ancient 'Israel' as a pilgrimage people singularly united in covenant with God and participating in the drama of eternally true redemption. Land, society, politics—in short the deep spaces of ancient 'Israel'—were laden with cultural meanings enacted within a long tradition of cultural expectations and the specific social realities of mid-century American Protestantism and the Albrightean school.[33]

28. Leona Glidden Running and David Noel Freedman, *William Foxwell Albright: A Twentieth-Century Genius* (New York: The Two Continents Publishing Group and Morgan Press, 1975), p. 316. On the Biblical Colloquium, see Long, *Planting and Reaping*, pp. 15-70.

29. Noll, 'Looking on the Bright Side', pp. 2-5.

30. Letter, John Bright to William Foxwell Albright, April 30, 1956. In the unpublished *Albright Papers*, American Philosophical Society, Philadelphia.

31. G. Ernest Wright and Floyd V. Filson, *The Westminster Historical Atlas to the Bible* (Westminster Aids to the Study of the Scriptures; Philadelphia: Westminster Press, 1946; rev. edn, 1956). All quotes are from the revised edition.

32. William P. Brown, 'Introduction to John Bright's *A History of Israel*', in Bright, *History* (4th edn, 2000), pp. 1-22 (1).

33. When Bright's work was reissued posthumously in 2000, at least one reviewer recast it as

3. *Cover Art*

The illustration on the front cover of the latest edition of John Bright's *History* (there were no illustrations in earlier editions) visually represented this conjunction of materiality, immaterial essence, and theological proclamation. At the same time, the image drew the book and its readers into a vernacular stream of Christian pilgrimage and pious longings that, like the Bible-centered historiography of John Bright, routinely transformed West Asia into a space cleared for the gift of pristine religious experience.

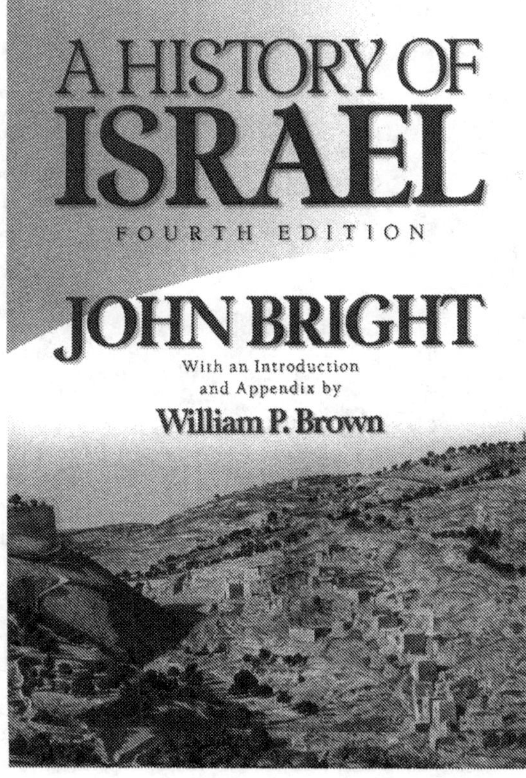

Figure 39. Cover design. Reproduced from John Bright, *A History of Israel*. ©2000 Westminster John Knox Press. Used by permission.

a newly relevant political intervention in the ongoing debates about biblical historiography. The 'history of Israel's faith', wrote Bright's colleague James Luther Mayes, no longer represented consensus in the field, but was nonetheless 'a refreshing alternative to the secularism and skepticism of much current writing about Israel's history' (from the promotional comment, printed on the book cover).

The designer used a cropped version of *Jerusalem and the Valley of Jehoshaphat from the Hill of Evil Counsel*, an 1854 painting by Pre-Raphaelite English artist Thomas Seddon.[34] Like many European artists at the time, Seddon traveled to Ottoman Palestine to draw inspiration from a land that, after many centuries of neglect, was presumed to evince the former glory of biblical life.[35] Intending to document various scenes from biblical history, Seddon finally gathered his energies for a six-month stay in Jerusalem, which despite his efforts to avoid rapture, brought a 'revulsion of feeling' that swept him tearfully into the 'vivid reality' of Christ.[36]

Outside the city walls, encamped 'on the hill south of Mount Zion, looking up the Valley of Jehoshaphat', Seddon first sketched the prospect that would eventually result in his famous painting.

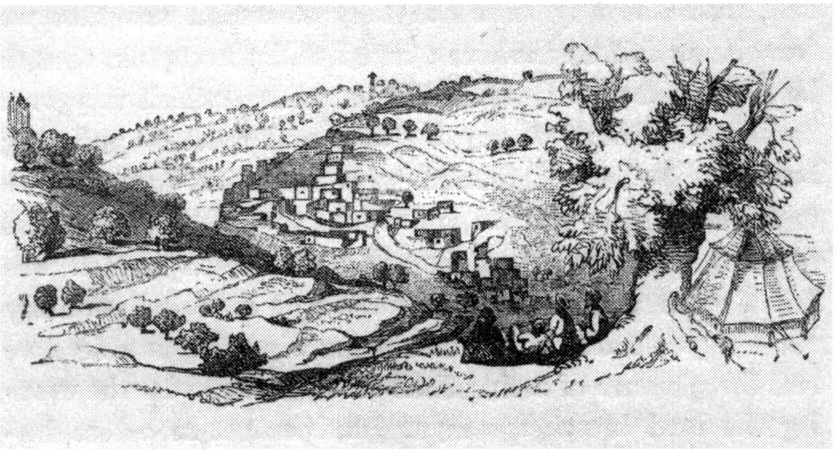

Figure 40. Artist's sketch, 'The Valley of Jehoshaphat', from Thomas Seddon, *Memoir and Letters of the Late Thomas Seddon, Artist* (1858), p. 8.

In describing the scene for his diary, Seddon peeled away the distasteful distractions of Ottoman Jerusalem and exposed a landscape swept virtually clean

34. See Allen Staley, *The Pre-Raphaelite Landscape* (Oxford Studies in the History of Art and Architecture; Oxford: Clarendon Press, 1973), pp. 96-106, and specifically on Seddon's 'Jerusalem', pp. 100-103.

35. Thomas Seddon, *Memoir and Letters of the Late Thomas Seddon, Artist* (ed. John Pollard Seddon; London: James Nisbet & Co., 1858), p. 85. On Orientalist painters, see Gerald M. Ackerman, *American Orientalists* (The Orientalists, 10; Paris: ACR Edition, 1994); John Davis, *The Landscape of Belief: Encountering the Holy Land in Nineteenth-Century American Art and Culture* (The Princeton Series in Nineteenth-Century Art, Culture, and Society; Princeton, NJ: Princeton University Press, 1996); Philippe Jullian, *The Orientalists: European Painters of Eastern Scenes* (trans. Helga and Dinah Harrison; Oxford: Phaidon, 1977); Lynne Thornton, *The Orientalists. Painter-Travellers, 1828–1908* (Paris: ACR Edition, 1983).

36. Seddon, *Memoir*, pp. 41, 91, 126.

of modernity and made sacred with biblical memory. In front, he wrote, 'is the Mount of Olives, with the village of Siloam creeping round the foot of the nearer mount, which is the Mount of Offence, where Solomon erected altars for his idolatrous wives. On the left is Mount Moriah (in shadow), with the commencement of the Temple wall—in the lower part still as Solomon built it with enormous stones…'.[37]

In this transformation of topography into scriptural landscape, Seddon may be compared, among many others, with William Thomson's *The Land and the Book*, an enormously popular and lavishly illustrated travelogue that presented the Holy Land as a 'divinely prepared tablet on which God's messages to men have been graven in ever-living characters'. Readers and fantasy travelers—everybody a new Moses—should 'put off the soiled sandals of worldliness and sin…' and enter that 'consecrated domain' in which 'the Land and the Book constitute the all-perfect text of the Word of God'.[38]

In the finished painting of Jerusalem, Seddon enacted a similar space of scriptural plenitude, a kind of visual Delphic oracle awaiting decipherment.

Figure 41. Thomas Seddon, *Jerusalem and the Valley of Jehoshaphat from the Hill of Evil Counsel*, 1854. Used by permission. Tate Gallery, London/Art Resource, New York.

37. Seddon, *Memoir*, p. 84.

38. William M. Thomson, *The Land and the Book: Or, Biblical Illustrations Drawn from the Manners and Customs, the Scenes and Scenery, of the Holy Land* (2 vols.; New York: Harper & Brothers, 1859; 3rd edn, 1880), p. 3.

One sees little earthly life, save the ornamental herdsman who, in the conventions of Orientalist paintings, languorously watches over a flock of goats. Unsettling light emanates high from the left, lending aridity to the unsubtle contrasts, the bare earth hard baked under searing sun. No human disorder, no filth, dust, poverty, or disease disturbs the view. No shrines of misguided piety (charges European travelers at the time frequently leveled at indigenous Christians) disfigure the scene. Seddon allows no hint of impulsive fanaticism (a trait those same travelers, even when entranced, ascribed derisively to Arabs and Muslims). The artist offers a calligraphy-like pattern of hills, terraces, and erosion that sweeps one's eye toward Olivet on the right and, it seems, into luminescent infinity.

Perhaps the scene bespeaks biblical heroes and events of time past, as does Seddon's caption for the ink sketch. Or the severe light of divine judgment, which religious tradition had long associated with this spot.[39] Or perhaps the scene suggests imminent disclosure of divinity—a wordless epiphany of searing light. In any case, Seddon transformed Ottoman Jerusalem into a suggestively effulgent space rescued from the backwater inconsequence, even neglect, of modernity.

By incorporating Seddon's painting into the cover design of John Bright's *History of Israel*, the publishers drew readers into this cultural stream of Christian geography and memory, but with a new twist.[40] The dome of the Al-Aqṣā mosque, which anyone familiar with nineteenth-century paintings and photographs would have recognized, has disappeared, along with the ornamental herdsman. The designer removed all vestiges of Arab, Muslim, or human presence for that matter. A reader-viewer hovers above the scene, contemplating a downward slope that rises up to a city wall, any city's wall, and then, to the right, dissolves into Seddon's calligraphy of line, shape, and color. Moreover, Seddon's landscape has been set against a massive white sphere rising over the horizon, an effect that recalls modern photographs of earth taken from the moon. The design is generic, offering no clue as to what one sees. Except that, positioned under the book's title, the art suggests a particular idea of what the Bible land should look like: a luminous place of stone and light that invites one to fill its empty topography with recollections of biblical events and the offerings of God. The graphic artist manages, with the help of Thomas Seddon, to suggest that the 'Israel' of the book's title fuses materiality of landscape with divine disclosure, just as John Bright writes of a singular people constituted in covenant with God, in the world but not of it, traversing time on a journey of faith.

39. Seddon, *Memoir*, p. 192. See W. Harold Mare, 'Jehoshaphat, Valley of', *ABD*, III, pp. 668-69.

40. Despite repeated efforts, I have received no responses from Westminster/John Knox Press to my questions about the process through which the publisher chose this design.

The cover art for Miller and Hayes' *History* evokes nothing of this particular fantasy-realism.

Figure 42. Cover design. Reproduced from *A History of Ancient Israel and Judah*. ©1986 J. Maxwell Miller and John H. Hayes. Used by permission of Westminster/John Knox Press.

Instead, a southward looking aerial photograph of '*Ein Duyk* and the Oasis of Jericho' invites contemplation of landscape as map. Green vegetation on the left (evidence of life giving springs, reflected in the place name, *Ein Duyk*) is sharply bounded by desert and starkly eroded hills to the right. Roads, dirt tracks, excavation sites and rectangular shapes register human activity, which is slight compared to the vastness of the natural topography. The photograph suggests a mental landscape of scientific reconnaissance, the pursuits of aerial photographers, geographers and archaeologists.

Despite appearances, however, the photo has other cultural roots in the socio-spatial practices of piety that grounds theology in the certaintistic language of science. Taken from the *Introductory Unit, Bible Lands Exhibit*, it is part of the *Wide Screen Project*, a comprehensive audio-visual package of maps, slides, sound tapes, study guides, and large-format photographs. The materials blend surface and aerial (later satellite) photography with up-to-date archaeological data to codify, teach, and illustrate the Bible—in a literalistic reading—as the principal historical record of biblical events.[41] At the same time, purchasers were promised religious benefits that come from surrogate travel to the Bible Land. 'More than a million pilgrims visited the Holy Land last year', readers of the Project's atlas, *The Student Map Manual*, were told, which is 'proof enough' of a widespread demand for 'maximal reality' and longing for religious experience in the land that gave birth to their faith. The millions more who never make the trip are no less deserving. 'Must the Bible remain less real for them?' the editor asked readers.[42]

In packaging study, travel, archaeology and cartography for an experience of maximal biblical 'reality', the atlas integrated two distinct socio-spatial practices: a Christian publisher aiming to strengthen religious commitment with biblical knowledge, and modern Israelis at work solidifying their patrimony. Printed by the Survey of Israel, the *Student Map Manual* presented maps that had been prepared by the Israeli government in connection with its on-going efforts to transform British Mandate Arab/Jewish (and indigenous Christian) Palestine into the landscape of modern Israel. In a frantic process beginning in the 1930s and accelerating after the War of Independence, official committees systematically replaced Arabic designations for thousands of villages, ruins, topographic features, flora and fauna with ancient and modern Hebrew names. Wherever possible, the committees sought to establish an irrefutable link between modern Jewish presence in the Land of Israel and ethnically and religiously Jewish life in pre-Muslim, and especially biblical, antiquity. In the view of Meron Benvenisti, this 'flawless Hebrew map' achieved over some years not only recorded the history of the victorious, but also documented Arab loss, what Palestinians now refer to as their 'catastrophe'.[43]

In effect, the *Student Map Manual* placed these Israeli maps, including their erasure of Arab presence, into the hands of Christian Bible students. Even though the manual indexed both Hebrew and Arabic place names, Jewish and biblical associations were the main features of the maps, and the index promulgated a system of 'main names' based on ancient or biblical authority, and failing that, on

41. See for example, *Regional Guide B1*, 'Sea of Galilee' (Jerusalem: Pictorial Archive, Est., 1978), an explanatory supplement to a package of seven laminated posters.

42. James Monson *et al.*, *Student Map Manual: Historical Geography of Biblical Lands* (Jerusalem: Pictorial Archives [Near Eastern History] Est., 1979), from the publisher's foreword.

43. Meron Benvenisti, *Sacred Landscape: The Buried History of the Holy Land since 1948* (trans. Maxine Kaufman-Lacusta; Berkeley: University of California Press, 2000), pp. 11-43.

'the appropriate Government Department of Antiquities'.[44] Moreover, names of sites were cross-referenced exclusively to authenticating excavations that had been codified by the Israeli-produced *Encyclopedia of Archaeological Excavations*.[45]

The *Wide Screen Project* thus integrated Bible study with modern archaeology—a primary goal—but also maintained the political significance of both. Up to the mid-twentieth century, it had been almost an exclusively Jewish and Christian enterprise to document cultural and material connections to ancient Palestine. Whether consciously or not, such pursuits reinforced exclusivist historical narratives and intervened in rival Jewish and Palestinian claims to patrimony that emerged, like mirror images, after 1948. By the late 1970s, when readings of the past by Israeli and Palestinian nationalists were becoming more stridently oppositional and entrenched, the *Student Map Manual* helped Christians imagine a spiritual patrimony, a Bible Land constructed in cultural affinity with Pre-Arab Palestine, Christianity, Judaism, and implicitly, the modern Jewish state.

When Miller and Hayes chose the cover photograph for their *History*, they may not have considered this particular cultural genealogy. More important for them, perhaps, was that the image encoded an aesthetic of modernity, of distance and objectivity, for which aerial observation is both metaphor and instrument in the service of historians who have 'trouble with miracles'. Like the authors' text, the photograph of *Ein Duyk* reaffirms an alliance between historiography and biblically oriented archaeology, and offers little of the fantasy-realism enacted by Thomas Seddon and the cover art of John Bright's *History*. At the same time, the textbook title and accompanying photograph reiterates, perhaps inadvertently, a widely accepted Anglo-European Orientalist practice: rendering West Asia exclusively as the locus of a biblical past, as the progenitor of Christian and Jewish—and no other's—cultural heritage.

4. *Cartography*

Miller and Hayes offered no maps that highlight the Bible's narratives of flight from Egypt, conquest of the Promised Land, and its apportionment among tribal groups. These particular themes have been among the stalwarts of biblical cartography, extending deep into the history of how Jews and Christians imagined the Holy Land from late antiquity to the modern era of elaborate atlases and printed Bibles. These maps became powerful instruments in the economic and political transformation of West Asia into what best served Anglo-European interests: a derelict garden awaiting reclamation as Christian or Jewish colony,

44. Monson, *Student Map Manual*, Section 15, 'Introduction to Indexes'.

45. Michael Avi-Yonah and Ephraim Stern (eds), *Encyclopedia of Archaeological Excavations in the Holy Land* (4 vols.; trans. from the Hebrew; Englewood Cliffs, NJ: Prentice–Hall, 1975–78).

as an outpost of western civilization, as a theologically delineated biblical land, as the taproot of European and American national identities.[46]

The omission of such cartographic illustrations, in the first instance, reflects the assessment by Miller and Hayes that the ancestral traditions enshrined in Genesis through Joshua offer little basis on which to construct a picture of premonarchical 'Israel'. The authors provide a few maps of relevance to general backgrounds—regionally based physical geography, for example—but none implies that readers (or historians) can define the physical and social realities of a biblical people before internal and external written sources give political definition to 'Judah' and 'Israel'.[47] Indeed, one map, 'Cities Conquered by the Israelites According to the Biblical Account', visually encodes the authors' skepticism toward the Bible's idealized narrative of origins. The authors project a geography of 'invading Hebrews', but they prominently mark seven locations mentioned in the Bible that have been excavated, and have 'produced very minimal evidence of occupation from the fifteenth through the thirteenth century BCE, or none at all'.[48]

In contrast, the maps chosen for inclusion in John Bright's *History* track not only the Hebrew ancestral traditions, but, like many popular and scholarly atlases, they adumbrate the narrative of Christian redemption from ancient 'Israel' to the early 'Church'. As iconic symbols, 'Israel' and the 'Church' trade the messiness of past events for the Christian claim of theological continuity between Old and New Testaments, or in Bright's terms, the Old Testament pilgrimage of faith that led to Christ.[49]

Of course, mapmakers did not put the matter so boldly. One map, for example, the 'Exodus from Egypt', represented, first, the biblical version of past events and second, a re-description of those events. 'The group that made the exodus', Bright wrote, received its 'distinctive faith' in the deserts of Egypt and later 'stood at Sinai, and subsequently moved on toward the Promised Land' where they 'engaged (themselves) to be the people of Yahweh and to

46. Kenneth Nebenzahl, *Maps of the Holy Land: Images of Terra Sancta through Two Millennia* (New York: Abbeville Press, 1986); Rehav Rubin, 'Ideology and Landscape in Early Printed Maps of Jerusalem', in *Ideology and Landscape in Historical Perspective: Essays on the Meanings of Some Places in the Past* (ed. Alan R.H. Baker and Gideon Biger; Cambridge Studies in Historical Geography, 18; Cambridge: Cambridge University Press, 1992), pp. 15-30; Robin A. Butlin, 'Ideological Contexts and the Reconstruction of Biblical Landscapes in the Seventeenth Century: Dr. Edward Wells and the Historical Geography of the Holy Land', in Baker and Biger (eds), *Ideology and Landscape*, pp. 31-62; Ruth Kark (ed.), *The Land That Became Israel: Studies in Historical Geography* (trans. Michael Gordon; Jerusalem: Magnes Press, 1989); Long, *Imagining the Holy Land*, pp. 165-202.

47. Miller and Hayes, *History*, maps of 'Eastern Mediterranean Seaboard', 'Palestine During Ancient Times', and 'Main Roads and Cities of Ancient Palestine', pp. 37, 41, 42.

48. Miller and Hayes, *History*, p. 73.

49. Bright, *History* (4th edn, 2000), pp. 463-64.

worship him alone'.[50] Another map, 'Tribal Claims During the Period of the Judges', visualized that same people of Yahweh as a kind of sub-division of 'covenant society', a society whose political and social realities were far less important to Bright than infusing the geography with the eternal promises of God.[51] Other maps plotted 'Palestine During the Ministry of Jesus' and 'The Journeys of Paul'.[52] Strictly speaking the last two topics lay beyond the limits of Bright's historiography, but not beyond the epilogue, which he entitled 'Toward the Fullness of Time'. And not, one might add, beyond his duties as a Presbyterian churchman attentive to the 'needs of the undergraduate theological student'.[53]

All of the appended maps were taken unaltered from *The Westminster Historical Atlas to the Bible*, an atlas and commentary that, it will be recalled, had been generated out of the activities of the Albright school and G. Ernest Wright's desire to integrate biblical archaeology with Protestant Christian theology. Indeed, 'the religious message' of the Bible, Wright and Filson wrote in the preface, 'cannot be truly understood without attention to the (providentially provided) setting and conditions of the revelation', which—here the authors mediate both Albright and St. Paul—came to a 'people who lived in the world, yet were never quite united with the world'.[54] Not surprisingly, John Bright 'especially recommended' the Westminster *Historical Atlas* to his readers.[55]

Of course, both Wright-Filson and Bright allowed for some uncertainty in the historical facts. On the map, 'The Exodus from Egypt', a dashed line marked the probable, not assured, route taken, and question marks register doubt about the exact location of some stops along the way. But no such ambiguity clung to the summits of Mount Sinai or Mount Nebo. Both peaks have been so tightly woven into biblical theology and romanticized Anglo-European explorations of the Holy Land that not even centuries of failed searches could dislodge the certainty of location that religious tradition assigns them, and with which cartographers regularly comply.[56]

50. Bright, *History* (4th edn, 2000), pp. 126 and 143, and pl. iii.

51. Bright, *History* (4th edn, 2000), pp. 144-82, and pl. iv.

52. Bright, *History* (4th edn, 2000), pls. xiv and xv.

53. Bright, *History* (4th edn, 2000), p. xviii.

54. Wright and Filson, *Historical Atlas* (rev. edn, 1956), p. 5. Compare Wright's dismissive picture of Canaan which ancient Israel righteously opposed (*Historical Atlas*, p. 36) with Albright's similar view (*Stone Age* [2nd edn, 1957], p. 281).

55. Bright, *History* (4th edn, 2000), p. xviii.

56. See, for example, Edward Robinson and Eli Smith, *Biblical Researches in Palestine, and in the Adjacent Regions: A Journey of Travels in the Year 1838* (3 vols.; Boston: Crocker & Brewster, 3rd edn, 1868), I, pp. 106-107, 570; Philip Schaff, *Through Bible Lands: Notes of Travel in Egypt, the Desert, and Palestine* (New York: American Tract Society, 1878), pp. 171-73; 302-303; George A. Barton, *A Year's Wandering in Bible Lands* (Philadelphia: Ferris & Leach, 1904), pp. 150-51; Wright and Filson, *Historical Atlas* (rev. edn, 1956), p. 38.

Bright recorded his discomfort, considering doubt about the location of Sinai, for example, to be unfortunate. No matter. Over all the events of Sinai 'there towers the figure of Moses...the great founder of Israel's faith'. Indeed, such events 'require a great personality behind them. And a faith as unique as Israel's demands a founder as surely as does Christianity or Islam, for that matter'. Furthermore, like Protestant travelers who sidestepped the problem of rival shrines that marked Jesus' burial place, Bright opined that knowing the exact location of Mount Sinai was not crucial for 'the history of Israel', especially since that history, for him, is a history of reified faith. 'There is no reason to doubt', Bright added, 'that it was there that Israel received that law and covenant which made her a people'.[57] And so, on the map, Mount Sinai gets no question mark, because its physical extent has been heavily infused with the abiding theological interests of religious communities.

A broader cultural dynamic may be seen in the map, 'Palestine During the Period of the Judges'.[58] In both its original and present context, this map presupposed the theological notion that early Israel was constituted as a tribal league, a 'people of Yahweh', a society bound together not by the machinery of centralized government, but in covenant with God.[59] It is this theological 'Israel' that the mapmakers illustrated while leaving a visual impression of a good many firm geographic boundaries around settled patrimonies. Moreover, the word 'Palestine' in the title, a change from previous editions, adds a sense of historical certainty and perhaps even political resonance that is lacking in the earlier title, '*Tribal Claims* During the Period of the Judges' (emphasis mine).[60] In any case, cartography (and Bright's reading of the biblical texts) visually imposed a sense of bounded sovereignty rooted in the modern Anglo-European experience of nation-states, despite Bright's use of the pre-statist notion of tribal league.[61] The mapmaker projected the bounded territories of a 'people of Israel' who, Bright wrote, were assembled out of disparate bands of in-migrants and unified by religious conviction. This, as it happens, is a story not entirely dissimilar to America's vernacular narratives of national beginnings.

Boldly shaded solid lines (marking 'known boundaries') and a few notched lines (for 'probable boundaries') represent what Bright described as the territories of ethnically mixed groups which had been absorbed into the ranks of desert invaders (the essential core of Israel).

57. Bright, *History* (4th edn, 2000), pp. 126-27, 125.

58. Bright, *History* (4th edn, 2000), pl. iv.

59. Bright, *History* (4th edn, 2000), pp. 144-82; Wright and Filson, *Historical Atlas* (rev. edn, 1956), p. 44.

60. The 'Tribal Claims' title appeared in the Wright-Filson *Atlas* and all previous editions of Bright's *History*.

61. See John W. Rogerson, 'Frontiers and Borders in the Old Testament', in *In Search of True Wisdom: Essays in Old Testament Interpretation in Honour of Ronald E. Clements* (ed. Edward Ball; JSOTSup, 300; Sheffield: Sheffield Academic Press, 1999), pp. 116-26.

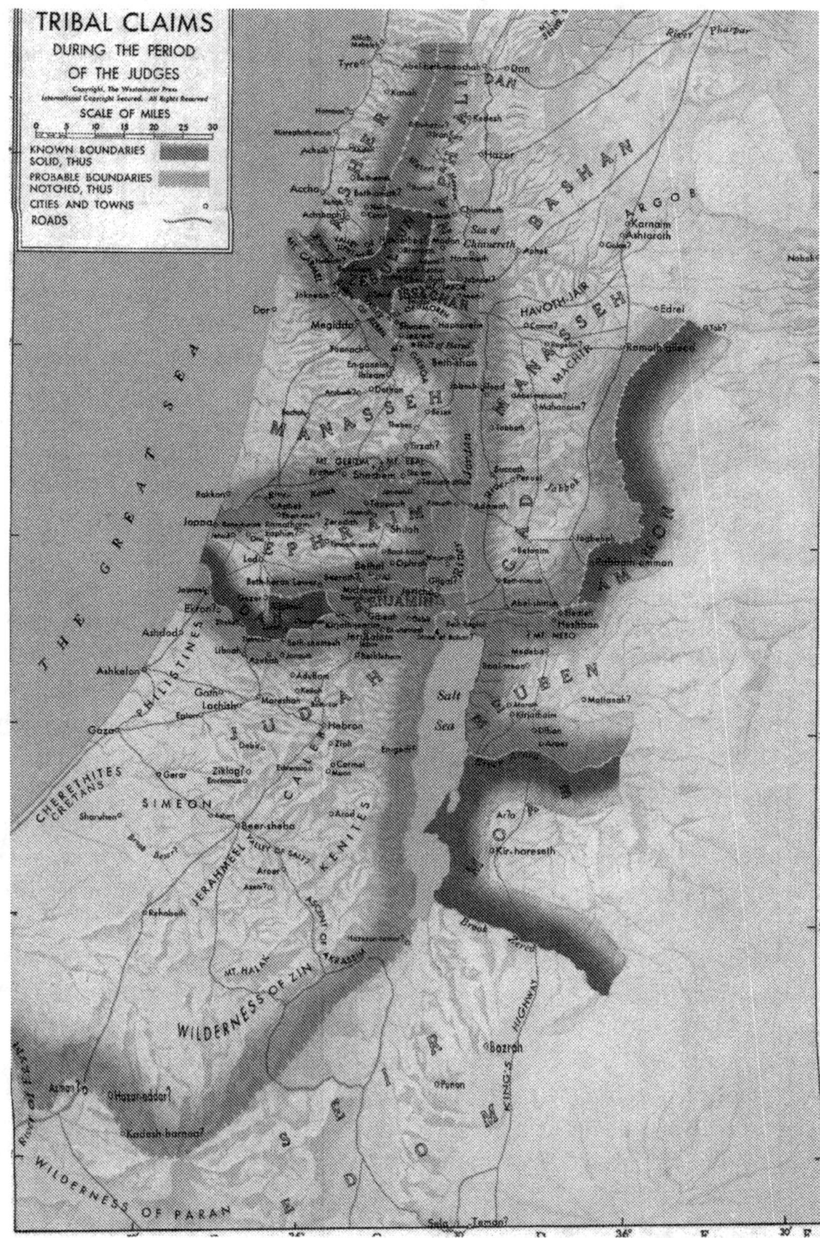

Map 2. 'Palestine During the Period of the Judges'. John Bright, *A History of Israel* (4th edn, 2000), pl. iv. Reproduced from *The Westminster Historical Atlas to the Bible* edited by G. Ernest Wright and Floyd V. Filson. Used by permission of Westminster/John Knox Press.

After the mixed multitudes swore allegiance to the God of Moses, he wrote, 'Israel's tribal structure assumed its classical form' with members for the most part 'in possession of the land they were to occupy for centuries to come'. Of course, according to Bright, 'some Canaanite enclaves remained...and fighting and friction were to go on for years'.[62]

However, no Canaanite enclaves appear on the Westminster *Atlas* map, which, following a long tradition in biblical geography, erased all traces of indigenous inhabitants, and—in this case—depicted only the decisive and meritorious outcome of what Bright called the 'bloody and brutal business' of the 'Holy War of Yahweh'. Bright seemed a little troubled by the morality of these events, even if perpetrated, as he added, only against those who *resisted* the Israelite onslaught.[63] But in the end, Bright (as both Albright and Wright had done) justified the bloody conquest, where it occurred, with reference to the victims' deficiencies, the 'extraordinarily debasing form of paganism' practiced by those peoples already living in the land. It was a paganism, Bright wrote, with which 'Israel...could never with good conscience make peace'.[64] Or, one may add, a cultural heterodoxy whose erasure from the triumphal narratives of Christians and Jews need not produce much guilt.[65]

Bright basically paraphrased the biblical account, and so his picture would have been familiar to readers of the Bible. But it also seems especially congenial to his American readers, whose narratives of national origins had long been shaped by biblical memory.[66] Early 'Israel' was a rag-tag mix of immigrants who, after a long process of expansive settlement and conquest, made a (nation-like) covenant society under God with ownership of territory unquestionably settled, despite on-going frictions and disputes with those relegated to 'Canaanite enclaves'. This socio-theological notion of early Israel's birth easily merges with the simplified myth of America's origin. Here, as every school child learns, religiously impassioned immigrants to North America wrested their patrimony in divinely sanctioned, often violent, confrontation with those who already lived in this (to the Europeans) new Promised Land.

In sum, Bright's construction of early Israel's history, along with maps selected from the Westminster *Atlas*, offer evidence of socio-spatial practices that transformed West Asia into a particular space, an Americanized nexus of memory, invention and geography sustained by attachments to ideas of exclusively biblical, Jewish and Christian monotheistic origins. This ancient Palestine was infused with the ambitions and truths of the Albright school, and filled with the desire to ground Protestant Christian theology in verifiable events of

62. Bright, *History* (4th edn, 2000), pp. 143.

63. Bright, *History* (4th edn, 2000), p. 142. Emphasis mine.

64. Bright, *History* (4th edn, 2000), pp. 118-19. See n. 54.

65. See Whitelam, *Invention of Israel*, pp. 37-175.

66. Of many accounts, see especially Sacvan Bercovitch, *The Puritan Origins of the American Self* (New Haven: Yale University Press, 1975); *idem*, 'The Biblical Basis of the American Myth', in *The Bible and American Arts and Letters* (ed. Giles Gunn; The Bible in American Culture, 3; Philadelphia: Fortress Press/Chico, CA: Scholars Press, 1983), pp. 219-29.

the past. It was also a memory-space where American readers could find cultural affinity with themes already expressed in popular narratives of American origins. At the same time, because modern cartographic projections so readily convey a sense of settled fact, the Westminster *Atlas* additions to Bright's historiography quietly reinforced his inclination to accept the Bible's narratives—its version of past events—as in the main trustworthy.

In contrast, Miller and Hayes illustrated Iron Age tribal presence in ancient Palestine with three maps, none of which encoded a theological notion of unified 'Israel' or suggested statist ideologies and sovereign control over territory. The maps entitled 'Domain of the Ephraim/Israel Tribes', 'The Galilee-Jezreel Tribes', and 'The Tribal Territory of Judah and Greater Judah', employed shadings and cross-hatching to suggest decentralization and instability, the permeable edges of 'domains', not fixed borders of patrimony, God-given or otherwise.[67]

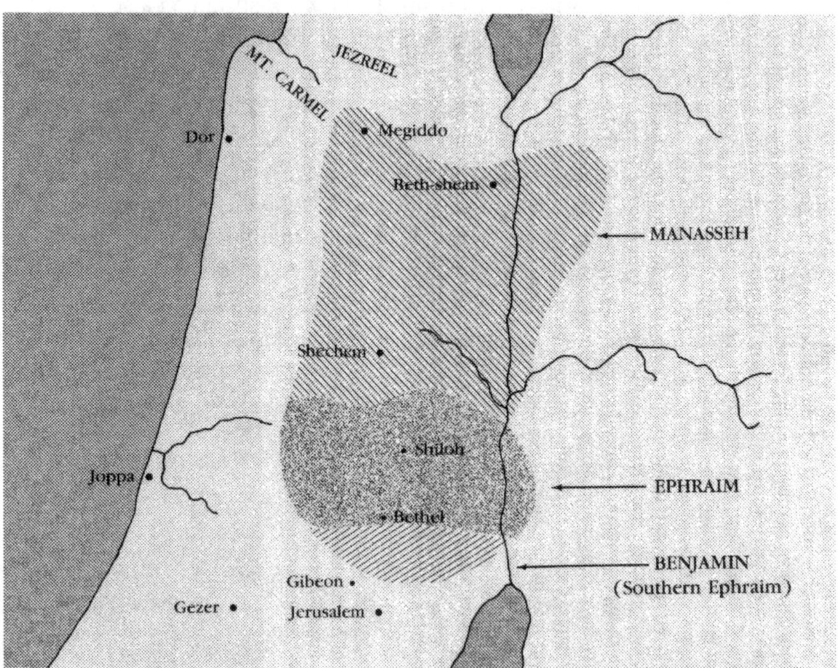

Map 3. 'Domain of the Ephraim/Israel Tribes'. Reproduced from *A History of Ancient Israel and Judah*, p. 95. ©1986 J. Maxwell Miller and John H. Hayes. Used by permission of Westminster/John Knox Press.

The authors imagined 'a heterogeneous population' sharing an 'essentially continuous religious and cultural scene', and within that, small socio-political units, such as the Israelite groups mentioned in the Book of Judges, but implic-

67. Miller and Hayes, *History*, maps 7, 8, and 10, pp. 95, 99, 104.

itly many others as well, moving around the central highlands of ancient Palestine. 'Loosely associated tribes dominated by Ephraim', Miller and Hayes wrote, spread about the north-central hill country and spilled into the trans-Jordanian highlands. These groups were not bound to the north-central Galilee-Jezreel tribes 'in any kind of formal tribal league'. And Reuben and Gad 'were never confined to a specific territory but ranged rather widely with their flocks'.[68]

In short, cartography in this case encoded the ambiguities Miller and Hayes found in the biblical texts, their skepticism toward the Bible's idealized narratives, and their refusal to enact in their historiography the exclusionary ideologies of Christian and Jewish monotheism. They constructed a physical extent—Iron Age Israel—filled not with the socially rooted interests of theological, nationalistic or ethnic unity, but with the interests of secular historiography and (perhaps valorized) pluralism. Their work sustained a sense of Iron Age Palestine as a place of decentralized social order, of heterogeneous tribal groups whose cultural realities, even religions, were more similar than different. Thus, Miller and Hayes opened the door to imagining ancient Israel's origins in ways that need not erase the histories of other Iron Age peoples, or foreclose their continuity with both Arabs and Jews who currently assert mutually exclusive claims to ethnic distinction and rights of primogeniture to the land.[69] The authors did not exactly walk through that door—their *History* still presumes that the overriding importance of West Asia, and writing its history, derives from its connection with the Bible, Judaism and Christianity. Yet, in their version of the Iron Age past events, ancient Palestine has not been nationalistically cleared of ethnic and religious diversity. And thereby the history of ancient Israel has not been rendered so easily compatible with modern claims to exclusive spiritual or political patrimony.

68. Miller and Hayes, *History*, pp. 83-85, 97, 100, 102, 111. See also map 13 and accompanying text, pp. 140-41, which depict Saul's 'domain' and the local authority he could occasionally assert. Also, maps 15 and 17, pp. 181 and 215, illustrate David's and Solomon's 'domains', the regions of limited and contested influence.

69. The unstated contemporary political importance of this matter may be judged from the intensity of recent debate over whether or not the material artifacts that archaeologists must interpret can establish anything like a distinctly 'Israelite' or 'proto-Israelite' presence in Iron Age Palestine. See, for example, William G. Dever, 'Ceramics, Ethnicity and the Question of Israel's Origins', *BA* 58 (1995), pp. 200-13; *idem*, '"Will the Real Israel Stand Up?" Archaeology and Israelite Historiography: Part I', *BASOR* 297 (1995), pp. 61-80; Keith W. Whitelam, 'The Identity of Early Israel: The Realignment and Transformation of Late Bronze-Age Palestine', *JSOT* 63 (1994), pp. 57-87; Thomas L. Thompson, 'Defining History and Ethnicity in the South Levant', in *Can a 'History of Israel' be Written?* (ed. Lester L. Grabbe; JSOTSup, 245; European Seminar in Historical Methodology, 1; Sheffield: Sheffield Academic Press, 1997), pp. 166-87.

5. *Retrospective*

By examining these examples of how historiography intersects with illustrative matter, I have tried to read modern biblical histories as artifacts of socio-spatial practices that continue to evolve so long as teachers, scholars, readers and publishers keep a particular version of biblical history in circulation. I asked how biblical historians transformed West Asia into something compatible with, and useful to, their own social and ideological interests, as well as those of the academic communities and audiences to whom they addressed their work. To this extent, I have made a start at setting John Bright, J. Maxwell Miller and John H. Hayes, along with their mentoring communities and publishers, within a cultural history of biblical scholarship that has yet to be written. It will be a narrative that blurs conventional distinctions between professional and vernacular appropriations of the biblical past. Its author(s) will show how Anglo-European biblical scholars—along with publishers, art designers, readers, entertainers, artists, merchants, politicians—joined cultural hands in managing, by inventing, an Oriental space called ancient 'Israel'. And for whom, and with what consequences, they did so.

Of Harems and Heroines

From 'Semiramis of Babylon' to 'Semiramis of Hammersmith'*

Julia M. Asher-Greve

For A.L.A.

Preface

Steven W. Holloway invited me to contribute an article to this volume on the following issues: to analyze the past and contemporary aversion of Assyriologists to incorporate feminist critiques of history and methodologies of gender studies into their research programs; to trace the general reluctance in our scholarly community to research women's histories; and finally, to situate the discussion within the collateral perspective of Orientalism.

In search of a theme, I encountered Semiramis in several recent publications and after further study realized her representations contain various aspects pertaining to my task. However, the more my research progressed, the more voluminous the material became and thus it was imperative to be rather selective.[1]

* I presented a different version of the Semiramis theme (visual and textual representation of an *exemplum*) at the interdisciplinary colloquium *Bild und Schrift* at Basel University in February 2005. I want to thank Thomas Späth and Adrian Stähli for their invitation, as well as their valuable comments and references. For various reasons I am indebted to Hannah Fournier (University of Waterloo, Canada), Lisa Hopkins (Sheffield Hallam University), Catherine Jenkins (Department for Drawings and Prints, Metropolitan Museum of Art, New York), Steven Holloway, Rivkah Harris, Thomas Segal (Baltimore), Jennifer Strasbaugh (Baltimore), Eva Strommenger, Alinari Archives (Florence), Stephanie Dalley (Oxford), Margherita E. Orselli (Tegna, Switzerland). My special thanks go to Rivkah Harris for sharing her personal experiences with me, to David J. Wille (Zürich) for his aid with literature on paintings and drawings, to the Paul Sacher Foundation (Basel) for help and advice concerning Arthur Honegger, and to the Zürich office of Sotheby's for information on the recently auctioned Semiramis painting by Il Guercino and to Sir Denis Mahon for granting me permission to reproduce photographs from his 1949 article on Guercino's Semiramis paintings. I also wish to thank the staff of the University Library of Basel University who helped finding rare books and articles. And last, I wish to express my gratitude to my husband, Arthur Lawrence Asher, by dedicating this article to him. Without his support research for this article would have been much more arduous.

1. To limit references to a reasonable amount I do not cite general works on feminist and gender theory, philosophy (including philosophy of women and gender), and history; interested readers will find relevant literature in bibliographies of cited literature. Because of the vastness of the literature on the themes discussed, I cite recent publications for the most part, many containing extensive bibliographies; concerning Semiramis literature I can mention only a selection of works.

Semiramis is a topic with a wide range of audiences; she is featured or alluded to in a great number of works in extremely diverse arts and studies. Already in antiquity, Semiramis, like Babylon, was used as metaphor for an entire concept alluding to political gynecocracy as well as lascivious, evil feminine sexuality. Comparable to Cleopatra,[2] fascination with Semiramis can be traced from ancient Greek literature and painting (Aetion) to contemporary poetry (Hans Magnus Enzensberger, see below), painting (Markus Lüpertz)[3] and websites. This enduring interest, according to the Assyriologist Georges Roux, can only be justified because the more one studies this '*diablesse*' the more fascinating she becomes.[4] As others before and since, Roux attributes abiding fascination to the dark side of Semiramis, although this was just one and not always the most important aspect of her multi-faceted character.

This study is divided into two parts: in the first I trace representations of Semiramis from Herodotus to the end of the twentieth century CE, in the second

For historical information and dates I used *Der neue Pauly: Enzyklopädie der Antike* (16 vols.; ed. Hubert Cancik and Helmuth Schneider; Stuttgart and Weimar: J.B. Metzler, 1996–2003); *EB: A History of Women in the West* (5 vols.; ed. George Duby and Michelle Perrot; Cambridge, MA and London: Harvard University Press, 1992–94); Eugen Joseph Weber, *A Modern History of Europe: Men, Cultures, and Societies from the Renaissance to the Present* (New York: W.W. Norton, 1971). For general information and dates I consulted for composers and opera *The New Grove Dictionary of Music and Musicians* (29 vols.; ed. Stanley Sadie; New York: Grove's Dictionaries/London: Macmillan, 2nd edn, 2001) and for visual arts and artists *The Dictionary of Art* (34 vols.; ed. Jane Turner; London: Macmillan, 1996) and *Allgemeines Lexikon der bildenden Künstler von der Antike bis zur Gegenwart: Unter Mitwirkung von 300 Fachgelehrten des In- und Auslandes* (37 vols.; ed. Ulrich Thieme and Felix Becker; Leipzig, 1907–50). Personal preference played a role in some of my choices but my selections are predominantly based on importance of author, artist, or issue. However, the selection is also influenced by availability of material as some is in collections not open to the public, only available in a few libraries or archives, or unpublished (this concerns rare books, paintings, drawings, prints, plays, opera librettos, stage sets, music scores, and letters).

2. *Cléopâtre dans le miroir de l'art occidentale: Musée Rath, Genève du 25 mars au 1er août 2004* (ed. Claude Ritschard and Allison Morehead; Geneva: Musées d'art et d'histoire/Milano: 5 Continents, 2004). Because no comparable work exists I intend to publish a book on Semiramis representations and interpretations throughout the ages.

3. David Cohen, *Markus Lüpertz 'Semiramis': September 12–November 16, 2002* (New York: Knodler & Company, 2002). Lüpertz's *Semiramis* series consists of fifteen colorful abstract oil paintings titled *Waterfall, Adrian, Portal, Green Bed, Red Roses, Cascade, Dew Drops, Sea Fragment, Juniper*, etc.; Lüpertz was inspired by 'The Hanging Gardens of Babylon' rather than Semiramis. Cohen mentions several possible sources of inspiration but not Arnold Schönberg's *15 Gedichte aus 'Das Buch der hängenden Gärten'*, op. 15; the poems Schönberg set to music are by Stefen George.

4. Georges Roux, 'Sémiramis, la reine mystérieuse d'Orient', in *Initiation à l'orient ancien: De Sumer à la Bible* (ed. Jean Bottéro; Points: Histoire, H170; Paris: Editions du Seuil, 1992), pp. 184-204 (202); see also Cesare Questa, *Semiramide redenta: Archetipi, fonti classiche, censure antropologiche nel melodramma* (Letteratura e antropologia, 2; Urbino: QuattroVenti, 1989), pp. 13-14.

I discuss possible interrelations between ancient Near Eastern studies, Orientalism, feminist and gender discourse. Both parts are pertinent to the discourse on women's sexuality, place and role in the polity.

1. *Model of Exceptionality*

Feminist historians consider the idea of exceptional women a phenomenon of 'andro-normative' historiography. Gerda Lerner argues 'the bias of patriarchally framed selection has tended to make only those women 'notable' and 'worthy' who did what men did and what men recognize as important',[5] and Margaret R. Sommerville states in *Sex and Subjugation: Attitudes to Women in Early Modern Society* that 'exceptional women were just exceptions to the normal rule'.[6] I will show that both arguments are true for Semiramis because her place in cultural history rests on her 'man-like' deeds as well as on trespassing societal rules and boundaries set for women, in particular when her sexual *persona* is the focus of discussion. Contrary to exceptional men, sexuality of exceptional women is nearly always a topic.

1.1. *Who was Semiramis? From Herodotus to Dante*

When Semiramis entered history in Herodotus' *Historiae* (1.185) over three centuries had passed since the death of queen Sammuramat, her alleged model, who probably died during the reign (809–782 BCE) of her son Adad-nērārī III (see below 2.1). Herodotus begins his universal history with the statement that he publishes his research so that the works of humans will be remembered. Semiramis is remembered by just one sentence mentioning her rule and the building of a dam, brief when compared to other women in his *Historiae*.[7] Considering Herodotus' interest in fantastic and extraordinary stories it is unlikely he had heard the stories about Semiramis which were reported by Diodorus Siculus three centuries later but which were claimed to have previously been reported by Herodotus' contemporary Ctesias who was the personal physician of Artaxerxes II Mnemon (404–359/58 BCE).[8] Ctesias may have done an 'over-imaginative' elaboration of genuine Assyrian sources, but this was probably

5. Gerda Lerner, *The Creation of Feminist Consciousness: From the Middle Ages to Eighteen-Seventy* (Oxford: Oxford University Press, 1993), p. 16.

6. Margaret R. Sommerville, *Sex and Subjugation: Attitudes to Women in Early Modern Society* (London and New York: E. Arnold, 1995), p. 42.

7. For a recent analysis of Herodotus' view of women, see Reinhold Bichler, 'Herodots Frauenbild und seine Vorstellung über Sexualität der Völker', in *Geschlechterrollen und Frauenbild in der Perspektive antiker Autoren* (ed. Robert Rollinger and Christoph Ulf; Innsbruck: Studien-Verlag, 2002), pp. 13-56.

8. On Ctesias, see now Dominique Lenfant, *La Perse; l'Inde; autre fragments: Ctesias de Cnide: Textes établi, traduit et commenté* (Collection des universités de France. Série grecque, 435; Paris: Les Belles Lettres, 2004).

the reason for the popularity of his *Persica;* other works popular in antiquity were romances and novels featuring Semiramis and Ninus, whose love story may derive from the Assyrian king Sennacherib's love for one of his wives (see below 2.1).[9]

Depending on context and line of argumentation, authors and artists made use of the complex and ambiguous stories circulating around Semiramis, Ninus and their son. Classical authors were not only interested in ruling queens but particularly in men who became dependent on women, incapable of fulfilling their vocation and thus providing women the chance to play a role in politics and portraying man in the traditional role of women that was considered an 'unnatural' situation. Although gynecocracy was generally associated with 'Asia' or 'barbarians',[10] Semiramis was primarily admired for her competence and accomplishments as ruler and warrior. This is evident in the so-called *tractati de mulieribus*, catalogues of short biographies of outstanding women that are known since Homeric times.[11] The oldest surviving catalogue is *Tractatus de mulieribus claris in bello* by an anonymous author dating to the end of the second or beginning of the first millennium BCE; fragments of forerunners are preserved. *Tractatus de mulieribus* is a collection of fourteen short biographies of four Greek and ten non-Greek warrior queens. All were allegedly historical women ruling before the early part of the fifth century BCE, most as widows and regents for minor sons; all are said to be extremely beautiful, intelligent and wise, as well as successful at men's work of warrior and ruler, but to use deception as a weapon. No mythological woman or Amazon is included. For each biography the author mentions his source, which for Semiramis (the first entry) is Ctesias. Only Semiramis's exemplary deeds are listed, with no mention of abusing power, trespassing sexual behavior codes, murdering her husband, or incest with her son. The final words are: 'she was conspired against by her son Ninyas and dies, having lived for 62 years and ruled for 42'.[12] Deborah Gera argues that biographies of historical queens were assembled not because they were women, but because they were important in the history of their countries.[13]

The most famous surviving ancient description of Semiramis is Diodorus Siculus in his *Bibliotheke* (Book 2) dating in the first century BCE. All books

9. Lenfant, *La Perse*, pp. xlii-xlv, li-liv; Stephanie Dalley and A.T. Reyes, 'Mesopotamian Contacts and Influence in the Greek World', in *The Legacy of Mesopotamia* (ed. S. Dalley; Oxford: Oxford University Press, 1998), pp. 85-124 (110, 118).

10. Johannes Nollé, 'Frauen wie Omphale? Überlegungen zu "politischen" Ämtern von Frauen im kaiserzeitlichen Kleinasien', in *Reine Männersache? Frauen in Männerdomänen der antiken Welt* (ed. Maria H. Dettenhofer; Köln: Böhlau, 1994), pp. 229-59 (230-31).

11. Deborah Levine Gera, *Warrior Women: The Anonymous* Tractatus de mulieribus (Mnemosyne, bibliotheca classica batava. Supplementum, 162; Leiden: E.J. Brill, 1997), pp. 26-27, 32-34. My summary is based on Gera and Lenfant, *La Perse*, p. 64.

12. Gera, *Warrior Women*, p. 6.

13. Gera, *Warrior Women*, p. 19.

and almost all articles summarize or refer to Diodorus' extensive description of Semiramis, whom he considered the most important of all women. Diodorus ends his biography with the statement 'such, then is the account that Ctesias of Cnidus has given about Semiramis'. However, Sabine Comploi recently argued that Diodorus' portrait of Semiramis cannot be considered as merely a summary of Ctesias, because the seven references to Ctesias only concern, aside from the dates of Semiramis' life and reign, the measurements of buildings.[14] According to Comploi, Diodorus did not 'quote' from his sources but used them freely, selecting and altering according to his didactic concept that history is written for the instruction of the readers, whose 'understanding of the failures and successes of other men, ...is acquired by the study of history (and) affords a schooling that is free from actual experiences of ill' (Diodorus 1.1-2). For Diodorus, a successful ruler has to be a good ruler, whereas a bad and godless ruler should be punished; his characters, including Semiramis, are exemplary.[15]

Comparison of Diodorus' biography of Semiramis with other classical references shows important differences.[16] One is Diodorus' explanation that Semiramis acted out of fear of losing power and position if she re-married, and therefore took lovers and had them killed (2.13.4). Nevertheless, Diodorus describes Semiramis as a successful and good ruler, endowed with 'understanding, daring and all other qualities which contribute to distinction' (2.6.5).

Although Semiramis continued to be represented as an exemplary ruler, there were also derogative remarks about gynecocracy, particularly in reference to the Orient. The names of dominant women such as Omphale, Cleopatra and Semiramis were part of the Roman vocabulary of political abuse, e.g., in his speech to the Roman senate, Cicero criticized Gabinus' government with reference to Semiramis: 'Then Syria: is this new Semiramis (= Gabinus) to be retained any longer there?'[17]

The images of Semiramis mentioned by Diodorus can be associated with Neo-Assyrian art representing kings but not queens.[18] Pliny mentions a paint-

14. For a recent analysis of Diodorus' Semiramis biography, see Sabine Comploi, 'Die Darstellung der Semiramis bei Diodorus Siculus', in *Geschlechterrollen und Frauenbild*, pp. 223-71; cf. Lenfant, *La Perse*, pp. 22-51.

15. For the differences in Semiramis narratives of classical authors, see S. Comploi, 'Darstellung der Semiramis', pp. 232-35; Lenfant, *La Perse*, pp. 22, 66-69. For detailed analysis of classical sources, see also Anna Maria G. Capomacchia, *Semiramis una femminilità ribaltata* (Storia delle religioni, 4; Rome: 'L'Erma' di Bretschneider, 1986); Questa, *Semiramide redenta*.

16. See, e.g., Capomacchia, *Semiramis una femminilità ribaltata*; Lenfant, *La Perse*, pp. 65-69.

17. Cicero, *Pro Caelio. De provinciis consularibus. Pro Balbo* (trans. Richard Gardner; LCL; London: Heinemann and Cambridge, MA: Harvard University Press, 1958), 4.9 (pp. 550-51); Jasper Griffin, 'Propertius and Antony', *Journal of Roman Studies* 67 (1977), pp. 17-26 (17 with nn. 4, 5); Nollé, 'Frauen wie Omphale?'

18. Diodorus mentions an image showing Semiramis on horseback, a bronze statue (2.8.7),

ing by the late fourth-century BCE painter Aetion representing *Semiramis Rising from Slavery to Royal Power*;[19] a *sujet* probably derived from a story told by a certain Athenaeus and mentioned by Diodorus (2.20.4): Semiramis was a courtesan who, because of her beauty, rose to queen. She asked Ninus to let her rule for five days, imprisoned him and seized the throne.

To my knowledge, the only certain ancient depiction of Semiramis (identified by inscription) is on a fourth-century CE relief found at Aphrodisias.[20] Semiramis faces an altar holding a staff and a branch resembling much earlier (third-millennium BCE) Mesopotamian date clusters (dates were and are a product of Western Asia).[21] Semiramis is depicted in Roman dress without any 'orientalizing' features. In earlier images on two mosaics from Asia Minor dating from around 200 CE, a male figure, presumably Ninos, is shown holding a portrait of Semiramis, a motif linked to the ancient Greek Ninos novel only preserved in fragments.[22]

The life-story of Semiramis was altered, augmented, and reinterpreted. Among the rather bizarre inventions attributed to Semiramis are castration and the chastity belt; also added to her biography is a stepson named Trebata, and a brother who is an augur.

According to a tenth-century epitaph, Semiramis expelled her stepson Trebata from his father Ninus' kingdom; Trebata then sought refuge in Germany where he founded Trèves, known today as Trier. In later chronicles Trebata becomes Semiramis' son, the incest motif is added, as is Semiramis' pursuit of

and a rock relief (2.13.2). For visual representation of Assyrian kings, see Ursula Magen, *Assyrische Königsdarstellungen – Aspekte der Herrschaft: Eine Typologie* (Baghdader Forschungen, 9; Mainz: Philipp von Zabern, 1986); for images of queens, see Tallay Ornan, 'The Queen in Public: Royal Women in Neo-Assyrian Art', in *Sex and Gender in the Ancient Near East: Proceedings of the 47th Rencontre assyriologique internationale, Helsinki, July 2-6, 2001* (ed. Simo Parpola and Robert M. Whiting; Helsinki: The Neo-Assyrian Text Corpus Project, 2002), pp. 461-76.

19. G. Bröker and W. Müller, 'Aëtion (I)', *Künstlerlexikon der Antike* (2 vols.; ed. Rainer Vollkommer; München and Leipzig: K.G. Saur, 2001–), I, p. 5-6; C. Hobey-Hamsher, 'Aetion', *Dictionary of Art*, I, p. 184.

20. Kenan T. Erim, *Aphrodisias, City of Venus Aphrodite* (London: Muler, Blond & White), p. 101 (above left); cf. Dalley and Reyes, 'Mesopotamian Contact and Influence', fig. 56 (left).

21. Dalley and Reyes, 'Mesopotamian Contact and Influence', pp. 118-19, fig. 56. For the images of Mesopotamian date clusters, see Julia M. Asher-Greve, *Frauen in altsumerischer Zeit* (Bibliotheca mesopotamica, 18; Malibu, CA: Undena, 1985), pl. 2.

22. Doro Levi, 'The Novel of Ninus and Semiramis', *Proceedings of the American Philosophical Society* 87 (1944), pp. 420-28; *idem*, *Antioch Mosaic Pavements* (2 vols.; Committee for the Excavation of Antioch and its Vicinity. Publications, 4; Princeton, NJ: Princeton University Press, 1947), I, pp. 117-18, 177, II, pl. 20; Marie-Henriette Quet, 'Romans grecs, mosaïques romaines', in *Le monde du roman grec: Actes du colloque international tenu à l'Ecole normale supérieure (Paris 17-19 décembre 1987)* (ed. Marie-François Baslez, Philippe Hoffmann, and Monique Trédé; Paris: Presses de l'Ecole normale supérieure, 1992), pp. 125-60 (129-35), figs. 2, 4.

Trebata to Troy or Trier, where Trebata finally kills her. This legend, narrated in many medieval chronicles, had the purpose of providing an etymology for 'Treveri' (Trèves, Trier) as well as to ascribe Trier's foundation to 'biblical times' and thus provide proof for the city's ancientness over Rome.[23]

At about the same time as the circulation of the Trebata epitaph, an unknown Provencal poet created another Semiramis myth.[24] Written in dialogue, the poem has two main protagonists: deified Semiramis and her brother, an augur. The brother accuses and condemns Semiramis, now a goddess, of an adulteress relationship with a bull, a reference to the myth of Europa and Zeus. She defends herself by explaining that the bull was Jupiter who pressed his love and desire on her:

> 'If the god played, this does not condemn his deed—there is no judgment against divine seducer, such an adulterer smiled at me without blame. Who, even if he wished, could deny me the right to sin with Jove? Who has come back from the garden, if the god willed otherwise? When the blessed one ravished me, we both sinned guiltlessly. When goddesses yield to voluptuousness, law is wholly overcome'.[25]

Remarkable are the poet's efforts to explain and excuse Semiramis' profligate behavior in contrast to the medieval representation generally describing her as the worst female sinner in history. According to Irene Samuel, in the Middle Ages Semiramis becomes 'a prime *exemplum* of vicious pagan womanhood,... a classical symbol of war, and a harlot'.[26] Saint Augustine, Jerome, and Orosius describe Semiramis as the most cruel, inhuman, and dissolute woman of the world with an unnatural lust of power, an incestuous mother with abnormal sexuality, who, together with her son Ninus, were the first idolaters.[27]

Dante condemned Semiramis together with Cleopatra to hell:[28]

> She was so broken to lascivious vice
> She licenced lust by law, in hopes to cover
> Her scandal of unnumbered harlotries.
> This was Semiramis; 'tis written of her

23. Ilse Haari-Oberg, *Die Wirkungsgeschichte der Trierer Gründungssage vom 10. bis 15. Jahrhundert* (Europäische Hochschulschriften. Reihe III, Geschichte und ihre Hilfswissenschaften, 607; Bern: Europäischer Verlag der Wissenschaften, 1994).

24. Peter Dronke, 'Semiramis, the Recreation of Myth', in *Poetic Individuality in the Middle Ages: New Departures in Poetry, 1000–1150* (Westfield Publications in Medieval Studies, 1; Oxford: Clarendon Press, 1970), pp. 66-113.

25. Dronke, 'Semiramis', p. 75.

26. Irene Samuel, 'Semiramis in the Middle Ages: The History of a Legend', *Medievalia et humanistica* 2 (1943), pp. 32-44 (41).

27. Samuel, 'Semiramis in the Middle Ages'. The incest motif is first mentioned in Justinus, *Epitome of the Philippic History of Pompeius Trogus*, 1.2.

28. Dante Alighieri, *The Comedy of Dante Aligheri, the Florentine. Cantica I: Hell (L'inferno)* (trans. Dorothy L. Sayers; Harmondsworth, Middlesex: Penguin Books, 1949), pp. 98-99, ll.55-63.

> That she was wife to Ninus and heiress, too,
> Who reigned in the land the Soldan now rules over.
> Lo! She that slew herself for love, untrue
> To Sychaeus' ashes. Lo! Tost on the blast,
> Voluptuous Cleopatra, whom love slew.

With 'it is written of her' Dante indicates he cites from a source, which is, according to Irene Samuel, Orosius' *Universal History* in which Semiramis is represented as anti-model.[29]

Edward Said—although conceding that Dante is not troubled by placing pagans, Muslims, and Christians in the same category of hell—claims that Dante had an 'Orientalist vision' because 'empirical data about the Orient or about parts of it count for very little'.[30] Said makes no specific reference that may have changed Dante's representation. However, concerning Semiramis, Dante did not select the most abominable sins attributed to her by earlier writers.

In the Middle Ages Semiramis is represented as a woman of many sexual vices; her sexuality is described as that of a powerful man giving in to all his desires. This masculinization is implicit in the incestuous relationship with her son, portrayed as her victim.[31] In this context it is of interest that centuries later during the trial of Marie Antoinette, the court was so frustrated that her answers would hardly justify the death sentence, she was finally accused of incest with her son.[32]

Semiramis is not only found guilty because she abused her position and power but implicitly also because she did not behave like a women and mother, and emasculated her son. Medieval Semiramis is constructed as pagan anti-model for Christian women, and in particular for queens regnant and women regents, many of whom made special efforts to conform with the ideals of Christian womanhood. Nevertheless a woman's reign often instigated groundless gossip and rumors about her unsuitable sexual behavior.[33]

29. Samuel, 'Semiramis in the Middle Ages', p. 33.

30. Edward W. Said, *Orientalism: Western Conceptions of the Orient* (London: Routledge & Paul Kegan, 2003 [1978]), p. 69.

31. On Semiramis and incest between mothers and sons in the Middle Ages, see Elizabeth Archibald, *Incest and the Medieval Imagination* (Oxford: Clarendon Press, 2001), pp. 68, 91-93, 104-44.

32. Carolly Erickson, *To the Scaffold: The Life of Marie Antoinette* (New York: William Morrow & Co., 1991), pp. 334-67, esp. p. 343.

33. On gender roles, warrior women, and queens in the Middle Ages, see, e.g., *A History of Women in the West.* II. *Silences of the Middle Ages* (ed. Christiane Klapisch-Zuber; Cambridge, MA and London: The Belknap Press of Harvard University Press, 1992); Sharon L. Jansen, *The Monstrous Regiment of Women: Female Rulers in Early Modern Europe* (New York: Palgrave, 2002) [with comprehensive index of queens, female monarchs and regents, including biographies of many]; Christine Reinle, 'Exempla weiblicher Stärke? Zu den Ausprägungen des mittelalterlichen Amazonenbildes', *Historische Zeitschrift* 270 (2000), pp. 1-38.

1.2. *Equivocality: Famous Woman, Worthy Woman, femme forte, and femme fatale*

In the third volume of *A History of Women*, the editors Natalie Zemon Davis and Arlette Farge comment that from the Renaissance to the age of Enlightenment women 'figured to an extraordinary degree in the realm of discourse and representation, myth and sermon, science and philosophy', and that 'paradoxically, the abundant and repetitious discourse on women was part of a strategy to establish order in the universe'.[34] This order meant to keep women generally in closely defined boundaries, ruling in their own right or as regents was only possible in polities organized as kingdoms or principalities.[35]

Medieval ideas about women such as Semiramis did not vanish with the Renaissance, although they were attacked in the 'debate about women' (also known as *querelle des femmes*) beginning at the end of the fourteenth century and lasting throughout the early modern period (c. 1500–1750).[36]

One of the most discussed and influential of texts is Boccaccio's (1313–75) *Famous Women* (*De mulieribus claris*).[37] In its final version, it comprises 106 chronologically-ordered biographies of predominantly classical women; Semiramis' follows second after Eve. *Famous Women* is the first post-classical collection of women biographies in Western literature; its popularity lasted throughout the fifteenth century. Boccaccio's portraits of women acquiring fame through talent and accomplishments presaged Renaissance ideas, although his notions about women expressed in the preface, conclusion and some comments remain medieval. The selection includes positive and negative models of power; Boccaccio is not only interested in their achievements but particularly in their sexuality. This is also evident in the Semiramis biography which is divided into two parts, her life and a lengthy moraliz-

34. Natalie Zemon Davis and Arlette Farge, 'Women as Historical Actors', in *A History of Women in the West*, III: *Renaissance and Enlightenment Paradoxes* (ed. N.Z. Davis and A. Farge; Cambridge, MA and London: The Belknap Press of Harvard University Press, 1993), pp. 1-7 (1).

35. Davis, 'Women in Politics', in *History of Women in the West*, III, pp. 167-83.

36. Merry E. Wiesner, *Women and Gender in Early Modern Europe* (New Approaches to European History, 20; Cambridge and New York: Cambridge University Press, 2nd edn, 2000), pp. 20-30; this book includes a comprehensive bibliography; *Geschlechterstreit am Beginn der europäischen Moderne: Die Querelle des Femmes* (ed. Gisela Engel, Friederike Hassauer, Brita Rand, Heide Wunder; Kulturwissenschaftliche Genderstudien, 6; Königstein im Taunus: Ulrike Helmer, 2004).

37. Stephen D. Kolsky, *The Genealogy of Women: Studies in Boccaccio's* De mulieribus claris (Studies in the Humanities: Literature–Politics–Society, 62; New York: Peter Lang, 2003); for a recent text edition and translation, see Giovanni Boccaccio, *Famous Women* (ed. and trans. Virginia Brown; The I Tatti Renaissance Library, 1; Cambridge, MA and London: Harvard University Press, 2001). My discussion is based on this translation.

ing comment.[38] The 'biographical' part consists of an amalgam of classical and Christian sources, which are, according to Virginia Brown, Valerius Maximus (see below), Justinus, Eusebius (Jerome), Orosius, and Paulinus Minorita.[39]

Boccaccio begins with the marriage to Ninus and Semiramis. There is no mention of Semiramis' first husband, her outstanding qualities, or that Ninus appointed her as regent. Instead she gains power after her husband's death through deception by disguising herself as her son. Boccaccio concedes that 'belying her sex, she preserved both kingship and military discipline while accomplishing many great deeds worthy of even the most powerful man', and that 'her accomplishments would be extraordinary and praiseworthy and deserving of perpetual memory for a vigorous male, to say nothing of a women'. Upon this accolade follows 'but with one unspeakable act of seduction Semiramis stained them all. Like others of her sex, this unhappy female was constantly burning with carnal desire…' The list of crimes are sexual and include incest. According to Boccaccio,

> 'it is believed that she [Semiramis] gave herself to many men. Among her lovers—and this is something most beastly than human—was her own son Ninyas… What heinous crime this was! The pestilence of lust, heedless of time and circumstances, flies about amidst the pressing concerns of kings, bloody battles (not to mention in time of peace) and, monstrously, in sorrow and in exile'.[40]

For Boccaccio the appropriate end was that she was killed by her son because she became pregnant by him.

The ambivalence in Boccaccio's text is also evident in some illustrations.[41] In a German edition from 1473, (fig. 43) Semiramis is depicted three times in one picture: in bed with her son Ninias, nearly naked in underpants accompanied by two court ladies also in underpants but wearing a coat, and thirdly as a statue on a column in full armor with crown and long hair indicating her gender.[42]

38. For the text, see Boccaccio, *Famous Women*, pp. 17-25; for a recent analysis, see Kolsky, *Genealogy of Women*, pp. 86, 157-66.

39. Boccaccio, *Famous Women*, p. 481; according to V. Brown, 'Introduction', in *Famous Women*, pp. xi-xxv (xvii), there are no thorough investigations of Boccaccio's sources.

40. Boccaccio, *Famous Women*, II § 13ff.

41. On ambiguities in Boccaccio's text, see Kolsky, *Genealogy of Women*, pp. 169-72.

42. *Semiramis* from Giovanni Boccaccio, *De mulieribus claris*, translated into German by Heinrich Steinhövel, printed by Johann Zainer, Ulm 1473, illustration in Kristina Domanski, 'Verwirrung der Geschlechter—Zum Rollentausch als Bildthema im 15. Jahrhundert', in *Frauen in der frühen Neuzeit: Lebensentwürfe in Kunst und Literatur* (ed. Anne-Marie Bonnet and Barbara Maria Schellewald; Atlas, Bonner Beiträge zur Kunstgeschichte, Neue Folge, 1; Köln: Böhlau, 2004), fig. 32.

Figure 43. *Semiramis*. After Giovanni Boccaccio, *De mulieribus claris* (1473).

This tri-partite image ridicules the rule of women.[43] A very different image in an edition from 1539 (fig. 44)[44] shows Semiramis in a domestic scene and again as statue in full armor on a column with an adoring warrior standing next to the monument.

Figure 44. *Semiramis*. After *Ioannis Boccatii Certaldo insigne opus de Claris Mulieribus* (1539); woodcuts by Jacob Kallenberg.

43. Domanski, 'Verwirrung der Geschlechter', pp. 37-83 (78-80); In this context it is of interest that sexually suggestive scenes were already depicted in medieval churches: Daniela Hammer-Tugendhat, 'Aspekte der subversiven Funktion von Kunst', in *Weiblichkeit in geschichtlicher Perspektive: Fallstudien und Reflexionen zu Grundproblemen der historischen Frauenforschung* (ed. Ursula A.J. Becher and Jöm Rüsen; Suhrkamp Taschenbuch Wissenschaft, 725; Frankfurt a.M.: Suhrkamp, 1988), pp. 150-73. Another novelty in this period is the motif of 'woman with mirror and comb' (p. 154) that is later used in Semiramis representations.

44. This edition published by Mathias Apiarus with woodcuts by Jacob Kallenberg is the only complete sixteenth-century Latin text; Brown, 'Introduction', p. xxi.

Boccaccio's *Famous Women* provided the model for numerous anthologies and images of collections and visual representations of *exempla*, also known as typologies or series of Worthy Women (*Femmes Fortes*). Many of these books were dedicated to women (see below).[45] Just as Boccaccio had created his compendium of famous women as counterpart to Petrarch's compendium of famous men,[46] the canon of the so-called Nine Worthy Women (French: *neuf preuses)* constitutes the counterpart to the Nine (male) Worthies.[47] The original series of Nine Worthy Women consisted of Semiramis and eight Amazon queens,[48] each considered a virile heroine, symbolizing warrior qualities comparable to those of knights. In the Renaissance being 'man-like'—not physically but in spirit and soul (*psyche*)—was considered the highest praise for a woman. *Queene Semiramys* is typically described in the old English poem *The ix. Ladies worthie* as

> Lo here Semiramys Queene of great Babylon
> Most generous gem and floure of lonely favor
> Whose excellent power fro Mede unto septentrion
> Flourished in her regally as mighty conqueror
> Subdued al Barbary: and Zorast that king of honor
> She skue in Ethiop, and conquered Armony in Inde,
> In which non entred but Alexaner and she as I finde.[49]

Figure 45. *Semiramis* from a set of playing cards, French, second half of 15th century. After Romain Merlin, *Origines des cartes à jouer* (1869), pl. F.

45. Martine Vasselin, 'Histoires déformées, miroirs déformants: l'image artistique des héroines au XVIe siècle', *Nouvelle revue du XVIe siècle* 12 (1994), pp. 33-62 (35-39).

46. Boccaccio, *Famous Women*, p. 9 (Preface §§ 1-4); Kolsky, *Genealogy of Women*, pp. 40-47.

47. Horst Schröder, *Der Topos der Nine Worthies in Literatur und bildender Kunst* (Göttingen: Vandenhoeck & Ruprecht, 1971), pp. 168-82; see also Vasselin, 'Histoire déformées, mirrors déformants'.

48. Sinope (Antiope), Hippolyte, Melanippe, Lampedo, Penthesilea, Tomyris; see Schröder, *Topos der Nine Worthies*, pp. 168-72.

49. Quoted from Schröder, *Topos der Nine Worthies*, pp. 181-82.

In Renaissance art Semiramis appears as one of the Nine Worthy Women in painting, on *gobelins* (tapestries), playing cards, ceramics, and the Worthies were also enacted in pageantries.[50] Semiramis is pictured as contemporary queen wearing a crown[51]

Figure 46. *Semiramis*, detail from the fresco cycle of *Nine Worthy Women* attributed to Giacomo Jaquerio and assistants in the Sala Baronale of the Castle of Manta, Cueno, *c*. 1420/30 (1994, Mauro Magliani for Alinari; courtesy of Alinari Archives/Bridgeman).

50. Schröder, *Topos der Nine Worthies*, pp. 183-202; pls. 2, 4, 7.

51. See *Semiramis* from set of playing card, French, second half of the fifteenth century (in Schröder, *Topos der Nine Worthies*, pl. 2).

(Figs. 48) or occasionally a helmet.[52] Like the other Worthies she is identified by a heraldic shield.[53] Her shield is adorned with three golden chairs symbolizing Assyria, Babylonia, and Chaldea. (Fig. 46, hanging behind her figure on a tree). The name is usually inscribed on the picture; some paintings also carry subtexts (fig. 46).[54] Similar to the representation on the relief from Antioch, Renaissance iconography of Semiramis contains no sign of her Oriental origin or sexual infamy. As *exemplum* of Worthy Woman she transcends such 'facts'. Her name even became a popular epithet of Christian female sovereigns, such as Margareta (I) of Denmark (1375–1412) who was called 'Semiramis of the North' because she conquered Norway and Sweden, or Isabella of Castille (1474–1504) called 'Semiramis of Christianity'.

A number of female monarchs and regents ruled in fifteenth- and particularly in sixteenth-century Europe, prompting debate about women and power, in particular in England where no queen had ruled in her own right since the early Middle Ages, and in France where Salic law prevented women from succession to the throne but not from reigning as regents.[55] Rulership of women contradicted traditional views about their place in the polity and their presumed incapability to play a public role; it was also considered not in accordance with the 'law of nature'. A woman's use of power was regarded differently than that of a man. If a ruling queen or princess acted like a woman this would not conform with her role as monarch, but if she acted like a male monarch this would be viewed as inappropriate for a woman.[56] While the sexual life of male rulers was rarely an issue of

52. See *Semiramis* (middle) on a maiolica dish from Venice, 1543, Victoria and Albert Museum, London (in Bernard Rackham, *Catalogue of Italian Maiolica: Victoria and Albert Museum* [2 vols.; London: Her Majesty's Stationary Office, rev. edn, 1977], pl. 156, no. 967).

53. See Schröder, *Topos der Nine Worthies*, pl. 2.

54.

> (Semiramis) de Babiloyne/Fu dame de soubz tout le trone,/Onc tel fame ne vesquy,/ Rise subiuga et vainqui:/De midy a setenterion/Mist tout a sa subiection/Gent Scicie et gent Barberie/ Soumist tout a sa segnurie/Et Zoroastrun le fort roy/Ocist elle per son arroy.

Quoted from Schröder, *Topos der Nine Worthies*, p. 187.

55. For discussion of views about female monarchs and regents, see, e.g. Pierre Ronzeaud, 'La femme au pouvoir ou le monde à l'envers', *XVIIe Siècle* 108 (1975), pp. 9-33; Constance Jordan, 'Woman's Rule in Sixteenth-Century British Political Thought', *Renaissance Quarterly* 40 (1987), pp. 421-51; Susan Dunn-Hensley, 'Whore Queens: The Sexualized Female Body and the State', in *'High and Mighty Queens' of Early Modern England: Realities and Representation* (ed. Carole Levin, Jo Eldridge Carney and Debra Barrett-Graves; New York: Palgrave Macmillan, 2003), pp. 101-16; C. Levin, *'The Heart and Stomach of a King': Elizabeth I and the Politics of Sex and Power* (New Cultural Studies; Philadelphia: University of Pennsylvania Press, 1994); see also the articles in *Geschlechterstreit am Beginn der europäischen Moderne*, part 2: 'Hof und Herrschaft', pp. 104-65.

56. Jordan, 'Woman's Rule in Sixteenth-Century British Political Thought'; Jansen, *Monstrous Regiment of Women*; Lisa M. Hopkins, *Writing Renaissance Queens: Texts by and about Elizabeth I and Mary, Queen of Scots* (Newark, DE: University of Delaware Press/London:

theoretical debates, there is much discussion about female monarchs' 'sex'. Defamation and slander of reigning queen's sexual life was common, which could continue beyond their death and become part of their legend.[57]

This double standard was criticized by Christine de Pizan (c. 1364–1429) who also attacked Boccaccio's portrayal of Semiramis. Pizan was the first woman to defend Semiramis and to re-interpret her as exemplary woman, the first in history to accomplish so much.[58] Pizan disregarded Boccaccio's preoccupation with Semiramis' sexuality, and argues that the incestuous marriage, the principal charge against Semiramis, was a bold political maneuver to consolidate power, but she omits mention of the concluding event of matricide.[59]

Another explanation is proposed by the sixteenth-century French poetess Louise Labé (1526?–66). According to Labé the enormity of love's power transformed Semiramis' fate, who is 'simultaneously positive and negative and full of contradictions, …a model of military greatness fallen, a monarch and commandant transformed into a passive, languishing woman who invites admiration and pity because she is vulnerable though powerful'.[60] Labé attributes Semiramis' incest to Amour's power und unpredictability: Love conquered not only Semiramis but also Mars, thus Semiramis cannot be considered culpable.[61] In 1716 a third French woman, Magdaleine-Angélique Poisson Gomez took up the theme in a play portraying Semiramis differently than did her male predecessors, Gabriel Gilbert in 1646 and Nicolas Desfontaines in 1647 (see below), by relieving Semiramis of responsibility for her husband's death.[62]

Associated University Presses, 2002), pp. 29-42 ('"Monstrous Regiment": Theorizing Female Rule'); Paulie Puppel, 'Gynaecocratie: Herrschaft hochadeliger Frauen in der Frühen Neuzeit', in *Geschlechterstreit am Beginn der europäischen Moderne*, pp. 152-65.

57. For example, the sexuality of Mary I. and Elizabeth I. of England, Catherine II. of Russia was vilified; see, e.g., Jordan, 'Woman's Rule in Sixteenth-Century British Political Thought'; Levin, *'The Heart and Stomach of a King'*, pp. 1-5, 65-90; Dunn-Hensley, 'Whore Queens'; Jansen, *Monstrous Regiment of* Women, pp. 229-30 nn. 1 and 2; compare also the new study by Oliver Gajda, *Katharina II. von Russland im Diskurs der Sexualität: Mittelbare Einflüsse narrativer Fiktion auf Geschichtsschreibung* (Akademische Abhandlungen zur Geschichte; Berlin: Verlag für Wissenschaft und Forschung, 2002), pp. 11-16.

58. Christine de Pizan, *The Book of the City of Ladies* (trans. Rosalind Brown-Grant; Penguin Classics; London: Penguin Books, 1999), pp. 35-37; Kolsky, *Genealogy of Women*, pp. 7-15.

59. Daniel Kempton, 'Christine de Pizan's *Cité des dames* and *Trésor de la cité*: Towards a Feminist Scriptural Practice', in *Political Rhetoric, Power, and Renaissance Women* (ed. Carole Levin and Patricia Ann Sullivan; SUNY Series in Speech Communication; Albany, NY: State University of New York Press, 1995), pp. 15-37 (22-23).

60. Phyllis Rugg Brown, 'Louise Labé and Semiramis: A Feminist Reading', *Women in French Studies* 5 (1997), pp. 107-22. For Louise Labé, see M.-M. Fontaine, 'Labé, Louise (avant 1524–1566)', in *Dictionnaire des littératures de langue française* (4 vols.; ed. Jean-Pierre de Beaumarchais, Daniel Couty and Alain Rey; Paris: Bordas, rev. edn, 1994), pp. 1235-36.

61. Brown, 'Louise Labé and Semiramis'.

62. See *NGDO*, IV, p. 311; Carmen C. Esteves, *The Dramatic Portrayal of Semiramis in Virues, Calderon and Voltaire* (PhD dissertation, The City University of New York, 1985; Ann Arbor, MI:

Numerous works written during the reign of Elizabeth I contain associations of the English queen with Semiramis. According to Lisa M. Hopkins, 'this connection...allows a figure ostensibly associated with praise of Elizabeth to activate some of the darker aspects of her reign', in particular the Empress of Babylon in Thomas Dekker's *The Whore of Babylon* and Titania in Shakespeare's *A Midsummer Night's Dream*.[63] Shakespeare also evokes the example of Semiramis in *Titus Andronicus* where Tamora, the Queen of the Goths is compared with Semiramis: [64]

> To wait upon this new-made empress,
> To wait, said I? To wanton with this queen,
> This goddess, this Semiramis, this nymph,
> This siren, that will charm Rome's Saturnine,
> And see his shipwreck and his commonweal's.[65]

Susan Dunn-Hensley argues that 'more than any of Shakespeare's other queens, Tamora illustrates male fear of the transgressive, contaminating female', comparisons with Semiramis, known for her promiscuity and cruelty, link 'Tamora with the forces of disorder that threatens the lives of men and the stability of civilization', and Shakespeare not only singles out the vices attributed to Semiramis, but portrays a woman's reign as contrary to civilized society.[66] Concerning the implicit allusions in *A Midsummer Night's Dream*, Hopkins suggests they are a 'critique of the image created by the queen's [Elizabeth I] iconography' and of 'the mythmaking process that surrounded the queen in general'.[67]

In the nineteenth century, Elizabeth I was still referred to as a Semiramis, as in George Borrow's letter to the Rev. A. Bradham from 1839.[68]

Women sovereigns were also the cause of numerous compendia of *Femmes Fortes*, heroines and other celebrated women, some dedicated to queens and

UMI), p. 125. I have not been able to get a copy of Gomez's *Sémiramis, tragédie politique*. For Gomez and her works, see *Dictionnaire des littératures de langue française*, II, p. 1028.

63. This was recently studied by Lisa M. Hopkins, 'The Dark Side of the Moon: Semiramis and Titania'. I wish to thank Lisa Hopkins for giving me a copy of her manuscript and permitting me to quote from it.

64. See, e.g., Lisa Jardine, *Still Harping on Daughters* (New York: Harvester Wheatsheaf, 1989); Katherine Eggert, *Showing like a Queen: Female Authority and Literary Experiment in Spenser, Shakespeare, and Milton* (Philadelphia: University of Pennsylvania Press, 2000); Theodora A. Jankowski, *Women in Power in Early Modern Drama* (Urbana, IL: University of Illinois Press, 1992); Hopkins, 'The Dark Side of the Moon'.

65. Quoted from *The Complete Works of William Shakespeare: With Thirty-Two Full Page Plates from Modern Stage Production* (London, New York, Toronto: Oxford University Press, 1955), p. 743, Act II, Scene I, ll. 20-24.

66. Jansen, *Monstrous Regiment of Women.* For discussion of views on women as monarchs, see Dunn-Hensley, 'Whore Queens'.

67. Hopkins, 'The Dark Side of the Moon'.

68. Online:http://www.worldwideschool.org/library/books/hst/biography/LettersofGeorgeBorrow/chap91.html

princesses.[69] In cycles of *Femme Fortes* and heroines, archetypal and exemplary women are defined in opposition to ordinary woman as feminine version of masculine equivalents. Because the virtues of women *exempla* were considered 'man-like' they are often designated as androgynous in recent studies. But 'acting like a man' must be differentiated from an androgynous character or persona that incorporates both femininity and masculinity. Some authors argue Semiramis used deception in masking her femininity by wearing trousers, however, according to Diodorus (2.6.6), when still married to her first husband Onnes, an officer of king Ninus, Semiramis, 'devised a garb which made it impossible to distinguish whether the wearer of it was a man or woman', and, because it was so well suited to travel and combat, the Medes later adapted it (for men). When discussing female rulers it is important to distinguish between androgyny and political tasks because the latter were considered men's acts but could be successfully fulfilled by women without having to be androgynous. This is evident in the iconography of Semiramis who, apart from a sword or helmet, is predominantly portrayed as a beautiful, feminine woman but—contrary to Cleopatra—hardly ever partially or totally nude.[70] Heroines are interchangeable because the common denominator of the heroic personage is their 'exemplarity'. Selecting from a corpus of ancient goddesses, queens, and other famous heroines, compendia and series vary and Semiramis can be replaced with another 'warrior' queen or the queen of Saba.[71] As *exemplum* Semiramis was considered the "oldest and most famous 'model' of successful female rulership.

69. E.g., *Die Galerie der starken Frauen = La galerie des femmes fortes: Die Heldin in der französischen und italienischen Kunst des 17. Jahrhunderts* (ed. Bettina Baumgärtel and Silvia Neyster; München: Klinkhardt & Biermann, 1995); Christa Schlumbohm, 'Die Glorifizierung der Barockfürstin als "Femme Forte"', in *Europäische Hofkultur im 16. und 17. Jahrhundert: Vorträge und Referate gehalten anlässlich des Kongresses des Wolfenbütteler Arbeitskreises für Renaissanceforschung und des Internationalen Arbeitskreises für Barockliteratur in der Herzog August Bibliothek Wolfenbüttel vom 4. bis 8. September 1979* (3 vols.; ed. August Buck *et al.*; Wolfenbütteler Arbeiten zur Barockforschung, 9; Hamburg: Hauswedell, 1981), II, pp. 113-22.

70. See also *Galerie der Starken Frauen*, pp. 318-24; Gerhard Hojer and Peter O. Krückmann, *Anton Raphael Mengs: Königin Semiramis erhält die Nachricht vom Aufstand in Babylon* (Neues Schloss Bayreuth; ed. Kulturstiftung der Länder in Verbindung mit der Bayrischen Verwaltung der staatlichen Schlösser, Gärten und Seen; Berlin and München: Kulturstiftung der Länder, Freistaat Bayern, 1995). For Cléopatra, see most recently Claude Ritschard and Allison Morehead, *Cléopâtre dans le miroir de l'art occidentale: Musée Rath, Genève du 25 mars au 1er août 2004* (Geneva: Musées d'art et d'histoire/Milano: 5 Continents, 2004).

71. In publications of opera librettos Semiramis is occasionally depicted with bare breasts and in lascivious poses, see, e.g., Wendy Heller, *Emblems of Eloquence: Opera and Women's Voices in Seventeenth-Century Venice* (Berkeley: University of California Press, 2003), pp. 232-34, fig. 7. Because Semiramis is hardly ever represented as an Oriental queen, I disagree with Mary D. Garrard that Semiramis represents the 'barbaric "other"' ('Historical Feminism and Female Iconography', in *Artemisia Gentileschi: The Image of the Female Hero in Italian Baroque Art* [Princeton, NJ: Princeton University Press, 1989], pp. 141-79 [149]). Garrard is not the only scholar who tacitly equates Oriental with pagan and Western with Christian. Schröder, *Topos der Nine Worthies*, pp. 292-96; Vasselin, 'Histoire déformées, mirrors déformants'.

1.3. *Political Allegory or Tragic Heroine in Seventeenth- and Eighteenth-century Painting, Drama and Opera*

In times when several women ruled successively, as in sixteenth-century England and seventeenth-century France, debate about women's capability to successfully exercise power intensified and is indirectly reflected in various media in figures such as Semiramis. In the seventeenth century, several women ruled in their own right or as regents, among them Christina, Queen of Sweden from 1689–94, Mary II, Queen of Britain and Ireland from 1643–89, and two Regents of France, Maria de' Medici from 1610 to1617 and Anne of Austria from 1643–89.

In paintings, Semiramis continues to be represented as heroine or as allegory of good queenship. Simon Vouet, court painter of Louis XIII from 1627–49, included a Semiramis in the series of *Femmes Forte* in the *cabinet* of the Duchess de la Meilleraye in the Hôtel de l'Arsénal in Paris.[72] *Semiramis Holding a Sword* (1623–25) by Matteo Roselli was the central figure among the paintings of heroines and Worthy Women decorating the walls of the audience hall in the *Villa Poggio Imperiale*, the residence of archduchess Maria Magdalena of Austria in Florence who reigned as regent for her son.[73] The decoration of her audience hall was designed to convey the message that female rule is as effective as that of men.[74]

At about the same time, Rubens suggested to Maria de' Medici that he include an image of Semiramis in the cycle commissioned for the grand gallery of the *Hôtel de Luxembourg*; but Semiramis was rejected 'because of a certain lack of moderation in matters of exemplary chastity', to which Claude Fabri de Peiresc, who informed Rubens of Maria de' Medici's decision, adds 'I myself would not have caviled at such minutiae'.[75] However, Maria de' Medici did not object to the Semiramis metaphor included in the eulogy on the wedding of her daughter Henriette-Marie of France with Charles I of England: 'how satisfying for France, and how profitable for England, to be united so inseparable, by a bond more indissoluble than a Gordian knot, and by a friendship more firmly cemented than the walls Semiramis built in Babylon'.[76]

72. William R. Crelly, *The Painting of Simon Vouet* (Yale Publications in the History of Art, 14; New Haven and London: Yale University Press, 1962), p. 110, fig. 134; in 1645 Vouet also painted a series of *femmes illustres* for the rooms of Anne of Austria in the *Palais Royal*, now destroyed: Schlumbohm, 'Die Glorifizierung der Barockfürstin', pp. 113, 118.

73. *Galerie der Starken Frauen*, fig. 167, p. 322. Ilaria Hoppe, 'Räume von und für Frauen? Die Gemächer der Maria Magdalena von Österreich in der Villa Poggio Imperiale bei Florenz', in *Frauen in der frühen Neuzeit*, pp. 213-34.

74. Hoppe, 'Räume von und für Frauen?', pp. 231-33.

75. Jacques Thuillier and Jacques Foucart, *Ruben's Life of Marie de' Medici* (trans. Robert Erich Wolf; New York: Harry N. Abrams, 1970), pp. 27-31, 104; *Correspondance de Rubens et documents épistolaires concernant sa vie et ses oeuvres*, vol. 2: *1609–25 juillet 1622* (ed. Max Rooses and Charles Ruelens; Anvers: Jos. Maes, 1898), pp. 434-38; on Claude Fabri de Peiresc, see Rooses and Ruelens, *Correspondance*, II, pp. 233-35.

76. Quoted from Thuillier, *Ruben's Life of Marie de' Medici*, p. 9.

A room of the French queen Anne of Austria in the *château* of cardinal Richelieu at Indre-et-Loire was decorated with a series *femmes fortes* including Semiramis, who is also included in Pierre Le Moyne's illustrated *La Galerie des Femmes Fortes* published in 1647 and dedicated to Anne of Austria during her regency from 1643 to 1651.[77] Although not the first to hold this opinion, Le Moyne argued that gender was insignificant, even irrelevant in the case of rulers, and that female ruler's sexual extravagance and incest can be tolerated when it is used as political tool and not perverse sexual desire. This was also the opinion of Daniel Casper von Lohenstein, the author of the drama *Agrippina* (1665) that was published with extensive commentary containing numerous references comparing Agrippina with Semiramis as well as with contemporary female heads of state. Lohenstein, according to Jane O. Newman, acknowledged 'the realities of female rulership during this period and articulates a gender ideology strikingly at odds with any simplistic requirements of chastity, fidelity, and silence for women'. Newman comes to the conclusion that standards of sexual conduct for Semiramis, Agrippina, or in seventeenth-century Europe reflect the complex realities of women's political power.[78]

The Baroque age witnessed the discovery of the potential of Semiramis as tragic heroine. The first dramatization was probably Muzio Manfredi's popular *La Semiramis: Tragedia* followed by a second pastoral play *La Semiramis: Boscareccia* both published in 1593.[79] Manfredi used several motives of the Semiramis story: courtship, widowhood, incest motivated by political necessity, transvestism (a favorite theme in Baroque theater and opera),[80] and murder.

Playwrights took great freedom in using the Semiramis legend and several re-invented Semiramis with didactic intent. For example, Cristóbal de Virués (1550–1609) intended to instill desire for virtue with his version of Semiramis, Madeleine-Angélique Poisson Gomez's *Sémiramis* is subtitled *tragédie politique*, and Voltaire's *Sémiramis* (1748) is a vehicle to take revenge on his censor Crébillon who had written an unsuccessful Semiramis play.[81] Most Semiramis plays

77. Céline Richard-Jamet, 'Cléopâtre: *femme forte* ou femme fatale? Une place équivoque dans les galeries de *femmes fortes* aux XVIe et XVIIe siècles', in Ritschard and Morehead (eds.), *Cléopâtre dans le miroir de l'art occidentale*, pp. 42-44; M. John E. Schloder, 'Une artiste oublié: Nicolas Prévost, peintre de Richelieu', *Bulletin de la Société de l'histoire de l'art français* 1980 (1982), pp. 50-69 (65, 69 nn. 46, 47). Several paintings of the serie are missing, including Semiramis; Schlumbohm, 'Die Glorifizierung der Barockfürstin', pp. 113, 118-19.

78. Jane O. Newman, 'Sons and Mothers: Agrippina, Semiramis, and the Philological Construction of Gender Roles in Early Modern Germany (Lohenstein's Agrippina, 1665)', *Renaissance Quarterly* 49 (1996), pp. 77-113.

79. Linhard Bergel, 'Semiramis in the Italian and Spanish Baroque', *Forum italicum* 7 (June 1973), pp. 227-49; Heller, *Emblems of Eloquence*, pp. 227, 344 n. 28.

80. Heller, *Emblems of Eloquence*, pp. 220-62.

81. For analysis of various Semiramis plays, see Esteves, *Dramatic Portrayal of Semiramis*. For G. Gilbert's and N. Desfontaine's dramas, see Gwynne Edwards, 'Introduction', in Pedro

are tragedies thematizing the darker side of the queen's character, occasionally as concealed warning. Two French Semiramis dramas dating to the beginning of the regency (1643–51) of Anne of Austria, mother of Louis XIV, thematize passion and ambition: in Gabriel Gilbert's *Sémiramis* (1646) the heroine says her passion to rule ranks above love;[82] Nicolas Desfontaines portrays *La véritable Sémiramis* (1647) as an ambitious and vengeful woman who ends by taking her own life.[83]

Dramatic versions predominantly focus on tragic destiny and transgression of boundaries of female rulers and therefore end with death.[84] Voltaire presents a queen who, although deserving our compassion because her destiny lies in the hands of the gods, failed in her duty as wife and abused her power, but remorsefully sacrifices herself for her son thus fulfilling at least her duty as mother. Voltaire's *Sémiramis* is a moralizing story spiced with his ideas about power, society, and justice.[85]

A Semiramis tragedy, widely admired by Goethe and others,[86] is Calderón's *La hija del aire* (The Daughter of the Air), first performed in 1653 in the presence of the Spanish king Philip IV and his second wife Mariana of Austria. By the time Calderón wrote *La hija del aire*, he had become a monk and Philip IV was re-married to his young cousin whose beauty served as model for Semiramis.[87] Calderón, who omits lust and incest from the play, presents a strikingly beautiful, intelligent and ambitious Semiramis whose downfall (she dies in battle) results from her cruelty and incapability to conceive alternatives.[88] Calderón's substantial changes of the Semiramis legend, his 'powerful didactic tone', and the attention he gives to the theme of kingship indicate he may have chosen the Semiramis subject because of historical circumstances and written the play as warning to the king and his beautiful wife.[89]

Calderón de la Barca, *La hija del aire* (Colección Támesis. Série B: Textos, 9; London: Támesis Books, 1979), pp. xiii-lxxx (xxxiv).

82. B. Baumgärtel, 'Is the King Genderless? The Staging of the Female Regent as Minerva Pacifera', in *Women Who Ruled: Queens, Goddesses, Amazons in Renaissance and Baroque Art* (ed. Annette Dixon; London: Merrell, in association with The University of Michigan Museum of Art, 2002), pp. 97-118 (102).

83. Esteves, *Dramatic Portrayal of Semiramis*, pp. 124-25.

84. Bergel, 'Semiramis in the Italian and Spanish Baroque'; Esteves, *Dramatic Portrayal of Semiramis*.

85. Jean-Jacques Olivier, 'Introduction', in François Marie Arouet de Voltaire, *Sémiramis: Tragédie* (ed. J.-J. Olivier; Textes littéraires français, 5; Paris: Droz, 1946), pp. vii-xlix; Esteves, *Dramatic Portrayal of Semiramis*, pp. 135-57.

86. Wolfgang von Wurzbach, 'Einleitung des Herausgebers', to *Die Tochter der Luft* (*La hija del aire*), in *Calderons ausgewählte Werke* (10 vols.; ed. W. von Wurzbach; Leipzig: Hesse & Becker, 1910), II, pp. 113-23 (119-20); Edwards, 'Introduction', pp. xvi-xx.

87. Wurzbach, 'Einleitung', p. 118.

88. Esteves, *Dramatic Portrayal of Semiramis*, pp. 65-117.

89. Edwards, 'Introduction'.

Figure 47. Anton Raphael Mengs, *Semiramis erhält die Nachricht von Aufstand in Babylon*, painting, 1755, Inv. BayNS. G 104, Bayreuth, Neues Schloss, R. 5. Courtesy of Bayrische Verwaltung der staatlichen Schlösser, Gärten und Seen.

In the age of Enlightenment, female rulers and regents governed Russia with short intervals from 1725 to 1796 and the Austrian empire for the first time was ruled by a woman, Maria Teresa who reigned from 1749 to 1780. In paintings of the period Semiramis is no longer represented in cycles of *Femmes Fortes* but preferably as a singular ancient historical queen. Such paintings were commissioned by princesses, for example, Wilhelmina of Prussia, sister of Frederick II (the Great) of Prussia and wife of the Margrave of Bayreuth who also wrote a libretto for a Semiramis opera.[90] Wilhelmina commissioned *Semiramis Receiving Word of the Revolt of Babylon* (1755) by Anton Raphael Mengs, an allegory of Wilhelmina who had been instrumental in building a new residence and opera house in Bayreuth. Mengs' Semiramis[91] (fig. 47) owes much to Guercino's (Giovanni Francesco Barbieri) famous painting 1627–28 in Dresden that was destroyed in the second World War.[92]

90. Hojer and Krückmann, *Anton Raphael Mengs*, pp. 19, 37.

91. See Anton Raphael Mengs: '*Entwurf*' for *Semiramis* painting, 1755, Neues Schloss Bayreuth (in Hojer and Krückmann, *Anton Raphael Mengs*, fig. 9). The illustration shown here is an 'Entwurf' that, except for the colors, deviates little from the painting; see Hojer and Krückmann, *Anton Raphael Mengs*, p. 16.

92. For a detailed description and history of the painting, see Hojer and Krückmann, *Anton Raphael Mengs*, pp. 6-26.

Figure 48. Giovanni Francesco Barbieri, called 'Il Guercino': *Semiramis*, *c.* 1627–28, formerly in the Staatliche Gemäldegalerie, Dresden, destroyed in World War II. After Mahon, 'Guernico's Paintings of Semiramis' (1949), fig. 1. Used by permission of Sir Denis Mahon.

Guercino painted two more versions, one of which is now in the Boston Museum of Fine Arts (fig. 49),

Figure 49. Giovanni Francesco Barbieri, called 'Il Guercino': *Semiramis*, 1624, Museum of Fine Arts, Boston. After Mahon, 'Guernico's Paintings of Semiramis' (1949), fig. 3. Used by permission of Sir Dennis Mahon.

the other, (fig. 50), recently auctioned at Sotheby's, was originally commissioned in 1645 by Cardinal Cornaro for his Venetian palace.[93]

Figure 50. Giovanni Francesco Barbieri, called 'Il Guercino': 'Cornaro *Semiramis*', 1645. After Mahon, 'Guernico's Paintings of Semiramis' (1949), fig. 2. Used by permission of Sir Denis Mahon.

The differences between Guercino's two earlier versions (figs. 48, 49) and his Cornaro Semiramis (fig. 50) are striking. In the often copied earlier paintings, Semiramis is shown seated wearing a crown, her head, rendered in three-quarter profile, turns toward the messenger and with her right hand holds her hair indicating she was just engaged at her *toilette*. In the Cornaro painting (fig. 50), Semiramis is standing, her long, blond hair is combed by a maid, her crown is lying on a table; standing opposite the messenger she does not look directly at him but seems to contemplate while her hand indicates 'wait, I know what to do'. Guercino captured the moment between the message and her reaction to lead her army to Babylon. All three paintings render Semiramis as a Baroque princess wearing luxurious robes in either a 'Venus-type' posture (figs. 48, 49) or in a more 'masculine' pose as in the Cornaro *Semiramis* (fig. 50); only the Boston painting has a landscape background. (Fig. 49).

93. Sotheby's, *Old Master Paintings Evening Sale* (London, Thursday 7 July 2005), pp. 110-15, with illustrations pp. 111, 113. All three paintings by Guercino are discussed by Mahon, 'Guercino's Paintings of Semiramis', pp. 217-23.

Paintings such as Guercino's, Meng's, as well as others[94] show Semiramis receiving the news of the revolt in Babylon while doing her hair, a subject taken from a passage in Valerius Maximus' *Facta et dicta memorabilia* (9.3), or Polyaenus' *Strategemata* (8.26). Iconographically speaking, the motif 'woman combing or holding her hair' associates the 'warrior queen' Semiramis with a long tradition of sculptures and paintings with a feminine erotic aspect that originates in depictions of *Venus anadyomene*.[95]

In opera the Semiramis theme was particularly popular in the seventeenth and eighteenth centuries.[96] Voltaire's tragedy was set to music thirteen times; the most famous and only version still performed is Rossini's *Semiramide*.[97] There are about forty operas using Metastasio's *Semiramide riconosciuta* libretto. This was first set to music by Leonardo Vinci in 1729 and last by Giaccomo Meyerbeer in 1819.[98] Metastasio's librettos were dramas intended to instruct mankind 'under the guise of giving pleasure' and they were written so that they could also be read or performed on stage as spoken dramas because he preferred that to poor musical settings.[99]

Plays and opera not only provided entertainment analogous to contemporary movies and television but furnished for a substantial part of the audience the only education in literature and history.[100] Rarely is Semiramis represented as *femme fatale*; rather, her extraordinary beauty that attracted men is emphasized as is her ambition as ruler. Metastasio's portrayal made *Semiramide riconosciuta* also acceptable for special court performances:[101] it was chosen for the corona-

94. See *Galerie der Starken Frauen*, pp. 318-24; Hojer and Krückmann, *Anton Raphael Mengs*, pp. 11-14; Andor Pigler, *Barockthemen: Eine Auswahl von Verzeichnissen zur Ikonographie des 17. und 18. Jahrhunderts* (Budapest: Akadémiai Kiadó, 2nd enl. edn, 1974), p. 341; the painting Pigler lists by Laurent de la Hire (or Hyre) in Budapest (see: Wilhelm Eilers, *Semiramis: Entstehung und Nachhall einer altorientalischen Sage* [Österreichische Akademie der Wissenschaften, Philosophisch-historische Klasse Sitzungsberichte, 274, Abhandlung 2; Wien: Hermann Böhlaus Nachfolger, 1971], fig. 3) does not depict 'Ninus offering Semiramis the crown' but 'Cornelia rejecting the crown of the Ptolemies' (I thank István Németh, Department of Old Masters, Museum of Fine Arts Budapest for this information).

95. LIMC, II/1, pp. 54-57 (Aphrodite), pls.: II/2, pp. 40-43; VIII/1, pp. 206-207 (Venus), pls.: VIII/2, pp. 142-43.

96. Questa, *Semiramide redenta*, pp. 39-69; Heller, *Emblems of Eloquence*, pp. 220-62.

97. Ronald S. Ridgway, 'Voltaire', in *NGDO*, IV, p. 1041; Richard Osborne, 'Semiramide', in *NGDO*, IV, pp. 308-10; Mozart also played with the idea to set it to music; Questa, *Semiramide redenta*, p. 45 n. 16.

98. Don Neville, 'Semiramide riconosciuta', in *NGDO*, IV, pp. 310-11; see also Questa, *Semiramide redenta*, pp. 39-69.

99. Don Neville, 'Metastasio [Trapassi], Pietro', in *NGDO*, III, pp. 351-60; *idem*, 'Semiramide riconosciuta', in *NGDO*, IV, pp. 310-11.

100. Reinhard Strohm, *Die italienische Oper im 18. Jahrhundert* (Taschenbücher zur Musikwissenschaft, 25; Wilhelmshaven: Heinrichshofen, 1979), pp.11-15.

101. For analysis of Metastasio's libretto, see Questa, *Semiramide redenta*.

tion opera for Maria Theresa in 1743, and in 1748 Gluck was commissioned to compose a new *Semiramide riconosciuta* for the celebration of the peace treaty of Aix-la-Chapelle on the occasion of Maria Theresa's birthday. The war that was supposed to end with this treaty began after Maria Theresa's accession to the throne in 1740 with several monarchs not accepting female succession but claiming their own right to the Austrian succession. The figure of Semiramis was considered a politically appropriate allegory whose status as first reigning queen in history was comparable to Maria Theresa's as first female ruler of the Austrian empire. That the gender of a ruler is irrelevant is expressed in the final scene of *Semiramide riconosciuta*: when discovering that Semiramis, who throughout the opera reigns disguised in men's clothes as king Ninus, is in reality a woman, the chorus jubilantly sings 'live happy and be our queen, just as you have been our king so far'.[102] This homage is meant for Maria Theresa.

In the second half of the eighteenth-century Semiramis is primarily represented in opera whereas painters and their patrons were less interested in this theme. Changing tastes in decorating residences may be responsible, but the decline in numbers of Semiramis pictures may also be connected to the demise of Old Testament heroines from the pictorial repertoire in the wake of the anti-biblical Enlightenment philosophers.

1.4. *Semiramis in the 'Age of Orientalism'*

Semiramis continued to be a popular theme in opera; several were composed in the first quarter of the nineteenth century, e.g., by Cimarosa in 1799, Antonio Portugal (*La morte di Semiramide*, 1801), Charles-Simon Catel in 1802 (Paris Opéra), Meyerbeer in 1819, and Rossini in 1823.[103] For Giacomo Meyerbeer personal reasons—he discovered an affinity between his own situation as a German Jew living in Italy and Semiramis' life as a Babylonian immigrant in Assyria—made him choose Metastasio's libretto; it was very successful until it was replaced in 1823 by Rossini's *Semiramide*.[104]

Queen Victoria's accession to the British throne in 1837 prompted a renewed debate on female rulers; many saw it as a 'glaring anomaly'.[105] Victoria her-

102. Gerhard Croll, 'Glucks Debüt am Burgtheater', *Österreichische Musikzeitschrift* 31 (1976), pp. 194-202; Don Neville, 'Metastasio'; Questa, *Semiramide redenta*.

103. Osborne, 'Semiramide'; Neville, 'Semiramide riconosciuta'; Sylvan Suskin, 'Catel, Charles-Simon', in *NGDO*, I, pp. 772-74; David Cranmer, 'Portugal [Portugallo], Marcos Antonio', in *NGDO*, I, p. 1075.

104. Rainer Zimmermann, *Giacomo Meyerbeer: Eine Biographie nach Dokumenten* (Berlin: Henschel, 1991), pp. 103-107. In Metastasio's *Semiramide riconosciuta* (Semiramis Rediscovered) Semiramis is an Egyptian princess who falls in love, elopes with and marries an Indian prince. Her husband wants to kill her because an Iago-like intrigant tells him she is unfaithful. She flees to Assyria where she marries Ninus. She becomes queen and after many adventures and intrigues she is at the end reunited with her first husband (Neville, 'Semiramide riconosciuta').

105. Gail T. Houston, 'Reading and Writing Victoria: The Conduct Book and Legal Constitu-

self felt like a man when saluting her troops, and she and her consort Albert 'viewed themselves as exceptions to gender rules'.[106] Numerous new compendia of famous women were published, among them 'role model anthologies' following narrative conventions which include women transgressing gender codes for which Semiramis among others served as a warning example.[107] Such compendia of biographies still re-appear from time to time; one of the last was published in 1988.[108] In *The Way We Live Now* (1875) Anthony Trollope makes a satirical reference to such anthologies with 'Criminal Queens', a book written by the untalented but ambitious writer Lady Carbury who, in a letter addressed to a potential reviewer of her book, writes that 'the sketch of Semiramis is at any rate spirited, though I had to twist it about a little to bring her in guilty'.[109]

Gender, sexuality, and the place of women in the polity were widely debated in the nineteenth century; extremely controversial theories were discussed in all segments of society. According to the nineteenth-century ideal of the 'respectable woman', largely constructed by men belonging to the bourgeoisie and adopted by the aristocracy, she should be a faithful, loyal, nourishing, and supportive wife and mother, an ideal entwined with the concept of a nation embodied by female allegorical figures.[110] Towards the end of the century more and more women contradicted this ideal, fought for emancipation, better education, and voting rights; also the number of women working outside the home increased.[111]

tion of Female Sovereignty', in *Remaking Queen Victoria* (ed. Margaret Homans and Adrienne Munich; Cambridge Studies in Nineteenth-Century Literature and Culture, 10; Cambridge: Cambridge University Press, 1997), pp. 159-81 (163-64); *idem*, *Royalties: The Queen and Victorian Writers* (Victorian Literature and Culture Series; Charlottesville, VA and London: University Press of Virginia, 1999).

106. Houston, 'Reading and Writing Victoria', pp. 168-69.

107. Alison Booth, 'Illustrious Company: Victoria among Other Women in Anglo-American Role Model Anthologies', in *Remaking Queen Victoria*, pp. 59-76. In 'An Ode Written for the Coronation of Victoria' by Martin Farquhar Tupper (1810–89) Semiramis directly addresses Queen Victoria (published in *Jubilate!* [London, 1887]). For this reference, I thank Lisa Hopkins.

108. Antonia Fraser, *The Warrior Queens: Boadicea's Chariot* (London: George Weidenfeld & Nicholson, 1988). There are also numerous fictional Semiramis biographies and plays by little known nineteenth- and twentieth-century authors. In *Semiramis*, published in 1931 (Zürich, Leipzig, Wien: Amalthea Verlag), the author Gräfin Stephanie Üchtritz-Amade describes in the preface how she learned the 'truth about Semiramis' whom she intended to portray as a beautiful, blond-haired heroine in a dream where Semiramis appeared as a brown (haired), energetic woman with dark shadows under her eyes, wearing make-up and rather colorful, exotic clothes, her smile that of a wild beast of prey (pp. 6-7). Such descriptions, and also pictures of Oriental women, are typical anti-Semitic stereotypes.

109. Anthony Trollope, *The Way We Live Now* (ed. John Andrew Sutherland; Oxford World's Classics; Oxford: Oxford University Press, 1999 [1875]), pp. 1-2, 484 n. 1.1.

110. George L. Mosse, *Nationalism and Sexuality: Respectability and Abnormal Sexuality in Modern Europe* (New York: Howard Fertig, 1997 [1985]).

111. Generally, see *A History of Women in the West*, IV: *Emerging Feminism from Revolution*

Literary references to Semiramis reflect these changes. For example, in William Thackeray's *Vanity Fair* (1848), Miss Pinkerton, the head-mistress of an 'academy for young ladies' is introduced as 'that majestic lady, the Semiramis of Hammersmith'. This woman of 'high position' stands for 'eminent virtues', described as being 'calm', 'dignified', 'austere', 'godlike', 'pompous', and 'tedious'. Throughout the first chapter Thackeray refers to Miss Pinkerton variously as Semiramis or Minerva, both examples of *Femmes Forte*, but he is sarcastically ambivalent by alluding to Miss Pinkerton's 'masculine' authoritative behavior and learnedness. Thus the Semiramis metaphor is reduced to its 'masculine' aspect, but also has an indirect Oriental reference because Miss Pinkerton wears a 'large solemn turban'.[112]

Semiramis was so well known she could be mentioned in passing as in Alexandre Dumas' *The Black Tulip* (1850),[113] or used as a doll's name in Louisa M. Alcott's classic children's book *Little Men: Life at Plumfield with Jo's Boys* (1871).[114] Emilio Botta cited Semiramis in a letter to a French official as a reason to ask for more finances for his excavation.[115] Walter Scott refers to her in his description of the ideal Christian wife:[116]

> in the mirror of human history Woman is reflected with many colors and shades of character. Sometimes like Lucretia and Penelope, we see her virtuous and of unshaken fidelity; like Zenobia, learned; or fair as the Queen of Scots, or Helen, or Esther. Perhaps, like Judith, brave, or Deborah, or the wife Jael. It may be she sits upon a throne of kingdoms, and like Semiramis, and Cleopatra, and Elizabeth, and Victoria, wields the rod of empire…
>
> But where in life is her loveliness more appreciated, or her excellence better felt, or the complement of her destiny so completely filled up, as when at home she is seen, at early morn or dewy eve, a Christian wife approaching the beloved and honored object of her heart's dearest affections—her own husband—with the book of God, the holy Bible in her hand, that he may read and pray!

Scott continues that the 'Christian Wife' 'is the true glory of the United States' and 'the strength of the Republic—the sure foundation of our Highest national gran-

to World War (ed. Geneviève Fraisse and Michelle Perrot; Cambridge, MA and London: The Belknap Press of Harvard University Press, 1993).

112. William Makepeace Thackeray, *Vanity Fair* (Penguin English Library, EL35; Harmondsworth: Penguin Books, 1968 [1848]), pp. 39-55 (chapters 1 and 2).

113. Alexandre Dumas, *The Black Tulip* (ed. David Coward; The World's Classics; Oxford: Oxford University Press, 1993 [*La tulipe noire*, Paris, 1850]), p. 157.

114. Louisa May Alcott, *Little Men: Life at Plumfield with Jo's Boys* (London: Puffin Books, Penguin Group, 1994), p. 248.

115. Mogens Trolle Larsen, *The Conquest of Assyria: Excavations in an Antique Land 1840–1860* (London and New York: Routledge, 1996), p. 28; see also McCall, 'Rediscovery and Aftermath', in Dalley (ed.), *Legacy of Mesopotamia*, pp. 183-213 (198).

116. W. Scott, 'The Christian Wife at Home', *The Protestant Unionist* 1/1, Wednesday, September 25 (1844). http://www.mun.ca/rels/restmov/texts/wscott/tpu1844/TCWAT.HTM (viewed 1/29/06).

deur—the secret spring of our boundless prosperity... Ye daughter of Columbia—mother of great men—be such a woman'. Scott's 'call to the arms' directed at women is an example of how nationalism interacts with sexuality.[117]

Paintings of heroic Semiramis belonged to court culture and were largely commissioned for decoration of castles and palaces,[118] but most distinguished nineteenth-century artists either took commissions only for portraits or otherwise chose themes themselves. Paintings of warrior queens were not *en vogue*, however, it is surprising that Semiramis does not figure among the lurid women or so-called whores of Babylon, a favorite subject with nineteenth-century artists, because a number of these were previously represented in series of *femmes fortes* or heroines.[119]

Among the numerous paintings with an Oriental theme discussed by Frederick M. Bohrer only one features Semiramis: Edgar Degas' *Semiramis Building Babylon* dated between 1859 and 1861 (see fig. 26 above).[120] Bohrer notes that although Degas' notebooks contain a number of drawings of Assyrian art that he studied in the Louvre, his Semiramis painting exhibits just 'a certain ancient Near Eastern currency in artistic discourse, a degree of reference with little consistent visual definition to articulate it'.[121] The most obvious 'reference' for the Near Eastern archaeologist is the frieze-like composition, horizontal frame, profile view, Assyrianized chariot on the right edge, and Semiramis' headdress reminiscent of headdresses worn by Assyrian kings. Degas was also influenced by Egyptian and ancient Greek art.[122]

117. See Mosse, *Nationalism and Sexuality*; Andrew Parker, Mary Russo, Doris Sommer and Patricia Yaeger, 'Introduction', in their *Nationalisms and Sexualities* (New York and London: Routledge, 1992). See also Bran Dijkstra, *Idols of Perversity: Fantasies of Feminine Evil in Fin-de-Siècle Culture* (New York and Oxford: Oxford University Press, 1986), pp. 3-24.

118. The decoration of the *Salon de Venus* in the *Grand Appartement* of Louis XIV in Versailles contains a painting by René-Antoine Housse depicting *Nabuchodonosor et Sémiramis font élever les jardins de Babylone* (Claire Constans, *Les peintures* [3 vols.; Paris: Editions de la Réunion des musées nationaux, 1995], I, p. 472 no. 2669). *Scenes from the History of Semiramis* by an unknown painter originally decorated a Flemish palace (Musée Ingres, Mantauban/France [Collections du musée Ingres, *Les peintures anciennes, XIVe-XVIIe siècles*, no. 231]).

119. E.g., Semiramis does not feature in the relevant chapters in Dijkstra, *Idols of Perversity*, pp. 352-401.

120. Frederick N. Bohrer, *Orientalism and Visual Culture: Imagining Mesopotamia in Nineteenth-Century Europe* (Cambridge and New York: Cambridge University Press, 2003); see also *idem*, 'Inventing Assyria: Exoticism and Reception in Nineteenth-Century England and France', in this volume. Degas' painting is given slightly varying titles, I found: *Semiramis Constructing a Town (or City, or Babylon); Semiramis Founding a City (or Babylon), Semiramis Rebuilding Babylon.* According to Roy McMullen, *Degas: His Life, Times, and Work* (London: Secker & Warburg, 1985), p. 94, *Semiramis Building Babylon* is the correct title.

121. Bohrer, *Orientalism and Visual Culture*, pp. 88-89; according to Henrietta McCall, 'Rediscovery and Aftermath', p. 204, Degas' *Semiramis* 'owed nothing to the sculptures in the Louvre'.

122. Phoebe Pool, 'The History Pictures of Edgar Degas and their Background', *Apollo*

Figure 51. Edgar Degas, detail of *Semiramis Building Babylon*. After Lemoisne, *Degas et son œuvre* (1946), I, fig. facing p. 42.

Degas' *Semiramis* is also discussed by Zainab Bahrani in the context of Orientalist representations of women. Bahrani juxtaposes Degas' painting to Fernand Knopf's *Ishtar*—an image of a nude whose hips and thighs fuse into serpents that was designed as a cover for Péladan's play *Ishtar*. According to Bahrani, Degas' *Semiramis* stands 'on the other side of the spectrum of historical Orientalism' because she 'is an almost genderless figure in a scene where Babylon is depicted

(October 1964), pp. 308, 310-11; Eugénie de Keyser, *Degas: Réalité et métaphore* (Publications d'histoire de l'art et d'archéologie de l'Université catholique de Louvain, 25; Louvain-la-Neuve: Institut supérieur d'archéologie et d'histoire de l'art, 1981), pp. 23, 27, 40, 70, 83; Geneviève Monnier, 'La genèse d'une œuvre de Degas: *Sémiramis construisant une ville*', *Revue du Louvre et des Musées de France* 28 (1978), pp. 407-26 (409-10); for the recent discussion of this painting, see Jill De Vonyar and Richard Kendall, *Degas and the Dance* (New York: Harry N. Abrams, in association with the American Federation of Arts, 2002), pp. 45-47.

as a city founded by a woman', and that her entourage of women makes this scene appears to be a 'Sapphic Orient where gendered norms are inverted' (there is the face of a bearded man among the women; fig. 51).[123] Further, Bahrani suggests that one may speculate whether Degas did not include a horse in a very prominent position in the foreground as a reference to Pliny's statement about Semiramis' intercourse with a horse.[124] The source for Pliny's remark (*equum adamatum a samiramide usque in coitum iuba auctor est*)[125] is not very reliable because it is the Roman educated Juba II, king of Mauretania (25 BCE–23 CE) who among other topics wrote about Assyria.[126] Lord Byron ridiculed this story attributed to 'calumniated Queen Semiramis' in *Don Juan* (Canto V 60,8 and 61):

> That injured Queen, by chroniclers so coarse,
> Has been accused (I doubt not by conspiracy)
> Of an improper friendship for her horse,
> (Love like religion sometimes runs to heresy);
> This monstrous tale had probably its source
> (For such exaggerations here and there I see)
> In printing 'Courser' [= warhorse] by mistake for 'Courier':
> I wish the case would come before a jury here.

That Degas' representation of Semiramis alludes to her dark sides is also proposed by Eugénie de Keyser (not quoted by Bahrani). Keyser suggests that Semiramis' crimes are masked by the harmony and calm conveyed by the painting and goes on to say (my translation) that Semiramis' feminine sweetness and grace are deceptive, a lure.[127] On the contrary, Norma Broude sees in Semiramis a serene, contemplative figure and argues that Degas 'dealt thematically with aspects of behavior and personality in women that were normally not encouraged for them in his society. He presented, in historical terms, possibilities for female independence, and he extolled the creative powers of women'.[128]

The theme of the painting is unique and there has been much discussion about Degas' source of inspiration. Several scholars suggest Rossini's opera performed

123. See Monnier, 'La genèse d'une œuvre de Degas', p. 408, fig. 55 (study).

124. Zainab Bahrani, *Women of Babylon: Gender and Representation in Mesopotamia* (London and New York: Routledge, 2001), p. 176. Degas was one of the best educated painters of his generation, and he also read widely. His source for *Semiramis Building Babylon* might have been Diodorus, Plutarch, or Strabo rather than other classical or Christian authors, see also Pool, 'History Pictures of Edgar Degas', p. 310.

125. Pliny, *Naturalis Historia*, 8.68.

126. Duane W. Roller, *The World of Juba II and Kleopatra Selene: Royal Scholarship on Rome's African Frontier* (Routledge Classical Monographs; New York and London: Routledge, 2003), pp. 237-38.

127. Keyser, *Degas*, p. 70; for discussion of historical paintings of Degas, see Carol M. Armstrong, *Odd Man Out: Readings of the Work and Reputation of Edgar Degas* (Texts and Documents; Los Angeles: The Getty Research Institute, 2003), pp. 101-20 (unfortunately, Armstrong's analysis does not include the Semiramis painting).

128. Norma Broude, 'Degas's "Misogyny"', *ArtB* 59 (1977), p. 101.

in a new French version at the Paris Opéra on 9 July 1860.[129] However, neither the libretto nor the Paris Opéra stage setting is reflected in Degas painting. Jil De Vonyar and Richard Kendall argue that the painting emerged 'out of a complex dialogue with a topical theme, perhaps offering a rebuke to the excesses of the Opéra and its extravagant characterizations'.[130] The drawings Degas made in preparation for the *Semiramis* painting show he was strongly influenced by Piero della Francesca's Queen of Saba fresco in San Francisco in Arezzo which Degas saw in 1858.[131]

Figure 52. Piero della Francesca, detail of fresco cycle *La Leggenda della Via Croce*: *Adorazione del sacro legno* (queen of Saba), between 1447–52, San Francesco, Arezzo. Courtesy of Ministero per i Beni e le Attività Culturali—Soprintendenza per I Beni Architettonici e per il Paesaggio, per il Patrimonio Storico, Artistico et Etnoantropologico per la Provincia di Arezzo.

It may not have been accidental that the referential painting represents the queen of Saba because in *femmes fortes* cycles Semiramis and the queen of

129. Richard Osborne, *Rossini* (The Master Musicians Series; London and Melbourne: J.M. Dent & Sons, 1987), p. 283; R. Osborne, 'Semiramide'. Already McMullen, *Degas*, pp. 94-95, argued that Degas' *Semiramis* does not 'illustrate' Rossini's opera because Babylon already exists when the curtain rises.

130. De Vonyar and Kendall, *Degas and the Dance*, pp. 45-47.

131. Piero della Francesca, *L'opera completa di Piero della Francesca* (ed. Oreste Del Buono and Pierluigi De Vecchi; Classici dell'arte: Biblioteca universale delle arti figurative, 9; Milano: Rizzoli, 1967), p. 93, fig. 15b; Monnier, 'La genèse d'une œuvre de Degas', p. 410, fig. 58; Pool, 'History Pictures of Edgar Degas', p. 310. Degas spent about three years in Italy from 1856 to 1859.

Saba were interchangeable. Degas' preliminary sketches for Semiramis also show he experimented with the figure of Semiramis, various urban views, and the positions of the horses. The final painting resulting from one of the sketches (fig. 53) shows two horses, one in the foreground in front of the chariot that covers the body of the second horse.[132]

Figure 53. Edgar Degas, study for *Semiramis Building Babylon*, Musée du Louvre, Cabinet des Dessins, Paris. After Monnier, 'La genése d'une œuvre de Degas' (1978), p. 424 fig. 52.

I doubt that the horse attached in front of the chariot represents the sex object of Semiramis as others have suggested. Similarly, two horses are also depicted in Piero della Francesca's painting, (fig. 52), where the one in the foreground covers a second horse where only the head is visible.

Degas may allude to the political situation in France which would explain the choice of the unusual subject of *Semiramis Building Babylon.*[133] Several similarities can be seen between Semiramis and empress Eugénie: both were beautiful and strong-willed, both were regents (Eugénie was regent of France while Napoleon III commanded the French army during Italy's war of independence in 1859) and both liked power. Eugénie would have liked to remain regent and when Napoleon III became sick, she suggested to him that he abdicate and make her regent for their young son.[134] *Semiramis Building Babylon* may also

132. Edgar Degas: study for *Semiramis Building Babylon*, Musée du Louvre, Cabinet des Dessins, Paris; see Monnier, 'La genése d'une œuvre de Degas', p. 424, fig. 52.

133. To my knowledge, the only other painting showing Semiramis in the context of building construction is that of René-Antoine Houasse in Versailles (see above n. 118).

134. Jean Autin, *L'impératrice Eugénie, ou, L'empire d'une femme* (Mesnil-sur-l'Estrée:

allude to the rebuilding of Paris by Baron Georges Hausmann between 1852 and 1870.[135] Rather than an example of 'historical Orientalism', Degas' *Semiramis* marks the end of a long tradition of symbolic representations of Semiramis and is a tribute to the art and influence of Piero della Francesca and—with an ironic touch (for which Degas was known)—to the contemporary empress and the imperial project of rebuilding Paris.

Although the Semiramis subject ceased to interest important painters,[136] this was not the case with poets and composers. Ottorino Resphigi composed a *Semirâma* (1908–10);[137] the German Nobel prize winner (1910) Paul Heyse wrote a tragedy *Die Tochter der Semiramis* (The Daughter of Semiramis); Hugo von Hofmannsthal worked fifteen years on the Semiramis theme, a potential libretto Richard Strauss hoped to set to music but Hofmannsthal never finished it;[138] and Paul Valéry and Arthur Honegger created a 'ballet-melodrama' sometimes referred to as 'opera' (see below). More recently, in 1992, the renowned German poet Hans Magnus Enzensberger wrote a Semiramis drama based on Calderón's *La hija del air*.[139] By adding the theme of sexual adventures avoided by Calderón, Enzensberger attempts to save Calderón's drama for contemporary theater[140] and thus creates another Semiramis representation focusing on the woman-power-sexuality theme.

Less well known is Josephin Péladan who, among other plays, wrote a *Sémiramis* drama he describes as a re-interpretation of the legend, which was intended to 'show in Nineveh's martial and harsh (environment) the love in the heart of a woman without a plot, built upon the psychological art of Racine'.[141] The rarely performed drama first opened in 1904 or 1905 in the amphitheater in Nimes in a setting reminiscent of Assyrian palaces (fig. 54). Péladan's interest

Fayard, 1990), for Eugénie's regency, see pp. 162-69; Otto Friedrich, *Olympia: Paris in the Age of Manet* (New York: HarperCollins, 1992), pp. 65-66, 68.

135. During her regency, Eugénie supported and approved (against strong opposition) Baron Georges Hausmann's plans to extend the limits of Paris (Autin, *L'impératrice Eugenie*, p. 164).

136. After Degas, the best known representations of Semiramis are three neo-classical sculptures by William Wetmore Story (in the Dallas Museum of Art, Los Angeles County Museum, and Pennsylvania Academy of the Fine Arts). For Story's sculptures of 'heroines', see Theodore E. Stebbins, *The Lure of Italy: American Artists and the Italian Experience, 1760–1914* (Boston: Museum of Fine Arts, in association with Harry N. Abrams, 1992), p. 72.

137. John C.G. Waterhouse, 'Respighi, Ottorino', *NGDO*, III, p. 1295.

138. Hugo von Hofmannsthal, *Sämtliche Werke*. VI. *Dramen 4* (ed. Hans-Georg Dewitz; Frankfurt a.M.: S. Fischer, 1995), pp. 105-56.

139. Hans Magnus Enzensberger, *Die Tochter der Luft: Ein Schauspiel nach dem Spanischen des Calderón de la Barca* (Frankfurt a.M.: Suhrkamp, 1992).

140. Enzensberger, *Die Tochter der Luft*, pp. 125-30.

141. Joséph(in) Péladan, *Semiramis* (trans. Emil Schering; Peladans Werke, 2; München: G. Müller, 1918), p. xix-xx (preface to German edition); the only French version available to me is an edition without preface: Péladan, *Sémiramis: Tragédie en quatre actes représentée le 23 juillet 1905 pour l'inauguration du Theâtre Antique de la Nature à Champigny-la-Bataille* (Paris: Société du Mercure de France, 1905).

in ancient art is also evident in the image on the cover of the playbill that depicts a female figure with a so-called Assyrian *Mauerkrone* (fig. 55).[142]

Figure 54. Stage setting of first performance of Péladan's *Sémiramis* in the amphitheater at Nimes on 24 July 1904. After Péladan, *Semiramis* (1918).

Figure 55. Cover-page of Péladan, *Sémiramis, Theatre antique de la Nature Champigny, 23 juillet 1905* (Paris, 1905).

142. I found various dates for the first and probably only performance of Péladan's *Semiramis*.

Also unsuccessful was *Sémiramis* by Arthur Honegger and Paul Valéry, created for Ida Rubinstein, the beautiful actress, dancer and patron of the arts.[143] It remains unclear from available documents whether Rubinstein or Valéry choose the theme; however, the resulting *Gesamtkunstwerk*[144] with ballet, pantomime, speech, singing, orchestral music, elaborate stage sets and costumes suited Rubinstein's talent and ambitions as well as Valéry's theoretical ideas about theater.[145] The music by Arthur Honegger was commissioned by Ida Rubinstein and *Sémiramis* was first performed in 1934 in the Paris Opéra with Rubinstein playing and dancing Semiramis. Its fiasco was blamed by Honegger on the French theaters and Parisian audience, but the composer also mentioned lack of 'leisure to complete' the work.[146] After Honegger's death in 1955 his widow forbade performances and in 1992 his daughter withdrew publication permission of the score. The music for *Sémiramis*, according to Honegger-specialist Harry Halbreich, counts among Honegger's best works and is characterized by 'seductive orchestral sensuality' and 'Orientalism'.[147]

143. In a letter to Honegger, Valéry refers to '*notre Ida*' (Paul Sacher Foundation, Honegger archive). From the few letters of Valéry in the Paul Sacher Foundation (Basel) it is obvious that pleasing Ida Rubinstein was Honegger's primary task. Ida first appeared in Paris in 1909 in Diaghelev's 'scandalous' *Cléopatra*. She later left the *Ballet Russe* to form her own company of which she was director and principal star. One of the dancers wrote that she was an 'enigmatic personality of compelling appearance'...'we had the feeling of being in a company run by an Electress of some principality for her own amusement'. Honegger's collaboration with Rubinstein began in 1925; before *Sémiramis*, Rubinstein had commissioned four compositions by him. Rubinstein had particular demands for her own roles which also concerned music, and she had a decided preference for classical and tragic heroines dying a violent death. She may have had an interest in the ancient Near East as her yacht was christened 'Ishtar'. See Arthur Honegger, *I am a Composer* (trans. Wilson O. Clough and Allan Arthur Willman; London: Faber & Faber, 1966), pp. 108-109; Harry Halbreich, *Arthur Honegger* (trans. Roger Nichols; Portland, OR: Amadeus Press, 1999), pp. 25, 104-105, 474; Michael De Cossart, *Ida Rubinstein (1885–1960): A Theatrical Life* (Liverpool Historical Studies, 2; Liverpool: Liverpool University Press, 1987).

144. *Gesamtkunstwerk* according to Valéry differs from Wagner's concept in that the different artistic disciplines should remain independent and have equal importance; see Paul Valéry, *The Collected Works of Paul Valéry.* 3. *Plays* (ed. Jackson Mathews; Bollingen Series, 45; New York: Pantheon Books, 1960), pp. 265-68 (preface to Sémiramis).

145. Francis Fergusson, 'The Theater of Paul Valéry', in *Collected Works of Paul Valéry*, pp. vii-xix.

146. Valéry, *Collected Works of Paul Valéry*, pp. 373-74; Honegger, *I am a Composer*, p. 109.

147. H. Halbreich, *L'oeuvre d'Arthur Honegger: Chronologie, catalogue raisonné, analyses, discographie* (Paris: Honoré Champion, 1994), pp. 666-76; *idem*, *Arthur Honegger*, pp. 25, 104, 620. Marcel Delannoy, *Honegger* (Geneva and Paris: Slatkine, nouvelle édition, 1986), p. 134, writes about the music, that it is 'la lascivité assyrienne. Avec les chœurs, un lourd parfum monte des fameux jardins suspenduc. L'érotisme musical d'un Florent Schmitt [1870–1958, French composer] sauterait ici sur l'occasion. Mais Honegger préfère agir par un sombre envoûtement'. For Orientalism in music, see John M. MacKenzie, *Orientalism: History, Theory, and the Arts* (Manchester and New York: Manchester University Press, 1995), pp. 138-75 (MacKenzie does

Female power is the central theme of Valéry's *Sémiramis*, who desired that 'the music should create an atmosphere of power and sovereign pride'.[148] Perhaps Ida Rubinstein's personality inspired Valéry representation of Semiramis, a theme also of one of his early poems.[149] About his libretto Valéry wrote, he 'borrowed little more from the fable...than its title and a few broad features', and that the 'argument is one of the simplest'. But what follows consternates: after a victory over neighboring kings, triumphant Semiramis strides—like Assyrian rulers depicted on Assyrian wall reliefs—over captives covering the floor; caught by the beauty of one captive, Semiramis chooses him as lover to whom in love-making she behaves 'like a woman'. His male pride, however, demands her subjugation and he treats her with brutality and like a slave to which she reacts with outrage and kills him. In the final act Semiramis must die because she has loved; an ecstatic Semiramis longs to vanish into the supernatural, a wish fulfilled by the Sun who consumes her; nothing remains but a bare altar gleaming in the sun. Although Valéry considers his plot largely a product of his imagination, he suggests that 'set, accessories, and costumes be inspired by the archaeological documents'.[150] A substantial part of the play consists of descriptive, detailed instructions for stage settings, actor-dancers and the composer with the intention to present to the audience 'a single coherent structure of sounds, images, and meanings'. Some of these instructions read like descriptions of Neo-Assyrian art.[151]

Central to Valéry's narrative—as in previous representations of Semiramis—is the 'woman-power' theme from the viewpoint of a man.[152] The cause of the failure of this 'music-drama' was, as Francis Fergusson points out, a problem inherent in Valéry librettos characterized by 'a tension between the theoretical ideal and the perversity of the human image, which the public and all too human medium of the theater continually threatens to reveal'.[153]

According to Edward Said, Valéry's works are 'secondhand abstractions' of the Orient, and Valéry himself an Orientalist. As evidence Said cites Valéry:

> We owe to the Orient all the beginnings of our arts and of a great deal of our knowledge...if something new is coming out of there...I very much doubt. Besides, the real question in such matters is to *digest*. But that has always been...the great spe-

not discuss Honegger but some of his contemporaries). The only recording of Honegger's *Sémiramis* is an edited and shortened version performed by Leopold Hager and the Orchestre symphonique de RTL (*Timpani* 1 C 1916).

148. Fergusson, 'Theater of Paul Valéry', pp. xi-xi.

149. P. Valéry, *Poésies* (Collection Soleil, 54; Paris: Gallimard, 22nd edn, 1942), pp. 58-63 (*Air de Sémiramis* from *Album de vers anciens, 1891–93*).

150. Valéry, *Collected Works of Paul Valéry*, pp. 265-70 (preface to *Sémiramis*).

151. Valéry, *Collected Works of Paul Valéry*, pp. 272-309: *Sémiramis*.

152. Apparently Valéry's representation of Semiramis is just one manifestation of his complex notions about women and art; see Anne Mairesse, *Figures de Valéry* (Critiques littéraires; Paris: L'Harmattan, 2000), pp. 213-75 ('Valéry *fait* femme'), p. 260 (on Semiramis).

153. Fergusson, 'Theater of Paul Valéry', p. xiii.

> cialty of the European mind through the ages. Our role is therefore to maintain this power of choice, of universal comprehension, of the transformation of everything into our own substance, powers which have made us what we are. The Greeks and the Romans showed us how to deal with the monsters of Asia, how to treat them by analysis, how to extract their quintessence.[154]

Whether Valéry intended to 'deal with the monsters of Asia' in *Sémiramis* is not mentioned in his preface where he explains his wish that the first episode (armored Semiramis as triumphant queen with chained prisoners of war and other spoils of victory) 'might have a certain *universal meaning*' (my italics), ...recalls and makes manifest to the eye the character of wars between ancient peoples, which were often thought of as duels between rival deities. Yet it may be regarded as illustrating the thought that all great conflicts are conflicts of belief'.[155] Valéry does not elaborate on the meaning of the rest of his drama but for the reader the central theme is man's fear of powerful woman.

Valéry's inspirational sources for *Sémiramis* include Assyrian art, in particular in his instructions for stage setting, costumes, and attributes.[156] The ending, Semiramis being burned by the sun, could have been inspired by Dante's Semiramis in hell if it was not followed by her rising in the form of vapor which act alludes to Semiramis' metamorphosis described by Diodorus, the difference being that instead of living on as a bird she vanishes completely. Valéry explains that this is 'the necessary end of a fabulous destiny. Men will not believe that she ever existed'.[157] This statement is puzzling but any interpretations go beyond the scope of this paper.[158]

The history of representations of the figure of Semiramis shows how prevalent beliefs or individual views influence interpretation of sources as well as re-representation. Since antiquity, Semiramis was a construct with multivalent meaning for theoreticians, historians, writers, poets, composers, politicians, female monarchs, and artists with varied purpose and intention regarding gender, power, sexuality, as well as other themes such as strength, ambition,

154. Quoted from Said, *Orientalism*, pp. 250-51.

155. Valéry, *Collected Works of Paul Valéry*, pp. 268-69.

156. Said interprets works as autonomous entities without any sustained consideration of the intentions of the individual participants involved in the creation of an artwork (e.g., for *Sémiramis* these were Arthur Honegger, Ida Rubinstein, and Paul Valéry) which leads to gross misinterpretations; see also the critique by Paul John Frandsen, 'Aida and Edward Said: Attitudes and Images of Ancient Egypt and Egyptology', in *Assyria and Beyond: Studies Presented to Mogens Trolle Larsen* (ed. J.G. Dercksen; NINOL, 100; Leiden: Nederlands Instituut voor het Nabije Oosten, 2004), pp. 205-27 (225). Frandsen also remarks that, as Said's quotations are often cited out of context, he has 'overstepped the bounds of fairness' (p. 212).

157. Valéry, *Collected Works of Paul Valéry*, p. 309.

158. An aspect I do not discuss here are the various deaths invented for Semiramis. The specific meaning that 'death of a queen' has in literature is discussed by Peter-André Alt, *Der Tod der Königin: Frauenopfer und politische Souveränität im Trauerspiel des 17. Jahrhunderts* (Quellen und Forschungen zur Literatur- und Kulturgeschichte, 30; Berlin: W. de Gruyter, 2004).

weakness, tragedy, destiny, or merely beauty. Semiramis, like all female rulers represents 'exceptionality' as well as the human (female) condition. Therefore this ancient queen was evoked and cited as precedence (archetype) and *exemplum.*[159] *Exempla*, contrary to archetypes (*prototype*), intentionally present a model for others to follow. Virtue (value judgment) constitutes a quintessential element in *exempla*. This explains certain contradictions in representations of Semiramis because, as *exemplum*, she combines qualities and virtues that queens should follow, while her wanton sexual behavior could be ignored or rationalized by the precarious situation of a female sovereign. Several women writers understand Semiramis primarily as a symbol of their gender's capabilities, whereas for many men she symbolizes all they fear in the opposite gender (gynecocracy, sexual monster, a man-devouring and murdering woman). This negative image of woman trespassing the role prescribed for her gender has become a topos in the discourse of engendered Orientalism often without taking into account positive female representation as *exemplum*. Interpreting Semiramis representations as an expression of Western cultural bias, recent scholarship 're-constructs' (and misconstrues) Semiramis as just one more one-dimensional manifestation of Orientalism and epitome of Otherness.

2. *Orientalism, Assyriology, Engendering—and Semiramis*

When I sent out an email via Jack M. Sasson's mailing list in 2004 requesting information on women in our discipline from colleagues, John S. Holladay, Jr., emeritus professor in Toronto wrote back 'in general, I don't think people made such a fuss over people's gender and sexual preferences in those days as was fashionable just a few years ago. (I was hoping those days were over or fading past). My feeling on those earlier days is that it was more what they could pull off, though, undoubtedly, women had a much harder time being taken seriously and breaking through into the front pack. But lots of men had the same problem'.

Although there were several women in Assyriology and Mesopotamian archaeology before the second World War, readily-obtainable information did not suffice for a study for this volume. Of some women we know hardly more than their name and dissertation title. There are statements by some men indicating their notion about women, not only as colleagues, but I cannot attribute these to an Orientalist mindset. Nonetheless, an Orientalist attitude is detectable in some scholarly works.

159. An *exemplum* can also be an archetype, but the archetype as 'primal figure' and, contrary to the archetype as *exemplum*, exists as a 'first' and does not imply value judgment. See Régis Boyer, 'Archetypes', in *Companion to Literary Myths: Heroes and Archetypes* (ed. Pierre Brunel; trans. Wendy Allatson, Judith Hayward, Trista Selous; London and New York: Routledge, 1992), pp. 110-17 (110-14).

2.1. *Semiramis in Assyriology*

The hypothesis that Sammuramat, the 'palace woman' of the Assyrian king Šamši-Adad V (823–811) and mother of king Adad-nērārī III (810–783) was the model for Semiramis and that ancient Greek and Roman accounts reflect historical events is controversial in Assyriology.[160] However, identification of Sammuramat with Semiramis, something that, according to Giovanni Pettinato, 'today (1985) *all* scholars agree with' (my italics),[161] is reiterated in numerous works including encyclopedias that perpetuate this assumption as fact. Even relatively recently, some Assyriologists have contributed to the confusion between presumption and fact by using the name Semiramis instead of Assyrian Sammuramat as, for example, Erika Bleibtreu in an article on monuments inscribed with the names of Assyrian 'palace women',[162] or Marten Stol who refers to the 'fabulous but *very real* Semiramis' (my italics) as one of the 'powerful Assyrian queens'.[163] According to Moshe Weinfeld 'the Greek legend about Semiramis combines features of several queens and projects them upon one *glorious* woman' and 'the image of Semiramis and the legends about her *cannot be dissociated* from Sammuramat, the queen mother of Adad-nirari III, and together with those of Naqʾia/Zakūtu, the queen mother of Esarhaddon, all are clearly a product of Syro-Palestinian and Assyrian background' (my italics).[164] Stephanie Dalley and A.T. Reyes argue that 'Semiramis combined the name and historical figure of Sammuramat...with Naqia';[165] as evidence they cite the stele found in Anatolia recounting Sammuramat's deeds and cuneiform texts recording historical events presumably associated by Greek authors with Semiramis, her husband Ninus and son Ninyas.[166]

It is at least problematic to blur the borders between Assyrian records and Greco-Roman literature where historical and fictional stories are fused into a

160. For bibliography of older literature, see Giovanni Pettinato, *Semiramis: Herrin über Assur und Babylon: Biographie* (trans. Robert Steiger; Zürich: Artemis, 1988), pp. 309-10. Semiramis is listed in numerous encyclopedias and handbooks; recently, occasionally under Sammuramat.

161. Pettinato, *Semiramis*, pp. 32-33.

162. Erika Bleibtreu, 'Semiramis und andere Gemahlinnen assyrischer Könige', in *Nachrichten aus der Zeit: Ein Streifzug durch die Frauengeschichte des Altertums* (ed. Edith Specht; Reihe Frauenforschung, 18; Wien: Wiener Frauenverlag, 1992), pp. 57-72.

163. Marten Stol, 'Women in Mesopotamia', *JESHO* 39 (1995), pp. 123-44.

164. Moshe Weinfeld, 'Semiramis: Her Name and her Origin', in *Ah, Assyria...Studies in Assyrian History and Ancient Near Eastern Historiography Presented to Hayim Tadmor* (ed. Mordechai Cogan and Israel Ephʿal; Scripta hierosolymitana, 33; Jerusalem: Magnes Press, Hebrew University, 1991), pp. 99-103.

165. Dalley and Reyes, 'Mesopotamian Contact and Influence', pp. 95-96. After the completion of this article, I received an article by Stephanie Dalley, in which she discusses pre-hellenistic historical traces of the Semiramis legend: 'Semiramis in History and Legend', in *Cultural Borrowings and Ethnic Appropriations in Antiquity* (ed. Erich S. Gruen; Oriens et occidens, 8; Stuttgart: Franz Steiner, 2005), pp. 11-22.

166. Dalley and Reyes, 'Mesopotamian Contact and Influence', p. 96.

Semiramis figure. As Katherine Eggert states with regard to Shakespeare's historical dramas 'all literary work…involves remaking at least a literary, if not also a historical past'.[167] If Semiramis is an amalgam of historical Sammuramat and Naqʾia, she should be considered a fictional character modeled partly after historical figures and incorporating additional hearsay, gossip, rumors, and poetic imagination.[168]

Neo-Assyrian texts and visual arts featuring royal women are public documents;[169] in none is an Assyrian or Babylonian royal woman referred to as queen, Akkadian *šarratu*; this title only refers to the wives of rulers of Mari, Alalakh, Mitanni, Nuzi, Ugarit, Hatti, and Egypt, i.e. the wives of foreign rulers.[170] In Assyria and Babylonia some royal wives and consorts are designated 'palace woman' (MÍ.É.GAL), but this title is not exclusive to the first wife of a king, and some wives kept the title MÍ.É.GAL after the death of their husband.[171]

Of the 'royal wives' with an exceptional record, three were 'mother of the king':[172] Sammuramat, Naqʾia/Zakūtu, and Adad-guppi (possibly the prototype of Greek Nitokris); just two 'palace women' can be identified in the visual representations: Naqʾia/Zakūtu, wife of Sennacherib (704–681 BCE) and mother of Esarhaddon (680–669 BCE), and Libbāli-šarrat, the 'palace woman' of Assurbanipal (669–630 BCE).[173] Sennacherib describes another of his wives, Tašmētu-šarrat, on his palace wall at Nineveh as 'my beloved wife, whose features (the goddess) Bēlet-ilāni had made perfect above all women'.[174] Julian Reade suggests that this unusual public admiration by a king of one of his wives can be

167. Eggert, *Showing Like a Queen*, p. 132.

168. McCall, 'Rediscovery and Aftermath', p. 184; This was the case with Persian royal women; see Maria Brosius, *Women in Ancient Persia (559–331 BC)* (Oxford Classical Monographs; Oxford: Clarendon Press, 1996), pp. 1-5, 8, 9, 118-19.

169. Bleibtreu, 'Semiramis'; Sarah Chamberlin Melville, *The Role of Naqia/Zakutu in Sargonid Politics* (SAAS, 9; Helsinki: The Neo-Assyrian Text Corpus Project, 1999); idem, 'Neo-Assyrian Royal Women and Male Identity: Status as a Social Tool', *JAOS* 124 (2004), pp. 37-57; Ornan, 'The Queen in Public'.

170. *CAD* Š/II, pp. 72-75. The titles of Assyrian royal women are usually written as Sumerograms.

171. *CAD* E, p. 61, s.v. *ekallu *ša ekalli*; S. Parpola, 'The Neo-Assyrian Word for "Queen"', *SAAB* II/2 (1988), pp. 73-76.

172. The Akkadian title *ummi šarri* is often written with the Sumerogram AMA.LUGAL; *AHw*, III, pp. 1416-17 sub 2).

173. Bleibtreu, 'Semiramis'; Melville, *Role of Naqia/Zakatu*; Ornan, 'The Queen in Public'; see also Wolfgang Röllig, 'Nitokris von Babylon', in *Beiträge zur alten Geschichte und deren Nachleben: Festschrift für Franz Altheim zum 6.10.1968* (2 vols.; ed. Ruth Stiehl and Hans Erich Stier; Berlin: W. de Gruyter, 1969), I, pp. 127-35.

174. Julian E. Reade, 'Was Sennacherib a Feminist?', in *La femme dans le Proche-Orient antique: Compte rendu de la XXXIIIe Rencontre assyriologique internationale, Paris, 7-10 Juillet 1986* (ed. J.-M. Durand; Paris: Editions Recherche sur les civilisations,1987), pp. 139-45 (141).

interpreted as either that of a 'doting husband', or as a break by Sennacherib from tradition by acknowledging the support and influence of royal women.[175]

Generally Assyrian and Babylonian records remain silent about power, influence and public role of royal wives, queen mothers, and concubines. The exceptionality of their presence in text and images are indicative of the unusual role of some royal women, but whether the rare title 'mother of king' refers to status as (former) regency remains speculative.[176] Even if occasionally a queen mother may have governed as regent for her son, her rule was likely subsumed under her son's name; her name therefore would not be mentioned on most official records. This practice was also common in ancient Egypt and later in Europe. Another reason for the exclusion of female rule is its association with negative omens, which, however, indicates that women occasionally did in fact hold reigning power (the only known example is Kubaba of Kish who, according to the king-list, reigned in the third millennium).[177]

No cuneiform texts have been found that confirm sexual abuse of power, or perverse sexual behavior of royal women in Assyria or Babylonia.[178] But, contrary to ancient Egypt, ancient Mesopotamia is not as rich in monuments and names attracting public attention, compelling many Assyriologists to dispense reluctantly with their only queen imbued with popular fame. Thus Semiramis is also invoked in contexts other than studies of Neo-Assyrian queens or monarchies as, for example, in Volker Haas' study of ancient Mesopotamian eroticism and sexuality.[179] Already the title *Babylonischer Liebesgarten* serves widespread Orientalist clichés. In the preface Haas cites Semiramis stories from classical and Christian literature concerning her alleged 'monstrous' sexuality, omitting any mention of the tradition of positive model (*exemplum*). After introducing readers to ancient Mesopotamian eroticism and sexuality with stories about Semiramis' sexual excesses, Haas equates these with legends about Babylon's reputation as the capital of sexual lasciviousness. Haas' introduction contradicts his express purpose to 'familiarize' German-speaking readers with eroticism and sexuality in the '*Ancient Orient*' (my italics) by wetting their appetites with 'images of the Orient' that give credibility to biblical, classical, and medieval accounts. The book ends with a chapter on the Babylonian references in Ovid's *Metamorphoses*, thereby establishing the conceptual framework of Mesopotamian eroticism and sexuality by allusions to ancient Assyrians and Babylonians as barbarian or pagan Other. Instead of analyzing

175. Reade, 'Was Sennacherib a Feminist?', p. 141.

176. For Neo-Assyrian royal women, see now Melville, 'Neo-Assyrian Royal Women'.

177. J.M. Asher-Greve, 'Decisive Sex, Essential Gender', in Parpola and Whiting (eds.), *Sex and Gender in the Ancient Near East*, pp. 11-26 (19-20).

178. Gwendolyn Leick, *Sex and Eroticism in Mesopotamian Literature* (London: Routledge, 1994).

179. Volkert Haas, *Babylonischer Liebesgarten: Erotik und Sexualität im Alten Orient* (München: C.H. Beck, 1999).

the contexts of ancient Mesopotamian sources, Haas constructs a context of Oriental eroticism and sexuality that perpetuates generalizations about a sexualized Orient and thus is, in Said's sense, Orientalistic.[180]

The expression *Babylonischer Liebesgarten* is not exceptional in the Assyriological discourse of eroticism and sexuality that largely avoids Foucaultian, Lacanian, and gender theory. Consequently, according to Roux, Semiramis is

> un nom que peu de gens ignorant et qui, pour la plupart, évoque une reine d'Orient, légendaire et lascive, vaguement associé à Babylone et ses 'jardin suspend', …c'est une femme très belle et désiderable, sensuelle et cruélle… Une *super-femme*…double d'un super-homme un personnage *dont* l'aspect fortement androgyne.[181]

Julia Assante has analyzed such interpretations and concludes that their 'amassed authority' is rooted in 'sheer repetition, the extent of which has turned fabrication into fact', and that reiteration in popular and scholarly works is a 'form of academic sensationalism'.[182]

2.2. *Orientalism and 'Our Past'*

New interest in ancient Near Eastern cultures is apparently associated with interest in Orientalism.[183] Although Near Eastern archaeology is from its beginnings a product of British, French as well as post–1871 German imperialism, Near Eastern studies, according to Jerrold S. Cooper, were more stepchild than servant of imperialism because it did not provide any political methods of control or domination but was a beneficiary of imperialist policies.[184]

Investigation of the impact of European political and cultural developments on ancient Near Eastern scholarship began only recently. According to Matthew W. Stolper, ancient Mesopotamian civilization was treated differently from other Eastern histories because it had 'left traces in the Bible and the writings of Greece and Rome and the church fathers', and therefore was considered 'our' past.[185] Interrelation between 'our' past and ancestors and historiography

180. See Joan Goodnick Westenholz, 'Review of Volker Haas, *Babylonische Liebesgarten: Erotik und Sexualität im alten Orient* (München, 1999)', *NIN, Journal of Gender Studies in Antiquity* 2 (2001), pp. 119-32.

181. Roux, 'Sémiramis', pp. 184, 191. See also below, Bahrani's interpretation of Degas' *Semiramis* painting in *Women of Babylon*, p. 176.

182. Julia Assante, 'From Whores to Hierodules: The Historiographic Invention of Mesopotamian Female Sex Professionals', in *Ancient Art and its Historiography* (ed. Alice A. Donohue and Mark D. Fullerton; Cambridge and New York: Cambridge University Press, 2003), pp. 13-47 (14).

183. Ann C. Gunter, 'Introduction', in *The Construction of the Ancient Near East* (ed. A.C. Gunter; Culture & History, 11; Copenhagen: Akademisk Forlag, 1992), pp. 7-11 (7).

184. Jerrold S. Cooper, 'From Mosul to Manila: Early Approaches to Funding Ancient Near Eastern Studies Research in the United States', in Gunter (ed.), *Construction of the Ancient Near East*, pp. 133-64 (133-34).

185. Matthew W. Stolper, 'On Why and How', in Gunter (ed.), *Construction of the Ancient Near East*, pp. 13-22 (19).

has been analyzed by Josef Wiesehöfer in German scholars' representations of the wars between the Persians and the Greeks in the fifth century BCE.[186] Wiesehöfer shows how interpretations and re-interpretations were influenced by the predominant philosophy of history as well as political ideas and demands. The earlier negative representation of Persians was influenced by German idealization of the Greeks. Discovery of the linguistic relationship between Iranian and German languages elicited re-assessment and re-representation of Persians as members of the Aryan family, in contrast to negatively portrayed 'Semitic Orientals' held responsible for 'bastardizing' the Persians. Equally, works of ancient Near Eastern specialists were influenced by changing theory and political ideology.[187]

According to Said, 'almost from the earliest times in Europe the Orient was something more than what was empirically known about it' and he criticizes ancient Greek representation of Asia (i.e. Persians) for depicting the Orient as the hostile Other and for giving to Asia 'the feelings of emptiness, loss, and disaster that seem thereafter to reward Oriental challenges to the West; and also, the lament that in some glorious past Asia fared better, was itself victorious over Europe'.[188] The second aspect of the Orient, which Said attributes to ancient Greeks, is associated with Dionysus' Asian origin, 'the strangely threatening excesses of Oriental mysteries', and 'the eccentric god's terrible power'. Said concluded that 'Aeschylus *represents* Asia, makes her speak in the person of the aged Persian queen, Xerxes mother. It is Europe that articulates the Orient'. In his examination of the origin of representation of Otherness, Said not only totally excludes the pertinent historical background, he criticizes others for doing the same.[189]

Engendered studies focusing on interrelation between Orientalism and Assyriology are rare. An important contribution is Julia Assante's analysis of the historiography of interpretation of women associated with sex-professions. Assante argues that Westerns ideas about Oriental women influenced Assyriologists' interpretations of sexual images in art as well as translations of Sumerian

186. Josef Wiesehöfer, '"Denn es sind welthistorische Siege...": Nineteenth- and Twentieth-Century German Views of the Persian Wars', in Gunter (ed.), *Construction of the Ancient Near East*, pp. 61-83. For the interrelation between classics and politics, see also Ian Morris, 'Archaeologies of Greece', in *Classical Greece: Ancient Histories and Modern Archaeologies* (ed. I. Morris; Cambridge: Cambridge University Press, 1994), pp. 8-47.

187. J.M. Asher-Greve, 'Stepping into the Maelstrom: Women, Gender, and Ancient Near Eastern Scholarship', *NIN, Journal of Gender Studies in Antiquity* 1 (2000), pp. 1-22; J.M. Asher-Greve and A. Lawrence Asher, 'From Thales to Foucault...and Back to Sumer', in *Intellectual Life of the Ancient Near East: Papers Presented at the 43rd Rencontre assyriologique internationale, Prague, July 1-5, 1996* (ed. Jirí Prosecky; Prague: Academy of Science of the Czech Republic, Oriental Institute, 1998), pp. 29-40; Cooper, 'From Mosul to Manila', pp.133-35.

188. Said, *Orientalism*, pp. 55-56.

189. Said, *Orientalism*, p. 74.

and Akkadian terminology and texts.[190] However, there is evidence that such views also result from comparison with one's own culture. For example, the Egyptian scholar Rifāʿah Rāfiʿ al-Ṭahṭāwī, who spent five years in Paris from 1826 to 1831, describes the city as a paradise for women, purgatory for men, and hell for horses because he compared the social status of men, women and horses in France with that in his own society, concluding that French women dominate men and even horses.[191]

In nineteenth-century Europe gender and sexuality were important issues but discourse focused on Western societies' concerns about itself rather than notions about Oriental women.[192]

2.3. *'Our Past'—a Construct by Men?*

Concerning his work as an archaeologist, Seton Lloyd wrote 'one is, in a sense *making history*' (my italics).[193] What did he mean—that he discovers, un- or re-covers, or 'constructs' history? Unfortunately he never elaborated on this remark but it is highly unlikely that he meant constructing ('making') history by applying contemporary theory from diverse fields, an approach first debated much later in historical disciplines; it is more likely that he felt that history is 'made' by those who 'recover' a lost past. That ancient Mesopotamian history is a construct is implied decades later by the title of a book of essays published in 1992: *The Construction of the Ancient Near East.*[194] This title also suggests a contemporary paradigm for ancient Near Eastern studies to strengthen its appeal to students, the intended audience of this book.[195] If ancient Mesopotamia is not a concrete

190. Assante, 'From Whores to Hierodules', pp. 13-47.

191. Nina Berman, *Orientalismus, Kolonialisms und Moderne: Zum Bild des Orients in der deutschsprachigen Kultur um 1900* (Stuttgart: J.B. Metzlersche Verlagsbuchhandlung and Carl Ernst Poeschel, 1997), pp. 346-48. For Muslim views about Western woman, see also Francis Robinson in *Cambridge Illustrated History of the Islamic World* (ed. F. Robinson; Cambridge: Cambridge University Press, 1996), p. xviii. It may be unfair to compare al-Ṭahṭāwī's work with that of his contemporary Alexis de Tocqueville, but de Tocqueville gained his understanding of American society in less than a year's sojourn in the United States (for Tocqueville's voyage to the USA and the reception of his book, see André Jardin, *Tocqueville: A Biography* [trans. Lydia Davis and Robert Hemenway; London: Peter Halban, 1988], pp. 101-251, 534-36). The difference is due to the authors' intentions and audiences; al-Ṭahṭāwī reports on European customs for the entertainment of Arab readers, whereas de Tocqueville wanted to democratize French politics; however, contrary to al-Ṭahṭāwī's book which is hardly read in Europe, de Tocqueville's became a classic in the USA.

192. *History of Women, IV*; for discourses on love and sexuality, see also Peter Gay, *The Bourgeois Experience: Victoria to Freud.* I. *The Education of the Senses* (New York and Oxford: Oxford University Press, 1984); idem, *The Bourgeois Experience: Victoria to Freud.* II. *The Tender Passion* (New York and Oxford: Oxford University Press, 1986); *idem*, *The Bourgeois Experience: Victoria to Freud.* III. *The Cultivation of Hatred* (New York and London: W.W. Norton & Co., 1993).

193. Thorkild Jacobsen, 'Searching for Sumer and Akkad', in *CANE*, IV, pp. 2743-52 (2747).

194. *Construction of the Ancient Near East.*

195. Gunter, 'Introduction', in *Construction of the Ancient Near East*, p. 7.

phenomenon but a fabrication assembled (Latin: *con-struere*, 'built together') from parts, elements, and ideas, this construct could be 'deconstructed'. However, the expectations implicit in this 'post-modern' title is not fully realized in the articles, all written by men who also omit feminist critique and gender theory. The articles not only confirm that 'history is the story written by the winners' (generally men) but also continue a tradition of introductory works written by male scholars, e.g., Frankfort, Jacobsen, Kramer, Moortgat, Nissen, Oppenheim, Orthmann, Postgate, Roaf.[196] Just three written by women feature regularly in bibliographies for introductory classes: Eva Strommenger's *The Art of Mesopotamia* (London, 1964), Dominique Collon's *First Impressions* (London, 1987), and Amélie Kuhrt's *The Ancient Near East* (London, 1995).[197] Additionally, several books written by men were translated into other languages, rarely so with women's works.[198] Male scholars also wrote most books for general audiences, among them many excavators, e.g. Amiet, Andrae, Garelli, Jacobsen, Hrouda, Klengel, Koldewey, Kramer, Lloyd, Matthiae, Max von Oppenheim, Orthmann, Parrot, Woolley.[199] Several men also published autobiographies, e.g., Andrae, Delitzsch, Kramer, Lloyd, Mallowan, Parrot, Woolley. A similar picture is gained when perusing 'Studies in Honor or Memory of': whereas, for example, Albright, Birot, Frankfort, Jacobsen, Kramer (and, as an exception, Edith Porada) are honored and/or reminisced with several publications, not one is dedicated to Elizabeth Douglas van Buren who preceded Henri Frankfort as a founder of ancient Near Eastern art history and whose publications are still important in the study of ancient Near Eastern art. In general, few contributions by women to ancient Near Eastern studies, predominantly in art history, gained equal status with those of men. One reason is that women excluded from excavations and therefore from publishing excavation reports turned to analysis of the excavated artifacts.[200]

196. For a recent introductory history with a 'Guide to Further Reading', see Marc van de Mieroop, *A History of the Ancient Near East, ca. 3000–323 BC* (Blackwell History of the Ancient World, 1; Oxford: Blackwell, 2004).

197. This can be extended to editorship of important dictionaries, lexica, and series. An exception is *The Assyrian Dictionary* (*CAD*) that, following the retirement of Erica Reiner has been edited by Martha T. Roth. This is a prestigious position in Assyriology and behind the scenes I have heard a lot of derogatory remarks and criticism from men concerning the competence of both women (and occasionally their characters).

198. Eva Strommenger's *5000 Years of the Art of Mesopotamia* (trans. Christina Haglund; New York: Harry N. Abrams, 1964) is the translation of *Fünf Jahrtausende Mesopotamien* published by Hirmer Verlag (1962) and represents an exception.

199. Some women also wrote books for wider audiences: e.g., Gwendolyn Leick's several books for Routledge (London), Joan Oates' *Babylon* (Ancient Peoples and Places, 94; London: Thames & Hudson, 1979), and Stephanie Dalley's *Myths from Mesopotamia: Creation, the Flood, Gilgamesh, and Others* (Oxford and New York: Oxford University Press, 1989).

200. See, e.g., Mary Ann Levine, 'Creating their Own Niches: Career Styles among Women in Americanist Archaeology between the Wars', in *Women in Archaeology* (ed. Cheryl Claassen; Philadelphia: University of Pennsylvania Press, 1994), pp. 9-40.

2.4. *Sexualized Learning and Excavating*

'Love' has been a widely used metaphor for the motivation of scholars and excavators, thus masking personal motives such as self-interest, curiosity, banal necessity, ambition, or acquiring knowledge for status and superiority. The object of learning and research becomes a 'Beloved', a sexual metaphor comparable to the term 'love of country' associating nationalism with sexuality. Association of ideas with sexuality was not a nineteenth-century idea, according to Peter Gay; the opportunities religion provided for erotic investment through the ages were merely revised and augmented in the nineteenth century.[201] George L. Mosse argues that notions of modern nationalism also influenced the construction of bourgeois norms and sexual behavior.[202] As learning and scholarship became prestigious professions for men of the bourgeoisie, they were also invested with the appropriate norms and sexualities: professors and scholars were described as men with a desire for knowledge, loving their work as women should love men.[203] The success of these men reflected on the nation symbolized in proud motherly allegorical statues. Places where carnal desire could find fulfillment were alien spaces where professors fail, as in Heinrich Mann's *Professor Unrat*, better known as the film version *The Blue Angel.*

Associating love with learning implies desire to explore, penetrate, and possess a 'body' of knowledge like the body of a woman. The object and aim of scholarly desire is further feminized in allegorical female figures and the academic institution where 'love of learning' is pursued: 'alma mater', the nourishing, fostering mother.[204] Nourishing and fostering is traditionally the woman's task; in the academic lifestyle, women historically have been relegated to the role of helpmates of men pursuing their 'love for learning'. Feminized symbolism excluded 'real' women as men's equals which also affected the views of Assyriologists and archaeologists toward women. For instance, in his memoirs Walter Andrae recounts that when he became engaged, Robert Koldewey said that he was now lost for archaeology because an archaeologist had to be *married* to research alone. Describing his life at Assur, Andrae compares it to that of a monk but believes

201. Gay, *The Bourgeois Experience*, II, p. 312.

202. Mosse, *Nationalism and Sexuality*; see also Parker *et al.*, 'Introduction'; Joan B. Landes, *Visualizing the Nation: Gender, Representation, and Revolution in Eighteenth-Century France* (Ithaca, NY: Cornell University Press, 2001).

203. All allegories of sciences, arts, nations, countries, and cities are female figures. 'Love' for learning served numerous scholars as an excuse to withdraw from the tasks of daily life ('professor's syndrome'), and it was also appropriate for monks who could thus sublimate sexual desire with desire for knowledge. Gay, *The Bourgeois Experience*, II, argues that 'the energies that fuel the pleasures of love and its pains reach far beyond the domain normally assigned to it...that men and women construct their sublimations from materials they find ready-made around them' (p. 34), and that 'men eroticize and feminize their work' (p. 81).

204. E.g., the walls of a lecture hall at the Sorbonne in Paris are decorated with large paintings of female allegories symbolizing academic disciplines.

this 'logical and reasonable' considering the circumstances. Women are banned, stated Andrae in the late 1950s, less for the (male) archaeologist's sake than for their own, and patronizingly adds that there is much debate about women's participation in excavations and that he is not in favor of it.[205] Others also thought like Andrae. The late J.J. van Dijk told me that the best works in Assyriology were done by monks or men who lived like monks, and mentioned several who also published about women, marriage, priestess-prostitutes, and prostitution. It was not until feminist critique introduced 'situatedness' as an aspect of scholarly work that such studies were re-examined.[206]

Although women archaeologists have worked in Egypt since the late nineteenth century,[207] this was not the case at ancient Assyrian or Babylonian sites until after the second World War. Gertrude Bell worked on early Late Classical and Islamic sites, Jane Dieulafoy in Persia.[208] Few women directed an excavation. Like Thackeray's 'Semiramis of Hammersmith' those who did were often unmarried, independent, learned, competent, and authoritative (a necessity on excavations); these woman were also rather successful.[209] But women's intellect was also linked to 'loose' or 'dangerous' sexual behavior. Nietzsche wrote, 'when a woman displays scientific interest, then there is something out of order in her sexuality' and he considered women's fight for emancipation 'stupidity', 'damaging' and 'destructive'.[210]

Archaeological discovery was associated with masculine adventurousness and heroism,[211] and women like Bell were referred to as a 'masculine adventurer', a label she tried to counter through elegant dress and lady-like comportment,[212] whereas Jane Dieulafoy, the first women archaeologist in her own

205. Walter Andrae, *Lebenserinnerungen eines Ausgräbers* (Berlin: W. de Gruyter, 1961), pp. 206-207.

206. Asher-Greve, 'Stepping into the Maelstrom', pp. 1-22; Assante, 'From Whores to Hierodules'; J.G. Westenholz, 'Towards a New Conceptualization of the Female Role in Mesopotamian Society', *JAOS* 110/3 (1990), pp. 510-21; see also the essays in *Women in Archaeology*.

207. Edmund S. Meltzer, 'Egyptology', in *The Oxford Encyclopedia of Ancient Egypt* (3 vols.; ed. Donald B. Redford; Oxford: Oxford University Press), I, pp. 448-58. I thank Deborah Sweeney for this reference.

208. J.M. Asher-Greve, 'Gertrude L. Bell, 1868–1926', in *Breaking Ground: Pioneering Women Archaeologists* (ed. Getzel M. Cohen and Martha Sharp Joukowsky; Ann Arbor, MI: University of Michigan Press, 2004), pp. 142-97; Eve Gran-Aymerich, 'Jane Dieulafoy, 1851–1916', in *Breaking Ground*, pp. 34-67.

209. *Women in Archaeology*; Margaret Cool Root, 'Introduction: Women of the Field, Defining the Gendered Experience', in *Breaking Ground*, pp. 1-33.

210. Gay, *The Bourgeois Experience*, II, pp. 85-86; see also *idem*, I, pp. 69-225 ('Offensive Women and Defensive Men'); *idem*, III, pp. 288-367 ('The Powerful, Weaker Sex'); see also G. Fraisse, 'A Philosophical History of Sexual Difference', in Fraisse and Perrot (eds.), *A History of Women in the West*, IV, pp. 48-79.

211. Root, 'Introduction', p. 9.

212. Asher-Greve, 'Gertrude Bell'.

right, emphasized eccentricity by wearing men's clothes, even when attending an imperial performance in the Berlin Opera house where her masculine apparel was considered so scandalous that she could not be introduced to the emperor's wife.[213]

The presence of wives on excavation sites was unusual, angered some excavators, and resulted in derogative remarks. When John H. Haynes could no longer bear the solitude at Nippur and requested that his wife be brought, John P. Peters considered this a 'very risky matter' and suggested consideration of Cassandria A. Haynes's 'personal equation, her temperament, training', and even her 'physique'. While the men assigned to Nippur were sick and absented themselves, Mrs. Haynes remained alone with her husband for eight and a half months, including the hot summer; she took notes that provided the basis for the weekly reports to Philadelphia. During Mrs. Haynes sojourn at Nippur the 'Tablet Hill' was found and eventually Hilprecht himself came to Nippur for ten weeks. To Philadelphia he reported that Cassandria Haynes had been a bad influence and was responsible for many misunderstandings concerning the excavation. Although he credited Mrs. Haynes for making the explorers comfortable in the excavation house, Hilprecht was of the opinion that an excavation was no place for a woman because only science justified the costs of staying in Mesopotamia, and this only for 'determined...well-trained and equipped men'. As Bruce Kuklick remarks, Hilprecht did not report to Philadelphia the suicidal homosexual yearnings Clarence Stanley Fisher had for Valentine Geere, although this constituted the central personal problem in the Nippur team.[214] The Nippur excavations confirm that 'the behavior of the archaeologist is the greatest source of variability in the archaeological record'.[215]

At Ur, the presence of the widowed Katharine Keeling, later Lady Woolley, was resented by the men, although she worked unpaid, making drawings for the catalogue, helping with household work, and showing around visitors.[216] Woolley appreciated her presence and work, writing that 'lastly, I do think that the presence of a lady has a good moral effect on the younger fellows in the camp and keeps them up to standard'.[217] After their marriage Katharine Woolley

213. Johannes Renger, 'Die Geschichte der Altorientalistik und der vorderasiatischen Archäologie in Berlin von 1875 bis 1945', in *Berlin und die Antike: Architektur, Kunstgewerbe, Malerei, Skulptur, Theater und Wissenschaft vom 16. Jahrhundert bis heute* (Aufsätze) (ed. Willmuth Arenhövel and Christa Schreiber; Berlin: Deutsches Archäologisches Institut, 1979), pp. 151-92 (168); Gran-Aymerich, 'Jane Dieulafoy', pp. 52, 62.

214. Bruce Kuklick, *Puritans in Babylon: The Ancient Near East and American Intellectual Life, 1880–1930* (Princeton: Princeton University Press, 1996), pp. 84-89.

215. Michael B. Schiffer, *Formation Processes of the Archaeological Record* (Albuquerque, NM: University of New Mexico Press, 1987), p. 326.

216. H.V.F. Winstone, *Woolley of Ur: The Life of Sir Leonard Woolley* (London: Secker & Warburg, 1990), p. 138.

217. Winstone, *Woolley of Ur*, pp. 142-44.

accompanied her husband on his excavations at Ur, but her behavior towards her husband and members of the excavations teams is heavily criticized by Max Mallowan as well as Woolley's biographer.[218] Although Katharine Woolley served as Agatha Christie's model for the excavator's unsympathetic wife in *Murder in Mesopotamia* (1936), in her autobiography Christie describes Mrs. Woolley more benignly.[219]

Mentorship or patronage was and is a widespread practice in academic disciplines, and can be crucial in fields with as few positions as are available in Assyriology and archaeology.[220] Professionals who succeed are trusted to produce more professionals in their own image', writes Ian Morris,[221] and one can add that traditionally this form of 'reproduction' did not include women who rarely found mentors and lacked role models.[222] There is ample evidence that the situation did not change for women after the second World War. Rivkah Harris, who began her studies at the Oriental Institute of the University of Chicago in 1950 reports that, from the distance of today, she is amazed that she managed to get through with teachers like Landsberger, Jacobsen, and Gelb, and that she suffered from insomnia for the last two years before she got her doctorate and long afterwards. Oppenheim's comment on her pregnancy was 'you could have been first rate, but...'; he did not finish the sentence and refused to talk to her for months.[223] Eva Strommenger, who received her doctorate in the same year as Rivkah Harris (1954) wrote in 1994 that, like many other women of her generation, she experiences hidden as well as open discrimination and remains extremely worried that nothing has changed in regard to women's academic careers. Strommenger also comments on the practice of excluding women from directing excavations, and that in 1972 the 'establish-

218. Max Mallowan, *Mallowan's Memoirs* (London: Collins, 1977), pp. 36-38, 44, 45, 65-66; Winstone, *Woolley of Ur*, pp. 1, 131-32, 137-38, 146-49, 154-56, 159-62, 165, 170, 171-75, 188, 230-31, 240-42.

219. Agatha Christie, *An Autobiography* (London: Collins, 1977), pp. 376-78, 391-93, 400-403, 429-30; see also, Janet P. Morgan, *Agatha Christie: A Biography* (London: Collins, 1984), pp. 172-73, 178-79, 316. Leonard Woolley was apparently not troubled by his wife's personal demands on him, and it is at least doubtful that she had a major influence on his scientific interpretations. However, as Woolley was one of the most famous and pre-eminent archaeologists of his time, one could hardly criticize him. He was certainly envied by colleagues and some may have used his wife as a scapegoat. The history of excavation is populated with men of eccentric behavior or flawed characters, but none of the men has been as vilified in the literature as Mrs. Woolley or Mrs. Haynes. In both cases the cause of the husband's mistakes is attributed to a wife's character.

220. See also Morris, 'Archaeologies of Greece', pp. 8-47 (13-14).

221. Morris, 'Archaeologies of Greece', p. 14.

222. Claassen, 'Introduction', in *Women in Archaeology*, pp. 1-8 (5; see also 1). It is evident from the articles in *Women in Archaeology* that gender as well as mentorship is a significant element in archaeologists' careers.

223. Quoted from a personal letter I received from Rivkah Harris (dated 28 April 1994).

ment' was still of the opinion that one could not entrust a woman with an excavation. In this letter, addressed to the president of the commission for women at the university of Frankfurt am Main, Strommenger states that her personal experiences have '*exemplarischen Charakter*' (meaning they are representative and typical), that women are still prevented from qualifying as excavators, and, as this is often an important qualifying criterion for tenured positions, women are thus systematically disadvantaged and excluded.[224]

In academia, conservative views of gender roles are often linked to persistent intellectual bias *vis-à-vis* feminist critique and gender theory.[225] Although the paradigmatic importance of gender-based theory and methodology has been recognized by some scholars, the assumption still prevails that gender theory means studying women. This is evident in a number of articles published in the proceedings of the *Rencontre assyriologique internationle* in Helsinki in 2001[226] as well as in Simo Parpola's preface where he writes that he originally suggested the theme 'Sexuality and Asexuality in the Ancient Near East' because '*asexuality*' was intended to encourage research on this 'negative' side of sexuality, which was essential to a holistic understanding of the subject but had been neglected in previous research. The theme was, however, changed to 'Sex and Gender in the Ancient Near East' because this 'might appeal to more people and produce more papers', and 'sexuality can easily include asexuality, while gender opens up other avenues'.[227] This statement exemplifies many Assyriologist's and archaeologist's ignorance about the postulate of gender theory that analysis of all manifestations of sexuality is integral to gender analysis.

Epilogue

A diachronic survey of Semiramis representations in different media shows that, depending on context, her Oriental origin was irrelevant because the function of an *exemplum* role was essentially independent of ethnicity. Where wanton sexuality is concerned the opposition is predominantly pagan versus Christian, or women's versus men's sexuality rather than Orient versus Occi-

224. Letter dated 27 July 1994 by Eva Strommenger addressed to Prof. Dr. Elke Tharun, president of the 'Frauenkommission' of the University of Frankfurt am Main. I want to thank Eva Strommenger for sending me a copy of this letter. The same facts are mentioned in letters by Brigitte Groneberg and Eva Strommenger addressed to the 'Frauenbeauftragte' of the University of Munich in July1994.

225. Although feminist alternatives are proving to be particularly effective (Morris, 'Archaeologies of Greece', p. 44), integration into *Altertumswissenschaften* lags far behind other disciplines.

226. Parpola and Whiting (eds.), *Sex and Gender in the Ancient Near East.*

227. Parpola, 'Introduction', in Parpola and Whiting (eds.), *Sex and Gender in the Ancient Near East*, pp. xiii-xv.

dent. Selecting non-Christian *exempla* had the advantage of expressing views without fearing criticism, censorship, or even prosecution. But Semiramis was also a source for creative inspiration because of the multi-faceted character that she shares with other women not of Oriental origin. As articulated by John M. MacKenzie,

> 'Orientalist' interpretation misses the complexities and dualities of the Western representations of the East and adaptations of eastern forms… We find moral condemnation befogging intellectual clarity; and at times negating essential characteristics of the critical faculty; and we find an entire epoch condemned out of hand as though historical ages themselves can be divided into 'goodies' and 'baddies'. At its worst, this type of activity, surprisingly favorably hailed in some quarter, is reduced to the level of grotesquerie.[228]

Representations and interpretations of the Semiramis theme reflect the changes in the debates on woman, power, and female sexuality as well as academic *Zeitgeist*. Semiramis was considered an extremely exceptional historical figure, but references to her as Oriental queen are rare and already in antiquity of less importance than her gender, status and behavior as ruler, aspects that interrelate with Western societies' concerns about women's role in public and their sexuality. Writers, painters, and princesses seeking ancient precedents found few queens whose accomplishments matched those of Semiramis as builder, warrior, and political master. Perceived as an 'historical first' she became the archetype of female rulership and *exemplum* for women in power.

Because discourses about women and power generally include the aspect of sexuality, this is also a major topic in recent scholarly interpretations of Semiramis-representations, casting her as the quintessential Oriental and/or ultra-Other with sexually excessive behavior. That such studies have gained authoritative status through uncritical reiteration strengthens the tendency to use theory less as an analytical tool than as an ostensible form of evidence. As a consequence, interpretations of this figure across many academic disciplines are similar, a fact that is particularly striking considering that Semiramis-representations are rather heterogeneous. The complexity and muli-valency of the Semiramis character disappears through a *reduction* of her image or character to a stock dramatic figure in artificial conformity with—and dictated by—Orientalism discourse.

For more than two millennia, representations of Semiramis have oscillated between strong, wise, competent ruler on the one hand and beautiful, attractive, powerful, sexually abusive woman on the other, perspectives that closely equate with two current themes in academia: gender theory and Orientalism. Scholars of ancient Near Eastern languages and cultures tend to either adopt Said's critique of Orientalism uncritically[229] (e.g., Bahrani) or

228. MacKenzie, *Orientalism*, p. xvii.

229. As I demonstrated earlier with Said's treatment of Valéry, there are general flaws in Said's

accept the traditional view of (Oriental) women's lascivious sexuality (e.g., Haas, Roux).

Ignorance of manifestations of Orientalism in ancient Near Eastern studies is based on scholars' reluctance to examine critically the history of the discipline. What Ian Morris wrote about classical archaeology is also applicable to the other disciplines dedicated to the study of ancient cultures: 'a spectre is haunting archaeology—the spectre of history. Archaeologists study the whole of the human past, but grow uncomfortable when considering themselves as part of that past'.[230] The cause of the reluctance to *integrate* feminist critique and gender theory into ancient Near Eastern studies, however, is not Orientalism but rather continued domination by male scholars, many of whom still remain skeptical of the academic competence of women, as well as of alternative theories authored by women. Numerous Assyriologists and archaeologists would much rather see women in the role of *alma mater*, i.e. 'helpmate' than that of 'Semiramis of Hammersmith', i.e. learned, competent and authoritative.

critiques which perhaps can be best illustrated by quoting, in another context, Frandsen, 'Aida and Edward Said', p. 206:

> The unfortunate distortion of data in his analysis of *Aida*, given the status of the author, makes a follow-up essential…it is sad to note that I have rarely come across such a blatant manipulation of sources, and I am not the only one to think so. In his review of Said's book, the Scottish historian John M. MacKenzie highlights the chapter on *Aida* as the most obvious instance of the author's 'eclecticism' in the selection of data, a procedure that he subsequently brands as being marked by 'wilful misunderstandings'.

230. Morris, 'Archaeologies of Greece', p. 8.

Another Look 'Inside': Harems and the Interpretation of Women

Elna K. Solvang

In a 1995 essay Abraham Malamat searches for 'a word for the royal harem in the Bible'. He begins with the assumption that 'in the palaces of Jerusalem and in the capital cities in the Northern Kingdom special quarters were set aside to accommodate royal ladies, similar to the harems throughout the ancient Near East and later in the Islamic and Ottoman Empires'.[1] Since there is no term in biblical Hebrew—nor in Akkadian—comparable to the Arabic *harem*, Malamat searches for 'an informal expression',[2] 'one denoting the physical realm of the women's quarters deep within the palace'.[3]

Malamat borrows from Jean-Claude Margueron's observation regarding the floor plan of the palace at Mari that in addition to the sector of the palace, which Margueron labeled the House of the King (*Maison du Roi*), directly connected to the royal throne room, (Room 65) at the 'heart of the palace', there was a smaller but significant complex of rooms around another central area (Court 31) that connected directly to the large central space of Court 106. Margueron labeled this sector the 'Second House' (*Seconde Maison*) noting that it not only enjoyed a connection to the public space but that it could be closed off by shutting three doors and effectively kept under surveillance (*assuré d'une surveillance très efficace*).[4] Malamat also draws from Jean-Marie Durand's conclusion from the textual sources at Mari that *tubqum*, typically translated as 'corner', is better understood as representing space in the palace associated with the royal household and staff, including the 'servants of the *tubqum*',[5] and where, for example in ARM, X, 74.10-21, a royal wife would be out of public view.[6]

1. Abraham Malamat, 'Is There a Word for the Royal Harem in the Bible? The *Inside* Story', in *Pomegranates and Golden Bells: Studies in Biblical, Jewish, and Near Eastern Ritual, Law, and Literature in Honor of Jacob Milgrom* (ed. David P. Wright, David Noel Freedman and Avi Hurvitz; Winona Lake, IN: Eisenbrauns, 1995), pp. 785-87 (785).

2. Malamat, 'Is There a Word for the Royal Harem?', p. 787.

3. Malamat, 'Is There a Word for the Royal Harem?', p. 786.

4. Jean-Marie Durand and J.-C. Margueron, 'La question du harem royal dans le palais de Mari', *Journal des savants* (Octobre–Décembre 1980), pp. 253-80 (280).

5. *gerseqqû* (LÚ.GÌR.SIG$_5$.GA.MEŠ) *ša tubuqtim* (ARM, XXI, 398.38). See discussion in ARMT, XXI, pp. 523-24.

6. Inib-šarri, a daughter of Zimri-Lim, complains of being forced to sit *ina tubqim* while her

Adopting Akkadian *tubqum* as an idiomatic equivalent to Arabic *harem*, Malamat finds a comparable term in Hebrew—*pĕnîmâ*—a word typically translated 'inside'. Malamat concludes that 'on closer examination it specifically refers to the harem proper'.[7] In support of this conclusion Malamat points to Ps. 45.14-15 (MT). Here he asserts the bride is not just taken 'inside' the palace, but is led to the king.[8] Malamat suggests that the king has his own chamber inside the 'harem' and that this is where the king of Israel is in 2 Kgs 7.11-12 when the good news of the departure of the Arameans is passed '*into* the king's palace'.[9]

Malamat's essay presents an important challenge to scholars of Assyria and the Bible: Where and how does one locate a 'harem' in the ancient world without a word to label such a space or concept? More fundamentally, what is it we are looking for and how do we know when we have found it?

Any use of the term *harem* in reference to ancient Assyria and Israel introduces an analogy by which the physical remains and textual legacies of those societies are interpreted and daily life reconstructed based on Islamic models that came into existence centuries after the destruction of those ancient kingdoms. While analogies are critical for historians and textual interpreters alike, the harem analogy shows significant signs of weakness—and failure—in its usefulness for the study of the ancient societies of the Levant. Moreover, rarely do scholars of the ancient texts use actual data from harems in constructing the analogy. This essay will examine varying assumptions about 'harems' operating within the field of ancient Near Eastern scholarship, explore sources for understanding Islamic *harems*, and consider the 'fit' between these data and prevailing assumptions and the ancient archaeological and textual remains.

1. *An Outsider's View of the 'Inside'*

When it comes to understanding 'harems', most Assyriologists and biblical scholars are in the position of being double 'outsiders', i.e., (1) outsiders to the ancient societies we seek to understand and (2) outsiders to the Islamic language and culture where the concept of 'harem' has its roots and history. Even as we acknowledge the *Thousand and One Nights* as 'tales' and shake our heads in amazement and lower them in shame over the excessiveness of European Orientalist fantasies about ancient Babylon and Nineveh,[10] the portrait of 'harem'

rival, the favored wife, sits with the husband and publicly receives gifts and tribute. See discussion in Durand and Margueron, 'La question du harem royal', pp. 256-59.

7. Malamat, 'Is There a Word for the Royal Harem?', p. 787.

8. Malamat, 'Is There a Word for the Royal Harem?', p. 787.

9. וַיַּגִּידוּ בֵּית הַמֶּלֶךְ פְּנִימָה: NJPSV translation as cited in Malamat, 'Is There a Word for the Royal Harem?', p. 787.

10. Highlights in Henrietta McCall, 'Rediscovery and Aftermath', in *The Legacy of Mesopotamia* (ed. S. Dalley; Oxford: Oxford University Press, 1998), pp. 183-223. Roswitha Gost suggests that the part of the Ottoman Empire's self presentation to the western world was this image

operative in western culture is exclusively that of the Ottoman Empire.[11] Moreover, that portrait is still largely the product of the religious tensions, imperial projections and cultural pretensions in the European encounter with Islamic society. Leslie Peirce observes:

> We in the West are heir to an ancient but still robust tradition of obsession with the sexuality of Islamic society. The harem is undoubtedly the most prevalent symbol in Western myths constructed around the theme of Muslim sensuality. One of the most fertile periods for the production of texts and images treating this theme was the late sixteenth and the seventeenth centuries, and the most frequent subject was the court of the Ottoman sultan. Preoccupied with its own forms of monarchical absolutism, Europe elaborated a myth of oriental tyranny and located its essence in the sultan's harem. Orgiastic sex became a metaphor for power corrupted.[12]

Harem is derived from Arabic *ḥarām* meaning 'forbidden', 'unlawful'. In describing how the term is applied in Islamic society, Norman Penzer notes that in contrast to *ḥalāl*, 'that which is lawful', *ḥarām* designates an area—for example 'the whole region for a certain distance round Mecca and Medina'—where 'certain things allowed elsewhere are not permitted'.[13] In this context, Penzer points out, the 'word also signified "holy", "protected", "sacred", "inviolate", and lastly "forbidden". In its secular application the word was used in reference to that portion of a Muslim house occupied by the women, because it was their *ḥarām*, or sanctuary'.[14]

Western women—governesses and wives of ambassadors who resided for periods of time in Egypt and in Turkey—are one source of descriptions of life 'inside' Oriental harems. In the early eighteenth century, the letters of Lady Mary Wortley Montagu, wife of the British ambassador to Turkey, detailing her observations of life in Istanbul, fed the imagination and influenced many in European literary circles, including the poet Alexander Pope. Montagu provided positive reports of the wealth and culture of the Turkish court, including the women of the royal *harem*. Upon returning to England she also labored to convince British doctors to adopt the practice of vaccinating against smallpox that she had seen in Turkey.

Emmeline Lott's observations of life in an Egyptian household, in contrast, are full of disdain for the women of the harem. Lott was governess to the young

of absolute power on the part of the sultan and the mystery, wealth and beauty of the palace—particularly for a western audience who measured power in those terms (R. Gost, *Der Harem* [Köln: DuMont Buchverlag, 1993]).

11. Other models such as the Indian *purdah* and the Iranian *andarūn* are not discussed.

12. Leslie P. Peirce, *The Imperial Harem: Women and Sovereignty in the Ottoman Empire* (Studies in Middle Eastern History; New York: Oxford University Press, 1993), p. 3.

13. Norman Mosley Penzer, *The Ḥarēm: An Account of the Institution as it Existed in the Palace of the Turkish Sultans with a History of the Grand Seraglio from Its Foundation to the Present Time* (Philadelphia: J.B. Lippincott, 1937), p. 15.

14. Penzer, *The Ḥarēm*, p. 15.

son and chief heir of 'H.H. Ismael Pacha, the Viceroy of Egypt'. Encouraged by a Greek fellow traveler that she might 'by the influence of [her] example [as an English lady], be able to graft a few civilized customs on their Arab and Turkish manners',[15] Lott kept a diary of her experiences without 'appearing to take the least notice of their singular habits, and, to [her], outlandish customs'.[16] Two volumes of Lott's *Harem Life in Egypt and Constantinople* were published in 1865. Her stated purpose for their publication was

> to disclose to European society...[what] cannot but be considered as secret institutions for the corruption of women...to give a concise yet impartial and sympathetic account of the daily life of the far-famed Odalisques of the nineteenth century—those mysterious impersonifications [*sic*] of Eastern loveliness.[17]

The massive Topkapı Palace in Istanbul, the seat of the sultanate of the Ottoman Empire, is the chief model for the western portrait of the 'harem'. That image provides the background for Pierre Loti's book *Les désenchantées* (*The Disenchanted*), published in Paris in 1906. The book was supposedly based on conversations with women who escaped from harem life and who later told their story in the fine salons of Paris,[18] though in the introduction Loti releases himself from the bounds of non-fiction by declaring that 'this is an entirely imaginary story'.[19]

Alongside these tales, epistles and diaries which fed European fascination, fears and fantasies about the Topkapı Palace and 'harem' life, N.M. Penzer's study, *The Ḥarēm*, stands out for its attempt to discern 'the dividing line between fact and fiction',[20] to correct 'misunderstandings, exaggerations, distortions, and occasionally deliberate fabrications',[21] and to offer a view of the *harem* 'clearly defined as regards its scope, and described as fully as possible with the aid of a detailed plan and occasional photographs'.[22]

By the time Penzer conducted his study the Ottoman Empire had fallen and the Topkapı Palace stood empty, yet his systematic attempt to describe the history of the palace, the arrangement of its myriad of rooms and the functions carried on in the palace remains an important resource for developing a picture of the royal *harem* at Topkapı Palace. Penzer's study includes a survey of the whole Topkapı Palace. He is concerned that

15. Emmeline Lott, *The 'English Governess' in Egypt: Harem Life in Egypt and Constantinople* (London: Richard Bentley, 1865), I, p. 13.

16. Lott, *The 'English Governess' in Egypt*, I, p. 268.

17. Lott, *The 'English Governess' in Egypt*, I, pp. viii-ix.

18. Alev Lytle Croutier, *Harem: The World behind the Veil* (New York: Abbeville Press, 1989), p. 189.

19. 'C'est une histoire entierement imaginée'. Pierre Loti, *Les désenchantées* (The Project Gutenberg Ebook, by Michael S. Hart, http://www.gutenberg.net/etext05/7dech10.txt, accessed June 25, 2005).

20. Penzer, *The Ḥarēm*, p. 13.

21. Penzer, *The Ḥarēm*, p. 14.

22. Penzer, *The Ḥarēm*, p. 15.

> the enormous activities of the Palace seem to have almost entirely escaped general notice, and while idle curiosity has always centered on the *harem*, the fact that the Palace contained a great military School of State, over a dozen mosques, ten double kitchens, two bakeries, a flour-mill, two hospitals, and various kinds of baths, store-rooms, sports fields, etc., is almost wholly ignored.[23]

Western perceptions of the *harem* have viewed it as 'private' space organized around the sultan and heavily guarded to protect the sexual integrity of its occupants, where survival depended on beauty, seduction and intrigue. Within the vast Topkapı Palace complex, however, Penzer, describes the *harem* as

> a little world of its own, governed with the utmost deliberation and care, not by a man at all, but by a woman. Every member of it had her exact duties to perform, and was forced to comply with all the rules and regulations that in many respects were as strict and rigid as in a convent.[24]

Even Emmeline Lott reports being cautioned on her journey to Egypt that 'the sad monotony of the daily life you will be called upon to lead will be of such a melancholy, convent-like nature, that in my opinion it were better far that you had immured yourself within the cell of a nunnery, than entered the precincts of a Harem'.[25]

Penzer counsels that 'It is impossible to understand the *harem* unless we consider it merely as a single unit in a large and highly complicated system'.[26] Though spatially deep 'inside' the palace complex, with passage to and from the area well guarded, the activities of the residents of the *harem* were legitimate and integral to the palace and to the empire. To understand this 'complicated system' it is important to comprehend that the relationship between 'inside' and 'outside' in the Topkapı Palace does not conform to Western designations of space as outside/public/male vs. inside/private/female, where power is perceived to be invested in those who function 'outside'.[27] For the Topkapı Palace it is more helpful to follow authority as it flows out and circulates away from the central figures of the royal household—male and female. This conception of the relationship between 'inside' and 'outside' accounts for the legitimate authority accorded to the *valide sultan* (mother of the king) without reducing the authority of the sultan. Indeed, as Leslie Peirce points out:

23. Penzer, *The Ḥarēm*, p. 15.

24. Penzer, *The Ḥarēm*, p. 14.

25. Lott, *The 'English Governess' in Egypt*, I, p. 16.

26. Penzer, *The Ḥarēm*, p. 15.

27. Summarizing Bernard Lewis on metaphor and allusion in political language (B. Lewis, *The Political Language of Islam* [Chicago: University of Chicago Press, 1988], pp. 11-13, 22-23.), Peirce notes that 'power relationships in Islamic society are represented by spatial division more horizontal than vertical, in contrast to Western metaphors: instead of moving *up*, one moves *in* toward greater authority' (Peirce, *The Imperial Harem*, p. 9).

> While supreme authority in the Ottoman sultanate was exercised by a male, that authority in the late sixteenth century emanated from a household that was presided over by the female elder of the dynasty.[28]

The locks on the doors and guards posted along the walls of the Topkapı Palace preserved the inviolability of the *harem* space and its residents, thereby creating a tightly organized unit *inside* the palace complex that functioned to preserve and promote the interests of the dynasty *outside* the palace walls. Through the members of the royal *harem* the next generation of princes and princesses were born, educated, and established in marriages. The female members of the royal house advanced the image of the dynasty through acts of public beneficence. Under the supervision of the *valide sultan*, the *harem* trained women to serve the royal house, some of whom might assume positions of authority *in* the *harem* unit or be 'suitable wives for men near the top of the military/administrative hierarchies'[29] *outside* of the *harem*.

The flow of authority and power from 'inside' the *harem* and the palace to 'outside' does not make the Ottoman Dynasty less hierarchical than typically perceived in Western thought, but it does force reexamination of the perception that the *harem* was simply the private quarters of the palace, under the arbitrary rule of the sultan, where women resided. More importantly, it illuminates the networks along which royal power flowed and how these networks functioned as the basis for imperial rule. As Peirce describes it,

> The governing class of the Ottoman Empire in this period operated not so much on the basis of institutionally or functionally ascribed authority as through a complex of personal bonds and family and household connections. Functionally ascribed authority—authority devolving from one's office—certainly existed, but more important was the web of individual relations—of patronage and clientage, of teacher and student, of kinship and marriage—that brought one to that office and that one used in the exercise of one's official power.[30]

This system generated a large number of officials—male and female—who served the royal house and represented its imperial interests. It was by the effective manipulation of such a system that the royal family preserved its privilege and carried out its ruling responsibilities. Politics was inseparable from family life and even 'members of the dynastic family whose blood carried no right to royal power—concubine mothers, women from Christian territories enslaved and converted to Islam'—were participants in this rule.[31] The royal household was the center from which sovereignty flowed. Access to that center was strictly regulated and highly coveted. Peirce notes:

28. Peirce, *The Imperial Harem*, p. 24.
29. Peirce, *The Imperial Harem*, p. 139.
30. Peirce, *The Imperial Harem*, p. 149.
31. Peirce, *The Imperial Harem*, p. 17.

> Recognizing the importance of palace-based networks and factions and the importance of royal women in their formation, ambassadors strove not only to acquire information about these women but to establish ties to them.[32]

With access to and information about the 'inside' of the royal household tightly guarded, the royal *harem*'s role in Ottoman dynastic rule was subject to misinterpretation and attack. Within Islamic Ottoman society ideological challenges to the activities of women within the royal house were raised, among them the Muslim cleric Sunulla Enfendi in 1599, representing the view that such sovereignty was contrary to the teachings of the prophet Muḥammad[33] (though the involvement of women in other political acts such as works of charity and religious piety was not challenged). Western interpreters, convinced of the irresistible beauty of the *harem* residents, have regarded sexuality as the only source of power for these women and have judged that power to trespass a personal versus political boundary, thereby characterizing royal women's involvement in the affairs of state as 'meddling', 'illegitimate' and, frequently, indicative of a weak sultan. A simplistic, but common, perception in the East and the West attributes the decline of the Ottoman Empire to 'the excessive interference of harem women'.[34] Indeed, the expenses associated with the royal house had a devastating effect on the economy of the empire and the tax burden of its citizens, but those expenses were not merely for the women nor were they the result of 'interference'.[35] The legitimate role of the *harem* within the governance system of the Ottoman Empire and the *harem*'s contributions to the persistence and effectiveness of Ottoman imperial rule should not be ignored.

The above discussion of the meaning of *harem* and examination of the functioning of the Ottoman imperial *harem* is a mere glimpse at ways the *harem* has functioned in Islamic family life and imperial society. Much more can be learned from the accounts of those who grew up in *harems*[36] and more care-

32. Peirce, *The Imperial Harem*, p. 117.

33. Peirce, *The Imperial Harem*, pp. vii, 267.

34. Burak H. Sansal (professional national tour guide, Turkey), 'HAREM in the Ottoman Empire' (http://www.allaboutturkey.com/harem.htm, accessed June 25, 2005).

35. Penzer, commenting on the Court of the Divan in the Topkapı Palace where those admitted beyond the Inner Wall presented themselves before the sultan and his council, indicates that it was Suleiman the Magnificent's decision to stop attending the divan and to listen in on the proceedings through a grilled window from a room next door 'without the council's knowing if he were there or not' that was the act to which 'historians have traced the beginning of the decline of the Ottoman power' (Penzer, *The Ḥarēm*, p. 102).

36. Contemporary accounts include Fatima Mernissi, *Dreams of Trespass: Tales of a Harem Girlhood* (Reading, MA: Addison–Wesley Publishing Company, 1994). In *Haremlik*, Demetra Vaka Brown, a woman of Greek ancestry who grew up in Istanbul, while living in the United States 'heard Turkey spoken of with hatred and scorn, the Turks reviled as despicable, their women as miserable creatures, living in practical slavery for the base desires of men'. She asks

ful study is required to understand the development of the imperial *harem*. This discussion, however, does prompt reflection on the sources used in constructing the portrait of *harem* life that functions in the analogy with ancient monarchies.

First, it is necessary to consider whether the term 'harem' as used in the study of ancient Mesopotamia and Israel is consistent with the understanding of this term in Islamic culture and history. Is the distinction between *ḥarām* and *ḥalāl* applicable to palaces? Are scholars from Eastern and Western traditions speaking of the same concept when they speak of the 'harem?' Is the space occupied by women inside a Mesopotamian palace understood as 'sacred' and 'forbidden?'

Second, it must be acknowledged that there is no generic 'harem'. Though the term may refer to '1. a house or section of a house reserved for women members of a Muslim household. 2. The wives, concubines, female relatives, and servants occupying such a place. 3. A group of women sexual partners for one man',[37] the cultural and historical context is essential for understanding the reference.[38] Even within a culture, over time the 'harem' can vary in form and function. Peirce argues that it was 'changes in the nature of the Ottoman state and society', namely 'the growing importance of the imperial palace as the center of government' and 'changes in the system of succession to the throne', that resulted in the prominent role of the imperial *harem* in the sixteenth and seventeenth centuries.[39]

Third, it is important to recognize that when the term 'harem' is employed in Assyriology and biblical scholarship it generally appears without any further

herself, 'Could it possibly be as the Americans said, and I never have known it?' (D.V. Brown, *Haremlik: Some Pages from the Life of Turkish Women* [Boston: Houghton Mifflin, 1909], p. 13). The book reflects on her visits with girlhood friends, now married, and her desire 'to see for myself, and not only to see but to talk with the women, to ask them their thoughts about their lives and their customs' (Brown, *Haremlik*, p. 13). She not only challenges the Orientalism of the Western culture but struggles with her own romanticized notions of Turkish life and the points of conflict between Eastern and Western cultures. Interestingly, the publication of this book coincides with the adoption of a constitution in Turkey in 1908.

37. *The American Dictionary of the English Language* (Houghton Mifflin Company, 4th edn, 2000. Electronic version http://www.bartleby.com/61/46/H0064600.html accessed June 25, 2005).

38. Joan Goodnick Westenholz demonstrates convincingly the incompatibility between the 'culture-specific' term *harem* and the Mesopotamian context in her review of *La femme dans le Proche-Orient antique: XXXIIIe Rencontre assyriologique internationale (Paris, 7-10 Juillet 1986)* (ed. J.-M. Durand; Paris: Éditions Recherche sur les civilisations, 1987). She points to the 'diachronic, ethnic, and evidentiary disparities' among the references to 'harems' in the nine out of twenty-four articles in the volume that employ the term (J.G. Westenholz, 'Towards a New Conceptualization of the Female Role in Mesopotamian Society', *JAOS* 110/3 [1990], pp. 510-21 [514]).

39. Peirce, *The Imperial Harem*, p. x.

explanation; the assumption being that the reader is familiar enough with the concept from the general culture to complete the analogy. It is safe to presume that the Ottoman imperial harem is the point of comparison. When the term 'harem' appears with some descriptors, the characteristics most often mentioned—'closed',[40] 'locked', 'guarded', 'women in the service of the king'[41]—are those typically associated with the Topkapı Palace. That the use of the term 'harem' in the scholarly literature draws from the same pool of perceptions about Turkish *harems* as the general Western culture is evident in efforts at times to modify those perceptions by calling attention to how the 'harem' being discussed is 'unlike' Turkish *harems*.[42]

2.0. *Life on the 'Inside'*

Methodologically, both N.M. Penzer and Leslie Peirce place the *harem* at the center of their inquiry.[43] It is through this lens that they discover and explore the *harem*'s functioning *inside* the system of imperial rule. When the female residents of the *harem* are at the center—and not in a side-by-side comparison with the male residents of the palace—new insights concerning each emerge. Peirce notes that 'Perhaps the most important thing to be learned from placing royal women at the center stage of historical investigation is that they, like the men of the dynasty, gained or lost power in the context of family dynamics'.[44] Both Penzer and Peirce seek to circumvent the Orientalist portrayal of the *harem* and understand it in its own historical and cultural context.

Contemporary Assyriologists and biblical scholars are cautious to avoid the Orientalist excesses in depicting *harems*. They differ, however, in how to proceed from there. Some, like Malamat, see continuity in form between the ancient world and the Ottoman context.[45] Others, like Nele Ziegler, see similarity between the two contexts based on their difference from Western models of household and space.[46] Joan Goodnick Westenholz urges abandoning the term

40. Durand and Margueron, 'La question du harem royal', p. 260.

41. Durand and Margueron, 'La question du harem royal', p. 263.

42. For example, in describing 'The Women of the Palace at Mari' Bertrand Lafont uses the term 'harem' but instructs the reader 'not to yield to the temptation...to form visions of an oriental *Thousand and one Nights* harem with its eunuchs and odalisques' (B. Lafont, 'The Women of the Palace at Mari', in *Everyday Life in Ancient Mesopotamia* [ed. Jean Bottéro; trans. Antonia Nevill; Baltimore, MD: The Johns Hopkins Press, 2001], pp. 127-40 [136]).

43. This methodology is also seen in Tal Ilan's studies of women in the Second Temple Period (T. Ilan, *Integrating Women into Second Temple History* [Texts and Studies in Ancient Judaism, 76; Tübingen: Mohr Siebeck, 1999]).

44. Peirce, *The Imperial Harem*, p. viii.

45. Malamat, 'Is There a Word for the Royal Harem?', pp. 785-87.

46. Ziegler acknowledges that the Muslim *harem* and the Mesopotamian context are not the same reality, but argues that they both permit polygamy and share the concept of a closed

'harem' altogether in discussing ancient Mesopotamia.[47] The last of these is the most attentive to the Islamic context that defines the concept of *harem*. Still, might there be something to be gained—for a post-Orientalist understanding of *harems* and for determining any relevance they might have to the study of ancient Mesopotamian royal society—from actually studying those *harems*? Previous generations of scholars derived their knowledge of *harem* life from the general culture. This paper does not suggest that Ottoman imperial households provide the model for reconstructing ancient Assyrian monarchies but it is curious about whether a deeper understanding of women's lives in Ottoman *harems* can contribute insights and provide information useful in interpreting data about Neo-Assyrian palace life.

The paragraphs that follow examine three issues drawn from information about Ottoman *harems* and explore possible implications for understanding and reconstructing Assyrian palace mores and structures.

2.1. *The Transfer of Valuables*

In her account of life in a Cairo *harem* Emmeline Lott reports what she was told about a craftswoman who

> had been in the habit of taking quantities of jewellery into that Harem on several occasions, and, that, on that very morning, she had visited [a particular harem woman] for the purpose of calling for some watch-charms, keys, &c. that required to be repaired.[48]

As the story unfolds two interesting pieces of information are revealed: (1) it is through the jeweler that a young man receives information about his fiancée, information for which he rewards the jeweler and information that the jeweler has manipulated to her advantage, exploiting the negotiations and exchange of presents between the families of the bride and groom; (2) The transfer of valuables to jewelers is recognized by the *harem* women to be hazardous: 'it is no uncommon occurrence, where valuable ornaments are taken away by such individuals out of the Harems, that some of less value are substituted, or else they

living quarters (*d'habitat fermeé*) for wives and servants, unlike Christian communities and western European civilization in general (N. Ziegler, *La population feminine des palais d'après les Archives royales de Mari: Le harem de Zimri-Lim* [Florilegium marianum, 4; Mémoires de N.A.B.U., 5; Paris: SEPOA, 1999], p. 8). Similarly, Alfonso Archi comments: 'To label these women as the harem of the king is a permissible simplification: a specific term which defines a phenomenon entirely alien to our culture may be applied, in an approximate sense, to another phenomenon equally strange to us but similar in some ways to the first' (A. Archi, 'The Role of Women in the Society of Ebla', in *Sex and Gender in the Ancient Near East: Proceedings of the 47th Rencontre assyriologique internationale, Helsinki July 2-6, 2001, Part I* [ed. Simo Parpola and Robert M. Whiting; Helsinki: University of Helsinki Press, 2002], pp. 1-9 [4]).

47. Westenholz, 'Towards a New Conceptualization of the Female Role in Mesopotamian Society', pp. 510-21.

48. Lott, *The 'English Governess' in Egypt*, I, p. 172.

are purloined'.[49] Lott reports, however, no prohibition against the women of the *harem* calling for the jeweler and conducting such business.

This incident brings to mind ¶5 in the collection of Middle Assyrian Palace Decrees (MAPD) that forbids a woman of the palace (*sinniltu ša ēk*[*alle*]) from giving 'gold, silver or precious stones to a palace slave (*urad ēkalle*)'.[50] Ernst F. Weidner draws a parallel between this injunction and a passage in the MAPD[51] that forbids 'either a slave or a slave-girl' from 'receiv[ing] anything from the hand of a married woman' and permits the husband to determine whether or not to administer punishment: 'the nose and the ears of the slave or slave-girl shall be cut off...the man shall cut off his wife's ears' and the stolen goods shall be restored.[52] A. Kirk Grayson observes concerning the law that 'Besides being a measure dealing with simple theft, this edict was no doubt meant to forestall bribery and treasonous plots'.[53]

In the MAPD ¶5 a craftsman (*ēpiš šipre*) appears to be forbidden to receive the aforementioned gold, silver or precious stones from the hands of the palace slave.[54] The text is quite broken, but it does appear to be the responsibility of the 'palace commander' (*rab ēkalle*) to enforce the ban. The palace woman is to be detained (*la uššuru*). Severe disfigurement is threatened for at least one of the violators and someone who fails to report the violator to the king will be 'doused (with hot oil?)'.[55]

It could be that the woman of the palace is regarded as a thief and the palace slave and craftsman are viewed as her accomplices, as Driver suggests about the married woman in the MAPD,[56] however the woman of the palace does not receive the same punishment that the married woman does in the Middle Assyrian Laws and there does not appear to be any restitution made in the passage. In addition, while the married woman is forbidden to pass along anything (*mimma*) to a slave (male or female), the woman of the palace is forbidden from passing along 'gold, silver and precious stones' to the slave (*urad ēkalle*). The appearance of the craftsman in the text is curious since he appears to produce something (*šipra*) from the goods he receives from the slave, an unusual way for a slave to dispose of stolen property. While the fragmentary condition of the

49. Lott, *The 'English Governess' in Egypt*, I, p. 172.

50. Martha T. Roth, *Law Collections from Mesopotamia and Asia Minor* (SBLWAW, 6; Atlanta, GA: Scholars Press, 1995), p. 199 ¶5.

51. Ernst F. Weidner, 'Hof- und Harems-Erlasse assyrischer Könige aus dem 2. Jahrtausend v. Chr', *AfO* 17 (1954-56), pp. 257-93 (273).

52. G.R. Driver and John C. Miles, *The Assyrian Laws* (Ancient Codes and Laws of the Near East; Oxford: Clarendon Press, 1935), p. 383 ¶4.

53. A. Kirk Grayson, *Assyrian Royal Inscriptions*. I. *From the Beginning to Ashur-Resha-Ishi I* (RIMA; Wiesbaden: Otto Harrassowitz, 1972), p. 100.

54. Roth, *Law Collections from Mesopotamia and Asia Minor*, p. 199 ¶5.

55. Roth, *Law Collections from Mesopotamia and Asia Minor*, p. 199 ¶5.

56. Driver and Miles, *The Assyrian Laws*, p. 22.

tablet makes it impossible to reconstruct the specifics of the edict, the problem appears to lie with the role of the palace slave as intermediary in the transfer of valuables.

Lott's account of gold and jewelry transfers in a nineteenth-century *harem* draws attention to the problem of unscrupulous artisans and to the way in which slaves are taken advantage of. She reports learning that

> It happened only at the latter end of last year, that H.H. Hawwaia Hanem, a member of the late Viceroy Abbas Pacha's Harem, brought an action in the British Consular Court at Cairo...against Barbara Maggi and Luigi Maggi, to recover a valuable ornament, called *girlandu*, worth 2,500*l* [pounds sterling] which she had entrusted to the defendants to repair.
>
> The bride had found great fault with the quality of those articles, for, like a great portion of the modern 'bijoux' generally sold to the inmates of many of the Harems by those kind of women, they were perfect rubbish, being neither more nor less than metal covered with a thick plate of gold, and *for which the slaves pay almost fabulous sums.*[57] (*emphasis mine*)

There is no question that the MAPD are intended to serve the interests of the royal household, which may be why the palace women are enjoined from transferring valuables through slaves who could be less scrupulous or less knowledgeable about gems and precious metals. While the law does not spell out the proper channel for the transfer of such items it is clearly not through slaves.

What glimpse into palace life does this decree provide? Weidner, who first published and commented on these decrees—labeling them the 'Harem Edicts'— indicated that 'though admittedly limited in detail' the decrees could be used safely (*unbedenklich*) as a 'sketch of the life (*Leben*) and desires (*Treiben*) of the Assyrian royal court' during this period.[58] For Weidner, the decrees provided a look *inside* the 'harem' and 'the many historico-culturally interesting details' led him to conclude 'that everywhere in the Orient where the extension of western civilization could not penetrate, not much had changed up until the twentieth century'.[59] Hence, Weidner's translation and commentary on the Assyrian laws are based on his perception of 'orientalischer Potentaten' and their 'Harem'.[60]

Ancient Assyrian rulers have not become kinder or gentler in the fifty years since Weidner's commentary—there is no mistaking the harshness of the pun-

57. Lott, *The 'English Governess' in Egypt*, I, pp. 172-73.

58. Weidner, 'Hof- und Harems-Erlasse', p. 260.

59. 'Hier kann man sozusagen einmal einen Blick hinter die Kulissen tun, den die starren offiziellen Urkunden niemals gestatten würden, hier gewinnt man aus mancherlei kulturhistorisch interessanten Einzelheiten den Eindruck, dass sich bis ins 20. Jahrhundert überall im Orient, wohin die Ausstrahlungen abendländischer Zivilisation nicht dringen konnten, nicht allzu viel geändert hatte (Weidner, 'Hof- und Harems-Erlasse', p. 260).

60. Weidner, 'Hof- und Harems-Erlasse', p. 276.

ishments for violating the palace decrees—but knowledge of Assyrian palace life and of life *inside* some 'Oriental' *harems* has increased, as has self-awareness about Orientalist assumptions. It is possible that MAPD ¶5 does not share the 'spirit of Semitic culture, in which the woman was cut off from the public',[61] and that Assyrian palace women might legitimately possess gold, silver and precious gems and arrange for them to be crafted in some way—as long as they were transferred properly. While this proposal, like Weidner's, is only a possible sketch of the world in which the Palace Decree functioned, it actually looks *inside* an 'Oriental' *harem* for insights on what women's lives were like. The insights, however, also need to be tested against the available data from the Neo-Assyrian period.

It is clear from the dowry contracts and inventory lists found in the archives of the Neo-Assyrian palaces that royal women had gold, silver and precious gems in their possession. The domestic quarters of the North-West Palace at Nimrūd offers evidence of such wealth in a vaulted area below Room 74, presumed to be 'the treasuries of the royal ladies'.[62] Tombs II and III and Well 4 in Courtyard 80 'at the south-east corner of the domestic wing'[63] all contain a magnificent assortment of treasures including jewelry of gold and precious stones. Some of the items in the tombs are inscribed with the names of Atalia (wife of Sargon II), Yabâ (wife of Tiglath-pileser III) and Bānītu (wife of Shalmaneser V), but the bodies in the graves are not all queens; included are young women and some men.

The royal inventories of precious metals and stones found in the excavations at Nineveh track the receipt and dispersal of those valuables. References to the repair (*batqi*) of various items, including jewelry,[64] and items produced by someone as 'work for the king' (*dulli šarri*)[65] are included in the lists. The receipts do not identify the officer responsible for their maintenance nor is it possible to reconstruct the procedure by which this work was managed.[66] From their study of the location, content and possible chronology of these texts, Fales and Postgate conclude that 'during Sargon's reign at least, documentation of both receipts and disbursements of these precious metals was handled by a

61. '…den Geist des semitischen Kulturkreises, in dem die Frau von der Öffentlichkeit abgeschlossen war' (Weidner, 'Hof- und Harems-Erlasse', p. 258).

62. Joan Oates and David Oates, *Nimrud: An Assyrian Imperial City Revealed* (London: British School of Archaeology in Iraq, 2001), p. 67.

63. Oates and Oates, *Nimrud*, p. 100.

64. SAA, VII, 63 III' 7-8.

65. SAA, VII, 66 obv. 3 and 67 rev. II'1'.

66. There is a letter to the king from from 'Nabû-sāgib, the son of Parruṭu, a goldsmith of the household of the queen' in which he indicates that he has delivered some jewelry 'to the gate guard', Atanḫa-ilu, along with a letter, saying, 'Deliver them to the king, my lord!' Nabû-sāgib is inquiring whether the items have been delivered (SAA, XVI, 81 obv. 8-rev. 8).

single department closely attached to the royal palace'.[67] Interestingly, only one of these lists mentions the queen (*ša ēkalli* [MÍ-É.GAL])[68] and another list, after reporting a total of '12 minas 27 shekels of gold', indicates that 'the sample in the domestic quarter was not weighed' (*litku ina bītāne la ḫīṭi*).[69] The poor and incomplete condition of the surviving tablets makes it difficult to conclude for certain how the royal jewelry and gems were accounted for. The textual and archaeological information, though, do suggest that there might be more than 'a single department'. It would appear that neither the *rab ēkalli* nor the *šakintu* had this responsibility since the inventory lists were not among the collections of documents associated with those individuals.[70]

It is safe to assume that in all periods of Assyrian history gold, silver and precious gems were handled with care and that there were strictly enforced channels for their transfer; MAPD ¶5 makes this clear. The Nimrūd artifacts and the Nineveh documents offer a glimpse at the quality and value of the items possessed by members of the royal household—including women. The precise nature of how they were transmitted and the role that the giving and receiving of such items played in the politics of the royal household remain to be explored.

2.2. *The Activity of Palace Women*

It is commonly assumed that the seclusion of *harem* women from the general public is a sign of their exclusion from public matters. Their lives are typically perceived to be constructed around satisfying the sexual desires of the sultan/king and caring for the offspring of those relations. Efforts to advance their position in the female hierarchy and to promote their sons are typically ascribed to feminine jealousy and misbehavior. Their conversations are characterized as 'idle gossip'[71] and they are presumed to be uneducated and ignorant of the ways of the world. The Western 'outsider' commenting on a *harem* woman perceives that 'The veil and lattice of the Harem, even though established to guard her modesty and purity, have...[made] her a prisoner'.[72]

67. SAA, VII, p. XXIV.

68. SAA, VII, 70.

69. SAA, VII, 64 rev. II' 13.

70. Since both Assyrian men and women wore jewelry, including earrings, rings and bracelets, such items listed in administrative texts can not be securely assigned to female ownership without additional information.

71. G.Y. Holliday, 'Awakening Womanhood', in *Daylight in the Harem: A New Era for Moslem Women, Papers on Present-Day Reform Movements, Conditions and Methods of Work among Moslem Women, Read at the Lucknow Conference, 1911* (ed. Annie van Sommer and Samuel Marinus Zwemer; New York: Fleming H. Revell Company, 1911), pp. 117-29 (127).

72. 'Egypt, the Land of Bondage', in *Our Moslem Sisters: A Cry of Need from Lands of Darkness Interpreted by Those Who Heard It* (ed. A. van Sommer and S.M. Zwemer; New York: Fleming H. Revell Company, 1907), pp. 24-37 (31).

'Prisoner' might be an apt description of the restrictions on movement and public access, the presence of guards and the authority of the commander of the residence. But prisoners are taken *out of society* in an attempt to safeguard against their impact on the public. Their incarceration is a fall from social respectability and the work they perform in that context is of little concern or value to the general public. In contrast, the Ottoman imperial *harem* was located *inside* the center of social standing and imperial power. It was through entry into or connection with this community of women that citizens and foreigners sought to advance their cause and their own status.

Weidner perceived that the 'harem edicts' were needed to control the squabbling (*keifen*), blaspheming, and malicious remarks by palace women that were 'the order of the day, as it is wherever jealous women are together without anything to do'.[73] If the women of the *harem* had time on their hands, it was not because of enforced idleness, it was as a consequence of wealth and privilege that provided them attendants and servants of a variety of types and rankings. The Topkapı Palace sheltered a staff of thousands in all types of positions, including those who worked in the kitchen, the garden, the stables, the laundry, those who styled hair, made beds, served food, delivered messages, hauled water, cleaned, sewed and entertained.[74] The 'idle rich' might best characterize the families depicted in Demetra Vaka Brown's account of women in various Turkish *harems*. She writes of picnics, late night conversations watching the stars, evening board games, scented rose petals, slaves appearing at the clap of hands, lavish food spreads, afternoon naps, elegant clothing, multilingual conversations, exquisitely beautiful women, and handsome and thoughtful husbands. It is the type of opulence, leisure and privilege romanticized in Jane Austen novels and summoned to mind when one mentions locations such as Newport, RI, Monaco and The Hamptons. Brown can certainly be faulted for presenting too much of the 'poetry in everything'[75] in her description of the women of the *harem*, but her work also gives insight into the strict hierarchy of women and attendants that comprised the *harem* and to the various forms of social interaction among the ranking women. A report on Egyptian women in 'Our Moslim Sisters' observes that 'It seems like the irony of fate that these women who are kept in such strict seclusion should be so extravagantly fond of society. They welcome in the most hospitable manner any visitors of their own sex'.[76]

Emmeline Lott, who actually lived in the company of *harem* women, describes walks in the elegant gardens, yacht and barge rides on the Nile, car-

73. Weidner, 'Hof- und Harems-Erlasse', p. 279.

74. Lott reported for her context 'The census of the Harem is 150 to 200, slaves and eunuchs included' (Lott, *The 'English Governess' in Egypt*, I, p. 184).

75. Brown, *Haremlik*, p. 13.

76. 'Our Moslem Sisters', p. 34.

riage travel to visit the *harem* of the late viceroy, 'a whole bevy of slaves, both white and black [standing] about Her Highness, in the form of an everlasting crescent, awaiting the orders of their mistress',[77] daily arrangements of fresh flowers, evenings spent playing dominoes or 'having tales related to them, which often comprise incidents which had transpired in the Harems of the late Viceroys and their widows or daughters',[78] while their slaves listened sipping 'pure Mocha coffee' and 'munching away at *bonbons*, fruit, and the most luscious sweetmeats, and smoking cigarettes'.[79] While Lott sees no 'poetry' in anything related to the *harem*, such luxuries and services are in keeping with the categories of wealth and class from her British upbringing by which she judges the occupants of the *harem*. So it surprises her that 'their Highnesses [i.e. the chief wives] were about and stirring as early as four o'clock in the morning'.[80] Apparently 'On Mondays they employed themselves in cutting out pantaloons, dressing-gowns, &c. for their liege lord, which were then given to the German needlewoman to make up'.[81] Lott stands with her young pupil watching while 'the Lady Paramount (H.H. the first wife), under whose superintendence the whole of the household arrangements were carried on, entered the laundry'.[82] There, much to Lott's amazement, 'Her Highness, the first wife of H.H. Ismael Pacha, the richest prince in the universe, save His Imperial Majesty the Emperor of All the Russias, ...remained [working] all the live-long day every Tuesday, merely leaving the laundry to partake of her meals and to indulge in a short *siesta*'.[83]

The activity of the *harem* women was not all confined to domestic chores and amusements. Though she hardly approves, Lott discerns how the elite women in the *harem* were involved in 'political changes':

> But Ismael Pacha places his trust and confides his secrets to the care of the Princess Validè, his august mother, the clever intriguing widow of that singular Prince the late Ibrahim Pacha. Still, all the Princesses belonging to the other members of the Viceregal family of Egypt, both widows, wives, and daughters pay occasional visits to their Highnesses the three wives, with whom they generally pass the day; and their con-

77. Lott, *The 'English Governess' in Egypt*, I, p. 229.
78. Lott, *The 'English Governess' in Egypt*, I, p. 245.
79. Lott, *The 'English Governess' in Egypt*, I, pp. 245-46.
80. Lott, *The 'English Governess' in Egypt*, I, p. 236.
81. Lott, *The 'English Governess' in Egypt*, I, p. 239.
82. Lott, *The 'English Governess' in Egypt*, I, p. 249.
83. Lott, *The 'English Governess' in Egypt*, I, pp. 249-50. Lott's rigid class consciousness is troubled by the activity of the 'princesses' in contrast to the 'laziness' of the slaves from Africa of whom she said 'Their occupation during the best portion of the day consisted in lolling or rolling about the divans and mattresses which lay upon the ground, or squatting upon all fours, doubling themselves up like snips upon their boards or, clasped knives, which *pose plastique* **I was for ever** doomed to behold' (Lott, *The 'English Governess' in Egypt*, I, p. 215).

> versation, brief and curt though it may be, naturally turns upon the plans and actions of their liege lords, and then the Harem becomes the arena of
>
> 'That vermin slander, bred in abject minds,
> Of thoughts impure, by vile tongues animate,
> Canker of conversation'.[84]

Though Lott views such 'political changes which are hatched within [the *harem*] walls'[85] with suspicion, Peirce points to the significance of 'female networks sustained through formal visiting rituals [that] provided women with information and sources of power useful to their male relatives'.[86] Such information was not restricted to promoting the interests of individual men, since women of the Ottoman imperial *harem* had other economic, religious and political interests to advance that involved the brokering of information and power inside and outside the *harem* walls.

Though the inside of *harems* remained invisible to outsiders, in wealthy *harems*, the residents were apparently quite international, with slaves, musicians, teachers, and other personnel coming from around the Mediterranean, from Africa and from Europe. A variety of languages, customs, clothing and experiences were brought into the *harem* community. The *harem* was also the context in which women were educated for various domestic roles, in the religious traditions and, in some wealthy homes, in music, languages, literature and culture. A Miss M.M. Patrick, PhD, in her report on 'Educated Women of Turkey' at a conference on 'Present-Day Reform Movements, Conditions and Methods of [Christian] Work among Moslem Women', makes the observation that

> women in the harems have been an unknown quantity to the outside world... Thus seclusion and the Oriental setting have seemed the principal elements of their being, and have appeared to form such great disadvantages that various advantages have been lost sight of that are nevertheless connected with their legal and social relations.[87]

Among the 'advantages' that she reports is a woman's ability to control 'money that she has inherited, and after marriage...her dowry',[88] as well as the involvement of many women in trade, owing in part to the fact that 'the treasurer at the head of the royal harem has been a woman, in early days the Valideh Sultana, but later another woman was appointed for the position, who had under her control a regular bureau of trained scribes, all women'.[89] Patrick also points

84. Lott, *The 'English Governess' in Egypt*, I, p. 163.

85. Lott, *The 'English Governess' in Egypt*, I, p. 162.

86. Peirce, *The Imperial Harem*, p. 7.

87. M.M. Patrick, 'Among the Educated Women of Turkey', in *Daylight in the Harem*, pp. 71-89 (73-74).

88. Patrick, 'Among the Educated Women of Turkey', p. 76.

89. Patrick, 'Among the Educated Women of Turkey', p. 79.

to women's production of poetry and novels and their skill in music and painting. She also comments that 'The strict laws regarding harem life have obliged Mohammedan women to learn something of medicine, for there has always been a strong prejudice against men doctors entering the harems'.[90]

Patrick's observations are not made inside *harems*. In fact, they take place following the end of the Ottoman imperial harem in 1909 and are in the context of an appeal to Christians that 'The opportunity is ripe for a large social and educational development among Moslem women in Turkey'.[91] Nevertheless, her observation that gender segregation and separation can necessitate rather than eliminate women's education in the arts and sciences is an important one. It is in keeping with Peirce's characterization of the Topkapı Palace as a center for training women and men of a range of rankings and roles to care for the imperial house and to carry forward its business.[92] As the center of imperial rule, the Topkapı Palace needed to maintain its control over the East and its contacts with the West. The *harem* played a vital role in this and the elite among its residents needed to be trained and have staff to carry forward those responsibilities.

Lest there be any doubt that the education of royal women was an expectation of Assyrian palace life, we have the letter of Princess Šērūʾa-ēṭerat, Assurbanipal's sister, to Libbāli-šarrat, his wife, in which she chastises the crown princess for her failure to attend to her studies:

> Why don't you write your tablet and do your homework? (For) if you don't, they will say: 'Is this the sister of Šērūʾa-ēṭerat, the eldest daughter of the Succession Palace of Aššur-etel-ilāni-mukinni, the great king, mighty king, king of the world, king of Assyria?'[93]

Šērūʾa-ēṭerat is apparently worried that Libbāli-šarrat's lack of scholarly diligence will reflect poorly upon her.[94]

The correspondence of the royal women of Old Babylonian Mari provides extensive evidence of the education of royal women and the significance of their knowledge of political, cultic and economic matters for the safety and

90. Patrick, 'Among the Educated Women of Turkey', p. 84. Interestingly, Patrick's essay is published with a note by the editor amending Patrick's interpretation of women's property rights under Islamic law. The editor chafes at the implication that Islam might be the source of any advantage to women. The note indicates: 'The Quran does not provide for this right of woman to hold her own property, neither does it appear in the history of the founding of Islam. The inference is, that fathers and brothers have devised it to protect the women of their families whom they give in marriage, and that instead of reflecting credit on Islam, it reveals the low ideas which underlie the Moslem conception of marriage' (*Daylight in the Harem*, p. 90).

91. Patrick, 'Among the Educated Women of Turkey', p. 89.

92. E.g., the role of the *valide sultan* as 'mentor and guardian' (Peirce, *The Imperial Harem*, pp. 236-41).

93. SAA, XVI, 28 obv. 3-rev. 4.

94. See the commentary in SAA, XVI, p. xxviii.

wellbeing of the kingdom and the king. When reporting on the scheming of neighboring vassal kings (e.g., ARM, X, 5), the local weather (e.g., ARM, X, 25), problems in shipping goods (e.g., ARM, X, 18), omens (e.g., ARM, X, 6), or complaining about one another (e.g., Šimātum about Kirû's appropriation of a gardener in ARM, X, 95), their reports are matters of state, not 'idle gossip'. These royal women are vital to the networks of information and management through which the interests of the kingdom were carried out. If the *tubqum* in which Zimri-Lim's daughter Inib-šarri is made to reside (*ušēšibannima*) by her husband[95] is the 'harem' located 'deep within the palace',[96] it does not prevent her from knowing what was going on 'outside' that space and it does not prevent her from sending her message directly to the king. In addition to the contact the royal women had with scribes in preparing written correspondence, they also had contact with messengers and omen-takers, both male and female (e.g., ARM, X, 6 and 10).[97]

The content of the messages were, obviously, to be guarded from persons other than the designated recipient, but the transmission itself was public. The contacts included persons outside the royal family (e.g., ARM, X, 151) and are important within the larger network of reports and correspondence produced in the Mari kingdom. Commenting on the contacts of the elite women *inside* the Ottoman imperial *harem* with the *outside*, Peirce notes: 'this establishment of a constellation of contacts outside the palace was by no means surreptitious. Nor was it a uniquely "female" or "harem" paradigm for the organization of political patronage and the creation of political influence'.[98]

The Neo-Assyrian materials, likewise, provide indication of royal women's knowledge of and participation in administrative, legal, cultic and economic matters affecting other members of the royal house, individual citizens, temples and heads of state. In the archives in Nineveh there is correspondence from Nabû-nādin-šumi offering prayers for the life of Esarhaddon and for the life of the king's daughter (*mārrat šarri*).[99] Šaddītu, Esarhaddon's sister, purchases a garden, house, land and people for eight minas of silver.[100] A letter to the crown prince from Dadî, a priest, complains about the theft of household utensils worth twenty minas of silver that had been gifts from the queen mother and the king.[101] The queen mother receives reports in response

95. ARM, X, 74.17-18.

96. Malamat, 'Is There a Word for the Royal Harem?', p. 786.

97. Dossin notes that though the messenger in letter six is identified as *Ili-ḫaznāya, assinnu*, there is no agreement on whether this term denotes a 'eunuch' (ARM, X, p. 253, notes: letter 6 L. 5). The delivery of messages is not limited to eunuchs.

98. Peirce, *The Imperial Harem*, p. 148-49.

99. SAA, XVIII, 55.

100. SAA, VI, 251.

101. SAA, XIII, 154.

to her inquiries on cultic rituals and omens.[102] Na'id-Marduk reports to Queen Naq'ia on the Elamite attack that took out a bridge in the Sealand and assures her during this time of crisis that 'my lord should know that my heart is completely devoted to my lord's house'.[103] In one list of court officials at Nineveh, nine are specifically identified as assigned to the queen mother, including four eunuchs (LÚ.SAG), one treasurer, one bodyguard, a cohort commander and a chariot driver.[104] Among the female administrative personnel are thirteen *šakintē* (MÍ.GAR.MEŠ).[105] Tablets found in the royal library of the SW Palace at Nineveh record the purchase of people and property by Aḫī-ṭalli—who is identified as a *sekret ēkalli* (MÍ.ERIM-É.GAL) and a *šakintu* of the center city (*qabsi āli*).[106]

Not only did the interests and activities of the women of the palace extend far beyond the palace walls, but the royal 'household' was not limited to the activity of the king or restricted to the palace space. In MAPD ¶3, women working in the palace who reside with their husbands *outside* the palace are required to get the king's permission to return home on holidays; male staff—including royal eunuchs (*ša rēš šarre*) and doorkeepers (*mazziz pane*)—appear to require similar permission.[107] This suggests that the palace system is highly regulated but not sealed off. MAPD ¶3 does not indicate where in the palace such persons are assigned. In the Neo-Assyrian period Nabû-sagib, 'son of Parruṭu, a goldsmith of the household of the queen'[108] delivers gems to the king through the gate guard. Luukko and Van Buylaere observe that 'The passage also illustrates the strict policy of admission to the royal palace: it shows that a person belonging to the household of the queen could not automatically enter the royal palace, even if delivering important and valuable items'.[109] That raises the question of where the queen is located; is she *inside* or *outside* the royal palace? Does she live with the other women of the palace *inside* the palace—as in the Topkapı *harem*—or in a space separate from the other women, or even a different palace location altogether?[110]

102. SAA, XIII, 76, 77.

103. SAA, XVIII, 85 rev. 13'-15'.

104. SAA, VII, 5.

105. SAA, VII, 23.

106. SAA, VI, 88, 89, 90. CAD, Š/1 s.v. *šakintu*: 'The very large amounts of rations received by the *šakintu* (between three and ten times as much as those of the other women in [a] ration list) and the range and value of the business carried out by the *šakintu*, as well as etymological considerations (the analogy of *šaknu*) firmly establish the *šakintu* as the head of the [royal] harem', p. 166.

107. Roth, *Law Collections from Mesopotamia and Asia Minor*, p. 198 ¶3.

108. SAA, XVI, 81.2-3.

109. Luukko and van Buylaere, SAA, XVI, p. xxxvi.

110. In a letter to Esarhaddon there is reference to the palace of the queen in Kilīzi (Qaṣr Šimamuk) (SAA, XVI, 111).

The MAPD strictly regulate the entry and departure of palace personnel, male and female.[111] Violators are severely punished. Stephanie Dalley, who concludes that there was no 'harem' at Mari, hypothesizes that

> the royal harem as an institution probably came in during the Middle Assyrian period, several centuries later, when for the first time there were royal edicts that governed very strictly the behaviour of palace women and the behaviour of male palace staff towards them; at the same time a new code of public laws dealt savagely with women's rights and sexual behaviour, quite different from the laws of Hammurabi'.[112]

The brutal nature of the punishments and standards of the MAPD cannot be ignored. They have their parallels in the punitive measures of the Ottoman imperial *harem*. In the Ottoman context, strict regulation of the women of the *harem*—including their absence from public view—did not create an idle, detached or silent population. Should we assume such measures *did* have that result in the Middle Assyrian period? Even if it were the case for the Middle Assyrian period, the portrait of women's involvement is quite different in the Neo-Assyrian period.[113] It is clear that if the *harem* analogy is to be at all useful in Assyrian studies it cannot describe all periods of Assyrian history.

2.3. *Visibility and Invisibility*

The pattern of communication in the Mari and the Neo-Assyrian texts is consistent with the results of Samuel A. Meier's study of scribes and messengers in the ancient Near East. Commenting on the women, Meier concludes that it is 'inappropriate to perceive the female world as an isolated entity, dialogically involved only with itself... The harem, for example, did communicate with the world outside the walls of the palace, and men who dealt with the female scribes of both palace and cloister were often in debt to the women, having taken loans or rented fields'.[114] In Meier's view, the engagement of high-ranking women with members of the public is consistent with the term 'harem'. Leslie Peirce's close study of the Ottoman *harems*, Emmeline Lott's disparag-

111. MAPD ¶¶1, 3, 6, 9, 19, 20, 21, 22, and 23 all address the circulation of personnel in some way.

112. S. Dalley, *Mari and Karana: Two Old Babylonian Cities* (Piscataway, NJ: Gorgias Press, 2nd edn, 2002), p. 100.

113. There is not room in this essay to consider possible reasons for the differences. Sarah Chamberlin Melville examines the prominence of Naqʾia/Zakūtu and suggests it was orchestrated by Esarhaddon to secure his own position (S.C. Melville, *The Role of Naqia/Zakutu in Sargonid Politics* [SAAS, 9; Helsinki: Neo-Assyrian Text Corpus Project, 1999]). Peirce attributes changes in the Ottoman *harem* to 'a gradual transition from a state geared to expansion and led by a warrior sultan to a territorially stable bureaucratic state ruled by a sedentary palace sultan' (Peirce, *The Imperial Harem*, p. x).

114. Samuel A. Meier, 'Women and Communication in the Ancient Near East', *JAOS* 111 (1991), pp. 540-47 (546).

ing portrayal of an Egyptian *harem* and Demetra Vaka Brown's romanticized visits to Turkish *harems* all testify to the active engagement of women *inside* the *harem*s with the world *outside*.

The women of the Ottoman *harems* make their mark on the outside world but remain invisible to it. This invisibility appears to apply neither to the women of the Mari kingdom nor the Neo-Assyrian royal house. The Mari texts report Šibtu conducting royal responsibilities in the presence of other officials of the royal house[115] and royal daughters participating in official audiences.[116] In the Neo-Assyrian period there are inscriptions and artwork featuring royal women. Among these, Wilson points out, are 'ivory *pyxides*, or ointment boxes, [at Nimrūd] whereon both sexes are represented; one of these illustrates a musical feast perhaps presided over by a queen'.[117] Also at Nimrūd is a seal 'impression depicting a female worshipper before a scorpion-symbol...a symbol associated with the administration of the queen'.[118] If the location where it was found—Room HH—was 'the harem, of the Northwest Palace',[119] this seal not only fits the communication pattern that Meier describes,[120] but ties that communication to a visual image of the queen. At Sennacherib's palace at Nineveh, a colossal sphinx at a doorway is inscribed with a tribute to Tašmētu-šarrat, one of Sennacherib's wives.[121] Though *inside* the palace, its audience was everyone who passed into that space and it spelled out the way Sennacherib wished that audience to view this queen.

Sarah Chamberlin Melville argues that Esarhaddon intentionally and systematically promoted an image of his mother Naqʾia for public and court audiences as 'an authority figure who served as a bastion of strength for him: when he was ill or on a campaign Naqʾia could keep an eye on things; when he died she could see to it that Assurbanipal became king'.[122] Melville notes that this included 'placing his mother's image in two different temples in Assyria sometime during the last years of his reign'.[123]

115. ARM, X, 133.

116. ARM, X, 74.

117. J.V. Kinnier Wilson, *The Nimrud Wine Lists: A Study of Men and Administration at the Assyrian Capital in the Eighth Century, B.C.* (Cuneiform Texts from Nimrud, 1; London: British Schools of Archaeology in Iraq, 1972), p. xi.

118. Suzanne Herbordt, 'Neo-Assyrian Royal and Administrative Seals and their Use', in *Assyrien im Wandel der Zeiten: XXXIXe Rencontre assyriologique internationale Heidelberg 6.-10. Juli 1992* (ed. Hartmut Waetzoldt and Harald Hauptmann; Heidelberger Studien zum Alten Orient, 6; Heidelberg: Heidelberger Orientverlag, 1997), pp. 279-83 (282).

119. Herbordt, 'Neo-Assyrian Royal and Administrative Seals', p. 282.

120. Meier, 'Women and Communication', pp. 540-47.

121. Julian E. Reade, 'Was Sennacherib a Feminist?', in *La femme dans le Proche-Orient antique: XXXIIIe Rencontre assyriologique internationale (Paris, 7-10 Juillet 1986)* (ed. J.-M. Durand; Paris: Éditions Recherche sur les civilisations, 1987), pp. 139-45 (141).

122. Melville, *The Role of Naqia/Zakutu*, p. 36.

123. Melville, *The Role of Naqia/Zakutu*, p. 59.

Paula Albenda argues a similar propaganda goal for the bas-relief composition at Assurbanipal's North Palace at Nineveh that includes a portrayal of the king and queen dining together in an outdoor setting. In this scene, the queen is clearly visible and depicted in royal pose[124] seated across from her husband, while the head of the Elamite king Teumman swings from the branch of a tree behind her. The display of a military 'trophy' in the midst of this idyllic setting, Albenda concludes, is to extol the king for the 'benefits of peace' that are 'Ashurbanipal's ultimate attainment as a consequence of his military career'.[125] Whether or not one adopts Albenda's identification of the meal setting as 'in the harem quarters, in the "garden of happiness" ',[126] there is no question that the queen is a visible and essential element of Assurbanipal's monumental composition announcing his accomplishments in securing the peace and well-being of the royal house and, by extension, the kingdom.

While the faces of the women of the Ottoman *harem* were not visible to the general public, the women were nevertheless critical in creating the public face of the imperial household. Peirce notes that 'In a period when it was deemed politically useful for the sultan to remain aloof from his subjects, public promotion of royal women helped to compensate the populace for the paucity of sultanic ceremonial'.[127] Charitable works on the part of royal women, 'patronage of scholars as well as of calligraphers, artists, architects and other craftsmen'[128] and 'pious endowments for public hospitals, markets, trade centers, colleges, schools, libraries, hostels, aqueducts, fountains, and so on'[129] not only promoted the royal house but were essential to securing the peace and well-being of the empire.

Peirce's analysis of the activity of Ottoman *harem* women in promoting the image and interests of the imperial house encourages similar examination of the contributions of Assyrian royal women.[130] Westenholz has already urged that 'Basic investigatory work...be done on the subject of inscriptions by royal females'.[131] This involves placing women at the center of inquiry and examining

124. Pauline Albenda, 'Landscape Bas-Reliefs in the *Bīt-Ḫilāni* of Ashurbanipal', *BASOR* 224 (December 1976), pp. 49-72 (63).

125. Albenda, 'Landscape Bas-Reliefs in the *Bīt-Ḫilāni* of Ashurbanipal—Continued', *BASOR* 225 (February 1977), pp. 29-45 (45).

126. Albenda, 'Landscape Bas-Reliefs—Continued', p. 45.

127. Peirce, *The Imperial Harem*, p. 216.

128. Peirce, *The Imperial Harem*, p. 217.

129. Peirce, *The Imperial Harem*, p. 218.

130. Five areas of activity through which women contribute to royal administration are outlined in chapter one of Elna K. Solvang, *A Woman's Place is in the House: Royal Women of Judah and their Involvement in the House of David* (JSOTSup, 349; Sheffield: Sheffield Academic Press, 2003), pp. 16-50.

131. Westenholz, 'Towards a New Conceptualization of the Female Role in Mesopotamian Society', p. 519.

their visibility and activities within the royal system, including their interactions with the various male officials of the royal bureaucracy and with the general citizenry. Perhaps closer study of the royal women may also shed some light on when and how royal men contributed to the image of the royal house.[132] In the Ottoman context, all Ottoman princes after Mehmed III (d. 1603) were confined to the palace, 'to emerge only if and when they ascended the throne'.[133]

3. *The Results of 'Inside' Information*

The starting point for this essay was Malamat's use of 'harems throughout the ancient Near East and later in the Islamic and Ottoman Empires'[134] as an analogy to guide his search for a term and a space deep *inside* the palace designating 'the physical realm of the women's quarters'.[135] However this essay reverses the direction of Malamat's inquiry, looking first *inside* Ottoman *harems* to discover how they fit into their society, how they participate in the royal governance, how they are structured and regulated, and how they communicate with and influence the larger society. Sources for this exploration have ranged from scholarly analyses (e.g., Peirce and Penzer) to individual observations (e.g., Lott, Patrick, Brown). The goal has not been to produce an exhaustive study of *harems* but to gain sufficient knowledge to test the analogy between Ottoman *harems* and the ancient Assyrian context.

Women in both contexts function in highly stratified and regulated settings, live with other women (and some males), have the benefits of wealth, conduct business, and communicate with persons outside of their domicile. The *harem* of the Topkapı Palace is more than a space; it is a female institution crucial to the functioning of the Ottoman imperial house and its governance of the land. The term *harem* signals the sacredness of the space and the honor and obeisance due its members;[136] a status that is preserved by 'seclusion from the common gaze'.[137] The *harem* analogy applied to Mari and the Neo-Assyrian materials illuminates patterns of royal women's activities and their benefits for the kingdom that are similar to those of the Ottoman women. A hierarchy can be discerned in the data but it is not evident that these royal women function as a female institution in the same way as the Ottoman *harem*. Moreover, the palace women at Mari and in the Neo-Assyrian context do not appear to share the invisibility of the Ottoman women,[138] hence it is important to examine how

132. It might help explain why only three princes appear on the distribution lists to the 'harem of Zimri-Lim'. See Ziegler, *Le harem de Zimri-Lim*, p. 9.

133. Peirce, *The Imperial Harem*, p. 98, discussion on p. 21.

134. Malamat, 'Is There a Word for the Royal Harem?', p. 785.

135. Malamat, 'Is There a Word for the Royal Harem?', p. 786.

136. See the discussion of *harem* in Peirce, *The Imperial Harem*, pp. 3-5.

137. Peirce, *The Imperial Harem*, p. 8.

138. Westenholz argues that veiling in Islamic society is another point of 'lack of correspon-

visibility—rather than invisibility— factors into the functions they perform and into the image of the royal house that they project in the kingdom.

Even freed from its Orientalist baggage, the Ottoman *harem* analogy does not fit with the Mari and Neo-Assyrian data.[139] Applying the analogy to these contexts necessitates qualifying the term and the institution it represents and can result in missing or misreading the ancient sources. Hopefully this essay has demonstrated that it is precisely when the *harem* is studied in its *own* religious-sociological-political context that it can be useful in the discussion of the Mesopotamian sources and in developing hypotheses about ancient palace life and functioning.

dence' between the *harem* model and ancient Syrian and Assyrian practice (Westenholz, 'Towards a New Conceptualization of the Female Role in Mesopotamian Society', p. 515).

139. This essay does not intend to imply that the Middle Assyrian period fits the analogy, only that the Mari Old Babylonian and Neo-Assyrian periods clearly do not. This examination of the Ottoman *harem* has exposed differences between the historical periods represented in the available data. More attention needs to be given to examining the sources from the Middle Assyrian period and then to relating that portrait to the later periods in Mesopotamian social history.

Assyriology and the Bible

Biblical Historiography in the Persian Period: or How the Jews Took Over the Empire

Lester L. Grabbe

One of the purposes of scholarly discourse and discussion is to cast a critical eye over our own presuppositions and assumptions. There are fads and bandwagons in scholarship as much as in ordinary life. We look back at the consensus of a former generation and shake our heads, for advancement is often a generational sort of thing: it takes a new generation, without the baggage of the previous one, to see its follies and move in a new direction. We all have our blind spots, but this should not prevent us from pointing out that the scholarly stampede is heading straight for a cliff.

The importance of the Persian period for Jewish history has been widely recognized, but what has not been so widely recognized is the extent to which Jewish history has reflected the propaganda of the sources. For example, one can point to E. Yamauchi's *Persia and the Bible* where the biblical text—whether Ezra, Esther, or Daniel—is accepted as factual and used as a reliable historical source.[1] Although this is a clear and blatant example, it could be argued with some justice that this is exceptional: most writers on the Jews in the Persian period do not work on the basis of biblical fundamentalism. Yet the bias of the Jewish sources has been widely followed by scholars for the past century and more, at least with the book of Ezra, as I intend to demonstrate.

One of the features of Jewish literature in the Second Temple period is the theme of Jews in interaction with their rulers. 'Court literature' forms a significant niche in Jewish writings of this time. Some of this literature was either written in the Persian period or ostensibly relates to the Persian period. In this sense a number of biblical writings are relevant for Jewish historiography with regard to the Persian period. I shall focus specifically, first, on the Joseph story, Daniel, Esther, and Ahiqar, and then draw on them in taking a more detailed look at Ezra. These writings have been chosen for a specific reason: in looking at Jewish literature, scholars have not by and large taken the picture in the Joseph story, Esther, Daniel, and Ahiqar at face value; on the other hand, many critical scholars have been more tolerant of similar material in Ezra-Nehemiah.

1. Edwin M. Yamauchi, *Persia and the Bible* (Grand Rapids MI: Baker Book House, 1990). See my review in *JSJ* 22 (1991), pp. 295-98.

This will be one of my main points: material accepted as historical without much criticism in Ezra-Nehemiah has been—inconsistently—rejected for other writings.

1. *Past Scholarly Approaches and Schools*

If we go back to the late nineteenth century, we see the beginnings of what might be considered two streams of interpretation—'school' might imply something more formal that it really was—exemplified in the positions of Julius Wellhausen and Eduard Meyer.[2] In 1895 Wellhausen wrote an article on the return of the Jews from the Babylonian exile, in which he was skeptical of the alleged Persian documents in Ezra 4–7 and other points in the book of Ezra.[3] The next year Meyer published his lengthy study of the origins of Judaism, with its primary focus on the narratives in the book of Ezra (plus some material from Nehemiah).[4] He mentioned a number of scholars, including Wellhausen (but not particularly singling him out), and commented, 'At present, it seems, all critical scholars are in agreement that all the documents of the book of Ezra are forgeries, which at best contain only a badly distorted representation of the real situation'.[5] Among those who took this position of inauthenticity was the great Semitist Theodor Nöldeke.[6] Undaunted, Meyer proceeded to advance a lengthy argument in favor of authenticity for those in Ezra 4–6 (in his chapter 1), followed by a general study of Judah's history in the first part of the Persian period.

Shortly after Meyer's work appeared, Wellhausen reviewed it in a rather startling way; at least, Meyer was startled by the review.[7] Wellhausen's opening sentence was provocative ('This book is essentially directed against me'[8]),

2. A useful overview of the interchange between Wellhausen and Meyer is given by Reinhard Gregor Kratz, 'Die Entstehung des Judentums: Zur Kontroverse zwischen E. Meyer und J. Wellhausen', in *idem*, *Das Judentum im Zeitalter des Zweiten Tempels* (FAT, 42; Tübingen: Mohr Siebeck, 2004), pp. 6-22.

3. Julius Wellhausen, 'Die Rückkehr der Juden aus dem babylonischen Exil', *Nachrichten von der Königl. Gesellschaft der Wissenschaften in Göttingen*, Philologisch-historische Klasse (Berlin: Akademie der Wissenschaften, 1895), pp. 166-86.

4. Eduard Meyer, *Die Entstehung des Judenthums: Eine historische Untersuchung* (Halle: Max Niemeyer, 1896; repr. Hildesheim: Olms, 1965).

5. Meyer, *Entstehung*, p. 3: 'Gegenwärtig stimmen, wie es scheint, alle kritischen Forscher darin überein, dass alle aramäischen Urkunden des Buches Ezra Fälschungen sind, die im günstigsten Falle nur eine arg entstellte Darstellung des wirklichen Hergangs enthalten'. See also the brief survey in Charles C. Torrey, *Ezra Studies* (Chicago: University of Chicago Press, 1910; repr. edited with a prolegomenon by W.F. Stinespring; New York: Ktav Publishing House, 1970), pp. 142-45.

6. See the references given by Franz Rosenthal, *Die aramaistische Forschung seit Th. Nöldeke's Veröffentlichungen* (Leiden: E.J. Brill, 1964 [1939]), p. 63; Torrey, *Ezra Studies*, p. 142.

7. In the *Göttingische gelehrte Anzeigen* 159/2 (1897), pp. 89-97.

8. 'Dies Buch is wesentlich gegen mich gerichtet' (*Göttingische gelehrte Anzeigen* 159/2 [1897], p. 89).

and he continued in the same vein to give not only a negative review but also a rather sarcastic and cutting one. Meyer was clearly hurt by the review. His 25-page reply (to Wellhausen's seven-page review) was published as a single volume with *Entstehung des Judenthums*.[9] But he claims that he initially aimed for a low-key response. He says that he sent a short note of correction to the journal in which Wellhausen's review appeared, by which he thought 'to be able to dispose of the concerns' through letting the reader know that the basic outlook dominating the review was contrary to the facts; the reader could then make up his own mind without Meyer having to give a detailed response to all the 'careless, malicious, and misleading' statements perpetrated by Wellhausen.[10] Unfortunately, according to Meyer, the journal editorship returned the note with the statement that they did not print responses to reviews (except where there was a legal ruling to do so). Meyer also claims that the references to Wellhausen's 1895 publication were inserted into his book manuscript after it had been written.[11] To a reader not taking sides, Meyer seems to have had a point: no special concentration on Wellhausen is apparent in the book.

Although, as Meyer pointed out, the dominant view in German-speaking scholarship was against the authenticity of the alleged documents in Ezra, the clash of these two giants was emblematic of the positions held throughout the twentieth century. Indeed, Meyer would have been gratified to see how much his position became the prevailing one, at least among English-speaking scholars. C.C. Torrey also took a skeptical point of view about Ezra, as did L.W. Batten,[12] but—with some exceptions—commentators in the later twentieth century have generally followed the stories in the book of Ezra as essentially historical, especially (but not exclusively) in English-speaking scholarship: Mowinckel,[13] Rudolph, Myers, Clines, Wil-

9. Meyer, *Julius Wellhausen und meine Schrift Die Entstehung des Judentums: Eine Erwiderung* (Halle: Max Niemeyer, 1897). The version of *Die Enstehung des Judenthums* available to me is a reprint (Hildesheim: Olms, 1965) that includes the reply to Wellhausen at the end of the volume, in the same format as the original edition.

10. Meyer, *Julius Wellhausen und meine Schrift*, p. 251 (5):

> Damit glaubte ich die Angelegenheit erledigen zu können. Denn ich meinte, wenn ich nachwies, dass die Grundanschauung, von der die Recension beherrscht ist, mit den Thatsachen in Widerspruch steht, würde der Leser genügend gewarnt sein und sich, wenn er mein Buch zur Hand nahm, selbst ein Urtheil über ihren Werth bilden können, ohne das ich nöthig hätte, alle die Flüchtigkeiten, Gehässigkeiten und Entstellungen, die Wellhausen begangen hat, in einzelnen aufzuweisen.

11. Meyer, *Julius Wellhausen*, p. 250 (4).

12. C.C. Torrey, *The Composition and Historical Value of Ezra–Nehemiah* (BZAW, 2; Giessen: J. Ricker Buchhandlung, 1896); idem, *Ezra Studies*; Loring W. Batten, *A Critical and Exegetical Commentary on Ezra and Nehemiah* (ICC, 12; Edinburgh: T. & T. Clark, 1913).

13. Sigmund Mowinckel, *Studien zu dem Buche Ezra–Nehemia.* I. *Die nachchronische Redaktion des Buches. Die Liste* (Skrifter utgitt av Det Norske Videnskaps-Akademi i Oslo II.

liamson, Blenkinsopp.[14] Naturally, these commentators do not represent a unified view, and some have expressed greater reservations than others. But real skepticism appeared once again with L.C.H. Lebram and especially with A.H.J. Gunneweg.[15]

2. *Four Examples of Jewish Historiography*

As a preface to looking at the picture in the book of Ezra, this section will examine four other examples of texts that either ostensibly relate to the Persian period or probably arose in the Persian period, though on the surface they describe another time in history. Those ostensibly relating to the Persian period—even if written at quite another time—are the books of Esther and Daniel. Two others that may actually have originated in the Persian period (at least in their known form) are the stories of Joseph and Ahiqar.

One of the important points to emerge from the investigation of these four texts is a literary pattern of the Jewish hero's triumph and elevation to high office.[16] The full pattern can be reconstructed along the following lines:

Hist.-Filos. Klasse. Ny Serie, 3; Oslo: Universitetsforlaget, 1964); idem, *Studien zu dem Buche Ezra–Nehemia.* II. *Die Nehemia-Denkschrift* (Skrifter utgitt av Det Norske Videnskaps-Akademi i Oslo II. Hist.-Filos. Klasse. Ny Serie, 5; Oslo: Universitetsforlaget, 1964); idem, *Studien zu dem Buche Ezra–Nehemia.* III. *Die Ezrageschichte und das Gesetz Moses* (Skrifter utgitt av Det Norske Videnskaps-Akademi i Oslo II. Hist.-Filos. Klasse. Ny Serie, 7; Oslo: Universitetsforlaget, 1965). Mowinckel did not do a full study of the passages with the 'Persian documents', but he stated that he was convinced by Meyer (*Studien*, III, p. 114). In *Studien III* he also investigated specifically the Artaxerxes decree relating to Ezra (pp. 113-17).

14. Wilhelm Rudolph, *Esra und Nehemia samt 3. Esra* (HAT, 20: Tübingen: J.C.B. Mohr [Paul Siebeck], 1949); Jacob M. Myers, *Ezra. Nehemiah: Introduction, Translation and Notes* (AB, 14; Garden City, NY: Doubleday, 1965); David J.A. Clines, *Ezra, Nehemiah, Esther: Based on the Revised Standard Version* (NCBC; London: Marshall, Morgan & Scott/Grand Rapids MI: Eerdmans, 1984); H.G.M. Williamson, *Ezra, Nehemiah* (WBC, 16; Waco, TX: Word Books, 1985); Joseph Blenkinsopp, *Ezra–Nehemiah: A Commentary* (OTL; London: SCM Press, 1989).

15. Antonius H.J. Gunneweg, *Esra* (KAT, 19.1; Gütersloh: Gütersloher Verlagshaus Mohn, 1985); J.C.H. Lebram, 'Die Traditionsgeschichte der Ezragestalt und die Frage nach dem historischen Esra', in *Achaemenid History.* I. *Sources, Structures and Synthesis* (ed. Heleen Sancisi-Weerdenburg; Proceeding of the Groningen 1983 Achaemenid History Workshop; Leiden: Nederlands Instituut voor het Nabije Oosten, 1987), pp. 103-38. It was Gunneweg's arguments that led me to reevaluate my own perspective which up until the late 1980s had agreed with the credulous position. Although I had read Meyer, I had been unaware of Wellhausen's position and of his altercation with Meyer until recently. What is intriguing, though hardly surprising, is the fact that some of Wellhausen's points are the same ones that had arisen from my own study of the traditions in the book of Ezra.

16. The important article by W. Lee Humphreys ('A Life-Style for Diaspora: A Study of the Tales of Esther and Daniel', *JBL* 92 [1973], pp. 211-23) has much of interest about tales like those drawn on in my study; however, he does not suggest a particular literary pattern such as I outline here.

1. A low beginning state (in captivity, slavery, or at least a state of subordination to a foreign power).
2. An initial measure of success or even elevation to a position of status.
3. A major setback, with perhaps even a threat to the person's life.
4. The threat overcome (divine help usually explicitly mentioned or strongly implied).
5. The protagonist rewarded, often directly by the (non-Jewish) king or emperor, frequently with a high office in the government.

To illustrate how this pattern is replicated in the examples, the various elements in the stories discussed below will be numbered according to the model above.

The Story of Joseph (Genesis 37, 40–50)

The story of Joseph has been variously dated, but there are good arguments to connect the version in Genesis—the only one known to us, even if there might have been others—with the Persian period. The first argument is that the Pentateuch as a whole is probably the product of the Persian period.[17] The second is that various elements within the Joseph story seem to point to the Persian period as its context.[18] The story of Joseph follows the following pattern:

1. Joseph is sold into slavery.
2. Joseph obtains favor in Potiphar's household.
3. He is accused by Potiphar's wife and is imprisoned.
4. His fortune changes when he interprets the king's dreams with supernatural help.
5. Joseph is made second-in-charge over Egypt by the Pharaoh.

The Book of Esther

The dating of the book is not completely clear, some putting it in the Greek period, but it tells a story relating to the Persian period and clearly attempts to presume a Persian background. There are indications that the writer was familiar with the city of Susa, yet the story itself is evidently a fiction.[19] There are

17. The Jewish community at Elephantine evidently did not know the Pentateuch, since in the extensive documents relating to Jewish law and Jewish observances, there is no reference to the Pentateuch as such, not even to Moses. On the other hand, there are good reasons to think the Pentateuch was in much its present form by the end of the Persian period. See Lester L. Grabbe, *A History of the Jews and Judaism in the Second Temple Period.* I. *Yehud: A History of the Persian Province of Judah* (LSTS, 47; London and New York: T. & T. Clark International, 2004), pp. 331-43.

18. See especially Donald B. Redford, *A Study of the Biblical Story of Joseph (Genesis 37–50)* (VTSup, 20; Leiden: E.J. Brill, 1970).

19. The attempt by J. Stafford Wright ('The Historicity of the Book of Esther', in *New Per-*

some problems because the book of Esther exists in a variety of versions,[20] but for our purposes the central story is basically the same in the various versions. It is somewhat complicated because instead of only one protagonist, as in the story of Joseph, there are three: (a) Esther, (b) her uncle Mordecai, and (c) the Jewish community:

1. (a) Esther and (b) Mordecai are living in Susa as a part of (c) the Jewish diaspora.
2. (a) Esther is chosen as queen of Ahasuerus (Xerxes), and (b) Mordecai also comes to court.
3. Haman threatens the (c) entire Jewish community but also (b) Mordecai in particular [and (a) Esther by implication].
4. (a) Esther makes her identity known to Ahasuerus; (b) Mordecai's service to the king becomes known and Haman is executed.
5. (a) Mordecai is elevated next to the king; (b) Esther is given Haman's property; (c) the Jewish community is allowed to defend itself and establish a new festival.

The pattern is complicated, especially with regard to (c) the Jewish community which disappears in some cases, but it follows through for the most part with (a) Esther and (b) Mordecai. Queen Esther is not under direct threat under point 3 above, but there is still an implied threat. Similarly, as queen she cannot really move up in status, but she is given Haman's estate. Thus, the basic pattern is present for all three main actors in the story.

The Book of Daniel

The book of Daniel probably grew up from a set of tales that lie at the core of the book in chs. 2–6. These may well have circulated as a unit for a period of time, but the apocalyptic chs. 7–12 were eventually added, as well as probably chapter 1 to create a unit. Yet this only describes the Hebrew version, and we must keep in mind that other versions circulated, so far attested only in Greek.[21]

spectives on the Old Testament [ed. J. Barton Payne; Evangelical Theological Society Symposium Series, 3; Waco, TX: Word Books, 1970], pp. 37-47) to find historical material in the book is clearly apologetic and strains at harmonistic gnats while ignoring the great camels of contradiction that crash through the story.

20. The various versions are discussed by several recent studies: David J.A. Clines, *The Esther Scroll: The Story of the Story* (JSOTSup, 30; Sheffield: JSOT Press, 1984); Karen H. Jobes, *The Alpha-Text of Esther: Its Character and Relationship to the Masoretic Text* (SBLDS, 153; Atlanta GA: Scholars Press, 1996); Charles V. Dorothy, *The Books of Esther: Structure, Genre, and Textual Integrity* (JSOTSup, 187; Sheffield: Sheffield Academic Press, 1997); Kristin De Troyer, *The End of the Alpha Text of Esther: Translation and Narrative Technique in MT 8:1-17, LXX 8:1-17, and AT 7:14-41* (trans. Brian Doyle; SBLSCS, 48; Atlanta, GA: Society of Biblical Literature, 2000).

21. Recent studies on these include Sharon Pace Jeansonne, *The Old Greek Translation of*

It is the tales of 1–6—though not contradicted by 7–12—that provide the pattern of salvation. These mainly relate to (a) Daniel but in part include (b) his three friends Hananiah, Azariah, and Mishael. There is also more than one episode, which needs to be taken account of:

1. (a) Daniel and (b) his friends are taken captive to Babylonia (Daniel 1).
2. (a) Daniel and (b) friends are selected for training for the king's service, including service as 'magicians'.

First episode (Daniel 2):

3. The king threatens to put the 'magicians' to death, including (a) Daniel and (b) friends.
4. (a) Daniel interprets Nebuchadnezzar's dream (with the meaning revealed by God), and all the wisemen of Babylon are saved.
5. (a) Daniel is elevated to governor of Babylon and chief of the wisemen and (b) the friends are made sub-administrators over Babylon.

Second episode (Daniel 3):

3. (b) Daniel's friends refuse to worship Nebuchadnezzar's image and are cast into the fiery furnace.
4. (b) The friends are saved from the furnace, with divine help strongly implied.
5. (b) The friends' God is acknowledged and they are promoted.

Third episode (Daniel 5):

[3. It is implied that (a) Daniel has become obsolescent at the Babylonian court.]
4. (a) Daniel interprets the unseen writing when no one else can.
5. (a) Daniel is elevated to one of three just below the king.

Fourth episode (Daniel 6):

2. (a) Daniel is one of three ministers over the kingdom of 'Darius the Mede'.
3. The machinations of other ministers lead to (a) Daniel's being condemned and thrown into the lion's den.
4. An angel of God delivers (a) Daniel from being eaten or mauled by the lions.
5. (a) Daniel prospers during the reign of Darius and beyond.

Daniel 7–12 (CBQM, 19; Washington, DC: Catholic Biblical Association of America, 1988); T.J. Meadowcroft, *Aramaic Daniel and Greek Daniel: A Literary Comparision* (JSOTSup, 198; Sheffield: Sheffield Academic Press, 1995); Tim McLay, *The OG and Th Versions of Daniel* (SBLSCS, 43; Atlanta, GA: Scholars Press, 1996).

Although a number of different episodes are described in Daniel 1–6, they still follow the common pattern, with the possible exception of the 'handwriting on the wall' (Daniel 5). The aim of that story is somewhat different from the others in that it wants to focus on the *hubris* of Belshazzar and the conquest of Babylon rather than Daniel as such. Yet even here the pattern is implied, at least to a large extent. When we look at other tales in the Daniel tradition, the results are mixed but interesting. *Bel and the Dragon* are really polemics against idolatry, and Daniel's function is to be the clever servant of God who exposes the falsity of this worship. But when we come to the story of *Susanna*, we actually see the pattern replicated for the most part:

1. Susanna lives in the diaspora.
2. She is the daughter of righteous parents and marries a rich husband.
3. Her status and estate are threatened by two elders who wish to commit adultery with her but who then lie when she resists and tries to expose them.
4. Her reputation is saved when Daniel uncovers the lies of the two elders.

[5. She resumes her position and status in society.]

Ahiqar

Strictly speaking Ahiqar is not a Jewish book, at least in origin. It seems to have been an Aramaic tale that perhaps originated in the Neo-Assyrian period (which is its ostensible setting, in the reign of Esarhaddon). Yet it was taken over and 'Judaized' by the Jewish community. We have evidence from texts found among the Elephantine documents that the Jews had adopted it and made it their own, though it naturally continued to circulate in its non-Jewish form, leaving a number of different later Near Eastern versions.[22] This Judaizing of the book is further indicated by the book of Tobit which makes Ahiqar a kinsman of Tobit's family (Tobit 1.21-22). The Elephantine version is used where available, but it lacks the ending of the story for which the later versions need to be consulted.[23]

[1. Ahiqar is apparently a member of the diaspora Jewish community.]

2. Ahiqar is scribe and keeper of the seal of King Esarhaddon.

22. See the catalogue of these in Frederick C. Conybeare, J. Rendel Harris, and Agnes Smith Lewis, *The Story of Ahikar: From the Syriac, Arabic, Armenian, Ethiopic, Greek and Slavonic Versions* (London: C.J. Clay & Sons, 1898).

23. For an edition of the Elephantine version, see James M. Lindenberger, *The Aramaic Proverbs of Ahiqar* (The Johns Hopkins Near Eastern Studies; Baltimore, MD: The Johns Hopkins University Press, 1983). A convenient translation of some of the later versions is found in J.R. Harris, A.S. Lewis and F.C. Conybeare, 'The Story of Aḥiḳar', in *The Apocrypha and Pseudepigrapha of the Old Testament in English: With Introductions and Critical and Explanatory Notes to the Several Books* (2 vols.; ed. R.H. Charles; Oxford: Clarendon Press, 1913), II, pp. 715-84.

3. Nadan, Ahiqar's nephew, tells lies about him and gets him condemned to death. He survives only because his executioner, whom he had helped in the past, substitutes another condemned man and then hides Ahiqar.
4. When Esarhaddon is challenged by the Pharaoh in a contest of riddles, Ahiqar is revealed to be alive and is brought back to support Esarhaddon.
5. Ahiqar is restored to his former position and executes Nadan by starvation, lecturing him via the wisdom sayings that form the second half of the book.

Point 1 seems more or less to have disappeared and can be restored only by a certain presumption. This may well be because of the origin of the story elsewhere that was only subsequently borrowed into the Jewish context. Otherwise, though, it fits the pattern very well.

3. *The Central Example: the Book of Ezra*

There are basically two stories in the book of Ezra. The first is about the initial settlement and building of the temple in the early Persian period (Ezra 1–6). The other is the story of Ezra (Ezra 7–10 plus Nehemiah 8). The narrative of Ezra 1–6 has some problematic features, notably the reference to alleged correspondence and events much later in the Persian period.[24] Nevertheless, the story surprisingly shows a pattern similar to that reconstructed from the previous writings:

[1. The Jews are in exile with the temple destroyed and Jerusalem in a ruined state.]
2. Cyrus issues a decree and well over 40,000 Jews return and begin the rebuilding of the temple.
3. The 'enemies of Judah and Benjamin' (Ezra 4.1) complain to the authorities and get the construction of the temple (and city?) stopped.
4. At the urging of prophets, the building is resumed; a search is made and the earlier permission to build is not only confirmed by Darius but financial support is provided from the imperial treasury.
5. The temple is completed and dedicated.

At first sight, the Ezra story seems somewhat diverse from the comparative stories; however, a closer look reveals some interesting points, partly because the story is not just about (a) Ezra but also about the (b) community in the land of Judah, and the pattern is largely replicated:

1. (a) Ezra is living in the diaspora, while (b) the Jewish community is 'slaves' in its own land (Ezra 9.9).

24. My more detailed treatment of these points is found in the works listed in the next note.

2. (a) Ezra is allowed to return and bring the law, as well as bearing great gifts for (b) the community.
3. Both (a) Ezra and (b) the community are threatened by the revelation of intermarriage.
4. The (b) community leaders, followed by (a) Ezra, come up with a solution to cleanse the community of the 'evil'.
5. (b) The community is purified, [and (a) Ezra is free to carry out his duties of teaching the law, which is described in the continuation of the story in Nehemiah 8].

The following catalogues some of the main examples of tendentiousness in the book of Ezra. Since I have already written extensively on the perspectives and biases of the compiler of Ezra-Nehemiah,[25] I shall only summarize some of the points I have made in other writings.

The Persian king openly recognizes and declares the greatness of the Jewish God. This is of course well known from the book of Daniel where Nebuchadnezzar (Dan. 3.28-29; 4.31-34) proclaims the Jewish God. The Joseph story is more low key, but even here the Pharaoh acknowledges Joseph's claim that it was 'God' who revealed the meaning of the dream to Joseph (Gen. 41.38-39). The Cyrus decree recognizes 'YHWH God of Israel' (Ezra 1.2-4). The Artaxerxes rescript presents a devotion to 'the God in Jerusalem' that goes beyond the normal lip service paid to the god of another people (Ezra 7.19-23). We do have some examples in which Cyrus claimed to act in the name of Marduk or Sîn,[26] but these differed in that they were central gods of the Mesopotamian pantheon. The primary consideration, however, is that the main object of these decrees is not to acknowledge particular gods; rather, the inscriptions are about the Persian king and aim to make him palatable to the people who worship that particular god. The decrees in Ezra, on the other hand, are not about the king but about the Jewish people. Their aim is to show that their god is recognized and honored by the king. We have no parallels to this in Persian sources.

25. My more detailed treatment of Ezra can be found in the following: Grabbe, *Judaism from Cyrus to Hadrian*. I. *Persian and Greek Periods;* II. *The Roman Period* (Minneapolis, MN: Fortress Press, 1992); British edition in one-volume paperback (London: SCM Press, 1994), pp. 126-38; *idem*, 'What Was Ezra's Mission?', in *Second Temple Studies*, 2: *Temple Community in the Persian Period* (ed. Tamara C. Eskenazi and Kent H. Richards; JSOTSup, 175; Sheffield: Sheffield Academic Press, 1994), pp. 286-99; *idem*, *Ezra–Nehemiah* (Old Testament Readings; London: Routledge, 1998), pp. 125-53; *idem*, *History of the Jews and Judaism*, pp. 269-85, 324-31.

26. As a part of Cyrus's propaganda to the newly conquered peoples, he had himself proclaimed as the choice of Marduk in a decree to the Babylonians (Cyrus Cylinder, ll.10-15; see *COS* II, no. 124 pp. 314-16), while in Nippur he was presented as the choice of Sîn (Roland de Vaux, 'The Decrees of Cyrus and Darius on the Rebuilding of the Temple', in *Bible and the Ancient Near East* [trans. Damian McHugh; London: Darton, Longman & Todd, 1971], pp. 63-96 [68-69]).

The emperor himself intervenes on behalf of the Jews. It is not just middle-ranking or high Persian officials who exercise themselves in service of the Jews but the emperor himself. In the Joseph story Joseph deals with the Pharaoh and serves him directly. Daniel serves the kings of Babylonia and Persia, as does Ahiqar the Assyrian king. Esther is married to the king, and Mordecai has direct contact with him. Our attested examples from the Persian period, on the other hand, involve Persian officials, not usually the king.[27] Yet the decree for the Jews to return and build the temple is allegedly issued by Cyrus in his very first year when he was busy with all sorts of business in establishing the Persian empire (Ezra 1.2-4; 6.2-5). The message is clear: one of the main things on Cyrus's mind was to get the temple in Jerusalem built. Similarly, Artaxerxes himself intervenes to establish the Jewish law (Ezra 7). Darius's codification of Egyptian law is often cited as a parallel, but there are considerable differences. Darius acted with regard to a major power, not a minor province; the question of the Jewish law was long after the time of Darius; and Ezra is given great authority over the region of Transeuphrates without regard to the satrap.[28]

Finance from the imperial treasury is provided for the Jewish project. One of the alleged Persian activities that has been accepted without much question by many commentators is the amount of imperial wealth showered on the Jews. In this the Ezra stories actually differ somewhat from the parallels discussed above. In the other stories, the protagonist is usually rewarded with high office, and the Jewish community (where it is mentioned) is saved. But large sums of money do not seem to have been handed over (though Esther does get Haman's estate). Perhaps this represents a necessary shift in the narrative pattern: instead of focusing on high office the book of Ezra concentrates on financial support.

The province of Judah, and the Jews as a people, are given an extremely important position within the Persian empire. The other stories are mainly interested in individual Jews, usually people that reach a high position, but do not say much about the Jewish community as a whole. Esther makes the Jewish community one of the protagonists, though: it is threatened by the decree insti-

27. The Passover papyrus says that a communication had come from the king to the satrap of Egypt, but the fragmentary nature of the document means that we do not know precisely the significance of this. No letter from the king was found: did Hananiah only claim authority from the king when the communication actually came from a high official? Or was it perhaps a general decree from the king to the provinces which Hananiah has 'interpreted' for the Jews by filling in details about the Passover? For the text, see A.E. Cowley, *Aramaic Papyri of the Fifth Century B.C.* (Oxford: Clarendon Press, 1923; repr. Osnabruck: Otto Zeller, 1967), pp. 60-65 (text 21); Bezalel Porten and Ada Yardeni, *Textbook of Aramaic Documents from Ancient Egypt*. I. *Letters* (Texts and Studies for Students; Jerusalem: Hebrew University, 1986), pp. 54-55 (text A4.1).

28. On this last point, see Lisbeth S. Fried, '"You Shall Appoint Judges": Ezra's Mission and the Rescript of Artaxerxes', in *Persia and Torah: The Theory of Imperial Authorization of the Pentateuch* (ed. James W. Watts; SBLSS, 17; Atlanta GA: Society of Biblical Literature, 2001), pp. 63-89.

gated by Haman and it fights back when it has royal backing. The royal support in Esther gives it preeminence among the peoples of the empire, but it is in Ezra that Judah and the Jewish community really come into their own. We have no fewer than *four royal decrees* on behalf of the Jews: Cyrus issues a Hebrew decree about return and rebuilding of the temple (Ezra 1.2-4); an Aramaic decree was also supposed to have been written that not only commanded the building of the temple but even provided money from the imperial treasury (Ezra 6.2-5); Darius renews the order to build the temple and provides payment from the regional taxes (Ezra 6.6-12); Artaxerxes gives permission for the promulgation of the law (Ezra 7.12-26), bestows great authority on Ezra (Ezra 7.14, 25-26), grants tax exemptions on the cult personnel (Ezra 7.24) and provides generous—even *enormous*—wealth for the community (Ezra 7.21-22; 8.25-27). For Ezra brought with him seven times the annual income of the Transeuphrates region or the equivalent of *15 percent of the entire annual income of the whole empire*.[29]

It is important to keep in mind that we are looking at the text from a broad perspective to recognize its general bias. There are occasional examples to parallel some of the details in the text. For example, Jews now and then did rise to relatively high rank, as did members of other *ethnoi*, but it did not happen very often. One well attested figure was Tiberias Julius Alexander in the first century CE, who became governor of Judea, governor of Egypt, and a Roman general, though even he is said to have abandoned the religion of his ancestors.

It is sometimes argued (as Meyer does) that what the Persians did with the Jews was not unusual. It was merely Persian policy. It has long struck me how scholars will talk carelessly about 'Persian policy' without the slightest bit of evidence *except* measures alleged *by the biblical text* to have been taken with regard to the Jews or Judah. In this case, Meyer (and others) also cites the Gadatas inscription. Once again scholarly tendentiousness now become evident, at least in hindsight.

First, the idea that the Persians were especially benevolent should have occasioned skepticism. Scholars had long known that the Neo-Assyrians dominated, conquered, destroyed, taxed, and stole the wealth of the many peoples in their sphere of influence. When the Neo-Babylonians came along, they did the same.

29. According to Herodotus 3.91, the entire satrapy of Ebir-nari produced tribute of only about 350 talents of silver per year. A standard rate of gold-to-silver in the Persian empire seems to have been about 13 to 1 (Herodotus 3.95; A.D.H. Bivar, 'Coins', *OEANE*, II, p. 44). The gold and silver said to have been donated for the Jerusalem temple amounted to 650 talents of silver, 100 talents of gold, and various expensive vessels for the temple (100 one-talent vessels of silver and 20 gold vessels of a thousand darics each). This would make the 120 talents of gold (including the gold vessels) equivalent in silver to 1,560 talents, to make a total equivalent in silver of more than 2,300 talents. The entire Persian empire under Darius is said to have yielded 14,560 talents of silver a year (Herodotus 3.95), which would make Ezra's treasure the equivalent of 15 percent of the tribute income for that year.

So why should the Persians suddenly turn around and generously dole out imperial funds to help the conquered peoples? Of course, some of their inscriptions attest to their concern on behalf of their subject peoples, but these are paralleled in Neo-Assyrian and Neo-Babylonian inscriptions. The continuity of policy between the Persians and their great Mesopotamian predecessors was demonstrated more than two decades ago by Amélie Kuhrt.[30] Like the empires before them, the Persians conquered, subjugated, and taxed their subjects, including temples. Only in very exceptional cases do we have any evidence of special treatment of temples, and none of these seem to relate to peoples outside the center of the empire.

Secondly, as far as the Gadatas inscription is concerned, what is almost always ignored in citations of it is that its authenticity has long been questioned and debated. Now, a thorough treatment by a noted scholar (who originally cited it as a source) makes it very difficult to accept it as a Persian-period inscription.[31] But the main point is that there have always been doubts about it, yet this fact has almost always been overlooked by biblical scholars.

When these two assumptions are removed, there is no evidence for special Persian support for the Jews—except for the allegations in the Jewish sources themselves. If these are to be believed, the Jews held a special place in the Persian empire—one could almost say that they were in control. Joseph holds high office and practically controls the country for the Pharaoh who has turned it over to him. Daniel and his companions hold the rulership of the Babylonian empire just below Nebuchadnezzar, and later Belshazzar and 'Darius the Mede' elevate Daniel to a high administrative position. As the Persian queen Esther issues decrees and Mordecai is Xerxes's chief minister (Esther 9.29-32; 10.3). Ahiqar stands right beside the king. Ezra can write decrees and present them to the king simply for his rubber stamp (or so scholars have alleged). It is ironic that, in parallel to anti-Semitic charges of a Jewish conspiracy to take over various governments, the ancient Jewish sources have the Jews practically running the Near Eastern empires!

4. *Conclusions*

The late nineteenth century saw the rise of two main positions on the traditions in Ezra. Wellhausen exemplified the dominant, skeptical view of the book and its contents. Against this view Meyer advanced a rather more credulous posi-

30. Amélie Kuhrt, 'The Cyrus Cylinder and Achaemenid Imperial Policy', *JSOT* 25 (1983), pp. 83-97.

31. Pierre Briant, 'Histoire et archéologie d'un texte: La *Lettre de Darius à Gadatas* entre Perses, Grecs et Romains', in *Licia e Lidia prima dell'Ellenizzazione: Atti del Convegno internazionale—Roma 11-12 ottobre 1999* (ed. Mauro Giorgieri, M. Salvini, M.-C. Trémouille, P. Vannicelli; Monografie Scientifiche, Serie Scienze umane e sociali; Rome: Consiglio nazionale delle ricerche, 2003), pp. 107-44.

tion that saw a good deal of historicity in the book. What has been somewhat surprising is the extent to which Wellhausen's position has been abandoned, at least in English-speaking scholarship which has used Ezra as a fairly reliable source of history for the Persian period. This is remarkable partly because such an influential view as Wellhausen's was rejected but also because even some of Meyer's cautions have been thrown aside (e.g., Meyer found the alleged document in Ezra 7 to be a Jewish writing, contrary to many writers in the second half of the twentieth century). But just as scholarship on a number of issues has gone in a great circle away from Wellhausen, only to arrive back at his original position in the last few decades, so a number of writers have recently taken positions on Ezra much closer to Wellhausen's.

No doubt one of the reasons that a more credulous attitude was adopted toward Ezra was because of Meyer's stature as a historian. But another was probably a general reaction against the critical position of Wellhausen's circle of influence that saw many of his views rejected in Anglo-Saxon scholarship. The intellectual forces that produced the 'Albright school' were conducive to seeing the stories in Ezra as fairly reliable. If we could believe in the patriarchs and a unified conquest, we could certainly believe in Ezra and in the founding of the temple as described in Ezra 1–6. This is not to suggest an abandonment of biblical criticism, but assessments of specific issues are often heavily determined by prior theoretical stances. Part of the shift back towards Wellhausen has been due to an intellectual reassessment of critical historical method, but part also seems to be due to new discoveries that have by and large gone against the more credulous point of view that had prevailed through much of the last century.

Such a large enterprise as biblical scholarship is not monolithic, however, nor does it maintain a uniformly consistent position. What I have tried to show is that with regard to the book of Ezra, scholars seem to have lacked a sense of healthy skepticism. This is surprising because in other aspects of biblical scholarship, a critical attitude was hardly lacking: the tales of Daniel had long since been relegated to legend. Apart from a few conservative evangelicals, 'Darius the Mede' has been expunged from history. Esther is often labeled a 'historical novel'. Yet Ezra was looked at differently. One of the reasons was most likely the acceptance of the alleged Persian documents as authentic. This was despite the doubts of Wellhausen and even the great Semitist Nöldeke, but by this time Wellhausen's writings on Ezra were largely forgotten—at least, by English-speaking scholars—and only a few Aramaic specialists were likely to read Nöldeke. Yet one of the main reasons for this neglect of the other position seems to have been the influence of the *Entstehung des Judenthums*.

Eduard Meyer, who was not a biblical scholar, apparently succeeded in canalizing thought about Ezra for the next century. The fact that the main opponent known among English-speakers was Torrey—whose views were seen as extreme—probably helped. Wellhausen had not been completely forgotten, however; in any case, what Wellhausen had found could be rediscovered by others on their own if they were willing to ask critical questions. According to my assessment, there is a movement in scholarship toward a position on Ezra closer to Wellhausen's. In this, as in many other areas, Wellhausen is coming back into fashion.

Josiah in a New Light: Assyriology Touches the Reforming King

Lowell K. Handy

1. *Introduction*

One might think Josiah an odd choice for considering Assyriology's influence on a biblical ruler in so far as this king of Judah does not appear at all in any known authentic Akkadian text; however, there are reasons why he is ideal for this venue:

1. The influence of Assyriology on him can be quickly covered;
2. It is mostly tangential data that affects Josianic studies;
3. Assyriology has made significant changes in our understanding of Josiah.

Consider something as deceptively simple as the political world in which Josiah reigned. Until the decipherment of Akkadian, Bible scholars had almost exclusively used the narratives of Kings and Chronicles to reconstruct the political environment of Judah in the late seventh-century BCE. While classical historians had been employed to flesh out the biblical material, no clear notion of the history of the period was available.[1] If one consulted *Calmet's Dictionary of the Holy Bible* (a highly regarded, influential and multiply-translated reference work reprinted well into the nineteenth century) on the Assyrians of the Josianic period, one could have read, as recently as the ninth edition of 1847:

> He left the throne to Saosduchinus, who reigned twenty years. This is supposed by some to be the prince who is named Nabuchodonosor, in Judith, but without any probability. Saosduchinus was succeeded by Chyniladon, the Nabuchodonosor mentioned in the book of Judith, upon whose death the throne was filled by Sarachus, or Chynaladanus, who was, without doubt, the true Sardanapalus. Upon his accession to the throne, this prince committed the government of Chaldæa to Nabopolassar… [who] determined upon seizing the crown. For this purpose he formed an alliance

1. George Sale, *An Universal History, from the Earliest Account of Time to the Present: Compiled from Original Authors* (66 vols.; Dublin: George Faulkner, 1744), I, pp. 857-905, was a standard world history for the English-speaking world well into the nineteenth century. His extensive reconstruction of Assyrian history relied heavily on classical authors, but biblical texts trumped any other accounts available to him.

> with Astyages, otherwise Ahasueres, son of the king of Media, and with their united forces besieged Nineveh, took the city, and divided the monarchy of the Assyrians; Sarachus having burned himself to death in his palace, Nabopolassar had Nineveh and Babylon; Astyages had Media, and the neighboring provinces. Nabopolassar was father of Nebuchadnezzar, who took Jerusalem.[2]

This passage condenses the Assyrian histories available at that time, all of which appear to conflate Assyrian and Babylonian lineages. The major source for Assyrian history had been the Greek historians, Herodotus in particular, although biblical references were almost always taken to be more authoritative when splicing Hellenistic material with Bible texts. It should be noted that while most histories of Assyria composed prior to the time of modern assyriological publications made use of the book of Judith (hence the ability to splice together the Assyrian and Babylonian royalty), most Protestant historians rejected the entire book as fiction and her 'Nebuchadnezzar the Assyrian' as a fictional character.[3] As far as biblical histories based on Kings and Chronicles accounts of the reign of Josiah were concerned, the Assyrians had permanently left the region of Israel with the retreat of Sennacherib from Jerusalem during the reign of Hezekiah, and if Josiah had any dealings at all with Assyrians it entailed the 'Assyrians' known as Chaldeans who had hauled Manasseh off to their jail.

Things changed dramatically with the decipherment of Akkadian texts; Josiah's reign has since become incorporated into Assyrian history. Three of the major aspects of Assyriological influence on Josianic studies will be considered here:

1. An understanding of the deities that Josiah had removed from the cult;
2. A clarification of Josiah's political position in the history of the region;
3. A look at the influence of Neo-Assyrian palace reliefs on the visual art of Josiah.

2. *Josiah's Deities*

Considering the centrality of Josiah's religious activities to the biblical narratives, the influence of assyriological studies on the understanding of the biblical deities is imperative. From the early church onward, the fact that Josiah destroyed idols was a central concern in the church's reading of this ruler.[4] Idolatry was generally condemned, although what exactly was meant by an idol

2. *Calmet's Dictionary of the Holy Bible: With Biblical Fragments* (5 vols.; ed. Charles Taylor; London: Henry G. Bohn, 9th edn, 1847), I, p. 211.

3. See Sale, *Universal History*, I, p. 897.

4. On the early Jewish and Christian interpretations of King Josiah, see Lowell K. Handy, 'Josiah after the Chronicler', *PEGLAMBS* 14 (1994), pp. 95-103.

was, and remains, hotly debated.[5] Vituperative descriptions of idols in general have shifted though time and space, but the term 'idol' has always carried a negative connotation in biblical studies.[6]

In the two centuries prior to the publication of information made available by modern assyriological research, scholarly readings of the Josianic idols retained the interpretations of a long history of Christian commentaries. The early church's understanding of these idols reflected its own context within the paganism of Late Antiquity. Well into the nineteenth century, Catholic reconstructions of Josiah's deities derived from ancient Greek and Roman divine images. That the deities destroyed by Josiah were construed in classical religious terms reflected the European educational tradition of stressing Greek and Latin literature. Seventeenth- and eighteenth-century European attempts to identify classical gods with those of other ancient peoples accord with many of the classical writers themselves.[7] To a certain extent, this understanding of Josiah's idols has maintained its hold on the scholarly imagination.

Protestant scholars since the Reformation made a decided shift in visualizing the idolatry of Josiah's time: biblical idols at one time became synonymous with Catholic religious art. Margaret Aston's extensive research on the art of King Edward VI of England demonstrates how the notion of Josiah's idols shifted in the Reformation to an anti-Catholicism polemic: the portrait of little Edward contains a nice Josianic portrait with the king destroying, in this case, a statue of the Virgin Mary, though any Catholic saint would have sufficed.[8] This vision of Protestants as restorers of proper worship against Catholic idolatry colored Protestant descriptions of the evil idols at the time of Josiah well into the nineteenth century.

5. Tryggve N.D. Mettinger, *No Graven Image? Israelite Aniconism in its Ancient Near Eastern Context* (ConBOT, 42; Stockholm: Almqvist & Wiksell International, 1995), pp. 18-27, struggles with the basic question of what constitutes a divine image. Even which ancient religiously connected images should be designated as an 'idol', as opposed to decorative artwork, is a problem; see Christoph Dohmen, *Das Bilderverbot: Seine Entstehung und seine Entwicklung im Alten Testament* (BBB, 62; a.M.: Athenäum, 2nd edn, 1985), pp. 36-37.

6. The denunciation of idols and their worshipers begins its long tradition with the biblical prophets themselves; Michael B. Dick, 'Prophetic Parodies of Making the Cult Image', in *Born in Heaven, Made on Earth: The Making of the Cult Image in the Ancient Near East* (ed. Michael B. Dick; Winona Lake, IN: Eisenbrauns, 1999), pp. 1-53 (16-44). George Rawlinson, *The Kings of Israel and Judah* (New York: Anson D.F. Randolph, 1889), pp. 217-18, retained this approach.

7. See the entries on Astaroth, Astarté, and Baal (ou Bel) in *Encyclopédie, ou, dictionnaire raisonné des sciences, des artes et des métiers* (36 vols.; ed. Denis Diderot; Lasaunne and Berne, 1778), III, pp. 709-10, IV, pp. 177-78. This can be seen as well in the *Calmet* plates regarding the deities of Judah and Israel. Note already *The Chronography of George Synkellos: A Byzantine Chronicle of Universal History from the Creation* (trans. and ed. William Adler and Paul Tuffin; Oxford: Oxford University Press, 2002), p. 312.

8. Margaret Aston, *The King's Bedpost: Reformation and Iconography in a Tudor Group Portrait* (Cambridge: Cambridge University Press, 1993), pp. 94-96, pl. I.

Orientalizing came with European colonizing. Any foreign deities, especially those with sculptured images, came to be associated with gods mentioned in the Bible in the scholarly imagination. In the mid-nineteenth century edition of *Calmet's Dictionary of the Bible* we find classical deities identified with the newly popular Indian subcontinent deities, all of whom were brought to bear on the biblical pantheon in the extensive volumes of plates developed for the dictionary. Layard's first publication of Assyrian discoveries extended the equation of classical Greek and Roman deities to the images uncovered in Assyria.[9] It should be noted that there was debate among biblical scholars well prior to the decipherment of Akkadian as to whether Diodorus Siculus' assertion that Assyrians had enforced worship of their gods on their conquered peoples meant that the deities Josiah confronted were Assyrian in origin.[10]

The period of European intellectual activity immediately prior to the influx of excavated Mesopotamian artifacts in the 1840s had become fascinated with universalizing theories. Strongly patterned theories of religious history, in vogue since classical times, joined Islamic writings and the newly central notions of social evolution in influential works by Lord Herbert of Cherbury, Hume, Comte, Hegel and others. The academic construction of the religious history of any given people by means of a single universal outline was intellectually fashionable and highly praised.[11] This in turn promoted the reductionistic notion that all deities followed a standard transformation, beginning as natural phenomenon misunderstood by primitives (unlike the scholars studying them), and yielded the end result that all religions' histories are essentially the same. Thus, Josiah's idols were understood as pre-Enlightenment nature-deities on a trajectory through imperial patron gods towards displacement in monotheism.

Taking up the deities actually mentioned in the Josiah narratives, we can see a decided shift in understanding and envisioning of the idols. In the early nineteenth century the god Baʿal, by means of classical citations, had been identified as a Phoenician god with classical parallels.[12] The eighteenth- and nineteenth-century European fascination with Indian Hindu sculpture led some scholars to depict Baʿal as an expression of 'Oriental idol religion'. In this approach, Baʿal was usually identified as a Canaanite version of the sun god, and could also be

9. Austen Henry Layard, *Nineveh and its Remains: With an Account of a Visit to the Chaldean Christians of Kurdistan and the Yezidis, or Devil-Worshippers, and an Inquiry into the Manners and Arts of the Ancient Assyrians* (2 vols.; New York: George P. Putnam, 1849), II, pp. 341-46.

10. See Sale, *Universal History*, I, p. 372, who assumes that the Assyrians removed the local religion and installed an Assyrian cult on the basis of Syrian practices reported in classical sources.

11. See Geo Widengren, 'Evolutionism and the Problem of the Origin of Religion', *Ethnos* 10 (1945), pp. 72-96 (72-90), for a survey of this scholarship.

12. Uncited comments on early Baʿal references are from *Calmet's Dictionary of the Holy Bible*, I, pp. 225-26.

identified with Molech as yet another aspect or avatar of the same deity.[13] The impact of assyriological scholarship on this consensus basically generated two main theories: The first, and strangely quite popular interpretation, was that since we now 'know' that Bel is merely a classicizing title for a deity, 'Baʿal' was therefore not a distinct deity at all, but a title randomly attributed to any local divinity.[14] Thus, Josiah's destruction of Baʿal in 2 Kgs 23.4-5 reflects only the removal of the local nature deity of the highest order. The second theory maintained that the biblical entity Baʿal was the western incarnation of powerful deities of the Mesopotamian pantheon.[15] Thus, Baʿal could be the Assyrian Adad (by way of Syrian Hadad) as noted early on and still accepted by some scholars.[16] Also popular was Assyria's patron deity Aššur, incorrectly identified by Layard and Rawlinson iconograpically by the archer in the winged disk,[17] though a much more anthropomorphic image is now identified with the deity.[18] From this notion of 'Baʿal' as a title for the paramount deity of a region or people, there proceeded the idea that behind the 'Baʿal' of the Josiah narratives lurked the Assyrian (or maybe Babylonian) patron deity. Even though the Ras Shamra tablets have prompted some scholars to disassociate West Semitic Baʿal from direct Mesopotamian borrowing, these old theories still persist in academic literature.

Scholarly understanding of the biblical goddess Asherah was less influenced by Assyriology in its formative years than had been that of Baʿal. On the basis of classical sources, it was generally assumed well into the twentieth century that this was not a goddess but a sacred grove of trees or perhaps a pillar.[19] No

13. *Calmet's Dictionary of the Holy Bible*, s.v. 'Baal', I, p. 226.

14. See W. Robertson Smith, *The Religion of the Semites: The Fundamental Institutions* (New York: Schocken Books, 1972), p. 109, first prepared for publication in 1889 from the Burnett Lectures of 1888–89. So also A.S. Peake, 'Baal', in Hastings (ed.), *Dictionary of the Bible*, I, pp. 209-11 (210). See survey in Lowell K. Handy, *Among the Host of Heaven: The Syro-Palestinian Pantheon as Bureaucracy* (Winona Lake, IN: Eisenbrauns, 1994), pp. 99-100.

15. Layard, *Nineveh and its Remains*, II, p. 187, declared that Baal or Belus was 'the supreme deity amongst all the Semitic races', and was picked up by Greeks and Romans as their Zeus and Jupiter, p. 342.

16. Johannes Hehn, *Die biblische und die babylonische Gottesidee: Die israelitische Gottesauffassung im Licht der altorientalischen Religionsgeschichte* (Leipzig: J.C. Hinrichs'sche Buchhandlung, 1913), p. 88. See the discussion in Wolfgang Herrmann, 'Baal', in *DDDB*², pp. 132-39 (132). Once in print, the relationship continues to be cited; see 'Adad (a)', in *Encyclopedia of Ancient Deities* (ed. Russell Coulter and Patricia Turner; Chicago: Fitzroy Dearborn Publishers, 2000), p. 13.

17. Layard, *Nineveh and its Remains*, I, title page; George Rawlinson, *The Religions of the Ancient World, Including Egypt, Phoenicia, Assyria and Babylonia, Etruria, Persia, Greece, India, Rome* (New York: Charles Scribner's Sons, 1883), p. 40.

18. See Jeremy Black and Anthony Green, *Gods, Demons and Symbols of Ancient Mesopotamia: An Illustrated Dictionary* (Austin: University of Texas Press, 1992), p. 38, fig. 27.

19. *Calmet's Dictionary of the Holy Bible*, s.v. 'Ashtaroth or Astarte', I, pp. 212-13 (212);

doubt the nineteenth-century obsession with male deities in patriarchal societies played a part in the eclipse of Asherah, though occasionally late nineteenth- and early twentieth-century scholars would suggest that Asherah was another name for or title of Astarte.[20] While Assyriology did not really make much of a dent in the Asherah-as-grove theory, the increasingly popular notion that Asherah was Assyria's sex-and-war goddess Ishtar in West Semitic garb became highly popular, thereby creating a scenario in which Asherah came to be taken seriously as a goddess rather than as a ritual object.[21] When the Ras Shamra texts appeared, it was not nearly such a shock to discover that Asherah was indeed a goddess than it might have been a century earlier.[22] The use of comparative references to Ishtar in studies of Asherah in the latter part of the twentieth century remain standard academic fare.[23]

Which brings us to Astarte. For historians from ancient Greece to the nineteenth century, it was Greek sources that defined this deity.[24] For most ancient Greek writers she was a Phoenician goddess, though occasionally the Greek

Willougby C. Allen, 'Asherah', in Hastings (ed.), *Dictionary of the Bible*, I, p. 165. W.R. Smith, *Religion of the Semites*, pp. 187-88.

20. Astarte was known from classical literature and was deemed a goddess; the conflation of goddesses into a single fertility, mother, or earth goddess was a standard response in the nineteenth century. Job Orton, *A Short and Plain Exposition of the Old Testament with Devotional and Practical Reflections, for the Use of Families* (Charleston: Samuel Etheridge, 1805 [1788–91]), p. 582, nicely presents Asherah as a grove of trees in which Astarte was worshiped, thus becoming identified itself with Astarte. The notion that the goddess can be reduced to a stand of trees persists but should be avoided in scholarly circles; see JoAnn Hackett, 'Can a Sexist Model Liberate Us? Ancient Near Eastern "Fertility" Goddesses', *Journal of Feminist Studies in Religion* 5 (1989), pp. 65-76 (71-73).

21. Hehn, *Biblische und die babylonische Gottesidee*, p. 106. A survey of the interpretation of Asherah appears in Steve A. Wiggins, *A Reassessment of 'Asherah': A Study according to the Textual Sources of the First Two Millennia B.C.E.* (AOAT, 235; Kevelaer: Butzon & Bercker/ Neukirchen–Vluyn: Neukirchener Verlag, 1993).

22. See William L. Reed, *The Asherah in the Old Testament* (Fort Worth: Texas Christian University Press, 1949).

23. Assyrian iconography of Ishtar provides comparative illustrations for Asherah (see Black and Green, *Gods, Demons and Symbols*, p. 108, fig. 87). The diversity of locally worshipped Mesopotamian goddesses named Ishtar or designated with her ideogram is only occasionally brought into the question of the deity's relationship with Asherah or Astarte to the West. However, the relationship of these Ishtars to each other and to their worshippers should be recognized as something of a confusion to modern scholars. At least it is highlighted in some works; see, for example, Martti Nissinen, 'City as Lofty as Heaven: Arbela and Other Cities in Neo-Assyrian Prophecy', in *'Every City Shall Be Forsaken': Urbanism and Prophecy in Ancient Israel and the Near East* (ed. Lester L. Grabbe and Robert D. Haak; JSOTSup, 330; Sheffield: Sheffield Academic Press, 2001), pp. 172-209 (182-83, 187).

24. By the time of Sale, *Universal History*, I, p. 862, the equation of the *Dea Syria* with Phoenician Astarte and with the goddess/planet Venus in Assyrian religion had already been made. See also 'Astarté', in Diderot (ed.), *Encyclopédie*, III, p. 710.

classical curriculum overcame the sense of foreignness and Astarte was presented as one of several Greek fertility goddesses. Tradition-bound nineteenth-century European scholars could even put forward Astarte as a variant name or a title for Aphrodite. Interestingly, in the late nineteenth century, Assyrian Ishtar was triply identified with Astarte: (a) the names Ishtar and Astarte were presented as mere dialectal variants of the same name, (b) they were female so they were taken as obvious variants of the same universal fertility/earth/mother goddess, and (c) Herodotus' report of sex in the Assyrian temples clinched the aspect of sex attached to the goddess Aphrodite to this Semitic goddess in the minds of many academics.[25] Curiously, modern classical scholars have accepted this early line of thought; both Burkert and Budin accept Aphrodite as either a direct Mesopotamian import or a heavily-recast Ishtar.[26] From the mid-nineteenth century on, female figurines (especially if their breasts were exposed), excavated anywhere in the Levant, were published as 'Astarte plaques',[27] and while the goddess's name shows up in Ugaritic texts, these tablets offer little more help in defining the role for this deity than the classical texts already available, so Mesopotamian Ishtar remains a productive comparative model in Astarte studies.

What has Assyriology done to help us understand the deities in Josiah's reign? The theory that the gods Josiah ejected from the Jerusalem temple were Assyrian deities predated modern Assyriology, but once (a) there were pictures of Assyrian deities to give representational substance to the theory, and (b) it became clear that the Assyrians had retained control of much of the region significantly longer than previously thought, the Assyrian-overlord-gods theory became increasingly popular. This theory did not go unchallenged. In 1908, Cheyne, in a widely influential volume on Josiah's reform, insisted that the current vogue for identifying Assyrian deities in Josiah's reform was nonsense because the names of the gods in the 2 Kings 23 narrative were expressly those of North Arabian deities (his argument about the war between the Ara-

25. See survey in Lewis Bayles Paton, 'Ashtart (Ashtoreth), Astarte', in *Encyclopedia of Religion and Ethics* (13 vols.; ed. James Hastings; Edinburgh: T. & T. Clark, 1910), II, pp. 115-18 (115-16); Hehn, *Biblische und die babylonische Gottesidee*, p. 106. On the influence of 'cult prostitution' theories on biblical studies see Phyllis A. Bird, 'The End of the Male Cult Prostitute: A Literary-Historical and Sociological Analysis of Hebrew *qādēš-qĕdēšim*', in *Congress Volume; Cambridge 1995* (ed. John A. Emerton; VTSup, 66; Leiden: E.J. Brill, 1997), pp. 37-80 (38-45).

26. Walter Burkert, *Greek Religion* (Cambridge, MA: Harvard University Press, 1985), pp.152-53, and recently, *idem*, *Babylon, Memphis, Persepolis: Eastern Contexts of Greek Culture* (Cambridge, MA: Harvard University Press, 2004), pp. 32, 42-44, where Ishtar in the Epic of Gilgamesh is related to the Aphrodite of Greek myth; Stephanie L. Budin, 'A Reconsideration of the Aphrodite–Ashtart Syncretism', *Numen* 51 (2004), pp. 109-21.

27. The term has been used as a generic tag for excavated figurines for some time; for a pair of examples, see Hugues Vincent, *Canaan d'après l'exploration récente* (Études bibliques; Paris: J. Gabalda & Cie, 1907), pp. 160, 167, fig. 113; Kathleen M. Kenyon, *Archaeology in the Holy Land* (London: Ernest Benn/New York: W.W. Norton, 4th edn, 1979), p. 253.

bian Mizraim and the Judeans is then set out in what can now only be called painful detail).[28] The reaction to such arguments was to posit that the good king expelled Assyrian gods, but that the true identities of these deities were hidden behind North Arabian (or West Semitic/Canaanite) deity names.[29] Decades after the publication of the Ugaritic tablets this theory remains widely popular, as witness Spieckermann's *Juda unter Assur in der Sargonidenzeit*.[30]

3. *Josiah's Historical Context*

The reconstruction of the history of Josiah's reign has been greatly affected by assyriological material. Prior to the decipherment of the Akkadian texts, biblical scholars generally accepted the notion, extrapolated from the biblical book of Kings, that, following Hezekiah's capitulation to Sennacherib, the Assyrians were no longer involved in Judah's political life. Once Sennacherib leaves the assault on Jerusalem, Assyrians disappear from the biblical narrative; since the Bible formed the authoritative history of the world for most biblical (and, indeed, universal world history) western scholars well into the nineteenth century, this absence of conclusive evidence for Assyrians was accepted as evidence of absence of Assyrians from the Judean world. When attempts were made to reconstruct an Assyrian presence, it was of the garbled variety quoted at the beginning of this essay.

Assyriological information regarding the tortuous succession of Neo-Assyrian rulers through the latter half of the seventh century BCE constitutes the single most important influence on reconstructions of the reign of the historical Josiah. Akkadian historiographic documents still lack sufficient data to fill in the details of royal activities during the reigns of the final Assyrian kings, let alone their role in Judah. However, just knowing about Assurbanipal revolutionized the understanding of Josiah's position in his world. Clearly, at least at the beginning of the child-king's rule, he was still a vassal of Assurbanipal, though the Bible gives us no information about this relationship. As early as Layard's volume of 1849, illustrations from the time of Assurbanipal became available to the modern reader, but it was the publication in 1871 of George Smith's texts and translations of inscriptions relating to Assurbanipal that brought this contemporary of Josiah's to life.[31] Assurbanipal quickly became a

28. Thomas Kelley Cheyne, *The Decline and Fall of the Kingdom of Judah* (London: Adam & Charles Black, 1908), pp. 22-25.

29. This was the basic thrust of Theodor Oestreicher, *Das deuteronomische Grundgesetz* (BFCT, 27/4; Gütersloh: T. Bertelsmann, 1923), in which the entire Josianic reform becomes a political overthrowing of Assyrian influence.

30. Hermann Spieckermann, *Juda unter Assur in der Sargonidenzeit* (FRLANT, 129; Göttingen: Vandenhoeck & Ruprecht, 1982), pp. 307-70.

31. George Smith, *History of Assurbanipal: Translated from the Cuneiform Inscriptions* (London: Williams & Norgate, 1871).

sensation among European scholars. Extensive accounts of his reign appeared in all histories of Assyria; his military exploits and his library gratifyingly highlighted his superior royal status among ancient rulers.[32] Quickly associated with the Sardanapalus of the Hellenistic historians, he was just as quickly declared to be far more magnificent than the Greek rendition of him.[33] Thus it was assumed that it followed reasonably that Josiah reigned under this capable Assyrian king's domination at least until his (Assurbanipal's) death.

It has been suggested both that Josiah was a loyal Assyrian subject and that he was a rebel.[34] In fact, scholars still take their pick from these options since Josiah's status under the last of the Assyrian kings remains a *tabula rasa*. What is clear, however, is that relations among Nubians, Egyptians, Phoenicians and Assyrians early in Assurbanipal's reign place Judah in the center of an international tempest that could not have avoided affecting Judah.[35] If, as seems not

32. Note the extensively illustrated biography of Assurbanipal by François Lenormant, *Histoire ancienne de l'orient: Jusqu'aux guerres médiques* (6 vols.; Paris: A. Levy, 9th edn, 1885), IV, pp. 333-71 (the fall of Nineveh, pp. 371-83, is also pretty much all about Assurbanipal); see also Zénaïde A. Ragozin, *The Story of Assyria: From the Rise of the Empire to the Fall of Nineveh* (New York: G.P. Putnam's Sons, 1889), pp. 371-416; the book's frontispiece is a reproduction of an Assurbanipal lion hunt relief. George Smith, *Assyrian Discoveries: An Account of Explorations and Discoveries on the Site of Nineveh, during 1873 and 1874* (New York: Scribner, Armstrong, 1875), pp. 319-80, provided translations of the Assurbanipal inscriptions for a wider audience.

33. G. Smith, *Assyrian Discoveries*, p. 317; Ragozin, *Story of Assyria*, p. 416, who declared flatly that the Greek renditions could now be seen to be 'utterly worthless'.

34. Samuel Kinns, *Graven in the Rock, or: The Historical Accuracy of the Bible Confirmed by Reference to the Assyrian and Egyptian Monuments in the British Museum and Elsewhere* (London: Cassell & Company, 1891), p. 615, and John Kitto, 'Josiah', in *A Cyclopaedia of Biblical Literature* (3 vols.; ed. John Kitto and William Lindsay Alexander; Philadelphia: J.B. Lippincott, 3rd edn, 1866), II, p. 660, are typical of those scholars who saw Josiah remaining a loyal vassal to Assyria until his death. On the other hand, William Thomas Bullock, 'Josiah', in *Dr William Smith's Dictionary of the Bible, Comprising its Antiquities, Biography, Geography, and Natural History* (4 vols.; ed. William Smith, Horatio Balch Hackett and Ezra Abbot; Boston: Houghton, Mifflin & Co., 1894), II, pp. 1480-81 (1481), n. a, assumes Josiah was no longer serving Assyria; while Thomas Kelley Cheyne, 'Josiah', in *Encyclopaedia Biblica: A Critical Dictionary of the Literary, Political and Religious History, the Archaeology, Geography, and Natural History of the Bible* (4 vols.; ed. T.K. Cheyne and J. Sutherland Black; New York: Macmillan, 1903), II, pp. 2610-12 (2610), assumes Josiah is both independent of Assyria and intent on reconstructing the Davidic Empire, though he cites W.M. Müller as an exponent of the position that Josiah, governed by Assyria, attacked Necho in the end on Assyrian orders.

35. Attempts to make sense of the international situation of the mid-to-late seventh-century BCE are legion, but clearly there were a lot of players and Judah was situated between the ambitions of Egypt and Assyria; see, for three modern examples, Jay A. Wilcoxen, 'The Political Background of Jeremiah's Temple Sermon', in *Scripture in History and Theology: Essays in Honor of J. Coert Rylaarsdam* (ed. Arthur L. Merrill and Thomas W. Overholt; Pittsburgh Theological Monograph, 17; Pittsburgh: Pickwick Press, 1977), pp. 151-66; Gösta W. Ahlström, *The History of Ancient Palestine from the Palaeolithic Period to Alexander's Conquest* (ed. Diana

improbable, Psamtek I became ruler of an independent Egypt with the acquiescence of Assurbanipal, Josiah's Judah lodged between Assyrian and Egyptian empires that were allied and for the most part on peaceful terms. Assurbanipal probably died in 627, which makes it the twelfth year of Josiah's reign by most reckonings; this information has been connected to both 2 Chr 34.3 and the reform of Josiah.[36] Since the records for Assyrian kings after Assurbanipal are sketchy at best, it is usually assumed that Josiah, even if nominally still a vassal of Assyria, had retained a measure of political freedom.[37] Whether he revolted, played Egypt off against Assyria, or for the rest of his reign remained loyal to the Assyrians are all questions open to conjecture.

If one assumes that Josiah gained political freedom from Assyria following the death of Assurbanipal, then the 'reform' narratives must be read against a declining Assyrian presence. One possible reconstruction of this period in Judah's history finds Josiah scrambling to deal with political instability. In this age of hermeneutics of suspicion, the option most favored today is to read the cult reform as a *de facto* political revolt from Assyria; Josiah thus becomes the post-colonial restorer of local autonomy. If one wishes to stay with the apparent intent of the texts, Josiah's actions reflect his own religious piety, not primarily Middle Eastern geopolitics. Again, scholars who believe that the Josianic reform resulted as a reaction to Assyrian overlordship are not obliged to turn the demoted gods' names into Assyrian deity references in order to claim this as a reassertion of local control after years of political pressure (and, as is known from a modern setting, claims to tradition may not have any authentic connection to the past). Finally, there is the possibility, recently raised, that the reform narrative might in fact only reflect theological imperatives of the Babylonian Exile, but that is another matter.[38] Trajectories down this line of thought all deal with reactive activities taken by a minor ruler in the wake of Assyrian political withdrawal.

Edelman; JSOTSup, 146; Sheffield: Sheffield Academic Press, 1993), pp. 747-83, and Donald B. Redford, *Egypt, Canaan, and Israel in Ancient Times* (Princeton, NJ: Princeton University Press, 1992), pp. 430-53.

36. See the seminal article by Frank Moore Cross and David Noel Freedman, 'Josiah's Revolt against Assyria', *JNES* 12 (1953), pp. 56-58.

37. By this juncture there is a reliable list of the last rulers of Assyria; see Amélie Kuhrt, *The Ancient Near East: c. 3000–330 B.C.* (2 vols.; Routledge History of the Ancient World; London: Routledge, 1995), II, p. 479, table 28. Note that G. Smith, *Assyrian Discoveries*, p. 384, Lenormant, *Histoire ancienne*, pp. 371-83, and Ragozin, *Story of Assyria*, pp. 417-32, in 1875, 1885 and 1889, respectively, were all aware that the period in Assyrian history after Assurbanipal was largely unknown; they used a combination of Greek sources, biblical prophecies by Ezekiel and Nahum, and imagination to attempt to fill in the period.

38. It has long been suspected that Josiah's 'reform' reflected a writer's situation in the exilic or post-exilic world; see already Stanley Arthur Cook, 'Josiah', in *Encyclopedia Britannica: A Dictionary of Arts, Sciences, Literature and General Information* (29 vols.; Cambridge: Cambridge University Press, 11th edn, 1911), XV, p. 520.

A much more assertive Josiah materializes along another hypothetical trajectory. Here Josiah steps into a real political vacuum to recreate the United Monarchy incorporating both Israel and Judah. This theory gives new life to an *old idea*. Not only Josephus in antiquity, but Sir Walter Raleigh already by 1614 had posited the political recreation of David's kingdom by Josiah.[39] This reconstruction of events presupposes the cessation of Assyrian rule and retreat of Assyrians from *Samerina* province, raising the thorny issue of the 'myth of the empty land' regarding the territory of Israel, but this is not the place to treat the obvious problems with this thesis. In accordance with the 'retreat' theory, the collapse of Assyria leaves Israel, politically speaking, open land; for some scholars the presence of Egypt in the coastal areas raises the question of who was actually in control of the northern tribal areas, but the 'greater Josiah's kingdom' theory has held sway in some circles for the better part of the past century.[40] A glorious flowering of political, religious, literary, and moral life has been posited for this expansionist Josianic kingdom,[41] though in all fairness, one scholarly contingent has now moved the 'Josianic' revolution to the time of Hezekiah.[42]

Nevertheless, it is worth noting that the territory ascribed to Josiah has expanded and contracted like a balloon in historiographic reconstructions of the past century.[43] The knowledge that Assyria at the end of the seventh century BCE was imploding has left our imaginations free to envision Josiah as the heir to Assyrian control of the West. In 1887, Ernest Renan saw Josianic Judah as a small and unimportant state that might or might not have included Bethel; this was also the extent of Josiah's kingdom in A.S. Peake's 1900 reconstruction.[44]

39. Josephus, *Ant.* 10.68; Walter Raleigh, *The History of the World*, in *The Works of Sir Walter Ralegh, Kt, Now First Collected: To Which are Prefixed the Lives of the Author, Oldys and Birch* (8 vols.; Oxford: Oxford University Press, 1829), IV, p. 785. On the question of authorship and date of publication of the work ascribed to Raleigh see Christopher M. Armitage, *Sir Walter Ralegh: An Annotated Bibliography* (Chapel Hill, NC: University of North Carolina Press, 1987), p. 6. The Talmudic belief that Jeremiah reunited Israel and Judah through preaching has not really caught on.

40. The use of this model in John Bright, *A History of Israel* (Philadelphia: Westminster Press, 1959), pp. 297-98, through the book's four editions has guaranteed the longevity of the thesis.

41. Recently, Marvin A. Sweeney, *King Josiah of Judah: The Lost Messiah of Israel* (Oxford: Oxford University Press, 2001), surveyed the extent of possible Josianic literary flourishing in the context of an expanded and independent Judah under Josiah.

42. So, for example, Andrew G. Vaughn, *Theology, History, and Archaeology in the Chronicler's Account of Hezekiah* (SBLABS, 4; Atlanta, GA: Scholars Press, 1999), moves both archaeological and theological notions often ascribed to Josiah backwards to the time of Hezekiah.

43. This paragraph is based on L.K. Handy, 'The Rise and Fall of the *sogennant* Josianic Empire', *PEGLAMBS* 21 (2001), pp. 69-79 (72-74, 78-79). The accompanying maps, however, are not the same that appear in the article on p. 79.

44. Map based on a written description in Ernest Renan, *Histoire du peuple d'Israël* (5 vols.; Paris: Calmann Lévy, 1891), III, pp. 204-205. See also, A.S. Peake, 'Josiah', in Hastings (ed.), *Dictionary of the Bible*, II, p. 788.

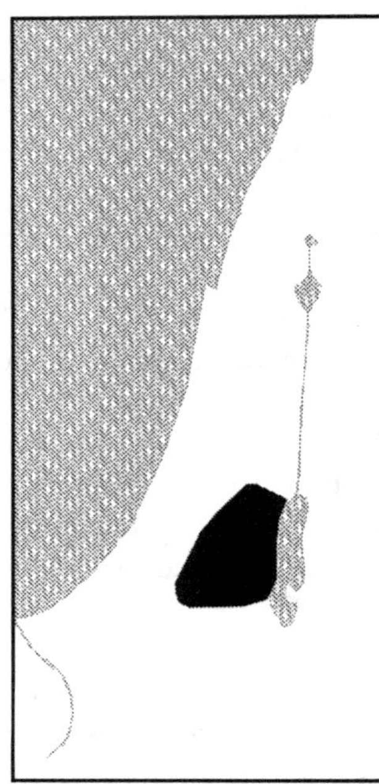

Map 4. Adapted from Ernest Renan, *Histoire du peuple d'Israël* (1891), III, pp. 204-205.

Map 5. After George Adam Smith, *Atlas of the Historical Geography of the Holy Land* (1915), map 36.

George Adam Smith in 1915 saw a reestablishment of the southern kingdom of Judah plus Bethel.[45] In 1959, John Bright envisioned Josiah retaking southern Israel and expanding the southern boundary well into Edom.[46]

Map 6. Adapted from Bright, *History of Israel* (1st edn, 1959), pp. 300-301.

In the Aharoni/Avi-Yonah atlas of 1968, the reconstruction of Josiah's kingdom reaches the largest extent in twentieth-century scholarship, though one suspects that the 1967 Israeli Six-Day War had something to do with the extensive incursion into Sinai.[47]

45. Map based on George Adam Smith, *Atlas of the Historical Geography of the Holy Land* (London: Hodder & Stoughton, 1915), map 36.

46. Map based on the written description in Bright, *History of Israel* (1st edn), pp. 300-301.

47. Map based on Yohanan Aharoni and Michael Avi-Yonah, *The Macmillan Bible Atlas* (New York: Macmillan, 1968), p. 102, map 158.

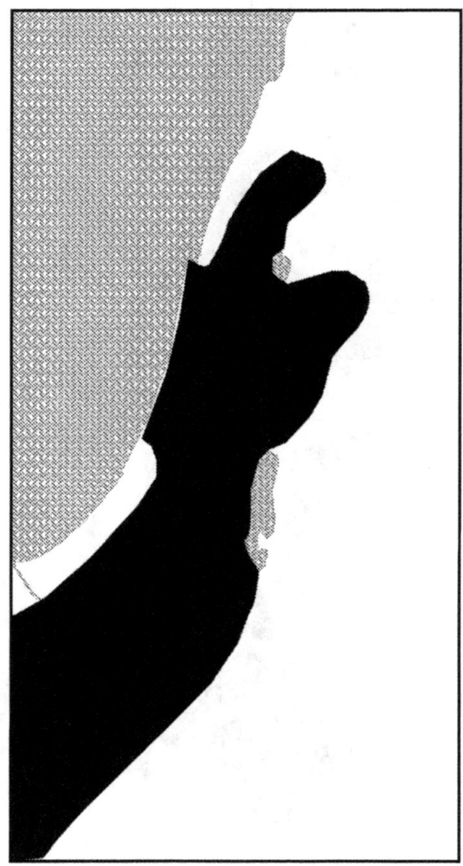

Map 7. After Aharoni and Avi-Yonah, *Macmillan Bible Atlas* (1968), p. 102, map 158.

Karl Hartmann's 1979 reconstruction essentially returns to the borders that were found in Smith,[48] while Na'aman's projection in 1991, as well as those of Finkelstein and Silberman in 2001, essentially return to the boundaries posited by Renan and Peake.[49]

48. Map based on Karl Hartmann, *Atlas-Tafel-Werk zu Bibel und Kirchengeschichte: Altes Testament und Geschichte des Judentums bis Jesus Christus* (5 vols.; Stuttgart: Quell Verlag, 1979), I, p. 52.

49. Map based on description of Josiah's territory reconstructed by Nadav Na'aman, 'The Kingdom of Judah under Josiah', *Tel Aviv* 18 (1991), pp. 3-71 (41-51). See also Israel Finkelstein and Neil Asher Silberman, *The Bible Unearthed: Archaeology's New Vision of Ancient Israel and the Origin of its Sacred Texts* (New York: Free Press, 2001), p. 258.

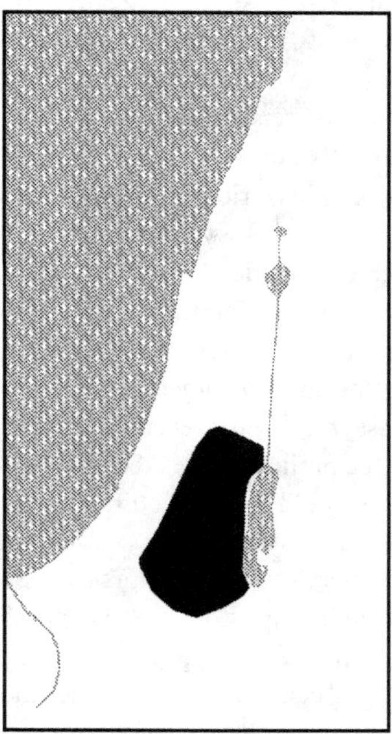

Map 8. After Hartmann, *Atlas-Tafel-Werk zu Bibel und Kirchengeschichte* (1979), I, p. 52.

Map 9. Adapted from Na'aman, 'Kingdom of Judah under Josiah', pp. 41-51.

The end of Josiah's reign and his soldierly death has also been reevaluated in light of Assyriology. The post-Assurbanipal position of Josiah *vis-à-vis* Assyrian overlordship remains a vexing conundrum. Prior to the decipherment of Akkadian texts, most scholars read Josiah's encounter with Pharaoh Necho in terms of Josiah protecting 'Israel' from Egyptian encroachment.[50] Late in the nineteenth century, in light of assyriological historiography, it became popular to assume that Josiah's loyalty to Assyria caused him to attempt to stop Necho from attacking the enfeebled Assyrian army.[51] However, the publication in 1923 by C.J. Gadd of the 'Babylonian Chronicle', portraying Pharaoh Necho as an ally and not an enemy of the last Assyrian king Aššur-uballiṭ II, obliged scholars to recast theories of Josiah as a subject in revolt with intent to stop Egyptian aid from reaching Assyria.[52] Most recently, an acknowledgement that there is real confusion within the biblical stories themselves and the actual politics of 609 BCE leaves this an open field for conjecture.

Finally, two political entities have been phased out of Josiah's immediate portrayal in light of Akkadian documents. First, the Scythians, so prevalent in reconstructions of the king's reign for 2000 years, based on Herodotus' history, have, with few exceptions, disappeared from academic reconstructions of Judah in the late seventh-century BCE.[53] Second, the Babylonians, routinely confounded by historians prior to the use of Neo-Assyrian documents with the Assyrian royal lineage and who were assumed, on the basis of Second Chronicles' story of Manasseh, to exercise control over the ruler of Judah, have for the most part been parsed by scholars into a separate political entity whose fateful impact on Judah follows the death of Josiah.

4. *Josiah's Image*

Finally, portrayals of Josiah in the visual arts have been influenced by reproductions of ancient Assyrian art since the late nineteenth century. Josiah in pictures

50. Already the established explanation by the Geneva Bible in 1560; *The Geneva Bible: A Facsimile of the 1560 Edition* (Madison, WI: University of Wisconsin Press, 1969), p. 177, n. to 2 Kgs 23.29.

51. So Archibald Henry Sayce, *The 'Higher Criticism' and the Verdict of the Monuments* (London: SPCK, 3rd edn, 1894), pp. 451-52.

52. C.J. Gadd, *The Fall of Nineveh: The Newly Discovered Babylonian Chronicles, No. 21,901, in the British Museum* (London: British Museum, 1923).

53. Rawlinson, *Kings*, p. 222, dismissed the Scythian invasion as having any real impact on Josiah's Judah, if there were such an invasion at all. Recently, Redford, *Egypt, Canaan, and Israel*, pp. 438-41, cautiously posits the possibility of such an invasion. Alfred J. Hoerth, *Archaeology and the Old Testament* (Grand Rapids, MI: Baker Books, 1998), pp. 358, 361, based on the work of Edwin M. Yamauchi, accepts the Scythian invasion found in Herodotus; Yamauchi, 'The Scythians: Invading Hordes from the Russian Steppes', *BA* 46 (1983), pp. 90-99. Akkadian sources record no such incursion and, perhaps more importantly, neither do Egyptian records.

prior to that period can be swiftly surveyed, primarily because he was never as popular a subject for the visual arts as were many other Old Testament figures like Adam and Eve, Abraham, Moses, David, Solomon, and even Esther. In the medieval church (and on into the Counter-Reformation), the king's story revolved around (a) the finding of the book of Deuteronomy, (b) the reading of that book by priests to the king, (c) the king's subsequent destruction of idols, and (d) his celebration of the Passover (usually depicted in relation to First Esdras).[54] In the Reformation, from whence Josiah's 'reform', Protestants envisioned themselves in Josiah, with biblical illustrators going so far as to portray Martin Luther and Frederick the Wise as Hilkiah and Josiah, respectively, in a 1572 Luther Bible.[55] This was a function of Protestant notions of the 'word' taking precedence over priests, kings, and idols. In the western church, whether Catholic or Protestant, Josianic portraiture was heavily self-reflective. So, for example, in a late seventeenth-century French Catholic print, a very Gallic king Josiah wearing classical and medieval royal garments, seated on his European canopied throne, listens to a visually clichéd Jewish priest read from a vast bound (and anachronistic) tome laid open on the back of a bent-over serf, before whom stand Romanesque soldiers and, in the background, a host of 'elders' who look suspiciously like Dominican monks.[56]

54. Aston, *The Kings's Bedpost*, pp. 37-48, surveys the medieval through Reformation Bible illustrations of Josiah.

55. Aston, *The Kings's Bedpost*, p. 42, fig. 30.

56. Anonymous artist; Nicolas Fontaine, *The History of the Old and New Testament, Extracted out of Sacred Scripture and Writings of the Fathers: To Which Are Added the Lives, Travels and Sufferings of the Apostles; with a Large and Exact* Historical Chronology *of All the Affairs and Actions Related in the Bible* (London: S. and J. Sprint, C. Brome, J. Nicholson, J. Pero & Benj. Tooke, 2nd corrected edn, 1699), pl. 129 (between pp. 164-65). Illustration courtesy of the Newberry Library, Chicago.

Figure 56. Fontaine, *History of the Old and New Testament* (1699), pl. 129.

Nor were German Catholics immune to this trope. Julius Schnorr von Carolsfeld's often reprinted engraving of Josiah depicts a stock-Jewish Hilkiah standing before a king more European than Oriental.[57] But during the nineteenth century, even when Neo-Assyrian artwork was beginning to appear in the popular press, orientalistic features colored biblical illustrations, with Josiah being

57. Julius Schnorr von Carolsfeld, *Das Buch der Bücher in Bildern: 240 Darstellungen, erfunden und gezeichnet* (Leipzig: Georg Wigand, 1908), pl. 123.

no exception. For example, Isabella Child published in 1855 a children's book illustration of Josiah and Hilkiah,[58] replete with a very Spanish looking *infanto* Josiah reflecting the European notion that the good kings of Judah were essentially Europeans. Hilkiah is attired in a typical Orientalist oversized turban and flowing, embroidered gown.

Assyrian palace reliefs influenced costume, coiffure, and hardware in the art surrounding Josiah. Nothing seems to have impressed artists so much as Assyrian chariots.[59] In a dramatic chariot scene included in a 1905 Russian Orthodox biblical commentary,[60]

Figure 57. Lopukhin, *Tolkovaia Bibliia* (1987 [1905]), I, p. 188.

58. Isabella Child, *The Child's Picture Bible* (New York: J.Q. Preble, 1855), p. 82, available online as part of the digitized Making of America series at http://www.hti.umich.edu/cgi/t/text/pageviewer-idx?cmoa;cc=moa;g=moagrp;xc=l;q1=1child%20s%20picture%20bible;rgn=full%20text;idno=afz0133.0001.001;didno=afz0133.0001.001;view=image;seq=00000084, accessed September 28, 2006. A cross and Bible displayed over the figures' heads places the 'good king' Josiah in the lineage of proper religious figures, in this case the ancestors of Jesus and readers of the Bible.

59. Examples appear in *Den Hellige Skrift, Indeholdende Det Gamle og Det Nye Testamentes Kanoniske Bøger: Tilligmed Det Gamle Testamentes Apokryphiske Bøger* (Philadelphia, 1891), p. 548, and William Brassey Hole, *Old Testament History* (London: Eyre & Spottiswoode, 1925), pl. facing p. 126.

60. A.P. Lopukhin, *Tolkovaia Bibliia, ili Kommentarii na vse knigi Sv. Pisaniia Vetkhago i Novago Zaveta* (St. Petersburg, 1905; repr. Stockholm: Institute of Bible Translation, 1987), I, p. 188. The author thanks Nina Shultz (née Schmit) for locating this picture and translating the Russian text on Josiah that it illustrates.

Assyrian reliefs have been used to portray Josiah in a recognizable Assyrian military chariot with proper martial personnel, a proper Assyrian shield and (at least for the upper portion of his body) Assyrian royal garb. Note also that the king is drawn with an authentic Assyrian royal beard and haircut. In this way, period props derived from ancient Assyrian reliefs converge dramatically to illustrate Josiah's death in the traditional Orthodox Churches' reconstruction of Josiah's death based on 2 Chr 35.23-24.

Some illustrators attempted to incorporate an ancient Near Eastern landscape into illustrations of the king. In a Joseph Adams' woodcut of Josiah and the reading of the law, we see a youthful Josiah listening to Hilkiah.[61]

Figure 58. 'Piety of Josiah', in *The Illuminated Bible* (1843–46), p. 408.

To give the picture a proper ancient Near Eastern landscape, and one that situates Judah culturally between Egypt and Mesopotamia, the background contains both an Egyptian temple and a ziggurat, traditional icons of Egypt and Mesopotamia, respectively. Use of Assyrian architectural features to establish

61. 'Piety of Josiah', in *The Illuminated Bible, Containing the Old and New Testaments, Translated out of the Original Tongues, and with the Former Translations Diligently Compared and Revised. With Marginal Readings, References, and Chronological Dates. Also, the Apocrypha. To which are Added, a Chronological Index. An Index of the Subjects Contained in the Old And New Testaments, Tables of Weights, Coins, Measures, a List of Proper Names, a Concordance, &c. Embellished with Sixteen Hundred Historical Engravings by J.A. Adams, More than Fourteen Hundred of which are from Original Designs by J.G. Chapman* (New York: Harper & Brothers, Publishers, 1843–46), p. 408.

Judah visually as an Assyrian vassal state or chronologically in Assyrian times is fairly rare in biblical illustrations; usually nothing more generically precise than Egyptianizing pillars appear in Josiah illustrations. Exceptionally, Steele Savage's 1932 Josiah reading the scroll to the elders has the king standing between two cherubim modeled after the winged bulls of Assyria.[62]

By the end of the 20th century, the artistic representations of biblical Josiah had taken a postmodernist turn. So, for instance, Barry Moser's portrait of Josiah, based on a photograph of a Jewish boy in a Nazi concentration camp, becomes an affirmation of tradition in the face of the Shoah. Josiah stands for those who kept the tradition alive; indeed the lost life of the Holocaust victim becomes eternally embodied in the Judean king.[63] Finally, Gloria Oostema's 1995 Josiah, for an infant's first picture Bible,[64] presents a happy child-King Josiah adorned in something of a Christmas-pageant vision of a generic shepherd-king who grasps an extremely large mallet for repairing a big temple. Here the colorful (purple) robes and cheerful child-king are geared to allow small children to identify with a Josiah engaged in 'religious' activity. By the twenty-first century, ancient Assyrian artistic influence on Josiah has been largely eschewed for more modern notions of representational art and postmodernist readings of the Bible.

62. In Jesse Lyman Hurlbut, *Hurlbut's Story of the Bible for Young and Old* (New York: Holt Rinehart & Winston, expanded edn, 1932), p. 374.

63. Barry Moser (illustrator), *The Holy Bible: Containing All the Books of the Old and New Testaments: King James Version* (New York: Penguin Group, 1999), p. 408. On the inspiration for the Josiah portrait, see Catherine Madsen, 'A Terrible Beauty: Moser's Bible', *Cross Currents* 50 (2000), pp. 136-45 (139).

64. Tracy L. Harrast, *My Baby and Me Story Bible* (Grand Rapids, MI: Zonderkidz, 1995), p. 77.

Babylon in Bethel—New Light on Jacob's Dream

Victor Avigdor Hurowitz

1. *Babylonian Motifs in the Story of Jacob's Dream*

Scholars have long realized that the story of Jacob's dream at Luz (Gen. 28.10-22) has Babylonian connections. These include:[1] (1) וראשו מגיע השמימה ('Its head reached unto the heavens'; Gen. 28.12), in the description of the סולם (stairway or ladder) resembles וראשו בשמים ('Its head was in heaven') in the description of the Tower of Babel (Gen. 11.4). Both these approximate the name of Marduk's temple in Babylon É.sag.íla, 'the house whose head is lifted', and numerous references in Mesopotamian inscriptions to lofty temples touching heaven;[2] (2) Jacob's exclamation וזה שער השמים ('And this is the gate of heaven'; Gen. 28.17) in reaction to his dream recalls the popular etymology Mesopotamian scribes gave to the name of the city Babylon, namely *Bābili* < *Bāb ilī* < KÁ.DINGIR.RA = 'gate of the god/s';[3] and (3) the stairway

1. See the critical commentaries *ad loc.* such as Moshe Weinfeld, *Genesis: The Pentateuch with a New Commentary* (Tel Aviv: S.L. Gordon, 1975), I, pp. 158-62 [Hebrew] and articles such as C. Houtman, 'What Did Jacob See in his Dream at Bethel? (Some Remarks on Genesis xxviii 10-22)', *VT* 27 (1977), pp. 337-51; M. Weinfeld, 'Zion and Jerusalem as Religious and Political Capital: Ideology and Utopia', in *The Poet and the Historian. Essays in Literary and Historical Biblical Criticism* (ed. Richard Elliott Friedman; HSS, 26; Chico, CA: Scholars Press, 1983), pp. 75-115, esp. pp. 107-108; Diana Lipton, *Revisions of the Night: Politics and Promises in the Patriarchal Dreams of Genesis* (JSOTSup, 288; Sheffield: Sheffield Academic Press, 1999), pp. 63-114. On the linkage between the stories of the Tower of Babel and of Jacob's dream see Yehuda Elitzur, 'The Tower of Babel and Jacob's Ladder', in *Israel and the Bible: Studies in Geography, History, and Biblical Thought* (ed. Y. Elitzur and Amos Frisch; Ramat Gan: Bar-Ilan University, 1999), pp. 44-48 [Hebrew].

2. See A.R. George, *Babylonian Topographical Texts* (OLA, 40; Leuven: Peeters, 1992), pp. 294-98; Frederick E. Greenspahn, 'A Mesopotamian Proverb and its Biblical Reverberations', *JAOS* 114 (1994), pp. 33-38. On the relationship between וראשו בשמים in the tower story and the description of building Babylon in *Enūma eliš* 6:60-62 and building Ešarra in the 'Pennsylvania Prism' of Esarhaddon, see E.A. Speiser, 'Word Plays of the Creation Epic's Version of the Founding of Babylon', *Orientalia* ns 25 (1956), pp. 317-23 = *Oriental and Biblical Studies. Collected Writings of E.A. Speiser* (ed. J.J. Finkelstein and Moshe Greenberg; Philadelphia: University of Pennsylvania Press, 1967), pp. 53-61. Speiser's suggestion applies to וראשו מגיע השמים in Jacob's dream as well.

3. See I.J. Gelb, 'The Name of Babylon', in *'I Studied Inscriptions from Before the Flood':*

in the vision (Gen. 28.12) resembles in form and function the Mesopotamian *ziggurat*, or stepped temple tower connecting the gods in heaven and man on earth, typical of Mesopotamian temples and probably the real-life background of the Tower of Babel.

Years after first recognizing these affinities, two new data were adduced, anchoring the dream more firmly in Mesopotamia, but not particularly in Babylon. On the one hand, the *hapax* סולם was recognized as semantically related and probably cognate to Akkadian *simmiltu*,[4] and Jacob's stairway was compared with the heavenly stairway found in the Akkadian myth 'Nergal and Ereshkigal'.[5] On the other hand, the angels going up and down on the stairway have been compared with a passage in that myth in which the divine emissary Namtar and the god Nergal make several ascents and descents on a *simmilat šamāmi* between the heaven and netherworld, reaching at the end of their journey the gate of heaven or the gate of Ereshkigal, queen of the netherworld.[6] The difference between the mythical stairway and Jacob's is that the Mesopotamian stairway has two gates, the gate of Anu, Enlil and Ea at the top, and the gate of Ereshkigal at the bottom, while the biblical stairway has only one gate. Absence of the lower gate in the biblical story stems naturally from the fact that its stairway is 'stood up on the ground' (מוצב ארצה) and does not seem to continue downward into the underworld. One may assume that the biblical author truncated the lower stairs because of theological aversion to Sheol, denying it as a venue of divine-human contact. The angels have

Ancient Near Eastern, Literary, and Linguistic Approaches to Genesis 1–11 (ed. Richard S. Hess and David Toshio Tsumura; Sources for Biblical and Theological Study, 4; Winona Lake, IN: Eisenbrauns, 1994), pp. 266-69; George, *Babylonian Topographical Texts*, pp. 253-56.

4. On the problem of the etymological connection between these two lexemes see most recently Paul V. Mankowski, *Akkadian Loanwords in Biblical Hebrew* (HSS, 47; Winona Lake, IN: Eisenbrauns, 2000), pp. 115-18. Even if the Hebrew word is not related etymologically to the Akkadian word (as suggested by B. Landsberger), there is no doubt they can act as synonyms and function identically in their literary uses; see most recently C. Cohen, 'The Literary Motif of Jacob's Ladder (Gen. 28:12) according to the Interpretation of Ibn-Ezra and in Light of Parallels in Akkadian Literature', in *Shai le-Hadassah: Studies in Hebrew and Jewish Languages, Eshel Beer-Sheva* (ed. Y. Ben-Toulila; Researches in Jewish Studies, 5; Beer-Sheva: Ben-Gurion University of the Negev, 1997), pp. 15-26.

5. See CAD S, pp. 273-76. The word *simmiltu* designates a ladder in the modern sense (two wooden poles standing upright connected horizontally by cross beams serving as steps), a staircase, and mountain terraces (resembling steps). For ladders (Sumerian kun.sag, Akkadian *simmiltu*) to heaven and the underworld see Wayne Horowitz, *Mesopotamian Cosmic Geography* (Mesopotamian Civilizations, 8; Winona Lake, IN: Eisenbrauns, 1998), pp. 66, 115, 144, 250, 267, 287-88, 353, 359-60.

6. See O.R. Gurney, 'The Sultantepe Tablets (Continued) VII: The Myth of Nergal and Ereshkigal', *AnSt* 10 (1960), pp. 105-31, esp. p. 108, col. 1 ll.16'-17'; p. 118, col. 4 l.26'; p. 122, col. 5 l.13'; p. 124, col. 6 ll.18-19; A.R. Millard, 'The Celestial Ladder and the Gate of Heaven (Genesis xxviii. 12, 17)', *ExpTim* 78 (1966), pp. 86-87.

no business in the netherworld, so their descent ends with the Earth's surface where their activities are well attested.

Another inner-biblical connection between the stories of the dream and the Tower is the semantic and phonetic similarity between dispersing the builders of the Tower throughout the world mentioned three times (הפיצם ויפץ פן נפוץ; Gen. 11.4, 8, 9) and the promise that Jacob would 'break out' (ופרצת Gen. 28.14) to the west, east, north and south. We must note, however, that this promise occurs in the J part of the narrative, while the remaining Babylonian and Mesopotamian elements appear in Elohistic passages.[7]

Even the cultic customs mentioned in Jacob's Bethel sojourn have some Mesopotamian parallels. Pouring oil on the pillar (Gen. 28.18; cf. 31.13) was compared long ago with the custom of Assyrian kings who restore dilapidated temples to replace the inscriptions and anoint them with oil.[8] My late teacher Raphael Kutscher suggested that the dream by the stone is to be related to the Mesopotamian association of dream incubation with the dream god ᵈZaqar (previously read as Anzaqar), whose name means 'god of the standing stone'.[9] Finally, Diana Lipton has suggested that the dream itself, in which Jacob sees part of a temple, reflects the Mesopotamian custom of authorizing construction of temples by means of a royal dream vision in which the king is shown the plan of the temple.[10]

In what follows I wish to introduce two new parallels between Jacob's dream and some Mesopotamian sources connected specifically with Babylon. These parallels have gone unnoticed, but they are most striking, and, in my opinion, no less impressive than the parallels already pointed out. I will then comment briefly on the significance of finding in the Bethel foundation legend ideas which are specifically Babylonian.

(1) The first parallel comes from an inscription published in 1985 of Nabopolassar, King of Babylon (605–625 BCE), father of Nebuchadrezzar II of biblical fame.[11] This text celebrates the construction of Imgur-Enlil—an inner wall

7. Even if Gen. 28.14 is regarded as an addition of an independent editor and not necessarily J, it would still not be identical with the author of the Tower story.

8. See CAD Š/1, p. 326, s.v. *šamnu* g1'; Sylvie Lackenbacher, *Le roi bâtisseur: Les récits de construction assyriens des origins à Teglathphalasar III* (Études assyriologiques, 11; Paris: Editions Recherche sur les civilizations, 1982), pp. 157-58, 228.

9. See R. Kutscher, 'The Mesopotamian God Zaqar and the Pillar of Jacob's Dream', *Beer Sheva* 3 (5748 [= 1987]), pp. 125-30 [Hebrew].

10. See Lipton, *Revisions of the Night*, pp. 65, 80-92.

11. See Farouk N.H. Al-Rawi, 'Nabopolassar's Restoration Work on the Wall *Imgur-Enlil* at Babylon', *Iraq* 47 (1985), pp. 1-13. The text has been studied by Paul-Alain Beaulieu, 'Nabopolassar and the Antiquity of Babylon', in *Hayim and Miriam Tadmor Festschrift Volume* (ed. Israel Ephʿal, Amnon Ben-Tor, Peter Machinist; Eretz Israel, 27; Jerusalem: Israel Exploration Society, 2003), pp. 1*-9*; Walter Farber, 'The City Wall of Babylon—a Belt Cord?', *N.A.B.U.* 1991, no. 72; Andrew R. George, 'The City Wall of Babylon—a Belt Cord', *N.A.B.U.* 1991 no. 101.

within the city of Babylon, that surrounded the holy compound in which stood the Etemenanki ziggurat (temple-tower) and the Esagila temple.[12] Col. 2 ll.8-21 provide a poetic description of the wall and the area that it encompasses. The text below is divided and arranged so as to emphasize the literary structure of the passage:

Imgur-Enlil dūra rabâ ša Bābilim
pulukku *reštā ša ištu ṣâtim šūpû*
kisurrâ *šuršudu ša labar dūr ūmē*
qinnâ zaqru ša šitnunu šamāmi
tukšu dannu ēdil pî māt ayyābi
tarbaṣu šumdulu *ša Igīgī*
kisallu palkâ *ša Anunnakī*
mēlīt šamāmi // simmilat ganzir
nanzāz Lugal-girra u Meslamtea
ibrat ša Ištar šarrat rabītim
maškan tilpanu *ša Dagan qurādu*
tarbaṣu karāšu *ša qarradu Ninurta*
bīt kidinni ša Anum u Enlil
ašar uṣurāt naklāti ša Ea bēli rubê
qaqqar niṣirtim ša ilī rabîtim
ša Igīgī u Anunnakī ina nūg libbīšunu ukinnū temēnšu /nakliš uštaṣbû /ullû rēšūšu

Imgur-Enlil, the great wall of Babylon

The ancient boundary marker which has been famous since the beginning of time,
The firm frontier as old as time itself,
The lofty eyrie as high as the heavens,
The strong shield which blocks the entry of the enemy lands,
The wide enclosure of the Igīgī,
The spacious courtyard of the Anunnakī,
The step up to heaven, // The stairway down to the netherworld,
The station of Lugal-girra and Meslamtaea,
The sanctuary of Ištar the great lady,
The maidan of the warrior Dagan,
The courtyard of the hero Ninurta's camp,
The place of asylum of Anu and Enlil,
The place of the clever plans of Ea lord of Eridu,

A reserved land of the great gods,
Which the Igīgī and Anunnakī had joyfully laid its foundations, completed artistically, and raised high its head.[13]

The most important line for us is the middle line according to the structure indicated here (col. 2 l.15). It contains two parallel cola and stands alone, isolated

12. For the walls of Babylon in the sixth century BCE see George, *Babylonian Topographical Texts*, p. 141, fig. 7.

13. Al-Rawi, 'Nabopolassar's Restoration', pp. 3-4.

and emphasized betwixt and between the other verses that appear in couplets.[14] This bi-colon line describes the wall as *mēlīt šamāmi // simmilat ganzir*, 'the step of heaven//staircase of the netherworld'. The word *mēlītu* means 'step', like Hebrew מעלה,[15] so the meaning of the two cola when combined will be 'a stepped stairway stretching from the heaven to the netherworld'. The similarity to Jacob's stairway planted on the earth with its head reaching to the heavens is obvious. In the description of the wall and the precinct it encloses, reality mingles with myth. On the one hand, a real wall surrounds the sacred area of the earthly city of Babylon. The wall is very high and its foundations deep. On the other hand, building the wall and the city quarter inhabited by gods is attributed to the gods of heaven and earth, lending a mythological dimension to the description, and making the walls' dimensions cosmic dimensions. The mythological dimension of the wall is enhanced if we take into account another passage describing King Nabopolassar who built the wall:

ṣābit alle ša Igīgī
zābil ***tupšikku*** *ša Anunnakī*

The one who grasps the hoe of the Igīgī
The one who carries the brick hod of the Anunnakī[16]

This unusual depiction of a king, in which the temporal monarch performs a divine task, raises obvious associations with *Enūma eliš* 6.59 which describes the construction of Babylon:

Anunnakī itrukū alla
šattu ištiat ***libbitašu*** *iltabnū?*

The Anunnakī pulled the hoe
For one year they molded its bricks.[17]

14. I have indicated in bold face type and underlining the main words and expressions which create the coupling of the verses. For the center line and the two couplets adjoining it see George, *Babylonian Topographical Texts*, p. 368. He cites this passage as a parallel to one found in the Description of Babylon, *Tintir* 5.85-86:

300 parak Igigi u 600 parak Anunnakki
180 ibrat Ištar 180 manzāza Lugal-girra u Meslamtea
300 socles of the Igigi and 600 socles of the Anunnakki
180 open-air shrines of Ištar and 180 standing places of Lugal-girra and Meslamtea

George, *Babylonian Topographical Texts*, p. 68. This parallel emphasizes the importance of the line describing the wall as a stepped staircase as an addition to a traditional literary topos.

15. George, *Babylonian Topographical Texts*, p. 368, translates simply 'place of ascent', without specifying any particular architectural form. Horowitz, *Cosmic Geography*, p. 267 translates 'incline', and perhaps he is referring to a ramp.

16. Al-Rawi, 'Nabopolassar's Restoration', p. 4, col. 3 ll. 7-8.

17. All passages from *Enūma eliš* are cited according to W.G. Lambert and Simon B. Parker, *Enuma Eliš: The Babylonian Epic of Creation, the Cuneiform Text* (Oxford: Clarendon Press, 1966).

The connotation of this text is that King Nabopolassar, when building the walls of Babylon, is doing the gods' work and recapitulating their task in primeval days when they first built that famous city.[18]

The words which describe the top and base of the wall are not the usual words for heavens and earth *šamû* and *erṣetu*, but *šamāmu* and *ganzir* which are rare, poetic terms suited more to cosmic regions than to mundane geography. Nonetheless, they are applied here to a wall of this world, built of bricks.

Among the several attested appearances of *simmiltu*, only here does this word apply specifically to the topography of Babylon. This stairway, which links the Heavens and the Underworld is none other than the stairway mentioned in the 'Nergal and Ereshkigal' myth, and, lo and behold, the stairway stands specifically in Babylon and is part of Babylon herself.

(2) The second parallel to the Genesis narrative of Jacob's ladder occurs in the fifth tablet of *Enūma eliš*, a text well known for many years.[19] This tablet relates how Marduk, having defeated Ti᾽āmat, and having created the world within her cleaved corpse, offers to build a resting place for the gods. In tablet 5.119-30 we read:

elēna Apsî šubat tarmâni
miḫrit Ešarra ša abnû anāku elkun
šapliš Ašrata udannina qaqqarša
lūpušma bīta lū šubat lalêja
qerbuššu māḫāzašu lušaršidma
kummī luddâ lukīn šarrūtī
<u>*enūma ultu Apsî tellâ ana puḫri*</u>
<u>*ašruššu lū nubattakun ana maḫār puḫurkun*</u>
<u>*enūma ultu šamāmi turrudā ana [puḫri]*</u>
<u>*ašruššu lū nubattakun ana maḫār puḫurkun*</u>
lubbīma šumšu Bābilī bītāti ilī rabûti
[nīni qerbuššu nipp[uš ...]-tum

Above Apsû, the place where you placed your dwelling,
A copy of Ešarra that I have made above you,
Below, in Ašrata I strengthened the ground.
I shall build a house, may it be my place of pleasure.

18. Building the walls of Babylon is attributed to Marduk (Bēl) himself by the Hellenistic historian Berossus. See Stanley Mayer Burstein, *The Babyloniaca of Berossus* (Sources and Monographs. Sources from the Ancient Near East, 1/5; Malibu, CA: Undena, 1978), p. 17.

19. See B. Landsberger, J.V. Kinnier Wilson, 'The Fifth Tablet of *Enuma Eliš*', *JNES* 20 (1961), pp. 154-79 (164-66); George, *Babylonian Topographical Texts*, pp. 255-56. The fifth tablet was previously known only partially, and L.W. King thought that the manuscript containing this passage did not belong to *Enūma eliš* but to some other composition. Cf. L.W. King, *The Seven Tablets of Creation, or the Babylonian and Assyrian Legends concerning the Creation of the World and of Mankind* (Luzac's Semitic Text and Translation Series, 12; London: Luzac, 1902), I, pp. 197-200. In any case, the full reconstruction of the text uncovering the parallel became possible only after the publication of the Sultantepe manuscript by Landsberger and Kinnier-Wilson.

> Within it I shall found its holy precinct.
> I shall assign my chapels, I shall establish my kingship.
> When you ascend from Apsû to the divine assembly
> In its place, may it be your lodging place before your assembly.
> When you descend from the heavens
> In its place, may it be your lodging before your assembly.
> I shall call it Babylon, the houses of the great gods.
> We, within it, shall do/make [...][20]

This passage mentions neither a stairway nor a *simmiltu*, and this absence may have hidden from scholars the striking similarity it has with Jacob's dream. Even so, it contains certain important elements reminiscent of the dream. First and foremost is the gods going up and down between heaven and Earth. This parallels the ascending and descending gods in 'Nergal and Ereshkigal' already mentioned, which was done, as we have seen, on a stairway, and, *mutatis mutandis*, the angels going up and down the staircase in Jacob's dream. In addition, whereas 'Nergal and Ereshkigal' mentions the messenger's ascent in one passage and the descent in another, *Enūma eliš* mentions them both in a single breath. Interestingly, here too the ascent is mentioned before the descent, just as in Jacob's dream, a detail that was of concern to many exegetes.[21]

A second similarity between *Enūma eliš* and the biblical narrative is the name given to the place, É.MEŠ DINGIR.MEŠ GAL.MEŠ (*bītāti ilī rabûti*), 'houses of the great gods' (5.129). This is parallel, of course, to Jacob's words of astonishment when awaking from his vision אין זה כי אם בית אלהים ('This is none other than the House of God'; Gen. 28.17), as well as the language of his vow 'This stone which I have set up as a pillar will be a house of God'. Perhaps it may be connected as well to the name of the place בית אל as is written 'and he called that place בית אל' (Gen. 28.19).

A third, most striking parallel, is that the place built is to be a 'lodging', *nubattu*, for the gods, *Enūma eliš* 5.128. The building plan is carried out in tablet 6.51-52 where the gods say to Marduk:

> Let us make a dais the name of which will be called:
> 'May in your shrine our lodging (*nubattani*) be; may we rest within it'.[22]

The word *nubattu*, which Landsberger and Kinnier-Wilson translated as 'night's resting place' is derived from the verb *bâtu* which happens to be the inter-dialectic equivalent of the Hebrew verb *lûn*, and proof of synonymity comes from Targum Onqelos which renders וילן as ובת. If so, the gods' lodging in Babylon at night is parallel to what is said about Jacob, 'he lodged there (וילן) because

20. Lambert and Parker, *Enuma Eliš*, s.v.

21. But cf. Rashbam *ad loc.* (Gen. 28.12) who says 'according to the plain meaning one must not precisely interpret the verse which puts ascending before descending, because it is only natural to mention ascent before descent'.

22. Lambert and Parker, *Enuma Eliš*, s.v.

the sun had set'. Obviously, the one who lodges in Luz-Bethel was Jacob, while the lodgers in Babylon are the gods of heaven and earth, but this demythologization, turning the divine lodgers into a human has somewhat of a precedent in the dream itself in which the 'gods' of the myths become simply angels of God. We might see in the same vein the stone that Jacob erects as a pillar. This stone was obviously considered the pillar to be erected in the future temple to be built in Bethel, and if so we have found that the cult object in this temple was erected by a human, and this is a demythologization in comparison with Babylon which was founded and even built by the gods.

The fourth parallel with *Enūma eliš* tablet 5 is that Marduk mentions twice *ašruššu*, 'in this place', and in another line Babylon is called *Ašrata*,[23] a fancy title of heaven derived from *ašru*, 'place', and these are parallel to the *Leitwort* מקום that appears three times before the dream in Gen. 28.11 and three times in the response to the dream in vv. 16, 17 and 19.

Finally, we may add to all these linguistic and thematic parallels, that in both *Enūma eliš* 5.119-30 and 6.51-52 the gods commit themselves to build a temple, and this promise resembles Jacob's vow that the stone will be a house of God. Similarly, in both stories the party who undertakes building the temple also gives it a name.

It becomes clear, therefore, that the account of Jacob's dream contains hardly a detail without some prominent linguistic or thematic parallel to Babylon in general and the myth of its primeval foundation in particular. I suggest that this is a clear example of appropriating traditions of one city and applying them to another. Transferring traditions from one sacred city to another is not without parallel or surprising in ancient Near Eastern literature. The Babylonians themselves applied to their own city traditions and theological concepts from other cities, and in particular those of Eridu and Nippur.[24] Likewise, Nippur's traditions were appropriated by the Assyrians who adapted and transferred them to their own cap-

23. This term is derived from *ašru*, 'place', and designates a part of heaven. But, according to Horowitz, *Cosmic Geography*, pp. 121-22, the ground of *Ašrata* is the *terra firma* upon which Babylon stands.

24. See W.G. Lambert, 'Nippur in Ancient Ideology', in *Nippur at the Centennial. Papers Read at the XXXVe Rencontre assyriologique internationale, Philadelphia, 1988* (ed. Maria deJong Ellis; Occasional Publications of the Samuel Noah Kramer Fund, 14; Philadelphia: Babylonian Section, The University Museum, 1992), pp. 119-26; J.G. Westenholz, 'The Theological Foundation of the City, The Capital City and Babylon', in *Capital Cities: Urban Planning and Spiritual Dimensions. Proceedings of the Symposium Held on May 27-29 Jerusalem, Israel* (ed. J.G. Westenholz; Jerusalem: Bible Lands Museum, 1998), pp. 43-45; Stefan M. Maul, 'Reflection and Navel: The Ancient Middle Eastern Capital City of the World', http://prelectur.stanford.edu/lectures/maul/capitals.html, English translation of 'Die altorientalische Hauptstadt: Abbild und Nabel der Welt', in *Die orientalische Stadt: Kontinuitat. Wandel. Bruch, 1 Internationale Colloquium der Deutschen Orient-Gesellschaft. 9.-10. Mai 1996 in Halle/Salle* (ed. Gernot Wilhelm; Colloquien der Deutschen Orient-Gesellschaft, 1; Saarbrücker Druckerei und Verlag, 1997), pp. 109-24.

ital, Assur. Babylon's traditions were also applied to other cities. The Neo-Assyrians appropriated the Babylonian *Enūma eliš* even while replacing Marduk with their imperial god Aššur. Now, conversion of *Enūma eliš* into an Assyrian ideological composition would have necessitated replacing the city of Babylon in tablets 5 and 6 with a different city, even though evidence for such a switch has not been preserved in extant tablets. At the same time, however, we should mention E.A. Speiser's important suggestion that the description of building Ešarra, the god Aššur's temple in the city Assur mentioned in a prism of Esarhaddon, was based on the construction of Babylon as described in *Enūma eliš* 6.61-62.[25] Similarly, in Uruk the new temple of Anu was built according to the measurements and blueprint of Esagila, perhaps with the intent to syncretize Anu and Marduk.[26] It is likely that traditions of Mesopotamian cities somehow reached Israel and her sacred cities such as Jerusalem, and in our case, Bethel. Put simply, the rule at work is that what is good for one capital city and its temple is good for another.[27] Just as the people of Uruk modeled the Anu temple in their city along the lines of the Marduk temple in Babylon, so the biblical writer transferred to Bethel the theological outline of Babylon, and in particular its role as a lodging place for gods going up and down a staircase between heaven and earth.

And let us be precise! It is reasonable to assume that in the case of Bethel we are not dealing with a general, nonspecific Mesopotamian background, but with a specifically Babylonian background. That is to say, several of the Mesopotamian traditions reflected in the Tower of Babel account and the stairway in Bethel came specifically from Babylon and not from some other, undetermined location. Admittedly, the concept of a connection between heaven and earth embodied in a defined geographical location is connected to the widespread concept of the capital city as the bond between heaven and earth. This general concept is expressed in idioms such as DUR.AN.KI, 'bond of heaven and earth' which is one of Nippur's most ancient by-names, or *markas šamê u erṣeti* (connection of heaven and earth), or *ṣerret Igīgī u Anunnakī* (lead-rope of gods of the heaven and gods of the earth), or *puluk šamê u erṣetim* (boundary marker of heaven and earth), etc.[28] These expressions were applied to various cities

25. See Speiser, 'Word Plays in the Creation Epic's Version of the Founding of Babylon', pp. 317-23.

26. See A.R. George, 'The Bricks of E-sagil', *Iraq* 57 (1995), pp. 173-97, esp. 194.

27. See M. Weinfeld, 'Zion and Jerusalem', pp. 75-116. One should remember as an analogy the well known transfer of Canaanite Mount Ṣāpôn to Mount Zion or the imposition of Mount Sinai motifs on Mount Zion. See, for example, R.E. Clements, *God and Temple: The Idea of the Divine Presence in Ancient Israel* (Oxford: Basil Blackwell, 1965), pp. 3-11.

28. See George, *Babylonian Topographical Texts*, pp. 261-62; J.G. Westenholz, 'The Foundation Myths of Mesopotamian Cities: Divine Planners and Human Builders', in *Mites de fundació de ciutats al món antic (Mesopotàmia, Grècia i Roma)* (ed. Pedro Azara, Ricardo Mar and Eva Subias Pascual; Actes del Colloqui, Monografies, 2; Barcelona: Museu d'Arqueologia de Catalunya, 2001), pp. 59-68.

including Babylon, Nippur and Assur. However, imaging this concept in the picture of a stairway on the one hand and gods going up and down on the other is not a common device. Similarly, the concept of the stairway between heaven and earth is found in mythology, but from among the real Mesopotamian cities only the walls of Babylon are known thus far to have merited this title in Nabopolassar's inscription. Also, the motif of gods traveling between heaven and earth is found in various myths, but only in *Enūma eliš* are they connected with a specific city, and that city was Babylon. Finally, the 'gate of heaven' occurs in myths, but from among known Mesopotamian cities only Babylon is identified as the gate of heaven. If so, we should not say that Bethel is described theologically as a typical capital city, but rather that Bethel is depicted as a reflection of Babylon.

2. *The Historical Background of the Story*

The special link between Babylon and Bethel is certainly interesting and important in its own right, but it may also have significance for the date of composition of the biblical account of Jacob's dream. This is not the place to discuss fully the ramifications of the link, and offer definitive conclusions. Suffice it, therefore, to present briefly several possibilities for dating the story on the basis of this link.

One possibility is that the account of the dream in Bethel was created at a time when Bethel was inhabited and Babylon ruled the world. Such a date turns on two assumptions: (1) a story about Bethel and its temple would be created only at a time when a functioning Israelite temple stood at the site, or when memory of such a temple lingered on and inspired hopes to restore it. According to this line of thought, it makes no sense to compose an aetiological *hieros logos* glorifying and sanctifying a city or temple which no longer stand, or have declined and sunk into oblivion to the extent that there was no longer hope to rebuild it. (2) Transferring theological motifs from one city to another or from one deity to another is a theo-political act connected to international competition over the primacy of a particular god over others.[29] Only when Babylon was at its pinnacle would there be reason to compete with it rather than with some other city. Babylon would not serve as a target of imitation if it were in ruins. If

29. Rivalry for supremacy in the Mesopotamian pantheon was quite ancient, and cannot be fully discussed in this context. Let us suffice in mentioning the rivalry between Enki and Eridu on the one side and Enlil and Nippur on the other, which evolved into a rivalry between Marduk and Babylon against Ninurta and Aššur. Eventually, Sîn and Ḫarrān joined the competition, as well as Nabû and Borsippa, and Anu and Uruk. In the Canaanite pantheon we find rivalry between ʾEl and Baʿal. This competition was joined by YHWH, God of Israel and Jerusalem or Bethel in our case. In all cases we find that myths concerning one god are rewritten on behalf of the competing god. Another characteristic of this competition is transference of the attributes of one god's temple to that of the other.

so, when did such circumstances exist? When, along with Babylonian domination in the world, was Bethel settled and its temple active?

These two circumstances existed under the Neo-Babylonian empire, following the destruction of Nineveh in 612 BCE and the rise of Babylon and the great building projects of Nabopolassar. If we accept Hanan Eshel's contention that Bethel was destroyed at the time of Josiah and restored for a short time after the destruction of Jerusalem as a replacement for that city,[30] then the window for composing the dream story will range somewhere from shortly after 586 BCE until the time of Darius I when the walls of Babylon were destroyed (521 BCE) or the end of the exile when Bethel ceased to be a temple-city. In other words, the Exilic period is one possible historical window for the account of Jacob's dream at Bethel.

Another possible date arises from Blenkinsopp's suggestion that Bethel was not totally destroyed at the time of Josiah but continued to function without interruption until the middle of the sixth century (perhaps until the time of the Megabyzus rebellion).[31] If this was the case, the window for composing the story could have opened earlier, but not before the fall of Nineveh in 612 BCE and the subsequent rise of Babylon to the rank of dominant imperial power in the ancient Near East. Also following Blenkinsopp, Bethel ceased to function before the return from the Exile. This window overlaps the previously mentioned window, but widens it by a quarter of a century.

A third possible date is based on the assumption of the continuous existence of Bethel from the time of Jeroboam I (following Blenkinsopp), and a different assumption about the need for a city to be politically supreme in order to serve as a theological model. Despite the apparently logical assumption that only a ruling city would be thought worthy of imitation, it does not stand up to the facts. It is a historical fact that certain cities were objects of theological imitation even though they were not the dominant imperial city or even within their own cultural sphere. Such were the cities Nippur and Eridu in Mesopotamia whose theological supremacy in the post-Kassite era was not related to their political position or military might. Eridu merited her position thanks to her antiquity and E-Abzu, temple of Ea, while Nippur enjoyed influence because it was the city of Enlil, supreme god in the Sumerian pantheon, from whose temple E-Kur legitimization flowed to Mesopotamian rulers. To be sure, we have already seen that even under the Neo-Assyrian empire the

30. See H. Eshel, 'The Historical Background of the Establishment of Temples to the God of Israel at Bethel and Samaria Following the Destruction of the First Temple', MA thesis, Faculty of Humanities, Jerusalem: The Hebrew University, 1989. Unavailable when writing this article was Klaus Koenen, *Bethel: Geschichte, Kult und Theologie* (OBO, 192; Freiburg, Switzerland: Universitätsverlag/Göttingen: Vandenhoeck & Ruprecht, 2003).

31. See Joseph Blenkinsopp, 'Bethel in the Neo-Babylonian Period', in *Judah and the Judeans in the Neo-Babylonian Period* (ed. Oded Lipschits and J. Blenkinsopp; Winona Lake, IN: Eisenbrauns, 2003), pp. 95-110.

city of Babylon was considered important,[32] and the Assyrians themselves appropriated its ideology, imposing it on the city Assur itself. In other words, the politically dominant city imitated the weaker, rival city. This raises the possibility that transferring traditions of Babylon to Bethel occurred earlier than the days of Neo-Babylonian domination of the world. It is possible that transferring its theological portrait to Bethel happened during the reigns of Sennacherib (705–681 BCE) or Esarhaddon (681–669 BCE), and that Bethel entered the international theological competition waged between Assur and Babylon at that time. We should remember that even at the time of Assyria's greatness in the seventh century, Babylon enjoyed a central religious importance that the Assyrians themselves saw fit to compete with. This wider window swallows up both the previous windows, widening them to a time span of one hundred eighty years (705–521 BCE).

But, there is even a fourth possibility for the dating of Jacob's dream. Since *Enūma eliš* was composed at the end of the second millennium BCE, apparently at the time of Nebuchadrezzar I (following Lambert), and since the ideas common to Bethel revealed above are based on it, it is possible that they were transferred and applied to Bethel as early as the time of Jeroboam I when the Bethel temple was either founded or converted into a royal temple for the Northern Kingdom of Israel. An early date for the narrative of Jacob's dream and the staircase falls within the accepted date of the Elohist source (E), namely the time of the Divided Monarchy.

As already stated, I cannot discuss definitively the question of the story's date, and I have no pretensions of having solved the question. One must bring into account additional factors such as the chronological background of the E source in its entirety, which is a vexed problem unto itself, and many archaeological problems relating to the identification of the site of Bethel and its history. At the same time, many will prefer, perhaps, the first of the options listed above; and that is because under Neo-Babylonian rule Israelite interest in Babylon would naturally increase, fuelling the desire to compete with her theologically, even if for reason of revenge and desire to prove superiority to the conqueror.

3. *The Significance of Babylon in Bethel in Canonical Context*

If the account of Jacob's dream is read together with the story of the Tower of Babel, as they stand in the extant Hebrew Bible, we find that Genesis contains two stories dealing with Babylon—one explicitly and the other implicitly.[33]

32. Although the Assyrians destroyed Babylon, they also rebuilt it. See Michael P. Streck, 'Der Wiederaufbau Babylons unter Asarhaddon und Assurbanipal in Briefen aus Ninive', *Altorientalische Forschungen* 29 (2002), pp. 205-33.

33. André Parrot has already suggested that it is impossible to distinguish between the name

Now, such a combination would seem to convey a message, although we must remember that the two stories are not the products of a single author (the tower story is attributed to J, while the staircase is relegated to E).[34] Not only are both stories related to Babylon, but they present opposite attitudes toward that city, which are effectively complementary, two sides of the same coin. The Tower of Babel story presents Babylon negatively, speaks about its abandonment because of divine intervention, and views the construction of the city and its tower as one sin of humankind in a chain of primordial transgressions starting in paradise and distancing humanity from God. The dream story, on the other hand, applies to an Israelite city and temple the central ideas in the Mesopotamian conception of Babylon; and the author obviously views them positively, using them to glorify the Israelite site. Those who have dealt with the simple theological significance of the staircase have described it as symbolizing a bridge linking humanity and God.[35] The theological import of the two stories in their canonical context is that the damage done to human-God relations by building the Tower of Babel before the birth of the Patriarchs was repaired at the time of Jacob by founding Bethel where the message of the dream will be realized. Humans cannot ascend to heaven by the tower of bricks they attempted to build in Babylon, but Israelites bridge the gap between heaven and earth by means of Bethel where one finds 'a staircase standing on the ground and its head reaches to heaven, and angels of God go up and down on it'.[36]

Babel (= gate of the gods) and 'the gate of heaven', and that the later helps understand the former. On the basis of the image of the ziggurat he contends that the Tower of Babel was the staircase and the temple supported by it was the gate of heaven. See A. Parrot, *La tour de Babel* (Cahiers d'archéologie biblique, 2; Neuchâtel: Delachaux & Niestlé, 1953), p. 55.

34. This division is not agreed upon by all scholars. So, for instance, M. Weinfeld, *Genesis*, p. 158, takes the entire pericope to be Elohistic apart from Gen. 28.13-14 which are an editorial insertion. But even Weinfeld did not attribute the story of the tower and the story of the dream to the same source. For the composition of the chapter see as well Alexander Rofé, *Introduction to the Composition of the Pentateuch* (Jerusalem: Academon, 1994), pp. 86-88 [Hebrew], and more recently J. Van Seters, 'Divine Encounter at Bethel (Gen 28,10-22) in Recent Literary-Critical Study of Genesis', *ZAW* 110 (1998), pp. 503-13. Y. Zakovitch claims that the author of the Bethel pericope knew the Tower of Babel story and mirrors it in response. See Y. Zakovitch, *Through the Looking Glass: Reflection Stories in the Bible* (Tel Aviv: Hakibbutz Hameuchad, 1995), pp. 60-62 [Hebrew]. I am grateful to Mr. Roni Goldstein for this reference.

35. See Cohen, 'The Literary Motif of Jacob's Ladder', pp. 15-26, who strengthens Ibn-Ezra's interpretation (on Gen. 28.12) 'that nothing will be held back from the Lord and what happens below (on earth) depend on what happens above (in heaven)'.

36. Cf. Y. Elitzur, 'The Tower of Babel and Jacob's Ladder', pp. 44-48 [Hebrew]. Despite some apologetic overtones, one can agree with his statement, 'This field in Bethel, seemingly empty, is the house of God whence ascends the true ladder between heaven and earth, whereas the towers of Babylon are nothing but brick and mortar (asphalt) monstrosities', p. 46.

Whose Truth and Whose Justice? The Uruk and Other Late Akkadian Prophecies re-Revisited

JoAnn Scurlock

SpTU, I, no. 3 (generally known as the *Uruk Prophecy*)[1] is a striking example of a genre of writings which bear comparison with biblical texts. In it, a sequence of eleven kings appears, all but three of whom are specifically said to be bad. In every case, the kings in question are not named but simply described as 'a king will arise'. For most of them, however, a few further details are provided to aid in identification.

Translation:

> **[... a king w]ill arise and rule the scattered land. {**King I**} [...a king] from the Sealand who exercised rulership in Babylon. [Aft]er him a king will arise. {**King II**} He will not provide justice for the land. He will not make a correct application of the laws. The traditional protective goddess of Uruk he will take away from Uruk and make her dwell in Babylon. He will make dwell in her sanctuary one not a protective goddess of Uruk and make her a present of people who are not her people.[2] He will impose a heavy tribute on the people of Uruk. He will lay Uruk waste, fill the canals with silt, and abandon the cultivated fields. After him a king will arise. {**King III**} He will not provide justice for the land. He will not make a correct application of the laws. Ditto, ditto, ditto, ditto. {**Kings IV-VII**} Ditto (After him a king will arise. {**King VIII**} He will not provide justice for the land. He will not make a correct application of the laws.) He will take the property of the land of Akkad to the land of Subartu. After him a king will arise. {**King IX**} He will not provide justice for the land. He will not make a correct application of the laws. He will rule the four quarters. At the mention of his name, the world will tremble. After him a king will arise in Uruk. {**King X**} He will provide justice for the land. He will make a correct application of the laws. He will establish the rites of Anu in Uruk. The traditional protective goddess of Uruk he will take away from Babylon and make her dwell in Uruk, in her sanctuary. He will make her a present of her people. He will rebuild the temples of Uruk. He will restore the sanctuaries. He will renew Uruk. He will rebuild the gates

1. For the text itself, see the original publication in Hermann Hunger, SpTU, I, no. 3. For further discussion of and bibliographical references to this text and the genre of texts to which it belongs, see Paul-Alain Beaulieu, 'The Historical Background of the Uruk Prophecy', in *The Tablet and the Scroll: Near Eastern Studies in Honor of William W. Hallo* (ed. Mark E. Cohen, Daniel C. Snell and David B. Weisberg; Bethesda, MD: CDL Press, 1993), pp. 41-52.
2. Literally a 'not protective goddess' and her 'not people'.

> of Uruk with lapis-lazuli. He will fill the canals and the cultivated fields with plenty and abundance. [Af]ter him a king, his son will arise in Uruk and rule the four quarters. {**King XI**} He will exercise [ruler]ship and kingship in Uruk. His dynasty will endure forever. [The king]s of Uruk will exercise rulership like the gods.[3]

The general purpose of the text would appear to be clear enough: a sequence of real kings in the past is used as a sort of omen allowing the prediction of hoped for events in the future. The idea of time as a linear sequence of cycles is the modern view, but it was also the original view of time traditional to mankind. Ancient attempts to predict the future from the past were predicated on the notion that apparently chance happenings were a coded message from the gods warning of events to come.[4] The science of omenology was, then, not as radically different in philosophy as one might suppose from the activities of a modern economist or historian. The object of being able to predict the future from the past is to avoid repeats of calamitous past events—i.e. you can prevent history from repeating itself and have a choice in the matter. Similarly, you could prevent the bad omen represented by a ghost crying in one's house, by performing the appropriate NAM.BÚR.BI (apotropaic ritual).

1. *The Uruk Prophecy: Previous Interpretations*

But if the general purpose of the *Uruk Prophecy* was to provide a sequence of real kings in the past to be used as a sort of omen that would allow the prediction of hoped-for events in the future, which of the events recounted were significant and which merely included to clue in the intended audience? And what exactly was the original prophecy predicting? I say original because the text indisputably refers to events which preceded the Persian conquest,[5] whereas the copy which we have can be dated to the Persian or Seleucid period.[6] This raises the further question of what it is doing in the archive in which it was found. At least six scholars to date have attempted to provide answers to one or all of these questions (see table below). King I is described as being from the Sealand and ruling in Babylon. Hunger and Kaufman[7] identify this king

3. SpTU, I, no. 3 r. 1-18. The obverse of the text is extremely fragmentary but also speaks of kings and their activities.

4. As pointed out by Robert D. Biggs, 'More Babylonian "Prophecies"', *Iraq* 29 (1967), pp. 117-32, historical omens are formatted as apodoses of a type typical of the corpus of Mesopotamian omens in general. What is odd is the usual absence of a prodosis in historical omens. Where such prodoses do exist, they seem to be drawn from astrology. So, for example, it would not be surprising to find *'If a star arises in the East, a king will arise in the land'.

5. See Peter Höffken, 'Heilszeitherrschererwartung in babylonischen Raum: Überlegungen im Anschluss an W 22 307.7', *WdO* 9 (1977), pp. 57-71.

6. W.G. Lambert, *The Background of Jewish Apocalyptic* (London: Athlone Press, 1978), p. 10.

7. Hermann Hunger and Stephen A. Kaufman, 'A New Akkadian Prophecy Text', *JAOS* 95 (1975), pp. 371-75.

with Marduk-balassu-iqbi (?–813 BCE) [8] or Baba-aḫa-iddina (812–? BCE) and Lambert with Marduk-apla-iddina II (721–710 BCE).[9] Cole, however, offers persuasive arguments that this king was intended to be Erība-Marduk (?–761? BCE).[10]

Uruk Prophecy King II is clearly the villain of the piece. He is supposed to have taxed Uruk to the point of utter ruin. His major crime, however was that he stole a statue of a divinity described as the traditional protective goddess of Uruk and took her to Babylon. This was not outright robbery; he gave the people of Uruk a replacement. The people of Uruk, however, did not want a new statue; they wanted the old statue back and took offense at this new protective goddess who, in their view, did not belong to Uruk and to whom they did not belong.

Hunger and Kaufman, followed by Goldstein,[11] Grayson,[12] and Beaulieu[13] argue that King II was Erība-Marduk. However, as far as we know the latter had a generally good reputation among later generations (even if quoted from Marduk-apla-iddina II who claimed descent from him, an opinion not necessarily shared at Uruk). Lambert prefers to see this king as Sargon II of Assyria (721–705 BCE).[14] Cole, basing himself on a new edition of SpTU, III, no. 58,[15] offers persuasive arguments that this evil king is instead to be identified with Nabû-šum-iškun (760–748 BCE), a Chaldean from the tribe of Bīt-Dakkūri.[16] Judging from the portrait given in SpTU, III, no. 58, the Chaldean was a sort of polytheistic analog to the anti-Christ, a Babylonian Antiochus IV, Caligula or Nero. Not only did he allegedly introduce every cultic innovation he could think of (including making the priests of Nabû eat leeks), but he burned people from Cuthah and Babylon alive just for amusement, plundered the Esagila under pretext of restoring it, and was in the midst of

8. All dates are cited from J.A. Brinkman in A. Leo Oppenheim, *Ancient Mesopotamia: Portrait of a Dead Civilization* (ed. Erica Reiner; Chicago: University of Chicago, rev. edn, 1977), pp. 335-46.

9. Lambert, *Background*, p. 11.

10. See Steven W. Cole, 'The Crimes and Sacrileges of Nabû-šuma-iškun', *ZA* 84 (1994), pp. 220-52 (245-46).

11. Jonathan A. Goldstein, 'The Historical Setting of the Uruk Prophecy', *JNES* 47 (1988), pp. 43-46.

12. A. Kirk Grayson, 'The Babylonian Origin of Apocalyptic Literature', *Atti dell'Istituto Veneto di Scienze, Lettere ed Arti* 146 (1989–90), pp. 203-18.

13. Beaulieu, 'Uruk Prophecy', p. 46.

14. Lambert, *Background*, p. 11.

15. SpTU, III, no. 58.

16. See Cole, 'Crimes and Sacrileges', pp. 220-52. This is now followed by P.-A. Beaulieu, *The Pantheon of Uruk during the Neo-Babylonian Period* (Cuneiform Monographs, 23; Leiden: Brill and Styx, 2003), pp. 131-33 who points out that the unhitching of seven lions from Ištar's chariot is mentioned both in SpTU, III, no. 58 and in Nabonidus's account of the 'swapping of statues'.

attacking an unsuspecting and peaceful people, described as 'lying in safe pastures', in direct violation of a sworn treaty, when the text breaks up into tiny fragments.

In the *Uruk Prophecy*, Kings III-VII are simply bad and except for King III not even dignified with anything other than 'ditto' which makes it difficult to be sure exactly how many kings were meant to have reigned before the next marked entry.[17] The point is obviously that nothing was good in the land as long as that statue was not back in the sanctuary where she belonged. About King VIII, who was also a bad king, it is noted that he took the property of the land of Akkad to the land of Subartu (i.e. Assyria). Goldstein identifies this king with Tiglath-pileser III (744–727 BCE).[18] Grayson takes Kings III-VIII whom he considers to be a single individual as Sennacherib (704–681 BCE).[19] Lambert identifies Kings III-VII as Sennacherib and King VIII as Esarhaddon (680–669 BCE).[20] Neither Tiglath-pileser III nor Esarhaddon is particularly associated with the plundering of Babylon. Indeed, the latter is renowned for having rebuilt the city after Sennacherib's destruction, but both Goldstein and Lambert assume the negative evaluation to be due to over-taxation.[21]

King IX was also bad but he ruled the four quarters (i.e. he was a universal ruler) and the world trembled at the mention of his name. Hunger and Kaufman identify this king with Tiglath-pileser III or Nabopolassar (625–605 BCE).[22] The latter possibility is seconded by Beaulieu.[23] Goldstein prefers to see King IX as Shalmaneser V (726–722 BCE),[24] Lambert as Assurbanipal (668–627 BCE)[25] and Grayson as Nebuchadnezzar II (604–562 BCE).[26]

Finally, King X appeared. He was a good king who performed construction work on the city and its temples and restored it to prosperity. More to the point, however, the statue of the traditional protective goddess finally came back home to her sanctuary and her people in his reign. For this king, Lambert suggests Nabopolassar[27] and Hunger and Kaufman Nebuchadnezzar II on the strength of an inscription which records Nebuchadnezzar II's attentions to the *šēdu* of Uruk and the *lamassu* of Eanna (the temple of Ištar of Uruk).[28] The identification of

17. See also Hunger and Kaufman, 'New Akkadian Prophecy', p. 373.

18. Goldstein, 'Uruk Prophecy', p. 46.

19. Grayson, 'Babylonian Origin', p. 208.

20. Lambert, *Background*, p. 11.

21. Goldstein, 'Uruk Prophecy', p. 46; Lambert, *Background*, p. 19 n. 17; cf. also Beaulieu, 'Uruk Prophecy', p. 48.

22. Hunger and Kaufman, 'New Akkadian Prophecy', p. 374

23. Beaulieu, 'Uruk Prophecy', p. 47.

24. Goldstein, 'Uruk Prophecy', p. 46.

25. Lambert, *Background*, p. 11.

26. Grayson, 'Babylonian Origin', p. 208.

27. Lambert, *Background*, p. 11.

28. Hunger and Kaufman, 'New Akkadian Prophecy', pp. 373-74.

King X with Nebuchadnezzar II is seconded by Beaulieu.[29] Goldstein would like to see this king as Marduk-apla-iddina II. He further argues that the text was intended as propaganda in support of the latter's revolt against Sargon II of Assyria and may thus be dated quite precisely to the years 721–710 BCE during which Marduk-apla-iddina II was in power.[30] It seems odd that, in this case, the text would have been cast in such an ambiguous way, particularly when it is understood to refer to genuine world conquerors like Tiglath-pileser III (allegedly King VIII) as 'that guy who robbed Babylon' and relatively insignificant and short-lived monarchs like Shalmaneser V (allegedly King IX) as world conquerors. How effective could this be as 'propaganda' when it is so obtuse that none but a handful of enlightened individuals will have had a clue as to what it was talking about?

King XI, the son of King X was the probable original directee of the prophecy. He will also be a good king, rule the four quarters and have a dynasty which lasts forever. Lambert assumes this king to be the son of Nabopolassar, i.e. Nebuchadnezzar II.[31] According to Hunger and Kaufman, followed by Beaulieu,[32] King XI would be Amēl-Marduk (561–560 BCE), son of Nebuchadnezzar II.[33] They further suggest that the propaganda value of this text lay in bolstering Amēl-Marduk's claim to the throne against his rival (and future successor by murder) Neriglissar. It is again not clear why, according to either interpretation, the text would have been issued as an ambiguously-worded prophecy since, assuming that the people of Uruk were trying to flatter currently ruling monarchs, they would have had no reason for concealment and could simply have predicted the eternal kingdom of their beloved ruler by name.

As for why this prophecy, which by no reconstruction offered to date actually came true (i.e. King XI, whoever he may have been, did not found a dynasty which lasted forever), was still being copied several empires later, only Beaulieu hazards a suggestion and that is that the *Uruk Prophecy* was intended as pro-Seleucid propaganda.[34] This would follow naturally from an assignment of Nebuchadnezzar II either to good King X or his son King XI, since Nebuchadnezzar II was regarded by the Seleucids as a sort of ancestor figure. Again, one wonders why in that case the text would not have given the names of the kings to which it refers rather than being phrased as a riddling prophecy.

29. Beaulieu, 'Uruk Prophecy', p. 46. See also idem, *Pantheon*, pp. 119, 129-38.

30. Goldstein, 'Uruk Prophecy', p. 46.

31. Lambert, *Background*, p. 11.

32. Beaulieu, 'Uruk Prophecy', p. 46.

33. Hunger and Kaufman, 'New Akkadian Prophecy', p. 374.

34. Beaulieu, 'Uruk Prophecy', pp. 48-50.

2. *The Evil Empire?*

For modern ideological reasons, none of the previous scholarship on the subject has dared to suggest that the hero of the *Uruk Prophecy*, King X, might be an Assyrian rather than a Babylonian. Indeed, Grayson[35] goes so far as to see the origin of apocalyptic literature in now lost Babylonian prophecies predicting the overthrow of the hated Assyrians. Goldstein further seeks to read into this prophecy from Uruk a condemnation of Assyrian kings whom he regards as the enemies of Israel: Tiglath-pileser III who was allegedly responsible for the 'apostasy' of Ahaz, Shalmaneser V who ended the northern kingdom and in particular Sargon II of Assyria who carried off the ten tribes into captivity. In so doing, Goldstein reads into his texts modern prejudices which view the defeat of Assyria by Babylonia as the first of a series of epic struggles in which Western democracy and rule of law triumph over Oriental despotism and terror. Other examples of this Orientalist trope include Alexander the Great's defeat of Darius III at Gaugamela and Publius Cornelius Scipio's victory over Hannibal Barca at Zama.[36]

As Western cultural ancestors, Neo-Babylonian rulers are far outclassed by Persians like Cyrus, whom even the Greeks admired, and do not usually come off much better than the Assyrians, but there are surprising exceptions. For example, Kvanvig[37] argues that the *Uruk Prophecy* shows Nebuchadnezzar II to have been the Mesopotamian equivalent of the messiah of the Hebrew Scriptures.[38] What is more, she asserts that the prophet Daniel saw Nebuchadnezzar as the model for the Son of Man and the Neo-Babylonian empire for the kingdom of heaven.[39] That Daniel would have seen as 'heavenly' an empire that left Jerusalem a smoking ruin and the man who ordered the deliberate torching of Solomon's temple as the type example of the messiah beggars belief. In any case, it is quite obvious that none of the earthly kingdoms mentioned in Daniel is good, and Kvanvig's alleged Messiah does not die as a sacrifice for mankind but is instead slain as the first prophesied beast whose body is thrown into the fire to be burnt up as a warning and example to the others.[40]

That Sennacherib was the subject of no little vituperation on the part of biblical prophets and viscerally hated by the citizens of Babylon whose city

35. Grayson, 'Babylonian Origin', p. 208.

36. On Orientalist views of the ancient Near East in general, and their application among early Assyriologists and the incident of Ahaz and Tiglath-pileser III in particular, see Steven W. Holloway, *Aššur is King! Aššur is King! Religion in the Exercise of Power in the Neo-Assyrian Empire* (CHANE, 10; Leiden: E.J. Brill, 2002), pp. 107-108 n. 120.

37. Helge S. Kvanvig, *Roots of Apocalyptic: The Mesopotamian Background of the Enoch Figure and the Son of Man* (WMANT, 61; Neukirchen–Vluyn: Neukirchner Verlag, 1988).

38. Kvanvig, *Roots*, pp. 489-90.

39. Kvanvig, *Roots*, pp. 484-91.

40. Daniel 7.11.

he destroyed in revenge for the murder of his son is unquestioned, and his demise at the hands of his own sons is reported in the Bible with what may safely be described as glee.[41] It is also quite probable that Cyrus, who is referred to as the Lord's anointed in Second Isaiah and whose Cyrus Cylinder boasts of the return home of statues of Mesopotamian divinities from Babylonian captivity would have been considered a 'good king' by most if not all of those he conquered. However, it would be a serious mistake to assume that resentment over Assyrian meddling would have dimmed the traditional hatred of old population centers such as Nippur (the ancient home of the pre-Marduk head of the Mesopotamian pantheon), and Uruk (where writing was actually invented) for the upstart Amorite city of Babylon which, under Samsuiluna in the seventeenth century BCE, had taken the fateful step of diverting the river Euphrates, leaving downstream users such as Nippur, Ur and Uruk to starve for lack of water.[42]

Neither does the dislike for Sennacherib translate to a blanket condemnation of Assyrian kings in the Bible. It is Ahaz and not Tiglath-pileser III who receives the blame in 2 Kings for introducing cultic innovations and those from Damascus whose ruler the Assyrian king has just executed.[43] 2 Chronicles outrageously slanders Tiglath-pileser by insisting that he provided no help whatsoever and that Damascus actually won the war.[44] The effect is, however, to remove any

41. 2 Kgs 19.37.

42. For Samsuiluna's reign as a time of famine in Sippar in Northern Babylonia, see C. Janssen, 'Samsu-iluna and the Hungry *Nadītums*', *Northern Akkad Project Reports* 5 (1991), pp. 3-39. Assuming the famine in question to be due to drought, the obvious solution for the kings in Babylon will have been to take more water from the Euphrates to save the capital and the northern cities, leaving downstream users with little or no water to irrigate their own fields. Alternatively, the decision to starve the south of water was made for political reasons but had the unhappy effect of flooding and ruining the fields of Sippar, thus producing an unintentional and artificial famine in the north. For these suggestions and a map of the affected region, see H. Gasche, *La Babylonie au 17ᵉ siècle avant notre ère: Approche archéologique, problèmes et perspectives* (Mesopotamian History and Environment Memoirs, 1; Ghent: University of Ghent, 1989). Cf. also Elizabeth C. Stone, 'Economic Crisis and Social Upheaval in Old Babylonian Nippur', in *Mountains and Lowlands: Essays in the Archaeology of Greater Mesopotamia* (ed. Louis D. Levine and T.C. Young; Bibliotheca Mesopotamica, 7; Malibu, CA: Undena Publications, 1977), pp. 267-89. For whatever reason, relations with the southern part of the country were very bad, as we know from Samsuiluna year dates mentioning campaigns in the area. For details, see Rosel Pientka, *Die spätaltbabylonische Zeit: Abiešuḫ bis Samsuditana, Quellen, Jahresdaten, Geschichte* (2 vols.; IMGULA, 2; Münster: Rhema-Verlag, 1998), I, pp. 6-14. Interesting to note in this connection is a reference from Seleucid Uruk to Ahiqar, the legendary vizier of Esarhaddon (see Lambert, *Background*, p. 16).

43. 2 Kings 16. For a full discussion of this incident, see Steven W. Holloway, 'The Case for Assyrian Religious Influence in Israel and Judah: Inference and Evidence' (PhD dissertation, University of Chicago, 1992), pp. 432-33, 447-56 (with a more conventional interpretation).

44. 2 Chr 28.16-23.

possibility that the changes in cult for which Ahaz is being criticized[45] were Assyrian-inspired. Shalmaneser V is not even mentioned, and Sargon's removal of Israelites is noted without adverse commentary. Indeed, in 2 Kings 17.24-28, the Assyrian is credited with attempting unsuccessfully to restore the worship of Yahweh to Ephraim. As for the alleged hero Marduk-apla-iddina II, Isaiah's reported comment on his mission to Hezekiah is that it was a sign that Babylon would one day destroy Jerusalem, a prophecy which Hezekiah accepted because he thought that he personally would not be adversely affected.[46]

3. *The Uruk Prophecy: A New Interpretation*

In any case, even if Assyrian kings had been Oriental despots (an imaginary beast) and the sworn enemy of prophets such as Isaiah, the author of the *Uruk Prophecy* neither knew of this nor cared. In his rather myopic view of things, goodness and evil were determined by the presence or absence of a particular statue from its rightful sanctuary. The reason we are hearing this tale of kings arising in the land is that the statue in question was, at the time of composition of the prophecy, once again missing. The people of Uruk were understandably devastated but hopeful that history would repeat itself and that they would eventually get it back, this time permanently.

To know, then, who the original good King X was, the question we really need to ask is not which Mesopotamian monarch, if any, represents the *Uruk Prophecy* messiah but what statue this is we are talking about. We have a hint in the inscriptions of Nabonidus who describes the removal of a statue from Uruk in the time of Erība-Marduk (which is almost correct) and its replacement by a deity 'inappropriate for Eanna' an injustice which was rectified after a long interval by a predecessor whose name is unfortunately lost in a lacuna.[47] Nabonidus adds that the goddess in question, who is never named in the *Uruk Prophecy*,[48] was Ištar of Uruk but also somehow 'Ištar, the lady of Elam, the princess who dwells in Susa', a description which suggests that it was from Elam that the goddess was ultimately returned to Uruk.[49]

45. It is probably not insignificant that 2 Chronicles omits the one change which is actually said in 2 Kings to have been inspired by Tiglath-pileser. That is the removal of the royal throne from inside the temple complex and the king's entrance. Both the throne and the private entrance sound like cultically improper innovations in line with Ahaz's alleged appropriation of the original altar for his own personal use. To a Mesopotamian, this would be a fairly obvious case of what the reformer Urukagina called 'the fields of the ensi encroaching upon the fields of Ningirsu' and it is quite believable that Tiglath-pileser would have ordered him to stop.

46. 2 Kgs 20.12-19.

47. Hunger and Kaufman, 'New Akkadian Prophecy', p. 374 erroneously state that Nabonidus named Nebuchadnezzar as the returnee—the name is, in fact, broken.

48. Beaulieu, 'Uruk Prophecy', p. 48 attributes this to the author's being more interested in Anu than in Ištar.

49. Beaulieu, 'Uruk Prophecy', p. 45.

Nabonidus' narrative permits us to deduce that in addition to the story we are hearing from the author of the *Uruk Prophecy* there was an alternative and complementary version of events in which another group of people, presumably Elamites, had a goddess who was stolen by a thieving King II (acting on behalf of wicked Uruk) and who was subsequently returned by a just and good King X to her proper sanctuary in Elam. But can we do any better than to say that the disputed divinity was a goddess of the Ištar variety?

Amazingly, yes. The fact that the *Uruk Prophecy* was still being copied as late as the Persian or even early Hellenistic period means that the statue was still in Elam as of that point. As luck would have it, one of the major divinities of Elymais, as Elam was called in the Hellenistic period, was a goddess of the Ištar type whose name was Nanaya, a divinity otherwise well known from Uruk.[50] Perhaps originally a separate goddess with her own shrine in the Eanna complex,[51] Nanaya appears alongside Uṣur-amāssa and Urkayītu in contexts which suggest that all three were manifestations of Ištar as mistress of Uruk.[52]

Sargon II of Assyria describes Nanaya as the daughter of the moon god Sîn. In later periods she seems to have become a goddess of the moon in her own right (and equated with Artemis or Diana).[53] In first-millennium Babylonia, Nanaya also acquired a husband, the ancient Mesopotamian god Nabû of Borsippa who was syncretized in the Hellenistic period with Apollo.[54]

Armed with this knowledge, there is only one king whom King X can be, and that is the Assyrian king Assurbanipal who discovered in Elam a statue of the goddess Nanaya which had been stolen, as he claims, 1,635 years earlier from the city of Uruk.[55] Naturally, he returned her, along with her friends Uṣur-amāssa and Urkayītu who had been carried off with her,[56] and the people of Uruk were, obviously, very grateful.

But how well does this work with the other kings who arose in the land before good King X? Admirably. If King X is Assurbanipal, King IX would be Esarhaddon, who extended the Assyrian empire to include Egypt and may have campaigned as far as Afghanistan in the East[57] which may not be a world

50. See Claus Ambos, 'Nanaja—eine ikonographische Studie zur Darstellung einer altorientalischen Göttin in hellenistisch-parthischer Zeit', *ZA* 93 (2003), pp. 231-55 (248-55).

51. See Joan Goodnick Westenholz, 'Nanaya: Lady of Mystery', in *Sumerian Gods and their Representations* (ed. Irving L. Finkel and Mark J. Geller; Cuneiform Monographs, 7; Groningen: Styx, 1997), pp. 57-84.

52. Beaulieu, *Pantheon*, p. 179, cf. 182-89.

53. For references, see Ambos, 'Nanaya', p. 234 and Marten Stol, 'Nanea', in *DDDB*², pp. 612-14.

54. See previous note.

55. Rassam Cyl. vi 107-24 (Streck, VAB 7, II, pp. 58-60).

56. K 3101a+ 2664+2628 ll.21-35 (Streck, VAB 7, II, pp. 220-22).

57. Personal communication from Erle Leichty.

empire but by ancient standards is pretty close. King VIII who destroyed Babylon and carried its plunder to Assyria is obviously Sennacherib who was indeed Assurbanipal's grandfather. Evil King II is definitely Nabû-šum-iškun, which leaves room for Nabû-nāṣir, Nabû-nādin-zēri, Nabû-šum-ukīn, Nabû-mukîn-zēri and Marduk-apla-iddina II as bad Kings III-VII.

And what about the prophecy part of the prophecy? Sadly for the people of Uruk, in a classic case of 'Whose goddess is it anyway?', the Elamites had by the reign of the Assyrian king Assurbanipal convinced themselves that Nanaya was an Elamite goddess. From their perspective, therefore, Assurbanipal's act of repatriation of Nanaya to Uruk was outright godknappery by the Elamite version of evil, thieving, King II. Thus when, in his accession year, Nabopolassar found himself in the unenviable position of trying to do the miraculous to defeat Assyria with precious little assistance from the old population centers of Babylonia, and saw fit to enlist Elamite help,[58] the price for that help was that Nanaya had to return to Elam. From the Elamite point of view, as expressed in Babylonian Chronicle 2, Nabopolassar was a good King X returning to Elam the Elamite goddess wickedly stolen from them by the Assyrians (i.e. Assurbanipal) and given to Uruk.[59] From the point of view of Uruk, by contrast, Nabopolassar's act will have been a repetition of the earlier theft of the statue by Nabû-šum-iškun. It was not until the reigns of Seleucus I (305–281 BCE) and Antiochus I (280–261 BCE), according to their own account, that the people of Uruk managed to recover the contents of tablets detailing the rites of Ištar and Anu which had been 'plundered' by Nabopolassar and shipped along with Nanaya to Elam, presumably to ensure the proper performance of her cult.[60]

Nabopolassar will certainly have promised the people of Uruk a replacement, and we know that his son Nebuchadnezzar II did indeed make them a new statue. However, the replacement of the old statue of Nanaya, which was going to stay in Elam, with a spanking new statue of 'Ištar of Elam' will not have acted as damage control as intended but on the contrary have further inflamed public opinion in Uruk.

But there is another twist to our story. If the *Uruk Prophecy*'s thieving King II who took the statue in the first place was indeed Nabû-šum-iškun, then Assurbanipal's claim that the statue of Nanaya which he returned had been stolen 1,635 years before its repatriation by him to Uruk would seem to be more than a little chronologically challenged. The name of the Elamite monarch who,

58. On this point, see also Elizabeth C. Carter and Matthew W. Stolper, *Elam: Surveys of Political History and Archaeology* (University of California Publications: Near Eastern Studies, 25; Berkeley: University of California Press, 1984), p. 53.

59. A.K. Grayson, *Assyrian and Babylonian Chronicles* (Texts from Cuneiform Sources, 5; Locust Valley, NY: J.J. Augustin, 1975), p. 88, Chronicle 2 ll.16-17.

60. See Beaulieu, 'Uruk Prophecy', p. 47.

according to Assurbanipal, took Nanaya to Elam is given in K 2631(+) obv. 12[61] as Kutir-Naḫḫunte, presumably the king of that name who ended the Kassite dynasty (ca. 1145 BCE) and also carried off the statue of Marduk from Babylon.[62] This is still far short of the 1,635 years claimed by Assurbanipal. The Assyrian text is, however, broken, and it is conceivable that the lost lines originally provided an account of various thefts of the statue culminating in her abduction by the Elamite king. In any case, for there to have been a statue of Nanaya for Nabû-šum-iškun (mid-eighth-century BCE) to wickedly purloin, there must have been more than one statue[63] or, to be more precise, more than one set of statues representing the triad of Nanaya, Uṣur-amāssa and Urkayītu.

Taking the simplest possible reconstruction, the original dispute over whose goddess Inanna of Uruk actually was dates from some time before the Ur III period, not a bad match for Assurbanipal's 1,635 years. This quarrel is enshrined in the Ur III literary composition *Enmerkar and Ensuḫgiriana, Lord of Aratta*[64] in which the later potentate claims Inanna of Uruk as his own goddess. The lord of Aratta boasts that he gave Inanna a lapis lazuli house in contrast to the mere brick house she had while in Uruk, to which Uruk counters that Aratta may have given her a lapis lazuli house, but Uruk was her house when she first set foot on earth.[65]

Areas to the east of Mesopotamia were not the only claimants for this much-admired goddess. Meli-Šipak[66] (ca. 1176ạ1162 BCE) abducted Nanaya as bride for Nabû of Borsippa, or more precisely his concubine, since Nabû already had a wife, Tašmētum. At this point, the original statue will have been moved to Babylon or Borsippa, and we may presume that a replacement statue was manufactured and left in Uruk. Let us call this latter statue Nanaya Replacement 1. The statue which was stolen by Kutir-Naḫḫunte was, then, the original which apparently remained in Elam until rescued by Assurbanipal.

Nanaya Replacement 1, however, was not so fortunate. Nabû of Borsippa was not to be left concubineless, so evil King 2 of the *Uruk Prophecy*, Nabû-šum-iškun, stole the remaining statue of Nanaya and took her to Babylon,[67]

61. Nab. 1 i 8-13 (Langdon, VAB 4, pp. 218-20).

62. Marduk was rescued and came back to Babylonia in the reign of Nebuchadnezzar I; Nanaya seems, however, to have remained in Elam.

63. See Westenholz, 'Nanaya', p. 75.

64. For the date of this cycle, see Beaulieu, *Pantheon of Uruk*, pp. 106-107.

65. Herman L.J. Vanstiphout, *Epics of Sumerian Kings: The Matter of Aratta* (SBLWAW, 20; Atlanta, GA: Society of Biblical Literature, 2003), pp. 31-32 ll.58-59, p. 33 ll.79-80. The interpretation adopted here follows that of C. Wilcke ('Epic, Play or What? Or: How was the "Epic" of "Enmerkar and Ensuḫgiriana" Performed?', paper read at the 215th American Oriental Society meeting held in Philadelphia, 2005).

66. There is a *kudurru* showing Nanaya that is dated to the reign of this monarch. His son and successor, Marduk-apla-iddina I mentions her as married to Nabû; see Westenholz, 'Nanaya', p. 71.

67. Nabû-šum-iškun is known to have celebrated a sacred marriage for Nanaya as husband of Nabû; see Westenholz, 'Nanaya', p. 73.

presumably leaving yet another replacement statue, Nanaya Replacement 2, in Uruk. During Sennacherib's wars with Babylonia, the Elamites murdered Aššur-nādin-šumi, who had been turned over to them by the Babylonians, and put Nergal-ušēzib on the throne in Babylon.[68] In the process, they will not have failed to run off with Nanaya Replacement 1. Uruk, meanwhile, which had had the ill grace to side with Babylon, was plundered and deprived of Nanaya Replacement 2 by the troops of Sennacherib (the *Uruk Prophecy*'s bad King VIII who took the property of the land of Akkad to the land of Subartu).[69]

Over the course of the next fifteen years, the gods of Akkad taken by the Elamites were gradually returned to their original owners. The Elamites hardly needed two sets of statues of Nanaya and her friends, and Uruk had gotten back its 'gods' (presumably Nanaya Replacement 1) as of 681 BCE, even before the death of Sennacherib.[70] Esarhaddon subsequently returned Nanaya Replacement 2 to Uruk from Assyria,[71] leaving Uruk with two sets of statues of Nanaya one of which (Nanaya Replacement 2) will have been quietly retired. This act of generosity on the part of Esarhaddon was enough for the author of the *Uruk Prophecy* to acknowledge him as world conqueror but not enough to avoid the label of bad King IX.

By now we should be beginning to understand why the people of Uruk were being so bloody-minded about having the correct statue. After so long a wait, Assurbanipal's return of the original goddess must have seemed like an impossible dream come true. And just as they were getting used to being back in possession of the real goddess, along came thieving Nabopolassar, who sent the beloved original statue right back to Elam. Had he at least had the decency to leave Uruk with Nanaya Replacement 1, things might have blown over but

68. Grayson, *Chronicles*, Chronicle 1 ii 39-45.

69. Daniel David Luckenbill, *The Annals of Sennacherib* (OIP, 2; Chicago: University of Chicago Press, 1924), p. 87:31-33; Grayson, *Chronicles*, Chronicle 1 ii 48-iii 3. The Chronicle passage is a bit confusing here, but iii 2-3 should probably be interpreted as 'after the Elamites came and (the Assyrians) carried off the gods of Uruk and its people...'. See J.A. Brinkman, *Prelude to Empire: Babylonian Society and Politics 747–626 B.C.* (Occasional Publications of the Babylonian Fund, 7; Philadelphia: Distributed by the Babylonian Fund, University Museum, 1984), p. 62 n. 299.

70. Grayson, *Chronicles*, Chronicle 1 iii 28-29. These gods are returning from Elam. Beaulieu, *Pantheon*, p. 225 notes that the reading is unsure. However, Elam will fit the traces and Aššur will not.

71. Borger, Ash. 84 AsBbA r. 43 specifically mentions Uṣur-amāssa and a letter from Mār-Ištar to Esarhaddon describes modifications made to the statues of Nanaya and Uṣur-amāssa preparatory to their return (Beaulieu, *Pantheon*, pp. 198, 227). This is not to be confused with the Elamite return of Ištar of Agade in 674, correcting Brinkman, *Prelude*, p. 76 n. 369. Agade may or may not be Babylon, but it is unlikely to have been Uruk, which was never part of Akkad. In any case, Esarhaddon is explicit that the return was from Assyria and not Elam (Borger, Ash. 74 Uruk A: 22-23 and SAA, X, no. 349; see Westenholz, 'Nanaya', p. 74 n. 136).

Nabû evidently could not be asked to part with his concubine, so off she went to Borsippa[72] and Uruk got Nanaya Replacement 3 from Nebuchadnezzar II, who had the temerity to insist that this was a 'restoration' of the original cult of Ištar of Uruk.[73]

Given this context, the fuss over Assurbanipal is quite understandable but why is Nabû-šum-iškun being made out to be such a goat? He admittedly stole Nanaya Replacement 1, but Replacement 1 was just a replacement, so why is Nabû-šum-iškun the personification of evil and not Meli-Šipak who actually stole the original statue for Nabû of Borsippa, leaving her at the mercy of marauding Elamites?

This brings us back to a problem which we ignored except for a brief mention in passing and that is the fact that Nabonidus clearly places the theft of what we are now calling Nanaya Replacement 1 not in the reign of Nabû-šum-iškun but instead in that of his predecessor Erība-Marduk. The difference all this makes is that both Nabû-šum-iškun and Erība-Marduk were Chaldeans whereas Meli-Šipak was not. Moreover, Nabû-šum-iškun and Erība-Marduk were from different tribes, the former from Bīt-Dakkūri and the latter from Bīt-Yakīn. Is this an accident? I wonder.

If the Urukeans attributed the theft of the original statue unjustly to Nabû-šum-iškun (rather than Meli-Šipak), it may be because they wished to lay the blame on a Chaldean. More curious is the quarrel over which Chaldean it was. The local Chaldean tribe of Bīt-Amukkani also produced a king of Babylon, namely Nabû-mukîn-zēri. This ruler could easily have been fingered by Uruk, whose relations with Bīt-Amukkani were not always of the smoothest. This raises several possibilities one or more of which may be relevant. Perhaps Bīt-Dakkūri was chosen because of its close association with Babylon and Borsippa (for whose god Nanaya was the stolen bride). Alternatively, the choice may have been intended to flatter the Assyrians. As Cole notes, quite a bit of the diatribe against the king of sacrilege strikes cords with very similarly worded Assyrian royal propaganda on the subject of how benevolent Assyrian kings were to Babylonia and how various local monarchs were wicked oppressors of the poor and the weak, stealers of temple property and everything else vile.[74] In view of these similarities, it is probable that the image of evil King II owes more than a little to Assurbanipal's self-promotion as the righter of wrongs committed by Chaldeans, especially those from the tribe of Bīt-Dakkūri for which tribe Assyrian kings seem to have had special animus, no doubt because it had a long history of on-and-off bad relations with the cities of Babylon and Borsippa whom the Assyrians wished to court.[75] Finally, the possibility remains

72. Langdon, VAB 4, p. 92 ii 18-19, 186ff. vi 4-57; see Westenholz, 'Nanaya', p. 75.
73. See Beaulieu, *Pantheon*, p. 129, cf. 135.
74. See Cole, 'Crimes and Sacrileges', pp. 246-51.
75. See in particular, Borger, Ash. 52 Nin. A iii 62-70.

that statue-stealing Nabopolassar, who was also a Chaldean, was specifically from the tribe of Bīt-Dakkūri.

In favor of this last possibility is Nabonidus's insistence that it was the people of Uruk themselves who sinned against their goddess, causing her to leave voluntarily during the reign of Erība-Marduk.[76] Nabonidus is well known for trying to exonerate his predecessors by shoving their misdeeds off onto others (for example, the Medes take responsibility for the destruction of Ḫarrān).[77] Bīt-Dakkūri and Bīt-Yakīn were not always on the best of terms, so was Nabonidus seeking to whitewash Nabû-šum-iškun of Nabopolassar's Bīt-Dakkūri and to transfer any possible blame from him to Erība-Marduk of the rival Chaldean tribe of Bīt-Yakīn?

In any case, the people of Uruk could take comfort in the fact that the theft of Nabopolassar had been foretold by that of Nabû-šum-iškun and, consequently, working from within the eschatological framework of the *Uruk Prophecy*, the eventual return of the goddess by a future Assurbanipal was assured. Previous interpreters of the *Uruk Prophecy* have claimed that the people of Uruk really loved Nabopolassar and Nebuchadnezzar and wanted to show their support for the son of their benefactor.[78] On the contrary, the original purpose of the prophecy will have been to predict the overthrow of the Neo-Babylonian dynasty.[79] This subversive desire, in turn, explains why the Urukeans were so coy about naming names. If the statue was stolen by a Chaldean and returned by an Assyrian, was not this an omen that the statue which had been re-stolen by a Chaldean would also be re-returned by an Assyrian, and in particular King XI, the son of King X? This was the ill-fated Sîn-šar-iškun (623–612 BCE) to whom the people of Uruk were dating their correspondence and legal documents as late as 619 BCE and for whose eventual victory over Nabopolassar and Nebuchadnezzar II they were praying. The return of the original statue by Assurbanipal was in reward for Uruk taking the Assyrian king's side against his brother Šamaš-šum-ukīn,[80] so Uruk had every reason to expect that Sîn-šar-iškun would repeat his father's generosity if they helped him to defeat Nabopolassar. To sum up what we have discovered thus far:

76. See Beaulieu, *Pantheon*, p. 131. Beaulieu believes the people of Uruk to be indeed guilty of sacrilege against their own goddess; see Beaulieu, *Pantheon*, p. 134.

77. Langdon, VAB 4, p. 218 i 8-13.

78. Hunger and Kaufman, 'New Akkadian Prophecy', p. 374.

79. For the Dynastic Prophecy as also anti-Seleucid propaganda, see Grayson, 'Babylonian Origin', p. 210; cf. L. Matouš, 'Review of A.K. Grayson, *Babylonian Historical-Literary Texts*', *Orientalistische Literaturzeitung* 75 (1980), pp. 28-30 (29).

80. For the loyalty of Uruk to Assurbanipal during the revolt of Šamaš-šum-ukīn, see Grant Frame, *Babylonia 689–627 B.C.: A Political History* (PIHANS, 69; Leiden: Nederlands Instituut voor het Nabije Oosten, 1992), pp. 134, 136, 157-62.

Table 6. Proposed Identifications of the Kings in the *Uruk Prophecy*

Kings of the *Uruk Prophecy*	**King I**	**King II**	**King III**	**King IV**	**King V**	**King VI**
Hunger & Kaufman	Marduk-balassu-iqbi or Baba-aḫa-iddina	Erība-Marduk				
Lambert	Marduk-apal-iddina II	Sargon II	Sennacherib	Sennacherib	Sennacherib	Sennacherib
Goldstein		Erība-Marduk	Nabû-nāṣir	Nabû-nādin-zēri	Nabû-šum-ukīn	Nabû-mukîn-zēri
Grayson	Sealands Dynasty	Erība-Marduk	Sennacherib	Sennacherib	Sennacherib	Sennacherib
Beaulieu						
Cole	Erība-Marduk	Nabû-šum-iškun				
Scurlock	Erība-Marduk	Nabû-šum-iškun	Nabû-nāṣir	Nabû-nādin-zēri	Nabû-šum-ukīn	Nabû-mukîn-zēri

Kings of the *Uruk Prophecy*	**King VII**	**King VIII**	**King IX**	**King X**	**King XI**
Hunger & Kaufman			Tiglath-pileser III or Nabopolassar	Nebuchadnezzar II	Amēl-Marduk
Lambert	Sennacherib	Esarhaddon	Assurbanipal	Nabopolassar	Nebuchadnezzar II
Goldstein		Tiglath-pileser III	Shalmaneser V	Marduk-apal-iddina II	
Grayson	Sennacherib	Sennacherib	Nebuchadnezzar II		
Beaulieu			Nabopolassar	Nebuchadnezzar II	Amēl-Marduk
Cole					
Scurlock	Marduk-apla-iddina II	Sennacherib	Esarhaddon	Assurbanipal	Sîn-šar-iškun

So it didn't happen, did it? Then why was this prophecy still being copied in the Persian or even the Seleucid period? The virtue of cryptic prophecies like the *Uruk Prophecy* is that they do not actually say that Sîn-šar-iškun is going to defeat Nabopolassar which when it does not happen automatically unmasks them as false prophecy. What this one does say is that when a Chaldean steals a statue from Uruk, after some suitable interval of time, a king and his son will come along and make everything right again. If that king and his son were not Assurbanipal and Sîn-šar-iškun, then why not Cyrus and Cambyses or Darius and Xerxes?

Cyrus II (538–530 BCE) was a wily politician and masterful propagandist. He succeeded in being accepted as God's anointed simply for allowing those among the Jewish community who desired it to return and rebuild the temple in Jerusalem, and for punching a small hole in the walls of Babylon.[81] To Uruk's ears, the music will have been Cyrus's claim, expressed in the Cyrus Cylinder, to be a returner of purloined statues and a successor to Assurbanipal.[82] Here, at last, was good King X of the prophecy. Unfortunately, whatever else he may have done, and there are indications that a large part of the revivification of the cult of Anu in Uruk actually took place under Persian rather than Seleucid patronage,[83] Cyrus was first and foremost a ruler of Elamite Anšan and an unlikely person to have robbed the Elamites of a statue they held so dear.

So what about Darius I (521–486 BCE) and Xerxes I (485–465 BCE)? The anti-Chaldean tone of the *Uruk Prophecy* will have been encouraged by a government which was having significant False Dimitri problems in Babylon in the form of alleged sons of Nabonidus. For these Mazdean rulers, this condescension will not, however, have translated to returning statues, stolen or otherwise, of what Xerxes refers to in the Akkadian version of his *daiva*-inscription[84] as 'evil ones', denying them thus even the status of gods. Alexander (330–323 BCE) was a polytheist and a heroic figure generally admired by all, but he died in Babylon planning his next conquest with no time left for petty quarrels over errant goddesses.

Enter the Seleucids. One almost feels sorry for these Macedonian Greeks who, as was the general policy of the successors of Alexander, followed Herodotus's lead in observing that 'every person thinks his own customs are best' by trying as little as possible to impose their culture on the conquered. In their eagerness to be seen as liberators and to profit from any lingering resentment of Babylonia at their treatment by Persian kings, they posed as successors of the last independent dynasty whose history they commissioned Berossus to celebrate.[85] This policy may have played reasonably well in Babylon, but claiming to be successors of Nebuchadnezzar II in particular will have had about as positive a reception in Uruk and among the Jewish population of Babylonia as Saddam Hussein's self-styling as successor to Nebuchadnezzar had in America and Israel. In its final form, then, the *Uruk Prophecy* was an anti-Seleucid piece of subversive literature dreaming of a king and his son who would come

81. The available sources are in disagreement as to the amount of damage done by Cyrus to Babylon, but it would appear to have been minimal. See Paul-Alain Beaulieu, *The Reign of Nabonidus, King of Babylon 556–539 B.C.* (YNER, 10; New Haven: Yale University Press, 1989), pp. 224-26.

82. See the translation of Mordechai Cogan in *COS*, II, pp. 314-16. It is interesting to note that Cyrus mentions Assurbanipal but not Nebuchadnezzer II as the predecessor whose inscriptions he found in the course of repairing the walls of Babylon.

83. Beaulieu, 'Uruk Prophecy', p. 48.

84. For a translation, see A.L. Oppenheim, 'Babylonian and Assyrian Historical Texts', in *ANET* (1969), pp. 316-17 no. 4.

85. For details, see Beaulieu, 'Uruk Prophecy', pp. 49-50.

to finally set things aright flourishing under the very noses of Seleucid officials in the clever disguise of the vague language of prophecy.[86]

4. *Šamaš-šum-ukīn Chronicle*

The recognition that evil King II is Nabû-šum-iškun also allows us to understand another text which has previously defied attempts at interpretation, namely Grayson's Šamaš-šum-ukīn Chronicle.[87] This text quotes 'non-integrated lines' from another source which describe in standard chronicle format the reigns of four kings. First there is Aššur-nādin-šumi (699–694 BCE) followed by Šamaš-šum-ukīn (667–648 BCE) and then, after a double line on the tablet, Širiqti-Šuqamuna (985 BCE) followed by Nabû-šum-iškun (750–748 BCE). Quite puzzling is the fact that the earlier pair of kings is mentioned last and that no indication is given as to why these particular monarchs were chosen for excerption. Grayson suggests that Širiqti-Šuqamuna and Nabû-šum-iškun might have been included because they were of Assyrian ancestry.[88]

In fact, the text in question, despite its wording, is either a reflection on the past events which it chronicles or another prophecy of the sort which we have been examining. In either case, the two sets of kings whose chronicle entries it quotes fall into a pattern readily recognizable from the Dynastic Prophecy. In both cases, the first king is one who met his end at the hands of Elamites (Aššur-nādin-šumi was turned over to Elamites by the Babylonians and Širiqti-Šuqamuna was the last king of the Bazi dynasty which preceded a dynasty of Elam). The second of each pair was a king who was not a native of Babylon but who ruled there and who came to a bad end (Šamaš-šum-ukīn, an Assyrian like Aššur-nādin-šumi and Nabû-šum-iškun, a Chaldean from Bīt-Dakkūri). In short, the sequence Širiqti-Šuqamuna, Nabû-šum-iškun could be seen in retrospect as having predicted the sequence Aššur-nādin-šumi, Šamaš-šum-ukīn which is why the earlier pair appears last. Put in Babylonian commentary style: 'Aššur-nādin-šumi, Šamaš-šum-ukīn: (That is because) Širiqti-Šuqamuna, Nabû-šum-iškun'. In Persian context, the sequence has a further value, since it could be seen as having predicted that the fall of the Assyrians to Nabopolassar and his Elamite allies would be followed as the night the day by the fall of another Chaldean who ruled in Babylon (Nabonidus) to Cyrus II of Anšan.

Curious in this regard is the fact that the fall of Nineveh as described by Ctesius, bears comparison with the tale of Belshazzar's feast in Daniel, and seems to have incorporated details[89] of a Persian account of the death

86. Nanaya seems to have had a great increase in popularity in the Parthian period—can we hope that these Iranian highlanders at last fulfilled the greatest hopes of the people of Uruk?

87. Grayson, *Chronicles*, pp. 128-30, Chronicle 15.

88. Grayson, *Chronicles*, p. 33.

89. See John D.A. Macginnis, 'Ctesias and the Fall of Nineveh', *Sumer* 45 (1987–88), pp. 40-43.

of Šamaš-šum-ukīn, Esarhaddon's eldest son (*ša Aššur-aḫa-iddina apalšu* = Sardanapalus) in the flames of his palace. The source for this Persian account is probably a tradition known to us from a document produced by an Aramaic speaking community originally inhabiting Rāšu in the borderland between Elam and Babylonia. Ironically, they appear to have been removed from Elam by Assurbanipal in the course of the very campaign which culminated in the return of Nanaya to Uruk.[90] These Arameans were apparently settled by Assurbanipal in the province of Samaria where they converted to their own unique version of Yahwism and from whence they fled to Egypt in the face of Josiah's cultic reforms. We encounter them in the beginning of the third century BCE, writing in Demotic script, but still devotees of Nanaya, still lamenting the fall of Nineveh, and still telling tales of the good Assurbanipal and his wicked and suicidal brother Šamaš-šum-ukīn.[91] If the gruesome death of Sardanapalus was indeed an event which was believed to have presaged the fall of Babylon to Cyrus in the reign of Nabonidus, Persian interest in the story would be obvious.

Alternatively, the Šamaš-šum-ukīn Chronicle is actually Seleucid in date and intended as a prophecy. In this case, the sequence Širiqti-Šuqamuna, Nabû-šum-iškun, Aššur-nādin-šumi, Šamaš-šum-ukīn would have presaged the fall of the Assyrians to the Chaldeans and their subsequent defeat by the Persians by way of predicting that the Seleucids would suffer the fate of the Chaldeans whom they aspired to emulate. It would in this case be anti-Seleucid propaganda along the same lines as the *Uruk Prophecy*.

5. *Conclusion*

In short, the *Uruk Prophecy* is subversive literature, a genre of which we have very little from ancient Mesopotamia from any period. Moreover it has a direct connection to other local products such as the Šamaš-šum-ukīn Chronicle. The reason for the similarities between these texts on the one hand and the Book of Daniel on the other is that they form a few precious relics of what may once have been a fair body of literature[92] which was subversive and underground and talked in riddles about mysterious kings who arose in the land (a.k.a. ominous past events) which, if properly understood, predicted the overthrow of hated local rulers.

90. Rassam Cyl. v 63-68 (Streck, VAB 7, pp. 46-48).

91. See Richard C. Steiner, 'The Aramaic Text in Demotic Script (1.99)', in *COS*, I, pp. 309-27.

92. From the late Neo-Assyrian empire onwards, Aramaic provided a *lingua franca* allowing easy communication between intellectuals living in population centers in Assyria and Babylonia with their counterparts in Greater Syria and Egypt. Scrolls are comparatively light and easy to transport; unfortunately they are also perishable which means that most of what was written in this language will have been lost.

We must not be too hasty in assuming that the author of the Book of Daniel would have taken no notice of such things. In trying to decode the will of Yahweh on the subject of whether or not it was a good idea to revolt against the ostensibly sure-to-be-victorious Antiochus IV, the babblings of idolaters need not have been considered irrelevant. Yahweh was known to choose strange instruments or, as the saying goes, 'out of the mouths of babes'. Thus, if the dialectic represented by the *Uruk Prophecy* was or could be seen as referring to the same events which a Jewish scholar wished to see as predicted (e.g. the overthrow of the Seleucids), there is no reason that it could not have been taken up and incorporated into his argument as corroborative evidence.[93] That the link may have existed at a purely political level makes the common use of prophetic language all the more interesting. It is high time that lingering Orientalist prejudices on the subject of Assyrians not be allowed to blind scholarship to hidden treasures such as these.

93. Note that Iberian Jewish or Muslim writers used Christian apocalyptic texts to predict the end of Christian domination. See Marya T. Green-Mercado, 'Morisco Jofores: Apocalyptic Prophecies and the Ottoman–Habsburg Rivalry in Sixteenth-Century Spain', paper read at the 2004 Middle East History and Theory Conference, Chicago.

Bibliography

Abdel-Malek, Anouar, 'Orientalism in Crisis', *Diogenes* 44 (1963), pp. 103-40.

Abduh, Ibrahim, *Jaridat al-Ahram: Tarikh wa fann 1875–1964* (Cairo: Mu'assasat Sijill al-'Arab, 1964).

Abou-Ghazi, Dia M., 'Ahmed Kamal 1849–1923', *ASAE* 64 (1981), pp. 1-5.

—'Egyptian Museum', *ASAE* 67 (1991), p. 9.

Abu El-Haj, Nadia, *Facts on the Ground: Archaeological Practice and Territorial Self-Fashioning in Israeli Society* (Chicago: University of Chicago Press, 2001).

Ackerman, Gerald M., *American Orientalists* (The Orientalists, 10; Paris: ACR Edition, 1994).

Adas, Michael, *Machines as the Measure of Men: Science, Technology, and Ideologies of Western Dominance* (Cornell Studies in Comparative History; Ithaca, NY: Cornell University Press, 1989).

Adler, Cyrus, 'The Beginnings of Semitic Studies in America', in *Oriental Studies Published in Commemoration of the Fortieth Anniversary (1883–1923) of Paul Haupt as Director of the Oriental Seminary of the Johns Hopkins University, Baltimore, MD* (ed. Cyrus Adler and Aaron Ember; Baltimore, MD: The Johns Hopkins Press, 1926), pp. 317-28.

—*I Have Considered the Days* (Philadelphia: The Jewish Publication Society of America, 1941).

—'Museum Collections to Illustrate Religious History and Ceremonials', in *Report of the U.S. National Museum, under the Direction of the Smithsonian Institution, for the Year Ending June 30, 1893* ([Washington, DC]: Smithsonian Institution, 1893), pp. 757-68.

—'On a Study-Collection of Casts of Assyrian and Babylonian Antiquities in the National Museum at Washington', *JAOS* 13 (1889), p. ccxxxiv.

—'Report on the Section of Oriental Antiquities in the U.S. National Museum, 1888', in *Report of the U.S. National Museum, under the Direction of the Smithsonian Institution, for the Year Ending June 30, 1888* ([Washington, DC]: Smithsonian Institution, 1890), pp. 93-95.

—'Report on the Section of Oriental Antiquities in the U.S. National Museum, 1889', in *Report of the U.S. National Museum, under the Direction of the Smithsonian Institution, for the Year Ending June 30, 1889* ([Washington, DC]: Smithsonian Institution, 1891), pp. 289-92.

—'Report on the Section of Oriental Antiquities in the U.S. National Museum, 1892', in *Report of the U.S. National Museum, under the Direction of the Smithsonian Institution, for the Year Ending June 30, 1892* ([Washington, DC]: Smithsonian Institution, 1893), pp. 111-13.

—'Two Persepolitan Casts in the U.S. National Museum', in *Report of the U.S. National Museum, under the Direction of the Smithsonian Institution, for the Year Ending June 30, 1893* ([Washington, DC]: Smithsonian Institution, 1893), pp. 751-53.

Adler, Cyrus, and Immanuel Moses Casanowicz, 'Biblical Antiquities: A Description of the Exhibit at the Cotton States International Exposition, Atlanta, 1895', in *Report of the U.S. National Museum, under the Direction of the Smithsonian Institution, for the Year Ending June 30, 1896* ([Washington, DC]: Smithsonian Institution, 1896). pp. 953-1023.

Adler, Cyrus, and Ira Robinson (ed.), *Selected Letters* (2 vols.; Philadelphia and New York: Jewish Publication Society of America and Jewish Theological Seminary of America, 1985).

Aharoni, Yohanan, and Michael Avi-Yonah, *The Macmillan Bible Atlas* (New York: Macmillan, 1968).

Ahlström, Gösta W., *The History of Ancient Palestine from the Palaeolithic Period to Alexander's Conquest* (ed. Diana Edelman; JSOTSup, 146; Sheffield: Sheffield Academic Press, 1993).

Ajami, Fouad, *The Dream Palace of the Arabs: A Generation's Odyssey* (New York: Pantheon Books, 1998).

Albenda, Pauline, 'Landscape Bas-Reliefs in *Bīt-Ḫīlāni* of Ashurbanipal', *BASOR* 224 (December 1976), pp. 49-72.

—'Landscape Bas-Reliefs in the *Bīt-Ḫīlāni* of Ashurbanipal—Continued', *BASOR* 225 (February 1977), pp. 29-48.

Albright, William Foxwell, 'Abram the Hebrew: A New Archaeological Interpretation', *BASOR* 163 (1961), pp. 36-54.

—*Archaeology and the Religion of Israel* (Baltimore, MD: The Johns Hopkins University Press, 1940; 2nd edn, Garden City, NY: Doubleday, 1967).

—*From the Stone Age to Christianity: Monotheism and the Historical Process* (Baltimore, MD: The Johns Hopkins University Press, 1940; 2nd edn, Garden City, NY: Doubleday, 1957).

—'Review of F.M.Th. Böhl, *King Hammurabi of Babylon in the Setting of his Time (about 1700 B.C.)*', *BO* 5 (1948), pp. 125-27.

—*Yahweh and the Gods of Canaan: A Historical Analysis of Two Contrasting Faiths* (Winona Lake, IN: Eisenbrauns, 1990 [1968]).

Alcott, Louisa May, *Little Men: Life at Plumfield with Jo's Boys* (London: Puffin Books, 1994).

Alexander, Robert L., 'Courbet and Assyrian Sculpture', *ArtB* 47 (1965), pp. 447-52.

Allen, Willougby C., 'Asherah', in Hastings (ed.), *Dictionary of the Bible*, I, p. 165.

Allingham, William, *The Music Master: A Love Story: And Two Series of Day and Night Songs* (London: George Routledge & Co., 1855).

Al-Rawi, Farouk N.H., 'Nabopolassar's Restoration Work on the Wall *Imgur-Enlil* at Babylon', *Iraq* 47 (1985), pp. 1-13.

Alt, Peter-André, *Der Tod der Königin: Frauenopfer und politische Souveränität im Trauerspiel des 17. Jahrhunderts* (Quellen und Forschungen zur Literatur- und Kulturgeschichte, 30; Berlin: W. de Gruyter, 2004).

Altick, Richard D., *The English Common Reader: A Social History of the Mass Reading Public, 1800–1900* (Chicago: University of Chicago Press, 1957).

—*The Shows of London* (Cambridge, MA: Belknap Press, 1978).

Ambos, Claus, 'Nanaja—eine ikonographische Studie zur Darstellung einer altorientalischen Göttin in hellenistisch-parthischer Zeit', *ZA* 93 (2003), pp. 231-55.

Amishai-Maisels, Ziva, *Gauguin's Religious Themes* (Outstanding Dissertations in the Fine Arts; New York: Garland, 1985).

Anderson, Irvine H., *Biblical Interpretation and Middle East Policy: The Promised Land, America, and Israel, 1917–2002* (Gainesville, FL: University Press of Florida, 2005).

Andrae, Walter, *Lebenserinnerungen eines Ausgräbers* (Berlin: W. de Gruyter, 1961).

André-Salvini, Béatrice, 'Introduction aux publications de P.E. Botta et de V. Place', in Fontan and Chevalier (eds.), *De Khorsabad à Paris*, pp. 166-72.

—' "Où sont-ils ces remparts de Ninive?" Les sources de connaissance de l'Assyrie avant les fouilles', in Fontan and Chevalier (eds.), *De Khorsabad à Paris*, pp. 22-43.

Andrew, Christopher M. and A.S. Kanya-Forstner, *The Climax of French Imperial Expansion 1914–1924* (Stanford: Stanford University Press, 1981).

Anon, *Degas* (New York: Metropolitan Museum of Art, 1988: exhibition catalogue).

—'Art in Scotland and the Provinces', *Art-Journal* (December 1865), p. 371.

—'Art Notes', *Art-Journal* (October 1880), pp. 317-19.

—'Bibles', *ILN*, 5 October 1861, p. 344.

—'Chautauqua: 1882', *The Chautauquan: A Weekly Newsmagazine* 2 (1882), pp. 368-70.

—'Dalziel's [*sic*] Bible Gallery', *Art-Journal* (December 1880), pp. 365-66.

—*Degas* (New York: Metropolitan Museum of Art, 1988: exhibition catalogue).

—'Egypt, the Land of Bondage', in *Our Moslem Sisters: A Cry of Need from Lands of Darkness Interpreted by Those Who Heard It* (ed. Annie van Sommer and Samuel Marinus Zwemer; New York: Fleming H. Revell Company, 1907), pp. 24-37.

—'Fine Arts: Exhibition of the Royal Academy', *ILN*, 6 May 1865, p. 439.

—'Fine Arts: Gift Books', *Athenaeum*, 13 November 1880, p. 646.

—'Fine Arts: Royal Academy', *Athenaeum*, 25 May 1861, pp. 698-700.

—'Fine Arts: Royal Academy', *Athenaeum*, 6 May 1865, pp. 626-29.

—'Fine Arts', *ILN*, 27 November 1880, p. 518.

—'Musée de Ninive', *L'Illustration*,15 May 1847, pp. 167-70.

—'New Music', *ILN*, 13 May 1865, p. 459.

—'Ninive', *Le Tour du Monde* 7 (1863), p. 318.

—'Nineveh', *Penny Magazine* 14 no. 851 (1845), p. 264.

—'Nineveh and Persepolis', *Art-Journal* 12 (1850), p. 225.

—'Our Weekly Gossip', *Athenaeum* no. 901, 1 February, 1845, pp. 120-21.

— 'Picture Sales', *Art-Journal* (July 1861), pp. 214-15.

—'Review of A. Keith, *Evidence of the Truth of the Christian Religion* (New York: J. & J. Harper, 1835)', *The Methodist Magazine and Quarterly Review* 21 (1839), pp. 215-22.

—'Reviews', *Art-Journal* 15 (1853), pp. 235-36.

—'The Royal Academy Exhibition', *Art-Journal* (June 1880), pp.186-88.

—'The Royal Academy Exhibition', *Art-Journal* N.S. 14 (1875), pp. 247-52.

—'Royal Academy Exhibition (Third Notice)', *The Times*, 18 May 1865, p. 6.

—'The Royal Academy: Second Exhibition of Works by Old, and Deceased, Masters', *Art-Journal* (February 1871), pp. 49-50.

—'Society for the Encouragement of the Fine Arts', *ILN*, 19 January 1861, p. 53.

—*Athenaeum*, No. 1298, 11 September 1852, p. 979.

—*ILN*, 28 October 1865, p. 424.

—*ILN*, 6 May 1865, p. 443.

—*Le magasin pittoresque* 16 (1848), pp. 131-34; 17 (1849), pp. 193-94; 20 (1852), pp. 241-44.

—*The Times*, 18 November 1880, p. 12.

—*The Times*, 28 December 1880, p. 9.

Anquetil-Duperron, Abraham-Hyacinthe, *Législation orientale, ouvrage dans lequel, en montrant quels sont en Turquie, en Perse et dans l'Indoustan, les principes fondamentaux du gouvernement, on prouve*... (Amsterdam: Marc-Michel Rey, 1778).

Arav, Rami, 'Archaeology in the Service of Ideology in Israel', in *'A Land Flowing with Milk and Honey': Visions of Israel from Biblical to Modern Times* (ed. Leonard J. Greenspoon and Ronald A. Simkins; Studies in Jewish Civilization, 11; Omaha, NE: Creighton University Press, 2001), pp. 85-104.

Archi, Alphonso, 'The Role of Women in the Society of Ebla', in *Sex and Gender in the ancient Near East*, pp. 1-9.

Archibald, Elizabeth, *Incest and the Medieval Imagination* (Oxford: Clarendon, 2001).

Armitage, Christopher M., *Sir Walter Ralegh: An Annotated Bibliography* (Chapel Hill, NC: University of North Carolina Press, 1987).

Armstrong, Carol M., *Odd Man Out: Readings of the Work and Reputation of Edgar Degas* (Texts and Documents; Los Angeles: The Getty Research Institute, 2003).

Arnold, Bill T., and Bryan Beyer (eds.), *Readings from the Ancient Near East: Primary Sources for Old Testament Study* (Grand Rapids, MI: Baker Academic, 2002).

Arnold, Bill T., and David B. Weisberg, 'Babel und Bibel und Bias: How Anti-Semitism Distorted Friedrich Delitzsch's Scholarship', *Bible Review* 18 (2002), pp. 32-40.

—'A Centennial Review of Friedrich Delitzsch's "Babel und Bibel" Lectures', *JBL* 121 (2002), pp. 441-57.

Aro, Sanna, and Robert M. Whiting (eds.), *The Heirs of Assyria: Proceedings of the Opening Symposium of the Assyrian and Babylonian Intellectual Heritage Project, Held in Tvärminne, Finland, October 8-11, 1998* (Melammu Symposia, 1; Helsinki: The Neo-Assyrian Text Corpus Project, 2000).

Aruri, Naseer Hasan, and Muhammed A. Shuraydi (eds.), *Revising Culture, Reinventing Peace: The Influence of Edward W. Said* (New York: Olive Branch Press, 2001).

Ashcroft, Bill, and D.P.S. Ahluwalia, *Edward Said: The Paradox of Identity* (London and New York: Routledge, 1999).

—, Gareth Griffiths and Helen Tiffin, *Post-Colonial Studies: The Key Concepts* (Routledge Key Guides; London and New York: Routledge, 2000).

Asher-Greve, Julia M., 'Decisive Sex, Essential Gender', in *Sex and Gender in the Ancient Near East*, pp. 11-26.

—*Frauen in altsumerischer Zeit* (Bibliotheca mesopotamica, 18; Malibu, CA: Undena, 1985).

—'Gertrude L. Bell, 1868–1926', in *Breaking Ground: Pioneering Women Archaeologists* (ed. Getzel M. Cohen and Martha Sharp Joukowsky; Ann Arbor, MI: University of Michigan Press, 2004), pp. 142-97.

—'Stepping into the Maelstrom: Women, Gender, and Ancient Near Eastern Scholarship', *NIN, Journal of Gender Studies in Antiquity* 1 (2000), pp. 1-22.

Asher-Greve, Julia M., and A. Lawrence Asher, 'From Thales to Foucault...and Back to Sumer', in *Intellectual Life of the Ancient Near East: Papers Presented at the 43rd Rencontre assyriologique internationale, Prague, July 1-5, 1996* (ed. Jirí Prosecky; Prague: Academy of Science of the Czech Republic, Oriental Institute, 1998), pp. 29-40.

Assante, Julia, 'From Whores to Hierodules: The Historiographic Invention of Mesopotamian Female Sex Professionals', in *Ancient Art and its Historiography* (ed. Alice A. Donohue and Mark D. Fullerton; Cambridge and New York: Cambridge University Press, 2003), pp. 13-47.

Assmann, Jan, *Moses the Egyptian: The Memory of Egypt in Western Monotheism* (Cambridge, MA and London: Harvard University Press, 1997).

Aston, Margaret, *The King's Bedpost: Reformation and Iconography in a Tudor Group Portrait* (Cambridge: Cambridge University Press, 1993).

Atil, Esin, Charles Newton, and Sarah Searight, *Voyages and Visions: Nineteenth-Century European Images of the Middle East from the Victoria and Albert Museum* (Washington, DC: Smithsonian Institution Traveling Exhibition Service/London: Victoria and Albert Museum in Association with University of Washington Press, Seattle and London, 1995).

Auerbach, Jeffrey A., *The Great Exhibition of 1851: A Nation on Display* (New Haven: Yale University Press, 1999).

Autin, Jean, *L'impératrice Eugénie, ou, L'empire d'une femme* (Mesnil-sur-l'Estrée: Fayard, 1990).

Avgouli, Maria, 'The First Greek Museums and National Identity', in *Museums and the Making of 'Ourselves': The Role of Objects in National Identity* (ed. Flora E.S. Kaplan; London: Leicester University Press, 1994).

Avi-Yonah, Michael (ed.), *A History of Israel and the Holy Land* (New York and London: Continuum, 2001).

Avi-Yonah, Michael, and Ephraim Stern (eds.), *Encyclopedia of Archaeological Excavations in the Holy Land* (4 vols.; Englewood Cliffs, NJ: Prentice–Hall, 1975–78).

Bacon, Roger, *The Greek Grammar of Roger Bacon and a Fragment of his Hebrew Grammar* (ed. Edmon Nolan and Samuel Abraham Hirsch; Cambridge: Cambridge University Press, 1902).

Badawi, Ahmad, *Rifaa Rafii al-Tahtawi* (Cairo, 2nd edn, 1959).

Badger, R. Reid, 'Chicago 1893: World's Columbian Exposition', in Findling and Pelle (eds.), *Historical Dictionary of World's Fairs and Expositions*, pp. 122-32.

Bahrani, Zainab, *The Graven Image: Representation in Babylonia and Assyria* (Archaeology, Culture, and Society; Philadelphia: University of Pennsylvania Press, 2003).

—*Women of Babylon: Gender and Representation in Mesopotamia* (London and New York: Routledge, 2001).

Balboni, L.A., *Gl'Italiani nella civiltà Egiziana de secolo XIX: Storia, biografie, monografie* (3 vols.; Alexandria: V. Penasson, 1906).

Ballantyne, Andrew, 'Knight, Haydon, and the Elgin Marbles', *Apollo* 128 (1988), pp. 155-59.

Balston, Thomas, *John Martin 1789–1854: His Life and Works* (London: Gerald Duckworth, 1947).

Banks, Edgar James, *Bismya, or The Lost City of Adab* (New York: J.P. Putnam's Sons, 1912).

Bar-Gal, Yoram, *Moledet we-ge'ografyah be-me'ah šanot ḥinuk Ṣiyoni* (Tel-Aviv: ʿAm ʿOved, 1993).

Barr, James, *History and Ideology in the Old Testament: Biblical Studies at the End of a Millennium* (New York: Oxford University Press, 2000).

Barton, George A., *Archaeology and the Bible* (Philadelphia: American Sunday-School Union, 1916).

—*Archaeology and the Bible*. Part I: *The Bible Lands, their Exploration, and the Resultant Light on the Bible and History;* Part II: *Translations of Ancient Documents Which Confirm or Illuminate the Bible* (Green Book Fund, 17; Philadelphia: American Sunday-School Union, 7th rev. edn, 1937).

—'Harper, Robert Francis (Oct. 18, 1864–Aug. 5, 1914)', in *DAB*, VIII, pp. 284-85.

—'Ward, William Hayes (June 25, 1835–Aug. 28, 1916)', in *DAB*, XIX, pp. 442-43.

—*A Year's Wandering in Bible Lands* (Philadelphia. Ferris & Leach, 1904).

Batten, Loring W., *A Critical and Exegetical Commentary on Ezra and Nehemiah* (ICC, 12; Edinburgh: T. & T. Clark, 1913).

Baumgärtel, Bettina, 'Is the King Genderless? The Staging of the Female Regent as Minerva Pacifera', in *Women Who Ruled: Queens, Goddesses, Amazons in Renaissance and Baroque Art* (ed. Annette Dixon; London: Merrell, in association with The University of Michigan Museum of Art, 2002), pp. 97-118.

Baumgärtel, Bettina, and Silvia Neysters (eds.), *Die Galerie der starken Frauen = La galerie des femmes fortes: Die Heldin in der französischen und italienischen Kunst des 17. Jahrhunderts* (München: Klinkhardt & Biermann, 1995).

Baxandall, Michael, *Painting and Experience in Fifteenth Century Italy: A Primer in the Social History of Pictorial Style* (Oxford: Clarendon Press, 1972).

Beaulieu, Paul-Alain, 'The Historical Background of the Uruk Prophecy', in *The Tablet and the Scroll: Near Eastern Studies in Honor of William W. Hallo* (ed. Mark E. Cohen, Daniel C. Snell and David B. Weisberg; Bethesda, MD: CDL Press, 1993), pp. 41-52.

—'Nabopolassar and the Antiquity of Babylon', in *Hayim and Miriam Tadmor Festschrift Volume* (ed. Israel Eph'al, Amnon Ben-Tor, Peter Machinist; Eretz Israel, 27; Jerusalem: Israel Exploration Society, 2003), pp. 1*-9*.

—*The Pantheon of Uruk during the Neo-Babylonian Period* (Cuneiform Monographs, 23; Leiden: Brill and Styx, 2003).

—*The Reign of Nabonidus, King of Babylon 556–539 B.C.* (YNER, 10; New Haven: Yale University Press, 1989).

Beaumarchais, Jean-Pierre de, Daniel Couty and Alain Rey (eds.), *Dictionnaire des littératures de langue française* (4 vols.; Paris: Bordas, rev. edn, 1994).

Behdad, Ali, *Belated Travellers: Orientalism in the Age of Colonial Dissolution* (Post-Contemporary Interventions; Durham, NC: Duke University Press, 1994).

Bendiner, Kenneth, *The Art of Ford Madox Brown* (University Park, PA: Pennsylvania State University Press, 1998).

Benjamin, Walter, *Gesammelte Schriften* (7 vols.; ed. Rolf Tiedemann and Hermann Schweppenhäuser; Frankfurt a.M.: Suhrkamp, 1972–89).

—*Illuminations* (trans. Harry Zohn; New York: Schocken Books, 1969).

Bennett, Mary, *Artists of the Pre-Raphaelite Circle: The First Generation: Catalogue of Works in the Walker Art Gallery, Lady Lever Art Gallery and Sudley Art Gallery* (London and Liverpool: Lund Humphries and National Museums and Galleries on Merseyside, 1996).

Benvenisti, Meron, *Sacred Landscape: The Buried History of the Holy Land since 1948* (trans. Maxine Kaufman-Lacusta; Berkeley: University of California Press, 2000).

Bercovitch, Sacvan, 'The Biblical Basis of the American Myth', in *The Bible and American Arts and Letters* (ed. Giles Gunn; The Bible in American Culture, 3; Philadelphia: Fortress Press/Chico, CA: Scholars Press, 1983), pp. 219-29.

—*The Puritan Origins of the American Self* (New Haven: Yale University Press, 1975).

Bergamini, Giovanni, ' "*Spoliis Orientis onustus*": Paul-Emile Botta et la découverte de la civilisation assyrienne', in Fontan and Chevalier (eds.), *De Khorsabad à Paris*, pp. 68-85.

Bergel, Lienhard, 'Semiramis in the Italian and Spanish Baroque', *Forum italicum* 7 (June 1973), pp. 227-49.

Berman, Nina, *Orientalismus, Kolonialisms und Moderne: Zum Bild des Orients in der deutschsprachigen Kultur um 1900* (Stuttgart: J.B. Metzlersche Verlagsbuchhandlung and Carl Ernst Poeschel, 1997).

Bernal, Martin, *Black Athena: The Afroasiatic Roots of Classical Civilization*. I. *The Fabrication of Ancient Greece 1785–1985* (New Brunswick, NJ: Rutgers University Press, 1987).

Bernhardsson, Magnus Thorkell, 'Reclaiming a Plundered Past: Archaeology and Nationalism in Modern Iraq, 1808–1941' (PhD dissertation, Yale University, 1999).

Berrebi, Eric-Henry, 'Sardanapale, ou l'impossible étreinte', *L'écrit-voir, revue d'histoire des arts* 8 (1986), pp. 37-49.

Bersani, Leo and Ulysse Dutoit, *The Forms of Violence: Narrative in Assyrian Art and Modern Culture* (New York: Schocken Books, 1985).

Beyerlin, Walter (ed.), *Near Eastern Religious Texts Relating to the Old Testament* (OTL; trans. John Bowden; Philadelphia: Westminster Press, 1978).

Bhabha, Homi K., 'DissemiNation: Time, Narrative, and the Margins of the Modern Nation', in *Nation and Narration* (ed. H.K. Bhabha; London and New York: Routledge, 1990), pp. 291-322.

—*The Location of Culture* (London and New York: Routledge, 1994).

Bhabha, Homi K., and W.J. Thomas Mitchell (eds.), *Edward Said: Continuing the Conversation* (Chicago: University of Chicago Press, 2004).

Bichler, Reinhold, 'Herodots Frauenbild und seine Vorstellung über Sexualität der Völker', in *Geschlechterrollen und Frauenbild in der Perspektive antiker Autoren* (ed. Robert Rollinger and Christoph Ulf; Innsbruck: Studien-Verlag, 2002), pp. 13-56.

Bidayat al-qudama wa hidayat al-hukama (trans. Mustafa al-Zawarbi, Muhammad Abd al-Raziq and Abdallah Abu al-Suud; Bulaq: Dar al-Tiba'ah al-Amiriyya, 1254/ 1838; 2nd edn, 1282/1865).

Biggs, Robert D., 'More Babylonian "Prophecies" ', *Iraq* 29 (1967), pp. 117-32.

Birch, Samuel, 'Inaugural Address', in *Transactions of the Second Session of the International Congress of Orientalists, Held in London in September 1874* (ed. Robert K. Douglas; London: Trübner & Co., 1876), pp. 1-3.

—(ed.), *Records of the Past: Being English Translations of the Assyrian and Egyptian Monuments* (12 vols.; London: Samuel Bagster, 1873–81).

Bird, Phyllis A., 'The End of the Male Cult Prostitute: A Literary-Historical and Sociological Analysis of Hebrew *qādēš-qĕdēšim*', in *Congress Volume; Cambridge 1995* (ed. John A. Emerton; VTSup, 66; Leiden: E.J. Brill, 1997), pp. 37-80.

Birot, Maurice, 'Données nouvelles sur la chronologie du règne de Zimri-Lim', *Syria* 55 (1978), pp. 333-43.

Bissell, Edwin Cone, *Biblical Antiquities: A Hand-Book for Use in Seminaries, Sabbath-Schools, Families and by All Students of the Bible* (Green Fund Book, 5; Philadelphia: American Sunday-School Union, 1888).

Black, Jeremy, and Anthony Green, *Gods, Demons and Symbols of Ancient Mesopotamia: An Illustrated Dictionary* (Austin: University of Texas Press, 1992).

Bleibtreu, Erika, 'Semiramis und andere Gemahlinnen assyrischer Könige', in *Nachrichten aus der Zeit: Ein Streifzug durch die Frauengeschichte des Altertums* (ed. Edith Specht; Reihe Frauenforschung, 18; Wien: Wiener Frauenverlag, 1992), pp. 57-72.

Blenkinsopp, Joseph, 'Bethel in the Neo-Babylonian Period', in *Judah and the Judeans in the Neo-Babylonian Period* (ed. Oded Lipschits and J. Blenkinsopp; Winona Lake, IN: Eisenbrauns, 2003), pp. 95-110.

—*Ezra–Nehemiah: A Commentary* (OTL; London: SCM Press, 1989).

Boccaccio, Giovanni, *De mulieribus claris* (Ulm: Johann Zainer, 1473).

—*Famous Women* (ed. and trans. Virginia Brown; The I Tatti Renaissance Library, 1; Cambridge, MA and London: Harvard University Press, 2001).

—*Ioannis Boccati de Certaldo insigne opus* De claris mulieribus (with woodcuts by Jacob Kallenberg; Berne: Mathias Apiarus, 1539).

Böhl, F.M.Th., *King Hammurabi of Babylon in the Setting of his Time (about 1700 B.C.)* (Amsterdam: Noord-Hollandsche uitgevers maatschappij, 1946).

Bohrer, Frederick N., 'Eastern Medi(t)ations: Exoticism and the Mobility of Difference', *History and Anthropology* 9 (1996), pp. 293-307.

—'Inventing Assyria: Exoticism and Reception in Nineteenth-Century England and France', *ArtB* 80 (1998), pp. 336-56.

—'A New Antiquity: The English Reception of Assyria' (PhD dissertation, University of Chicago, 1989).

—*Orientalism and Visual Culture: Imaging Mesopotamia in Nineteenth-Century Europe* (Cambridge and New York: Cambridge University Press, 2003).

—'The Printed Orient: The Production of A.H. Layard's Earliest Works', in Gunter (ed.), *The Construction of the Ancient Near East*, pp. 85-105.

—'The Times and Spaces of History: Representation, Assyria, and the British Museum', in *Museum Culture: Histories, Discourses, Spectacles* (ed. Daniel Sherman and Irit Rogoff; Media & Society, 6; Minneapolis, MN: University of Minnesota Press, 1994), pp. 197-222.

Boone, Joseph A., 'Vacation Cruises; Or, the Homoerotics of Orientalism', in *Feminist Postcolonial Theory: A Reader* (ed. Reina Lewis and Sara Mills; New York: Routledge, 2003), pp. 460-86.

Booth, Alison, 'Illustrious Company: Victoria among Other Women in Anglo-American Role Model Anthologies', in *Remaking Queen Victoria* (ed. Margaret Homans and Adrienne Munich; Cambridge Studies in Nineteenth-Century Literature and Culture, 10; Cambridge: Cambridge University Press, 1997), pp. 59-76.

Borger, R., 'Altorientalische Lexikographie: Geschichte und Probleme zur Vollendung von W. von Soden, Akkadisches Handwörterbuch', *Nachrichten der Akademie der Wissenschaften in Göttingen.* I. *Philologisch-historische Klasse* (1984/2), pp. 70-114.

—*Beiträge zum Inschriftenwerk Assurbanipals: Die Prismenklassen A, B, C = K, D, E, F, G, H, J und T sowie andere Inschriften* (Wiesbaden: Harrassowitz Verlag, 1996).

—*Handbuch der Keilschriftliteratur* (3 vols.; Berlin: W. de Gruyter, 1967).

—*Die Inschriften Asarhaddons, Königs von Assyrien* (AfOB, 9; Graz: im Selbstverlage des Herausgebers, 1956).

—'Wolfram von Soden (19. 6. 1908–6. 10. 1996)', *AfO* 44–45 (1997–98), pp. 588-94.

Boscawen, William St. Chad, *The Bible and the Monuments: The Primitive Hebrew Records in the Light of Modern Research* (London: Eyre & Spottiswoode, 1895).

Bosworth, C.E., 'The Study of Islam in British Scholarship', in *Mapping Islamic Studies: Genealogy, Continuity and Change* (ed. Azim Nanji; Religion and Reason, 38; Berlin and New York: Mouton de Gruyter, 1997), pp. 45-67.

Botta, Paul-Emile, 'Découvertes archéologiques faites à Ninive, en 1843 et 1845', *Le magasin pittoresque* 12 (1844), pp. 283-86.

—*Lettres de M. Botta sur ses découvertes à Khorsabad, près de Ninive* (Paris: Imprimerie royale, 1845).

—*M. Botta's Letters on the Discoveries at Nineveh, Translated from the French by C.T.* (London: Longman, Brown, Green, & Longmans, 1850).

Botta, Paul-Emile, and Eugène Flandin, *Monument de Ninive découvert et décrit* (5 vols.; Paris: Imprimerie nationale, 1849–50).

Bottéro, Jean, *Le problème des Ḫabiru à la 4e Rencontre assyriologique internationale* (Paris: Imprimerie nationale, 1954).

Bottéro, Jean, and André Finet, *Répertoire analytique des tomes I à V* (ARM, XV; Paris: Imprimerie nationale, 1954).

Boyer, Régis, 'Archetypes', in *Companion to Literary Myths: Heroes and Archetypes* (ed. Pierre Brunel; trans. Wendy Allatson, Judith Hayward, Trista Selous; London and New York: Routledge, 1992), pp. 110-17.

Bradner, Lester, 'The Order of the Sentence in the Assyrian Historical Inscriptions', *Hebraica* 8 (1891), pp. 1-14.

Breasted, James Henry, *The Oriental Institute of the University of Chicago: A Beginning and a Program* (Oriental Institute Communications, 1; Chicago: University of Chicago Press, 1922) = *AJSLL* 38 (1922), pp. 233-328.

Breckenridge, Carol A., and Peter van der Veer (eds.), *Orientalism and the Postcolonial Predicament: Perspectives on South Asia* (New Delhi and New York: Oxford University Press, 1994).

Briant, Pierre, 'Histoire et archéologie d'un texte: La *Lettre de Darius à Gadatas* entre Perses, Grecs et Romains', in *Licia e Lidia prima dell'Ellenizzazione: Atti del Convegno internazionale—Roma 11-12 ottobre 1999* (ed. Mauro Giorgieri, M. Salvini, M.-C. Trémouille and P. Vannicelli; Monografie Scientifiche, Serie Scienze umane e sociali; Rome: Consiglio nazionale delle ricerche, 2003), pp. 107-44.

Bright, John, *A History of Israel* (Philadelphia: Westminster Press, 1959).

—*A History of Israel* (Louisville, KY: Westminster/John Knox, 4th edn, 2000 [1959]).

Brinkman, J.A., in A. Leo Oppenheim, *Ancient Mesopotamia: Portrait of a Dead Civilization* (ed. Erica Reiner; Chicago: University of Chicago, rev. edn, 1977), pp. 335-46.

—*Prelude to Empire: Babylonian Society and Politics 747–626 B.C.* (Occasional Publications of the Babylonian Fund, 7; Philadelphia: Distributed by the Babylonian Fund, University Museum, 1984).

British Museum Archives, Minutes of Trustee Meetings, Sub. Comm., 22 Jan 1848, f. 399-402; Comm., 29 Jan 1848, f. 7443-46.

Bröker, G., and W. Müller, 'Aëtion (I)', *Künstlerlexikon der Antike* (2 vols.; ed. Rainer Vollkommer; München and Leipzig: K.G. Saur, 2001–), I, p. 5-6.

Bronkhurst, Judith, in *The Pre-Raphaelites* (ed. Leslie Parris; London: Tate Gallery and Penguin Books, 1984).

Brosius, Maria, *Women in Ancient Persia (559–331 BC)* (Oxford Classical Monographs; Oxford: Clarendon Press, 1996).

Broude, Norma, 'Degas's "Misogyny" ', *ArtB* 59 (1977), p. 101.

Brown, Chandos M., *Benjamin Silliman: A Life in the Young Republic* (Princeton, NJ: Princeton University Press, 1989).

Brown, Demetra Vaka, *Haremlik: Some Pages from the Life of Turkish Women* (Boston: Houghton Mifflin, 1909).

Brown, Ford Madox, *The Diary of Ford Madox Brown* (ed. Virginia Surtees; New Haven: Yale University Press, 1918).

—*Exhibition of Work, and Other Paintings, by Ford Madox Brown, at the Gallery, 191 Piccadilly* (London: Gallery, 1865).

Brown, Francis, *Assyriology: Its Use and Abuse in Old Testament Study* (New York: Charles Scribner's Sons, 1885).

Brown, Phyllis Rugg, 'Louise Labé and Semiramis: A Feminist Reading', *Women in French Studies* 5 (1997), pp. 107-22.

Brown, Virginia, 'Introduction', in *Famous Women* (ed. and trans. Virginia Brown; The I Tatti Renaissance Library, 1; Cambridge, MA and London: Harvard University Press, 2001), pp. xi-xxv.

Brown, William P., 'Introduction to John Bright's *A History of Israel*' and 'An Update in the Search of Israel's History', in Bright, *History of Israel* (4th edn, 2000), pp. 1-22.

Brugsch, Heinrich, *Mein Leben und mein Wandern* (Berlin: Allgemeiner Verein für Deutsche Literatur, 2nd edn, 1894 [1893]).

Brunner, Hellmut and Walter Beyerlin (eds.), *Religionsgeschichtliches Textbuch zum Alten Testament* (Grundrisse zum Alten Testament. Das Alte Testament Deutsch, 1; Göttingen: Vandenhoeck & Ruprecht, 1975).

Bryson, Norman, 'Art in Context', in *Studies in Historical Change* (ed. Ralph Cohen; Charlottesville, VA and London: University Press of Virginia, 1992), pp. 18-42.

Buckingham, James S., *The Buried City of the East, Nineveh: A Narrative of the Discoveries of Mr Layard and M. Botta at Nimroud and Khorsabad; with Descriptions of the Exhumed Sculptures, and Particulars of the Early History of the Ancient Ninevite Kingdom* (London: Office of the National Illustrated Library, 1851).

Budge, E.A. Wallis, *Assyrian Sculptures in the British Museum: Reign of Ashur-Nasir-Pal, 885–860 B.C.* (London: Printed by Order of the Trustees [of the British Museum], 1914).

—*The Rise and Progress of Assyriology* (London: Martin Hopkinson, 1925).

Budin, Stephanie L., 'A Reconsideration of the Aphrodite–Ashtart Syncretism', *Numen* 51 (2004), pp. 109-21.

Bullock, William Thomas, 'Josiah', in *Dr William Smith's Dictionary of the Bible, Comprising its Antiquities, Biography, Geography, and Natural History* (4 vols.; ed. William Smith, Horatio Balch Hackett and Ezra Abbot; Boston: Houghton, Mifflin & Co., 1894), II, pp. 1480-81.

Burckhardt, Jacob, *Reflections on History* (trans. M.D. Hottinger; Indianapolis, IN: Liberty Classics, 1979).

—*Weltgeschichtliche Betrachtungen* (ed. Jakob Oeri; Berlin and Stuttgart: W. Spemann, 1905).

Burge, Robert, 'Pablo Picasso's *Man with a Sheep*', *Source: Notes in the History of Art* 2 (1982), pp. 21-26.

Burkert, Walter, *Babylon, Memphis, Persepolis: Eastern Contexts of Greek Culture* (Cambridge, MA: Harvard University Press, 2004).

—*Greek Religion* (Cambridge, MA: Harvard University Press, 1985).

Burmeister, Karl Heinz, *Sebastian Münster: Versuch eines biographischen Gesamtbildes* (Basler Beiträge zur Geschichtswissenschaft, 91; Basel and Stuttgart: Helbing & Lichtenhahn, 1963).

Burne-Jones, Georgiana, *Memorials of Edward Burne-Jones* (2 vols.; London: Macmillan & Co., 1904).

Burnett, Stephen G., *From Christian Hebraism to Jewish Studies: Johannes Buxtorf (1564–1629) and Hebrew Learning in the Seventeenth Century* (Studies in the History of Christian Thought, 68; Leiden and New York: Brill, 1996).

Burrows, Mathew, ' "Mission civilisatrice": French Cultural Policy in the Middle East, 1860–1914', *Historical Journal* 29 (1986), pp. 109-35.

Burstein, Stanley Mayer, *The Babyloniaca of Berossus* (Sources and Monographs. Sources from the Ancient Near East, 1/5; Malibu, CA: Undena, 1978).

Buruma, Ian and Avishai Margalit, *Occidentalism: The West in the Eyes of its Enemies* (New York: Penguin Press, 2004).

Butler, Janet, 'A Pre-Raphaelite Shibboleth: Joseph', *Journal of Pre-Raphaelite Studies* 3/1 (1982), pp. 78-90.

Butlin, Robin A., 'Ideological Contexts and the Reconstruction of Biblical Landscapes in the Seventeenth and Early Eighteenth Centuries: Dr Edward Wells and the Historical Geography of the Holy Land', in *Ideology and Landscape in Historical Perspective: Essays on the Meanings of Some Places in the Past* (ed. Alan R.H. Baker and Gideon Biger; Cambridge Studies in Historical Geography, 18; Cambridge: Cambridge University Press, 1992), pp. 31-62.

Byron, George Gordon Byron, Baron, *The Complete Poetical Works* (7 vols.; ed. Jerome J. McGann; Oxford and New York: Clarendon Press/Oxford University Press, 1981).

—*The Poetical Works of Lord Byron* (ed. William Michael Rossetti; London: Moxon, 1870).

Cameron, George G., 'Leroy Waterman (1875–1972)', *AfO* 26 (1978–79), pp. 244-45.

Campbell, C.J., *Campbell's Visitor's Guide to the International Exhibition and Handy Book of London* (London: C.J. Campbell, 1862).

Campbell, John, *The Hittites: Their Inscriptions and their History* (London: J.C. Nimmo, 1891).

Cancik, Hubert and Helmuth Schneider (eds.), *Der neue Pauly: Enzyklopädie der Antike* (16 vols.; Stuttgart and Weimar: J.B. Metzler, 1996–2003).

Capomacchia, Anna Maria G., *Semiramis una femminilità ribaltata* (Storia delle religioni, 4; Rome: 'L'Erma' di Bretschneider, 1986).

Carena, Omar, *History of the Near Eastern Historiography and its Problems 1852–1985*. Part 1: *1852–1945* (trans. E. Schmitz and L. Tosco; AOAT, 218/1; Kevelaer: Butzon & Bercker/Neukirchen–Vluyn: Neukirchener Verlag, 1989).

Carrier, James G., *Occidentalism: Images of the West* (Oxford and New York: Clarendon Press, 1995).

Carter, Elizabeth C., and Matthew W. Stolper, *Elam: Surveys of Political History and Archaeology* (University of California Publications: Near Eastern Studies, 25; Berkeley: University of California Press, 1984).

Carter, Paul, *The Road to Botany Bay: An Essay in Spatial History* (New York: Knopf, 1987).

Carter, Robin Borglum, *Mary's Story* (Corpus Christi, TX: privately published, 2005).

Célestin, Roger, *From Cannibals to Radicals: Figures and Limits of Exoticism* (Minneapolis, MN: University of Minnesota Press, 1996).

Çelik, Zeynep, *Displaying the Orient: Architecture of Islam at Nineteenth-Century World's Fairs* (Comparative Studies on Muslim Societies, 12; Berkeley: University of California Press, 1992).

—'Speaking Back to Orientalist Discourse at the World's Columbian Exposition', in *Noble Dreams, Wicked Pleasures: Orientalism in America, 1870–1930* (ed. Holly Edwards; Princeton, NJ: Princeton University Press and Sterling and Francine Clark Art Institute, 2000), pp. 76-97.

Çelik, Zeynep, and Lila Kinney, 'Ethnography and Exhibitionism at the Expositions Universelles', *Assemblages* 13 (1990), pp. 34-59.

Césaire, Aimé, *Discourse on Colonialism* (trans. Joan Pinkham; New York: MR, 1972).

Cezar, Mustafa, *Müzeci ve ressam Osman Hamdi Bey* (Türk Kültürüne Hizmet Vakfi sanat yayinlari, 1; Istanbul: Türk Kültürüne Hizmet Vakfi, 1987).

Chambers, Iain, and Lidia Curti (eds.), *The Post-Colonial Question: Common Skies, Divided Horizons* (New York: Routledge, 1996).

Chardin, Jean, *The Travels of Sir John Chardin into Persia and the East-Indies. The First Volume, Containing the Author's Voyage from Paris to Ispahan: To Which is Added, the Coronation of This Present King of Persia, Solyman the Third* (London: Printed for Moses Pitt..., 1686).

Charpin, Dominique, *Hammu-rabi de Babylone* (Paris: Presses universitaires de France, 2003).

—'Toponymie amorrite et toponymie biblique: La ville de Ṣîbat/Ṣobah', *RA* 92 (1998), pp. 79-92.

—' "Ein umherziehende Aramäer war mein Vater": Abraham im Lichte der Quellen aus Mari', in *'Abraham, unser Vater': Die gemeinsamen Wurzeln von Judentum, Christentum und Islam* (ed. R.G. Kratz and Tilman Nagel; Göttingen: Wallstein Verlag, 2003), pp. 40-52.

Charpin, Dominique, and Jean-Marie Durand, 'La suzeraineté de l'empéreur (*sukkalmaḫ*) d'Elam sur la Mésopotamie et le "nationalisme" amorrite', in *Mésopotamie et Elam: Actes de la XXXVIème Rencontre assyriologique internationale*, Gand, 10-14 juillet 1989 (ed. L. De Meyer and H. Gasche; Mesopotamian History and Environment, Occasional Publications, [IV]/I; Ghent: The University, 1991), pp. 59-66.

Charpin, Dominique, and Nele Ziegler, *Mari et le Proche-Orient à l'époque amorrite: Essai d'histoire politique* (Florilegium marianum, 5; Mémoires de N.A.B.U., 6; Paris: SEPOA, 2003).

Chavalas, Mark W., 'Assyriology and Biblical Studies: A Century of Tension', in Chavalas and Younger, Jr (eds.), *Mesopotamia and the Bible*, pp. 21-67.

Chavalas, Mark W., and K. Lawson Younger, Jr (eds.), *Mesopotamia and the Bible: Comparative Explorations* (JSOTSup, 341; Sheffield: Sheffield Academic Press, 2002).

Cheyne, Thomas Kelley, *The Decline and Fall of the Kingdom of Judah* (London: Adam & Charles Black, 1908).

—'Josiah', in *Encyclopaedia Biblica: A Critical Dictionary of the Literary, Political and Religious History, the Archaeology, Geography, and Natural History of the Bible* (4 vols.; ed. T.K. Cheyne and J. Sutherland Black; New York: Macmillan, 1903), II, pp. 2610-12.

Child, Isabella, *The Child's Picture Bible* (New York: J.Q. Preble, 1855), available online as part of the digitized Making of America series at http://www.hti.umich.edu/cgi/b/bib/bibperm?q1=AFZ0133, accessed September 28, 2006.

Childs, Brevard S., *Biblical Theology in Crisis* (Philadelphia. Westminster Press, 1970).

Choueri, Youssef M., *Arab History and the Nation-State: A Study in Modern Arab Historiography 1820–1980* (Exeter Arabic and Islamic Series; London: Routledge, 1989).

Christie, Agatha, *An Autobiography* (London: Collins, 1977).

Çiğ, Muazzez, 'Atatürk and the Beginnings of Cuneiform Studies in Turkey', *JCS* 40 (1988), pp. 211-16.

Cicero, *Pro Caelio. De provinciis consularibus. Pro Balbo* (trans. Richard Gardner; LCL; London: Heinemann and Cambridge, MA: Harvard University Press, 1958).

Claassen, Cheryl, 'Introduction', in Claasen (ed.), *Women in Archaeology*, pp. 1-8.

Claassen, Cheryl (ed.), *Women in Archaeology* (Philadelphia: University of Pennsylvania Press, 1994).

Clark, Samuel, and George Grove, *The Bible Atlas of Maps and Plans to Illustrate the Geography and Topography of the Old and New Testaments and the Apocrypha, with Explanatory Notes* (London: Society for Promoting Christian Knowledge, 1868).

Clark, Samuel, and Nicholas Penny (eds.), *The Arrogant Connoisseur: Richard Payne Knight, 1751–1824: Essays on Richard Payne Knight together with a Catalogue of Works Exhibited at the Whitworth Art Gallery, 1982* (Manchester: Manchester University Press, 1982).

Clements, R.E., *God and Temple: The Idea of the Divine Presence in Ancient Israel* (Oxford: Basil Blackwell, 1965).

Clines, David J.A., *The Esther Scroll: The Story of the Story* (JSOTSup, 30; Sheffield: JSOT Press, 1984).

—*Ezra, Nehemiah, Esther: Based on the Revised Standard Version* (NCBC; London: Marshall, Morgan & Scott/Grand Rapids, MI: Eerdmans, 1984).

Cogan, Mordechai, and Israel Eph'al (eds.), *Ah, Assyria…: Studies in Assyrian History and Ancient Near Eastern Historiography Presented to Hayim Tadmor* (Scripta hierosolymitana, 33; Jerusalem: Magnes Press, 1991).

Cohen, C., 'The Literary Motif of Jacob's Ladder (Gen. 28:12) according to the Interpretation of Ibn-Ezra and in Light of Parallels in Akkadian Literature', in *Shai le-Hadassah: Studies in Hebrew and Jewish Languages, Eshel Beer-Sheva* (ed. Y. Ben-Toulila; Researches in Jewish Studies, 5; Beer-Sheva: Ben-Gurion University of the Negev, 1997), pp. 15-26.

Cohen, David, *Markus Lüpertz 'Semiramis': September 12–November 16, 2002* (New York: Knodler & Company, 2002).

Cohn, Bernard S., *Colonialism and its Forms of Knowledge: The British in India* (Princeton Studies in Culture/Power/History; Princeton, NJ: Princeton University Press, 1966).

Cole, Juan Ricardo, *Colonialism and Revolution in the Middle East: Social and Cultural Origins of Egypt's Urabi Movement* (Princeton, NJ: Princeton University Press, 1993).

Cole, Steven W., 'The Crimes and Sacrileges of Nabû-šuma-iškun', *ZA* 84 (1994), pp. 220-52.

Coleman, Edward D., and Joseph Reider, 'A Bibliography of the Writings and Addresses of Cyrus Adler 1882–1933', in *Lectures, Selected Papers, Addresses, by Cyrus Adler, with a Bibliography* (Philadelphia: privately printed, 1933), pp. 364-445.

Coleman, Lyman, *An Historical Text Book and Atlas of Biblical Geography* (Philadelphia: J.B. Lippincott, rev. edn, 1867).

Collins, John J., 'The Zeal of Phineas: The Bible and the Legitimation of Violence', *JBL* 122 (2003), pp. 3-21.

Comploi, Sabine, 'Die Darstellung der Semiramis bei Diodorus Siculus', in *Geschlechterrollen und Frauenbild in der Perspektive antiker Autoren* (ed. Robert Rollinger and Christoph Ulf; Innsbruck: Studien-Verlag, 2002), pp. 223-71.

Constans, Claire, *Les peintures* (3 vols.; Paris: Editions de la Réunion des musées nationaux, 1995).

Conybeare, Frederick C., J. Rendel Harris and Agnes Smith Lewis, *The Story of Ahikar: From the Syriac, Arabic, Armenian, Ethiopic, Greek and Slavonic Versions* (London: C.J. Clay & Sons, 1898).

Cook, Stanley Arthur, 'Josiah', in *EB*[11], XV, p. 520.

Coombes, Annie, 'The Recalcitrant Object: Culture Contact and the Question of Hybridity', in *Colonial Discourse/Postcolonial Theory* (ed. Francis Barker, Peter Hulme and Margaret Iversen; The Essex Symposia; Manchester and New York: Manchester University Press, 1994), pp. 89-114.

Cooper, Jerrold S., 'American School of Oriental Research in Baghdad', in *The Oxford Encyclopedia of Archaeology* (5 vols.; Oxford: Oxford University Press, 1997), I, pp. 92-94.

—'Assyrian Prophecies, the Assyrian Tree, and the Mesopotamian Origins of Jewish Monotheism, Greek Philosophy, Christian Theology, Gnosticism, and Much More', *JAOS* 120 (2000), pp. 430-44.

—'From Mosul to Manila: Early Approaches to Funding Ancient Near Eastern Studies Research in the United States', in Gunter (ed.), *The Construction of the Ancient Near East*, pp. 133-64.

—'Posing the Sumerian Question: Race and Scholarship in the Early History of Assyriology', *AuOr* 9 (1991), pp. 47-66.

—'Sumerian and Aryan: Racial Theory, Academic Politics and Parisian Assyriology', *RevHistRel* 210 (1993), pp. 169-205.

Cooper, Robyn, 'The Popularisation of Renaissance Art in Victorian England: The Arundel Society', *Art History* 1 (1978), pp. 263-92.

Cooper, Walter Gerald, *The Cotton States and International Exposition and South, Illustrated: Including the Official History of the Exposition* (Atlanta, GA: The Illustrator Company, 1896).

Cooperman, Bernard Dov (ed.), *Jewish Thought in the Sixteenth Century* (Harvard Judaic Texts and Studies, 2; Cambridge, MA: Harvard University Press, 1983).

Coulter, Russell, and Patricia Turner (eds.), 'Adad (a)', in *Encyclopedia of Ancient Deities* (Chicago: Fitzroy Dearborn Publishers, 2000).

Courbet, Gustave, *Letters of Gustave Courbet* (ed. and trans. Petra ten-Doesschate Chu; Chicago: University of Chicago Press, 1992).

Cowley, A.E., *Aramaic Papyri of the Fifth Century B.C.* (Oxford: Clarendon Press, 1923; repr. Osnabruck: Otto Zeller, 1967).

Crane, Walter, *An Artist's Reminiscences* (London: Methuen, 1907).

Cranmer, David, 'Portugal [Portugallo], Marcos Antonio', in *NGDO*, I, p. 1075.

Crelly, William R., *The Painting of Simon Vouet* (Yale Publications in the History of Art, 14; New Haven and London: Yale University Press, 1962).

Croffut, Bessie Nicholls, 'Exposition, Cotton-States and International', in *Appleton's Annual Cyclopaedia and Register of Important Events of the Year 1895: Embracing Political, Military, and Ecclesiastical Affairs; Public Documents; Biography, Statistics, Commerce, Finance, Literature, Science, Agriculture, and Mechanical Industry* (42 vols.; New York: D. Appleton & Company, 1868–1903), XXXV, pp. 269-77.

Croll, Gerhard, 'Glucks Debüt am Burgtheater', *Österreichische Musikzeitschrift* 31 (1976), pp. 194-202.

Cromer, Evelyn Baring, Earl of, *Modern Egypt* (2 vols.; New York: Macmillan, 1908).

Crosby, Howard, 'The Moabite Stone', *Palestine Exploration Society* 1 (1871), pp. 17-21.

Cross, Frank Moore, and David Noel Freedman, 'Josiah's Revolt against Assyria', *JNES* 12 (1953), pp. 56-58.

Croutier, Alev Lytle, *Harem: The World behind the Veil* (New York: Abbeville Press, 1989).

Crozet, Pascal, 'La trajectoire d'un scientifique égyptien au XIXe siècle: Mahmoud al-Falaki (1815–1885)', in Roussillon (ed.), *Entre réforme sociale*, pp. 285-310.

Cummings, Frederick, 'Benjamin Robert Haydon and the Critical Reception of the Elgin Marbles' (PhD dissertation, University of Chicago, 1967).

Dalley, Stephanie (ed.), *The Legacy of Mesopotamia* (Oxford: Oxford University Press, 1998).

—*Mari and Karana: Two Old Babylonian Cities* (Piscataway, NJ: Gorgias Press, 2nd edn, 2002).

—*Myths from Mesopotamia: Creation, the Flood, Gilgamesh, and Others* (Oxford and New York: Oxford University Press, 1989).

—'Nineveh, Babylon and the Hanging Gardens: Cuneiform and Classical Sources Reconciled', *Iraq* 56 (1994), pp. 45-58.

—'Semiramis in History and Legend', in *Cultural Borrowings and Ethnic Appropriations in Antiquity* (ed. Erich S. Gruen; Oriens et occidens, 8; Stuttgart: Franz Steiner, 2005), pp. 11-22.

Dalley, Stephanie, and A.T. Reyes, 'Mesopotamian Contact and Influence in the Greek World', in *The Legacy of Mesopotamia* (ed. S. Dalley; Oxford: Oxford University Press, 1998), pp. 85-124.

Dalziel, Edward, and George Dalziel, *The Brothers Dalziel: A Record of Fifty Years' Work in Conjunction with Many of the Most Distinguished Artists of the Period 1840–1890* (London: Methuen & Co., 1901).

Dalziels' Bible Gallery (London: George Routledge & Sons, 1881).

Daniel, Glyn, *A Hundred and Fifty Years of Archaeology* (London: Gerald Duckworth, 1978).

Daniell, David, *The Bible in English: Its History and Influence* (New Haven and London: Yale University Press, 2003).
Daniels, Peter T., 'Methods of Decipherment', in *The World's Writing Systems* (ed. P.T. Daniels and William Bright; New York and Oxford: Oxford University Press, 1996), pp. 141-59.
—' "Shewing of Hard Sentences and Dissolving of Doubts": The First Decipherment', *JAOS* 108 (1988), pp. 419-36.
Dante Alighieri, *The Comedy of Dante Aligheri, the Florentine. Cantica I: Hell (L'inferno)* (trans. Dorothy L. Sayers; Harmondsworth, Middlesex: Penguin Books, 1949).
David, Elisabeth, *Mariette Pacha 1821–1881* (Paris: Pygmalion and G. Watelet, 1994).
Davis, John, 'Holy Land, Holy People? Photography, Semitic Wannabes, and Chautauqua's Palestine Park', *Prospects* 17 (1992), pp. 241-71.
—*The Landscape of Belief: Encountering the Holy Land in Nineteenth-Century American Art and Culture* (The Princeton Series in Nineteenth-Century Art, Culture, and Society; Princeton, NJ: Princeton University Press, 1996).
Davis, Natalie Zemon, 'Women in Politics', in Davis and Farge (eds.), *A History of Women in the West*, III, pp. 167-83.
—'Women as Historical Actors', in Davis and Farge (eds.), *A History of Women in the West*, III, pp. 1-7.
Davis, Natalie Zemon, and Arlette Farge (eds.), *A History of Women in the West*, III: *Renaissance and Enlightenment Paradoxes* (Cambridge, MA and London: The Belknap Press of Harvard University Press, 1993).
Davis, Thomas W., *Shifting Sands: The Rise and Fall of Biblical Archaeology* (Oxford and New York: Oxford University Press, 2004).
Dawson, Warren R., and Eric P. Uphill, *Who Was Who in Egyptology* (rev. M.I. Bierbrier; London: Egypt Exploration Society, 3rd edn, 1995).
De Cossart, Michael, *Ida Rubinstein (1885–1960): A Theatrical Life* (Liverpool Historical Studies, 2; Liverpool: Liverpool University Press, 1987).
De Odorico, Marco, *The Use of Numbers and Quantifications in the Assyrian Royal Inscriptions* (SAAS, 3; Helsinki: The Neo-Assyrian Text Corpus Project, 1995).
De Vonyar, Jill and Richard Kendall, *Degas and the Dance* (New York: Harry N. Abrams, in association with the American Federation of Arts, 2002).
Dearman, J. Andrew, 'J. Maxwell Miller, Scholar and Teacher: A Sketch', in *The Land That I Will Show You: Essays on the History and Archaeology of the Ancient Near East in Honor of J. Maxwell Miller* (ed. J. Andrew Dearman and M. Patrick Graham; JSOTSup, 343; Sheffield: Sheffield Academic Press, 2001), pp. 16-35.
Deimel, Anton, *Šumerisches Lexikon* (4 vols.; Rome: Pontifical Institute Press, 1928–33).
Delacroix, Eugène, *Journal* (3 vols.; ed. André Joubin; Paris: Plon, 1932).
—'Des variations du beau', in *Ecrits sur l'art* (ed. François-Marie Deyrolle and Christophe Denissel; Paris: Librairie Séguier, 1988 [1857]).
Delannoy, Marcel, *Honegger* (Geneva and Paris: Slatkine, nouvelle édition, 1986).
Delanoue, Gilbert, *Moralistes et politiques musulmans dans l'Egypte du XIX*[e] *siècle (1798–1882)* (2 vols. Textes arabes et études islamiques, 15; Cairo: Institut français d'archéologie orientale du Caire, 1982).
Delany, Martin Robison, *Principia of Ethnology: The Origin of Races and Color, with an Archaeological Compendium of Ethiopian and Egyptian Civilization, from Years of Careful Examination and Enquiry* (Philadelphia: Harper, 1879).
Delitzsch, Friedrich, *Assyrische Lesestücke: Nach den originalen Theils revidirt Theils zum ersten Male herausgegeben, und durch Schrifttafeln eingeleitet* (Leipzig: J.C. Hinrichs, 1876).

—*Babel and Bible: A Lecture on the Significance of Assyriological Research for Religion. Delivered before the German Emperor* (trans. Thomas J. McCormack; Chicago: Open Court Publishing Co., 1902).

—*Babel und Bibel: Ein Vortrag* (Leipzig: J.C. Hinrichs, 1902).

—*Die große Täuschung: Kritische Betrachtungen zu den alttestamentlichen Berichten über Israels Eindringen in Kanaan, die Gottesoffenbarung vom Sinai und die Wirksamkeit der Propheten* (Stuttgart: Deutsche Verlags-Anstalt, 1920).

Dever, William G., 'Ceramics, Ethnicity and the Question of Israel's Origins', *BA* 58 (1995), pp. 200-13.

—'The Identity of Early Israel: A Rejoinder to Keith W. Whitelam', *JSOT* 72 (1996), pp. 3-24.

—' "Will the Real Israel Stand Up?" Archaeology and Israelite Historiography: Part I', *BASOR* 297 (1995), pp. 61-80.

Dick, Michael B., 'Prophetic Parodies of Making the Cult Image', in *Born in Heaven, Made on Earth: The Making of the Cult Image in the Ancient Near East* (ed. M.B. Dick; Winona Lake, IN: Eisenbrauns, 1999), pp. 1-53.

Diderot, Denis (ed.), *Encyclopédie, ou, dictionnaire raisonné des sciences, des arts et des métiers* (36 vols.; Lasaunne and Berne, 1778).

Diehl, Charles, *America and German Scholarship 1770–1870* (New Haven: Yale University Press, 1978).

Dijkstra, Bram, *Idols of Perversity: Fantasies of Feminine Evil in Fin-de-Siècle Culture* (New York and Oxford: Oxford University Press, 1986).

Dinsmoor, William B., 'Early American Studies of Mediterranean Archaeology,' *Proceedings of the American Philosophical Society* 87/1 (1943), pp. 70-104.

Dohmen, Christoph, *Das Bilderverbot: Seine Entstehung und seine Entwicklung im Alten Testament* (BBB, 62; Frankfurt a.M.: Athenäum, 2nd edn, 1985).

Domanski, Kristina, 'Verwirrung der Geschlechter—Zum Rollentausch als Bildthema im 15. Jahrhundert', in *Frauen in der frühen Neuzeit: Lebensentwürfe in Kunst und Literatur* (ed. Anne-Marie Bonnet and Barbara Maria Schellewald; Atlas, Bonner Beiträge zur Kunstgeschichte, Neue Folge, 1; Köln: Böhlau, 2004), pp. 37-83.

Donner, Fred M., 'Pioneers in Medieval Near Eastern Studies: Philip K. Hitti', *al-Usur al-Wusta* 8 (1996), pp. 48-52.

Doré, Gustave, *The Doré Gallery: Containing Two Hundred and Fifty Beautiful Engravings Selected from the Doré Bible, Milton, Dante's Inferno, Dante's Purgatorio and Paradiso, Atala, Fontaine, Fairy Realm, Don Quixote, Baron Munchausen, Croquemitaine*... (London: Cassell, Petter, Galpin & Co, 1870).

Dorothy, Charles V., *The Books of Esther: Structure, Genre, and Textual Integrity* (JSOTSup, 187; Sheffield: Sheffield Academic Press, 1997).

Dossin, Georges, 'Les archives épistolaires du palais de Mari', *Syria* 19 (1938), pp. 105-25 [= *Recueil Georges Dossin: Mélanges d'assyriologie, 1934–1959* (*Akkadica*. Supplementum, 1; Leuven: Peeters, 1983), pp. 102-32].

—'La correspondance de Zimrilim, dernier roi de Mari (vers 2000 avant J.-C.)', in *Comptes-rendus des séances de l'Académie des Inscriptions et Belles-Lettres, année 1937* (Paris: Auguste Picard, 1937), pp. 12-20.

—'Une révélation du dieu Dagan à Terqa', *RA* 42 (1948), pp. 125-34 [= *Recueil Georges Dossin*, pp. 169-79].

Dougherty, Raymond Philip, *Temple Records from Erech, Reign of Nabonidus, 555–538 B.C.* (YOS, Babylonian Texts, 6; New Haven: Yale University Press, 1920).

Douin, Georges, *Histoire du règne du Khédive Ismaïl*, 3 vols. in 4 (Cairo: Reale Società di geografia d'Egitto; 1933–39).

Drioton, Etienne, 'Le Musée de Boulac', *Cahiers d'histoire égyptienne* 3/1 (November 1950), pp. 1-12.

Driver, G.R., and John C. Miles, *The Assyrian Laws* (Ancient Codes and Laws of the Near East; Oxford: Clarendon Press, 1935).

Droixhe, Daniel, *La linguistique et l'appel de l'histoire (1600–1800): Rationalisme et révolutions positivistes* (Geneva: Droz, 1978).

Dronke, Peter, 'Semiramis, the Recreation of Myth', in *Poetic Individuality in the Middle Ages: New Departures in Poetry, 1000–1150* (Westfield Publications in Medieval Studies, 1; Oxford: Clarendon Press, 1970), pp. 66-113.

Dröse, Ruth, *Der Zyklus 'Bilder aus dem altjüdischen Familienleben' und sein Maler Moritz Daniel Oppenheim* (Hanau: CoCon-Verlag, 1996).

Du Maurier, George, *The Young George Du Maurier: A Selection of his Letters 1860–67* (ed. Daphne Du Maurier; London: Peter Davies, 1951).

Duby, George and Michelle Perrot (eds.), *A History of Women in the West* (5 vols.; Cambridge, MA and London: Harvard University Press, 1992–94).

Dumas, Alexandre, *The Black Tulip* (ed. David Coward; The World's Classics; Oxford: Oxford University Press, 1993 [*La tulipe noire*, Paris, 1850]).

Duncan, Russell, 'Atlanta 1895: Cotton States and International Exposition', in Findling and Pelle (eds.), *Historical Dictionary of World's Fairs and Expositions*, pp. 139-41.

Dunn-Hensley, Susan, 'Whore Queens: The Sexualized Female Body and the State', in *'High and Mighty Queens' of Early Modern England: Realities and Representation* (ed. Carole Levin, Jo Eldridge Carney and Debra Barrett-Graves; New York: Palgrave Macmillan, 2003), pp. 101-16.

Durand, Jean-Marie, *Le culte d'Addu d'Alep et l'affaire d'Alahtum* (Florilegium marianum, 7; Mémoires de N.A.B.U., 8; Paris: SEPOA, 2002).

—*Les documents épistolaires du palais de Mari* (3 vols. ; LAPO, 16-18; Paris: Les Editions du Cerf, 1997–2000).

—'Réalités amorrites et traditions bibliques', *RA* 92 (1998), pp. 3-39.

—'Unité et diversités au Proche-Orient à l'époque amorrite', in *La circulation des biens, des personnes et des idées dans le Proche-Orient ancien* (ed. D. Charpin and Francis Joannès; Actes de la XXXVIIIème Rencontre assyriologique internationale, Paris, 8-10 juillet 1991; Paris: Éditions Recherche sur les civilisations, 1992), pp. 97-128.

Durand, Jean-Marie (ed.), *La femme dans le Proche-Orient antique: Compte rendu de la XXXIIIe Rencontre assyriologique internationale, Paris, 7-10 Juillet 1986* (Paris: Editions Recherche sur les civilisations,1987).

—*Mari, Ebla, et les Hourrites: Dix ans de travaux, première partie: Actes du colloque international (Paris, mai 1993)* (Amurru, 1; Paris: Editions Recherche sur les civilisations, 1996).

Durand, Jean-Marie, and D. Charpin (eds.), *Mari, Ebla, et les Hourrites: Dix ans de travaux, deuxième partie: Actes du colloque international (Paris, mai 1993)* (Amurru, 2; Paris: Editions Recherche sur les civilisations, 2001).

Durand, Jean-Marie, and Jean-Claude Margueron (eds.), *Actes du colloque internationale du C.N.R.S. 620*, 'A propos d'un cinquantenaire: Mari, bilan et perspectives' (Strasbourg, 29, 30 juin, 1er juillet 1983), in *MARI* 4 (1985).

—'La question du harem royal dans le palais de Mari', *Journal des savants* (Octobre–Décembre 1980), pp. 253-80.

Dykstra, Darrell I., 'A Biographical Study in Egyptian Modernization: Ali Mubarak (1823/4–93)' (2 vols.; PhD dissertation, University of Michigan, 1977).

Earll, R. Edward, 'Report upon the Exhibit of the Smithsonian Institution, Including the

U.S. National Museum, at the Centennial Exposition of the Ohio Valley and Central States, held at Cincinnati, Ohio, in 1888', in *Report of the U.S. National Museum, under the Direction of the Smithsonian Institution, for the Year Ending June 30, 1889* ([Washington, DC]: Smithsonian Institution, 1891), pp. 154-89.

Ebach, Jürgen, 'Panbabylonismus', in *Handbuch religionswissenschaftlicher Grundbegriffe* (4 vols.; ed. Burkhard Gladigow, Hubert Cancik and Karl-Heinz Kohl; Stuttgart: W. Kohlhammer, 1998).

Ebers, Georg, *Egypt: Descriptive, Historical, and Picturesque* (2 vols.; trans. Clara Bell; London: Cassell, 1878–79).

—*Richard Lepsius: A Biography* (trans. Z.D. Underhill; New York: W.S. Gottsberger, 1887).

Edmond, Charles (Karol Edmund Chojecki), *L'Egypte à l'exposition universelle de 1867* (Paris: Dentu, 1867).

Edwards, Gwynne, 'Introduction', in Pedro Calderón de la Barca, *La hija del aire* (Colección Támesis. Série B: Textos, 9; London: Támesis Books, 1979), pp. xiii-lxxx.

Eggert, Katherine, *Showing like a Queen: Female Authority and Literary Experiment in Spenser, Shakespeare, and Milton* (Philadelphia: University of Pennsylvania Press, 2000).

Eilers, Wilhelm, *Semiramis: Entstehung und Nachhall einer altorientalischen Sage* (Österreichische Akademie der Wissenschaften, Philosophisch-historische Klasse Sitzungsberichte, 274, Abhandlung 2; Wien: Hermann Böhlaus Nachfolger, 1971).

Eisenstein, Elizabeth L., *The Printing Press as an Agent of Change: Communications and Cultural Transformations in Early-Modern Europe* (2 vols.; Cambridge and New York: Cambridge University Press, 1979).

Elazar, Daniel J., 'Covenant as the Basis of the Jewish Political Tradition', in *Kinship and Consent: The Jewish Political Tradition and its Contemporary Uses* (ed. D.J. Elazar; Ramat Gan: Turtledove, 1981), pp. 21-56.

—'Kinship and Consent in the Jewish Community: Patterns of Continuity in Jewish Communal Life', *Tradition: A Journal of Orthodox Jewish Thought* 14/4 (Fall 1974), pp. 63-79.

Elazar, Daniel J., and Stuart A. Cohen. *The Jewish Polity: Jewish Political Organizations from Biblical Times to the Present* (Bloomington, IN: Indiana University Press, 1985).

Elitzur, Yehuda, 'The Tower of Babel and Jacob's Ladder', in *Israel and the Bible: Studies in Geography, History, and Biblical Thought* (ed. Y. Elitzur and Amos Frisch; Ramat Gan: Bar-Ilan University, 1999), pp. 44-48 [Hebrew].

Ellis, Marc H., 'Edward Said and the Future of the Jewish People', in *Revising Culture, Reinventing Peace: The Influence of Edward W. Said* (ed. Naseer Hasan Aruri and Muhammed A. Shuraydi; New York: Olive Branch Press, 2001), pp. 38-72.

Ellul, Jacques, *Index des communications et mémoires publiés par l'Institut d'Egypte (1859–1952)* (Cairo: IFAO, 1952).

Elzea, Betty, *Frederick Sandys 1829–1904: A Catalogue Raisonné* (Woodbridge, Suffolk: Antique Collectors' Club, 2001).

Elzea, Rowland, *The Samuel and Mary Bancroft Jr. and Related Pre-Raphaelite Collections* (Wilmington, DE: Delaware Art Museum, 1978).

Engel, Gisela, Friederike Hassauer, Brita Rand and Heide Wunder (eds.), *Geschlechterstreit am Beginn der europäischen Moderne: Die Querelle des Femmes* (Kulturwissenschaftliche Genderstudien, 6; Königstein im Taunus: Ulrike Helmer, 2004).

Enzensberger, Hans Magnus, *Die Tochter der Luft: Ein Schauspiel nach dem Spanischen des Calderón de la Barca* (Frankfurt a.M.: Suhrkamp, 1992).

Erasmus, Desiderius, 'Apology against the Dialogue of Latomus', in *Collected Works of Erasmus*. LXXI. *Controversies* (ed. J.K. Sowards; trans. Martin Lowry; Toronto: University of Toronto Press, 1993), pp. 31-84.

Ergil, Tülay, *Museums of Istanbul / Istanbul Müzerleri* (Istanbul: Istanbul Egitim ve Kültür Vakfi, 1993).

Erickson, Carolly *To the Scaffold: The Life of Marie Antoinette* (New York: William Morrow & Co., 1991).

Erim, Kenan T., *Aphrodisias, City of Venus Aphrodite* (London: Muler, Blond & White).

Erpenius, Thomas, *Grammatica Arabica, quinque libris methodicè explicata* (Leiden: In Officina Raphelengiana, 1613).

Eshel, H., 'The Historical Background of the Establishment of Temples to the God of Israel at Bethel and Samaria Following the Destruction of the First Temple', MA thesis, Faculty of Humanities, Jerusalem: The Hebrew University, 1989.

Esposito, Donato, 'From Ancient Egypt to Victorian London: The Impact of Ancient Egyptian Furniture on British Art and Design 1850–1900', *Decorative Arts Society Journal* 27 (2003), pp. 80-94.

Esteves, Carmen C., *The Dramatic Portrayal of Semiramis in Virues, Calderon and Voltaire* (PhD dissertation, The City University of New York, 1985; Ann Arbor, MI: UMI).

Faber, Paul, Anneke Groeneveld and Hein Reedijk, *Beelden van de Oriënt: Fotografie en toerisme, 1860–1900 = Images of the Orient: Photography and Tourism, 1860–1900* (Amsterdam: Fragment in samenwerking met Museum voor Volkenkunde Rotterdam, 1986).

Fabian, Johannes, 'Presence and Representation: The Other and Anthropological Writing', *Critical Inquiry* 16 (1990), pp. 753-72.

—*Time and the Other: How Anthropology Makes its Object* (New York: Columbia University Press, 1983).

Fahmi, Zaki, *Safwat al-asr fi tarikh wa rusum mashahir rijal fi Misr* (2 vols.; Cairo: Matbaʿat al-Iʿtimad, 1926).

Fales, Frederick Mario (ed.), *Assyrian Royal Inscriptions: New Horizons in Literary, Ideological, and Historical Analysis. Papers of a Symposium held in Cetona (Siena), June 26-28, 1980* (Orientis antiqui collectio, 17; Rome: Istituto per l'Oriente, 1981).

Fales, Frederick Mario, and Bernard J. Hickey (eds.), *Austen Henry Layard tra l'Oriente e Venezia: Symposium internazionale, Venezia, 26-28 ottobre 1983* (Roma: 'L'Erma' di Bretschneider, 1987).

Farber, Walter, 'The City Wall of Babylon—a Belt Cord?', *N.A.B.U.* 1991, no. 72.

Farnie, D.A., *East and West of Suez, 1854–1956* (Oxford: Clarendon Press, 1969).

Farwell, Beatrice, 'Sources for Delacroix's *Death of Sardanapalus*', *ArtB* 40 (1958), pp. 66-71.

Fay, C.R., *Palace of Industry: A Study of the Great Exhibition and its Fruits* (Cambridge: Cambridge University Press, 1951).

Feaver, William, *The Art of John Martin* (Oxford: Clarendon Press, 1975).

Feige, Michael, 'ʾArkeʾologyah, ʾantropologyah, wa-ʿirot ha-pitoḥ: ʿiṣovu šel ha-maqom ha-Yisraʾeli', *Zion* (1998), pp. 441-59.

Feldman, Marian, 'Review of Zainab Bahrani, *The Graven Image: Representation in Babylonia and Assyria*', *JAOS* 124 (2004), pp. 599-601.

Fergusson, Francis, 'The Theater of Paul Valéry', in Paul Valéry, *The Collected Works of Paul Valéry*. III. *Plays* (ed. Jackson Mathews; Bollingen Series, 45; New York: Pantheon Books, 1960), pp. vii-xix.

Fergusson, James, *The Palaces of Nineveh and Persepolis Restored* (London: John Murray, 1851).

Ferrari, Roberto C., 'The Unexplored Correspondence of Simeon Solomon', *The Journal of Pre-Raphaelite Studies* N.S. 12 (Spring 2003), pp. 23-34.

Field, James A., Jr, *America and the Mediterranean World, 1776–1882* (Princeton, NJ: Princeton University Press, 1969).

Findley, Carter, 'Ottoman Occidentalist', *American Historical Review* 103 (1998), pp. 15-49.

Findling, John E., and Kimberly D. Pelle (eds.), *Historical Dictionary of World's Fairs and Expositions, 1851–1988* (New York: Greenwood Press, 1990).

Finet, André, 'Yahvé au royaume de Mari', in *Circulation des monnaies, des marchandises et des biens* (ed. Rika Gyselen; Res orientales, 5; Bures-sur-Yvette: Groupe pour l'étude de la civilisation du moyen-orient, 1993), pp. 15-22.

Finkelstein, Israel and Neil Asher Silberman, *The Bible Unearthed: Archaeology's New Vision of Ancient Israel and the Origin of its Sacred Texts* (New York: Free Press, 2001).

Finnie, David H., *Pioneeers East: The Early American Experience in the Middle East* (Cambridge, MA: Harvard University Press, 1967).

Flandin, Eugène, 'Voyage archéologique à Ninive: L'architecture assyrienne', *Revue des deux mondes* 10/2 (1845), pp. 642-60.

—'Voyage archéologique à Ninive: La sculpture assyrienne et les bas-reliefs de Khorsabad', *Revue des deux mondes* 10/2 (1845), pp. 768-85.

Fleming, Daniel E., *Democracy's Ancient Ancestors: Mari and Early Collective Governance* (Cambridge and New York: Cambridge University Press, 2004).

—'Mari and the Possibility of Biblical Memory', *RA* 92 (1998), pp. 41-78.

Fletcher, James Phillips, *Notes from Nineveh, and Travels in Mesopotamia, Assyria and Syria* (2 vols.; London: Henry Colburn, 1850).

Fliedner, Stephan, *Ali Mubarak und seine Hitat: Kommentierte Übersetzung der Autobiographie und Werkbesprechung* (Islamkundliche Untersuchungen, 140; Berlin: K. Schwarz, 1990).

Fontaine, M.-M., 'Labé, Louise (avant 1524–1566)', in *Dictionnaire des littératures de langue française* (4 vols.; ed. Jean-Pierre de Beaumarchais, Daniel Couty and Alain Rey; Paris: Bordas, rev. edn, 1994), pp. 1235-36.

Fontaine, Nicolas, *The History of the Old and New Testament, Extracted out of Sacred Scripture and Writings of the Fathers: To Which Are Added the Lives, Travels and Sufferings of the Apostles; with a Large and Exact* Historical Chronology *of All the Affairs and Actions Related in the Bible* (London: S. & J. Sprint, C. Brome, J. Nicholson, J. Pero & Benj. Tooke, 2nd corrected edn, 1699).

Fontan, Elisabeth, 'Introduction', in Fontan and Chevalier (eds.), *De Khorsabad à Paris*, pp. 12-15.

Fontan, Elisabeth, and Nicole Chevalier (eds.), *De Khorsabad à Paris: La découverte des Assyriens* (Louvre, Département des Antiquités Orientales: Notes et documents des musées de France, 26; Paris: Réunion des Musées nationaux, 1994).

Foster, Benjamin R., 'Barton, George Aaron (12 Nov. 1859–28 June 1942)', in *ANB*, II, pp. 291-92.

—'Clay, Albert Tobias (4 Dec. 1866–14 Sept. 1925)', in *ANB*, V, pp. 17-18.

—'Haupt, Paul (25 Nov. 1858–15 Dec. 1926)', in *ANB*, X, pp. 320-21.

—'Salisbury, Edward Elbridge (6 Apr. 1814–5 Feb. 1901)', in *ANB*, XIX, pp. 206-208.

—'Torrey, Charles Cutler (20 Dec. 1863–12 Nov. 1956)', in *ANB*, XIX, pp. 756-57.

—'Yale and the Study of Near Eastern Languages in America, 1770–1839', in *The United States and the Middle East: Cultural Encounters* (ed. Abbas Amanat and Magnes T. Bernhardsson; YCIAS Paper Series; New Haven: Yale Center for International and Area Studies, 2002), pp. 6-16.

Foster, Karen Polinger, 'The Hanging Gardens of Nineveh', *Iraq* 66 (2004), pp. 207-20.

Fox, Aley, *Art Pictures from the Old Testament: Sunday Reading for the Young: A Series of Ninety Illustrations from Original Drawings* (London: Society for Promoting Christian Knowledge, 1894).

Fox, Nili Sacher, *In the Service of the King: Officialdom in Ancient Israel and Judah* (MHUC, 23; Cincinnati: Hebrew Union College Press, 2000), pp. 9-42.

Frahm, Eckart, *Einleitung in die Sanherib-Inschriften* (AfOB, 26; Vienna: Institut für Orientalistik der Universität Wien, 1997), pp. 21-28.

—'Images of Ashurbanipal in Later Tradition', in *Hayim and Miriam Tadmor Festschrift Volume* (ed. Israel Eph'al, Amnon Ben-Tor, Peter Machinist; Eretz Israel, 27; Jerusalem: Israel Exploration Society, 2003), pp. 37*-48*.

—'Wie "christlich" war die assyrische Religion?', *WdO* 31 (2000–2001), pp. 31-45.

—'Zwischen Dichtung und Wahrheit: Assur und Assyrien in den Augen der Nachwelt', in *Wiedererstehendes Assur: 100 Jahre deutsche Ausgrabungen in Assyrien* (ed. Joachim Marzahn and Beate Salje; Mainz am Rhein: Philipp von Zabern, 2003), pp. 19-28.

Fraisse, Geneviève, 'A Philosophical History of Sexual Difference', in Fraisse and Perrot (eds.), *A History of Women in the West*, IV, pp. 48-79.

Fraisse, Geneviève, and Michelle Perrot (eds.), *A History of Women in the West*, IV: *Emerging Feminism from Revolution to World War* (Cambridge, MA and London: The Belknap Press of Harvard University Press, 1993).

Frame, Grant, *Babylonia 689–627 B.C.: A Political History* (PIHANS, 69; Leiden: Nederlands Instituut voor het Nabije Oosten, 1992).

Frandsen, Paul John, 'Aida and Edward Said: Attitudes and Images of Ancient Egypt and Egyptology', in *Assyria and Beyond: Studies Presented to Mogens Trolle Larsen* (ed. Jan Gerrit Dercksen; NINOL, 100; Leiden: Nederlands Instituut voor het Nabije Oosten, 2004), pp. 205-27.

Frank, Carl, *Lamastu, Pazuzu und andere Dämonen: Ein Beitrag zur babylonisch-assyrischen Dämonologie* (MAOG, 14/2; Leipzig: Otto Harrassowitz, 1941).

Fraser, Antonia, *The Warrior Queens: Boadicea's Chariot* (London: George Weidenfeld & Nicholson, 1988) [paperback editions by Mandarin (1993), Arrow Books (1997), and Phoenix Press (2003)].

Freedman, David Noel, 'W.F. Albright as an Historian', in *The Scholarship of William Foxwell Albright: An Appraisal* (ed. Gus W. Van Beek; HSS, 33; Atlanta, GA: Scholars Press, 1989), pp. 33-43.

French, John C., *History of the University Founded by Johns Hopkins* (Baltimore, MD: The Johns Hopkins University Press, 1946).

Freud, Sigmund, *Vorlesungen zur Einführung in die Psychoanalyse*, in *Gesammelte Werke* (18 vols.; ed. Anna Freud *et al.*; London: Imago Publishing Co., 1940 [1917]).

Fried, Lisbeth S., ' "You Shall Appoint Judges": Ezra's Mission and the Rescript of Artaxerxes', in *Persia and Torah: The Theory of Imperial Authorization of the Pentateuch* (ed. James W. Watts; SBLSS, 17; Atlanta, GA: Society of Biblical Literature, 2001), pp. 63-89.

Friedman, Jerome, *The Most Ancient Testimony: Sixteenth-Century Christian-Hebraica in the Age of Renaissance Nostalgia* (Athens, OH: Ohio University Press, 1983).

Friedrich, Otto, *Olympia: Paris in the Age of Manet* (New York: HarperCollins, 1992).

Fuchs, Andreas, *Die Inschriften Sargons II. aus Khorsabad* (Göttingen: Cuvillier Verlag, 1994).

—'Review of Walter Mayer, *Politik und Kriegskunst der Assyrer*', *AfO* 44–45 (1997–98), pp. 409-17.

Gadd, C.J., *The Fall of Nineveh: The Newly Discovered Babylonian Chronicles, No. 21,901, in the British Museum* (London: British Museum, 1923).

—*The Stones of Assyria: The Surviving Remains of Assyrian Sculpture, their Recovery, and their Original Positions* (London: Chatto & Windus, 1936).

Gaffarel, Jacques, *Unheard-of Curiosities Concerning the Talismanical Sculpture of the Persians; the Horoscope of the Patriarkes; and the Reading of the Stars. Written in French by James Gaffarel. And Englished by Edmund Chilmead* (London: Printed by G.D. for H. Moseley, 1650 [Paris 1646]).

Gage, John, *Goethe on Art* (London and Berkeley: Scolar Press, 1980).

Gajda, Oliver, *Katharina II. von Russland im Diskurs der Sexualität: Mittelbare Einflüsse narrativer Fiktion auf Geschichtsschreibung* (Akademische Abhandlungen zur Geschichte; Berlin: Verlag für Wissenschaft und Forschung, 2002).

Gamboni, Dario, 'Histoire de l'art et "reception": Remarques sur l'état d'une problematique', *Histoire de l'art* 35-36 (October 1996), pp. 9-14.

Gandhi, Leela, *Postcolonial Theory: A Critical Introduction* (New York: Columbia University Press, 1998).

Garnot, Jean Sainte Fare, *Mélanges Mariette* (IFAO, Bibliothèque d'études, 32; Cairo: Institut français d'archéologie orientale, 1961).

Garrard, Mary D., *Artemisia Gentileschi: The Image of the Female Hero in Italian Baroque Art* (Princeton, NJ: Princeton University Press, 1989).

Gasche, H., *La Babylonie au 17ᵉ siècle avant notre ère: Approche archéologique, problèmes et perspectives* (Mesopotamian History and Environment Memoirs, 1; Ghent: University of Ghent, 1989).

Gay, Peter, *The Bourgeois Experience: Victoria to Freud*. I. *The Education of the Senses* (New York and Oxford: Oxford University Press, 1984).

—*The Bourgeois Experience: Victoria to Freud*, II: *The Tender Passion* (New York and Oxford: Oxford University Press, 1986).

—*The Bourgeois Experience: Victoria to Freud*, III: *The Cultivation of Hatred* (New York and London: W.W. Norton & Co., 1993).

Gelb, I.J., 'Mari', *AJSLL* 52 (1935), pp. 43-44.

—'The Name of Babylon', in *'I Studied Inscriptions from Before the Flood': Ancient Near Eastern, Literary, and Linguistic Approaches to Genesis 1–11* (ed. Richard S. Hess and David Toshio Tsumura; Sources for Biblical and Theological Study, 4; Winona Lake, IN: Eisenbrauns, 1994), pp. 266-69.

—'An Old Babylonian List of Amorites', *JAOS* 88 (1968), pp. 39-46.

Geneva Bible, The: A Facsimile of the 1560 Edition (Madison, WI: University of Wisconsin Press, 1969).

George, Andrew R., *Babylonian Topographical Texts* (OLA, 40; Leuven: Peeters, 1992).

—'The Bricks of E-sagil', *Iraq* 57 (1995), pp. 173-97.

—'The City Wall of Babylon – a Belt Cord', *N.A.B.U.* 1991, no. 101.

Gera, Deborah Levine, *Warrior Women: The Anonymous* Tractatus de mulieribus (Mnemosyne, bibliotheca classica batava. Supplementum, 162; Leiden: E.J. Brill, 1997).

Gesenius, Wilhelm, *Geschichte der hebräischen Sprache und Schrift: Eine philologisch-historisch Einleitung in die Sprachlehren und Wörterbücher der hebräischen Sprache* (Leipzig: Friedrich Christian Wilhelm Vogel, 1815).

Girardot, Norman R., 'Max Müller's Sacred Books and the Nineteenth-Century Production of the Comparative Science of Religions', *HR* 41 (2002), pp. 213-50.

Glazer, Nathan, *American Judaism* (Chicago: University of Chicago Press, 2nd edn, 1972).

Gleeson White, *English Illustration: 'The Sixties' 1855–70* (London: A. Constable & Co., 1897).

Gobineau, Arthur, *Oeuvres* (3 vols.; ed. Jean Gaulmier and Jean Boissel; Bibliothèque de la Pléiade, 306; Paris: Gallimard, 1983).

Goby, J.-E., 'Travaux de premier Institut d'Egypte (1798–1801)', *Bulletin de la Société française d'égyptologie* 66 (March 1973), p. 36.

Goldman, Paul, 'The Dalziel Brothers and the British Museum', *The Book Collector* 45 (1996), pp. 341-50.

—*Victorian Illustrated Books 1850–1870: The Heyday of Wood-Engraving* (London: British Museum Press, 1994).

Goldstein, Jonathan A., 'The Historical Setting of the Uruk Prophecy', *JNES* 47 (1988), pp. 43-46.

Gonick, Larry R., *Cartoon History of the Universe, Book 1* (San Francisco: Rip Off Press, 1978).

Goode, G. Brown, 'The Collection of Oriental Antiquities, and The Collection of Religious Ceremonial Objects', in *Annual Report of the Board of Regents of the Smithsonian Institution, Showing the Operations, Expenditures, and Condition of the Institution for the Year Ending June 30, 1893* (1895), pp. 135-37.

—'Cotton States and International Exposition at Atlanta, Ga.', in *Annual Report of the Board of Regents of the Smithsonian Institution, Showing the Operations, Expenditures, and Condition of the Institution for the Year Ending June 30, 1895* (1897), p. 47-48.

—*The Exhibit of the Smithsonian Institution at the Cotton States Exposition, Atlanta, 1895* (Washington, DC: Smithsonian Institution, 1895).

Gordis, Robert, 'Democratic Origins in Ancient Israel: The Biblical *'ēdāh*', in *Alexander Marx: Jubilee Volume on the Occasion of his Seventieth Birthday* (New York: Jewish Theological Seminary of America, 1950), pp. 369-88.

Gordon, David C., *Images of the West: Third World Perspectives* (Totowa, NJ: Rowman & Littlefield, 1989).

Gordon, Robert P., 'The Legacy of Lowth: Robert Lowth and the Book of Isaiah in Particular', in *Biblical Hebrew, Biblical Texts: Essays in Memory of Michael P. Weitzman* (ed. Ada Rapoport-Albert and Gillian Greenberg; JSOTSup, 333; Hebrew Bible and its Versions, 2; Sheffield: Sheffield Academic Press, 2001), pp. 57-76.

Gost, Roswitha, *Der Harem* (Köln: DuMont Buchverlag, 1993).

Gottwald, Norman K., *All the Kingdoms of the Earth: Israelite Prophecy and International Relations in the Ancient Near East* (New York: Harper & Row, 1964).

Grabar, Oleg, in *Luminaries, Princeton Faculty Remembered* (ed. Patricia H. Marks; Princeton, NJ: Association of Princeton Alumni, 1996), pp. 119-24.

Grabbe, Lester L., *Ezra–Nehemiah* (Old Testament Readings; London: Routledge, 1998).

—*A History of the Jews and Judaism in the Second Temple Period*. I. *Yehud: A History of the Persian Province of Judah* (LSTS, 47; London and New York: T. & T. Clark International, 2004), pp. 331-43.

— *Judaism from Cyrus to Hadrian*. I. *Persian and Greek Periods*; II: *The Roman Period* (Minneapolis, MN: Fortress Press, 1992).

—'Review of E. Yamauchi, *Persia and the Bible*', *JSJ* 22 (1991), pp. 295-98.

—'What Was Ezra's Mission?', in *Second Temple Studies, 2: Temple Community in the Persian Period* (ed. Tamara C. Eskenazi and Kent H. Richards; JSOTSup, 175; Sheffield: Sheffield Academic Press, 1994), pp. 286-99.

Gran, Peter, *Islamic Roots of Capitalism: Egypt 1760–1840* (Modern Middle East Series, 4; Austin: University of Texas Press, 1979).

Gran-Aymerich, Eve, 'Jane Dieulafoy, 1851–1916', in *Breaking Ground: Pioneering Women Archaeologists* (ed. Getzel M. Cohen and Martha Sharp Joukowsky; Ann Arbor, MI: University of Michigan Press, 2004), pp. 34-67.

Grant, Asahel, *The Nestorians, or the Lost Tribes: Containing Evidence of their Identity, an*

Account of their Manners, Customs, and Ceremonies, together with Sketches of Travel in Ancient Assyria, Armenia, Media, and Mesopotamia and Illustrations of Scripture Prophecy (London: John Murray, 2nd edn, 1843 [New York, 1841]).

Grayson, A. Kirk, *Assyrian and Babylonian Chronicles* (Texts from Cuneiform Sources, 5; Locust Valley, NY: J.J. Augustin, 1975).

—*Assyrian Royal Inscriptions*. I. *From the Beginning to Ashur-Resha-Ishi I* (RANE; Wiesbaden: Otto Harrassowitz, 1972).

—'The Babylonian Origin of Apocalyptic Literature', *Atti dell'Istituto Veneto di Scienze, Lettere ed Arti* 146 (1989–90), pp. 203-18.

—*Royal Inscriptions of Mesopotamia, Assyrian Periods* (3 vols.; Toronto: University of Toronto Press, 1987–96).

Greenhalgh, Paul, *Ephemeral Vistas: The Expositions universelles, Great Exhibitions, and World's Fairs, 1851–1939* (Studies in Imperialism; Manchester: Manchester University Press, 1988).

Green-Mercado, Marya T., 'Morisco Jofores: Apocalyptic Prophecies and the Ottoman–Habsburg Rivalry in Sixteenth-Century Spain', paper read at the 2004 Middle East History and Theory Conference, Chicago.

Greenspahn, Frederick E., 'Introduction', in *Essential Papers on Israel and the Ancient Near East* (ed. F.E. Greenspahn; New York and London: New York University, 1991), pp. 1-14.

—'A Mesopotamian Proverb and its Biblical Reverberations', *JAOS* 114 (1994), pp. 33-38.

Gregory, Derek, *Geographical Imaginations* (Oxford: Blackwell, 1994).

Gressmann, Hugo (ed.), *Altorientalische Texte und Bilder zum Alten Testamente* (Tübingen: J.C.B. Mohr [Paul Siebeck], 1909).

—(ed.), *Altorientalische Texte und Bilder zum Alten Testament* (Berlin and Leipzig: W. de Gruyter, 2. völlig neugestaltete und stark vermehrte Auflage, 1926–1927).

Grice, Ettalene Mears, *Chronology of the Larsa Dynasty* (YOS, Researches, 4/1; New Haven: Yale University Press, 1919).

—'Review of Clay, *Empire of the Amorites*', *Yale Divinity News* 17/4 (May, 1921), p. 3.

—'Review of W. Lansdell Wardle, *Israel and Babylon*', *AJA* 30 (1926), pp. 470-71.

—'Tablets from Ur and Larsa, Dated in the Larsa Dynasty', PhD dissertation, published as *Records from Ur and Larsa Dated in the Larsa Dynasty* (YOS, Babylonian Texts, 5; New Haven: Yale University Press, 1919).

—'Yale Babylonian Collection', *Little Blue Bulletin*, May, 1922, p. 8.

Griffin, Jasper, 'Propertius and Antony', *Journal of Roman Studies* 67 (1977), pp. 17-26.

Grigsby, Darcy Grimaldo, 'Rumor, Contagion and Colonization in Gros's *Plague-Stricken of Jaffa* (1804)', *Representations* 51 (1995), pp. 1-46.

Groot, Joanna de, ' "Sex" and "Race": The Construction of Language and Image in the Nineteenth Century', in *Sexuality and Subordination: Interdisciplinary Studies of Gender in the Nineteenth Century* (ed. Susan Mendus and Jane Rendall; London and New York: Routledge, 1989), pp. 89-128.

Grossman, Grace Cohen and Richard E. Ahlborn, *Judaica at the Smithsonian: Cultural Politics as Cultural Model* (Smithsonian Studies in History and Technology, 52; Washington, DC: Smithsonian Institution Press, 1997).

Gruenwald, Ithamar, ' "How Much Qabbalah in Ancient Assyria?"—Methodological Reflections on the Study of a Cross-Cultural Phenomenon', in *Assyria 1995: Proceedings of the 10th Anniversary Symposium of the Neo-Assyrian Text Corpus Project, Helsinki, September 7-11, 1995* (ed. S. Parpola and R.M. Whiting; Helsinki: The Neo-Assyrian Text Corpus Project, 1997), pp. 115-27.

Guichard, Michaël, 'Les aspects religieux de la guerre à Mari', *RA* 93 (1999), pp. 27-48.

Gunneweg, Antonius H.J., *Esra* (KAT, 19.1; Gütersloh: Gütersloher Verlagshaus Mohn, 1985).

Gunter, Ann C. (ed.), *The Construction of the Ancient Near East* (Culture & History, 11; Copenhagen: Akademisk Forlag, 1992).

—'Introduction', in Gunter (ed.), *Construction of the Ancient Near East*, pp. 7-11.

Gurney, O.R., 'The Sultantepe Tablets (Continued) VII: The Myth of Nergal and Ereshkigal', *AnSt* 10 (1960), pp. 105-31.

Haari-Oberg, Ilse, *Die Wirkungsgeschichte der Trierer Gründungssage vom 10. bis 15. Jahrhundert* (Europäische Hochschulschriften. Reihe III, Geschichte und ihre Hilfswissenschaften, 607; Bern: Europäischer Verlag der Wissenschaften, 1994).

Haas, Volkert, *Babylonischer Liebesgarten: Erotik und Sexualität im Alten Orient* (München: C.H. Beck, 1999).

Habachi, Labib, *The Obelisks of Egypt: Skyscrapers of the Past* (Cairo: American University in Cairo Press, 1984).

Habib, Tawfiq, 'Dars al-athar fi al-Jamia al-Misriyya', *Al-Muqtataf* 72 (1928), pp. 438-39.

—'Tarikh al-kashf an al-athar al-misriyya wa amal al-marhum Ahmad Kamal Basha', *Al-Hilal* 32 (1 November 1923), pp. 135-41.

Hackett, JoAnn, 'Can a Sexist Model Liberate Us? Ancient Near Eastern "Fertility" Goddesses', *Journal of Feminist Studies in Religion* 5 (1989), pp. 65-76.

Hadley, James, 'The Book of Nabataean Agriculture', *The New Englander* 21 (1862), pp. 505-36, available online at http://cdl.library.cornell.edu/moa/browse.journals/nwng.

Halbreich, Harry, *Arthur Honegger* (trans. Roger Nichols; Portland, OR: Amadeus Press, 1999).

—*L'oeuvre d'Arthur Honegger: Chronologie, catalogue raisonné, analyses, discographie* (Paris: Honoré Champion, 1994).

Hallo, William W., 'Biblical History in its Near Eastern Setting: The Contextual Approach', in *Scripture in Context: Essays on the Comparative Method* (ed. Carl D. Evans, W.W. Hallo and John B. White; Pittsburgh Theological Monograph Series, 34; Pittsburgh: Pickwick Press, 1980), pp. 1-26.

—*The Book of the People* (Brown Judaic Studies, 225; Atlanta, GA: Scholars Press, 1991), pp. 23-34.

—'Compare and Contrast: The Contextual Approach to Biblical Literature', in *The Bible in the Light of Cuneiform Literature: Scripture in Context III* (ed. W.W. Hallo, Bruce William Jones, and Gerald L. Mattingly; Ancient Near Eastern Texts and Studies, 8; Lewiston: Edwin Mellen Press, 1990), pp. 1-30.

—'Introduction: Ancient Near Eastern Texts and their Relevance for Biblical Exegesis', in *COS*, I, pp. xxiii-xxviii.

—'Introduction: The Bible and the Monuments', in *COS*, II, pp. xxi-xxvi.

—'Sumer and the Bible', in *COS*, III, pp. xlix-liv.

Hallo, William W., and K. Lawson Younger, Jr (eds.), *The Context of Scripture*. I. *Canonical Compositions from the Biblical World*; II. *Monumental Compositions from the Biblical World*; III. *Archival Documents from the Biblical World* (Leiden: E.J. Brill, 1997–2002).

Hamilakis, Yannis, and Eleana Yalouri, 'Antiquities as Symbolic Capital in Modern Greek Society', *Antiquity* 70 (1996), pp. 117-29.

Hamilton, Mark W., 'The Past as Destiny: Historical Visions in Samʾal and Judah under Assyrian Hegemony', *HTR* 91 (1998), pp. 215-50.

Hammer-Tugendhat, Daniela, 'Aspekte der subversiven Funktion von Kunst', in *Weiblichkeit in geschichtlicher Perspektive: Fallstudien und Reflexionen zu Grundproblemen der historischen Frauenforschung* (ed. Ursula A.J. Becher and Jöm Rüsen; Suhrkamp Taschenbuch Wissenschaft, 725; Frankfurt a.M.: Suhrkamp, 1988), pp. 150-73.

Handlin, Oscar, and Mary F. Handlin, *The Wealth of the American People: A History of American Affluence* (New York: McGraw–Hill, 1975).

Handy, Lowell K., *Among the Host of Heaven: The Syro-Palestinian Pantheon as Bureaucracy* (Winona Lake, IN: Eisenbrauns, 1994).

—'Josiah after the Chronicler', *PEGLAMBS* 14 (1994), pp. 95-103.

—'The Rise and Fall of the *sogennant* Josianic Empire', *PEGLAMBS* 21 (2001), pp. 69-79.

Hanisch, Ludmila, and Hanne Schönig, 'Ausgegrenzte Kompetenz: Porträts vertriebener Orientalisten und Orientalistinnen 1933–1945', *Orientwissenschaftliche Hefte* 1 (2001), pp. 15-141.

Harbsmeier, Michael, 'Before Decipherment: Persepolitan Hypotheses in the Late Eighteenth Century', in Gunter (ed.), *Construction of the Ancient Near East*, pp. 23-59.

Harlé, Diane Sarofim, 'The Unknown Nestor L'Hôte', in *Travellers in Egypt* (ed. Paul Starkey and Janet Starkey; London: I.B. Tauris, 1998), pp. 121-29.

Harley, John B., 'Historical Geography and the Cartographic Illusion', *Journal of Historical Geography* 15 (1989), pp. 80-91.

—'Maps, Knowledge and Power', in *The Iconography of Landscape: Essays on the Symbolic Representation, Design and Use of Past Environments* (ed. Denis Cosgrove and Stephen Daniels; Cambridge: Cambridge University Press, 1988), pp. 277-312.

Harper, Robert Francis (ed.), *Assyrian and Babylonian Literature: Selected Translations. With a Critical Introduction* (The World's Great Books, Aldine edition; New York: D. Appleton & Company, 1901).

Harrast, Tracy L., *My Baby and Me Story Bible* (Grand Rapids, MI: Zonderkidz, 1995).

Harrelson, Sam B., *Asia has Claims upon New England: Assyrian Reliefs at Yale* (New Haven: Yale University Art Gallery, 2006).

Harris, J.R., A.S. Lewis and F.C. Conybeare, 'The Story of Aḥiḳar', in *The Apocrypha and Pseudepigrapha of the Old Testament in English: With Introductions and Critical and Explanatory Notes to the Several Books* (2 vols.; ed. R.H. Charles; Oxford: At the Clarendon Press, 1913), II, pp. 715-84.

Hartmann, Karl, *Atlas-Tafel-Werk zu Bibel und Kirchengeschichte: Altes Testament und Geschichte des Judentums bis Jesus Christus* (5 vols.; Stuttgart: Quell Verlag, 1979).

Hartog, François, *The Mirror of Herodotus: The Representation of the Other in the Writing of History* (trans. Janet Lloyd; New Historicism, 5; Berkeley: University of California Press, 1988).

Hasan, Muhammad Abd al-Ghani, and Abd al-Aziz al-Disuqi, *Rawdat al-madaris: Nashatuha wa ittijahatuha al-adabiyya wa al-ilmiyya dirasah naqdiyya tahliliyya* (Cairo: Al-Hay'a al-Misriyya al-Amma lil-Kitab, 1975).

Haskell, Francis, *Rediscoveries in Art: Some Aspects of Taste, Fashion and Collecting in England and France* (Wrightsman Lectures, 7; London: Phaidon Press, 1976).

Hastings, James, *A Dictionary of the Bible Dealing with its Language, Literature, and Contents Including the Biblical Theology* (4 vols.; ed. James Hastings; New York: Charles Scribner's Sons/Edinburgh: T. & T. Clark, 1899).

Haupt, Paul, 'Excavations in Assyria and Babylonia', in *Report of the U.S. National Museum, under the Direction of the Smithsonian Institution, for the Year Ending June 30, 1888* ([Washington, DC]: Smithsonian Institution, 1890), pp. 95-104.

Hauser, Stefan R., 'German Research on the Ancient Near East and its Relation to Political and Economic Interests from *Kaiserreich* to World War II', *Princeton Papers, Interdisciplinary Journal of Middle Eastern Studies* 10–11 (2004), pp. 155-80.

—'History, Races, and Orientalism: Eduard Meyer, the Organization of Oriental Research, and Ernst Herzfeld's Intellectual Heritage', in *Ernst Herzfeld and the Development of Near Eastern Studies, 1900–1950* (ed. Ann Clyburn Gunter and S.R. Hauser; Leiden: E.J. Brill, 2005), pp. 505-59.

—'Orientalismus', in *Der neue Pauly,* XV, pp. 1239-43.

Hawkins, Hugh, *Pioneer: A History of the Johns Hopkins University, 1874–1889* (Ithaca, NY: Cornell University Press, 1960).

Hayes, John H., and J. Maxwell Miller (eds.), *Israelite and Judean History* (Philadelphia: Westminster Press, 1977).

Hazlitt, Gooden and Fox, *John Martin 1789–1854* (London, 1975: exhibition catalogue).

Hehn, Johannes, *Die biblische und die babylonische Gottesidee: Die israelitische Gottesauffassung im Licht der altorientalischen Religionsgeschichte* (Leipzig: J.C. Hinrichs'sche Buchhandlung, 1913).

Heilmann, Regina, *Paradigma Babylon: Rezeption und Visualisierung des Alten Orients im Spielfilm: Ein Beitrag der vorderasiatischen Archäologie zur Orientalismus-Forschung* (Orient-Archäologie; Deutsches Archäologisches Institut [forthcoming]).

—' "Those Old Assyrian Legends": Zur Rezeption des Alten Orients im wiederentdeckten Kurzfilm *La Regina di Ninive* (Italien 1991)', in *Nineveh: Papers of the XLIXe Rencontre assyriologique internationale, London, 7-11 July 2003* (2 vols.; ed. D. Collon and A.R. George; London: British School of Archaeology in Iraq, 2005), I, pp. 257-64.

Heller, Wendy, *Emblems of Eloquence: Opera and Women's Voices in Seventeenth-Century Venice* (Berkeley: University of California Press, 2003).

Hellige Skrift, Den, Indeholdende Det Gamle og Det Nye Testamentes Kanoniske Bøger: Tilligmed Det Gamle Testamentes Apokryphiske Bøger (Philadelphia, 1891).

Herbelot de Molainville, Barthélemy d', *Bibliothèque orientale, ou Dictionaire universel, contenant généralement tout ce qui regarde la connoissance des peuples de l'Orient. Leurs histoires et traditions véritables ou fabuleuses. Leurs religions, sectes et politique. Leurs gouvernement, loix, coûtumes, moeurs, guerres, & les révolutions de leurs empires. Leurs sciences, et leurs arts... Les vies et actions remarquables de tous leurs saints, docteurs, philosophes, historiens, poëtes, capitaines, & de tous ceux qui se sont rendus illustres parmi eux, par leur vertu, ou par leur savoir. Des jugemens critiques, et des extraits de tous leurs ouvrages* (Paris: Compagnie des Libraires, 1697).

Herbordt, Suzanne, 'Neo-Assyrian Royal and Administrative Seals and their Use', in *Assyrien im Wandel der Zeiten: XXXIX*[e] *Rencontre assyriologique internationale, Heidelberg 6.-10. Juli 1992* (ed. Hartmut Waetzoldt and Harald Hauptmann; Heidelberger Studien zum Alten Orient, 6; Heidelberg: Heidelberger Orientverlag, 1997), pp. 279-83.

Herbst, Jurgen, *The German Historical School in American Scholarship: A Study in the Transfer of Culture* (Ithaca, NY: Cornell University Press, 1965).

Herrmann, Wolfgang, 'Baal', in *DDDB*², pp. 132-39.

Hess, Richard S., 'Ancient Near Eastern Studies', in *Interpreting the Old Testament. A Guide for Exegesis* (ed. Craig C. Broyles; Grand Rapids, MI: Baker Academic, 2001), pp. 201-20.

Heyworth-Dunne, James, *Introduction to the History of Education in Modern Egypt* (London: Luzac, 1968).

Hilal, Amal, 'Les premiers égyptologues égyptiens et la réforme', in Roussillon (ed.), *Entre réforme sociale et mouvement national*, p. 346.

Hinsley, Curtis M., 'Revising and Revisioning the History of Archaeology: Reflections on Region and Context', in *Tracing Archaeology's Past: The Historiography of Archaeology* (ed. Andrew L. Christenson; Publications in Archaeology [Southern Illinois

University at Carbondale. Center for Archaeological Investigations]; Carbondale, IL: Southern Illinois University Press, 1989), pp. 79-96.

—'The World as Marketplace: Commodification of the Exotic at the World's Columbian Exposition, Chicago, 1893', in *Exhibiting Cultures: The Poetics and Politics of Museum Display* (ed. Ivan Karp and Steven Lavine; Washington, DC: Smithsonian Institution Press, 1991), pp. 344-65.

Hirsch, S.A., 'Roger Bacon and Philology', in *Roger Bacon Essays* (ed. Andrew George Little; New York: Russell & Russell, 1972 [Oxford University Press, 1914]), pp. 101-51.

History and Description of the Great Exhibition of the World's Industry (4 vols.; London: Tallis, 1851).

Hitchcock, Edward, *Reminiscences of Amherst College, Historical, Scientific, Biographical and Autobiographical; Also, of Other and Wider Life Experiences* (Northampton, MA: Bridgman & Childs, 1863).

Hobey-Hamsher, C., 'Aetion', in Jane (ed.), *Dictionary of Art*, I, p. 184.

Hoerth, Alfred J., *Archaeology and the Old Testament* (Grand Rapids, MI: Baker Books, 1998).

Hoffenberg, Peter H., *An Empire on Display: English, Indian, and Australian Exhibitions from the Crystal Palace to the Great War* (Berkeley: University of California Press, 2001).

Höffken, Peter, 'Heilszeitherrschererwartung in babylonischen Raum: Überlegungen im Anschluss an W 22 307.7', *WdO* 9 (1977), pp. 57-71.

Hofmannsthal, Hugo von, *Sämtliche Werke*. VI. *Dramen 4* (ed. Hans-Georg Dewitz; Frankfurt a.M.: S. Fischer, 1995).

Hojer, Gerhard and Peter O. Krückmann, *Anton Raphael Mengs: Königin Semiramis erhält die Nachricht vom Aufstand in Babylon* (Neues Schloss Bayreuth; ed. Kulturstiftung der Länder in Verbindung mit der Bayrischen Verwaltung der staatlichen Schlösser, Gärten und Seen; Berlin and München: Kulturstiftung der Länder, Freistaat Bayern, 1995).

Hole, William Brassey, *Old Testament History* (London: Eyre & Spottiswoode, 1925).

Holliday, G.Y., 'Awakening Womanhood', in Sommer and Zwemer (eds.), *Daylight in the Harem*, pp. 117-29.

Holloway, Steven W., *Aššur is King! Aššur is King! Religion in the Exercise of Power in the Neo-Assyrian Empire* (CHANE, 10; Leiden: E.J. Brill, 2002).

—'Austin's Asiatic Antiquities: The First Cuneiform Inscriptions Published in America' [51st Rencontre assyriologique internationale conference volume, forthcoming].

—'Biblical Assyria and Other Anxieties in the British Empire', *Journal of Religion & Society* [http://moses.creighton.edu/JRS/] (2001).

—'The Case for Assyrian Religious Influence in Israel and Judah: Inference and Evidence' (PhD dissertation, University of Chicago, 1992).

—'Nineveh Sails for the New World: Assyria Envisioned in Nineteenth-Century America', *Iraq* 66 (2004), pp. 243-56.

—'The Quest for Sargon, Pul, and Tiglath-Pileser in the Nineteenth Century', in Chavalas and Younger, Jr (eds.), *Mesopotamia and the Bible*, pp. 68-87.

Holly, Michael Ann, *Past Looking: Historical Imagination and the Rhetoric of the Image* (Ithaca, NY: Cornell University Press, 1996).

Holub, Robert C., *Reception Theory: A Critical Introduction* (London and New York: Methuen, 1984).

Holy Bible, The: Containing the Old and New Testaments according to the Authorized Version with the Marginal References and the Usual Various Readings, also Notes,

Reflections, Questions, Improved Readings, Improved Divisions of Chapters, the Chronological Order, Metrical Portions Distinguished, and Various Other Advantages, without Disturbing the Usual Order of the Books, Verses, and Chapters/by The Rev. Ingram Cobbin, M.A.; illustrated with Numerous Descriptive Engravings (New York: Samuel Hueston, 1851).

Hommel, Fritz, *Der babylonische Ursprung der ägyptischen Kultur, nachgewiesen* (München: G. Franz, 1892).

Honegger, Arthur, *I am a Composer* (trans. Wilson O. Clough and Allan Arthur Willman; London: Faber & Faber, 1966).

Hopkins, A.G., 'The Victorians and Africa: A Reconsideration of the Occupation of Egypt, 1882', *Journal of African History* 27 (1986), p. 379.

Hopkins, Lisa M., 'The Dark Side of the Moon: Semiramis and Titania', unpublished manuscript based on paper 'Viragoes and Voluptuaries: Classical Precedents and Elizabeth's Iconography' delivered at the conference on *Gloriana's Rule* at the University of Oporto, June 2003.

—*Writing Renaissance Queens: Texts by and about Elizabeth I and Mary, Queen of Scots* (Newark, DE: University of Delaware Press/London: Associated University Presses, 2002).

Hoppe, Ilaria, 'Räume von und für Frauen? Die Gemächer der Maria Magdalena von Österreich in der Villa Poggio Imperiale bei Florenz', in *Frauen in der frühen Neuzeit: Lebensentwürfe in Kunst und Literatur* (ed. Anne-Marie Bonnet and Barbara Maria Schellewald; Atlas, Bonner Beiträge zur Kunstgeschichte, Neue Folge, 1; Köln: Böhlau, 2004), pp. 213-34.

Horowitz, Wayne, *Mesopotamian Cosmic Geography* (Mesopotamian Civilizations, 8; Winona Lake, IN: Eisenbrauns, 1998).

Hourani, Albert, *A History of the Arab Peoples* (Cambridge, MA: Harvard University Press, 1991).

House of Commons, 'Minutes of... the Select Committee on the National Gallery', *Parliamentary Papers 1852–53* (1853), XXXI, pp. 9050ff.

Houston, Gail T., 'Reading and Writing Victoria: The Conduct Book and Legal Constitution of Female Sovereignty', in *Remaking Queen Victoria* (ed. Margaret Homans and Adrienne Munich; Cambridge Studies in Nineteenth-Century Literature and Culture, 10; Cambridge: Cambridge University Press, 1997), pp. 159-81.

—*Royalties: The Queen and Victorian Writers* (Victorian Literature and Culture Series; Charlottesville, VA and London: University Press of Virginia, 1999).

Houtman, C., 'What Did Jacob See in his Dream at Bethel? (Some Remarks on Genesis xxviii 10-22)', *VT* 27 (1977), pp. 337-51.

Howard, D.M., Jr, 'Review of Hallo and Younger (eds.), *The Context of Scripture*', *JETS* 47 (2004), pp. 137-40.

Hueffer, Ford Madox [Ford Madox Ford], *Ford Madox Brown: A Record of his Life and Work* (London: Longmans, Green & Co., 1896).

Hulme, Peter, *Colonial Encounters: Europe and the Native Caribbean, 1492–1797* (London and New York: Methuen, 1986).

Humphreys, W. Lee, 'A Life-Style for Diaspora: A Study of the Tales of Esther and Daniel', *JBL* 92 (1973), pp. 211-23.

Hunger, Hermann, *Spätbabylonische Texte aus Uruk, Teil I* (Ausgrabungen der Deutschen Forschungsgemeinschaft in Uruk-Warka, 9; Berlin: Gebr. Mann Verlag, 1976).

Hunger, Herman and Stephen A. Kaufman, 'A New Akkadian Prophecy Text', *JAOS* 95 (1975), pp. 371-75.

Hunter, F. Robert, *Egypt under the Khedive, 1805–1879: From Household Government to Modern Bureaucracy* (Pittsburgh: University of Pittsburgh Press, 1984).

Huntington, Samuel P., 'The Clash of Civilizations?', *Foreign Affairs* 72 (1993), pp. 22-49.

—*The Clash of Civilizations and the Remaking of World Order* (New York: Simon and Schuster, 1996).

Hureaux, Alain Daguerre de and Stéphane Guégan, *l'ABCdaire de Delacroix et l'orient* (Paris: Flammarion: Institut du monde arabe, 1994).

Hurlbut, Jesse Lyman, *Hurlbut's Story of the Bible for Young and Old* (New York: Holt, Rinehart & Winston, expanded edn, 1932).

—*Manual of Biblical Geography: A Text-Book on Bible History* (Chicago: Rand McNally, 1884).

Hussain, Asaf, Robert Olson and Jamil Qureshi (eds.), *Orientalism, Islam, and Islamists* (Brattleboro, VT: Amana Books, 1984).

Hussey, Mary Inda, 'Some Sumerian-Babylonian Hymns of the Berlin Collection', *AJSLL* 23 (1906–1907), pp. 142-76.

—*Sumerian Tablets in the Harvard Semitic Museum* (2 vols.; Harvard Semitic Series, 3-4; Cambridge, MA: Harvard University Press, 1912, 1915).

—, Albrecht Götze and J.J.A. van Dijk, *Early Mesopotamian Incantations and Rituals* (YOS, 11; New Haven: Yale University Press, 1985).

Ilan, Tal, *Integrating Women into Second Temple History* (Texts and Studies in Ancient Judaism, 76; Tübingen: Mohr Siebeck, 1999).

Illuminated Bible, The, Containing the Old and New Testaments, Translated out of the Original Tongues, and with the Former Translations Diligently Compared and Revised. With Marginal Readings, References, and Chronological Dates. Also, the Apocrypha. To which are Added, a Chronological Index. An Index of the Subjects Contained in the Old And New Testaments, Tables of Weights, Coins, Measures, a List of Proper Names, a Concordance, &c. Embellished with Sixteen Hundred Historical Engravings by J.A. Adams, More than Fourteen Hundred of which are from Original Designs by J.G. Chapman (New York: Harper & Brothers, Publishers, 1843–46).

Inglis, Alison, in *Queen of Sheba: Treasures from Ancient Yemen* (ed. St John Simpson; London: British Museum Press, 2002).

International Geographical Union, Commission on History of Geographic Thought, *Geography through a Century of International Congresses* (Caen: International Geographical Union, 1972).

Itzkowitz, Norman, *Ottoman Empire and Islamic Tradition* (Chicago and London: University of Chicago Press, 1972).

Jacobs, Joseph and Lucien Wolf, *Catalogue of the Anglo-Jewish Historical Exhibition, 1887, Royal Albert Hall* (London: Office of the *Jewish Chronicle*, 1888).

Jacobsen, Thorkild, 'Primitive Democracy in Ancient Mesopotamia', *JNES* 2 (1943), pp. 159-72.

—'Searching for Sumer and Akkad', in *CANE*, IV, pp. 2743-52.

—*Toward the Image of Tammuz and Other Essays on Mesopotamian History and Culture* (ed. W.L. Moran; HSS, 21; Cambridge, MA: Harvard University Press, 1970).

—*The Treasures of Darkness: A History of Mesopotamian Religion* (New Haven and London: Yale University Press, 1976).

Jahn, Johann, 'A View of Studying Languages', in *Dissertations on the Importance and Best Method of Studying the Original Languages of the Bible by Jahn and Others, Translated from the Originals, and Accompanied with Notes* (trans. Moses Stuart; Andover: Flagg & Gould, 1821).

Jankowski, Theodora A., *Women in Power in the Early Modern Drama* (Urbana, IL: University of Illinois Press, 1992).

Jansen, Sharon L., *The Monstrous Regiment of Women: Female Rulers in Early Modern Europe* (New York: Palgrave, 2002).

Janssen, C., 'Samsu-iluna and the Hungry *Nadītums*', *Northern Akkad Project Reports* 5 (1991), pp. 3-39.

Jardin, André, *Tocqueville: A Biography* (trans. Lydia Davis and Robert Hemenway; London: Peter Halban, 1988).

Jardine, Lisa, *Still Harping on Daughters: Women and Drama in the Age of Shakespeare* (New York: Harvester Wheatsheaf, 1989).

Jastrow, Morris, 'In Memoriam: William Hayes Ward (1835–1916)', *JAOS* 36 (1916), pp. 233-41.

Jean, Charles-François, *La littérature des babyloniens et des assyriens* (Paris: Libraire orientaliste Paul Geuthner, 1924).

Jeansonne, Sharon Pace, *The Old Greek Translation of Daniel 7–12* (CBQM, 19; Washington, DC: Catholic Biblical Association of America, 1988).

Jefferson, Thomas and Cyrus Adler (ed.), *The Life and Morals of Jesus of Nazareth, Extracted Textually from the Gospels in Greek, Latin, French, and English* (Washington, DC: Government Printing Office, 1904).

Jenkins, Ian, *Archaeologists and Aesthetes in the Sculpture Galleries of the British Museum, 1800–1939* (London: British Museum Press, 1992).

Jenkyns, Richard, *Dignity and Decadence: Victorian Art and the Classical Inheritance* (Cambridge, MA: Harvard University Press, 1992).

Jeremias, Alfred, *Das Alte Testament im Lichte des alten Orients* (Leipzig: J.C. Hinrichs, 3. völlig neu bearbeitete Auflage, 1916).

—*Das Alte Testament im Lichte des alten Orients* (Leipzig: J.C. Hinrichs, 4. völlig erneuerte Auflage, 1930).

—*Das Alte Testament im Lichte des alten Orients: Handbuch zur biblisch-orientalischen Altertumskunde* (Leipzig: J.C. Hinrichs, 1904).

—*Das Alte Testament im Lichte des alten Orients: Handbuch zur biblisch-orientalischen Altertumskunde* (Leipzig: J.C. Hinrichs, 2. neu bearbeitete Auflage, 1906).

—*The Old Testament in the Light of the Ancient East: Manual of Biblical Archaeology* (2 vols.; ed. C.H.W. Johns; trans. C.L. Beaumont from the 2nd German edn; Theological Translation Library, 28-29; London: Williams & Norgate; New York: Putnam, 1911).

Jirat-Wasiutyński, Vojtech, 'Gauguin's Self Portraits and the Oviri: The Image of the Artist, Eve, and the Fatal Woman', *Art Quarterly* NS 2 (1979), pp. 172-90.

Jobes, Karen H., *The Alpha-Text of Esther: Its Character and Relationship to the Masoretic Text* (SBLDS, 153; Atlanta, GA: Scholars Press, 1996).

Johanning, Klaus, *Der Bibel–Babel–Streit: Eine forschungsgeschichtliche Studie* (Europäische Hochschulschriften, Reihe 23, Theologie, 343; Frankfurt a.M.: Peter Lang, 1988).

Johnson, Lee, 'The Etruscan Sources of Delacroix's *Death of Sardanapalus*', *ArtB* 42 (1960), pp. 296-300.

—*The Paintings of Eugène Delacroix: A Critical Catalogue* (7 vols.; Oxford: Clarendon Press, 1981–2002).

—'Toward Delacroix's Oriental Sources', *Burlington Magazine* 120 (1978), pp. 144-51.

Johnstone, Christopher, *John Martin* (London: Academy Editions: 1974).

Joll, Evelyn, *Cecil Higgins Art Gallery: Watercolours and Drawings* (Bedford, UK: Cecil Higgins Art Gallery, 2002).

Jones, Owen, and Joseph Bonomi, *Description of the Egyptian Court Erected in the Crystal Palace* (London: Crystal Palace Library and Bradbury & Evans, 1854).

Jordan, Constance, 'Woman's Rule in Sixteenth-Century British Political Thought', *Renaissance Quarterly* 40 (1987), pp. 421-51.

Jullian, Philippe, *The Orientalists: European Painters of Eastern Scenes* (Oxford: Phaidon, 1977).

Kabbani, Rana, *Europe's Myths of Orient* (Bloomington, IN: Indiana University Press, 1986).

Kaiser, Otto *et al.* (eds.), *Texte aus der Umwelt des Alten Testaments* (4 vols.; Gütersloh: G. Mohn, 1982–2001).

Karim, Ahmad Izzat Abd al-, *Tarikh al-talim fi Misr min nihayat hukm Muhammad Ali ila awail hukm Tawfiq 1848–1882* (3 vols.; Cairo: Matbaʿat al-Nasr, 1945).

Kark, Ruth, *American Consuls in the Holy Land, 1832–1914* (America-Holy Land Monographs; Detroit, MI: Wayne State University Press, 1994).

Kark, Ruth (ed.). *The Land That Became Israel: Studies in Historical Geography* (trans. Michael Gordon; Jerusalem: Magnes Press, 1989).

Kasson, John F., *Amusing the Million: Coney Island at the Turn of the Century* (American Century Series; New York: Hill & Wang, 1978).

Keimer, Louis, 'Le Musée égyptologique de Berlin', *Cahiers d'histoire égyptienne,* ser. 3, fasc. 1 (November 1950), pp. 30-36.

Keiser, Clarence Elwood, 'Cuneiform Labels and Tags from the Third Millennium B.C.', PhD dissertation published as *Cuneiform Bullae of the Third Millennium B.C.* (BRM, 3; New Haven: Yale University Press, 1914).

Keith, Alexander, *Evidence of the Truth of the Christian Religion, Derived from the Literal Fulfillment of Prophecy; Particularly as Illustrated by the History of the Jews, and by the Discoveries of Recent Travellers* (New York: J. & J. Harper, repr. of the 6th Edinburgh edn, 1832).

Kemp, Wolfgang, 'Review of John Shearman, *Only Connect: Art and the Spectator in the Italian Renaissance*', *ArtB* 76 (1994), pp. 364-67.

Kempton, Daniel, 'Christine de Pizan's *Cité des dames* and *Trésor de la cité*: Towards a Feminist Scriptural Practice', in *Political Rhetoric, Power, and Renaissance Women* (ed. Carole Levin and Patricia Ann Sullivan; SUNY Series in Speech Communication; Albany, NY: State University of New York Press, 1995), pp. 15-37.

Kennedy, Valerie, *Edward Said: A Critical Introduction* (Oxford and Malden, MA: Polity Press in association with Blackwell, 2000).

Kenyon, Kathleen M., *Archaeology in the Holy Land* (London: Ernest Benn/New York: W.W. Norton, 4th edn, 1979).

Keyser, Eugénie de, *Degas: Réalité et métaphore* (Publications d'histoire de l'art et d'archéologie de l'Université catholique de Louvain, 25; Louvain-la-Neuve: Institut supérieur d'archéologie et d'histoire de l'art, 1981).

Khalaf, Samir, 'The Background and Causes of Lebanese/Syrian Immigration to the United States before World War I', in *Crossing the Waters: Arabic-Speaking Immigrants to the United States before 1940* (ed. Eric J. Hooglund; Washington, DC and London: Smithsonian Institution Press, 1987), pp. 17-35.

Kim, Uriah Y., *Decolonizing Josiah: Toward a Postcolonial Reading of the Deuteronomistic History* (The Bible in the Modern World, 5; Sheffield: Sheffield Phoenix Press, 2005).

King, L.W., *The Seven Tablets of Creation, or the Babylonian and Assyrian Legends concerning the Creation of the World and of Mankind* (Luzac's Semitic Text and Translation Series, 12; London: Luzac, 1902).

Kinnier Wilson, J.V., *The Nimrud Wine Lists: A Study of Men and Administration at the Assyrian Capital in the Eighth Century B.C.* (Cuneiform Texts from Nimrud, 1; London: British School of Archaeology in Iraq, 1972).

Kinns, Samuel, *Graven in the Rock, or: The Historical Accuracy of the Bible Confirmed by Reference to the Assyrian and Egyptian Monuments in the British Museum and Elsewhere* (London: Cassell & Company, 1891).

Kippenberg, Hans Gerhard, *Die Entdeckung der Religionsgeschichte: Religionswissenschaft und Moderne* (München: Verlag C.H. Beck, 1997), pp. 45-51.

Kirshenblatt-Gimblett, Barbara, *Destination Culture: Tourism, Museums, and Heritage* (Berkeley: University of California Press, 1998).

—'A Place in the World: Jews and the Holy Land at World's Fairs', in *Encounters with the 'Holy Land': Place, Past and Future in American Jewish Culture* (ed. Jeffrey Shandler and Beth S. Wenger; Brandeis Series in American Jewish History, Culture, and Life; Philadelphia and Hanover: National Museum of American Jewish History: Center for Judaic Studies; University of Pennsylvania Library; distributed by University Press of New England), pp. 60-82.

Kitto, John, 'Josiah', in *A Cyclopaedia of Biblical Literature* (3 vols.; ed. John Kitto and William Lindsay Alexander; Philadelphia: J.B. Lippincott, 3rd edn, 1866), II, p. 660.

Kittredge, J.E., 'Archaeological Museum', *Chautauqua Assembly Herald* 6/16 (1881), p. 5.

—'Chautauqua's Archaeological Society', *Chautauqua Assembly Herald* 8/12 (1883), pp. 6-7.

Klapisch-Zuber, Christiane (ed.), *A History of Women in the West*. II. *Silences of the Middle Ages* (ed. Christiane Klapisch-Zuber; Cambridge, MA and London: The Belknap Press of Harvard University Press, 1992).

Koenen, Klaus, *Bethel: Geschichte, Kult und Theologie* (OBO, 192; Freiburg, Switzerland: Universitätsverlag/Göttingen: Vandenhoeck & Ruprecht, 2003).

Kolsky, Stephen D., *The Genealogy of Women: Studies in Boccaccio's* De mulieribus claris (Studies in the Humanities: Literature–Politics–Society, 62; New York: Peter Lang, 2003).

Kramer, Samuel Noah, *In the World of Sumer: An Autobiography* (Detroit, MI: Wayne State University Press, 1986).

—'Léon Legrain (1878–1963)', *AfO* 21 (1966), pp. 261-62.

Kratz, Reinhard Gregor, 'Die Entstehung des Judentums: Zur Kontroverse zwischen E. Meyer und J. Wellhausen', in *Das Judentum im Zeitalter des Zweiten Tempels* (FAT, 42; Tübingen: Mohr Siebeck, 2004), pp. 6-22.

Krengel-Strudthoff, Inge, 'Archäologie auf der Bühne—das wiedererstandene Ninive: Charles Keans Ausstattung zu *Sardanapalus* von Lord Byron', *Kleine Schriften der Gesellschaft für Theatergeschichte* 31 (1981), pp. 1-24.

Kritzeck, James, and R. Bayley Winder, 'Philip K. Hitti', in *The World of Islam: Studies in Honour of Philip K. Hitti* (ed. J. Kritzeck and R.B. Winder; London: Macmillan & Co., 1959), pp. 1-37.

Kuhrt, Amélie, *The Ancient Near East c. 3000–330 B.C.* (2 vols.; Routledge History of the Ancient World; London: Routledge, 1995).

—'The Cyrus Cylinder and Achaemenid Imperial Policy', *JSOT* 25 (1983), pp. 83-97.

Kuklick, Bruce, *Puritans in Babylon: The Ancient Near East and American Intellectual Life, 1880–1930* (Princeton, NJ: Princeton University Press, 1996).

Künzl, Hannelore, *Der Einfluss des alten Orients auf die europäische Kunst besonders im 19. und 20. Jh.* (Cologne [Inaug.-Diss.], 1973).

Kupper, Jean-Robert, 'Dans les jardins de Carkémish...', in *Recueil d'études à la mémoire d'André Parrot* (ed. D. Charpin and J.-M. Durand; Florilegium marianum, 6; Mémoires de N.A.B.U., 7; Paris: SEPOA, 2002), pp. 195-200.

—*Les nomades en Mésopotamie au temps des rois de Mari* (Bibliothèque de la Faculté de philosophie et lettres de l'Université de Liège, 142; Paris: Société d'Edition «Les Belles Lettres», 1957).

Kutscher, R., 'The Mesopotamian God Zaqar and the Pillar of Jacob's Dream', *Beer Sheva* 3 (5748 [= 1987]), pp. 125-30 [Hebrew].

Kvanvig, Helge S., *Roots of Apocalyptic: The Mesopotamian Background of the Enoch Figure and the Son of Man* (WMANT, 61; Neukirchen–Vluyn: Neukirchner Verlag, 1988).

Kwok, Pui-lan, *Discovering the Bible in the Non-Biblical World* (Bible & Liberation Series; Maryknoll, NY: Orbis Books, 1995).

—*Postcolonial Imagination and Feminist Theology* (Louisville, KY: Westminster/John Knox Press, 2005).

Lackenbacher, Sylvie, *Le roi bâtisseur: Les récits de construction assyriens des origins à Teglathphalasar III* (Etudes assyriologiques, 11; Paris: Editions Recherche sur les civilizations, 1982).

Lafont, Bertrand, 'International Relations in the Ancient Near East: The Birth of a Complete Diplomatic System', *Diplomacy and Statecraft* 12 (2001), pp. 39-60.

—'Relations internationales, alliances et diplomatie au temps des royaumes amorrites: Essai de synthèse', in Durand and Charpin (eds.), *Mari, Ebla, et les Hourrites* (Amurru, 2), pp. 213-328.

—'The Women of the Palace at Mari', in *Everyday Life in Ancient Mesopotamia* (ed. Jean Bottéro; trans. Antonia Nevill; Baltimore, MD: The Johns Hopkins Press, 2001), pp. 127-40.

Lambert, W.G., *The Background of Jewish Apocalyptic* (London: Athlone Press, 1978).

—'Nippur in Ancient Ideology', in *Nippur at the Centennial. Papers Read at the XXXVe Rencontre assyriologique internationale, Philadelphia, 1988* (ed. Maria deJong Ellis; Occasional Publications of the Samuel Noah Kramer Fund, 14; Philadelphia: Babylonian Section, The University Museum, 1992), pp. 119-26.

Lambert, W.G., and Simon B. Parker, *Enuma Eliš: The Babylonian Epic of Creation, the Cuneiform Text* (Oxford: Clarendon Press, 1966).

Landes, David S., *Bankers and Pashas: International Finance and Economic Imperialism in Egypt* (Harvard University. Research Center in Entrepreneurial History. Studies in Entrepreneurial History; Cambridge, MA: Harvard University Press, 1958).

Landes, Joan B., *Visualizing the Nation: Gender, Representation, and Revolution in Eighteenth-Century France* (Ithaca, NY: Cornell University Press, 2001).

Landsberger, Benno, *The Conceptual Autonomy of the Babylonian World* (trans. T. Jacobsen, B.R. Foster and H. von Siebenthal; Monographs on the Ancient Near East, 1/4; Malibu, CA: Undena, 1976).

—'Die Eigenbegrifflichkeit der babylonischen Welt: Ein Vortrag', *Islamica* 2 (1926), pp. 355-72.

—*Die Eigenbegrifflichkeit der babylonischen Welt: Ein Vortrag* (Libelli, 142*; Darmstadt: Wissenschaftliche Buchgesellschaft, 1965), pp. 1-18.

—'Einige unerkannt gebliebene oder verkannte Nomina des Akkadischen', *WZKM* 57 (1961), pp. 1-23.

Landsberger, Benno, and J.V. Kinnier Wilson, 'The Fifth Tablet of *Enuma Eliš*', *JNES* 20 (1961), pp. 154-79.

Lane-Poole, Stanley, *The Life of the Right Honourable Stratford Canning Viscount Stratford de Redcliffe: From his Memoirs and Private and Official Papers* (2 vols.; New York: AMS Press, 1976 [1888]).

Langdon, Stephen, *Die neubabylonischen Königsinschriften* (trans. Rudolf Zehnpfund; VAB, 4; Leipzig: J.C. Hinrichs, 1912).

Lanier, Sidney, *Poems of Sidney Lanier: Edited by His Wife, with a Memorial by William Hayes Ward* (New York: Charles Scribner's Sons, 1884).

Larsen, Mogens Trolle, 'The "Babel/Bible" Controversy and its Aftermath', in *CANE*, I, pp. 95-106.

—*The Conquest of Assyria: Excavations in an Antique Land 1840–1860* (London and New York: Routledge, 1996).

—'Hincks versus Rawlinson: The Decipherment of the Cuneiform System of Writing', in *Ultra terminum vagari: Scritti in onore di Carl Nylander* (ed. Börje Magnusson *et al.*; Rome: Quasar, 1997), pp. 339-56.

—'Orientalism and Near Eastern Archaeology,' in *Domination and Resistance* (ed. Daniel Miller, Michael R. Rowlands and Christopher Tilley; One World Archaeology, 3; London and New York: Routledge, 1989), pp. 229-39.

—'Orientalism and the Ancient Near East', in *The Humanities between Art and Science: Intellectual Developments, 1880–1914* (ed. Michael Harbsmeier and M.T. Larsen; Copenhagen: Akademisk Forlag, 1989), pp. 181-202.

—'Seeing Mesopotamia', in Gunter (ed.), *Construction of the Ancient Near East*, pp. 107-32.

Layard, Austen Henry, *Discoveries in the Ruins of Nineveh and Babylon, with Travels in Armenia, Kurdistan and the Desert: Being the Result of a Second Expedition Undertaken for the Trustees of the British Museum* (London: John Murray, 1853).

—*Nineveh and its Remains, with an Account of a Visit to the Chaldean Christians of Kurdistan and the Yezidis, or Devil-Worshippers, and an Inquiry into the Manners and Arts of the Ancient Assyrians* (2 vols.; New York: George P. Putnam, 1850 [London, 1849]).

—*Sir A. Henry Layard, G.C.B., D.C.L., Autobiography and Letters from his Childhood until his Appointment as H.M. Ambassador at Madrid, Edited by the Hon. William N. Bruce, with a Chapter on his Parliamentary Career by the Rt Hon. Arthur Otway* (2 vols.; London: John Murray, 1903).

Leask, Nigel, *British Romantic Writers and the East: Anxieties of Empire* (Cambridge Studies in Romanticism; Cambridge and New York: Cambridge University Press, 1992).

Lebram, J.C.H., 'Die Traditionsgeschichte der Ezragestalt und die Frage nach dem historischen Esra', in *Achaemenid History*. I. *Sources, Structures and Synthesis* (ed. Heleen Sancisi-Weerdenburg; Proceeding of the Groningen 1983 Achaemenid History Workshop; Leiden: Nederlands Instituut voor het Nabije Oosten, 1987), pp. 103-38.

Leduc-Adine, Jean-Pierre, 'Exotisme et discours d'art au XIXe siècle', in *L'exotisme: Actes du colloque de Saint-Denis de la Réunion* (ed. Alain Buisine, Norbert Dodille and Claude Duchet; Paris: Diffusion Didier-Erudition, 1988), pp. 457-65.

Lehmann, Reinhard G., *Friedrich Delitzsch und der Babel–Bibel–Streit* (OBO, 133; Freiburg, Switzerland: Universitätsverlag/Göttingen: Vandenhoeck & Ruprecht, 1994).

Leick, Gwendolyn, *Sex and Eroticism in Mesopotamian Literature* (London: Routledge, 1994).

Lemaire, André, 'Mari, la Bible et le monde nord-ouest sémitique', *MARI* 4 (1985), pp. 549-58.

—'Les textes prophétiques de Mari dans leurs relations avec l'Ouest', in Durand (ed.), *Mari, Ebla, et les Hourrites* (Amurru, 1), pp. 427-38.

Lemoisne, Paul-André, *Degas et son œuvre* (4 vols.; Les artistes et leurs œuvres, études et documents; Paris: Paul Brame and C.M. de Hanke, 1946).

Lenfant, Dominique, *La Perse; l'Inde; autre fragments: Ctesias de Cnide: Textes établi, traduit et commenté* (Collection des universités de France. Série grecque, 435; Paris: Les Belles Lettres, 2004).

Lenormant, François, *Histoire ancienne de l'orient: Jusqu'aux guerres médiques* (6 vols.; Paris: A. Levy, 9th edn, 1885).

Lerner, Gerda, *The Creation of Feminist Consciousness: From the Middle Ages to Eighteen-Seventy* (Oxford: Oxford University Press, 1993).

Levavasseur, Charles, 'Notice sur Paul-Emile Botta', in Paul-Emile Botta, *Relation d'un voyage dans l'Yémen, entrepris en 1837 pour le Muséum d'histoire naturelle de Paris* (Paris: B. Duprat, 1880), pp. 1-34.

Levi, Doro, *Antioch Mosaic Pavements* (2 vols.; Committee for the Excavation of Antioch and its Vicinity. Publications, 4; Princeton, NJ: Princeton University Press, 1947).

—'The Novel of Ninus and Semiramis', *Proceedings of the American Philosophical Society* 87 (1944), pp. 420-28.

Levin, Carole, *'The Heart and Stomach of a King': Elizabeth I and the Politics of Sex and Power* (New Cultural Studies; Philadelphia: University of Pennsylvania Press, 1994).

Levine, Mary Ann, 'Creating their Own Niches: Career Styles among Women in Americanist Archaeology between the Wars', in Claasen (ed.), *Women in Archaeology*, pp. 9-40.

Lewis, Bernard, *The Crisis of Islam: Holy War and Unholy Terror* (New York: Modern Library, 2003).

—*The Political Language of Islam* (Chicago: University of Chicago Press, 1988).

Lewis, Reina, *Gendering Orientalism: Race, Femininity and Representation* (Gender, Racism, Ethnicity; London and New York: Routledge, 1996).

—*Rethinking Orientalism: Women, Travel and the Ottoman Harem* (London: I.B. Tauris, 2004).

Lewy, Hildegard, 'Assyria c. 2600–1816 B.C.', in *CAH*[3] I/2, pp. 729-70.

Lindenberger, James M., *The Aramaic Proverbs of Ahiqar* (The Johns Hopkins Near Eastern Studies; Baltimore, MD: The Johns Hopkins University Press, 1983).

Lipton, Diana, *Revisions of the Night: Politics and Promises in the Patriarchal Dreams of Genesis* (JSOTSup, 288; Sheffield: Sheffield Academic Press, 1999).

Little, Douglas, *American Orientalism: The United States and the Middle East since 1945* (Chapel Hill, NC: University of North Carolina Press, 2002).

Liverani, Mario, 'Ancient Near Eastern Cities and Modern Ideologies', in *Die orientalische Stadt: Kontinuität, Wandel, Bruch: 1. Internationales Colloquium der Deutschen Orient-Gesellschaft, 9.-10. Mai 1996 in Halle/Saale* (ed. Gernot Wilhelm; Colloquien der Deutschen Orient-Gesellschaft, 1; Saarbrücken: Saarbrücker Druckerei und Verlag, 1997), pp. 85-107.

Livingstone, David N., *The Geographical Tradition: Episodes in the History of a Contested Enterprise* (Oxford and Cambridge, MA: Blackwell, 1992).

—*Putting Science in its Place: Geographies of Scientific Knowledge* (Chicago: University of Chicago Press, 2003).

Livre d'or de l'Institut égyptien: Publié à l'occasion du centenaire de la fondation de L'Institut égyptien, 6 mai 1859–5 mai 1899 (Le Mans: Imprimerie de l'Institut de bibliographie, 1899).

Lloyd, Seton, *Foundations in the Dust: The Story of Mesopotamian Exploration* (London and New York: Oxford University Press, rev. edn, 1980).

Lochnan, Katharine A., Douglas E. Schoenherr and Carole Silver (eds.), *The Earthly Paradise: Arts and Crafts by William Morris and his Circle from Canadian Collections* (Toronto: Art Gallery of Ontario and Key Porter Books, 1993).

Lockman, Zachary, *Contending Visions of the Middle East: The History and Politics of Orientalism* (Cambridge and New York: Cambridge University Press, 2004).

Long, Burke O., 'Bible Maps and America's Nationalist Narratives' [forthcoming].

—*Imagining the Holy Land: Maps Models and Fantasy Travels* (Bloomington, IN: Indiana University Press, 2003).

—*Planting and Reaping Albright: Politics, Ideology, and Interpreting the Bible* (University Park, PA: Pennsylvania State University Press, 1997).

Longman, Tremper, *Fictional Akkadian Autobiography: A Generic and Comparative Study* (Winona Lake, IN: Eisenbrauns, 1991).

Lopukhin, A.P., *Tolkovaia Bibliia, ili Kommentarii na vse knigi Sv. Pisaniia Vetkhago i Novago Zaveta* (Stockholm: Institute of Bible Translation, 1987 [St. Petersburg, 1905]).

Loti, Pierre, *Les désenchantées* (The Project Gutenberg Ebook, by Michael S. Hart, http://www.gutenberg.net/etext05/7dech10.txt, accessed June 25, 2005).

Lott, Emmeline, *The 'English Governess' in Egypt: Harem Life in Egypt and Constantinople* (2 vols.; London: Richard Bentley, 1865).

Louca, Anouar, *Voyageurs et écrivains égyptiens en France au XIX*[e] *siècle* (Etudes de littérature étrangère et comparée, 61; Paris: Didier, 1970).

Lowe, Lisa, *Critical Terrains: French and British Orientalisms* (Ithaca, NY: Cornell University Press, 1994).

Luckenbill, Daniel David, *The Annals of Sennacherib* (OIP, 2; Chicago: University of Chicago Press, 1924).

Lukács, György, *Theorie des Romans* (trans. Anna Bostock; Cambridge, MA: M.I.T. Press, 1971).

Luthi, Jean-Jacques, *Le français en Egypte: Essai d'anthologie* (Beirut: Maison Naaman pour la Culture, 1981).

Lutz, Henry Frederick, *Early Babylonian Letters from Larsa* (YOS, Babylonian Texts, 2; New Haven: Yale University Press, 1917).

Lynch, William Francis, U.S.N., *Narrative of the United States' Expedition to the River Jordan and the Dead Sea* (Philadelphia: Lea & Blanchard, 8th rev. edn, 1852).

Lyon, David Gordon, in the section 'Semitic, 1880–1929', in Samuel Eliot Morison, *The Development of Harvard University since the Inauguration of President Eliot, 1869–1929* (Cambridge, MA: Harvard University Press, 1930), pp. 231-40.

Lyons, F.S.L., *Internationalism in Europe 1815–1914* (Aspects européens, 14. Série C. Etudes politiques; Leiden: Sijthoff, 1963).

Macfie, A.L., *Orientalism* (London: Longman, 2002).

Macginnis, John D.A., 'Ctesias and the Fall of Nineveh', *Sumer* 45 (1987–88), pp. 40-43.

Machinist, Peter, 'The Question of Distinctiveness in Ancient Israel: An Essay', in Cogan and Eph'al (eds.), *Ah, Assyria*..., pp. 196-212.

MacKenzie, John M., *Orientalism: History, Theory, and the Arts* (Manchester and New York: Manchester University Press, 1995).

Macleod, Dianne Sachko, *Art and the Victorian Middle Class: Money and the Making of Cultural Identity* (Cambridge: Cambridge University Press, 1996).

Madsen, Catherine, 'A Terrible Beauty: Moser's Bible', *Cross Currents* 50 (2000), pp. 136-45.

Magen, Ursula, *Assyrische Königsdarstellungen—Aspekte der Herrschaft: Eine Typologie* (Baghdader Forschungen, 9; Mainz: Philipp von Zabern, 1986).

Mahon, Denis, 'Guercino's Paintings of Semiramis', *ArtB* 31 (1949), pp. 217-23.

Maigne, Vincenette, 'Exotisme: Evolution en diachronie du mot et de son champ sémantique', in *Exotisme et création: Actes du colloque internationale (Lyons 1983)* (Paris: L'Hermès, 1985), pp. 7-16.

Mairesse, Anne, *Figures de Valéry* (Critiques littéraires; Paris: L'Harmattan, 2000).

Majdi, Salih, *Hilyat al-zaman bimanaqib khadim al-watan: Sirat Rifaa Rafii al-Tahtawi* (ed. Jamal al-Din al-Shayyal; Cairo: Maktabat Mustafa al-Babi al-Halabi, 1958).

Malamat, Abraham, 'Is There a Word for the Royal Harem in the Bible? The *Inside* Story', in *Pomegranates and Golden Bells: Studies in Biblical, Jewish, and Near Eastern Ritual, Law, and Literature in Honor of Jacob Milgrom* (ed. David P. Wright, David Noel Freedman and Avi Hurvitz; Winona Lake, IN: Eisenbrauns, 1995), pp. 785-87.

Mallowan, Max, *Mallowan's Memoirs* (London: Collins, 1977).

Malul, Meir, *The Comparative Method in Ancient Near Eastern and Biblical Legal Studies* (AOAT, 227; Kevelaer: Butzon & Bercker/Neukirchen–Vluyn: Neukirchener Verlag, 1990).

Mankowski, Paul V., *Akkadian Loanwords in Biblical Hebrew* (HSS, 47; Winona Lake, IN: Eisenbrauns, 2000), pp. 115-18.

Manuel, Frank Edward, *The Broken Staff: Judaism through Christian Eyes* (Cambridge and London: Harvard University Press, 1992).

Marchand, Suzanne L., *Down from Olympus: Archaeology and Philhellenism in Germany, 1750–1970* (Princeton, NJ: Princeton University Press, 1996).

Mare, W. Harold, 'Jehoshaphat, Valley of', *ABD*, III, pp. 668-69.

Mariette, Auguste, *Album de musée du Boulaq* (Cairo: Mourès, 1871).

—*Aperçu de l'histoire d'Egypte depuis les temps les plus reculés jusqu'à la conquête musulmane (Kitab Qudama al-Misriyyin)* (Alexandria: Imprimerie de Mourès, Rey, 1864).

—*Description du parc égyptien: Exposition universelle de 1867* (Paris: Dentu, 1867).

—*Exposition universelle de Paris 1878: La galerie de l'Egypte ancienne à l'exposition rétrospective du Trocadéro* (Paris: F. Pichon, 1878).

—*Furjat al-mutafarrij ʿalá al-Intiqih Khanah al-Khidiwiyah al-kaʾinah bi-Bulaq Misr al-mahamiyah, wa-hiyya ʿibarah ʿan wasf nukhbat al-athar al-qadima al-misriyya al-mawjuda fi khazinat al-tuhaf al-ilmiyya al-misriyya* (Cairo: Matbaʿat Wadi al-Nil, 1286 / 1869).

—*Notice des principaux monuments exposés dans les galeries provisoires du Musée d'antiquités égyptiennes de S.A. le Vice-Roi à Boulaq* (Alexandria and Cairo, 1st–6th edn, 1864–76).

—*Oeuvres diverses* (40 vols.; ed. Gaston Maspero; Bibliothèque égyptologique, contenant les oeuvres des égyptologues français, 18; Paris: E. Leroux, 1893–1915).

—*Le Sérapeum de Memphis* (Paris: F. Vieweg, 1882).

—*Une visite au musée de Boulaq ou description des principaux monuments conservés dans les salles de cet établissement* (Paris: A. Franck, 1869).

Mariette, Edouard, *Lettres et souvenirs personnels (avec un portrait de Mariette Pacha)* (Paris: H. Jouve, 1904).

Markley, Robert, *Dying Planet: Mars in Science and the Imagination* (Durham, NC and London: Duke University Press, 2005).

Martin, John, *A Description of the Picture, Belshazzar's Feast, Painted by Mr J. Martin...* (London, 42nd edn, 1825).

—*Descriptive Catalogue of the Picture of The Fall of Nineveh* (London: George Woodfall, 1828).

Maspero, Gaston, *Guide du visiteur au Musée du Caire* (Cairo: Imprimerie de l'Institut français d'archéologie orientale, 4th edn, 1915).

—'Mariette (1821–1881): Notice biographique', in Mariette, *Oeuvres diverses*, I, pp. i-ccxxiv.

Mathieu, Pierre-Louis, 'La bibliothèque de Gustave Moreau', *Gazette des Beaux-Arts* ser. 6, 91 (1978), pp. 155-62.

Matouš, L., 'Review of A.K. Grayson, *Babylonian Historical-Literary Texts*', *Orientalistische Literaturzeitung* 75 (1980), pp. 28-30.

Matthews, Victor H. and Don C. Benjamin, *Old Testament Parallels: Laws and Stories from the Ancient Near East* (New York: Paulist Press, 1991; 2nd fully rev. and expanded edn, 1997).

Mauer, Gerlinde and Ursula Magen, 'Schriftenverzeichnis Karlheinz Deller', in *Ad bene et fideliter seminandum: Festgabe für Karlheinz Deller zum 21. Februar 1987* (ed. G. Mauer and U. Magen; AOAT, 220; Kevalaer: Butzon & Bercker/Neukirchen–Vluyn: Neukirchener Verlag, 1988), pp. 1-23, with additions at http://assyriologie.uni-hd.de/Deller.pdf.

Maul, Stefan M., 'Reflection and Navel: The Ancient Middle Eastern Capital City of the World', http://prelectur.stanford.edu/lectures/maul/capitals.html, English translation of 'Die altorientalische Hauptstadt: Abbild und Nabel der Welt', in *Die orientalische Stadt: Kontinuitat. Wandel. Bruch, 1 Internationale Colloquium der Deutschen Orient-Gesellschaft. 9.-10. Mai 1996 in Halle/Salle* (ed. Gernot Wilhelm; Colloquien der Deutschen Orient-Gesellschaft, 1; Saarbrücker Druckerei und Verlag, 1997), pp. 109-24.

Mayer, Walter, *Politik und Kriegskunst der Assyrer* (ALASPM, 9; Münster: Ugarit-Verlag, 1995).

McCall, Henrietta, 'Rediscovery and Aftermath', in Dalley (ed.), *Legacy of Mesopotamia*, pp. 183-213.

McCall, Henrietta, and Jonathan Tubb, *I Am the Bull of Nineveh: Victorian Design in the Assyrian Style* (London: PDC Publishers [privately printed], 2003).

McClintock, Anne, *Imperial Leather: Race, Gender and Sexuality in the Colonial Contest* (London and New York: Routledge, 1995).

McCullough, Edo, *World's Fair Midways: An Affectionate Account of American Amusement Areas from the Crystal Palace to the Crystal Ball* (New York: Exposition Press, 1966).

McLay, Tim, *The OG and Th Versions of Daniel* (SBLSCS, 43; Atlanta, GA: Scholars Press, 1996).

McLean, Ruari, *Joseph Cundall: A Victorian Publisher; Notes on his Life and a Check-List of his Books* (Pinner: Private Libraries Association, 1976).

McMullen, Roy, *Degas: His Life, Times, and Work* (Boston: Houghton Mifflin, 1984).

Meade, C. Wade, *Road to Babylon: Development of U.S. Assyriology* (Leiden: E.J. Brill, 1974).

Meadowcroft, T.J., *Aramaic Daniel and Greek Daniel: A Literary Comparision* (JSOTSup, 198; Sheffield: Sheffield Academic Press, 1995).

Meek, Theophile James, 'The Challenge of Oriental Studies to American Scholarship', *JAOS* 63 (1943), pp. 83-93.

—'The Code of Hammurabi', in *ANET* (1950), pp. 163-80.

Meier, Samuel A., 'Women and Communication in the Ancient Near East', *JAOS* 111 (1991), pp. 540-47.

Melchert, H. Craig (ed.), *The Luwians* (Handbuch der Orientalistik. Erste Abteilung, Nahe und der Mittlere Osten, 68; Leiden and Boston: Brill, 2003).

Melman, Billie, *Women's Orients—English Women and the Middle East, 1718–1918: Sexuality, Religion, and Work* (Ann Arbor, MI: University of Michigan Press, 1992).

Meltzer, Edmund S., 'Egyptology', in *The Oxford Encyclopedia of Ancient Egypt* (3 vols.; ed. Donald B. Redford; Oxford: Oxford University Press), I, pp. 448-58.

Melville, Sarah Chamberlin, 'Neo-Assyrian Royal Women and Male Identity: Status as a Social Tool', *JAOS* 124 (2004), pp. 37-57.

—*The Role of Naqia/Zakutu in Sargonid Politics* (SAAS, 9; Helsinki: Neo-Assyrian Text Corpus Project, 1999).

Mémoires du congrès international des Orientalistes, 1re session, Paris (3 vols.; Paris: Maisonneuve, 1873–76).

Ménant, M. Joachim, *Annales des rois d'Assyrie, traduites et mises en ordre sur le texte assyrien* (Paris: Maisonneuve, 1874).

Mendenhall, George E., 'Ancient Oriental and Biblical Law', *BA* 17 (1954), pp. 26-46.

Mercer, Samuel A.B., *A Brief Autobiography* (privately printed, 1958).

—*The Tell el-Amarna Tablets* (2 vols.; Toronto: Macmillan Co. of Canada, 1939).

Merlin, Romain, *Origine des cartes à jouer: Recherches nouvelles sur les naïbis, les tarots et sur les autres espèces des cartes* (Paris: l'auteur, 1869).

Mernissi, Fatima, *Dreams of Trespass: Tales of a Harem Girlhood* (Reading, MA: Addison–Wesley Publishing Company, 1994).

Merrill, Selah, 'Assyrian and Babylonian Monuments in America', *Bibliotheca Sacra* 32 (1875), pp. 320-49.

Mettinger, Tryggve N.D., *No Graven Image? Israelite Aniconism in its Ancient Near Eastern Context* (ConBOT, 42; Stockholm: Almqvist & Wiksell International, 1995).

Meyer, Eduard, *Die Entstehung des Judenthums: Eine historische Untersuchung* (Halle: Max Niemeyer, 1896; repr. Hildesheim: Olms, 1965).

—*Julius Wellhausen und meine Schrift Die Entstehung des Judentums: Eine Erwiderung* (Halle: Max Niemeyer, 1897).

Michaelis, Johann David, *Abulfedae Descriptio Aegypti, arabice et latine: ex codice parisiensi* (Gottingen: J.C. Dieterich, 1776).

—*Arabische Grammatik, nebst einer arabische Chrestomathie, und Abhandlung vom arabischen Geschmack, sonderlich in der poetischen und historischen Schreibart* (Göttingen: V. Vosziegel, 2nd edn, 1781).

—*Fragen an eine Gesellschaft gelehrter Männer, die auf Befehl Ihro Majestät des Königes von Dännemark nach Arabien reisen* (Frankfurt: Johann Gottlieb Garbe, 1762).

Michel, Cécile, *Old Assyrian Bibliography of Cuneiform Texts, Bullae, Seals and the Results of the Excavations at Aššur, Kültepe/Kaniš, Acemhöyük, Alişar and Boğazköy* (Old Assyrian Archives, Studies, 1; PIHANS, 97; Leiden: Nederlands Instituut voor het Nabije Oosten, 2003).

Midway Types: A Book of Illustrated Lessons about the People of the Midway Plaisance, World's Fair, 1893 (Chicago: American Engraving Co., 1893).

Mignan, Robert, *Travels in Chaldæa, Including a Journey from Bussorah to Bagdad, Hillah, and Babylon, Performed on Foot in 1827: With Observations on the Site and Remains of Babel, Seleucia, and Ctesiphon* (London: Henry Colburn & R. Bentley, 1829).

Millard, A.R., 'The Celestial Ladder and the Gate of Heaven (Genesis xxviii. 12, 17)', *ExpTim* 78 (1966), pp. 86-87.

Miller, Edward, *That Noble Cabinet: A History of the British Museum* (London: A. Deutsch, 1973).

Miller, J. Maxwell, 'The Fall of the House of Ahab', *VT* 17 (1967), pp. 307-24.

—'The Israelite Occupation of Canaan', in *Israelite and Judean History* (ed. John H. Hayes and J. Maxwell Miller; OTL; Philadelphia: Westminster Press, 1977), pp. 213-84.

—'Jebus and Jerusalem: A Case of Mistaken Identity', *ZDPV* 90 (1974), pp. 115-27.

—'The Rest of the Acts of Jehoahaz (I Kings 20 22.1-38)', *ZAW* 80 (1968), pp. 337-42.

—'W.F. Albright and Historical Construction', *BA* 42 (1979), pp. 37-45.

Miller, J. Maxwell, and John H. Hayes, *A History of Ancient Israel and Judah* (Philadelphia: Westminster Press, 1986).

Milloué, L. de, *Petit guide illustré au Musée Guimet* (Paris: Ernest Leroux, 1894).

Milman, H.H., *The History of the Jews, from the Earliest Period down to Modern Times* (3 vols.; London: John Murray, 1829).

—'Review of A.H. Layard, *Nineveh and its Remains*', *Quarterly Review* 84 no. 167 (1848), pp. 106-53.

Mitchell, Timothy, *Colonising Egypt* (Cambridge Middle East Library; Cambridge: Cambridge University Press, 1988).

—'Orientalism and the Exhibitionary Order', in *The Visual Culture Reader* (ed. Nicholas Mirzoeff; London and New York: Routledge, 1998), pp. 293-303.

—'The World as Exhibition', *Comparative Studies in Society and History* 31 (1989), pp. 217-36.

Mohl, Jules, *Vingt-sept ans d'histoire des études orientales: Rapports faits à la Société Asiatique de Paris de 1840 à 1867* (2 vols.; Paris: Reinwald, 1879–80).

Monckton, Norah, 'Architectural Backgrounds in the Pictures of John Martin', *Architectural Review* 104 (1948), pp. 81-84.

Monnier, Geneviève, 'La genèse d'une œuvre de Degas: *Sémiramis construisant une ville*', *Revue du Louvre et des Musées de France* 28 (1978), pp. 407-26.

Monson, James *et al.*, *Student Map Manual: Historical Geography of Biblical Lands* (Jerusalem: Pictorial Archive [Near Eastern History] Est., 1979).

Montgomery, James A., and Joseph Reider, 'Cyrus Adler, 1863–1940', *JAOS* 61 (1941), pp. 193-94.

Montgomery, Mary Williams, *Briefe aus der Zeit des babylonischen Königs Hammurabi (ca. 2250 v. Chr.)*, Inaugural-Dissertation Berlin [1901] (Leipzig: A. Pries, 1901).

Montgomery, Mary Williams, and Robert J. Casey, *Give the Man Room: The Story of Gutzon Borglum* (Indianapolis, IN: Bobbs-Merrill, 1952).

Moorish Palace and its Startling Wonders, The—The Chief Attraction of Midway Plaisance—World's Columbian Exposition 1893 (Chicago: Metcalf Stationery Co., 1893).

Moran, William L., 'The Hebrew Language in its Northwest Semitic Background', in *The Bible and the Ancient Near East: Essays in Honor of William Foxwell Albright* (ed. G. Ernest Wright; New York: Doubleday, 1961), pp. 59-84.

Morgan, Janet P., *Agatha Christie: A Biography* (London: Collins, 1984).

Morris, Ian, 'Archaeologies of Greece', in *Classical Greece: Ancient Histories and Modern Archaeologies* (ed. I. Morris; Cambridge: Cambridge University Press, 1994), pp. 8-47.

Morrison, Theodore, *Chautauqua: A Center for Education, Religion, and the Arts in America* (Chicago: University of Chicago Press, 1974).

Moscrop, John James, *Measuring Jerusalem: The Palestine Exploration Fund and British Interests in the Holy Land* (London and New York: Leicester University Press, 2000).

Moser, Barry (illustrator), *The Holy Bible: Containing All the Books of the Old and New Testaments: King James Version* (New York: Penguin Group, 1999).

Mosse, George L., *Nationalism and Sexuality: Respectability and Abnormal Sexuality in Modern Europe* (New York: Howard Fertig, 1997 [1985]).

Mouelhy, Ibrahim el, 'L'Egypte à l'exposition de Philadelphie (1876)', *Cahiers d'histoire égyptienne* 1 (1948), pp. 316-26.

Mouliou, Maria, 'Ancient Greece, its Classical Heritage, and the Modern Greeks: Aspects of Nationalism in Museum Exhibitions', in *Nationalism and Archaeology* (ed. John A. Atkinson, Iain Banks and Jerry O'Sullivan; Scottish Archaeological Forum; Glasgow: Cruithne Press, 1996), pp. 174-99.

Moulton, Warren J., 'The American Palestine Exploration Society', *Annual of the American Schools of Oriental Research* 3 (1928), pp. 55-78.

Movers, F.C., *Die Phönizier* (2 vols.; Bonn and Berlin: Eduard Weber, 1841–50).

Mowinckel, Sigmund, *Studien zu dem Buche Ezra–Nehemia*. I. *Die nachchronische Redaktion des Buches. Die Liste* (Skrifter utgitt av Det Norske Videnskaps-Akademi i Oslo II. Hist.-Filos. Klasse. Ny Serie, 3; Oslo: Universitetsforlaget, 1964).

—*Studien zu dem Buche Ezra–Nehemia*. II. *Die Nehemia-Denkschrift* (Skrifter utgitt av Det Norske Videnskaps-Akademi i Oslo II. Hist.-Filos. Klasse. Ny Serie, 5; Oslo: Universitetsforlaget, 1964).

—*Studien zu dem Buche Ezra–Nehemia*. III. *Die Ezrageschichte und das Gesetz Moses* (Skrifter utgitt av Det Norske Videnskaps-Akademi i Oslo II. Hist.-Filos. Klasse. Ny Serie, 7; Oslo: Universitetsforlaget, 1965).

Mubarak, Ali, *Al-Khitat al-tawfiqiyya al-jadida* (20 vols.; Cairo: al-Matbaʿah al-Kubra al-Amiriyah, 1305–1306/1886–89).

Müller, F. Max, 'Notice sur Jules Mohl', in Mohl, *Vingt-sept ans d'histoire des études orientales*, I, pp. ix-xlvii.

Muller, Richard A., 'The Debate over the Vowel Points and the Crisis in Orthodox Hermeneutics', *The Journal of Medieval and Renaissance Studies* 10 (1980), pp. 53-72.

Myers, Jacob M., *Ezra. Nehemiah: Introduction, Translation and Notes* (AB, 14; Garden City, NY: Doubleday, 1965).

Na'aman, Nadav, 'The Kingdom of Judah under Josiah', *Tel Aviv* 18 (1991), pp. 3-71.

Nadar (Gaspar Félix Tournachon), 'Les contemporains de Nadar: Courbet', *Journal amusant*, 11 December 1858.

Naff, Alixa, *Becoming American: The Early Arab Immigrant Experience* (Middle East Research Institute Special Studies; Philadelphia: Middle East Research Institute, University of Pennsylvania, 1985).

Nebenzahl, Kenneth, *Maps of the Holy Land: Images of Terra Sancta through Two Millennia* (New York: Abbeville Press, 1986).

Neugebauer, Otto, 'The Chronology of the Hammurabi Age', *JAOS* 61 (1941), pp. 58-61.

Neuman, Abraham A., *Cyrus Adler: A Biographical Sketch* (Philadelphia: The Jewish Publication Society of America, 1942).

Neville, Don, 'Metastasio [Trapassi], Pietro', in *NGDO*, III, pp. 351-60.

—'Semiramide riconosciuta', in *NGDO*, IV, pp. 310-11.

Newman, Jane O., 'Sons and Mothers: Agrippina, Semiramis, and the Philological Construction of Gender Roles in Early Modern Germany (Lohenstein's Agrippina, 1665)', *Renaissance Quarterly* 49 (1996), pp. 77-113.

Niebuhr, Carsten, *Beschreibung von Arabien aus eigenen Beobachtungen und in Lande selbst gesammleten Nachrichten* (Kopenhagen: N. Moeller, 1772).

—*Reisebeschreibung nach Arabien und andern umliegenden Ländern* (Kopenhagen: N. Moeller, 1774).

Nietzsche, Friedrich, *Thus Spake Zarathustra* (trans. Thomas Common; New York: Heritage Press, 1970).

Nikou, Mehrangiz N., 'Egypt's Architectural Representation in the 1867 Paris International Exposition and Napoleon III's Aspiration for a French Arab Kingdom', unpublished paper presented at the convention of the Middle East Studies Association, Orlando, Florida, 16-19 November 2000.

Nippel, Wilfried, 'Facts and Fiction: Greek Ethnography and its Legacy', *History and Anthropology* 9 (1996), pp. 125-38.

Nir, Yeshayahu, *The Bible and the Image: The History of Photography in the Holy Land 1839–1899* (Philadelphia: University of Pennsylvania Press, 1985).

Nissinen, Martti, 'City as Lofty as Heaven: Arbela and Other Cities in Neo-Assyrian Prophecy', in *'Every City Shall Be Forsaken': Urbanism and Prophecy in Ancient Israel and the Near East* (ed. Lester L. Grabbe and Robert D. Haak; JSOTSup, 330; Sheffield: Sheffield Academic Press, 2001), pp. 172-209.

Nochlin, Linda, 'The Imaginary Orient', in *The Politics of Vision: Essays on Nineteenth-Century Art and Society* (Icon Editions; New York: Harper & Row, 1989), pp. 33-59.

—and Sarah Faunce, *Courbet Rediscovered* (New York: Brooklyn Museum, 1988: exhibition catalogue).

Noll, Kurt L., 'Looking on the Bright Side of Israel's History: Is There Pedagogical Value in a Theological Presentation of History?', *Biblical Interpretation* 7 (1999), pp. 1-27.

Nollé, Johannes, 'Frauen wie Omphale? Überlegungen zu "politischen" Ämtern von Frauen im kaiserzeitlichen Kleinasien', in *Reine Männersache? Frauen in Männerdomänen der antiken Welt* (ed. Maria H. Dettenhofer; Köln: Böhlau, 1994), pp. 229-59.

Nott, Josiah Clark and George R. Gliddon, *Types of Mankind: Or, Ethnological Researches Based upon the Ancient Monuments, Paintings, Sculptures, and Crania of Races, and upon their Natural, Geographical, Philological and Biblical History: Illustrated by Selections from the Inedited Papers of Samuel George Morton and by Additional Contributions from L. Agassiz, W. Usher, and H.S. Patterson* (Philadelphia: J.B. Lippincott Grambo & Co., 6th edn, 1854).

Nusayr, Ayda Ibrahim, *Kutub al-arabiyya nushirat fi Misr fi al-qarn al-tasi ashar* (Cairo: American University in Cairo Press, 1990).

Oates, Joan, *Babylon* (Ancient Peoples and Places, 94; London: Thames & Hudson, 1979).

—and David Oates, *Nimrud: An Assyrian Imperial City Revealed* (London: British School of Archaeology in Iraq, 2001).

Obermann, Heiko A., *The Roots of Anti-Semitism in the Age of the Renaissance and Reformation* (trans. James I. Porter; Philadelphia: Fortress Press, 1984).

Oestreicher, Theodor, *Das deuteronomische Grundgesetz* (BFCT, 27/4; Gütersloh: T. Bertelsmann, 1923).

Ogden, Charles J., 'Proceedings of the American Oriental Society at the Meeting in Washington, DC, 1928', *JAOS* 48 (1928), pp. 326-52.

Olivier, Jean-Jacques, 'Introduction', in Voltaire, *Sémiramis: Tragédie* (ed. J.-J. Olivier; Textes littéraires français, 5; Paris: Droz, 1946), pp. vii-xlix.

Oppenheim, Moritz Daniel, *Bilder aus dem altjüdischen Familienleben: Nach Original-Gemälden von Moritz Oppenheim. Mit Einführung und Erläuterungen von Rabbiner Dr Emil Levy* (Berlin: L. Lamm, 1913).

Oppert, Jules, 'L'immortalité de l'âme chez les Chaldéens', *Annales de philosophie chrétienne* 87 (1874), pp. 210-33.

Oren, Dan A., *Joining the Club: A History of Jews and Yale* (New Haven: Yale University Press, 1985).

Orfalea, Gregory, *Before the Flames: A Quest for the History of Arab Americans* (Austin: University of Texas Press, 1988).

Ornan, Tallay, 'The Queen in Public: Royal Women in Neo-Assyrian Art', in Parpola and Whiting (eds.), *Sex and Gender in the Ancient Near East*, pp. 461-76.

Orton, Job, *A Short and Plain Exposition of the Old Testament with Devotional and Practical Reflections, for the Use of Families* (Charleston: Samuel Etheridge, 1805 [1788–91]).

Osborne, Richard, *Rossini* (The Master Musicians Series; London and Melbourne: J.M. Dent & Sons, 1987).

—'Semiramide', in *NGDO*, IV, pp. 308-10.

Paley, Morton D., *The Apocalyptic Sublime* (New Haven: Yale University Press, 1986).

Panaino, Antonio, and Giovanni Pettinato (eds.), *Ideologies as Intercultural Phenomena: Proceedings of the Third Annual Symposium of the Assyrian and Babylonian Intellectual Heritage Project, held in Chicago, USA, October 27-31, 2000* (Melammu Symposia, 3; Milan: Università di Bologna/Roma: IsIAO, 2002).

Papers Read at the Anglo-Jewish Historical Exhibition, Royal Albert Hall, London, 1887 (Publications of the Anglo-Jewish Historical Exhibition, 1; London: Office of the 'Jewish Chronicle', 1888).

Parables of Our Lord and Saviour Jesus Christ, The: With Pictures by John Everett Millais. Engraved by the Brothers Dalziel (London: Routledge, Warne & Routledge, 1864).

Pardee, Dennis, 'Review of Carl D. Evans, W.W. Hallo and John B. White (eds.), *Scripture in Context: Essays in the Comparative Method*', *JNES* 44 (1985), pp. 220-22.

—'Review of S.B. Parker (ed.), *Ugaritic Narrative Poetry*', *JNES* 60 (2001), pp. 142-45.

—'Ugaritic Studies at the End of the 20th Century (review of W.G.E. Watson and N. Wyatt [eds.], *Handbook of Ugaritic Studies*)', *BASOR* 320 (2000), pp. 49-86.

Parker, Andrew, Mary Russo, Doris Sommer, Patricia Yaeger, 'Introduction', in their *Nationalisms and Sexualities* (New York and London: Routledge, 1992).

Parker, Simon B., 'The Ancient Near Eastern Literary Background of the Old Testament', in *The New Interpreter's Bible* (ed. Leander E. Keck; Nashville: Abingdon Press, 1994), I, pp. 228-43.

—*Stories in Scripture and Inscriptions: Comparative Studies on Narratives in Northwest Semitic Inscriptions and the Hebrew Bible* (New York and Oxford: Oxford University Press, 1997).

Parpola, Simo, *Assyrian Prophecies* (SAA, 9; Helsinki: Helsinki University Press, 1997).

—'The Assyrian Tree of Life: Tracing the Origins of Jewish Monotheism and Greek Philosophy', *JNES* 52 (1993), pp. 161-208.

—'Assyrians after Assyria', *Journal of the Assyrian Academic Society* 12/2 (2000), pp. 1-16, and available online at http://www.aanf.org/America/assyrians/assyrians_assyria.htm, accessed September 28, 2006.

—'Introduction', in Parpola and Whiting (eds.), *Sex and Gender in the Ancient Near East*, pp. xiii-xv.

—'Monotheism in Ancient Assyria', in *One God or Many? Concepts of Divinity in the Ancient World* (ed. Barbara Nevling Porter; Transactions of the Casco Bay Assyriological Institute, 1; Chebeague, ME: Casco Bay Assyriological Institute, 2000), pp. 165-209.

—'The Neo-Assyrian Word for "Queen"', *SAAB* II/2 (1988), pp. 73-76.

—'The Originality of the Teachings of Zarathustra in the Light of Yasna 44', in *Sefer Moshe: The Moshe Weinfeld Jubilee Volume: Studies in the Bible and the Ancient Near East, Qumran, and Post-Biblical Judaism* (ed. Chaim Cohen, Avi Hurvitz and Shalom M. Paul; Winona Lake, IN: Eisenbrauns, 2004), pp. 373-83.

Parpola, Simo, and Robert M. Whiting (eds.), *Sex and Gender in the Ancient Near East: Proceedings of the 47th Rencontre assyriologique internationale, Helsinki, July 2-6, 2001* (Helsinki: The Neo-Assyrian Text Corpus Project, 2002).

Parrot, André, *Nineveh and Babylon* (trans. Stuart Gilbert and James Emmons; The Arts of Mankind, 2; London: Thames & Hudson, 1991).

—*La tour de Babel* (Cahiers d'archéologie biblique, 2; Neuchâtel: Delachaux & Niestlé, 1953).

—'La vie d'un chef d'état au IIe Millénaire', in *Institut de France: Séance publique annuelle (mardi 25 octobre. 1966)* (Paris: Institut de France, 1966), pp. 3-11.

Paton, Lewis Bayles, 'Ashtart (Ashtoreth), Astarte', in *Encyclopedia of Religion and Ethics* (13 vols.; ed. James Hastings; Edinburgh: T. & T. Clark, 1910), II, pp. 115-18.

Patrick, H.H., 'Among the Educated Women of Turkey', in Sommer and Zwemer (eds.), *Daylight in the Harem*, pp. 71-89.

Pauthier, J.P. Guillaume, *Hymnes sanscrits, persans, égyptiens, assyriens et chinois; Chi-king; ou, Livre des vers* (Bibliothèque orientale: publiée sous la direction d'un comité scientifique international: chefs d'oeuvre littéraires de l'Inde, de la Perse, de l'Egypte et de la Chine, 2; Paris: Maisonneuve, 1872).

Pavan, Massimiliano, 'Antonio Canova e la discussione sugli "Elgin Marbles"', *Rivista dell'Instituto nazionale d'archelogia e storia dell'Arte* NS 11-12 (1974–75), pp. 219-344.

Peake, A.S., 'Baal', in Hastings (ed.), *Dictionary of the Bible* (4 vols.; ed. James Hastings; New York: Charles Scribner's Sons/Edinburgh: T. & T. Clark, 1899), I, pp. 209-11.

—'Josiah', in Hastings (ed.), *Dictionary of the Bible*, II, p. 788.

Peirce, Leslie P., *The Imperial Harem: Women and Sovereignty in the Ottoman Empire* (Studies in Middle Eastern History; New York: Oxford University Press, 1993).

Péladan, Joséph(in), *Semiramis* (trans. Emil Schering; Peladans Werke, 2; München: Georg Müller, 1918).

—*Sémiramis: Tragédie en quatre actes représentée le 23 juilliet 1905 pour la inauguration du Théâtre Antique de la Nature à Champigny-la-Bataille* (Paris: Société du Mercure de France, 1905).

Peleg, Yaron, *Orientalism and the Hebrew Imagination* (Ithaca, NY: Cornell University Press, 2005).

Penzer, Norman Mosley, *The Ḥarēm: An Account of the Institution as It Existed in the Palace of the Turkish Sultans with a History of the Grand Seraglio from its Foundation to the Present Time* (Philadelphia: J.B. Lippincott, 1937).

Perez, Nissan N., *Focus East: Early Photography in the Near East (1839–1885)* (New York and Jerusalem: Harry N. Abrams, in association with The Domino Press and The Israel Museum, Jerusalem, 1988).

Perkins, Kenneth J., 'Three Middle Eastern States Helped America Celebrate its Centennial in Philadelphia', *Aramco World* (November–December 1976), pp. 9-13.

Petrie, W.M. Flinders., *Seventy Years in Archaeology* (London: S. Low, Marston & Co., 1931).

Pettinato, Giovanni, *Semiramis: Herrin über Assur und Babylon: Biographie* (trans. Robert Steiger; Zürich: Artemis, 1988).

Phelps, Elizabeth Stuart, and Herbert D. Ward, *The Master of the Magicians* (Boston: Houghton, Mifflin & Company, 1890).

Picard, Alfred, *Exposition universelle internationale de 1889 à Paris: Rapport général*. II. *Travaux de l'Exposition universelle de 1889* (Paris: Imprimerie nationale, 1891).

Picart, Bernard, *Cérémonies et coutumes religieuses de tous les peuples du monde*. I. *Cérémonies des juifs & des chrétiens catholiques* (Amsterdam: Chez J.F. Bernard, 1723).

Pientka, Rosel, *Die spätaltbabylonische Zeit: Abiešuḫ bis Samsuditana, Quellen, Jahresdaten, Geschichte* (2 vols.; IMGULA, 2; Münster: Rhema-Verlag, 1998).

Piero della Francesca, *L'opera completa di Piero della Francesca* (ed. Oreste Del Buono and Pierluigi De Vecchi; Classici dell'arte: Biblioteca universale delle arti figurative, 9; Milano: Rizzoli, 1967).

Pigler, Andor, *Barockthemen: Eine Auswahl von Verzeichnissen zur Ikonographie des 17. und 18. Jahrhunderts* (Budapest: Akadémiai Kiadó, 2nd enl. edn, 1974),

Pillet, Maurice, *Khorsabad: Les découvertes de V. Place en Assyrie* (Paris: Leroux, 1918).

Pinches, T.G., 'Review of E. Grice, *Chronology of the Larsa Dynasty*', *JRAS* (1920), pp. 611-15.

Pipes, Daniel, *Militant Islam Reaches America* (New York: W.W. Norton, 2002).

—*Sandstorm: Middle East Conflicts & America* (Lanham, MD and Philadelphia: University Press of America and Foreign Policy Research Institute, 1993).

—*Slave Soldiers and Islam: The Genesis of a Military System* (New Haven: Yale University Press, 1981).

Pittman, Holly, 'Review of Zainab Bahrani, *The Graven Image: Representation in Babylonia and Assyria*', *ArtB* 87 (2005), pp. 342-43.

Pizan, Christine de, *The Book of the City of Ladies* (trans. Rosalind Brown-Grant; Penguin Classics; London: Penguin Books, 1999).

Poliakov, Léon, *The History of Anti-Semitism*. I. *From the Time of Christ to the Court Jews* (trans. Richard Howard; New York: Vanguard, 1965).

Pool, Phoebe, 'The History Pictures of Edgar Degas and their Background', *Apollo* (October 1964), pp. 306-11.

Porten, Bezalel and Ada Yardeni, *Textbook of Aramaic Documents from Ancient Egypt*. I. *Letters* (Texts and Studies for Students; Jerusalem: Hebrew University, 1986).

Postes en Egypte, Les: Notices publiées à l'occasion du Xe Congrès Postal Universel et du soixante-dixième anniversaire de la fondation des postes égyptiennes (Cairo: Imprimerie nationale, 1934).

Poynter, Edward John, *Painting, Classic, Early Christian, Italian and Teutonic* (Illustrated Handbooks of Art History; London: Samson Low, Marston, Searle & Rivington, 1882).

Poynter, Edward John, and Percy Rendell Head, *Classic and Italian Painting* (Illustrated Text-Books of Art Education; New York: Scribner & Welford/London: Sampson, Low, Marston & Co., 1880).

Prakash, Gyan, '*Orientalism* Now', *History and Theory* 34 (1995), pp. 199-212.

Pratt, Mary Louise, *Imperial Eyes: Travel Writing and Transculturation* (London and New York: Routledge, 1992).

Préaud, Maxime, 'Picart, Bernard', in *Grove Art Online* (Oxford University Press, 2005).

Prideaux, Humphrey, *The Old and New Testament Connected in the History of the Jews and Neighbouring Nations, from the Declension of the Kingdoms of Israel and Judah to the Time of Christ* (2 vols.; London. R. Knaplock & J. Tonson, 1716–18).

Prior, Michael, *The Bible and Colonialism: A Moral Critique* (The Biblical Seminar, 48; Sheffield: Sheffield Academic Press, 1997).

Pritchard, James B. (ed.), *The Ancient Near East: Supplementary Texts and Pictures Relating to the Old Testament* (Princeton, NJ: Princeton University Press, 1969).

—(ed.) *The Ancient Near East in Pictures Relating to the Old Testament* (Princeton, NJ: Princeton University Press, 1954)

—(ed.), *Ancient Near Eastern Texts Relating to the Old Testament* (Princeton, NJ: Princeton University Press, 1950; 2nd edn, 1955, 3rd edn, 1969).

—'Introduction', in *ANET*, pp. xiii-xviii.

Provan, Ian W., 'The End of (Israel's) History—A Review Article on K.W. Whitelam's *The Invention of Ancient Israel*', *JSS* 42 (1998), pp. 283-300.

—V. Philips Long and Tremper Longman III, *A Biblical History of Israel* (Louisville, KY: Westminster/John Knox Press, 2003).

Puppel, Paulie, 'Gynaecocratie: Herrschaft hochadeliger Frauen in der Frühen Neuzeit', in *Geschlechterstreit am Beginn der europäischen Moderne: Die Querelle des Femmes* (ed. Gisela Engel, Friederike Hassauer, Brita Rand, Heide Wunder; Kulturwissenschaftliche Genderstudien, 6; Königstein and Taunus: Ulrike Helmer, 2004), pp. 152-65.

Putnam, Frederick W., *Oriental and Occidental, Northern and Southern Portrait Types of the Midway Plaisance: A Collection of Photographs of Individual Types of Various Nations from All Parts of the World Who Represented, in the Department of Ethnology, the Manners, Customs, Dress, Religions, Music and other Distinctive Traits and Peculiarities of their Race, with Interesting and Instructive Descriptions Accompanying Each Portrait* (Portrait Types Art Series; St. Louis: Thompson Publishing Co., 1894).

Questa, Cesare, *Semiramide redenta: Archetipi, fonti classiche, censure antropologiche nel melodramma* (Letteratura e antropologia, 2; Urbino: QuattroVenti, 1989).

Quet, Marie-Henriette, 'Romans grecs, mosaïques romaines', in *Le monde du roman grec: Actes du colloque international tenu à l'Ecole normale supérieure (Paris 17-19 décembre 1987)* (ed. Marie-François Baslez, Philippe Hoffmann, and Monique Trédé; Paris: Presses de l'Ecole normale supérieure, 1992), pp. 125-60.

Rackham, Bernard, *Catalogue of Italian Maiolica: Victoria and Albert Museum* (2 vols.; London: Her Majesty's Stationary Office, rev. edn, 1977).

Radner, Karen, 'Traders in the Neo-Assyrian Period', in *Trade and Finance in Ancient Mesopotamia: Proceedings of the First MOS Symposium (Leiden 1997)* (ed. J.G. Dercksen; PIHANS, 84; Istanbul: Nederlands Historisch-Archaeologisch Instituut te Istanbul, 1999), pp. 101-26.

Radwan, Abu al-Futuh, *Tarikh Matbaat Bulaq: wa-lamhat fi tarikh al-tiba'ah fi buldan al-Sharq al-Awsat* (Cairo: al-Matba'ah al-Amiriyya, 1953).

Rafii, Abd al-Rahman al-, *Asr Ismail* (2 vols.; Cairo: Maktabat al-Nahda al-Misriyya, 2nd edn, 1948).

Ragozin, Zénaïde A., *The Story of Assyria: From the Rise of the Empire to the Fall of Nineveh* (New York: G.P. Putnam's Sons, 1889).

Raleigh, Walter, *The History of the World*, in *The Works of Sir Walter Ralegh, Kt, Now First Collected: To Which are Prefixed the Lives of the Author, Oldys and Birch* (8 vols.; Oxford: Oxford University Press, 1829).

Ranke, Leopold von, *Zur Kritik neuerer Geschichtschreiber: Eine Beylage zu desselben romanischen und germanischen Geschichten* (Leipzig and Berlin: G. Reimer, 1824).

Rassam, Hormuzd, *Asshur and the Land of Nimrod: Being an Account of the Discoveries Made in the Ancient Ruins of Nineveh, Asshur, Sepharvaim, Caleh, Babylon, Borsippa, Cuthah, and Van. Including a Narrative of Different Journeys in Mesopotamia, Assyria, Asia Minor, and Koordistan* (Cincinnati and New York: Curtis & Jennings, 1897).

Rauwerda, Antje M., 'Rushdie Affair', in *A Historical Companion to Postcolonial Thought in English* (ed. Prem Poddar and David Johnson; New York: Columbia University Press, 2005), pp. 431-32.

Rawlinson, George, *The Five Great Monarchies of the Ancient Eastern World; Or, the History, Geography, and Antiquities of Chaldaea, Assyria, Babylon, Media, and Persia, Collected and Illustrated from Ancient and Modern Sources* (4 vols.; London: John Murray, 1862–67).

—*The Kings of Israel and Judah* (New York: Anson D.F. Randolph, 1889).

—*The Religions of the Ancient World, Including Egypt, Phoenicia, Assyria and Babylonia, Etruria, Persia, Greece, India, Rome* (New York: Charles Scribner's Sons, 1883).

Rawlinson, Henry C., *Outlines of Assyrian History from the Inscriptions of Nineveh: The Twenty-Ninth Annual Report of the Royal Asiatic Society of Great Britain* (London: John W. Parker & Son, 1852).

Ray, Gordon N., *The Illustrator and the Book in England from 1790 to 1914* (New York: Pierpont Morgan Library/Oxford: Oxford University Press, 1976).

Reade, Julian E., 'Reflections on Layard's Archaeological Career', in Fales and Hickey (eds.), *Layard tra l'Oriente e Venezia*, pp. 47-53.

—'Les relations anglo-françaises en Assyrie', in Fontan and Chevalier (eds.), *De Khorsabad à Paris*, pp. 116-34.

—'Was Sennacherib a Feminist?', in Durand (ed.), *La femme dans le Proche-Orient antique*, pp. 139-45.

Redford, Donald B., *Egypt, Canaan, and Israel in Ancient Times* (Princeton, NJ: Princeton University Press, 1992).

—*A Study of the Biblical Story of Joseph (Genesis 37–50)* (VTSup, 20; Leiden: E.J. Brill, 1970).

Reed, William L., *The Asherah in the Old Testament* (Fort Worth: Texas Christian University Press, 1949).

Reff, Theodore, *The Notebooks of Edgar Degas: A Catalogue of the Thirty-Eight Notebooks in the Bibliothèque Nationale and Other Collections* (2 vols.; Oxford: Clarendon Press, 1976).

Reid, Donald Malcolm, 'The Egyptian Geographical Society: From Foreign Laymen's Society to Indigenous Professional Association', *Poetics Today* 14 (1993), pp. 539-72.

—*Whose Pharaohs? Archaeology, Museums, and Egyptian National Identity from Napoleon to World War I* (Berkeley: University of California Press, 2002).

Reiner, Erica, *An Adventure of Great Dimension: The Launching of the Chicago Assyrian Dictionary* (Transactions of the American Philosophical Society, 92/3; Philadelphia: American Philosophical Society, 2002).

Reinle, Christine, 'Exempla weiblicher Stärke? Zu den Ausprägungen des mittelalterlichen Amazonenbildes', *Historische Zeitschrift* 270 (2000), pp. 1-38.

Renan, Ernest, *Histoire du peuple d'Israël* (5 vols.; Paris: Calmann Lévy, 1887–93).

Renger, Johannes, 'Die Geschichte der Altorientalistik und der Vorderasiatischen Archäologie in Berlin von 1875 bis 1945', in *Berlin und die Antike: Architektur, Kunstgewerbe, Malerei, Skulptur, Theater und Wissenschaft vom 16. Jahrhundert bis heute* (Aufsätze) (ed. Willmuth Arenhövel and Christa Schreiber; Berlin: Deutsches Archäologisches Institut, 1979), pp. 151-92.

Report of the President, *Bulletin of Yale University*, Second Series No. 7 (June 1906).

Rhoné, Arthur, *L'Egypte à petites journées: Le Caire d'autrefois* (Paris: Société générale d'éditions, new edn, 1910).

Rich, Claudius J. *Memoir on the Ruins of Babylon* (London: Longman, Hurst, Rees, Orme & Brown, 1815).

—*Narrative of a Journey to the Site of Babylon in 1811: Now First Published: Memoir on the Ruins with Engravings from the Original Sketches* (London: Duncan, 1839).

—*Narrative of a Residence in Koordistan, and on the Site of Ancient Nineveh; with Journal of a Voyage down the Tigris to Bagdad and an Account of a Visit to Shirauz and Persepolis, Edited by his Widow* (2 vols.; London: James Duncan, 1836).

—*Second Memoir on Babylon: Containing an Inquiry into the Correspondence between the Ancient Description of Babylon and the Remains Still Visible on the Site* (London: Longman, Hurst, Rees, Orme & Brown etc., 1818).

Richard-Jamet, Céline, 'Cléopâtre: *femme forte* ou femme fatale? Une place équivoque dans les galeries de *femmes fortes* aux XVIe et XVIIe siècles', in Ritschard and Morehead (eds.), *Cléopâtre dans le miroir de l'art occidentale*, pp. 37-52.

Rida, Muhammad Rashid, *Tarikh al-Ustadh al-Imam al-Shaykh Muhammad Abduh: wa-fihi tafsil siratuhu wa-khulasat sirat muqiz al-Sharq al-hakim wa-al-Islam Jamal al-Din al-Afghani* (3 vols.; Cairo: Matbaʿat al-Manar, 1324–50/1906–31).

Ridgway, Ronald S., 'Voltaire', in *NGDO*, IV, p. 1041.

Rieser, Andrew Chamberlin, *The Chautauqua Moment: Protestants, Progressives, and the Culture of Modern Liberalism* (New York: Columbia University Press, 2003).

Ritchie, Lionel Alexander, 'Keith, Alexander (1792–1880)', in *Oxford Dictionary of National Biography: From the Earliest Times to the Year 2000* (60 vols.; ed. H.C.G. Matthew and Brian Harrison; Oxford and New York: Oxford University Press, 2004), XXXI, p. 56.

Ritschard, Claude, and Allison Morehead (eds.), *Cléopâtre dans le miroir de l'art occidentale: Musée Rath, Genève du 25 mars au 1er août 2004* (Geneva: Musées d'art et d'histoire/Milano: 5 Continents, 2004).

Ritter, Helmut, 'Carl Heinrich Becker als Orientalist', *Der Islam* 24 (1937), pp. 175-85.

Ritterband, Paul, and Harold S. Wechsler, *Jewish Learning in American Universities: The First Century* (Modern Jewish Experience; Bloomington, IN: Indiana University Press, 1994).

Rizk, Yunan, 'Al-Ahram: A Diwan of Contemporary Life', *al-Ahram Weekly*, 12-18 August 1993.

Roberts, J.J.M., 'The Ancient Near Eastern Environment', in *The Hebrew Bible and its Modern Interpreters* (ed. Douglas A. Knight and Gene M. Tucker; Philadelphia: Fortress Press/Chico, CA: Scholars Press, 1985), pp. 75-121.

Robinson, Edward and Eli Smith, *Biblical Researches in Palestine, and in the Adjacent Regions: A Journey of Travels in the Year 1838* (3 vols.; Boston: Crocker & Brewster, 3rd edn, 1868–71).

Robinson, Francis (ed.), *The Cambridge Illustrated History of the Islamic World* (Cambridge: Cambridge University Press, 1996).

Robinson, Ira, 'Adler, Cyrus (13 Sept. 1863–7 Apr. 1940)', in *ANB Online* (Oxford University Press, 2005).

Robson, Eleanor, *Mathematics in Ancient Iraq: A Social History* (Princeton, NJ: Princeton University Press [forthcoming]).

Rodinson, Maxime, 'The Western Image and Western Studies of Islam', in *The Legacy of Islam* (ed. Joseph Schacht and C.E. Bosworth; Oxford: Clarendon Press, 2nd edn, 1974), pp. 9-62.

Rofé, Alexander, *Introduction to the Composition of the Pentateuch* (Jerusalem: Academon, 1994).

Rogers, Robert William, *Cuneiform Parallels to the Old Testament* (New York: Eaton & Mains, 1912).

—*Cuneiform Parallels to the Old Testament* (New York: Abingdon Press, 2nd edn, 1926).

—*A History of Babylonia and Assyria* (2 vols.; New York and Cincinnati: Abingdon Press, 6th edn, 1915).

Rogerson, John W., 'Frontiers and Borders in the Old Testament', in *In Search of True Wisdom: Essays in Old Testament Interpretation in Honour of Ronald E. Clements* (ed. Edward Ball; JSOTSup, 300; Sheffield: Sheffield Academic Press, 1999), pp. 116-26.

Roller, Duane W., *The World of Juba II and Kleopatra Selene: Royal Scholarship on Rome's African Frontier* (Routledge Classical Monographs; New York and London: Routledge, 2003).

Röllig, Wolfgang, 'Nitokris von Babylon', in *Beiträge zur alten Geschichte und deren Nachleben: Festschrift für Franz Altheim zum 6.10.1968* (2 vols.; ed. Ruth Stiehl and Hans Erich Stier; Berlin: W. de Gruyter, 1969), I, pp. 127-35.

Rollinger, Robert, and Christoph Ulf (eds.), *Geschlechterrollen und Frauenbild in der Perspektive antiker Autoren* (Innsbruck: Studien-Verlag, 2002).

—(eds.), *Commerce and Monetary Systems in the Ancient World: Means of Transmission and Cultural Interaction: Proceedings of the Fifth Annual Symposium of the Assyrian and Babylonian Intellectual Heritage Project, Held in Innsbruck, Austria, October 3rd-8th 2002* (Melammu Symposia, 5; Stuttgart: Steiner, 2004).

Ronzeaud, Pierre, 'La femme au pouvoir ou le monde à l'envers', *XVIIe Siècle* 108 (1975), pp. 9-33.

Rooses, Max, and Charles Ruelens (eds.), *Correspondance de Rubens et documents épistolaires concernant sa vie et ses oeuvres* (6 vols.; Anvers: Veuve de Backer, 1887–1909).

Root, Margaret Cool, 'Introduction: Women of the Field, Defining the Gendered Experience', in *Breaking Ground: Pioneering Women Archaeologists* (ed. Getzel M. Cohen and Martha Sharp Joukowsky; Ann Arbor, MI: University of Michigan Press, 2004), pp. 1-33.

Rosenthal, Donald, 'A Mughal Portrait Copied by Delacroix', *Burlington Magazine* 119 (1977), pp. 505-506.

Rosenthal, Franz, *Die aramaistische Forschung seit Th. Nöldeke's Veröffentlichungen* (Leiden: E.J. Brill, 1964 [1939]).

Roth, Martha T., *Law Collections from Mesopotamia and Asia Minor* (SBLWAW, 6; Atlanta, GA: Scholars Press, 1995).

Rothenberg, Jacob, *'Descensus ad terram': The Acquisition and Reception of the Elgin Marbles* (Outstanding Dissertations in the Fine Arts; London and New York: Garland, 1977).

Roussillon, Alain (ed.), *Entre réforme sociale et mouvement national: identité et modernisation en Egypte (1882–1962): Actes du colloque 'Réforme social en Egypte' qui s'est tenu du 10 au 13 décembre 1992 à l'Institut français d'archéologie orientale, Le Caire* (Cairo: CEDEJ, 1995).

Roux, Georges, 'Sémiramis, la reine mystérieuse d'orient', in *Initiation à l'Orient ancien: De Sumer à la Bible* (ed. Jean Bottéro; Points: Histoire, H170; Paris: Editions du Seuil, 1992), pp. 184-204.

Rubin, Rehav, 'Ideology and Landscape in Early Printed Maps of Jerusalem', in *Ideology and Landscape in Historical Perspective: Essays on the Meanings of Some Places in the Past* (ed. Alan R.H. Baker and Gideon Biger; Cambridge Studies in Historical Geography, 18; Cambridge: Cambridge University Press, 1992), pp. 15-30.

Rudolph, Wilhelm, *Esra und Nehemia samt 3. Esra* (HAT, 20: Tübingen: J.C.B. Mohr [Paul Siebeck], 1949).

Rule, William Harris, *Oriental Records: Monumental. Confirmatory of the Old Testament Scriptures* (London: Samuel Bagster & Sons, 1877).

Running, Leona Glidden and David Noel Freedman, *William Foxwell Albright: A Twentieth-Century Genius* (New York: The Two Continents Publishing Group and Morgan Press, 1975).

Ruskin, John, *The Works of John Ruskin* (39 vols.; ed. Edward T. Cook and Alexander Wedderburn; London: G. Allen/New York: Longmans, Green, & Co., 1903–12).

Russell, John Malcolm, 'Bulls for the Palace and Order in the Empire: The Sculptural Program of Sennacherib's Court VI at Nineveh', *ArtB* 69 (1987), pp. 520-39.

—*From Nineveh to New York: The Strange Story of the Assyrian Reliefs in the Metropolitan Museum and the Hidden Masterpiece at Canford School* (New Haven: Yale University Press, 1997).

Rydell, Robert W., *All the World's a Fair: Visions of Empire at American International Expositions, 1876–1916* (Chicago: University of Chicago Press, 1984).

—'A Cultural Frankenstein? The Chicago World's Columbian Exposition of 1893', in *Grand Illusions: Chicago's World's Fair of 1893* (ed. Neil Harris *et al.*; Chicago: Chicago Historical Society, 1993), pp. 142-70.

Rydell, Robert W., and Nancy Gwinn (eds.), *Fair Representations: World's Fairs and the Modern World* (European Contributions to American Studies, 27; Amsterdam: VU University Press, 1994).

Sabat, Khalil, *Tarikh al-tibaa fi al-sharq al-arabi* (Maktabat al-dirasat al-tarikhiyah; Cairo: Dar al-Maʿarif, 2nd edn, 1966).

Sachar, Howard Morley, *The Course of Modern Jewish History* (A Delta Book; New York: Dell, 1981).

Sadie, Stanley (ed.), *The New Grove Dictionary of Music and Musicians* (29 vols.; New York: Grove's Dictionaries/London: Macmillan, 2nd edn, 2001).

—(ed.), *The New Grove Dictionary of Opera* (4 vols.; London and New York: Macmillan, 1992).

Saggs, H.W.F., 'Assyriology and Biblical Studies', in *Dictionary of Biblical Interpretation* (ed. John H. Hayes; Nashville: Abingdon Press, 1999), I, pp. 69-83.

—*The Encounter with the Divine in Mesopotamia and Israel* (Jordan Lectures in Comparative Religion, 12; London: Athlone Press, 1978).

—'Introduction', to Layard, *Nineveh and its Remains* (London and New York: Routledge & Kegan Paul, 1970 [London, 1849]), pp. 1-64.

Said, Edward W., *Culture and Imperialism* (New York: Knopf, 1993).

—'Invention, Memory, and Place', *Critical Inquiry* 26 (Winter, 2000), pp. 175-92.

—*Orientalism* (New York: Vintage Books, 1978).

—*Orientalism: Western Conceptions of the Orient* (London: Routledge & Paul Kegan, 2003 [1978]).

Said, Edward W., and David Barsamian, *Culture and Resistance: Conversations with Edward W. Said* (Cambridge, MA: South End Press, 2003).

Sale, George, *An Universal History, from the Earliest Account of Time to the Present: Compiled from Original Authors* (66 vols.; Dublin: George Faulkner, 1744).

Saleh, Mohamed and Hourig Sourouzian, *The Egyptian Museum Cairo: Official Catalogue* (trans. Peter Der Manuelian and Helen Jacquet-Gordon; Cairo: Organisation of Egyptian Antiquities, the Arabian Republic of Egypt/Mainz: Verlag Philipp von Zabern, 1987).

Samārah, ʿĀdil, and Aḥmad Ḥusayn (eds.), *Naqd al-thaqāfawīyah al-burjwāzīyah al-kuluniyālīyah fī utruḥāt Idwārd Saʿīd* (Rām Allāh: Markaz al-Mashriq al-ʿĀmil lil-Dirāsāt al-Thaqāfīyah wa-al-Tanmawīyah, 2000).

Sami, Amin, *Al-Talim fi Misr fi sanatay 1914 wa 1915: wa-bayan tafsili li-nashr al-taʿlim al-awwali wa-al-ibtidaʿi bi-anha' al-diyar al-Misriyya, mumahhadan la-hu bi-shadharat min kitab al-taʿlim* (Cairo: Matbaʾat al-Maʿarif, 1917).

Sammarco, Angelo, *Histoire de l'Egypte moderne depuis Mohammed Ali jusqu'à l'occupation britannique (1801–1882)* (Cairo: Imprimerie de L'Institut français d'archéologie orientale, 1937).

—*Gli italiani in Egitto: il contributo italiano nella formazione dell'Egitto moderno* (Alexandria: Edizioni del fascio, 1937).

Samuel, Irene, 'Semiramis in the Middle Ages: The History of a Legend', *Medievalia et humanistica* 2 (1943), pp. 32-44.

Sandars, Frank Knight, 'The Yale Period', *The Biblical World* 27 (1906), pp. 177-81.

Sanna, Marianne, 'Gottheil, Richard James Horatio (13 Oct. 1863–22 May 1936)', in *ANB*, IX, pp. 323-24.

Sansal, Burak H., 'HAREM in the Ottoman Empire' (http://www.allaboutturkey.com/harem.htm, accessed June 25, 2005).

Sarna, Jonathan D., 'Cyrus Adler and the Development of American Jewish Culture: The "Scholar-Doer" as a Jewish Communal Leader', *American Jewish History* 78 (1989), pp. 382-94.

Sasson, Jack M., 'About "Mari and the Bible"', *RA* 92 (1998), pp. 91-123.

—'The King and I: A Mari King in Changing Perceptions', *JAOS* 118 (1998), pp. 453-70.

—'The King's Table: Food and Fealty in Old Babylonian Mari', in *Food and Identity in the Ancient World* (ed. Cristiano Grottanelli and Lucio Milano; History of the Ancient Near East. Studies, 9; Padua: S.A.R.G.O.N. Editrice e Libreria, 2004), pp. 179-215.

—'On Choosing Models for Recreating Israelite Pre-Monarchic History', *JSOT* 21 (1981), pp. 3-24.

—'On Reading the Diplomatic Letters in the Mari Archives', in Durand and Charpin (eds.), *Mari, Ebla, et les Hourrites* (Amurru, 2), pp. 329-38.

—'Two Recent Works on Mari', *AfO* 27 (1980), pp. 127-35.

Saulcy, Félicien de, 'Musée du Caire', *Revue archéologique* NS 9 (May 1864), pp. 313-22.

Sayce, Archibald Henry, *The 'Higher Criticism' and the Verdict of the Monuments* (London: SPCK, 3rd edn, 1894).

—*The Hittites: The Story of a Forgotten Empire* (London: Religious Tract Society, 4th rev. and enl. edn, 1888).

Sayce, Archibald Henry, (ed.). *Records of the Past: Being English Translations of the Ancient Monuments of Egypt and Western Asia*. New Series (6 vols.; London: Samuel Bagster & Sons, 1888–92).

Schaff, Philip, *Through Bible Lands: Notes of Travel in Egypt, the Desert, and Palestine* (New York: American Tract Society, 1878).

Schiffer, Michael B., *Formation Processes of the Archaeological Record* (Albuquerque, NM: University of New Mexico Press, 1987).

Schlenther, Boyd Stanley, *Charles Thomson: A Patriot's Pursuit* (Newark, DE: University of Delaware Press, 1990).

Schloder, M. John E., 'Une artiste oublié: Nicolas Prévost, peintre de Richelieu', *Bulletin de la Société de l'histoire de l'art français* 1980 (1982), pp. 50-69.

Schlumbohm, Christa, 'Die Glorifizierung der Barockfürstin als "Femme Forte" ', in *Europäische Hofkultur im 16. und 17. Jahrhundert: Vorträge und Referate gehalten anlässlich des Kongresses des Wolfenbütteler Arbeitskreises für Renaissanceforschung und des Internationalen Arbeitskreises für Barockliteratur in der Herzog August Bibliothek Wolfenbüttel vom 4. bis 8. September 1979* (3 vols.; ed. August Buck *et al.*; Wolfenbütteler Arbeiten zur Barockforschung, 9; Hamburg: Hauswedell, 1981), II, pp. 113-22.

Schmökel, Hartmut, *Geschichte des alten Vorderasien* (Handbuch der Orientalistik. 1 Abt., Der Nahe und der Mittlere Osten; 2. Bd., 3. Abschnitt; Leiden: E.J. Brill, 1957).

Schnorr von Carolsfeld, Julius, *Das Buch der Bücher in Bildern: 240 Darstellungen, erfunden und gezeichnet* (Leipzig: Georg Wigand, 1908).

—*Schnorr's Bible Pictures: Scripture History Illustrated in One Hundred and Eight Wood Cuts from Original Designs* (London: Williams & Norgate, 1860).

Schott, Albert, *Die Vergleiche in den akkadischen Königsinschriften* (MVAG, 30; Leipzig: J.C. Hinrichs, 1925).

Schrader, Eberhard, *The Cuneiform Inscriptions and the Old Testament* (2 vols.; trans. Owen C. Whitehouse from the 2nd German edn; Theological Translation Fund Library, 33, 38; London and Edinburgh: Williams & Norgate, 1885, 1888).

—*Die Keilinschriften und das Alte Testament* (Giessen: J. Ricker, 1872; 2. umgearb. und sehr verm. Aufl., 1883).

Schrader, Eberhard, Heinrich Zimmern and Hugo Winckler, *Die Keilinschriften und das Alte Testament*. I. *Geschichte und Geographie*. II. *Religion und Sprache* (Berlin: Reuther & Reichard, 3. Aufl. mit Ausdehnung auf die Apokryphen, Pseudepigraphen und das Neue Testament, 1902–1903).

Schröder, Horst, *Der Topos der Nine Worthies in Literatur und bildender Kunst* (Göttingen: Vandenhoeck & Ruprecht, 1971).

Schueller, Malini Johar, *U.S. Orientalisms: Race, Nation, and Gender in Literature, 1790–1890* (Ann Arbor, MI: University of Michigan Press, 1998).

Schwab, Raymond, *Vie d'Anquetil-Duperron, suivie des usages civils et religieux des Parses par Anquetil-Duperron* (Paris: E. Leroux, 1934).

Schwanitz, Wolfgang G., 'The German Middle Eastern Policy, 1871–1945', *Princeton Papers, Interdisciplinary Journal of Middle Eastern Studies* 10–11 (2001), pp. 1-23.

Scott 2000 Standard Postage Stamp Catalogue, Countries of the World. II. *Countries C-F* (Sidney, OH: Scott Publishing Co., 156th edn, 2000).

Seddon, Thomas, *Memoir and Letters of the Late Thomas Seddon, Artist* (ed. John Pollard Seddon; London: James Nisbet & Co., 1858).

Segovia, Fernando F., *Decolonizing Biblical Studies: A View from the Margins* (Maryknoll, NY: Orbis Books, 2000).

Segovia, Fernando F., and Mary Ann Tolbert (eds.), *Teaching the Bible: The Discourses and Politics of Biblical Pedagogy* (Maryknoll, NY: Orbis Books, 1998).

Seznec, Jean, *John Martin en France* (All Souls Studies, 4; London: Faber & Faber, 1964).

Shakespeare, William, *The Complete Works of William Shakespeare: With Thirty-Two Full Page Plates from Modern Stage Production* (London, New York, Toronto: Oxford University Press, 1955).

Shankar, S., 'Post-Postcolonial Theory', in *Encyclopedia of Postcolonial Studies* (ed. John C. Hawley; Westport, CT: Greenwood Press, 2001), pp. 359-63.

Shanks, Hershel, 'The Storm over the Bone Box', *BAR* 29 (2003), pp. 27-39, 83.

Sharafuddin, Mohammed, *Islam and Romantic Orientalism: Literary Encounters with the Orient* (London and New York: I.B. Tauris, 1994).

Shavit, David, *The United States in the Middle East: A Historical Dictionary* (New York: Greenwood Press, 1988).

Shavit, Jacob, *History in Black: African-Americans in Search of an Ancient Past* (London and Portland, OR: Frank Cass, 2001).

Shaw, William Bristol, 'Wolfe, Catharine Lorillard (March 1828–Apr. 4, 1887)', in *DAB*, XX, pp. 449-50.

Shayyal, Jamal Al-Din al-, *A History of Egyptian Historiography in the Nineteenth Century* (Alexandria University. Faculty of Arts. Publication, 15; Alexandria: Alexandria University Press, 1960).

Sheehi, Stephen P., 'Edward Said', in *Encyclopedia of Postcolonial Studies* (ed. John C. Hawley; Westport, CT: Greenwood Press, 2001), pp. 392-97.

Shuckford, Samuel, *The Sacred and Profane History of the World Connected, from the Creation of the World to the Dissolution of the Assyrian Empire at the Death of Sardanapalus, and to the Declension of the Kingdoms of Judah and Israel under the Reigns of Ahaz and Pekah* (2 vols.; London: R. Knaplock & J. Tonson, 1728–30).

Sidey, Tessa, *Prints in Focus: Birmingham Museums and Art Gallery* (Birmingham: Birmingham Museums and Art Gallery, 1997).

Siegel, Thomas J., 'Professor Stephen Sewall and the Transformation of Hebrew at Harvard', in *Hebrew and the Bible in America: The First Two Centuries* (ed. Shalom Goldman; Brandeis Series in American Jewish History, Culture, and Life; Hanover, NH: University Press of New England for Brandeis University Press and Dartmouth College, 1993), pp. 228-45.

Silber, Evelyn, *The Sculpture of Epstein: With a Complete Catalogue* (Oxford: Phaidon, 1986).

Silberman, Neil Asher, 'Between Athens and Babylon: The AIA and the Politics of American Near Eastern Archaeology, 1884–1997', in *Excavating our Past: Perspectives on the History of the Archaeological Institute of America* (ed. Susan Heuck Allen; Colloquia and Conference Papers, 5; Boston: Archaeological Institute of America, 2002), pp. 115-22.

—*Digging for God and Country: Exploration, Archaeology, and the Secret Struggle for the Holy Land, 1799–1917* (New York: Knopf, 1982).

—'Promised Lands and Chosen Peoples: The Politics and Poetics of Archaeological Narrative', in *Nationalism, Politics, and the Practice of Archaeology* (ed. Philip L. Kohl and Clare P. Fawcett; Cambridge and New York: Cambridge University Press, 1995), pp. 249-62.

Simoën, Jean-Claude, *Egypte éternelle: les voyageurs photographes au siècle dernier* (Paris: J.C. Lattès, 1993),

Smith, Clyde Curry, 'Some Footnotes to the History of Assyriology: Leonard William King of the British Museum and the University of Pennsylvania', in *If a Man Builds a Joyful House: Assyriological Studies in Honor of Erle Verdun Leichty* (ed. Ann K. Guinan *et al.*; Cuneiform Monographs, 31; Leiden; Boston: Brill, 2006), pp. 431-41.

Smith, George, *Assyrian Discoveries: An Account of Explorations and Discoveries on the Site of Nineveh, during 1873 and 1874* (New York: Scribner, Armstrong, 1875).

—*The Chaldean Account of Genesis, Containing the Description of the Creation, the Fall of Man, the Deluge, the Tower of Babel, the Times of the Patriarchs, and Nimrod: Babylonian Fables, and Legends of the Gods from the Cuneiform Inscriptions* (New York: Scribner, Armstrong & Co., 1876).

—'The Chaldean History of the Deluge', *The* [*London*] *Times*, no. 27551, 4 December 1872.

—'The Chaldean Story of the Deluge', *The* [*London*] *Times*, no. 27552, 5 December 1872.

—*History of Assurbanipal: Translated from the Cuneiform Inscriptions* (London: Williams & Norgate, 1871).

Smith, George Adam, *Atlas of the Historical Geography of the Holy Land* (London: Hodder & Stoughton, 1915).

Smith, Mark S., 'Ugaritic Studies and the Hebrew Bible, 1968–1998 (with an Excursus on Judean Monotheism and the Ugaritic Texts)', in *Congress Volume: Oslo 1998* (ed. André Lemaire and Magne Sæbø; VTSup, 80; Leiden: E.J. Brill, 2000), pp. 327-52.

—*Untold Stories: The Bible and Ugaritic Studies in the Twentieth Century* (Peabody, MA: Hendrickson, 2001).

Smith, Neil, *Uneven Development: Nature, Capital, and the Production of Space* (Oxford: Blackwell, 1990).

Smith, W. Robertson, *The Religion of the Semites: The Fundamental Institutions* (New York: Schocken Books, 1972).

Smith, William, *Dr William Smith's Dictionary of the Bible: Comprising its Antiquities, Biography, Geography, and Natural History* (4 vols.; New York: Hurd & Houghton, rev. edn, 1869).

Smith, William, and George Grove, *An Atlas of Ancient Geography, Biblical & Classical: To Illustrate the Dictionary of the Bible and the Classical Dictionaries* (London: John Murray, 1874).

Smithsonian Institution, *The Books of the Fair: Materials about World's Fairs, 1834–1916, in the Smithsonian Institution Libraries* (intro. Robert W. Rydell; Smithsonian Institution Libraries Research Guide, 6; Chicago: American Library Association, 1992).

Snodgrass, Judith, *Presenting Japanese Buddhism to the West: Orientalism, Occidentalism, and the Columbian Exposition* (Chapel Hill, NC: University of North Carolina Press, 2003).

Soden, Wolfram von, *Der Aufstieg des Assyrerreiches als geschichtliches Problem* (Der Alte Orient, 37/1-2; Leipzig: J.C. Hinrichs, 1937).

Soja, Edward W., *Postmodern Geographies: The Reassertion of Space in Critical Theory* (London and New York: Verso, 1989).

—*Thirdspace: Journeys to Los Angeles and Other Real-and-Imagined Places* (Oxford: Blackwell, 1996).

Solvang, Elna K., *A Woman's Place is in the House: Royal Women of Judah and their Involvement in the House of David* (JSOTSup, 349; Sheffield: Sheffield Academic Press, 2003).

Sommer, Annie van, and Samuel Marinus Zwemer (eds.), *Daylight in the Harem: A New Era for Moslem Women, Papers on Present-Day Reform Movements, Conditions and*

Methods of Work among Moslem Women, Read at the Lucknow Conference, 1911 (New York: Fleming H. Revell Company, 1911).

Spector, Jack J., *Delacroix: The Death of Sardanapalus* (Art in Context; New York: Viking Press, 1974).

Speiser, E.A., 'Word Plays of the Creation Epic's Version of the Founding of Babylon', *Orientalia* NS 25 (1956), pp. 317-23 = *Oriental and Biblical Studies. Collected Writings of E.A. Speiser* (ed. J.J. Finkelstein and Moshe Greenberg; Philadelphia: University of Pennsylvania Press, 1967), pp. 53-61.

Spieckermann, Hermann, *Juda unter Assur in der Sargonidenzeit* (FRLANT, 129; Göttingen: Vandenhoeck & Ruprecht, 1982).

Staley, Allen, *The Pre-Raphaelite Landscape* (Oxford Studies in the History of Art and Architecture; Oxford: Clarendon Press, 1973).

Standard Catalog of World Coins, 1801–1900 (Iola, WI: Krause, 2nd edn, 1998).

Standard Catalog of World Coins, 2001 (Iola, WI: Krause, 2000).

Stanhope, Philip, 5th Earl Stanhope, 'The Royal Academy', *Art-Journal* (June 1865), pp. 161-72.

Stebbins, Theodore E., *The Lure of Italy: American Artists and the Italian Experience, 1760–1914* (Boston: Museum of Fine Arts, in association with Harry N. Abrams, 1992).

Steiner, Richard C., 'The Aramaic Text in Demotic Script (1.99)', in *COS*, I, pp. 309-27.

Steinke, William A., 'An Archaeological Source for Delacroix's *Death of Sardanapalus*', *ArtB* 66 (1984), pp. 318-20.

Stol, Marten, 'Nanea', in *DDDB*[2], pp. 612-14.

—'Women in Mesopotamia', *JESHO* 39 (1995), pp. 123-44.

Stolper, Matthew W., 'On Why and How', in Gunter (ed.), *The Construction of the Ancient Near East*, pp. 13-22.

Stone, Elizabeth C., 'Economic Crisis and Social Upheaval in Old Babylonian Nippur', in *Mountains and Lowlands: Essays in the Archaeology of Greater Mesopotamia* (ed. Louis D. Levine and T.C. Young; Bibliotheca Mesopotamica, 7; Malibu, CA: Undena Publications, 1977), pp. 267-89.

Storr, Richard J., *The Beginnings of Graduate Education in America* (Chicago: University of Chicago Press, 1953).

—*Harper's University: The Beginnings; A History of the University of Chicago* (Chicago: University of Chicago Press, 1966).

Streck, Maximilian, *Assurbanipal und die letzten assyrischen Könige bis zum Untergange Nineveh's* (VAB, 7; Leipzig: J.C. Hinrichs, 1916).

Streck, Michael P., 'Der Wiederaufbau Babylons unter Asarhaddon und Assurbanipal in Briefen aus Ninive', *Altorientalische Forschungen* 29 (2002), pp. 205-33.

Strohm, Reinhard, *Die italienische Oper im 18. Jahrhundert* (Taschenbücher zur Musikwissenschaft, 25; Wilhelmshaven: Heinrichshofen, 1979).

Strommenger, Eva, *5000 Years of the Art of Mesopotamia* (trans. Christina Haglund; New York: Harry N. Abrams, 1964).

Stuart, Moses, *A Hebrew Grammar without the Points; Designed as an Introduction to the Knowledge of the Inflections and Idiom of the Hebrew Tongue* (Andover: Flagg & Gould, 1813).

Sugirtharajah, R.S., *The Bible and the Third World: Precolonial, Colonial, and Postcolonial Encounters* (Cambridge: Cambridge University Press, 2001).

—*Imagining Hinduism: A Postcolonial Perspective* (London and New York: Routledge, 2003).

—*The Postcolonial Bible* (The Bible and Postcolonialism, 1; Sheffield: Sheffield Academic Press, 1998).

—*Postcolonial Criticism and Biblical Interpretation* (Oxford: Oxford University Press, 2002).

—(ed.), *Vernacular Hermeneutics* (The Bible and Postcolonialism, 2; Sheffield: Sheffield Academic Press, 1999).

—*Voices from the Margin: Interpreting the Bible in the Third World* (Maryknoll, NY: Orbis Books, 1991).

Suleiman, Susan R., 'Introduction: Varieties of Audience-Oriented Criticism', in *The Reader in the Text* (ed. S.R. Suleiman and Inge Crosman; Princeton, NJ: Princeton University Press, 1980), pp. 3-45.

Suskin, Sylvan, 'Catel, Charles-Simon', in *NGDO*, I, pp. 772-74.

Swails, John W., 'Austen Henry Layard and the Near East, 1839–1880', PhD dissertation, University of Georgia, 1983.

Swayne, George C., *The History of Herodotus* (Edinburgh: William Blackwood & Sons, 1870).

Sweek, Joel, 'The Monuments, the *Babel–Bibel Streit* and Responses to Historical Criticism', in *The Pitcher is Broken: Memorial Essays for Gösta W. Ahlström* (ed. S.W. Holloway and L.K. Handy; JSOTSup, 190; Sheffield: Sheffield Academic Press, 1995), pp. 401-19.

Sweeney, Marvin A., *King Josiah of Judah: The Lost Messiah of Israel* (Oxford: Oxford University Press, 2001).

Synkellos, George, *The Chronography of George Synkellos: A Byzantine Chronicle of Universal History from the Creation* (trans. and ed. William Adler and Paul Tuffin; Oxford: Oxford University Press, 2002).

Tadmor, Hayim, *The Inscriptions of Tiglath-pileser III, King of Assyria: Critical Edition, with Introductions, Translations, and Commentary* (Jerusalem: Israel Academy of Sciences and Humanities, 1994).

Tadmor, Hayim, and Moshe Weinfeld (eds.), *History, Historiography, and Interpretation: Studies in Biblical and Cuneiform Literatures* (Jerusalem: Magnes Press, 1984).

Taeger, Fritz, *Das Altertum: Geschichte und Gestalt* (3 vols.; Stuttgart: W. Kohlhammer, 1939).

Ṭahṭāwī, Rifāʿah Rāfiʿ al-, *Al-Amal al-kamila li-Rifaa Rafi al-Tahtawi*. III. *Tarikh Misr wa al-arab qabla al-Islam* (ed. Muhammad Amara; Beirut: al-Muʾassassah al-ʿArabiyah lil-Dirasat wa-al-Nashr, 1974).

Talbot, William Henry Fox, 'The Legend of Ishtar Descending to Hades', *TSBA* 2 (1873), pp. 179-212.

Talmon, Shemaryahu, 'The "Comparative Method" in Biblical Interpretation—Principles and Problems', in *Congress Volume: Göttingen 1977* (ed. John A. Emerton; VTSup, 29; Leiden: E.J. Brill, 1978), pp. 320-56.

Taussig, Michael T., *Mimesis and Alterity: A Particular History of the Senses* (New York: Routledge, 1993).

Taylor, N.A., 'The Theological Seminary in the Configuration of American Higher Education: The Ante-Bellum Years', *History of Education Annual* 17 (1977), pp. 17-30.

Taylor, C. (ed.), *Calmet's Dictionary of the Holy Bible: With Biblical Fragments* (5 vols.; London: Henry G. Bohn, 9th edn, 1847).

Tedder, Henry Richard, 'Societies, Learned', in *EB*[11], XXV, pp. 309-19.

Temple, Robert K.G., *Crystal Sun: Rediscovering a Lost Technique of the Ancient World* (London: Arrow, 1999).

Tennyson, Alfred, *Poems* (London: Moxon, 1857).

Thackeray, William Makepeace, *The Paris Sketch Book of Mr M.A. Titmarsh: The Irish*

Sketchbook; and Notes of a Journey from Cornhill to Grand Cairo (New York: n.p., n.d.).

—'Roundabout Papers, Vol. V', *Cornhill Magazine* 2 (July 1860), pp. 122-28.

—*Vanity Fair* (Penguin English Library, EL35; Harmondsworth: Penguin Books, 1968 [1848]).

Thieme, Ulrich and Felix Becker (eds.), *Allgemeines Lexikon der bildenden Künstler von der Antike bis zur Gegenwart: Unter Mitwirkung von 300 Fachgelehrten des In- und Auslandes* (37 vols.; Leipzig, 1907–50).

Thomas, D. Winton (ed.), *Documents from Old Testament Times* (London and New York: Thomas Nelson and Sons, 1958).

Thomas, Nicholas, *Colonialism's Culture: Anthropology, Travel, and Government* (Princeton, NJ: Princeton University Press, 1994).

Thompson, Jason, *Sir Gardner Wilkinson and his Circle* (Austin: University of Texas Press, 1992).

Thompson, Thomas L., 'Defining History and Ethnicity in the South Levant', in *Can a 'History of Israel' be Written?* (ed. Lester L. Grabbe; JSOTSup, 245; European Seminar in Historical Methodology, 1; Sheffield: Sheffield Academic Press, 1997), pp. 166-87.

—*The Historicity of the Patriarchal Narratives* (BZAW, 133; Berlin: W. de Gruyter, 1974).

Thomson, William M., *The Land and the Book: Or, Biblical Illustrations Drawn from the Manners and Customs, the Scenes and Scenery, of the Holy Land* (2 vols.; New York: Harper & Brothers, 3rd edn, 1880).

Thornton, Lynne, *The Orientalists: Painter-Travellers, 1828–1908* (trans. Helga and Dinah Harrison; Paris: ACR Edition, 1983).

Thuesen, Peter J., *In Discordance with the Scriptures: American Protestant Battles over Translating the Bible* (Religion in America Series; Oxford: Oxford University Press, 1999).

Thuillier, Jacques and Jacques Foucart, *Ruben's Life of Marie de' Medici* (trans. Robert Erich Wolf; New York: Harry N. Abrams, 1970).

Thureau-Dangin, F., 'Iasmaḫ-Adad', *RA* 34 (1937), pp. 135-39.

Tibawi, Abdul Latif al-, 'English-Speaking Orientalists: A Critique of their Approach to Islam and Arab Nationalism', *Islamic Quarterly* 8 (1964), pp. 25-45, 73-88.

—'On the Orientalists Again', *Muslim World* 70 (1980), pp. 56-61.

—'Second Critique of the English-Speaking Orientalists and their Approach to Islam and the Arabs', *Islamic Quarterly* 23 (1979), pp. 3-54.

Tidrick, Kathryn, *Heart-Beguiling Araby* (Cambridge: Cambridge University Press, 1981).

Tigay, Jeffrey H., 'On Evaluating Claims of Literary Borrowing', in *The Tablet and the Scroll: Near Eastern Studies in Honor of William W. Hallo* (ed. Mark E. Cohen, Daniel C. Snell and David B. Weisberg; Bethesda, MD: CDL Press, 1993), pp. 250-55.

Toorn, Karel van der, *Family Religion in Babylonia, Syria and Israel: Continuity and Changes in the Forms of Religious Life* (SHCANE, 7; Leiden: E.J. Brill, 1996).

Toorn, Karel van der, Bob Becking and Pieter W. van der Horst (eds.), *Dictionary of Deities and Demons in the Bible* (Leiden: E.J. Brill: 2nd edn, 1999).

Torrey, Charles C., *The Composition and Historical Value of Ezra–Nehemiah* (BZAW, 2; Giessen: J. Ricker Buchhandlung, 1896).

—*Ezra Studies* (Chicago: University of Chicago Press, 1910; repr. edited with a prolegomenon by W.F. Stinespring; New York: Ktav Publishing House, 1970).

—'The Outlook for Oriental Studies', *JAOS* 38 (1918), pp. 107-20.

Tourneux, Maurice, *Eugène Delacroix devant ses contemporains, ses écrits, ses biographes, ses critiques* (Bibliothèque internationale de l'art; Paris: Librairie de l'art, 1886).

Trad, May, 'Journal d'entrée et catalogue général', *ASAE* 70 (1984–85), pp. 352-57.

Trafton, Scott, *Egypt Land: Race and Nineteenth-Century American Egyptomania* (Durham, NC and London: Duke University Press, 2004).

Tremayne, Arch, *Temple Records from Erech, Reign of Cyrus, 538–529 B.C.* (YOS, Babylonian Texts, 7; New Haven: Yale University Press, 1925).

Trigger, Bruce G., 'Alternative Archaeologies: Nationalist, Colonialist, Imperialist', *Man* NS 19 (1984), pp. 355-70.

Trollope, Anthony, *The Way We Live Now* (ed. John Andrew Sutherland; Oxford World's Classics; Oxford: Oxford University Press, 1999 [1875]).

Troyer, Kristin de, *The End of the Alpha Text of Esther: Translation and Narrative Technique in MT 8:1-17, LXX 8:1-17, and AT 7:14-41* (trans. Brian Doyle; SBLSCS, 48; Atlanta, GA: Society of Biblical Literature, 2000).

Turner, Bryan S., *Marx and the End of Orientalism* (Controversies in Sociology, 7; London: George Allen & Unwin, 1978).

—*Orientalism, Postmodernism and Globalism* (London and New York: Routledge, 1994).

Turner, Jane (ed.), *The Dictionary of Art* (34 vols.; London: Macmillan, 1992).

Üchtritz-Amade, Gräfin Stephanie, *Semiramis* (Zürich, Leipzig, Wien: Amalthea Verlag, 1931).

Uehlinger, Christoph, *Weltreich und 'eine Rede': Eine neue Deutung der sogenannten Turmbauerzählung (Gen 11, 1-9)* (OBO, 101; Freiburg, Switzerland: Universitätsverlag/Göttingen: Vandenhoeck & Ruprecht, 1990).

Ustorf, Werner, '*Wissenschaft*, Africa and the Cultural Process according to Johann Gottfried Herder (1744–1803),' in *European Traditions in the Study of Religion in Africa* (ed. Frieder Ludwig and Afe Adogame; Wiesbaden: Harrassowitz, 2004), pp. 117-27.

Vaczek, Louis and Gail Buckland, *Travellers in Ancient Lands: A Portrait of the Middle East, 1839–1919* (Boston: New York Graphic Society, 1981).

Valéry, Paul, *The Collected Works of Paul Valéry*. 3. *Plays* (ed. Jackson Mathews; Bollingen Series, 45; New York: Pantheon Books, 1960).

—*Poésies* (Collection Soleil, 54; Paris: Gallimard, 22nd edn, 1942).

Van de Mieroop, Marc, *A History of the Ancient Near East, ca. 3000–323 BC* (Blackwell History of the Ancient World, 1; Oxford: Blackwell, 2004).

—*King Hammurabi of Babylon: A Biography* (Blackwell Ancient Lives; London: Blackwell Publishing, 2004).

Van Seters, John, *Abraham in History and Tradition* (New Haven: Yale University Press, 1975).

—'Divine Encounter at Bethel (Gen 28,10-22) in Recent Literary-Critical Study of Genesis', *ZAW* 110 (1998), pp. 503-13.

Vandewalle, C.B., 'Roger Bacon dans l'histoire de la philologie', *La France franciscaine* 11 (1928), pp. 315-409; 12 (1929), pp. 45-90, 161-228.

Vanstiphout, Herman L.J., *Epics of Sumerian Kings: The Matter of Aratta* (SBLWAW, 20; Atlanta, GA: Society of Biblical Literature, 2003).

Vassalli, Luigi, *L'egittologo Luigi Vassalli (1812–1887): disegni e documenti nei Civici Istituti Culturali Milanesi* (Milan: Edizioni ET, 1994).

Vasselin, Martine, 'Histoires déformées, mirois déformants: l'image artistique des héroines au XVIe siècle', *Nouvelle revue du XVI*[e] *siècle* 12 (1994), pp. 33-62.

Vaughn, Andrew G., *Theology, History, and Archaeology in the Chronicler's Account of Hezekiah* (SBLABS, 4; Atlanta, GA: Scholars Press, 1999).

Vaux, Roland de, 'The Decrees of Cyrus and Darius on the Rebuilding of the Temple', in *Bible and the Ancient Near East* (trans. Damian McHugh; London: Darton, Longman & Todd, 1971), pp. 63-96.

Veenhof, Klaas R., '"Seeing the Face of God": The Use of Akkadian Parallels', *Akkadica* 94–95 (1995), pp. 33-37.

Venn, Couze, *Occidentalism: Modernity and Subjectivity* (London and Thousand Oaks, CA: Sage Publications, 2000).

Vincent, Hugues, *Canaan d'après l'exploration récente* (Etudes bibliques; Paris: J. Gabalda & Cie, 1907).

Volkoff, Oleg V., *Comment on visitait la vallée du Nil: les 'Guides' de l'Egypte* (Recherches d'archéologie, de philologie et d'histoire, 28; Cairo: IFAO, 1967).

Vollers, K., 'Le IXme congrès international des orientalistes tenu à Londres du 5 au 12 septembre 1892', *BIE,* ser. 3, 3 (November 1892), p. 193.

Vollkommer, Rainer (ed.), *Künstlerlexikon der Antike* (2 vols.; München and Leipzig: K.G. Saur, 2001–).

Voltaire, François-Marie Arouet de, *Sémiramis: Tragédie* (ed. J.-J. Olivier; Textes littéraires français, 5; Paris: Droz, 1946),

Vriezen, Th. C., 'The Study of the Old Testament and the History of Religion', in *Congress Volume in Rome 1968* (VTSup, 17; Leiden: E.J. Brill, 1969), pp. 1-24.

Waardenburg, Jacques D.J., 'The Study of Islam in Dutch Scholarship', in *Mapping Islamic Studies: Genealogy, Continuity and Change* (ed. Azim Nanji; Religion and Reason, 38; Berlin and New York: Mouton de Gruyter, 1997), pp. 68-94.

Wakeman, Geoffrey, *Victorian Book Illustration: The Technical Revolution* (Detroit, MI: Gale Research Company, 1973).

Walia, Shelley, *Edward Said and the Writing of History* (Postmodern Encounters; Duxford, Cambridge and Lanham, MD: Icon Books; Totem Books USA).

Wallins, Roger P., '*The Quarterly Review*', in *British Literary Magazines: The Romantic Age, 1789–1836* (4 vols.; ed. Alvin Sullivan; Historical Guides to the World's Periodicals and Newspapers; Westport, CT: Greenwood Press, 1983), II, pp. 359-67.

Ward, William Hayes, 'The Hamath Inscriptions', *Palestine Exploration Society* 2 (1873), pp. 19-26.

—*What I Believe and Why* (New York: Charles Scribner's Sons, 1915).

Warner, Nicholas (ed.), *An Egyptian Panorama: Reports from the 19th Century British Press* (Cairo: Zeitouna, 1994).

Wasilewska, Ewa, *The Forgotten American Indiana Jones* [forthcoming], a biography of E.J. Banks, a version of which is available online at http://www.worldandi.com/Public/2000/August/indy.html, accessed September 28, 2006.

Wasserman, Nathan, *Style and Form in Old-Babylonian Literary Texts* (Cuneiform Monographs, 27; Leiden: Brill and Styx, 2003).

Waterfield, Gordon, *Layard of Nineveh* (New York and Washington, DC: Frederick A. Praeger, 1963).

Waterhouse, John C.G., 'Respighi, Ottorino', *NGDO*, III, p. 1295.

Weber, Eugen Joseph, *A Modern History of Europe: Men, Cultures, and Societies from the Renaissance to the Present* (New York: W.W. Norton, 1971).

Wechsler, Harold S., 'Pulpit or Professoriate: The Case of Morris Jastrow', *American Jewish History* 74 (1985), pp. 338-55.

Weidner, Ernst F., 'Hof- und Harems-Erlasse assyrischer Könige aus dem 2. Jahrtausend v. Chr.', *AfO* 17 (1954–56), pp. 257-93.

Weiher, Egbert von, *Spätbabylonische Texte aus Uruk, Teil III* (Ausgrabungen der Deutschen Forschungsgemeinschaft in Uruk-Warka, 12; Berlin: Gebr. Mann Verlag, 1988).

Weinfeld, Moshe, *Genesis: The Pentateuch with a New Commentary* (Tel Aviv: S.L. Gordon, 1975) [Hebrew].

—'Semiramis: Her Name and her Origin', in Cogan and Eph'al (eds.), *Ah, Assyria...*, pp. 99-103.

—'Zion and Jerusalem as Religious and Political Capital: Ideology and Utopia', in *The Poet and the Historian. Essays in Literary and Historical Biblical Criticism* (ed. Richard Elliott Friedman; HSS, 26; Chico, CA: Scholars Press, 1983), pp. 75-115.

Weippert, Manfred, ' "König, fürchte dich nicht!" Assyrische Prophetie im 7. Jahrhundert v. Chr.', *Or* 71 (2002), pp. 1-54.

Weisberg, David B., 'The Impact of Assyriology on Biblical Studies', in *COS*, III, pp. xliii-xlviii.

Wellhausen, Julius, 'Review of E. Meyer, *Entstehung des Judenthums*', *Göttingische gelehrte Anzeigen* 159/2 (1897), pp. 89-97.

—'Die Rückkehr der Juden aus dem babylonischen Exil', *Nachrichten von der Königl. Gesellschaft der Wissenschaften in Göttingen*, Philologisch-historische Klasse (Berlin: Akademie der Wissenschaften, 1895), pp. 166-86.

Wendell, Charles, *The Evolution of the Egyptian National Image: From its Origins to Ahmad Lutfi al-Sayyid* (Berkeley: University of California Press, 1972).

Wesemael, Pieter van, *Architecture of Instruction and Delight: A Socio-Historical Analysis of World Exhibitions as a Didactic Phenomenon (1798–1851–1970)* (Rotterdam: 010 Publishers, 2001).

West, M.L., *The East Face of Helicon: West Asiatic Elements in Greek Poetry and Myth* (Oxford: Clarendon Press, 1997).

Westenholz, Joan Goodnick, 'The Foundation Myths of Mesopotamian Cities: Divine Planners and Human Builders', in *Mites de fundació de ciutats al món antic (Mesopotàmia, Grècia i Roma)* (ed. Pedro Azara, Ricardo Mar and Eva Subias Pascual; Actes del Colloqui, Monografies, 2; Barcelona: Museu d'Arqueologia de Catalunya, 2001), pp. 59-68.

—'Nanaya: Lady of Mystery', in *Sumerian Gods and their Representations* (ed. Irving L. Finkel and Mark J. Geller; Cuneiform Monographs, 7; Groningen: Styx, 1997), pp. 57-84.

—'Review of Volker Haas, *Babylonische Liebesgarten: Erotik und Sexualität im alten Orient* (München, 1999)', *NIN*, Journal of Gender Studies in Antiquity 2 (2001), pp. 119-32.

—'The Theological Foundation of the City, The Capital City and Babylon', in *Capital Cities: Urban Planning and Spiritual Dimensions. Proceedings of the Symposium Held on May 27-29 Jerusalem, Israel* (ed. J.G. Westenholz; Jerusalem: Bible Lands Museum, 1998), pp. 43-45.

—'Towards a New Conceptualization of the Female Role in Mesopotamian Society', *JAOS* 110 (1990), pp. 510-21.

Wheatley, Richard, 'The Jews in New York', *The Century Magazine* 43 (1892), pp. 323-42.

Whitelam, Keith W., 'The Identity of Early Israel: The Realignment and Transformation of Late Bronze-Age Palestine', *JSOT* 63 (1994), pp. 57-87.

—*The Invention of Ancient Israel: The Silencing of Palestinian History* (London and New York: Routledge, 1996).

—'Representing Minimalism: The Rhetoric and Reality of Revisionism', in *Sense and Sensitivity: Essays on Reading the Bible in Memory of Robert Carroll* (ed. Alastair G. Hunter and Philip R. Davies; JSOTSup, 348; Sheffield: Sheffield Academic Press, 2002), pp. 194-223.

Whiting, Robert M., 'Amorite Tribes and Nations of Second-Millennium Western Asia', in *CANE*, II, p. 1231-42.

Whiting, Robert M., (ed.), *Mythology and Mythologies: Methodological Approaches to Intercultural Influences: Proceedings of the Second Annual Symposium of the Assyrian and Babylonian Intellectual Heritage Project, Held in Paris, France, Oct. 4-7, 1999* (Melammu Symposia, 2; Helsinki: The Neo-Assyrian Text Corpus Project, 2001).

Widengren, Geo, 'Evolutionism and the Problem of the Origin of Religion', *Ethnos* 10 (1945), pp. 72-96.

Wiesehöfer, Josef, ' "Denn es sind welthistorische Siege…": Nineteenth- and Twentieth-Century German Views of the Persian Wars', in Gunter (ed.), *The Construction of the Ancient Near East*, pp. 61-83.

Wiesner, Merry E., *Women and Gender in Early Modern Europe* (New Approaches to European History, 20; Cambridge and New York: Cambridge University Press, 2nd edn, 2000).

Wiggins, Steve A., *A Reassessment of 'Asherah': A Study according to the Textual Sources of the First Two Millennia B.C.E.* (AOAT, 235; Kevelaer: Butzon & Bercker/Neukirchen–Vluyn: Neukirchener Verlag, 1993).

Wilcke, C., 'Epic, Play or What? Or: How was the "Epic" of "Enmerkar and Ensuḫgiriana" Performed?', paper read at the 215th American Oriental Society meeting held in Philadelphia, 2005.

Wilcoxen, Jay A., 'The Political Background of Jeremiah's Temple Sermon', in *Scripture in History and Theology: Essays in Honor of J. Coert Rylaarsdam* (ed. Arthur L. Merrill and Thomas W. Overholt; Pittsburgh Theological Monograph, 17; Pittsburgh: Pickwick Press, 1977), pp. 151-66.

Wildman, Stephen, *Visions of Love and Life: Pre-Raphaelite Art from the Birmingham Collection, England* (Alexandria, VA: Art Services International, 1995).

—*et al.*, *Waking Dreams: The Art of the Pre-Raphaelites from the Delaware Art Museum* (Alexandria, VA: Art Services International, 2004).

Wilhelm II, Emperor of Germany, *Das Königtum im alten Mesopotamien* (Berlin: W. de Gruyter, 1938).

Williamson, H.G.M., *Ezra, Nehemiah* (WBC, 16; Waco, TX: Word Books, 1985).

Willmott, Robert Aris, *Poets of the Nineteenth Century* (London: George Routledge & Co., 1857).

Wilmot-Buxton, Harry John and Edward John Poynter, *German, Flemish and Dutch Painting* (Illustrated Text-Books of Art Education; New York: Scribner & Welford/London: Samson Low, Marston, Searle & Rivington, 1881).

Winckler, Hugo, *Arabisch, Semitisch, Orientalisch: Kulturgeschichtlich-mythologische Untersuchung* (Berlin: W. Peiser, 1901).

—*Keilinschriftliches Textbuch zum Alten Testament* (Hilfsbücher zur Kunde des alten Orients, 1; Leipzig: E. Pfeiffer, 1892; 2. neu bearbeitete Aufl., 1903; 3. neubearb. Aufl. mit einer Einführung, 1909).

Wind, James P., *The Bible and the University: The Messianic Vision of William Rainey Harper* (Atlanta, GA: Scholars Press, 1987).

—'Harper, William Rainey (24 July 1856–10 Jan. 1906)', *ANB*, X, pp. 131-34.

Winstone, H.V.F., *Woolley of Ur: The Life of Sir Leonard Woolley* (London: Secker & Warburg, 1990).

Wolf, C. Umhau, 'Traces of Primitive Democracy in Ancient Israel', *JNES* 6 (1947), pp. 98-108.

Wood, Leon James, *Survey of Israel's History* (Grand Rapids, MI: Zondervan, 1970).

Worthington, Charles, 'Our Government Exhibit at the World's Fair', *The Chautauquan: A Weekly Newsmagazine* 16 (January, 1893), pp. 393-98.

Wright, G. Ernest, *The God Who Acts: Biblical Theology as Recital* (Studies in Biblical Theology, 8; London: SCM Press, 1952).

Wright, G. Ernest, and Floyd V. Filson, *The Westminster Historical Atlas to the Bible* (Westminster Aids to the Study of the Scriptures; Philadelphia: Westminster, 1946; rev. edn, 1956).

Wright, G. Ernest, and Reginald H. Fuller, *The Book of the Acts of God: Christian Scholarship Interprets the Bible* (Christian Faith Series; Garden City, NY: Doubleday, 1957).

Wright, J. Stafford, 'The Historicity of the Book of Esther', in *New Perspectives on the Old Testament* (ed. J. Barton Payne; Evangelical Theological Society Symposium Series, 3; Waco, TX: Word Books, 1970), pp. 37-47.

Wright, William *et al.*, *The Empire of the Hittites* (London: James Nisbet & Co., 1884).

Wurzbach, Wolfgang von, 'Einleitung des Herausgebers', to *Die Tochter der Luft* (*La hija del aire*), in *Calderons ausgewählte Werke* (ed. W. von Wurzbach; Leipzig: Hesse & Becker, 1910), II, pp. 113-23.

Yale University, *Doctors of Philosophy 1861–1960* (New Haven: Yale University Press, 1961).

Yamauchi, Edwin M., *Persia and the Bible* (Grand Rapids, MI: Baker Book House, 1990).

—'The Scythians: Invading Hordes from the Russian Steppes', *BA* 46 (1983), pp. 90-99.

Younger, K. Lawson, Jr, 'The "Contextual Method": Some West Semitic Reflections', in *COS*, III, pp. xxxv-lxii.

Younis, Adele L. and Philip M. Kayal, *The Coming of the Arabic-Speaking People to the United States* (Staten Island, NY: Center for Migration Studies, 1995).

Zakovitch, Y., *Through the Looking Glass: Reflection Stories in the Bible* (Tel Aviv: Hakibbutz Hameuchad, 1995) [Hebrew].

Zalesch, Saul E., 'Wolfe, Catharine Lorillard (8 Mar. 1828–4 Apr. 1887)', in *ANB*, XXIII, pp. 728-29.

Zettler, Richard L., 'Excavations at Nippur, The University of Pennsylvania, and the University's Museum', in *Nippur at the Centennial: Papers Read at the XXXV*[e] *Rencontre assyriologique internationale, Philadelphia, 1988* (ed. Maria deJong Ellis; Occasional Publications of the Samuel Noah Kramer Fund, 14; Philadelphia: University Museum, 1992), pp. 325-36.

Zhi, Yang, 'The Excavation of Adab', *Journal of Ancient Civilizations* 3 (1988), pp. 1-21.

Ziegler, Nele, *La population feminine des palais d'après les archives royales de Mari: Le harem de Zîmri-Lîm* (Florilegium marianum, 4; Mémoires de N.A.B.U., 5; Paris: SEPOA, 1999).

Zimmermann, Reiner, *Giacomo Meyerbeer: Eine Biographie nach Dokumenten* (Berlin: Henschel, 1991).

Zimmern, Heinrich, *Die Assyriologie als Hülfswissenschaft für das Studium des Alten Testaments und des Klassischen Altertums: Antritts-Vorlesung, gehalten in der Aula der Königl. Albertus-Universität zu Königsberg i. Pr. am 1. November 1889* (Königsberg i. Pr.: W. Koch, 1889).

Indexes

Index of References

Bible

CLASSICAL

ARCHIVAL MANUSCRIPTS

VISUAL ARTIFACTS

Index of Authors

Index of Subjects

www.ingramcontent.com/pod-product-compliance
Lightning Source LLC
LaVergne TN
LVHW020050110826
845155LV00021B/53

* 9 7 8 1 9 0 6 0 5 5 3 3 2 *